Algebra 1

Response to Intervention

© (Golden Gate Bridge, CA) holbox/Shutterstock; (Dome of Botanic Garden, Milwaukee, WI) Henryk Sadura/Shutterstock; (Bodie Island Lighthouse, NC) Dave Allen Photography/Shutterstock

Printed in the U.S.A.

ISBN 978-0-544-38197-1
3 4 5 6 7 8 9 10 0748 23 22 21 20 19 18 17 16 15
4500542869 B C D E F G

Contents

Introduction

Tier 2: Prerequisite Skills Module Pre-Tests

Tier 2: Prerequisite Skills Post-Tests

Tier 1: Reteach Worksheets

Response to Intervention

UNIT 1 QUANTITIES AND MODELING					
Student Edition Lessons	**Tier 1 Skills**	**Pre-Tests**	**Tier 2 Skills Strategic Intervention**	**Post-Tests**	**Tier 3 Skills Intensive Intervention**
Module 1 Quantitative Reasoning					Building Block (Tier 3) worksheets are available online for students who need additional support on prerequisite skills. See the teacher page of each Tier 2 Skill lesson for a list of Building Block skills.
1.1 Solving Equations	Reteach 1-1	Module 1	13 One-Step Equations	Skill 13	
1.2 Modeling Quantities	Reteach 1-2		17 Scale Factor and Scale Drawings	Skill 17	
1.3 Reporting with Precision and Accuracy	Reteach 1-3		19 Significant Digits	Skill 19	
			24 Writing Linear Equations	Skill 24	
Module 2 Algebraic Models					
2.1 Modeling with Expressions	Reteach 2-1	Module 2	2 Algebraic Expressions	Skill 2	
			13 One-Step Equations	Skill 13	
2.2 Creating and Solving Equations	Reteach 2-2		14 One-Step Inequalities	Skill 14	
			21 Two-Step Equations	Skill 21	
2.3 Solving for a Variable	Reteach 2-3		22 Two-Step Inequalities	Skill 22	
2.4 Creating and Solving Inequalities	Reteach 2-4				
2.5 Creating and Solving Compound Inequalities	Reteach 2-5				

UNIT 2 UNDERSTANDING FUNCTIONS					
Student Edition Lessons	**Tier 1 Skills**	**Pre-Tests**	**Tier 2 Skills Strategic Intervention**	**Post-Tests**	**Tier 3 Skills Intensive Intervention**
Module 3 Functions and Models					Building Block (Tier 3) worksheets are available online for students who need additional support on prerequisite skills. See the teacher page of each Tier 2 Skill lesson for a list of Building Block skills.
3.1 Graphing Relationships	Reteach 3-1	Module 3	6 Graphing Linear Nonproportional Relationships	Skill 6	
3.2 Understanding Relations and Functions	Reteach 3-2		7 Graphing Linear Proportional Relationships	Skill 7	
			10 Linear Functions	Skill 10	
3.3 Modeling with Functions	Reteach 3-3				
3.4 Graphing Functions	Reteach 3-4				
Module 4 Patterns and Sequences					
4.1 Identifying and Graphing Sequences	Reteach 4-1	Module 4	1 Add and Subtract Integer	Skill 1	
			2 Algebraic Expressions	Skill 2	
4.2 Constructing Arithmetic Sequences	Reteach 4-2		12 Multiply and Divide Integers	Skill 12	
4.3 Modeling with Arithmetic Sequences	Reteach 4-3				

ADDITIONAL ONLINE INTERVENTION RESOURCES

Tier 1, Tier 2, Tier 3 Skills

Personal Math Trainer will automatically create a standards-based, personalized intervention assignment for your students, targeting each student's individual needs!

Tier 2 Skills

Students scan QR codes with their smart phones to watch Math on the Spot tutorial videos for every Tier 2 skill.

UNIT 3 LINEAR FUNCTIONS, EQUATIONS, AND INEQUALITIES					
Student Edition Lessons	**Tier 1 Skills**	**Pre-Tests**	**Tier 2 Skills Strategic Intervention**	**Post-Tests**	**Tier 3 Skills Intensive Intervention**
Module 5 Linear Functions					Building Block (Tier 3) worksheets are available online for students who need additional support on prerequisite skills. See the teacher page of each Tier 2 Skill lesson for a list of Building Block skills.
5.1 Understanding Linear Functions 5.2 Using Intercepts 5.3 Interpreting Rate of Change and Slope	Reteach 5-1 Reteach 5-2 Reteach 5-3	Module 5	4 Constant Rate of Change 7 Graphing Linear Proportional Relationships 8 Interpreting the Unit Rate as Slope 11 Multi-Step Equations 20 Slope 23 Unit Rates	Skill 4 Skill 7 Skill 8 Skill 11 Skill 20 Skill 23	
Module 6 Forms of Linear Equations					
6.1 Slope-Intercept Form 6.2 Point-Slope Form 6.3 Standard Form 6.4 Transforming Linear Functions 6.5 Comparing Properties of Linear Functions	Reteach 6-1 Reteach 6-2 Reteach 6-3 Reteach 6-4 Reteach 6-5	Module 6	4 Constant Rate of Change 7 Graphing Linear Proportional Relationships 10 Linear Functions 20 Slope 21 Two-Step Equations 23 Unit Rates	Skill 4 Skill 7 Skill 10 Skill 20 Skill 21 Skill 23	
Module 7 Linear Equations and Inequalities					
7.1 Modeling Linear Relationships 7.2 Using Functions to Solve One-Variable Equations 7.3 Linear Inequalities in Two Variables	Reteach 7-1 Reteach 7-2 Reteach 7-3	Module 7	2 Algebraic Expressions 7 Graphing Linear Proportional Relationships 10 Linear Functions 24 Writing Linear Equations	Skill 2 Skill 7 Skill 10 Skill 24	

UNIT 4 STATISTICAL MODELS					
Student Edition Lessons	**Tier 1 Skills**	**Pre-Tests**	**Tier 2 Skills Strategic Intervention**	**Post-Tests**	**Tier 3 Skills Intensive Intervention**
Module 8 Multi-Variable Categorical Data					Building Block (Tier 3) worksheets are available online for students who need additional support on prerequisite skills. See the teacher page of each Tier 2 Skill lesson for a list of Building Block skills.
8.1 Two-Way Frequency Tables	Reteach 8-1	Module 8	15 Percent 25 Two-Way Frequency Tables	Skill 15 Skill 25	
8.2 Relative Frequency and Probability	Reteach 8-2		26 Two-Way Relative Frequency Tables	Skill 26	
Module 9 One-Variable Data Distributions					
9.1 Measures of Center and Spread	Reteach 9-1	Module 9	28 Measures of Center 29 Box Plots 30 Histograms	Skill 28 Skill 29 Skill 30	
9.2 Data Distributions and Outliers	Reteach 9-2				
9.3 Histograms and Box Plots	Reteach 9-3				
9.4 Normal Distributions	Reteach 9-4				
Module 10 Linear Modeling and Regression					
10.1 Scatter Plots and Trend Lines	Reteach 10-1	Module 10	9 Linear Associations 10 Linear Functions	Skill 9 Skill 10	
10.2 Fitting a Linear Model to Data	Reteach 10-2		18 Scatter Plots 24 Writing Linear Equations	Skill 18 Skill 24	

ADDITIONAL ONLINE INTERVENTION RESOURCES

Tier 1, Tier 2, Tier 3 Skills

Personal Math Trainer will automatically create a standards-based, personalized intervention assignment for your students, targeting each student's individual needs!

Tier 2 Skills

Students scan QR codes with their smart phones to watch Math on the Spot tutorial videos for every Tier 2 skill.

UNIT 5 LINEAR SYSTEMS AND PIECEWISE-DEFINED FUNCTIONS					
Student Edition Lessons	**Tier 1 Skills**	**Pre-Tests**	**Tier 2 Skills Strategic Intervention**	**Post-Tests**	**Tier 3 Skills Intensive Intervention**
Module 11 Solving Systems of Linear Equations					
11.1 Solving Linear Systems by Graphing 11.2 Solving Linear Systems by Substitution 11.3 Solving Linear Systems by Adding or Subtracting 11.4 Solving Linear Systems by Multiplying First	Reteach 11-1 Reteach 11-2 Reteach 11-3 Reteach 11-4	Module 11	2 Algebraic Expressions 6 Graphing Linear Nonproportional Relationships 7 Graphing Linear Proportional Relationships 10 Linear Functions	Skill 2 Skill 6 Skill 7 Skill 10	Building Block (Tier 3) worksheets are available online for students who need additional support on prerequisite skills. See the teacher page of each Tier 2 Skill lesson for a list of Building Block skills.
Module 12 Modeling with Linear Systems					
12.1 Creating Systems of Linear Equations 12.2 Graphing Systems of Linear Inequalities 12.3 Modeling with Linear Systems	Reteach 12-1 Reteach 12-2 Reteach 12-3	Module 12	2 Algebraic Expressions 10 Linear Functions 14 One-Step Inequalities 21 Two-Step Equations 22 Two Step Inequalities	Skill 2 Skill 10 Skill 14 Skill 21 Skill 22	
Module 13 Piecewise-Defined Functions					
13.1 Understanding Piecewise-Defined Functions 13.2 Absolute Value Functions and Transformations 13.3 Solving Absolute-Value Equations 13.4 Solving Absolute-Value Inequalities	Reteach 13-1 Reteach 13-2 Reteach 13-3 Reteach 13-4	Module 13	10 Linear Functions 11 Multi-Step Equations 22 Two-Step Inequalities 27 Absolute Value	Skill 10 Skill 11 Skill 22 Skill 27	

Response to Intervention

UNIT 6 EXPONENTIAL RELATIONSHIPS					
Student Edition Lessons	**Tier 1 Skills**	**Pre-Tests**	**Tier 2 Skills Strategic Intervention**	**Post-Tests**	**Tier 3 Skills Intensive Intervention**
Module 14 Rational Exponents and Radicals					Building Block (Tier 3) worksheets are available online for students who need additional support on prerequisite skills. See the teacher page of each Tier 2 Skill lesson for a list of Building Block skills.
14.1 Understanding Rational Exponents and Radicals 14.2 Simplifying Expressions with Rational Exponents and Radicals	Reteach 14-1 Reteach 14-2	Module 14	2 Algebraic Expressions 5 Exponents 16 Real Numbers	Skill 2 Skill 5 Skill 16	
Module 15 Geometric Sequences and Exponential Functions					
15.1 Understanding Geometric Sequences 15.2 Constructing Geometric Sequences 15.3 Constructing Exponential Functions 15.4 Graphing Exponential Functions 15.5 Transforming Exponential Functions	Reteach 15-1 Reteach 15-2 Reteach 15-3 Reteach 15-4 Reteach 15-5	Module 15	2 Algebraic Expressions 5 Exponents 11 Multi-Step Equations	Skill 2 Skill 5 Skill 11	
Module 16 Exponential Equations and Models					
16.1 Using Graphs and Properties to Solve Equations with Exponents 16.2 Modeling Exponential Growth and Decay 16.3 Using Exponential Regression Models 16.4 Comparing Linear and Exponential Models	Reteach 16-1 Reteach 16-2 Reteach 16-3 Reteach 16-4	Module 16	4 Constant Rate of Change 5 Exponents 15 Percent 18 Scatter Plots	Skill 4 Skill 5 Skill 15 Skill 18	

ADDITIONAL ONLINE INTERVENTION RESOURCES

Tier 1, Tier 2, Tier 3 Skills

Personal Math Trainer will automatically create a standards-based, personalized intervention assignment for your students, targeting each student's individual needs!

Tier 2 Skills

Students scan QR codes with their smart phones to watch Math on the Spot tutorial videos for every Tier 2 skill.

Response to Intervention

UNIT 7 POLYNOMIAL OPERATIONS					
Student Edition Lessons	**Tier 1 Skills**	**Pre-Tests**	**Tier 2 Skills Strategic Intervention**	**Post-Tests**	**Tier 3 Skills Intensive Intervention**
Module 17 Adding and Subtracting Polynomials					Building Block (Tier 3) worksheets are available online for students who need additional support on prerequisite skills. See the teacher page of each Tier 2 Skill lesson for a list of Building Block skills.
17.1 Understanding Polynomial Expressions 17.2 Adding Polynomial Expressions 17.3 Subtracting Polynomial Expressions	Reteach 17-1 Reteach 17-2 Reteach 17-3	Module 17	1 Add and Subtract Integers 2 Algebraic Expressions 5 Exponents	Skill 1 Skill 2 Skill 5	
Module 18 Multiplying Polynomials					
18.1 Multiplying Polynomial Expressions by Monomials 18.2 Multiplying Polynomial Expressions 18.3 Special Products of Binomials	Reteach 18-1 Reteach 18-2 Reteach 18-3	Module 18	2 Algebraic Expressions 5 Exponents 12 Multiply and Divide Integers	Skill 2 Skill 5 Skill 12	

UNIT 8 QUADRATIC FUNCTIONS					
Student Edition Lessons	**Tier 1 Skills**	**Pre-Tests**	**Tier 2 Skills Strategic Intervention**	**Post-Tests**	**Tier 3 Skills Intensive Intervention**
Module 19 Graphing Quadratic Functions					Building Block (Tier 3) worksheets are available online for students who need additional support on prerequisite skills. See the teacher page of each Tier 2 Skill lesson for a list of Building Block skills.
19.1 Understanding Quadratic Functions 19.2 Transforming Quadratic Functions 19.3 Interpreting Vertex Form and Standard Form	Reteach 19-1 Reteach 19-2 Reteach 19-3	Module 19	2 Algebraic Expressions 3 Algebraic Representations of Transformations 5 Exponents 10 Linear Functions	Skill 2 Skill 3 Skill 5 Skill 10	
Module 20 Connecting Intercepts, Zeros, and Factors					
20.1 Connecting Intercepts and Zeros 20.2 Connecting Intercepts and Linear Factors 20.3 Applying the Zero Product Property to Solve Equations	Reteach 20-1 Reteach 20-2 Reteach 20-3	Module 20	2 Algebraic Expressions 5 Exponents 10 Linear Functions	Skill 2 Skill 5 Skill 10	

UNIT 9 QUADRATIC EQUATIONS AND MODELING					
Student Edition Lessons	**Tier 1 Skills**	**Pre-Tests**	**Tier 2 Skills Strategic Intervention**	**Post-Tests**	**Tier 3 Skills Intensive Intervention**
Module 21 Using Factors to Solve Quadratic Equations					Building Block (Tier 3) worksheets are available online for students who need additional support on prerequisite skills. See the teacher page of each Tier 2 Skill lesson for a list of Building Block skills.
21.1 Solving Equations by Factoring $x^2 + bx + c$ 21.2 Solving Equations by Factoring $ax^2 + bx + c$ 21.3 Using Special Factors to Solve Equations	Reteach 21-1 Reteach 21-2 Reteach 21-3	Module 21	2 Algebraic Expressions 5 Exponents 21 Two-Step Equations	Skill 2 Skill 5 Skill 21	
Module 22 Using Square Roots to Solve Quadratic Equations					
22.1 Solving Equations by Taking Square Roots 22.2 Solving Equations by Completing the Square 22.3 Using the Quadratic Formula to Solve Equations 22.4 Choosing a Method for Solving Quadratic Equations 22.5 Solving Nonlinear Systems	Reteach 22-1 Reteach 22-2 Reteach 22-3 Reteach 22-4 Reteach 22-5	Module 22	2 Algebraic Expressions 5 Exponents 11 Multi-Step Equations	Skill 2 Skill 5 Skill 11	
Module 23 Linear, Exponential, and Quadratic Models					
23.1 Modeling with Quadratic Functions 23.2 Comparing Linear, Quadratic, and Exponential Models	Reteach 23-1 Reteach 23-2	Module 23	4 Constant Rate of Change 6 Graphing Linear Nonproportional Relationships 7 Graphing Linear Proportional Relationships 10 Linear Functions	Skill 4 Skill 6 Skill 7 Skill 10	

UNIT 10 INVERSE RELATIONSHIPS					
Student Edition Lessons	**Tier 1 Skills**	**Pre-Tests**	**Tier 2 Skills Strategic Intervention**	**Post-Tests**	**Tier 3 Skills Intensive Intervention**
Module 24 Functions and Inverses					Building Block (Tier 3) worksheets are available online for students who need additional support on prerequisite skills. See the teacher page of each Tier 2 Skill lesson for a list of Building Block skills.
24.1 Graphing Polynomial Functions 24.2 Understanding Inverse Functions 24.3 Graphing Square Root Functions 24.4 Graphing Cube Root Functions	Reteach 24-1 Reteach 24-2 Reteach 24-3 Reteach 24-4	Module 24	6 Graphing Linear Nonproportional Relationships 10 Linear Functions 31 Squares and Square Roots 32 Cubes and Cube Roots	Skill 6 Skill 10 Skill 31 Skill 32	

ADDITIONAL ONLINE INTERVENTION RESOURCES

Tier 1, Tier 2, Tier 3 Skills

Personal Math Trainer will automatically create a standards-based, personalized intervention assignment for your students, targeting each student's individual needs!

Tier 2 Skills

Students scan QR codes with their smart phones to watch Math on the Spot tutorial videos for every Tier 2 skill.

Using HMH Algebra 1 Response to Intervention

<table>
<tr><td></td><td>Print Resources</td><td>Online Resources</td></tr>
<tr><td>TIER 1</td><td>TIER 2 STRATEGIC INTERVENTION</td><td>TIER 1, TIER 2, AND TIER 3</td></tr>
<tr><td>Reteach worksheet
(one worksheet per lesson)
• Use to provide additional support for students who are having difficulty mastering the concepts taught in Algebra 1.</td><td>Skill Intervention worksheets
(one set per skill)
• Use for students who require intervention with prerequisite skills taught in Middle School.

Skill Intervention Teacher Guides
(one guide per skill)
• Use to provide systematic and explicit instruction, and alternate strategies to help students acquire mastery with prerequisite skills.</td><td>Personal Math Trainer
T1, T2, and T3 skills
• Assign the Personal Math Trainer, which will create standards-based practice for all students and customized intervention when necessary.

Progress Monitoring
• Use the Personal Math Trainer to assess a student's mastery of skills.</td></tr>
<tr><td>Progress Monitoring
• Use Student Edition Ready to Go On? Quizzes to assess mastery of skills taught in the Modules. Use for all students.
• Use Assessment Resources Module Quizzes to assess mastery of skills taught in the Modules. For students who are considerably below level, use Modified Quizzes. For all other students, use Level B.</td><td>Progress Monitoring
• Use Response to Intervention Module Pre-Tests or the Student Edition Are You Ready? Quizzes to assess whether a student has the necessary prerequisite skills for success in each Module.
• Use Response to Intervention Skill Post-Tests to assess mastery of prerequisite skills.</td><td> T2 skills
• Use Math on the Spot tutorial videos to help students review skills taught in Middle School.

 T3 skills
• Use Building Block Skills worksheets for struggling students who require additional intervention.</td></tr>
</table>

Recommendations for Intervention

Tier 1	For students who require small group instruction to review lesson skills taught in Algebra 1.
Tiers 2–3	For students who require strategic or intensive intervention with prerequisite skills needed for success in Algebra 1.
Tiers 1–3	Intervention materials and the *Personal Math Trainer* are designed to accommodate the diverse skill levels of students at all levels of intervention.

DIAGNOSIS

Tier 2 Module Pre-Tests *(RTI ancillary)*
Tier 2 Are You Ready? Quizzes *(Student Edition)*
Tier 1 Ready to Go On? Quizzes *(Student Edition)*

INTERVENE

Use **Tier 1** Reteach and/or **Tier 2** Skill Worksheets *(RTI ancillary)*.

- Uncluttered with minimum words to help all students, regardless of English acquisition
- Vocabulary presented in context to help English learners and struggling readers
- Multiple instructional examples for students to practice thinking-aloud their solutions

Use **Tier 2** Skill Teacher Guides *(RTI ancillary)*.

- Explicit instruction and key teaching points
- Alternate strategies to address the different types of learners
- Common misconceptions to develop understanding of skills
- Visual representations to make concept connections
- Checks to fine-tune instruction and opportunities for immediate feedback

MONITOR PROGRESS

Tier 2: Skill Post-Tests *(RTI ancillary)*
Tier 1–2: Assessment Readiness *(Student Edition)*
Tier 1–3: Leveled Module Quizzes *(Assessment Resources online)*

Use **Tiers 1–3** online additional intervention, practice, and review materials.

- Personal Math Trainer
- Math on the Spot videos
- Building Block Skills worksheets with Teacher Guides
- Differentiated Instruction with leveled Practice, Reading Strategies, and Success for English Learners worksheets

Name ________________ Date ____________ Class ____________

MODULE 1

Response to Intervention

Pre-Test: Skills 13, 17, 19, 24

1. Solve $3.1 = \frac{x}{2}$.

____

2. Solve the equation $-5 = 3s + 5$.

____

3. Moving Company A charges $45 on arrival and $25 an hour. The final bill was $470. How many hours did the movers work?

____

4. Sara is building a raised platform for her dining room. She made a scale drawing as shown below.

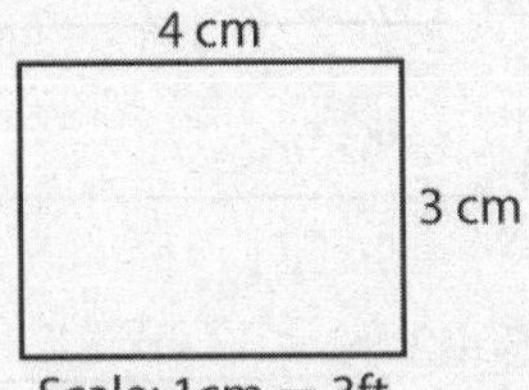

What is the perimeter of the platform?

____

5. A factory made 424 items in 4 hours at a constant rate. Plot the points on the graph to represent the total number of items made each hour.

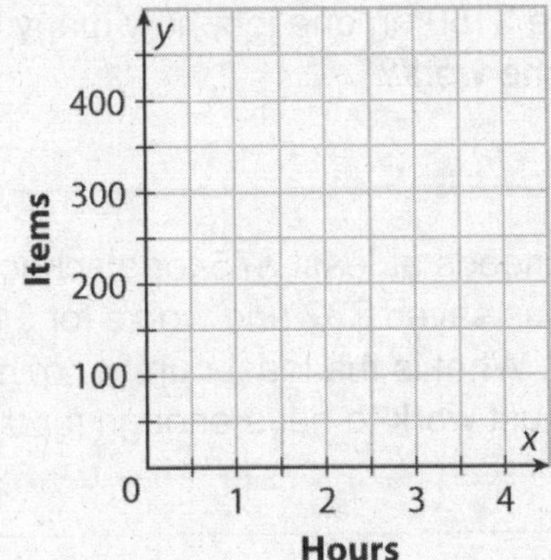

6. What is the best first step for solving the equation $5 = 3x - 4$?

   A Add 4 to both sides of the equation.

   B Subtract 4 from both sides of the equation.

   C Multiply both sides of the equation by 3.

   D Divide both sides of the equation by 3.

7. What is the solution for the equation $-6.4 = 5.0 + 2.4m$?

____

8. Write an equation that can be used to find the area *A* of a rectangular rug whose sides are 5 feet long and *s* feet long.

____

9. A tree that is 18 meters tall casts a shadow that is 6 meters long. At the same time, another tree casts a shadow that is 9 meters long. How tall is the second tree?

____

10. Which of the following is the most precise measurement?

    A 7 cm C 7.523 cm

    B 7.5 cm D 7.52 cm

11. Does each of the following numbers have 3 significant digits?

A	0.072	O Yes	O No
B	0.720	O Yes	O No
C	720	O Yes	O No
D	7200	O Yes	O No

Name ______________________ Date ______________ Class ______________

MODULE 2

Response to Intervention

Pre-Test: Skills 2, 13, 14, 21, 22

1. Evaluate $3(y - 5)$ for $y = 7$.

2. The expression $1.8C + 32$ can be used to convert Celsius temperatures to Fahrenheit. Evaluate the expression for $C = -5$.

3. Simplify $5w - 4 + 3w + 7$.

4. At a white sale, the price of a set of towels was described by $1.03(0.8p) + 5$ where p was the original price, 3% is the sales tax and 5 is the shipping cost. If the original price was \$22, what does the towel set cost on sale with sales tax and shipping?

5. Write an expression for the quotient of a number and 5 decreased by 4.

Solve each equation for *m*.

6. $3m = 19$

7. $m + 5 = 9$

8. $\frac{m}{2} = 14$

9. $m - 1.6 = 2$

10. An angle measure is $x°$. It is supplementary to an angle of 120°. What is the measure of angle x?

Solve each inequality for *x*.

11. $2x \geq 7$

12. $x - 5 < 2$

13. $1.3 + x \leq 9$

14. $\frac{x}{-4} > 5$

15. Roseanne has \$20 to spend on three gifts of equal price. Write and solve and inequality that shows the greatest amount she can spend on each gift.

Solve for *x*.

16. $3x + 5 = 17$

17. $4 - \frac{x}{2} = 3$

18. $0.8x + 0.5 = 3$

19. $5x - 3 \geq 9$

20. $4 + \frac{x}{7} \leq 10$

21. $0.9x - 3 < 7$

22. Diane charges \$10 for a house call plus \$35 an hour for electrical work. If she made \$150 on one job, how many hours did she work?

23. Ron needs at least \$75 for a school trip. He has saved \$32 and works for \$12 an hour. What is the least number of hours he must work to have enough for the trip?

Name ______________________ Date ______________ Class ______________

MODULE 3

Response to Intervention

Pre-Test: Skills 6, 7, 10

Complete.

1. Describe the graph of a linear function.

____

____

2. Complete the table for the equation $y = 2x + 1$.

x	−2	−1	0	1	2
y					

3. Does this graph show a nonproportional relationship? Explain your answer.

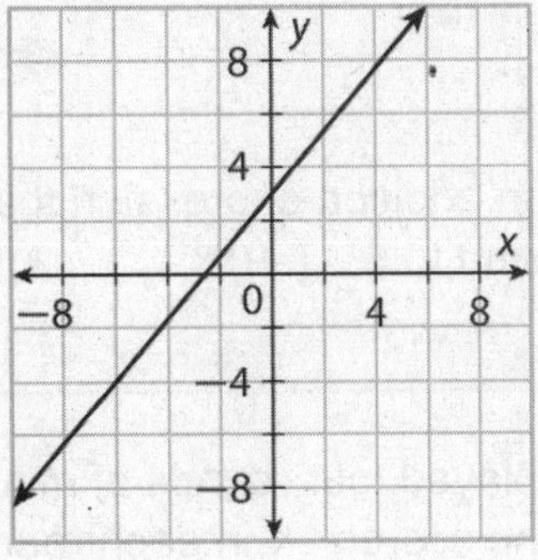

____

____

4. Determine which of the following equations shows a proportional relationship. Choose Yes or No for each.

A $y = -6x - 8$ ○ Yes ○ No

B $y = 5x$ ○ Yes ○ No

C $y = 0.3x$ ○ Yes ○ No

D $y = 4.6x + 1$ ○ Yes ○ No

5. The graph shows the flight of a weather balloon. What do the coordinates (3, 7.5) represent?

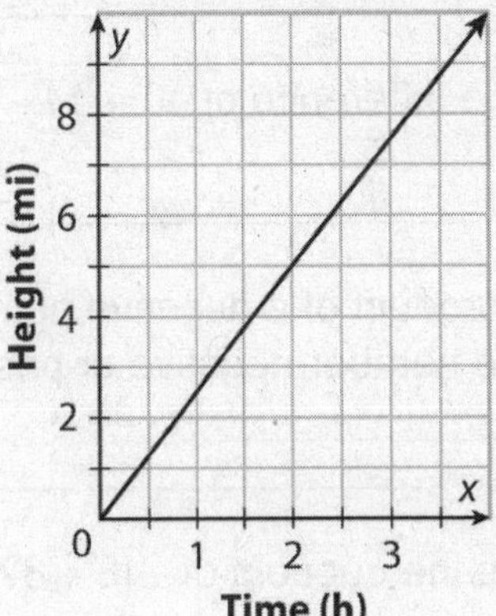

____

____

6. The total charge for renting a video camera for x hours is given by the equation $y = 4.5x + 5$. Complete the table.

x	1	2	3	4	5
y	9.5				

Name ______________________ Date ____________ Class ____________

MODULE 4

Response to Intervention

Pre-Test: Skills 1, 2, 12

Complete.

1. Write an expression for 8 less than 2 times a number.

2. Write an expression for the product of −7 and a number.

3. What is the sum of −7 + 12?

4. Find the difference of −6 − 4.

5. Is the product of a negative number and a positive number negative or positive?

6. What is the quotient of −48 ÷ 8?

7. Write an expression for 15 divided by a number.

8. One city has an elevation of 12 feet above sea level. A second city has an elevation of 4 feet below sea level. What is the difference in the elevations? Show your work.

9. What is the product of −8(9)?

10. What is the opposite of −6?

11. Evaluate $-0.8d + 7.2$ for $d = -1.2$.

12. Evaluate the following expression for $x = 5$ and $y = 4$.

$$6x - 5y + 2x - 7$$

13. Simplify the expression.

$$7(2x + 4) + 8$$

14. Write an addition expression that is equivalent to 6 − (−9).

15. Dawn played four rounds of miniature golf. She scored −4 in each round. What was her total score after four rounds?

16. Write the algebraic expression for 4 more than the product of 7 and a number.

17. What is quotient of −32 ÷ (−4)?

18. Jemima is going to subtract −3 − 5 on a horizontal number line. She places a point at −3. In what direction will the arrow point to show subtracting 5?

Name ______________________ Date ______________ Class ______________

MODULE 5

Response to Intervention

Pre-Test: Skills 4, 7, 8, 11, 20, 23

Use the table for 1–2.

x	2	4	6	8	10
y	10	20	30	40	50

1. What is the constant of proportionality?

____

2. Write an equation in the form of $y = kx$ to describe the relationship between x and y.

____

3. Graph the equation $y = \frac{1}{2}x$.

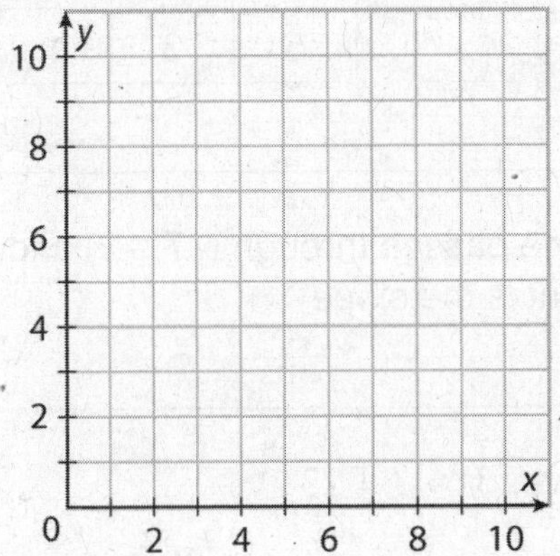

4. Is the equation $y = 0.75x$ a proportional relationship?

   ○ Yes ○ No

5. Solve: $2a - 3 = 9$.

____

6. Solve: $-3(b + 2) = -9$

____

Use the table for 7–8.

Distance Traveled

Time (min)	**Distance (mi)**
4	6
8	12
12	18
16	24

7. What is the unit rate?

____

8. How is the slope related to the unit rate?

____

9. A line passes through (–4, –6) and (4, 10). What is the slope?

____

10. Use the table to write an equation in slope-intercept form.

x	1	2	3	4	5
y	5	11	17	23	29

____

11. A box of 8 pencils costs \$1.84. At that rate how much would 20 pencils cost?

____

12. Ms. Cooper drove 18 miles in $\frac{1}{3}$ hour. What is her speed in miles per hour?

____

Name ______________________ Date ______________ Class ______________

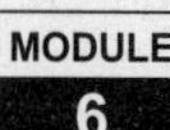

Response to Intervention

Pre-Test: Skills 4, 7, 10, 20, 21, 23

Use the table for 1–2.

T-Shirts Cost

Number of T-Shirts	Cost (dollars)
1	
2	
3	
4	52
5	

1. Complete the table. Each t-shirt costs the same amount.
2. Write an equation in the form of $y = kx$ to describe the relationship between the number of t-shirts, x, and the cost, y.

____

3. Does the graph show a proportional relationship?

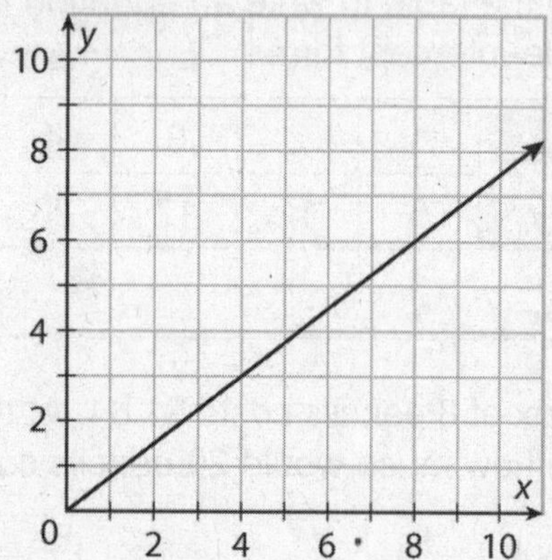

O Yes O No

4. Determine which equations form a linear function.

A $y = x + 3$ O Yes O No

B $y = x^2$ O Yes O No

C $y = \frac{x}{3}$ O Yes O No

5. Tell whether the slope is positive, negative, zero, or undefined.

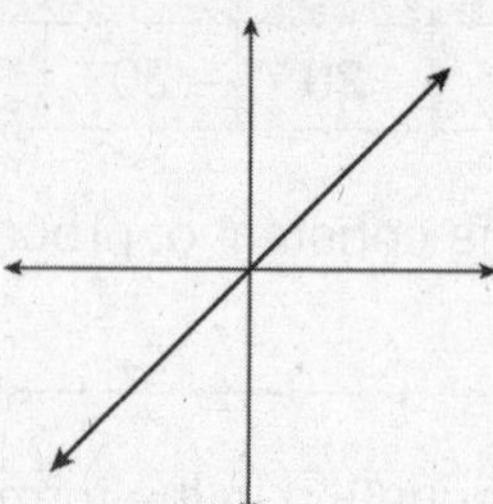

____

6. Use the table to write an equation in slope-intercept form.

x	2	3	4	5
y	7	5	3	1

____

7. A line passes through (–7, –2) and (1, 6). What is the slope?

____

8. Solve: $3k + 7 = 28$

____

9. Solve: $3.5m - 1.05 = 7$

____

10. A machine at a factory produces 30 toy cars every 2 minutes. What is the unit rate for producing a toy car using this machine?

____

11. A recipe calls for $\frac{1}{2}$ cup of water for every $\frac{1}{3}$ cup of milk. How many cups of water are needed per cup of milk?

____

Name ______________________ Date ______________ Class ______________

MODULE 7

Response to Intervention

Pre-Test: Skills 2, 7, 10, 24

Complete.

1. Evaluate $3a - 6b$ for $a = 3.5$ and $b = 2$.

____

2. Simplify the expression.

   $1.4s - 5t + 0.7s - 3.4t - 8.7$

____

3. Josie practices the piano 5 days a week for the same amount of time and 60 minutes on Saturdays. Write an expression to represent the total number of minutes Josie practices the piano each week. Let *m* represent the number of minutes practicing on weekdays.

____

4. Does the graph show a proportional relationship?

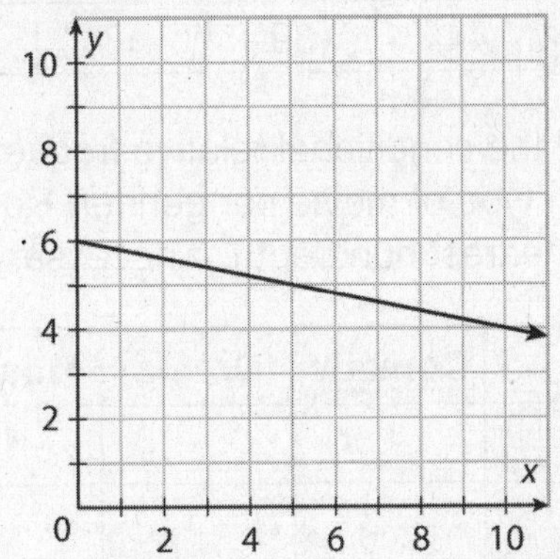

○ Yes ○ No

5. Determine if the relationship is a function.

Input	Output
3	5
4	7
5	7
6	8

○ Yes ○ No

6. The equation $25 - x$ represents the number of miles that are left in a drive. Complete the table.

x	*y*
0	
2	
4	
6	
8	

7. Maddie has read 30 pages of a book. Her plan is to read 40 pages each day from this point on. Write an equation in slope-intercept form to represent the situation.

____

8. Write the equation of the line in slope-intercept form that connects the set of data points.

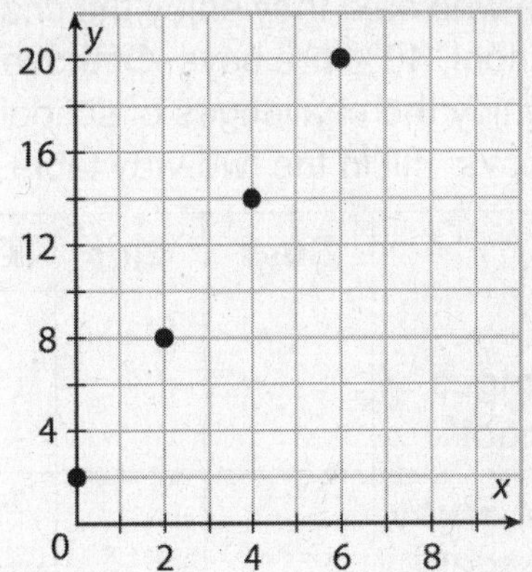

____

Name ____________________ Date ____________ Class ____________

MODULE 8

Response to Intervention

Pre-Test: Skills 15, 25, 26

Complete.

1. Aubrey bought a pair of boots that cost $72 before sales tax. The sales tax was 7%. What was the total cost of the boots?

   ____

2. In May, Sydney bicycled 240 kilometers. In June, she bicycled 312 kilometers. What was the percent increase?

   ____

3. Paul deposited $1,200 into an account that earns 1.5% in annual simple interest. If Paul does not make any deposits or withdrawals, how much money will Paul have in his account in 2 years?

   ____

4. In a survey of 200 students, 65% said they enjoy the challenges of school. Of those who said they enjoy the challenges of school, 40% are boys. Of those who do not enjoy the challenges of school, 70% are boys. Fill in the two-way table.

	Boys	Girls	TOTAL
Enjoy Challenges of School			
Do Not Enjoy Challenges of School			
TOTAL			

5. People were surveyed about inclement weather. They were asked if they prefer rain or snow. The two-way table is partially filled. Complete the table.

	Prefer Rain	Prefer Snow	TOTAL
Adults		16	45
Students	22		
TOTAL			120

Use this information for Problem 6.

Students in Grade 9 were asked to name their favorite type of movie from three choices. The table shows the data.

	Comedy	Drama	Musical	TOTAL
Boys	26	18	6	50
Girls	18	21	11	50
TOTAL	44	39	17	100

6. Find the conditional relative frequency for each type of movie per gender. Round to the nearest hundredth, if necessary.

	Comedy	Drama	Musical
Boys			
Girls			
TOTAL			

Name ______________________ Date ______________ Class ______________

MODULE 9

Response to Intervention

Pre-Test: Skills 28, 29, 30

Complete. Use the data set shown.

87, 93, 87, 96, 92

1. What is the mean?

____

2. What is the median?

____

3. What is the mode?

____

4. Terri wants to have a bowling score of at least 140 after 9 games. Her first 8 scores are shown below.

   136, 128, 142, 151, 137, 162, 136, 138

   What is the lowest she can score if she needs to have a mean score of at least 140?

____

Use the data set shown for 5–10.

5, 14, 11, 16, 7, 5, 18, 9

5. What is the median?

____

6. What is the lower quartile?

____

7. What is the upper quartile?

____

8. Complete the box plot.

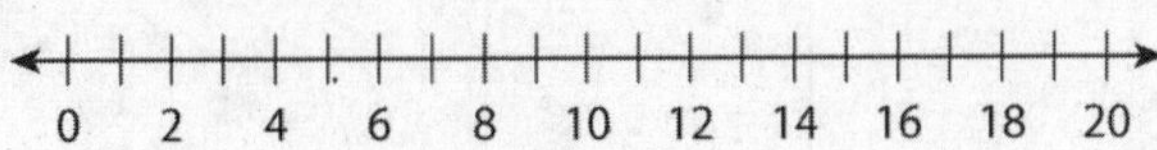

9. What is the range?

____

10. What is the interquartile range?

____

11. Each item at a garage sale was sold for an integer number of dollars. The histogram shows the costs for the items.

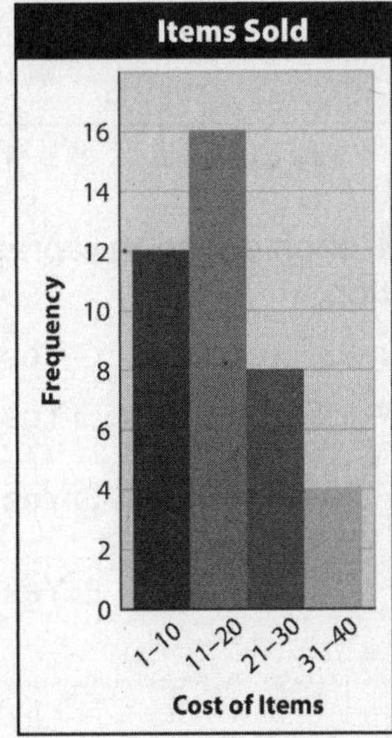

What percent of the items cost more than $10?

____

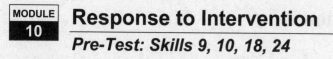

Name ______________________ Date ______________ Class ______________

MODULE 10

Response to Intervention

Pre-Test: Skills 9, 10, 18, 24

Complete.

1. Does the following show a linear association? Choose Yes or No.

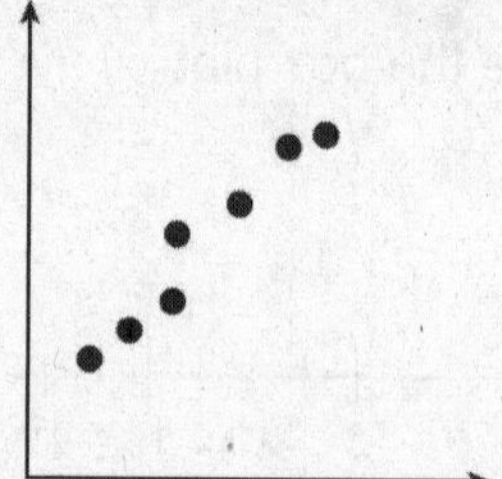

○ Yes ○ No

2. Draw the trend line.

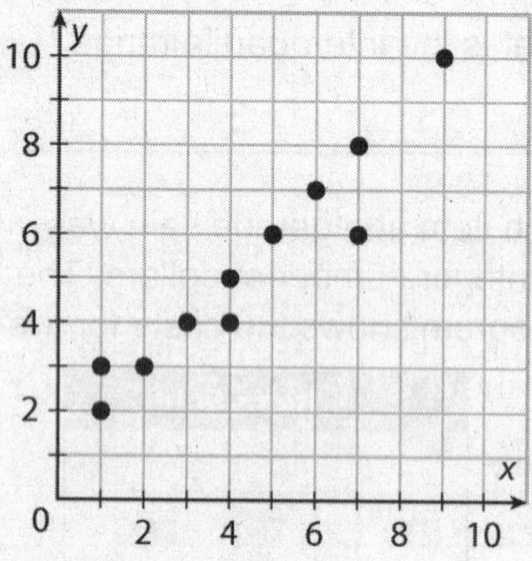

Determine if each equation represents a linear function.

3. $y = 8.5x + 3$ ○ Yes ○ No
4. $y = 7x^2 - 1.5$ ○ Yes ○ No
5. $y = \dfrac{2}{x}$ ○ Yes ○ No
6. $y = -9x + 7.2$ ○ Yes ○ No

7. Determine if the relationship is a function.

Input	Output
3	5
3	6
3	7
3	8

○ Yes ○ No

8. Determine if the following exhibits a cluster, outlier, or none.

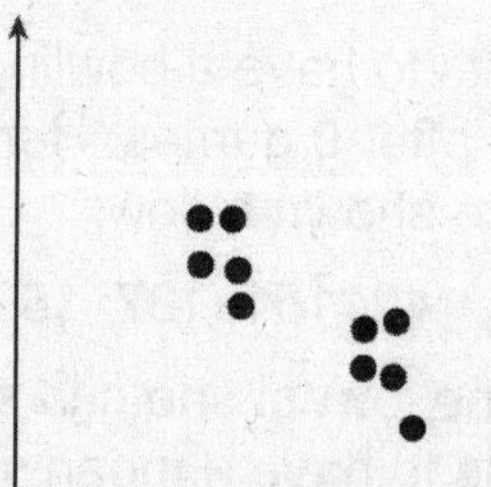

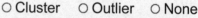

○ Cluster ○ Outlier ○ None

9. Mr. Davis earns \$1000 for 40 hours of work and \$1375 for 50 hours of work within the same month. Write an equation in slope-intercept form to represent the situation.

____

10. Write an equation that represents the data in the table.

Time (min)	2	4	6	8	10
Height (cm)	12	16	20	24	28

____

Name ______________________ Date ______________ Class ______________

MODULE 11

Response to Intervention

Pre-Test: Skills 2, 6, 7, 10

Complete.

1. Evaluate $21 + a$ for $a = -9$.

____

2. What is another way to write $\frac{b}{6}$?

____

3. Evaluate $2c - 4d + 3$ for $c = 6$ and $d = 8$.

____

4. A group of friends is going roller-skating. The entrance fee is \$5 per person, and the group is going to share a \$2-off coupon. Write an expression to represent the total cost.

____

5. Graph the equation $y = 0.75x + 1$.

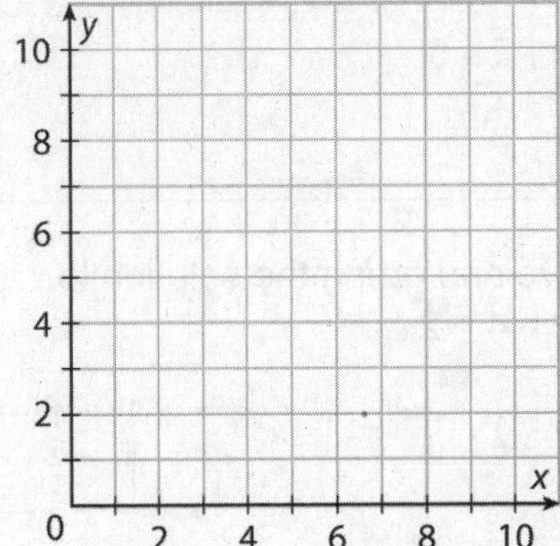

6. Does the line of the graph you drew for Problem 5 show a proportional relationship? Explain your answer.

____

____

7. Enzo's Pizzeria charges a delivery fee of \$0.40 per mile for up to 10 miles. Graph the equation that shows the total cost for up to 10 miles.

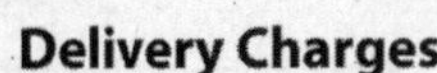

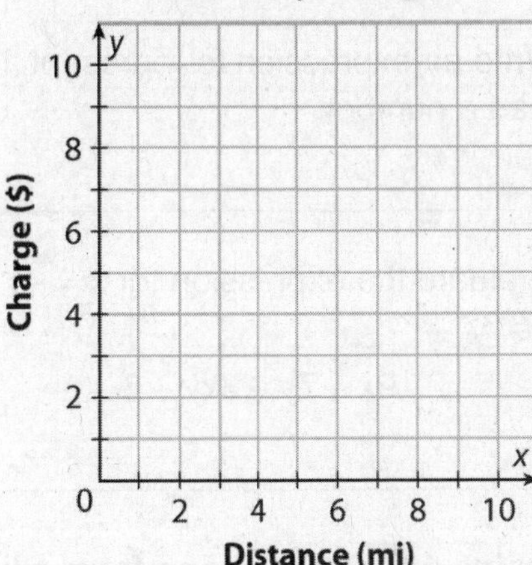

8. Does the line of the graph you drew for Problem 7 show a nonproportional relationship? Explain your answer.

____

____

9. Is this relationship a function?

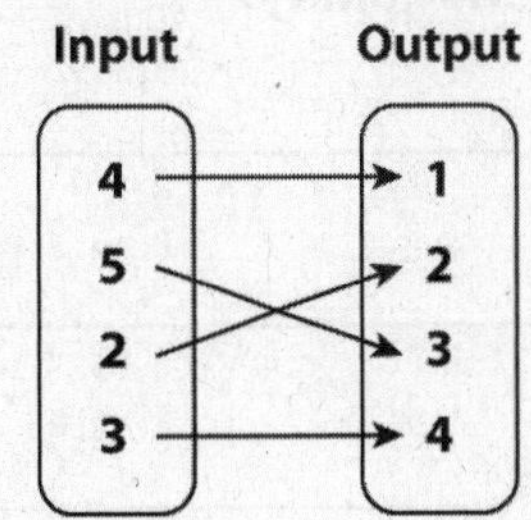

○ Yes ○ No

Name ________________ Date ________ Class ________

MODULE 12

Response to Intervention

Pre-Test: Skills 2, 10, 14, 21, 22

Complete.

1. Simplify the expression.

$$6(2e - 4) + 7$$

____

2. Write an expression to represent 15 less than a number.

____

3. Evaluate the expression for $x = -4$ and $y = 3$.

$$9x - 7y + 3xy - 6$$

____

Determine which equations form a linear function.

4. $y = -x + 2$ ○ Yes ○ No
5. $y = 3x - 4$ ○ Yes ○ No
6. $y = x^3$ ○ Yes ○ No
7. $y = \frac{x}{4} - \frac{2}{3}$ ○ Yes ○ No

Solve each inequality.

8. $3a > 12$ ______________

9. $\frac{b}{5} \leq 7$ ______________

10. $c - 7 > 8$ ______________

11. Graph the solution to the following inequality.

$$d + 2 > 8$$

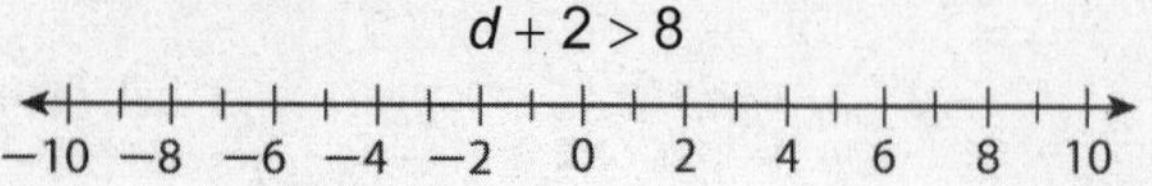

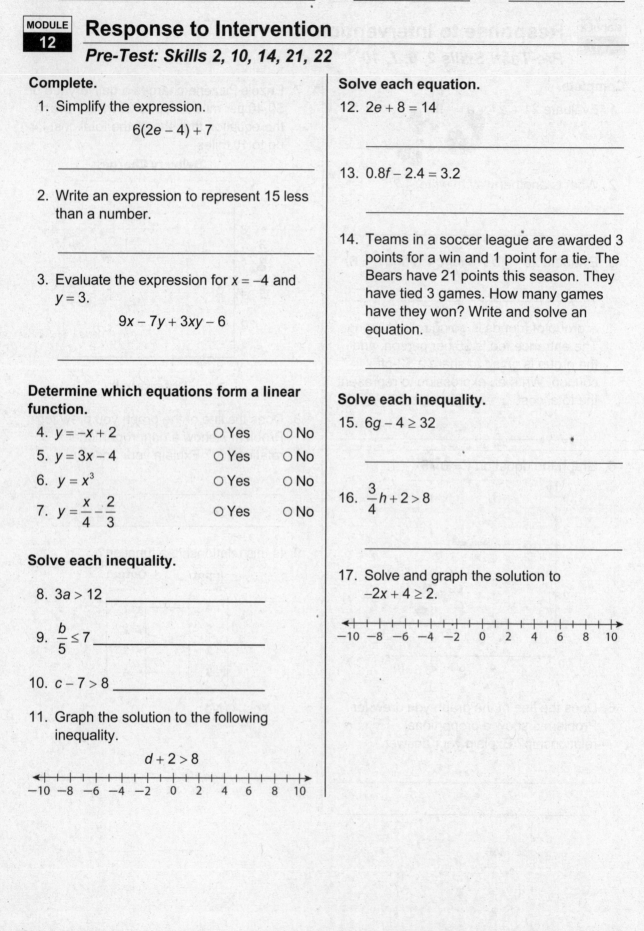

Solve each equation.

12. $2e + 8 = 14$

____

13. $0.8f - 2.4 = 3.2$

____

14. Teams in a soccer league are awarded 3 points for a win and 1 point for a tie. The Bears have 21 points this season. They have tied 3 games. How many games have they won? Write and solve an equation.

____

Solve each inequality.

15. $6g - 4 \geq 32$

____

16. $\frac{3}{4}h + 2 > 8$

____

17. Solve and graph the solution to $-2x + 4 \geq 2$.

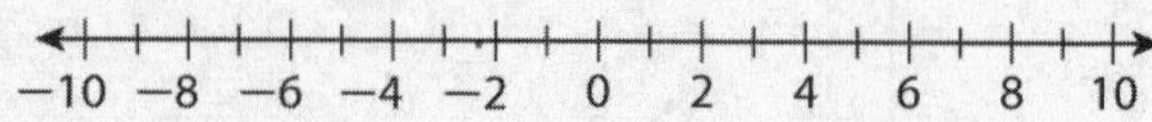

Name ____________ Date ________ Class ________

MODULE 13

Response to Intervention

Pre-Test: Skills 10, 11, 22, 27

Complete.

1. Is this relationship a function?

Input	Output
2	3
4	5
8	7

O Yes O No

2. Determine which equations form a linear function.

A. $y = 3x + 4$ O Yes O No

B. $y = x^2 - 2$ O Yes O No

C. $y = \frac{3}{x}$ O Yes O No

D. $y = \frac{x}{7}$ O Yes O No

3. Solve: $4a - 2 = 26$

____

4. Solve: $-3b + 9 = 12$

____

5. Solve: $2(c + 3) = -9$

____

6. Solve: $\frac{1}{3}d + 4 = 8$

____

7. Solve: $-3e + 2 = 5e - 4$

____

8. Rashad jogged more than 46 miles this week. He jogged 4 miles on Sunday. Write an inequality that can be used to find the number of miles that Rashad averaged the other 6 days of the week.

____

9. Solve: $4f - 6 \geq 30$

____

10. Solve: $-2g + 4 < 10$

____

11. Graph the solution to $4x - 2 \leq -10$.

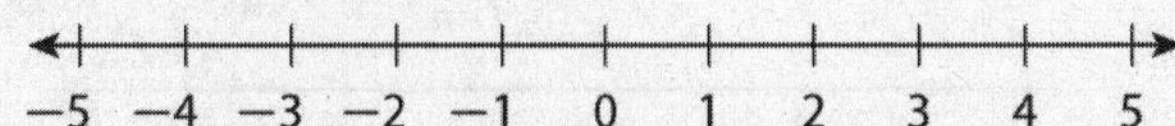

Find the absolute value.

12. $|2.4| =$ ________

13. $|-5| =$ ________

14. Dave's game score is less than −12 points. Does he need to score more than 12 points or less than 12 points to get his score back to 0? Explain your answer.

____

____

Name ______________________ Date ______________ Class ______________

MODULE 14

Response to Intervention

Pre-Test: Skills 2, 5, 16

Complete.

1. Decide which are like terms.

A $3a$ and $4b$ ○ Yes ○ No

B $-2c$ and $6c$ ○ Yes ○ No

C $0.75d$ and $3de$ ○ Yes ○ No

D $\frac{3}{8}f$ and $5f$ ○ Yes ○ No

2. Evaluate $2.7g$ for $g = 0.6$.

____

3. Evaluate $6h - 4j - 4 \div 2$ for $h = 8$ and $j = 2$.

____

4. Simplify the expression.

$$6(2k - 3) + 4k - 2$$

____

5. Write an expression to represent n split into 6 equal groups.

____

6. The freshmen at Fillmore High School are running a car wash for a fundraiser. They will charge \$8 per car. Supplies and advertising cost \$150 in all. They earned \$600 in profits. Write an equation to represent the number of cars that were washed.

____

7. Write $7 \cdot 7 \cdot 7 \cdot 7 \cdot 7$ in exponential form.

____

8. What is another way to represent 2^6?

____

Evaluate.

9. 6^0 ______________________

10. 12^1 ______________________

11. 7^4 ______________________

Simplify. Write your answer using base-10 numerals.

12. $6^2 \cdot 6^{-4}$

____

13. $2^{-3} \cdot 2^{-2}$

____

14. $\frac{4^4}{4^2}$

____

15. $\frac{8^3}{8^{-2}}$

____

16. Write $\frac{13}{20}$ as a decimal.

____

17. Write $0.\overline{8}$ as a fraction in simplest form.

____

Solve for *x*.

18. $x^2 = 81$ ______________________

19. $x^2 = \frac{4}{121}$ ______________________

20. $x^3 = 512$ ______________________

21. Approximate $\sqrt{45}$ to one decimal place without using a calculator.

____

Name ______________________ Date ______________ Class ______________

MODULE 15

Response to Intervention

Pre-Test: Skills 2, 5, 11

Complete.

1. Write an expression to represent 6 groups of a number.

____

2. Write three ways to represent 10 times n.

____

3. Evaluate $\frac{p}{4}$ for $p = 24$.

____

4. Simplify the expression.

$0.65(2q + 1.8)$

____

5. Nick bought 3 books that cost the same amount of money and a magazine that cost $2. Write an expression that can be used to represent the total amount of money that Nick spent.

____

6. Write 6^{-4} using repeated multiplication.

____

7. The number of people at a concert can be described by 10^4. How many people went to the concert?

____

Evaluate.

8. 9^0 ______________________

9. 7^1 ______________________

10. 3^5 ______________________

Simplify. Write your answer using base-10 numerals.

11. $5^3 \cdot 5^3$

____

12. $\frac{9^3}{9^5}$

____

13. $(3 \cdot 4)^3$

____

14. $(6^2)^2$

____

15. $(2^{-3})^5$

____

Solve.

16. $3r - 6 = 9$

____

17. $4s + 8 = 24$

____

18. $\frac{5}{6}t - 3 = -9$

____

19. $-2u - 7 = 5$

____

20. $4v - 2 = 2v + 8$

____

21. $6(w - 2) = 12$

____

Name ________________ Date ________ Class ________

MODULE 16

Response to Intervention

Pre-Test: Skills 4, 5, 15, 18

Complete.

1. Determine if each pair of ratios forms a proportion.

A $\frac{24}{3}$ and $\frac{56}{7}$ O Yes O No

B $\frac{60}{5}$ and $\frac{90}{6}$ O Yes O No

C $\frac{15}{27}$ and $\frac{20}{35}$ O Yes O No

D $\frac{18}{30}$ and $\frac{27}{45}$ O Yes O No

Use the table.

Number of Hours	Cost, in Dollars
1	8
2	16
3	24
4	32
5	40

2. What is the constant rate of change?

____

3. Write an equation in the form of $y = kx$ to describe the relationship between the number of hours, x, and the cost in dollars, y.

____

4. What is the value of 4^5?

____

5. Simplify $7^2 \cdot 7^{-5}$.

____

6. Tim bought 3 DVDs that cost a total of $45 before sales tax. The sales tax was 8%. What was the total cost of the DVDs?

____

7. In July there were 120 people at the town meeting. In August there were 72 people at the town meeting. What is the percent decrease?

____

8. Delia deposited $750 into a savings account that earns $2% annual simple interest. If Delia does not make any deposits or withdrawals, how much simple interest will Delia earn in 18 months?

____

9. Make a scatter plot using the data in the table.

Goals Scored	2	3	4	2	1	5	3	2	4	2	3	7
Goals Allowed	4	1	0	5	3	5	2	1	3	2	4	1

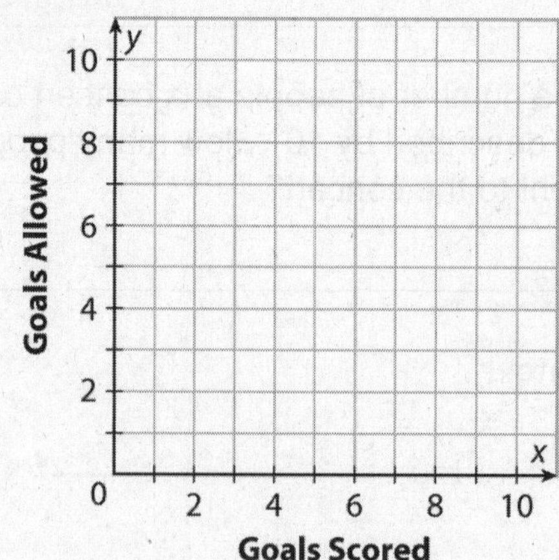

Name ______________________ Date ______________ Class ______________

MODULE 17

Response to Intervention

Pre-Test: Skills 1, 2, 5

Complete.

1. What is the opposite of 3?

2. What the absolute value of –5?

3. What is the sum of –7 + (–4)?

4. What is the sum of 8 + (–10)?

5. Darren is going to add 5 to –7 on a horizontal number line. He places a point at –7. In what direction will the arrow point to show adding 5?

6. The temperature was –3 °C at 9 P.M. By 2 A.M., the temperature had dropped by 6 °C. What was the temperature at 2 A.M.?

7. What addition expression is equivalent to 3 – (–7)?

8. Evaluate 4.6*a* for *a* = 1.5.

9. Evaluate 72 ÷ *b* for *b* = 6.

10. Write an expression to represent 18 less a number.

Simplify the expression.

11. $8(2c - 4) - 9$

12. $8 + 4d - 6e + 2 - 3d + 4e$

13. Evaluate for $f = -5$ and $g = 3$.

$$4f - 3g + 2f - 6$$

Write in exponential form. Use a whole number as the base.

14. $3 \cdot 3 \cdot 3 \cdot 3 \cdot 3 \cdot 3$ ______

15. $\frac{1}{6} \cdot \frac{1}{6} \cdot \frac{1}{6} \cdot \frac{1}{6} \cdot \frac{1}{6}$ ______

Evaluate.

16. 8^4 ______

17. 9^3 ______

18. 12^1 ______

Simplify. Write in exponential form.

19. $6^3 \cdot 6^4$ ______

20. $(5^3)^4$ ______

21. $(3^{-2})^{-4}$ ______

22. $(4 \cdot 5)^3$ ______

23. $\frac{5^2}{5^7}$ ______

Name ______________________ Date ______________ Class ______________

MODULE 18

Response to Intervention

Pre-Test: Skills 2, 5, 12

Complete.

1. Evaluate $0.36d$ for $d = 0.8$.

2. Evaluate $2.7 + e = 6.15$.

3. Evaluate $f - 4.6 = 2.53$.

4. Write an expression to represent 9 groups of a number.

5. Maureen bought 2 tops that cost *d* dollars and a pair of shoes. The shoes cost $20. Write an expression to represent the total amount, in dollars that Maureen spent.

Simplify the expression.

6. $9 - 3a + 4b + 2a - 3b + 4$

7. $7(3g - 2) + 4g$

Write in exponential form using a whole number as the base.

8. $9 \cdot 9 \cdot 9 \cdot 9 \cdot 9 \cdot 9 \cdot 9$

9. $\frac{1}{4} \cdot \frac{1}{4} \cdot \frac{1}{4} \cdot \frac{1}{4} \cdot \frac{1}{4} \cdot \frac{1}{4}$

Evaluate.

10. 4^0

11. 3^1

12. 5^4

Simplify. Write in exponential form.

13. $5^2 \cdot 5^6$

14. $\left(4^3\right)^2$

15. $\left(7^{-3}\right)^{-4}$

16. $(3 \cdot 2)^4$

17. $\frac{6^3}{6^{-6}}$

18. $\frac{8^{-2}}{8^4}$

Multiply.

19. $-4(7)$

20. $8(-5)$

21. $-6(-9)$

22. A diver was 10 feet below sea level. She descended 15 feet per minute for 3 minutes. What was her elevation after 3 minutes?

Divide.

23. $72 \div (-8)$

24. $-27 \div (-9)$

25. $\frac{24}{-6}$

26. The temperature at 3 A.M. was −12 °C. The temperature had changed by the same number of degrees each hour since 12 midnight, when the temperature was 0 °C. What was the change in temperature each hour?

Name ______________________ Date ____________ Class ____________

MODULE 19

Response to Intervention

Pre-Test: Skills 2, 3, 5, 10

Simplify the expression.

1. $5 + 6x - 8y + 2x - 9 + 3y$

____

2. $4(5a + 3) - 4a - 2$

____

Use the coordinate plane. Write the vertices of the image.

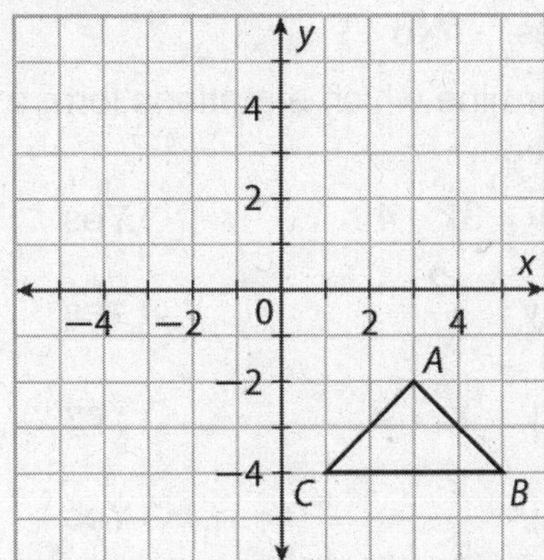

3. Translate triangle *ABC* 3 units left and 4 units up.

   A′ ________ *B′* ________ *C′* ________

4. Reflect triangle *ABC* across the *x*-axis.

   A′ ________ *B′* ________ *C′* ________

5. Reflect triangle *ABC* across the *y*-axis.

   A′ ________ *B′* ________ *C′* ________

6. Rotate triangle *ABC* 90° clockwise about the origin.

   A′ ________ *B′* ________ *C′* ________

7. Rotate triangle *ABC* 90° counterclockwise about the origin.

   A′ ________ *B′* ________ *C′* ________

8. Rotate triangle *ABC* 180° counterclockwise about the origin.

   A′ ________ *B′* ________ *C′* ________

Dilate triangle *DEF* using the origin as the center of dilation. Write the vertices of the dilated image.

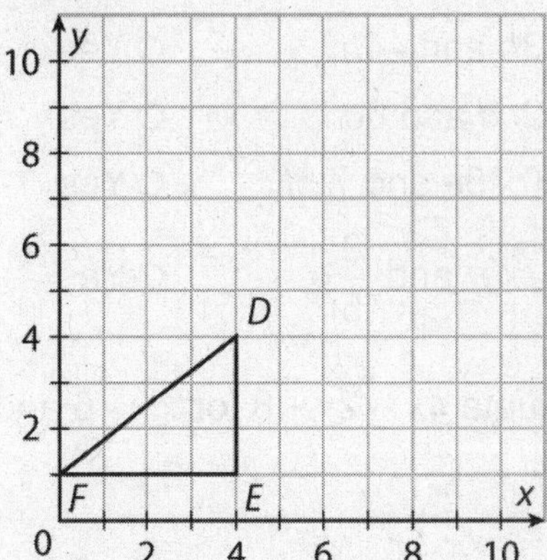

9. Scale of 2

   D′ ________ *E′* ________ *F′* ________

10. Scale of $\frac{1}{2}$

   D′ ________ *E′* ________ *F′* ________

Evaluate. Write your answer using base-10 numerals.

11. $(3^2)^3$ ______________________

12. $(2^{-3})^3$ ______________________

13. Is this relationship a function?

Input	Output
2	–3
3	4
4	7

○ Yes ○ No

Name ______________________ Date ______________ Class ______________

MODULE 20

Response to Intervention

Pre-Test: Skills 2, 5, 10

Complete.

1. What is another way to write $\frac{a}{4}$?

____

2. Decide which are like terms. Choose Yes or No.

A $3b$ and $-4b$ ○ Yes ○ No

B $2cd$ and $6c$ ○ Yes ○ No

C $0.75e$ and $7.5f$ ○ Yes ○ No

D $-4g$ and $\frac{3}{5}g$ ○ Yes ○ No

3. Evaluate $4x - 2y + 8$ for $x = -6$ and $y = 3$.

____

4. Evaluate $3(2x + 4y)$ for $x = 5$ and $y = 2$.

____

Simplify. Write the product using base-10 numerals.

5. $4^3 \cdot 4^2$ ______________________

6. $\frac{3^4}{3^8}$ ______________________

7. $(2^4)^2$ ______________________

8. $(3^{-2})^3$ ______________________

9. The number of marbles in a box can be described as $(3 \cdot 3)^4$. How many marbles are in the box?

____

10. Does this graph show a linear function?

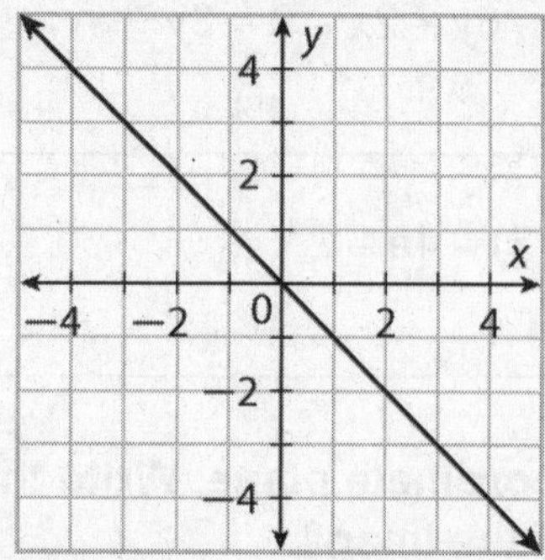

○ Yes ○ No

11. Determine which equations form a linear function.

A $y = 3x - 4$ ○ Yes ○ No

B $y = \frac{-2}{x}$ ○ Yes ○ No

C $y = x^2 + 2$ ○ Yes ○ No

D $y = \frac{x}{6}$ ○ Yes ○ No

12. The equation $y = 3x + 5$ represents the cost of buying pizza by the slice and a pitcher of lemonade. Complete the table.

Number of Slices, x	Cost in Dollars, y
3	
5	
7	
9	

Name ____________________ Date ____________ Class ____________

MODULE 21

Response to Intervention

Pre-Test: Skills 2, 5, 21

Write an expression.

1. 6 more than 2 times a number

2. 4 less than a number, split into 3 equal parts

3. A restaurant charges $40 per hour for renting its banquet room. In addition, each dinner costs $35. Write an expression to show the total cost for renting the banquet room.

4. Evaluate $2(3x + -2y)$ for $x = 3$ and $y = 6$.

Simplify. Write the product using base-10 numerals.

5. 2^9 ____________

6. $4^3 \cdot 4^4$ ____________

7. $(3^2)^{-2}$ ____________

8. $(5^{-2})^{-4}$ ____________

9. Write $8 \cdot 8 \cdot 8 \cdot 8$ in exponential form.

10. The number of pages in the book that Reggie is reading can be described as 7^3. How many pages long is Reggie's book?

Solve.

11. $4b - 6 = 20$

12. $3c + 9 = -6$

13. $\frac{2}{5}d - 4 = 8$

14. $-2e - 5 = -7$

15. $-5f + 3 = 12$

16. $0.42g + 3.36 = 2.52$

17. Caleb earned $12 per hour working at his mother's office. In addition, his mother gave Caleb $30 for a job well done. Caleb earned a total of $126 for the day. How many hours did Caleb work? Write and solve an equation.

18. There are 128 people still waiting in line to ride the flume. A total of 32 people have already taken their ride. Each car can hold 8 people. How many times will the flume cars be filled to accommodate all the people? Write and solve an equation.

Name ______________________ Date ______________ Class ______________

MODULE 22

Response to Intervention

Pre-Test: Skills 2, 5, 11

Complete.

1. Evaluate $18 + a$ for $a = -27$.

2. Evaluate $2.6b$ for $b = 2.5$.

3. Evaluate $3c + 4d - 2cd$ for $c = 6$ and $d = 3$.

4. Write an expression to represent 20 less a number.

5. Walt walks his dog the same number of times each day except Saturday when he walks his dog 4 times. Write an expression to represent how many times Walt walks his dog in a week.

Simplify. Write the product using base-10 numerals.

6. 6^0

7. 16^1

8. $9^{-2} \bullet 9^{-3}$

9. $\frac{7^6}{7^2}$

10. $\frac{6^2}{6^{-4}}$

11. $(4^4)^{-2}$

Solve.

12. $4b + 2 = 22$

13. $2c + 8 = -4$

14. $\frac{3}{8}d - 6 = 12$

15. $-5e + 2 = -18$

16. $4(f + 3) = -10$

17. $6(g - 4) = 18$

18. $4h + 8 = 2h - 6$

19. $-3j + 5 = 5j - 9$

Name ______________________ Date ______________ Class ______________

MODULE 23

Response to Intervention

Pre-Test: Skills 4, 6, 7, 10

Use the table.

x	3	6	9	12
y	10.5	21	31.5	42

1. What is the constant of proportionality?

____

2. Write an equation in the form of $y = kx$ to describe the relationship between x and y.

____

3. If $x = 20$, what is the value of y?

____

4. Graph the equation $y = 0.25x + 3$.

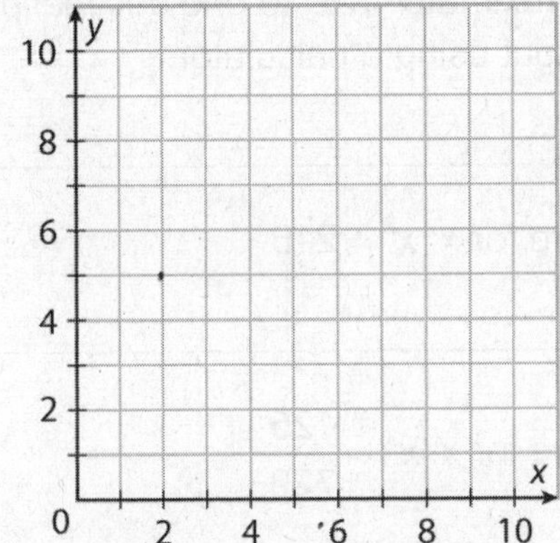

5. Determine if each shows a nonproportional relationship. Choose Yes or No for each.

A $y = 6x - 4$ ○ Yes ○ No

B $y = 5x$ ○ Yes ○ No

C $y = 0.9x$ ○ Yes ○ No

D $y = \frac{1}{3}x + 2$ ○ Yes ○ No

6. Graph the equation $y = 0.6x$.

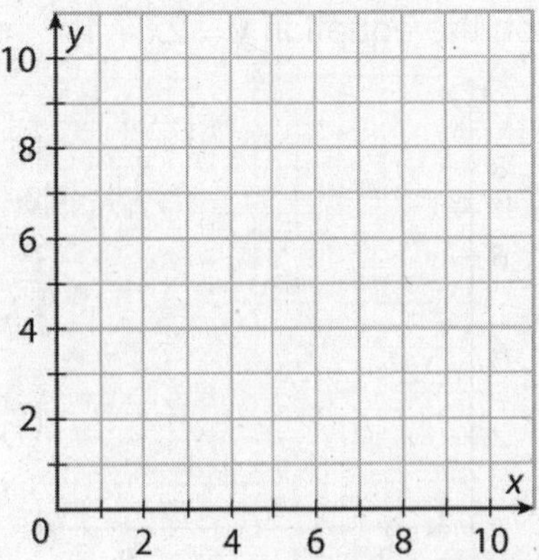

7. Determine if each shows a linear function.

A $y = x^2 + 2$ ○ Yes ○ No

B $y = 2x - 5$ ○ Yes ○ No

C $y = -x - 3$ ○ Yes ○ No

D $y = x^3 - 2$ ○ Yes ○ No

8. The equation $y = 8x + 10$ represents the number of minutes that Larry will exercise, where x represents the number of miles and 10 represents the number of minutes that Larry warms up. Complete the table.

x	y
0	
2	
4	
6	
8	

Name ______________________ Date ______________ Class ______________

MODULE 24

Response to Intervention

Pre-Test: Skills 6, 10, 31, 32

Complete.

1. Graph the equation $y = 2x + 1$.

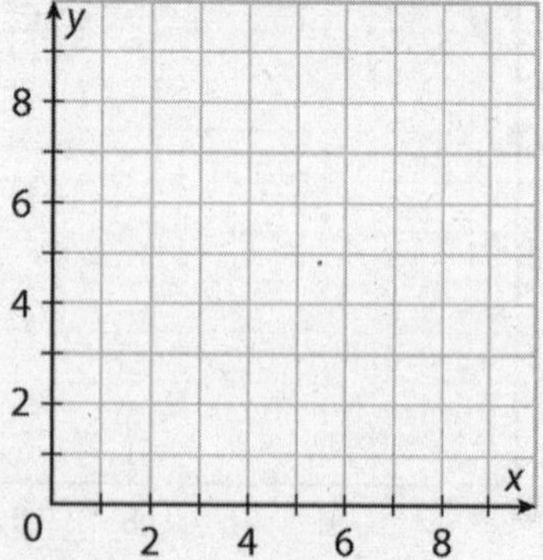

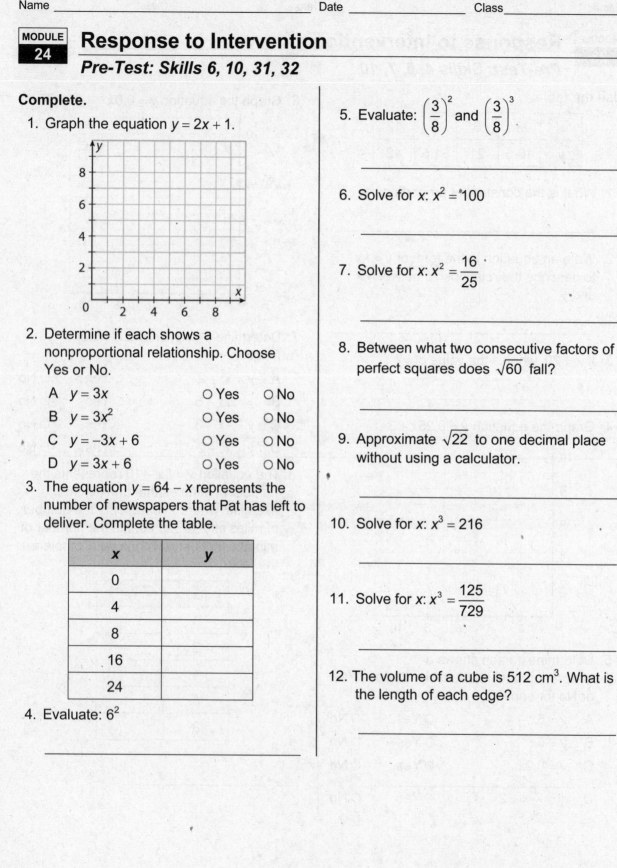

2. Determine if each shows a nonproportional relationship. Choose Yes or No.

   A $y = 3x$ O Yes O No
   B $y = 3x^2$ O Yes O No
   C $y = -3x + 6$ O Yes O No
   D $y = 3x + 6$ O Yes O No

3. The equation $y = 64 - x$ represents the number of newspapers that Pat has left to deliver. Complete the table.

x	y
0	
4	
8	
16	
24	

4. Evaluate: 6^2

____

5. Evaluate: $\left(\frac{3}{8}\right)^2$ and $\left(\frac{3}{8}\right)^3$.

____

6. Solve for x: $x^2 = 100$

____

7. Solve for x: $x^2 = \frac{16}{25}$

____

8. Between what two consecutive factors of perfect squares does $\sqrt{60}$ fall?

____

9. Approximate $\sqrt{22}$ to one decimal place without using a calculator.

____

10. Solve for x: $x^3 = 216$

____

11. Solve for x: $x^3 = \frac{125}{729}$

____

12. The volume of a cube is 512 cm^3. What is the length of each edge?

____

Name ______________________ Date ______________ Class ______________

SKILL 1

Response to Intervention

Post-Test: Add and Subtract Integers

1. What is the sum of –6 + –8?

____

2. What is the sum of 3 + (–7)?

____

3. What is the opposite of –4?

____

4. What is the absolute value of –6?

____

5. What is the difference of 6 – 9?

____

6. Find the difference.
   –4 – (–3)

   A –7 C 1

   B –1 D 7

7. The temperature at 9 P.M. was 4 °C. By 1 A.M., the temperature had dropped 7 °C. What was the temperature at 1 A.M.?

____

8. Erica is going to subtract 3 – (–4) on a number line. She places a point at 3. In what direction will the arrow point to show subtracting –4?

____

9. A football team gained 2 yards on its first play and lost 5 yards on its second play. Write an expression to represent this situation.

____

10. A group of hikers finished hiking at an elevation of –5 feet. The group started hiking at an elevation of 8 feet. What was the change, in feet, of the group's elevation?

____

11. What is the opposite of 3?

____

12. What is the difference of –5 – 7?

____

13. What addition expression is equivalent to 4 – (–8)?

____

14. Steve is going to add 2 to –6 on a number line. He places a point at –6. In what direction will the arrow point to show adding 2?

____

15. What is the sum of a number and its opposite?

____

16. A golfer plays two rounds. She scores –4 in the first round and –3 in the second round. What is her total score after two rounds?

____

17. Two absolute values are compared. Choose True or False for each comparison.

    A $|-3| > |4|$ ○ True ○ False

    B $|-5| > |2|$ ○ True ○ False

    C $|-4| < |-3|$ ○ True ○ False

    D $|2| < |-4|$ ○ True ○ False

Name ______________________ Date ____________ Class ____________

SKILL 2

Response to Intervention

Post-Test: Algebraic Expressions

1. Evaluate $15 + a$ for $a = -12$.

____

2. Evaluate $b - 9$ for $b = 5$.

____

3. Evaluate $0.8c$ for $c = 4$.

____

4. What is another way to write $\frac{d}{8}$?

____

5. Evaluate $48 \div e$ for $e = 6$.

____

6. Evaluate $5f + 3g - 8 \div 4$ for $f = 8$ and $g = 6$.

____

7. Decide which are like terms. Choose Yes or No.

A	$5g$ and $3h$	○ Yes	○ No
B	$6j$ and $5j$	○ Yes	○ No
C	$\frac{2}{5}k$ and $3k$	○ Yes	○ No
D	$0.6l$ and $0.75m$	○ Yes	○ No

8. Simplify the expression.
$3n + 4p - 5n + 2p - 6$

____

9. Mrs. Roberts bought 4 student movie tickets and one adult ticket that cost $12. Write an expression to represent the total cost of the tickets. Let *s* represent each student ticket.

____

10. Simplify the expression.
$5(3u - 4) + 6$

____

11. Simplify the expression.
$0.35(2v + 6) - v + 3$

____

12. Write an expression to represent *n* less than 10.

____

13. Write an expression to represent *n* split into 8 equal groups.

____

14. Write an expression to represent *n* and 3.

____

15. Evaluate the expression.
$8x - 4y + 2x + 4$ for $x = 3$ and $y = 4$.

____

16. Simplify the expression.
$6 + 4r - 5s + 2r - 4s + 2$

____

17. Write three ways to represent 8 times *m*.

____

____

18. To train for a race, Michele jogged 6 miles each day before the last two days before the race. She jogged 10 miles each of those two days. Write an expression to represent the number of miles that Michele jogged in preparation for the race. Let *d* represent the number of days.

____

Name ________________ Date ________________ Class ________________

SKILL 3

Response to Intervention

Post-Test: Algebraic Representations of Transformations

Use the coordinate plane. Write the vertices of the image.

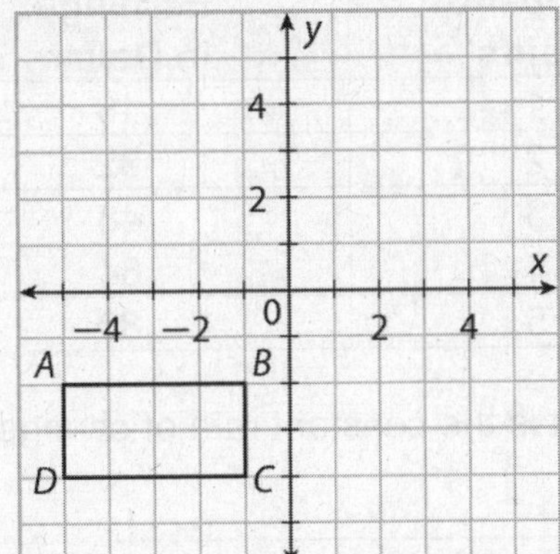

1. Translate rectangle *ABCD* 5 units right and 3 units up.

   *A'*___ *B'*___ *C'*___ *D'*___

2. Reflect rectangle *ABCD* across the *x*-axis.

   *A'*___ *B'*___ *C'*___ *D'*___

3. Reflect rectangle *ABCD* across the *y*-axis.

   *A'*___ *B'*___ *C'*___ *D'*___

4. Rotate rectangle *ABCD* 90° clockwise about the origin.

   *A'*___ *B'*___ *C'*___ *D'*___

5. Rotate rectangle *ABCD* 90° counterclockwise about the origin.

   *A'*___ *B'*___ *C'*___ *D'*___

6. Rotate rectangle *ABCD* 180° about the origin.

   *A'*___ *B'*___ *C'*___ *D'*___

7. Do any of the transformations above change the size of the rectangle? Explain.

   ____

   ____

   ____

Dilate triangle *LMN* using the origin as the center of dilation. Write the vertices of the dilated image.

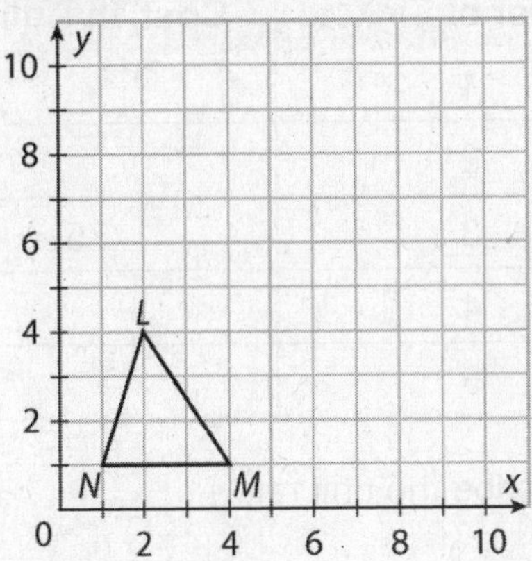

8. Dilate triangle *LMN* by a scale factor of 2.

   *L'*___ *M'*___ *N'*___

9. Dilate triangle *LMN* by a scale factor of $\frac{1}{4}$.

   *L'*___ *M'*___ *N'*___

10. Dilate triangle *LMN* by a scale factor of $1\frac{1}{2}$.

    *L'*___ *M'*___ *N'*___

11. Do any of the dilations above change the size of the triangle? Explain.

    ____

    ____

    ____

Name ______________________ Date ______________ Class ______________

SKILL 4

Response to Intervention

Post-Test: Constant Rate of Change

Use the table. Each ticket costs the same amount.

Number of Tickets	Cost, in Dollars
1	
2	
3	75
4	
5	

1. Describe the unit rate.

____

2. Complete the table.

3. What is the constant rate of change?

____

4. What is the cost for 12 tickets?

____

5. If Dan had $110, how many tickets could he buy?

____

6. Determine if each pair of ratios forms a proportion.

A $\frac{18}{2}$ and $\frac{45}{5}$ ○ Yes ○ No

B $\frac{50\text{ m}}{6\text{ s}}$ and $\frac{80\text{ m}}{10\text{ s}}$ ○ Yes ○ No

C $\frac{\$15}{3\text{ games}}$ and $\frac{\$25}{5\text{ games}}$ ○ Yes ○ No

D $\frac{26}{4}$ and $\frac{36}{6}$ ○ Yes ○ No

Use the table.

Number of Hours	Earnings, in Dollars
1	16
2	32
3	48
4	64
5	80

7. What is the constant rate of change?

____

8. What is the constant of proportionality?

____

9. Write an equation in the form of $y = kx$ to describe the relationship between x and y.

____

10. If Siobhan worked for 2.5 hours, what would her earnings be?

____

Use the table.

x	4	8	12	16
y	11	22	33	44

11. What is the constant of proportionality?

____

12. Write an equation in the form of $y = kx$ to describe the relationship between x and y.

____

Name ______________________ Date ______________ Class ______________

SKILL 5

Response to Intervention

Post-Test: Exponents

Complete.

1. Write $8 \cdot 8 \cdot 8 \cdot 8 \cdot 8 \cdot 8$ in exponential form.

2. The number of people in an auditorium can be described by 9^3. How many people are in the auditorium?

3. Write another way to represent 3^{-5}.

4. What is the value of 2^{-7}?

5. What is the value of 8^0?

6. What is the value of 15^1?

7. Write $\frac{1}{3} \cdot \frac{1}{3} \cdot \frac{1}{3} \cdot \frac{1}{3}$ in exponential form.

8. Simplify $8^2 \cdot 8^3$. Show your work.

9. Simplify $6^{-2} \cdot 6^{-3}$. Show your work.

10. Simplify $4^{-5} \cdot 4^3$. Show your work.

11. Simplify $9^2 \cdot 9^{-5}$. Show your work.

12. Simplify $\frac{5^6}{5^3}$. Show your work.

13. Simplify $\frac{2^3}{2^{-3}}$. Show your work.

14. Simplify $\frac{7^{-2}}{7^{-3}}$. Show your work.

15. The number of people at a parade can be described as $(8 \cdot 3)^3$. How many people are at the parade?

16. Simplify $(5 \cdot 2)^6$. Show your work.

17. Simplify $(7^2)^3$. Show your work.

18. Simplify $(4^{-3})^{-4}$. Show your work.

19. Simplify $(3^{-3})^3$. Show your work.

20. Simplify $(6^2)^{-4}$. Show your work.

Name ______________________ Date ______________ Class ______________

SKILL 6

Response to Intervention

Post-Test: Graphing Linear Nonproportional Relationships

Complete.

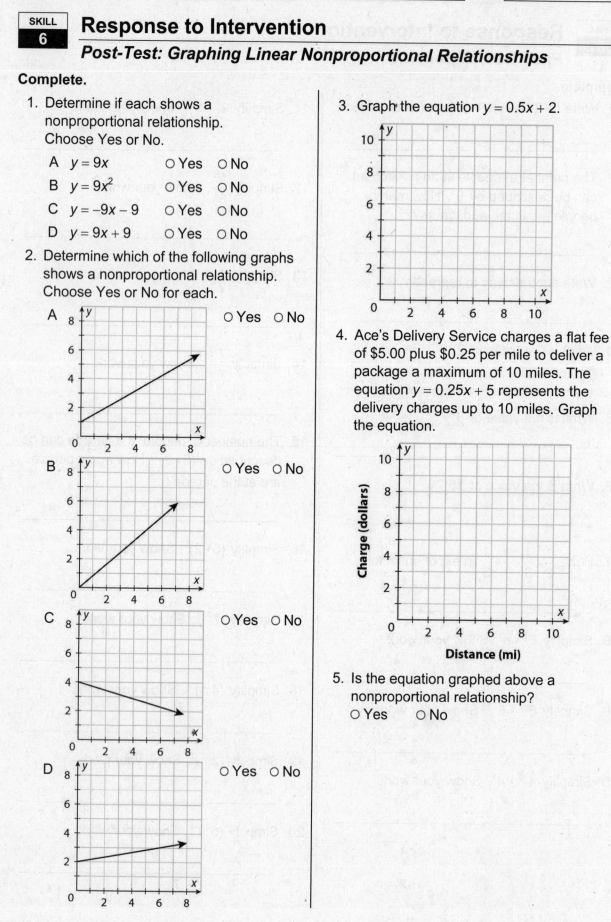

1. Determine if each shows a nonproportional relationship. Choose Yes or No.

   A $y = 9x$ ○ Yes ○ No

   B $y = 9x^2$ ○ Yes ○ No

   C $y = -9x - 9$ ○ Yes ○ No

   D $y = 9x + 9$ ○ Yes ○ No

2. Determine which of the following graphs shows a nonproportional relationship. Choose Yes or No for each.

   A 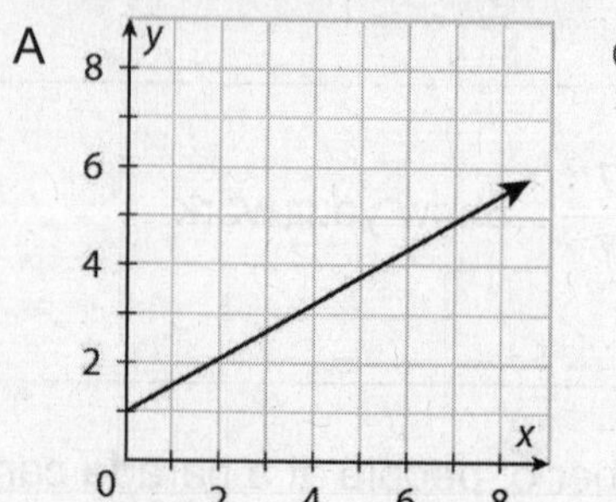 ○ Yes ○ No

   B 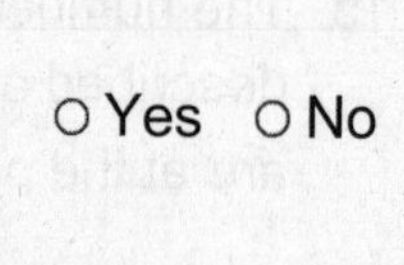 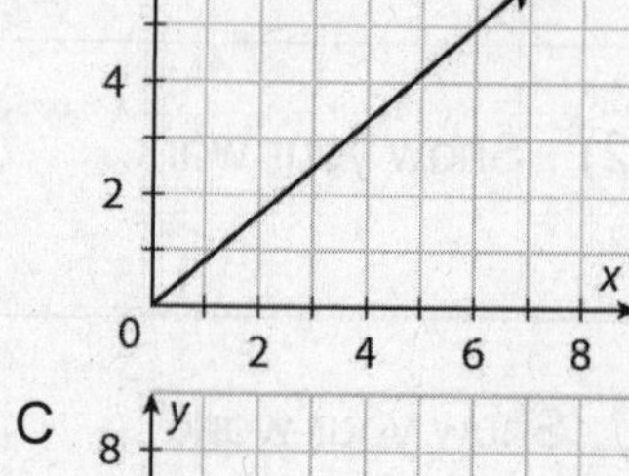 ○ Yes ○ No

   C 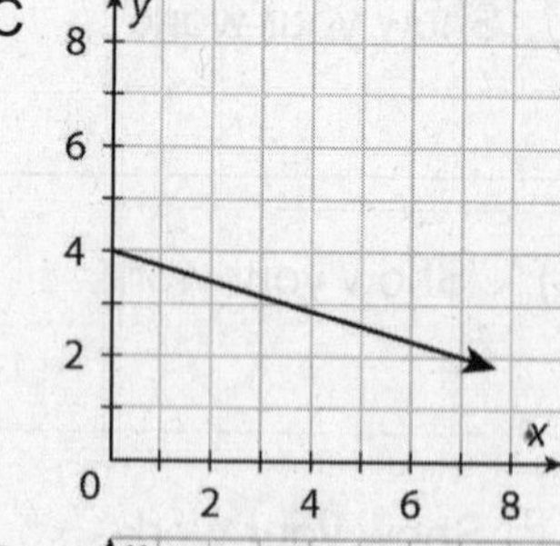 ○ Yes ○ No

   D 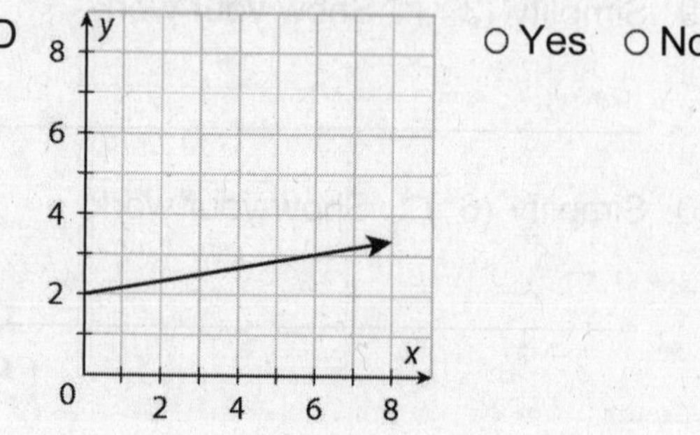 ○ Yes ○ No

3. Graph the equation $y = 0.5x + 2$.

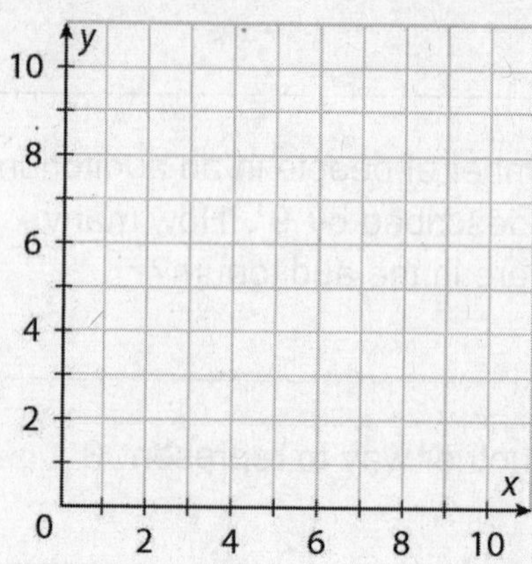

4. Ace's Delivery Service charges a flat fee of \$5.00 plus \$0.25 per mile to deliver a package a maximum of 10 miles. The equation $y = 0.25x + 5$ represents the delivery charges up to 10 miles. Graph the equation.

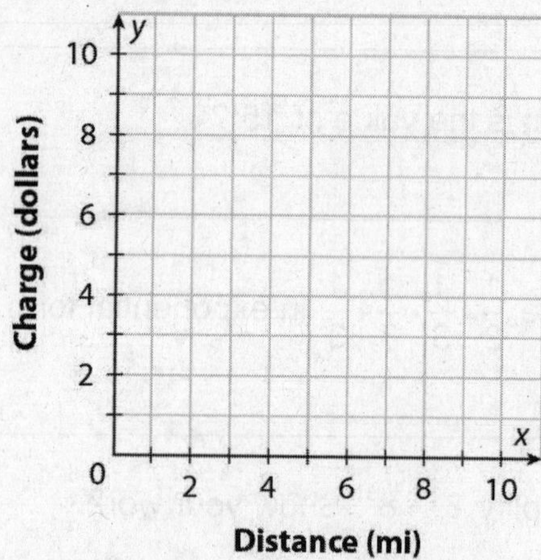

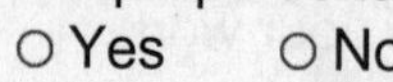

5. Is the equation graphed above a nonproportional relationship?
   ○ Yes ○ No

Name ______________________ Date ____________ Class ____________

SKILL 7

Response to Intervention

Post-Test: Graphing Linear Proportional Relationships

Choose the best answer.

1. Determine which of the following equations shows a proportional relationship. Choose Yes or No for each.

   A $y = 4x + 4$ ○ Yes ○ No

   B $y = 4x$ ○ Yes ○ No

   C $y = \frac{1}{4}x$ ○ Yes ○ No

   D $y = 0.4x$ ○ Yes ○ No

2. Determine which of the following graphs shows a proportional relationship? Choose Yes or No for each.

   A ○ Yes ○ No

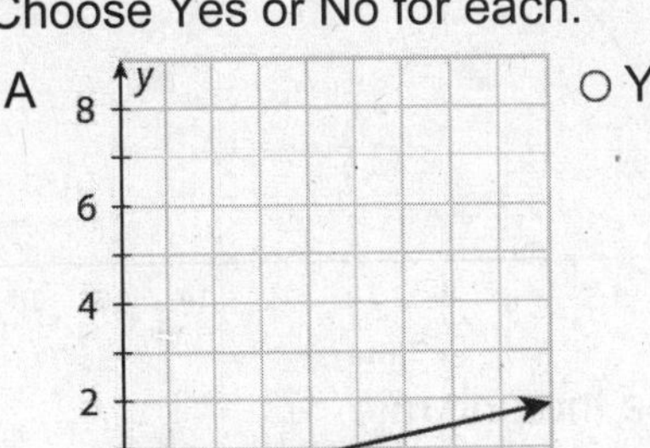
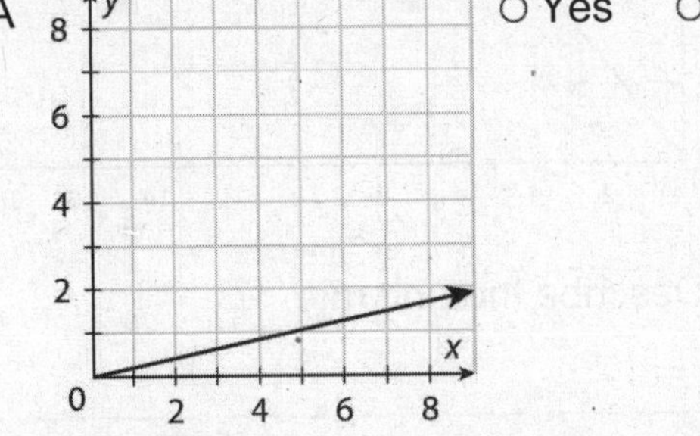

   B ○ Yes ○ No

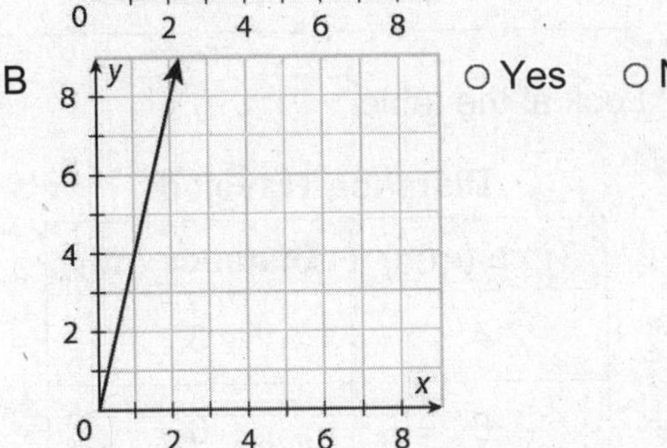

   C ○ Yes ○ No

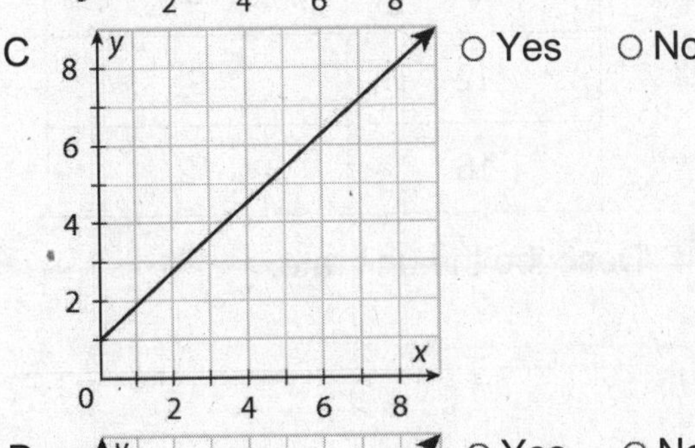

   D ○ Yes ○ No

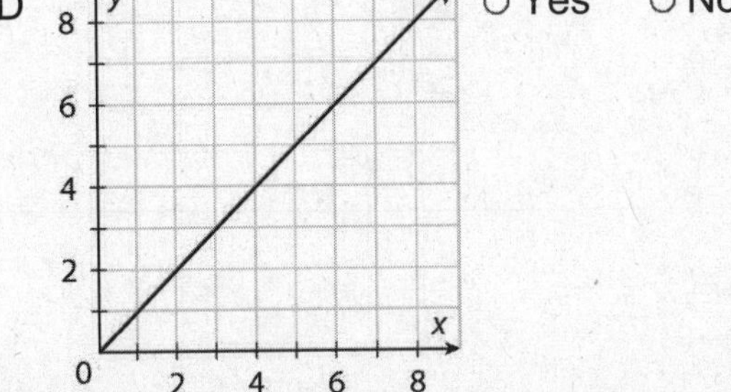

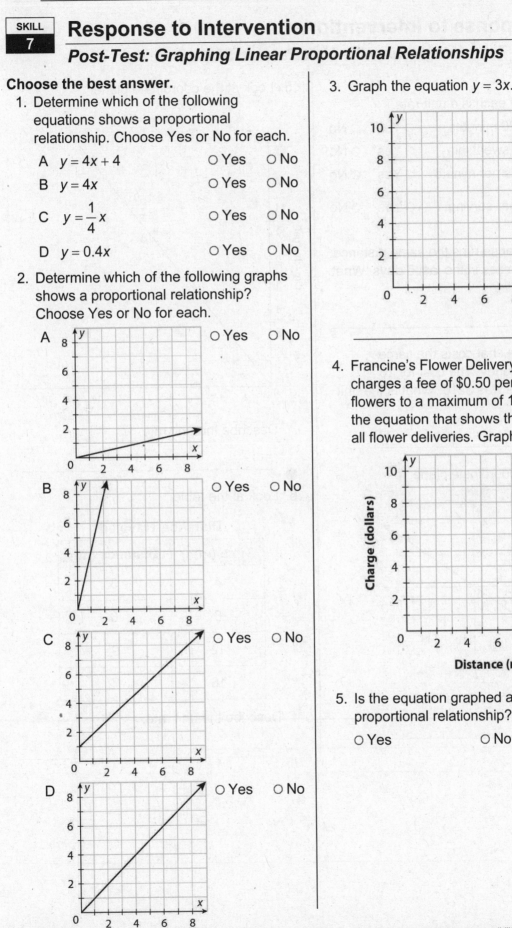

3. Graph the equation $y = 3x$.

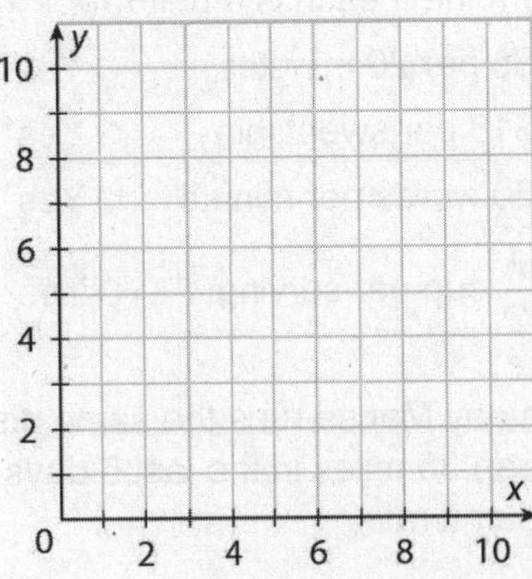

4. Francine's Flower Delivery Service charges a fee of $0.50 per mile to deliver flowers to a maximum of 10 miles. Graph the equation that shows the total cost for all flower deliveries. Graph the equation.

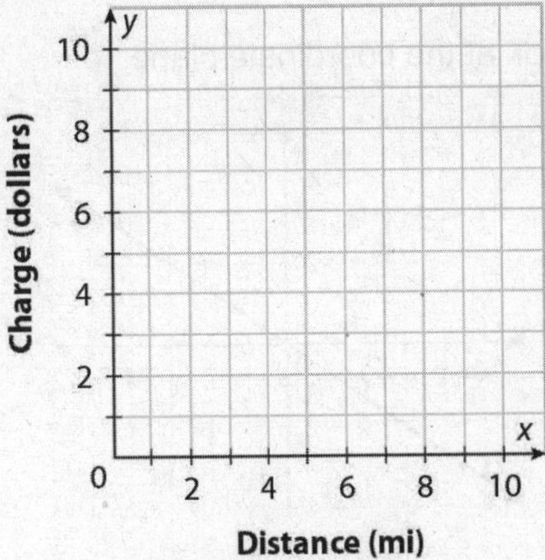

5. Is the equation graphed above a proportional relationship?

   ○ Yes ○ No

Name ______________________ Date ____________ Class ____________

SKILL 8

Response to Intervention

Post-Test: Interpreting the Unit Rate as Slope

Complete.

1. Determine if each is a unit rate.

A	\$5 per 20 minutes	O Yes	O No
B	\$18 per sweatshirt	O Yes	O No
C	60 words per minute	O Yes	O No
D	$\frac{1}{2}$ cup per serving	O Yes	O No

2. Each day Marisa runs the same distance. She ran 35 miles in the last 5 days. What is the unit rate?

____

3. Each baseball hat costs the same amount of money. The cost for 18 baseball hats was \$216. What is the unit price?

____

4. Look at the coordinate plane.

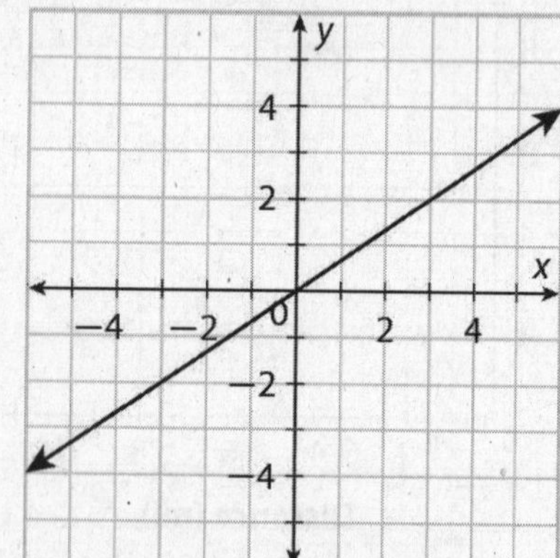

What is the slope of the line?

____

5. Look at the coordinate plane.

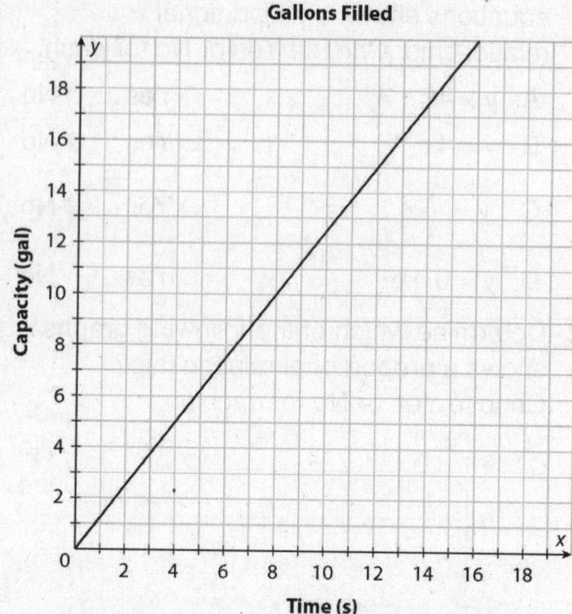

Describe the unit rate.

____

6. Look at the table.

Distance Traveled

Time (min)	Distance (mi)
4	3
8	6
12	9
16	12

Describe the unit rate.

____

Name ______________________ Date ______________ Class ______________

SKILL 9

Response to Intervention

Post-Test: Linear Associations

Complete.

1. Determine which of the following exhibit a linear association. Choose Yes or No for each.

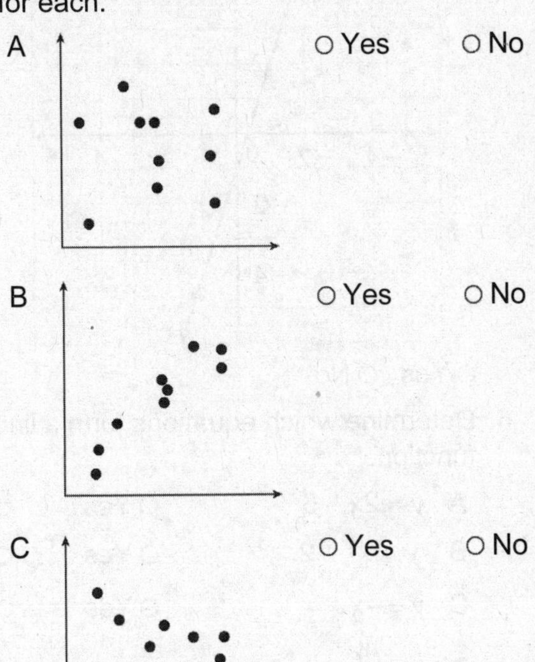

2. Determine which of the following shows a trend line. Choose Yes or No for each.

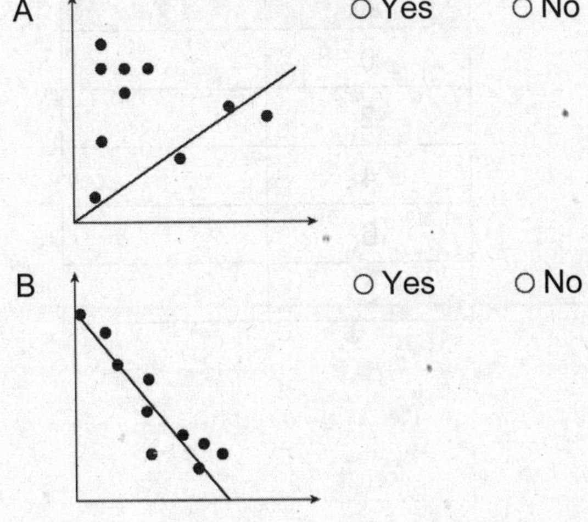

3. Draw the trend line.

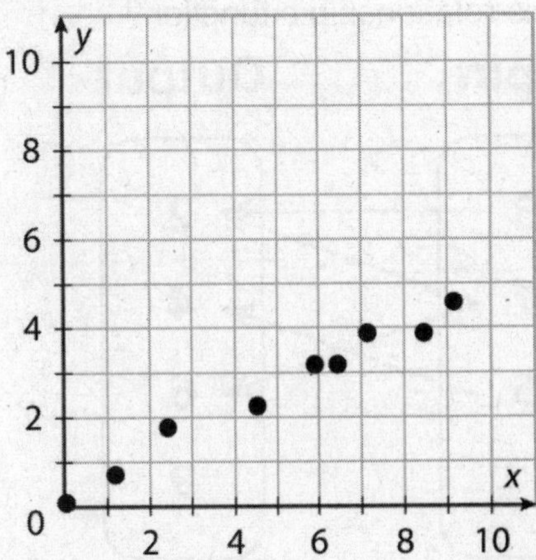

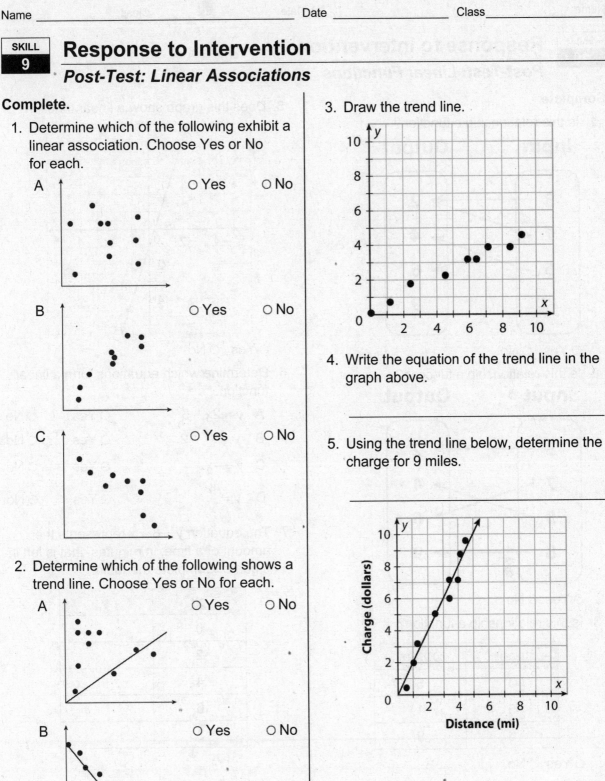

4. Write the equation of the trend line in the graph above.

____

5. Using the trend line below, determine the charge for 9 miles.

____

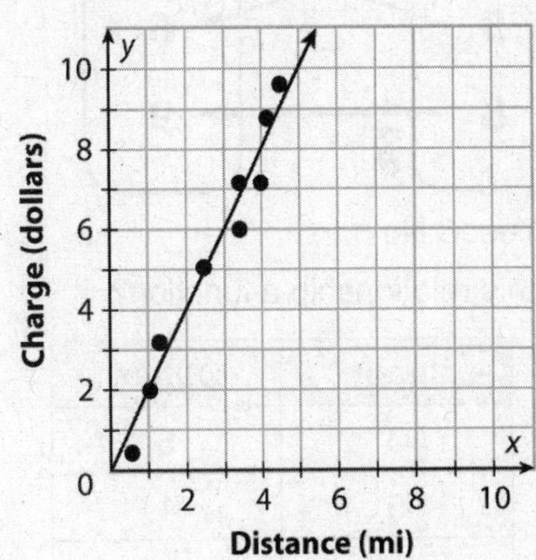

Name ______________________ Date ____________ Class ____________

SKILL 10

Response to Intervention

Post-Test: Linear Functions

Complete.

1. Is this relationship a function?

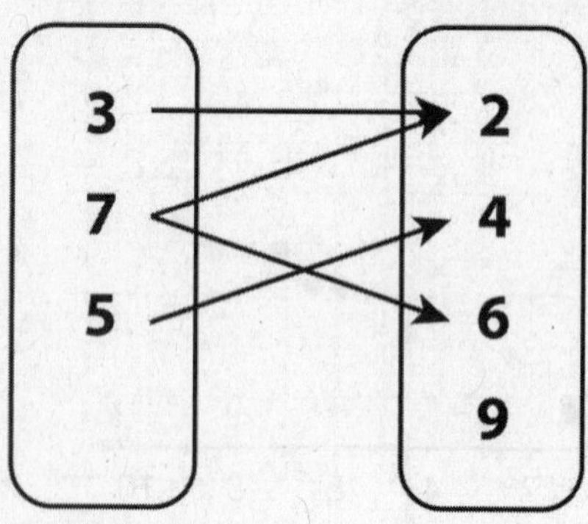

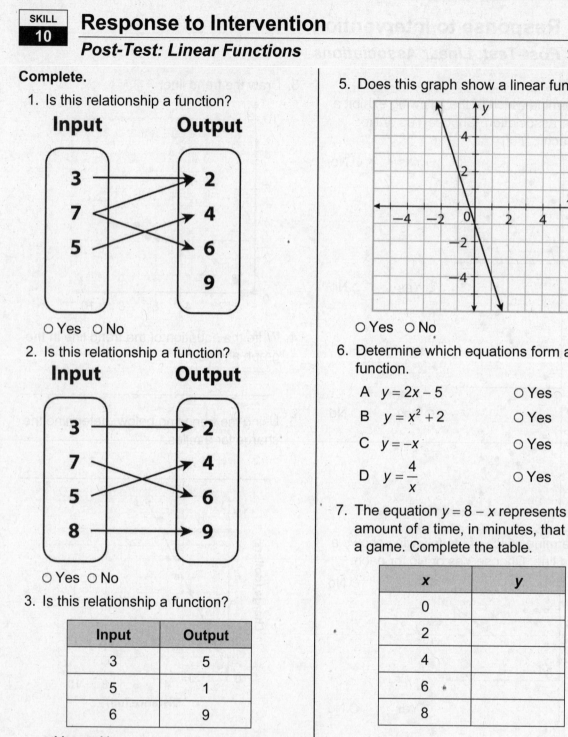

○ Yes ○ No

2. Is this relationship a function?

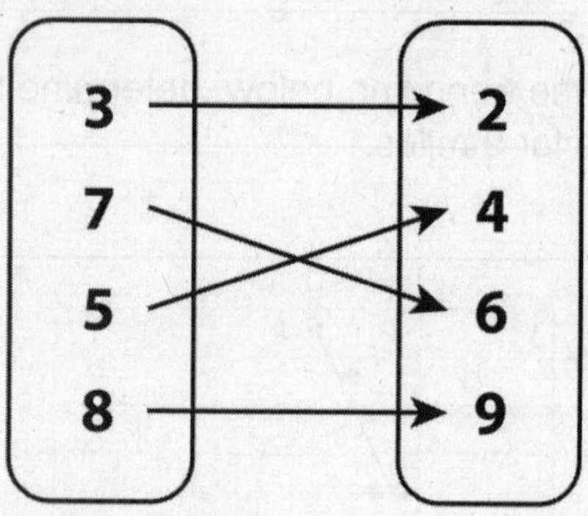

○ Yes ○ No

3. Is this relationship a function?

Input	Output
3	5
5	1
6	9

○ Yes ○ No

4. Describe a function.

____

____

5. Does this graph show a linear function?

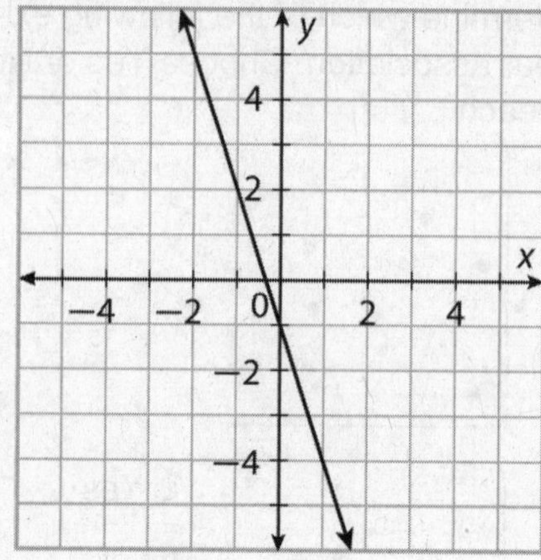

○ Yes ○ No

6. Determine which equations form a linear function.

A $y = 2x - 5$ ○ Yes ○ No

B $y = x^2 + 2$ ○ Yes ○ No

C $y = -x$ ○ Yes ○ No

D $y = \frac{4}{x}$ ○ Yes ○ No

7. The equation $y = 8 - x$ represents the amount of a time, in minutes, that is left in a game. Complete the table.

x	*y*
0	
2	
4	
6	
8	

Name ____________ Date ____________ Class ____________

SKILL 11

Response to Intervention

Post-Test: Multi-Step Equations

Complete.

1. What is the inverse operation of addition?

2. What is the inverse operation of division?

3. Solve: $5a + 4 = 19$

4. Solve: $3b - 2 = 7$

5. Solve: $-2c + 6 = 10$

6. Solve: $-4d - 6 = -10$

7. Solve: $\frac{3}{5}e - 2 = 5$

8. Solve: $-\frac{2}{3}f + 4 = 2$

9. Solve: $3(g - 2) = 8$

10. Solve: $5(h - 3) = 25$

11. Solve: $\frac{1}{4}j - 6 = 5$

12. Solve: $-3(k - 2) = -2$

13. Solve: $2m + 4 = 4m - 6$

14. Solve: $3n - 6 = n + 2$

15. Solve: $-4p + 6 = 3p - 1$

Name ______________________ Date ______________ Class ______________

SKILL 12

Response to Intervention

Post-Test: Multiply and Divide Integers

Complete.

1. What is the product of –3(5)?

2. What is the product of –4(3)?

3. What is the product of 6(–5)?

4. What is the product of 4(–7)?

5. Is the product of a negative integer times a positive integer positive or negative?

6. What is the product of –3(–9)?

7. What is the product of –5(–8)?

8. Is the product of two negative integers positive or negative?

9. Camilla played a game. She scored –8 on each of her first 4 turns. Write an expression that shows how to find Camilla's score after 4 turns.

10. Using the information in Question 9, what was Camilla's score after 4 turns?

11. What is the quotient of –16 ÷ 4?

12. What is the quotient of –35 ÷ 5?

13. What is the quotient of 48 ÷ (–6)?

14. What is the quotient of 63 ÷ (–7)?

15. If the dividend and divisor have the same sign, is the quotient positive or negative?

16. If the dividend and divisor have different signs, is the quotient positive or negative?

17. What is the quotient of –42 ÷ (–7)?

18. What is the quotient of –36 ÷ (–9)?

19. What is the quotient of $\frac{-14}{7}$?

20. What is the quotient of $\frac{-24}{-3}$?

21. A football team lost 9 yards on its last 3 plays. The team lost the same number of yards on each of the plays. Write an expression to show how many yards the team lost in each of the 3 plays.

Name ______________________ Date ______________ Class ______________

SKILL 13

Response to Intervention

Post-Test: One-Step Equations

Complete.

1. Write an equation for the following situation:

   8 times a number is equal to 56

   ____

2. Write an equation for the following situation:

   15 less than a number is equal to 12

   ____

3. Write an equation for the following situation:

   Nick has 12 books on each shelf. He has a total of 72 books. How many shelves are in the bookcase?

   ____

4. Write an equation for the following situation:

   Candice played two games. She scored 175 points in the first game. She scored 411 points in all. How many points did she score in the second game?

   ____

5. Solve: $0.82 + a = 1.51$

   ____

6. Solve: $\frac{3}{8} + b = \frac{3}{4}$

   ____

7. Solve: $c - 13 = 29$

   ____

8. Solve: $8d = -96$

   ____

9. Solve: $0.25e = 8$

   ____

10. Solve: $\frac{4}{5}f = \frac{2}{3}$

    ____

11. Solve: $\frac{g}{4} = 7$

    ____

12. Solve: $\frac{h}{6} = -3$

    ____

13. Mr. Thompson drives to work 5 days of the week. He drives the same distance each day. He drove 85 miles roundtrip last week for work. How many miles does Mr. Thompson drive each day for work? Write an equation and give the solution.

    ____

Name ______________________ Date ____________ Class ____________

SKILL 14

Response to Intervention

Post-Test: One-Step Inequalities

Complete.

1. Write an inequality for this situation:

   16 and a number is less than 28

   ____

2. Write an inequality for this situation:

   9 times a number is greater than or equal to 36

   ____

3. Solve:

   $1.3 + a < 5.2$

   ____

4. Solve:

   $\frac{1}{4} + b \geq \frac{11}{12}$

   ____

5. Solve: $c - 2.75 > 1.45$

   ____

6. Solve: $d - \frac{1}{3} < \frac{1}{6}$

   ____

7. Solve: $6e < 84$

   ____

8. Solve: $5f \geq -60$

   ____

9. Solve: $\frac{g}{7} > 9$

   ____

10. Solve: $-\frac{h}{4} > -12$

    ____

11. Airline passengers can put no more than 50 pounds into a suitcase before additional charges are added. Jill has 37.5 pounds in her suitcase already. Write an inequality to represent the situation.

    ____

12. Using the information in Problem 11, how many pounds can Jill still put into the suitcase?

    ____

13. Graph the solution to the following inequality:

    $3 + j \geq -2$

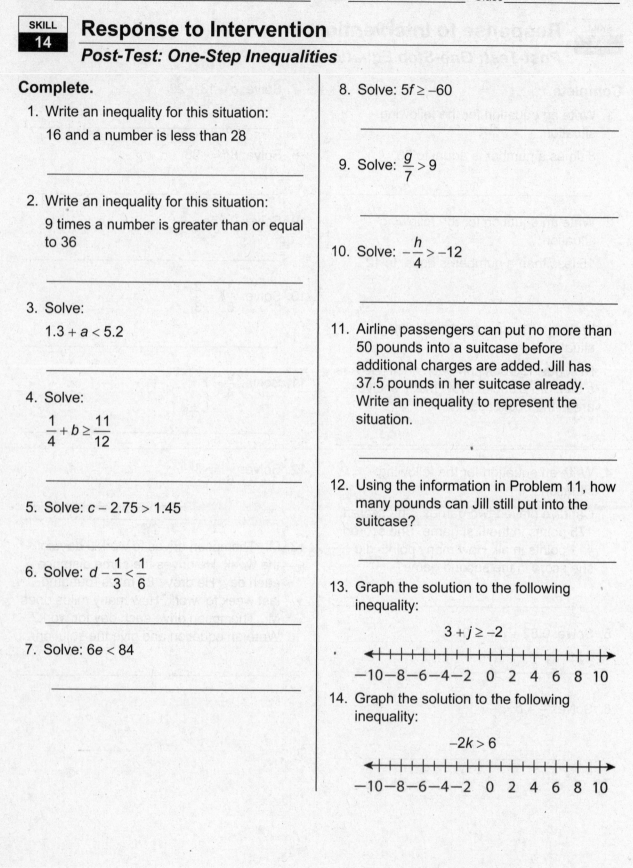

    −10 −8 −6 −4 −2 0 2 4 6 8 10

14. Graph the solution to the following inequality:

    $-2k > 6$

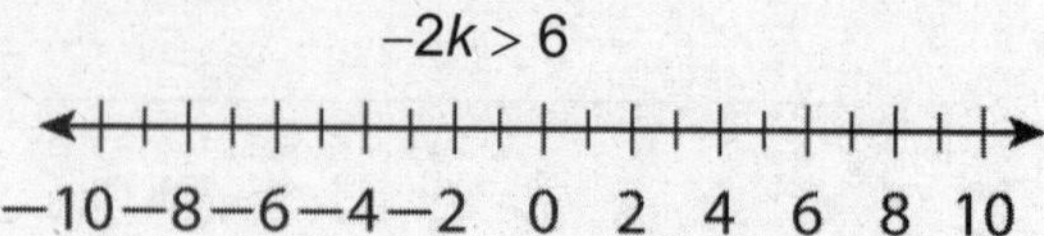

Name ______________________ Date ______________ Class ______________

SKILL 15

Response to Intervention

Post-Test: Percent

Complete.

1. James bought a game for $15. The sales tax is 8%. How much sales tax will James pay?

____

2. Miri bought 3 books for a total of $40. The sales tax on the books is 7%. How much will Miri pay for the books in all?

____

3. A computer game that normally costs $45 is on sale this week for 20% off. What is the sale price of the computer game?

____

4. The bike that Camila wants to buy normally costs $320. The bike is currently on sale for 15% off. What is the sale price of the bike?

____

5. The Tigers won 15 games last year. This year the Tigers have won 9 games. What is the percent decrease in the games that the Tigers have won?

____

6. The shirt that Jack wants to buy normally costs $36. He can buy the shirt for $27. What is the percent decrease on the cost of the shirt?

____

7. A fruit drink costs $0.10 for each glass. The Juice Shoppe charges $1.50 for each glass of fruit drink. What is the percent increase?

____

8. Alicia scored 240 points in a board game. She played again and scored 324 points. What was the percent increase in Alicia's scores?

____

9. Owen deposited $600 into a savings account that earns 3% annual simple interest. If Owen does not make any withdrawals or deposits, how much simple interest will he earn in 15 months?

____

10. Ms. Zimmer took out a $3,000 loan at 18% annual simple interest. If she pays back the loan in 6 months, how much simple interest will she pay?

____

11. The poster Chrissy wants to buy normally costs $7.50. The poster is on sale for 20% off and the sales tax is 5%. What is the total amount that Chrissy will pay for the poster?

____

Name ______________________ Date ______________ Class ______________

SKILL 16

Response to Intervention

Post-Test: Real Numbers

Complete.

1. Write $\frac{12}{25}$ as a decimal.

2. Write $\frac{11}{12}$ as a decimal.

3. Write 0.68 as a fraction in simplest form.

4. Write $0.6\overline{1}$ as a fraction in simplest form.

5. Solve for *x*: $x^2 = 144$

6. Solve for *x*: $x^2 = \frac{25}{121}$

7. Solve for *x*: $x^3 = 343$

8. Solve for *x*: $x^3 = \frac{8}{125}$

9. Approximate $\sqrt{70}$ to one decimal place without using a calculator.

10. Approximate $\sqrt{90}$ to one decimal place without using a calculator.

11. Use *real number, rational number, integer, whole number,* and *irrational number* to describe −18 in as many ways as possible.

12. Use *real number, rational number, integer, whole number,* and *irrational number* to describe $\sqrt{36}$ in as many ways as possible.

13. Use *real number, rational number, integer, whole number, and irrational number* to describe $\sqrt{15}$ in as many ways as possible.

14. Order from least to greatest:
$4\frac{3}{4}, \sqrt{21}, 4.65$

Name ______________________ Date ______________ Class ______________

SKILL 17

Response to Intervention

Post-Test: Scale Factor and Scale Drawings

Complete.

1. Which uses $\frac{4}{1} = \frac{x}{6}$ as the proportion to the find the actual distance between the city hall and the library? Choose Yes or No.

A ○ Yes ○ No

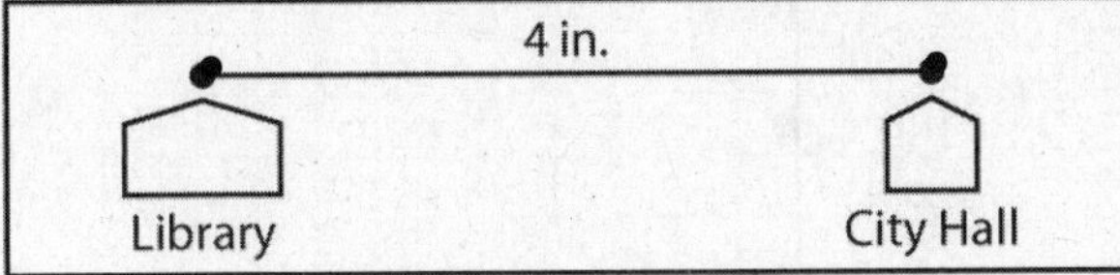

Scale: 1 inch = 6 miles

B ○ Yes ○ No

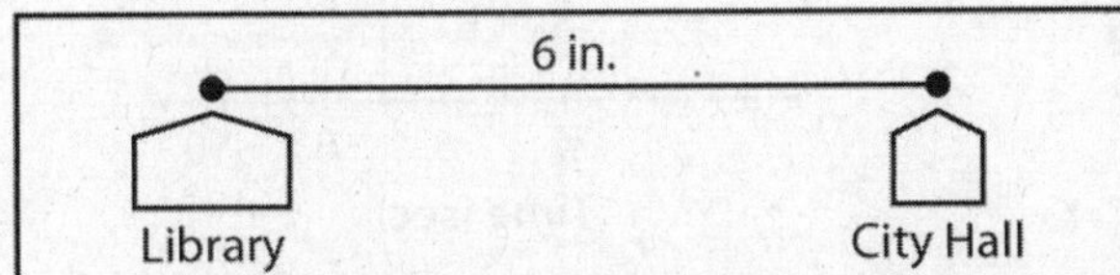

Scale: 4 inches = 1 mile

C ○ Yes ○ No

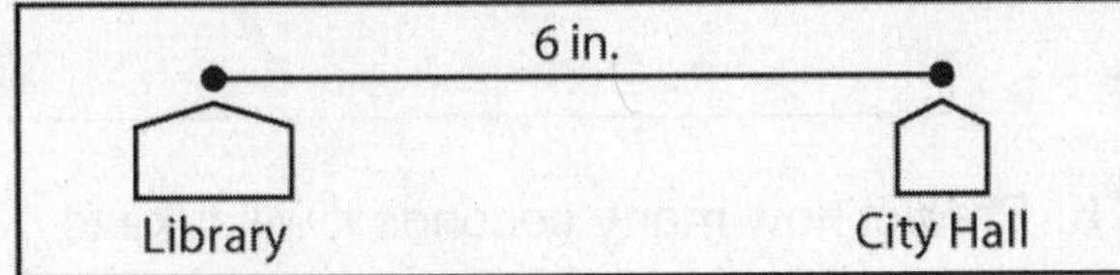

Scale: 1 inch = 4 miles

D ○ Yes ○ No

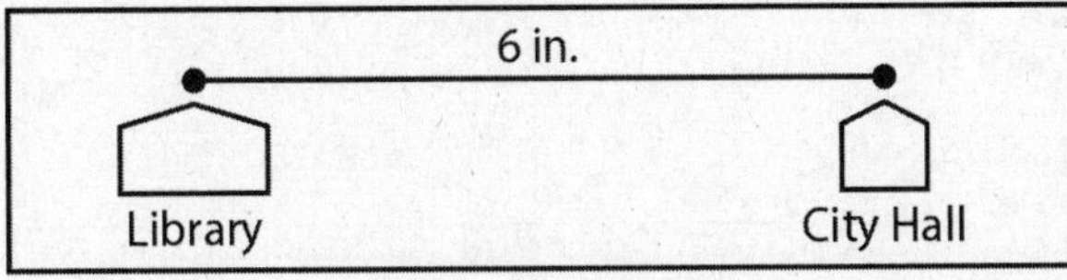

Scale: 2 inches = 8 miles

2. A scale drawing shows 1 inch = 3.5 feet. Fill in the table below using this ratio.

Blueprint length (in.)	Actual length (ft)
0.5	
1	
1.5	
	7
5	
7	
	35

Use the scale drawing to answer 3 and 4.

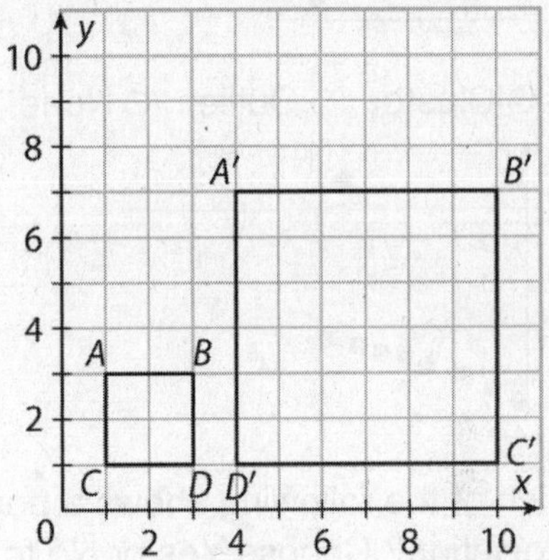

3. What is the scale factor used to draw $A'B'C'D'$? __________

4. What is the area of $A'B'C'D'$?

____

Name ______________________ Date ______________ Class ______________

SKILL 18

Response to Intervention

Post-Test: Scatter Plots

Choose the best answer.

1. Determine which of the following exhibit a cluster or outlier. Choose Cluster, Outlier, or None for each.

A ○ Cluster ○ Outlier ○ None

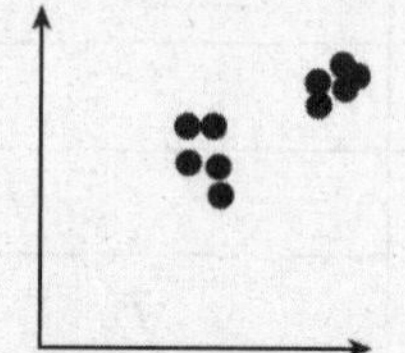

B ○ Cluster ○ Outlier ○ None

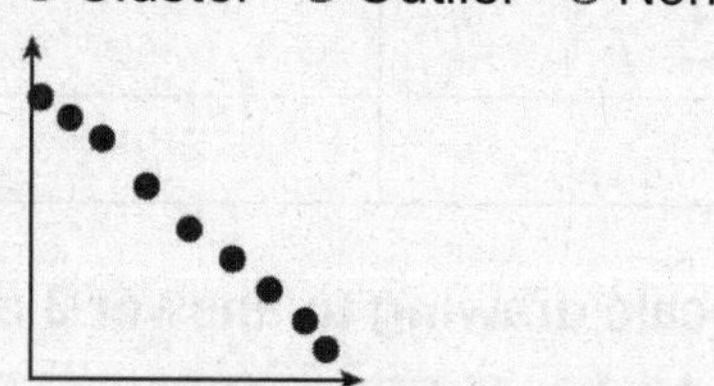

C ○ Cluster ○ Outlier ○ None

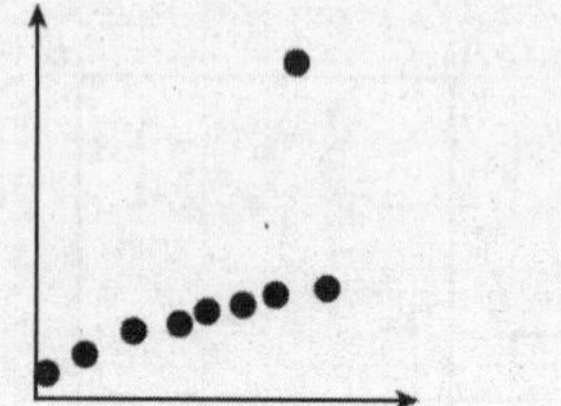

2. Which of the following shows a positive association? Choose Yes or No for each.

A ○ Yes ○ No

B ○ Yes ○ No

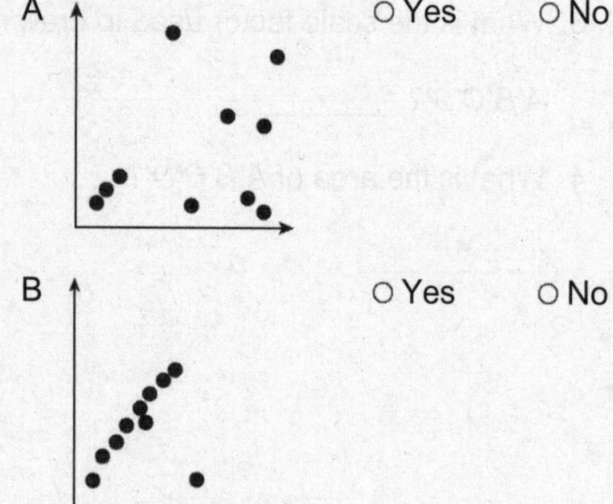

3. Make a scatter plot using the data in the table.

Time (sec)	1	5	4	4	2	5	1	3	2	2	3	3
Distance (ft)	2	9	8	9	4	8	1	5	3	5	7	6

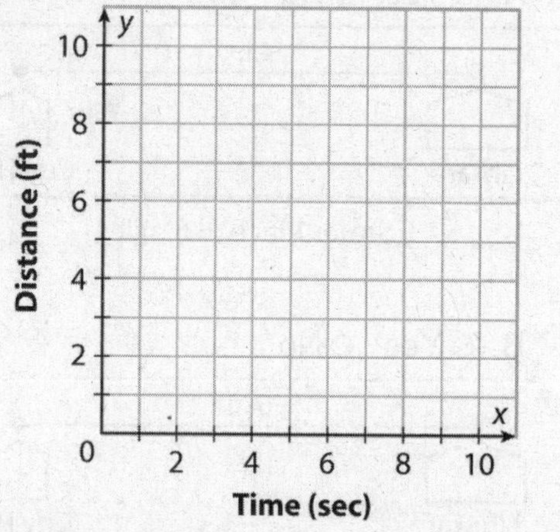

4. Draw the trend line on the scatter plot.

5. Predict how many feet will be traveled in 5 seconds.

____

6. Predict how many seconds it will take to travel 14 feet.

____

Name ________________________ Date ______________ Class ______________

SKILL 19

Response to Intervention

Post-Test: Significant Digits

Complete.

1. Choose the more precise measure.

   6 kg or 60 g

   ____

2. Choose the more precise measure.

   2 lb or 40 oz

   ____

3. Choose the more precise measure.

   3.82 ft or 3.7 ft

   ____

4. Choose the more precise measure.

   3.65 g or 4.3 mg

   ____

5. How many significant digits does 35,628 have?

   ____

6. How many significant digits does 40.92 have?

   ____

7. How many significant digits does 60,000 have?

   ____

8. How many significant digits does 0.0724 have?

   ____

9. How many significant digits does 0.06030 have?

   ____

10. Find the perimeter of the rectangle using the correct number of significant digits.

    Length: 12.8 cm; Width: 6.4 cm

    ____

11. Using the information in Problem 10, find the area using the correct number of significant digits.

    ____

12. Paige's backyard is rectangular. It has a length of 50 yards and a width of 80 feet. Find the perimeter of Paige's backyard using the correct number of significant digits.

    ____

13. Using the information in Problem 12, find the area using the correct number of significant digits.

    ____

Name ______________________ Date ____________ Class ____________

SKILL 20

Response to Intervention

Post-Test: Slope

Complete.

1. Tell whether the slope is positive, negative, zero, or undefined.

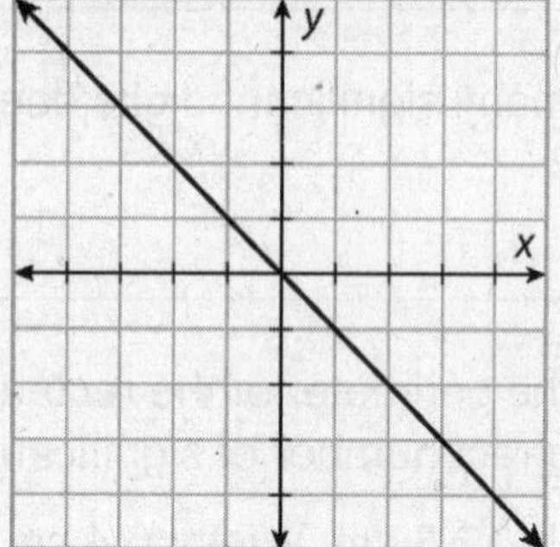

____

2. Tell whether the slope is positive, negative, zero, or undefined.

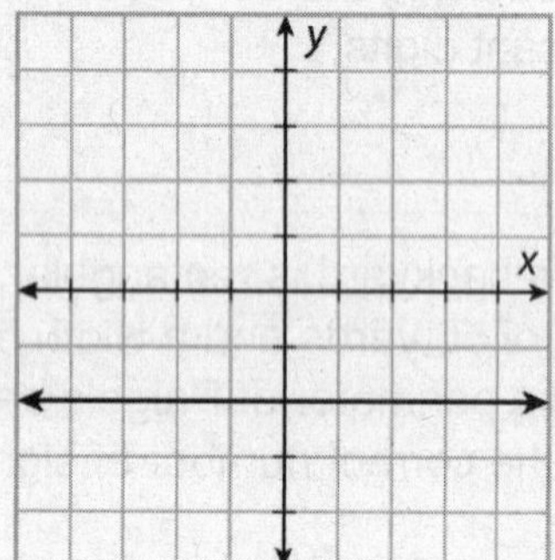

____

3. What is the slope?

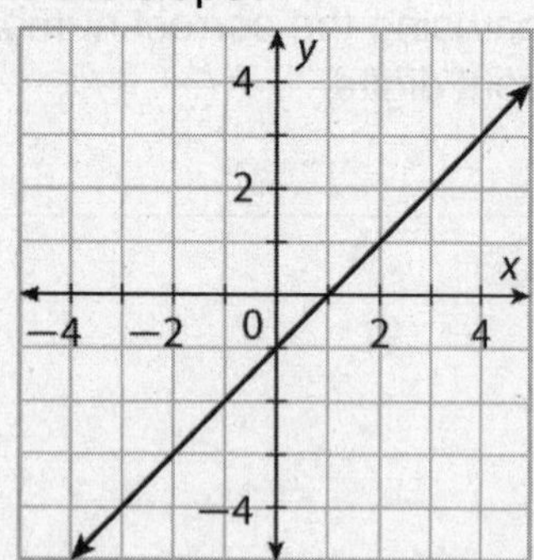

____

4. What type of line has an undefined slope?

____

5. What is the slope?

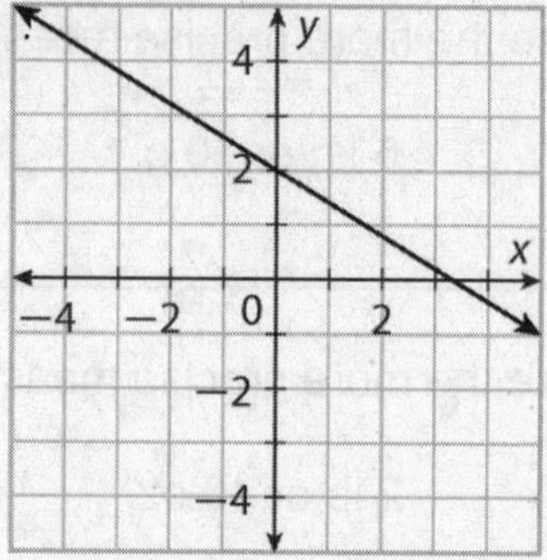

____

6. A line passes through (–2, –8) and (4, 10). What is the slope?

____

7. A line passes through (–6, 10) and (4, –10). What is the slope?

____

8. Use the table to write an equation in slope-intercept form.

x	1	2	3	4	5
y	3	5	7	9	11

____

9. Use the table to write an equation in slope-intercept form.

x	2	4	6	8	10
y	17	13	11	7	3

____

Name ______________________ Date ______________ Class ______________

SKILL 21

Response to Intervention

Post-Test: Two-Step Equations

Complete.

1. Samantha scored 15 points in her last basketball game. She made 3 free throws that are worth 1 point each. The rest of her points came on 2-point field goals. Write an equation that can be used to find the number of 2-point field goals that Samantha made.

____

2. Jeremy bought 3 pairs of pants that cost the same amount of money. He had a \$10 off coupon for the pants. Using the coupon, Jeremy spent \$35. Write an equation that can be used to find the cost of the pants before the coupon was applied.

____

3. Write a verbal description that can be represented by $6x + 8 = 32$.

____

____

____

4. Solve: $3a - 9 = 12$

____

5. Solve: $2b + 5 = 7$

____

6. Solve: $1.5c - 2.4 = 6$

____

7. Solve: $0.6d + 1.8 = 2.7$

____

8. Solve: $\frac{2}{5}e + 4 = 9$

____

9. Solve: $\frac{1}{4}f - 3 = 8$

____

10. Solve: $-2g - 5 = -3$

____

11. Solve: $-4h + 6 = 14$

____

12. Jackie made 6 playlists. Five of the playlists had the same number of songs. The sixth playlist had 22 songs. There were a total of 117 songs on the playlists. How many songs were on the each of the first 5 playlists? Write and solve an equation.

____

13. Erin bought a pair of shoes for 0.7 of the normal cost and a jacket that cost \$40. Erin spent \$75 altogether. What is the normal cost of the shoes? Write and solve an equation.

____

Name ______________________ Date ______________ Class ______________

SKILL 22

Response to Intervention

Post-Test: Two-Step Inequalities

Complete.

1. Wyatt has in his pocket 15 cents in nickels and a number of quarters. He has at least \$1.65 in his pocket. Write an inequality that can be used to find the number of quarters that Wyatt has in his pocket.

____

2. Ashley biked no more than 75 kilometers this week. She biked 15 kilometers on Saturday. Write an inequality that can be used to find the number of kilometers that Ashley averaged the other 6 days of the week.

____

3. Write a verbal description that can be represented by $3x + 9 < 24$.

____

____

____

4. Solve: $5j + 7 > 22$

____

5. Solve: $3k - 8 \leq 19$

____

6. Solve: $0.75l + 3.5 \geq 6.05$

____

7. Solve: $\frac{2}{3}m + 3 > 6$

____

8. Solve: $\frac{1}{4}n - 2 \leq 6$

____

9. Solve: $-2p - 4 \geq -8$

____

10. Solve: $-3q + 5 < 8$

____

11. Frank bought 6 DVDs and a poster at the mall. Each DVD cost the same amount and the poster cost \$8. Frank spent less than \$62. What is the maximum amount of money that Frank spent on each DVD? Write and solve an inequality.

____

12. Carly spent more than 180 minutes this week on her computer. She spent 45 minutes on Sunday and the same number of minutes each of the other 6 days. What is the minimum number of minutes that Carly spent on her computer each of the other 6 days? Write and solve an inequality.

____

13. Solve and graph the solution to $2x - 3 \geq 3$.

____

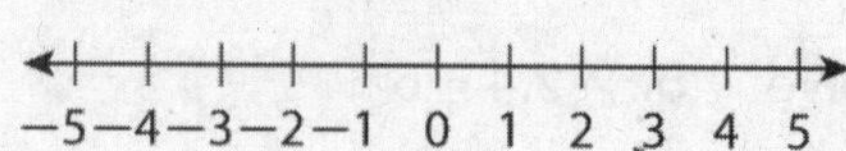

Name ______________________ Date ______________ Class ______________

SKILL 23

Response to Intervention

Post-Test: Unit Rates

Complete.

1. Is each a unit rate?

   A 30 miles per gallon ○ Yes ○ No

   B 36 points in 3 games ○ Yes ○ No

   C $2.75 per pound ○ Yes ○ No

2. Maggie baked 96 cookies in 4 batches. What is the number of cookies per batch?

   ____

3. An airplane can fly 270 miles in 30 minutes. How many miles can the airplane fly per minute?

   ____

4. Marco jogs 40.6 miles per week. He jogs every day. How many miles does Marco jog per day?

   ____

5. A carton of 6 eggs costs $1.44. At that rate, how much would a carton of 12 eggs cost?

   ____

6. A box of cereal costs $1.92 for 16 ounces. At that rate, how much would a 40-ounce box of cereal cost?

   ____

7. James has read 108 pages of a book in 3 days. At that rate, how many days would it take him to read 576 pages of the book?

   ____

8. Daisy made 6 phone calls in $\frac{1}{3}$ hour. At that rate, how many phone calls can she make in 1 hour?

   ____

9. Mrs. Lowry drove 20 miles in $\frac{2}{5}$ hour. What is Mrs. Lowry's speed in miles per hour?

   ____

10. A recipe calls for $\frac{3}{4}$ cup of water for every $\frac{2}{3}$ cup of pancake mix. How many cups of water are needed per cup of mix?

    ____

11. The table shows the costs of 3 packages of paper.

Number of Sheets	Price ($)
150	$0.90
250	$1.25
400	$2.20

    Which number of sheets is the best buy?

    ____

12. Using the information in the table, which unit price is the most expensive?

    ____

Name ______________________ Date ______________ Class ______________

SKILL 24

Response to Intervention

Post-Test: Writing Linear Equations

Complete.

1. A plumber charges $125 per hour plus a $50 fee for a house call. Write an equation in slope-intercept form to represent the situation.

____

2. Johann has traveled 15 miles from his station on the train. He will continue on the train at 80 miles per hour. Write an equation in slope-intercept form to represent the distance Johann will travel.

____

3. What is the equation from the data in the graph?

____

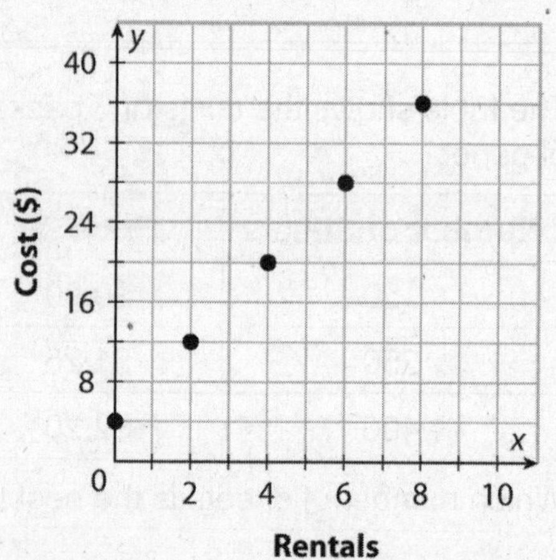

4. Mrs. Anderson earns $840 for 35 hours of work and $1320 for 50 hours of work within the same month. Write an equation in slope-intercept form to represent the situation.

____

5. Emma had 300 meters to run after running for 15 seconds. She had 50 meters to run after running for 65 seconds. Write an equation in slope-intercept form to represent the situation.

____

6. Write an equation that represents the data in the table.

Time (mo)	1	2	3	4	5
Weight (lb)	15	20	25	30	35

____

7. Write an equation that represents the data in the table.

Time (min)	2	4	6	8	10
Gallons	60	52	44	36	28

____

8. Write the equation of the line in slope-intercept form that connects the set of data points.

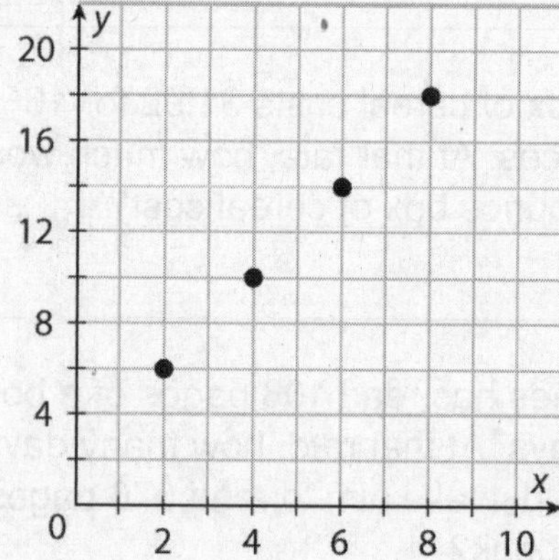

____

Name ______________________ Date ______________ Class ______________

SKILL 25

Response to Intervention

Post-Test: Two-Way Frequency Tables

Complete.

1. In a survey of 125 car owners, 16% said they own a hybrid. Of the car owners that own a hybrid, 80% said they would buy a hybrid the next time they need to buy a car. Of the car owners who do not own a hybrid, 40% said they would buy a hybrid the next time they need to buy a car. Fill in the two-way table.

	Will Buy Hybrid	Will Not Buy Hybrid	TOTAL
Own Hybrid			
Do Not Own Hybrid			
TOTAL			

2. At Greeley High School, 110 students were asked if they prefer basketball or volleyball. The two-way table is partially filled. Complete the table.

	Prefer Basketball	Prefer Volleyball	TOTAL
Boys		32	50
Girls	24		
TOTAL			110

Use the two-way table.

A total of 180 eighth-grade students were surveyed to determine if they prefer science or social studies. The data is displayed in the two-way table.

	Prefer Science	Prefer Social Studies	TOTAL
Boys	36	44	80
Girls	54	46	100
TOTAL	90	90	180

3. What is the relative frequency of a boy preferring science?

____

4. What is the relative frequency of a girl preferring science?

____

5. Is there an association between preferring science to social studies and gender? Explain your reasoning.

____

____

____

Name ______________________ Date ____________ Class ____________

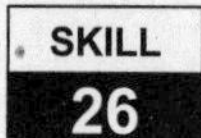

Response to Intervention

Post-Test: Two-Way Relative Frequency Tables

Complete.

1. Look at the frequency table.

Color	Red	Blue	Green	TOTAL
Frequency	36	24	15	75

Convert the frequency table into a relative frequency table. Use decimals.

Color	Red	Blue	Green	TOTAL
Frequency				

2. Complete the two-way frequency table.

	Cats	Dogs	Birds	TOTAL
Boys	8		3	24
Girls		12		
TOTAL	18		5	48

3. Convert the two-way frequency table into a two-way relative frequency table. Use decimals and round to the nearest hundredth, if necessary.

	Cats	Dogs	Birds	TOTAL
Boys				
Girls				
TOTAL				

4. Describe joint relative frequency.

____

____

5. Describe marginal relative frequency.

____

____

Ninth-grade students were asked to name their favorite subjects from three choices. The table shows the data.

	Alg. 1	World History	Sci.	TOTAL
Boys	18	30	12	60
Girls	14	10	16	40
TOTAL	32	40	28	100

6. Find the conditional relative frequency for each subject per gender. Round to the nearest hundredth, if necessary.

	Alg. 1	World History	Sci.
Boys			
Girls			
TOTAL			

7. Is there an association between preferring world history and gender? Explain your reasoning.

____

____

____

Name ______________________ Date ______________ Class ______________

SKILL 27

Response to Intervention

Post-Test: Absolute Value

Find the absolute value.

1. $|4| =$ _____

2. $|9| =$ _____

3. $|-3| =$ _____

4. $|-7| =$ _____

5. Describe absolute value.

____

____

Use this information to answer Questions 6 and 7.

Each player in a game starts with 0 points. After 1 round, Mike lost 10 points.

6. What is Mike's score written as an integer?

____

7. What is Mike's score written as an absolute value?

____

Compare. Use >, <, or =.

8. $|7|$ _____ $|9|$

9. $|5|$ _____ $|-3|$

10. $|-7|$ _____ $|-2|$

11. $|-5|$ _____ $|8|$

12. Belinda's game score is greater than –15 points. Does she need to score more than 15 points or fewer than 15 points to get her score back to 0? Explain your answer.

____

____

13. The temperature outside is less than –9 °C. Does the temperature need to increase by more than 9 °C or less than 9 °C to get back to 0 °C? Explain your answer.

____

____

Find the absolute value.

14. $|-3.4| =$ _____

15. $\left|5\frac{1}{3}\right| =$ _____

16. $|2.09| =$ _____

17. $\left|-6\frac{4}{5}\right| =$ _____

Compare. Use >, <, or =.

18. $|-3.5|$ _____ $|3.5|$

19. $\left|5\frac{1}{4}\right|$ _____ $\left|-6\frac{1}{2}\right|$

20. $\left|-\frac{5}{8}\right|$ _____ $\left|-\frac{7}{8}\right|$

21. $|-7.52|$ _____ $|4.39|$

Name ________________ Date ________ Class ________

SKILL 28

Response to Intervention

Post-Test: Measures of Center

Find the mode or modes of each data set.

1. 36, 54, 36, 57, 38, 54, 36

2. 70, 66, 80, 72, 64, 72, 80, 72

3. 42, 97, 58, 42, 61, 97, 73, 87, 95

Find the mean of each data set.

4. 57, 72, 48, 64, 83

5. 74, 68, 84, 93, 88, 91

6. Roger wants to have a mean score of at least 90 on his science quizzes. His scores are 88, 87, 92, and 86. What is the least score that he needs on his next science quiz to have a mean of at least 90?

Find the median of each data set.

7. 68, 92, 84, 77, 64

8. 89, 76, 64, 93, 88, 72

Identify the outlier in each data set. If there is no outlier, write *no outlier*.

9. 32, 57, 63, 58, 62

10. 76, 68, 82, 90, 64, 88

11. When there is an outlier does the mean or median better describe the data set? Explain your answer.

Use this information to answer 12–14.

The number of phone calls that Alicia makes each day is shown.

15, 10, 18, 8, 12, 15

12. What is the mode of the data?

13. What is the median of the data?

14. What is the mean of the data?

Name ______________________ Date ______________ Class______________

SKILL 29

Response to Intervention

Post-Test: Box Plots

Use the box plot to solve 1–5. All values are integers.

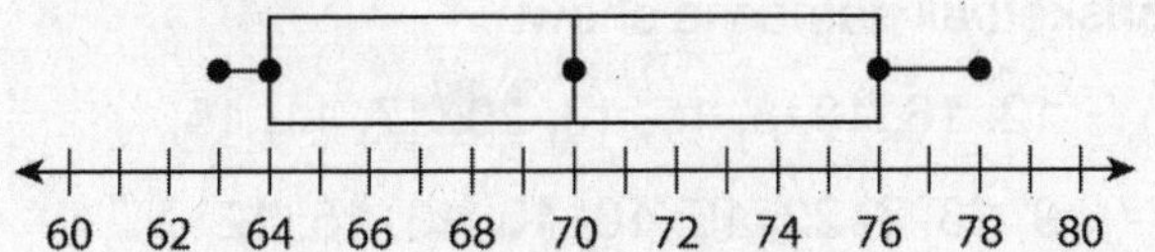

1. Greatest value ______________
2. Least value ______________
3. Lower quartile ______________
4. Median ______________
5. Upper quartile ______________

Use the data set below for 6–13.

48, 36, 30, 42, 40, 32, 42

6. Greatest value ______________
7. Least value ______________
8. Median ______________
9. Lower quartile ______________
10. Upper quartile ______________
11. Draw a box plot for the data.

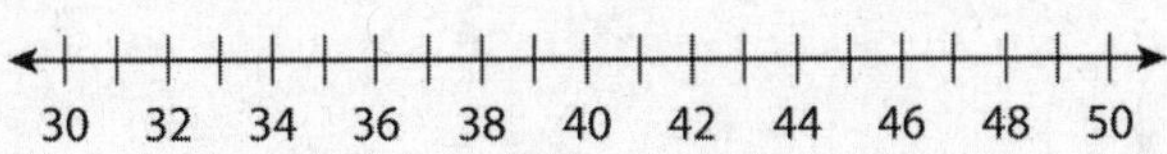

12. What is the range of the data set?

    ____

13. What is the interquartile range of the data set?

    ____

Use the data set below for 14–19.

8, 12, 6, 14, 16, 4, 16, 10

14. Median ______________
15. Lower quartile ______________
16. Upper quartile ______________
17. Draw a box plot for the data.

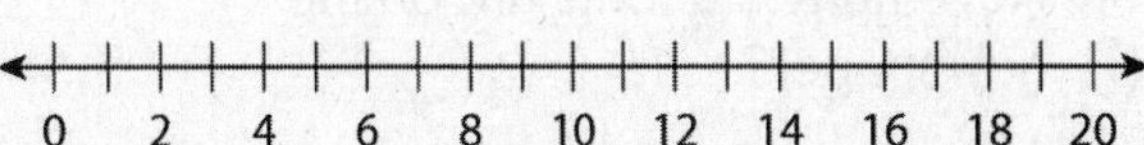

18. What is the range of the data set?

    ____

19. What is the interquartile range of the data set?

    ____

Name ______________________ Date ______________ Class ______________

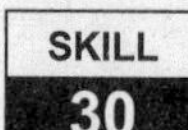

Response to Intervention

Post-Test: Histograms

Use the histogram to solve 1–4.
The histogram shows the number of letters that students on the school newspaper have in their last names.

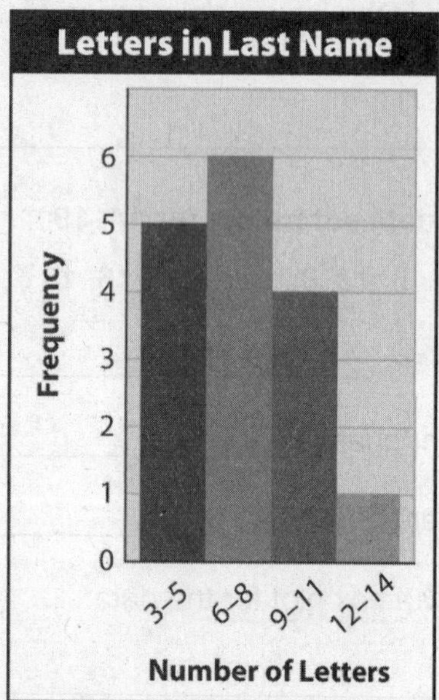

1. How many students are on the newspaper?

   ____

2. What percent of the students have less than 9 letters in their last names?

   ____

3. What percent of the students have 6–11 letters in their last names?

   ____

4. Could the median number of letters in a student's last name be 7? Explain your answer.

   ____

   ____

Use this information to solve 5 and 6.
The number of points that Kevin scored in his basketball games is shown.

12, 16, 10, 8, 15, 13, 20, 17, 11, 15,
9, 13, 7, 22, 16, 18, 10, 13, 15, 12

5. If you were to pick 4 intervals to use, what would they be? Explain your answer.

   ____

   ____

   ____

6. Make a histogram to represent the data.

Name ________________ Date ________________ Class ________________

SKILL 31

Response to Intervention

Post-Test: Squares and Square Roots

Evaluate.

1. $9^2 =$ ________________

2. $7^2 =$ ________________

3. $0.1^2 =$ ________________

4. $0.6^2 =$ ________________

5. $\left(\frac{2}{3}\right)^2 =$ ________________

6. $\left(\frac{1}{4}\right)^2 =$ ________________

7. Each side of a square is 15 inches. What is the area of the square?

____

Solve for *x*.

8. $x^2 = 25$ ________________

9. $x^2 = 64$ ________________

10. $x^2 = 0.81$ ________________

11. $x^2 = 0.04$ ________________

12. $x^2 = \frac{1}{49}$ ________________

13. $x^2 = \frac{9}{100}$ ________________

14. The area of a square drawing is 81 in^2. What is the length of each side of the drawing?

____

15. Is each number a square number? Choose Yes or No for each number.

A	24	O Yes	O No
B	49	O Yes	O No
C	64	O Yes	O No
D	88	O Yes	O No

Write the two perfect squares and their square roots that each of the following falls between.

16. $\sqrt{12}$ ________________

17. $\sqrt{45}$ ________________

18. $\sqrt{75}$ ________________

Approximate each square root to one decimal place without using a calculator.

19. $\sqrt{12}$ ________________

20. $\sqrt{45}$ ________________

21. $\sqrt{72}$ ________________

22. $\sqrt{90}$ ________________

23. The area of a square garden is 150 square feet. What is the length of each side of the garden, rounded to the nearest tenth?

____

Name ______________________ Date ____________ Class ____________

SKILL 32

Response to Intervention

Post-Test: Cubes and Cube Roots

Evaluate.

1. $1^3 =$ ______________

2. $5^3 =$ ______________

3. $0.4^3 =$ ______________

4. $0.8^3 =$ ______________

5. $\left(\frac{2}{3}\right)^3 =$ ______________

6. $\left(\frac{1}{4}\right)^3 =$ ______________

7. Each edge of a cube is 12 inches. What is the volume of the cube?

____

Solve for *x*.

8. $x^3 = 125$ ______________

9. $x^3 = 512$ ______________

10. $x^3 = 0.027$ ______________

11. $x^3 = 0.729$ ______________

12. $x^3 = \frac{1}{216}$ ______________

13. $x^3 = \frac{512}{729}$ ______________

14. The volume of a cube is 343 cm^3. What is the length of each edge?

____

15. Is each number a cube? Choose Yes or No for each number.

A	25	O Yes	O No
B	64	O Yes	O No
C	125	O Yes	O No
D	200	O Yes	O No

16. How many cube roots does each number have? Explain your answer.

____

____

____

17. If a number is a perfect cube, what do you know about its cube root?

____

____

18. Linda has a box that is shaped like a cube with a volume of 512 in^3. Tiffany has a box that is shaped like a cube with a volume of 216 in^3. How many inches greater are the edges of Linda's box than Tiffany's box?

____

Name ________________________ Date ______________ Class ______________

LESSON 1-1

Solving Equations

Reteach

Any addition equation can be solved by adding the opposite.
Any subtraction equation can be written as an addition.

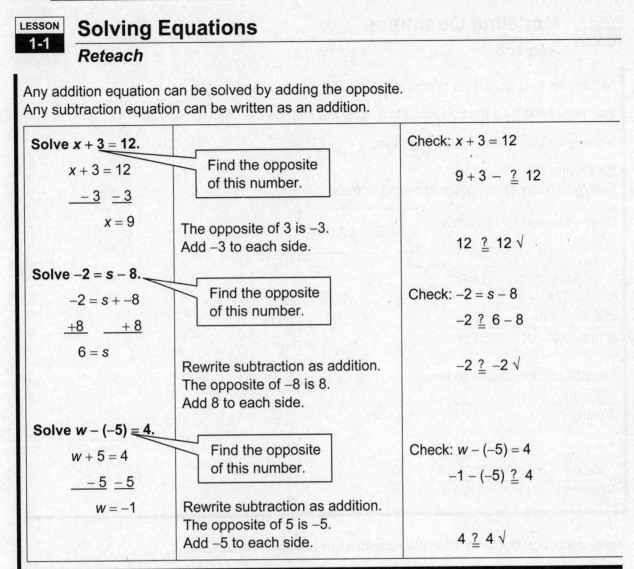

Solve $x + 3 = 12$. $x + 3 = 12$ $\underline{-3 \quad -3}$ $x = 9$	Find the opposite of this number. The opposite of 3 is –3. Add –3 to each side.	Check: $x + 3 = 12$ $9 + 3 \stackrel{?}{=} 12$ $12 \stackrel{?}{=} 12$ √
Solve $-2 = s - 8$. $-2 = s + -8$ $\underline{+8 \quad\quad +8}$ $6 = s$	Find the opposite of this number. Rewrite subtraction as addition. The opposite of –8 is 8. Add 8 to each side.	Check: $-2 = s - 8$ $-2 \stackrel{?}{=} 6 - 8$ $-2 \stackrel{?}{=} -2$ √
Solve $w - (-5) = 4$. $w + 5 = 4$ $\underline{-5 \quad -5}$ $w = -1$	Find the opposite of this number. Rewrite subtraction as addition. The opposite of 5 is –5. Add –5 to each side.	Check: $w - (-5) = 4$ $-1 - (-5) \stackrel{?}{=} 4$ $4 \stackrel{?}{=} 4$ √

Rewrite each subtraction as an addition. Solve.

1. $x - 7 = 12$ ______ ______
2. $y - (-1) = -5$ ______ ______
3. $-4 = p - 2$ ______ ______
4. $-7 = 4 - a$ ______ ______

Solve each equation. Check your answers.

5. $k + 10 = -6$ ______ ______
6. $-8 = g - 2$ ______ ______
7. $h - (-5) = 2$ ______ ______
8. $21 = d + 2$ ______ ______

Name ______________________ Date ____________ Class ____________

LESSON 1-2

Modeling Quantities

Reteach

Multiplying by 1 does not change the value of a number: $33 \bullet 1 = 33$

So, multiplying by a fraction equal to 1 does not change the value either: $33 \bullet \frac{5}{5} = 33$

Multiplying by 1 is like converting rates.

Example

Convert 150 feet per minute to miles per hour.

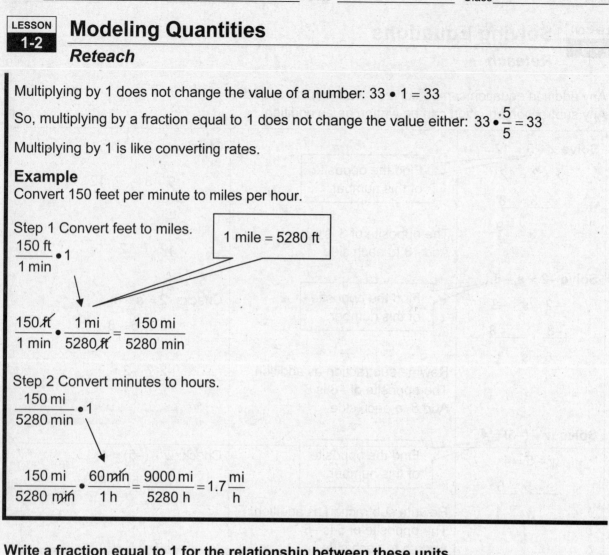

Step 1 Convert feet to miles.

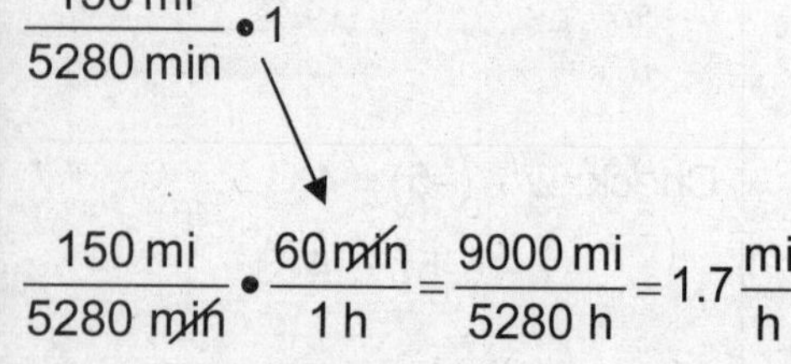

$$\frac{150 \text{ ft}}{1 \text{ min}} \bullet 1$$

$$\frac{150 \text{ ft}}{1 \text{ min}} \bullet \frac{1 \text{ mi}}{5280 \text{ ft}} = \frac{150 \text{ mi}}{5280 \text{ min}}$$

Step 2 Convert minutes to hours.

$$\frac{150 \text{ mi}}{5280 \text{ min}} \bullet 1$$

$$\frac{150 \text{ mi}}{5280 \text{ min}} \bullet \frac{60 \text{ min}}{1 \text{ h}} = \frac{9000 \text{ mi}}{5280 \text{ h}} = 1.7 \frac{\text{mi}}{\text{h}}$$

Write a fraction equal to 1 for the relationship between these units.

1. feet and yards

$\frac{\_\_\_\_ \text{ ft}}{\_\_\_\_ \text{ yd}} = 1$

2. meters and centimeters

$\frac{\_\_\_\_ \text{ m}}{\_\_\_\_ \text{ cm}} = 1$

3. fluid ounces and cups

$\frac{\_\_\_\_ \text{ fl oz}}{\_\_\_\_ \text{ c}} = 1$

Solve each proportion.

4. The 2004 Tour de France was 3391.1 kilometers. The winner won the race in a little over 83.5 hours. Fill in the blanks to find the winner's average speed in meters per hour.

$$\frac{3391.1 \text{ km}}{83.5 \text{ h}} \bullet 1 = \frac{3391.1 \text{ km}}{83.5 \text{ h}} \bullet \frac{\_\_\_\_}{\_\_\_\_} = \frac{\_\_\_\_ \text{ m}}{\_\_\_\_ \text{ h}} = \frac{\_\_\_\_ \text{ m}}{\text{h}}$$

5. A soft-serve ice cream machine makes 1200 gallons per hour. Convert this rate to cups per minute.

(Hint: 1 gallon = 16 cups) ______________________

Name ______________________________ Date _______________ Class _______________

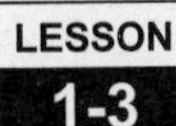

Reporting with Precision and Accuracy

Reteach

In measurements with different units and the same number of significant digits, the more precise measurement is the one with smaller units.

Seconds are more precise than hours.
Feet are more precise than miles.

If the units are the same, the more precise measurement has **more significant digits**.

Examples

Choose the more precise measurement in each pair.

3 ft; 36 in.	An inch is smaller than a foot. 36 inches is more precise.
5 lb; 81 oz	An ounce is smaller than a pound. 81 ounces is more precise.
0.68 c; 0.680 c	0.680 cups is more precise. (3 significant digits)
2450 h; 2405 h	2405 hours is more precise. (4 significant digits)

Determine which measurement is more precise.

1. 2 h; 180 min ________
2. 37.2 kg; 7.65 g ________
3. 2.5 in.; 2.50 in. ________
4. 0.08 qt; 7.203 qt ________

When calculating with measurements, the answer can be only as precise as the *least* precise measurement.

When you are **adding or subtracting,** find the number with the fewest decimal places. Round your answer to match.

When you are **multiplying or dividing,** find the least precise number and count its significant digits. Round your answer to the same number of significant digits.

Examples

Use the correct number of significant digits to rewrite the answer.

$2.5 \text{ ft} \times 3.01 \text{ ft} = 7.525 \text{ ft}^2$	Two significant digits: the answer is 7.5 ft^2.
$2.5 \text{ ft} + 3.01 \text{ ft} = 5.51 \text{ ft}$	One decimal place: the answer is 5.5 ft.
$2.5 \text{ ft} \div 3.01 \text{ ft} = 0.830565 \text{ ft}$	Two significant digits: the answer is 0.83 ft.

Simplify. Use the correct number of significant digits in your answer.

5. $12.8 \text{ c} \div 4 \text{ c}$ ________
6. $30.27 \text{ yd} + 5.1 \text{ yd}$ ________
7. $9.08 \text{ oz} - 4.2 \text{ oz}$ ________
8. $6.05 \text{ mi} \times 7 \text{ mi}$ ________

Name ______________________ Date ______________ Class ______________

Modeling with Expressions

Reteach

A **numerical expression** contains operations and numbers.	$4 + 3 - 1$ is a numerical expression.
An **algebraic expression** contains operations, numbers, and at least one variable.	$5x + 3 - 7y$ is an algebraic expression.
Terms are the parts of the expression that are separated by addition signs. Rewrite subtraction to show addition.	Rewrite $5x + 3 - 7y$ to show addition: $5x + 3 + (-7y)$. The terms are $5x$, 3, and $-7y$.
A **coefficient** is a number that multiplies a variable.	5 is the coefficient of x. -7 is the coefficient of y. 3 does not multiply a variable, so it is not a coefficient.

Example

Write an expression that reflects the situation.

Jacques has 8 more DVDs than Erik. Write an expression for the number of DVDs Jacques has.

Erik has d DVDs. Jacques has 8 more DVDs. The word "more" shows addition.

Jacques has $d + 8$ DVDs.

Write an expression for each situation.

1. Enrique collected 7 more than 2 times as many recyclable bottles, b, as Natasha collected. Write an expression for the number of bottles Enrique collected in all.

____

2. Mr. McKay bought b boxes of crackers for \$3 each and p pounds of cheese for \$4 per pound. How much did he spend in all?

____

3. Jean walked 1 mile to her friend's house, and then bicycled for 2 hours at m miles per hour. Write an expression for the total length of her trip.

____

Name ______________________ Date ______________ Class ______________

LESSON 2-2

Creating and Solving Equations

Reteach

To write an equation for a real-world problem, look for words that will help you solve the problem and translate them into parts of the equation. For example, the sum of two times a number and 8 is 18 as shown below.

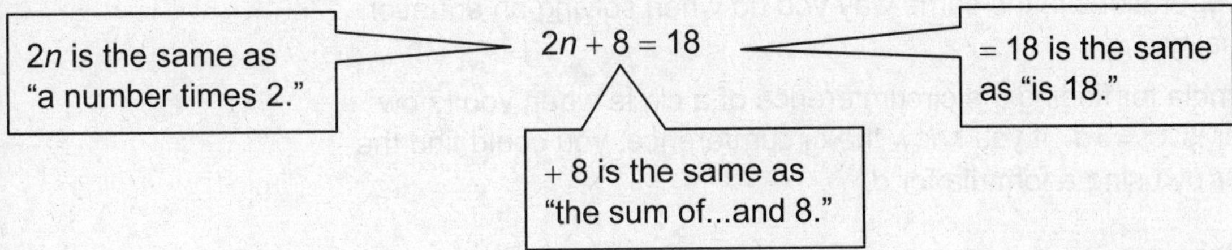
$2n$ is the same as "a number times 2."
$2n + 8 = 18$
= 18 is the same as "is 18."
+ 8 is the same as "the sum of...and 8."

Example

The Lions and Tigers played a football game. The Lions scored three more than three times the number of points the Tigers scored. The total number of points scored by both teams is 31. How many points were scored by each team?

points the Tigers scored	t
Lions scored three more than three times	$3t + 3$
total number of points scored by both teams is 31	$t + (3t + 3) = 31$

So the equation is $t + (3t + 3) = 31$. You can simplify and use Properties of Equality to solve.

Write an equation and solve each problem.

1. Mako runs m miles each day. De'Anthony runs twice as many miles as Mako. Altogether, they run 18 miles each day. How many miles does Mako run each day?

____

2. Bella's cell phone costs $18 per month plus $0.15 for every minute she uses the phone. Last month her bill was $29.25. For how many minutes did she use her phone last month?

____

3. Eric and Charlotte collected donations for the food bank. Charlotte collected 3 times the amount of Eric's donations minus $20. Eric and Charlotte combined their donations and spent half of the money on canned food. The rest of the money, $50, was donated to the food bank directly. How much money did each student collect?

____

Name ______________________ Date ____________ Class ____________

LESSON 2-3

Solving for a Variable

Reteach

Solving for a variable in a formula can make the formula easier to use. You can solve a formula, or literal equation, for any one of the variables.

To solve a literal equation or formula, underline the variable you are solving for, and then **undo** what has been done to that variable. Use inverse operations in the same way you do when solving an equation or inequality.

The formula for finding the circumference of a circle when you know diameter is $C = \pi d$. If you know the circumference, you could find the diameter by using a formula for d.

Examples

Solve $C = \pi \underline{d}$ for d. Since d is multiplied by π, use division to **undo** this.

$\frac{C}{\pi} = \frac{\pi \underline{d}}{\pi}$ Divide both sides by π.

$\frac{C}{\pi} = d$ or $d = \frac{C}{\pi}$

Solve $F = \left(\frac{9}{5}\right)\underline{C} + 32$ for C. What has been done to C? First **undo** adding 32.

$F - 32 = \left(\frac{9}{5}\right)\underline{C} + 32 - 32$ Subtract 32 from both sides.

$\left(\frac{5}{9}\right)(F - 32) = \left(\frac{5}{9}\right)\left(\frac{9}{5}\right)\underline{C}$ Multiply both sides by $\left(\frac{5}{9}\right)$, the reciprocal of $\left(\frac{9}{5}\right)$.

$\left(\frac{5}{9}\right)(F - 32) = C$ Simplify.

Solve each formula for the indicated variable.

1. $A = \frac{1}{2}bh$, for b

2. $A = lw$, for l

3. $R = \frac{2s - 6t + 5}{2}$, for s

_______________ _______________ _______________

4. $P = a + b + c$, for c

5. $I = \frac{1}{2}prt$, for t

6. $G = \frac{HJ}{K}$, for H

_______________ _______________ _______________

Solve each equation for the indicated variable.

7. $m + n + p + q = 360$, for n

8. $t = rs + s$, for s

9. $\frac{a}{b} = \frac{c}{d}$, for a

_______________ _______________ _______________

Name ______________________ Date ______________ Class ______________

LESSON 2-4

Creating and Solving Inequalities

Reteach

An inequality, such as $2x < 8$, has infinitely many numbers in its solution. For example, 2, 0, $-\frac{1}{2}$, and -350 are all values of x that make this inequality true.

Solve an inequality by UNDOING what has been done to x, using the same steps as you would use for an equality, with the *exception* given below.

Solving inequalities has one special rule *different* from solving equations.

Multiplying or dividing an inequality by a NEGATIVE number REVERSES the inequality sign.

Try some positive and negative numbers in $-3x < 15$.

Example

$-3x < 15$	Note that 6 and 8 make this true, but it is *not* true for -6 or -8.
$\frac{-3x}{-3} > \frac{15}{-3}$	Dividing by -3 REVERSES the inequality sign.
$x > -5$	This is still true for 6 and 8, and not true for -6 or -8.

Solve each inequality. Show your work.

1. $-3e - 10 \le -4$

2. $\frac{c}{2} + 8 > 11$

Solve each inequality.

3. $15 \le 3 - 4s$

4. $\frac{3}{4}j + 1 > 4$

5. $8c + 4 > 4(c - 3)$

6. $5(x - 1) < 3x + 10 - 8x$

7. $-8 + 4a - 12 > 2a + 10$

8. $0.6t - 3 < 15$

Name ______________________________ Date ________________ Class ________________

LESSON 2-5

Creating and Solving Compound Inequalities

Reteach

Two inequalities that are considered at the same time are compound inequalities. The two inequalities are joined by the word **AND** or by the word **OR**.

Tina estimates that she can sell her old bicycle for at least $50, but she thinks the most someone will pay her for it is $70. Write and graph a compound inequality to describe this.

Step 1 Write an inequality to describe the lowest price. Use *x* for the variable.

$50 \leq x$

Step 2 Write an inequality to describe the highest price. Use *x* for the variable.

$x \leq 70$

Step 3 Which word joins the inequalities?

AND

NOTE: Tina expects to make at least $50, **and**, at the same time, she expects to make no more than $70.

Step 4 Graph the inequalities on separate number lines.

Step 5 The word **AND** means **both** conditions must be satisfied. Graph the **overlap** of the number lines in Step 4 on a single number line.

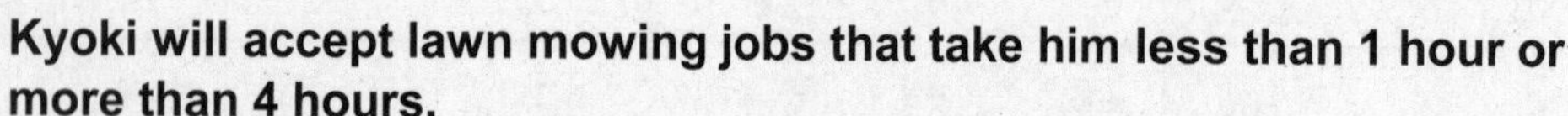

Kyoki will accept lawn mowing jobs that take him less than 1 hour or more than 4 hours.

1. Write two inequalities to describe the jobs Kyoki will take.

____.

2. Which word joins the inequalities? ______________________.

3. Graph both inequalities on the number line below.

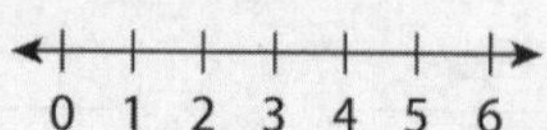

4. Complete the sentence below.

The word **OR** means ________________ condition must be satisfied. The single graph excludes certain numbers, but ________________ the rest of the numbers.

Name ________________________ Date ______________ Class ______________

LESSON 3-1

Graphing Relationships

Reteach

You can draw a graph to show a quick picture of a situation.

Ramon filled a balloon with water. The balloon popped and all the water spilled out.

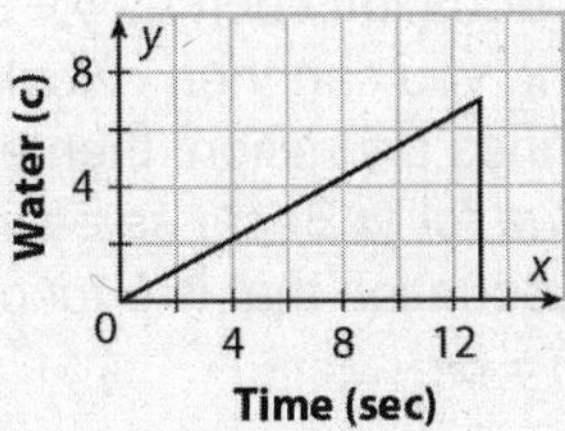

The graph shows that the level of water in the balloon goes up slowly when it is being filled. Then it pops and the water level goes down to 0 suddenly. This matches the situation.

Example

Cathy takes a walk with her dog. The dog runs away, continuing in the same direction, so Cathy goes back to her house to get help.

This graph shows Cathy's walk.

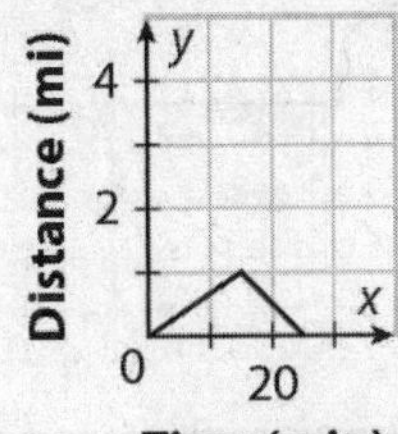

This graph shows the dog's walk.

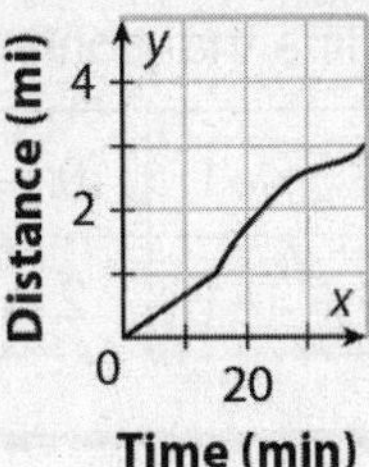

How are the graphs alike? How are they different?

They are alike until the dog runs away because Cathy and the dog were walking away from the house together. Then the line for Cathy goes down as she gets closer to her house. The line for the dog goes up because it is still running away.

Choose the graph that matches the situation.

1. A bus travels at 25 miles per hour. It slows and stops to pick up riders. The bus picks up riders at 2 stops. Graph ________.

A.

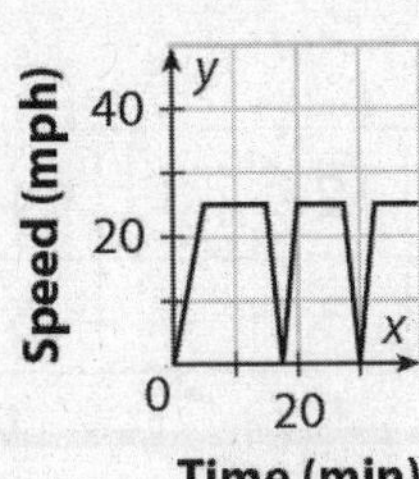

B.

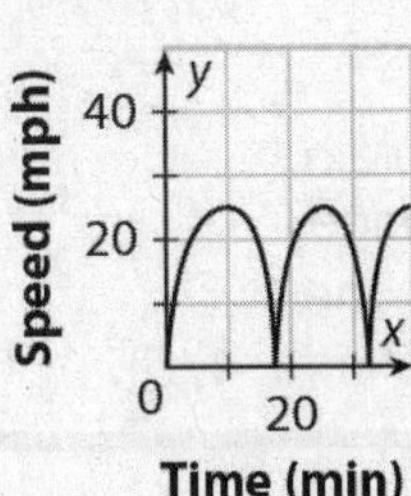

C.

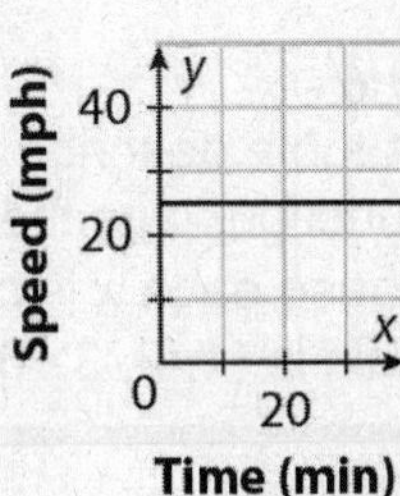

2. The cook put broth and vegetables into the pot. Later he added some meat. He let it cook for a while, then served it to diners one dish at a time. Graph ________.

A.

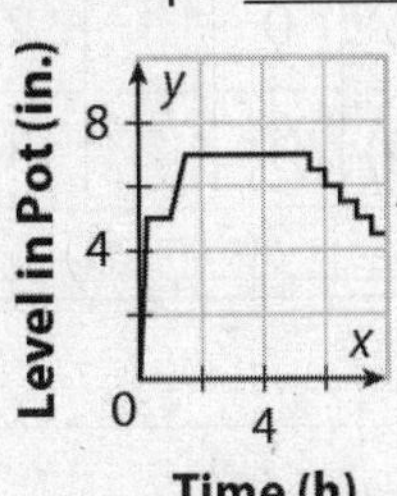

B.

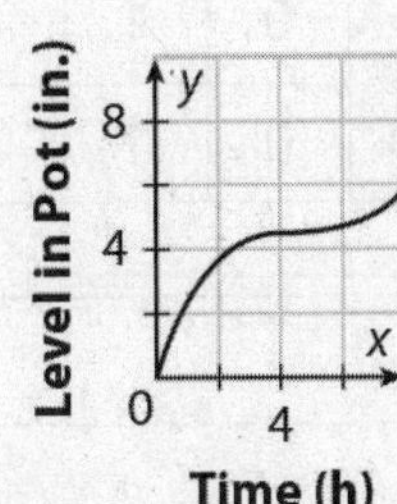

C.

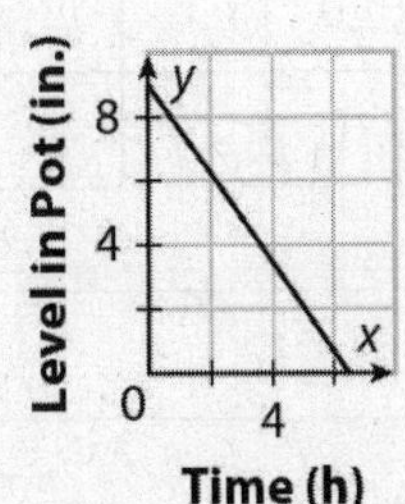

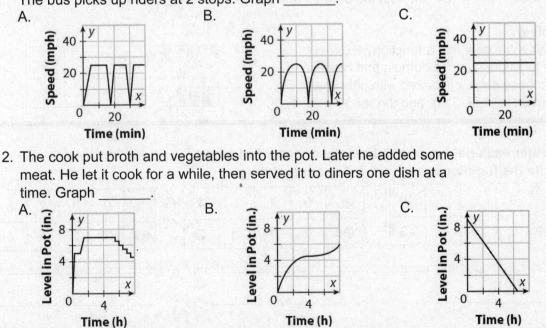

Name ______________________ Date ______________ Class ______________

LESSON 3-2

Understanding Relations and Functions

Reteach

An equation such as $y = 3x + 2$ defines a **function**. If you choose a value for x, you can then calculate a corresponding value for y. If the equation defines a function, then each value for x will correspond with *only one value for y*. Because each value for y depends on the chosen value for x, an equation that is a function can be written in function notation, such as $f(x) = 3x + 2$.

In function notation, the f next to the (x) does NOT mean to multiply. Say this as "the function of x is $3x + 2$" or "f of x equals $3x + 2$."

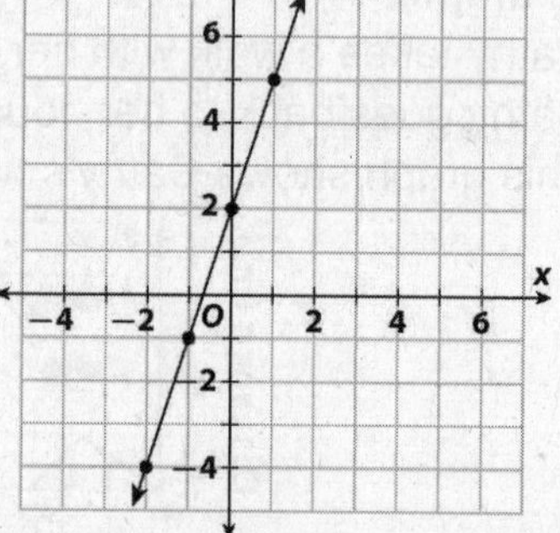

Example

To graph $f(x) = 3x + 2$, make a table of three or more values for x with the corresponding values for y. Then plot the ordered pairs and join them with a line that continues in both directions.

x	−2	−1	0	1
f(x)	−4	−1	2	5

Complete the table and graph the function $f(x) = -2x - 4$.

1.

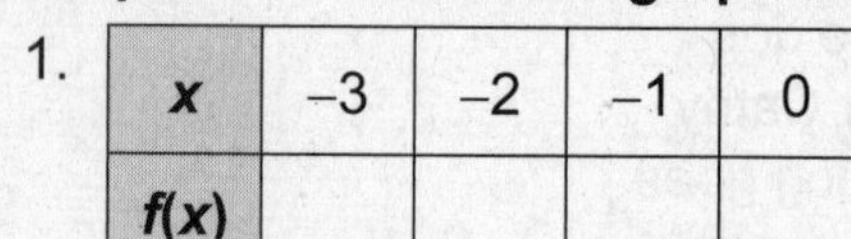

x	−3	−2	−1	0
f(x)				

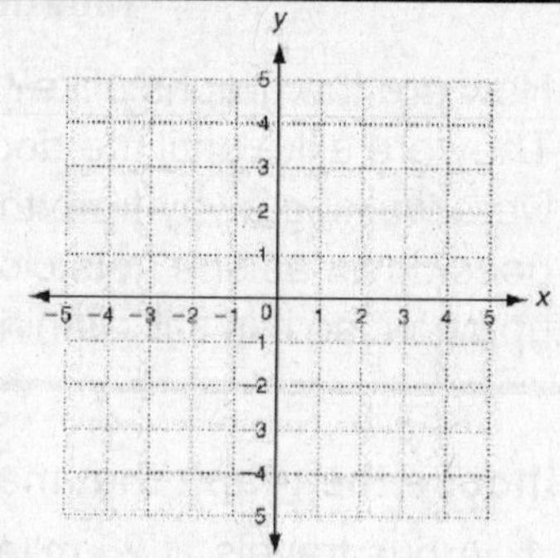

The **domain** of a function is the set of values for **x**.
The **range** of a function is the set of values for **y**.
In the function $f(x) = -2x - 4$, both the domain and the range are all real numbers.

Example

Does this table describe a function? Explain.
If it is a function, give the domain and range.
Yes, because each x is paired with only one y.
The domain is {1, 2, 3, 4}, and the range is {3, 4, 5}.

x	1	2	3	4
f(x)	3	3	4	5

Tell whether each pairing of numbers describes a function.
If so, write the function and give the domain and range.

2.

x	0	1	2	3
f(x)	0	−1	−2	−3

____

____

3.

x	0	1	1	4
f(x)	0	1	−1	2

____

____

4.

x	0	1	2	3
f(x)	1	2	3	4

____

____

Name ______________________ Date ______________ Class ______________

LESSON 3-3

Modeling with Functions

Reteach

To write a function for a situation, identify the independent variable and the dependent variable.

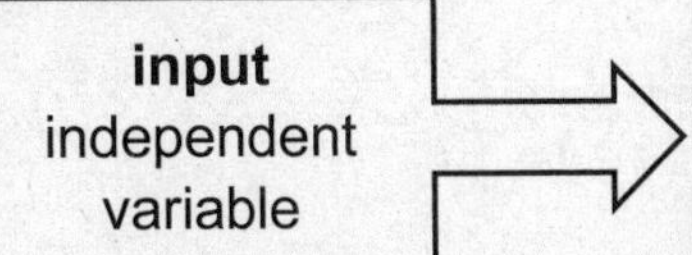

Function

output
dependent
variable

In a word problem, the output is usually the answer to the problem, but not always.

Example:

Nick earns $21 per hour. How much will he make working for 8 hours?

Think: 8 hours × $21 = the total amount Nick earns.

independent variable can change

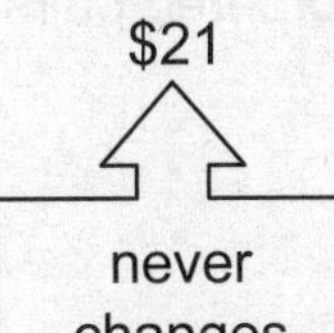

dependent variable changes when the independent variable changes

Nick can work any number of hours. This is the independent variable.
Nick will earn (number of hours × $21). The total depends on the number of hours. This is the dependent variable.

Identify the independent variable and the dependent variable in 1–3.

1. Brandie earns $8 per hour. How much will she earn working 7 hours?

   Think: ______________ × $8 = ______________________

   Independent variable: ______________________

   Dependent variable: ______________________

2. A cell phone company charges $0.15 per minute. Zach used his phone 103 minutes last month. How much will he be charged?

   Think: ______________ × $0.15 = ______________________

   Independent variable: ______________________

   Dependent variable: ______________________

3. Every serving of lasagna has 410 calories. Ed ate 3 servings. How many calories did he eat?

   Think: ______________ × 410 = ______________________

   Independent variable: ______________________

   Dependent variable: ______________________

Name ______________________ Date ______________ Class ______________

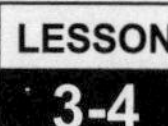

Graphing Functions

Reteach

To check whether an equation is a function, isolate the *y* variable on one side of the equation and simplify.

$$4x - 2y = -8$$

$$-2y = -4x - 8 \quad \text{Subtract } 4x \text{ from both sides.}$$

$$y = 2x + 4 \quad \text{Divide each term by } -2.$$

Write the equation as a function: $f(x) = 2x + 4$.

If the domain = {2, 3, 4}, substitute each value into the function and simplify to find the values of the range.

$f(x) = 2(2) + 4$	$f(x) = 2(3) + 4$	$f(x) = 2(4) + 4$
$f(x) = 4 + 4$	$f(x) = 6 + 4$	$f(x) = 8 + 4$
$f(x) = 8$	$f(x) = 10$	$f(x) = 12$

Use a table to find the ordered pairs. Graph the ordered pairs.

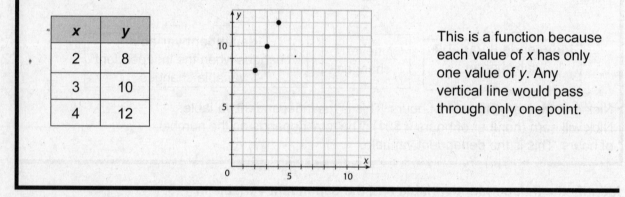

x	*y*
2	8
3	10
4	12

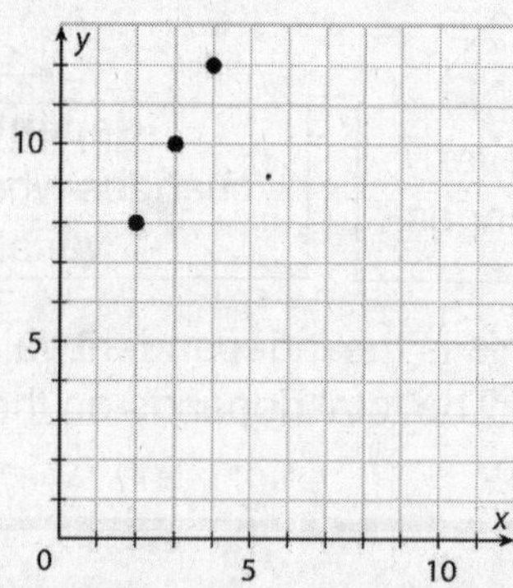

This is a function because each value of *x* has only one value of *y*. Any vertical line would pass through only one point.

Is this equation a function? Use the domain values to find the values for the range. Graph the points and tell whether it is a function or not.

1. $f(x) = 3x + 2$ for the domain {1, 2, 3, 4}

x	*y*

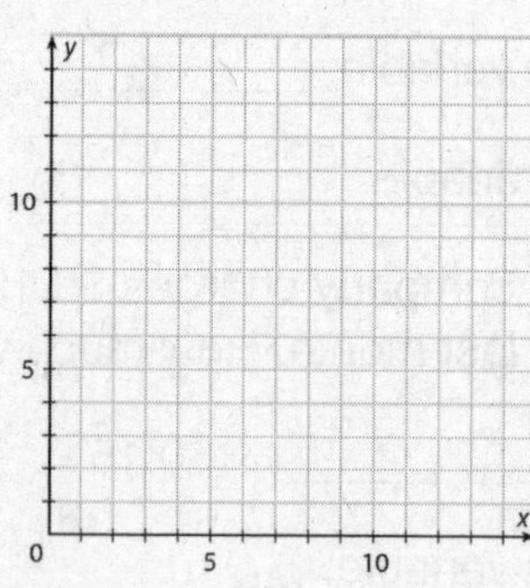

function? ______________

Use the vertical line test to tell if each graph shows a function.

2.

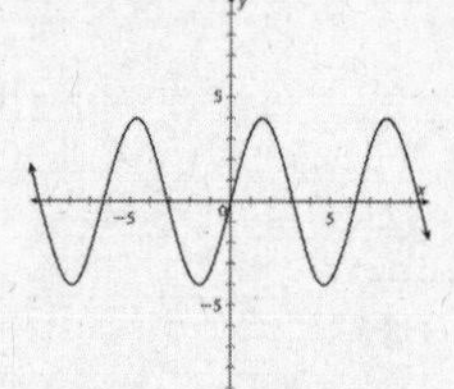

function? ______________

3.

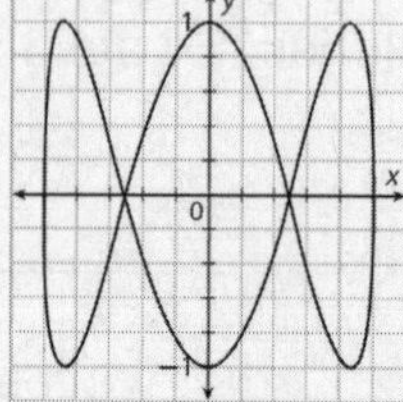

function? ______________

4.

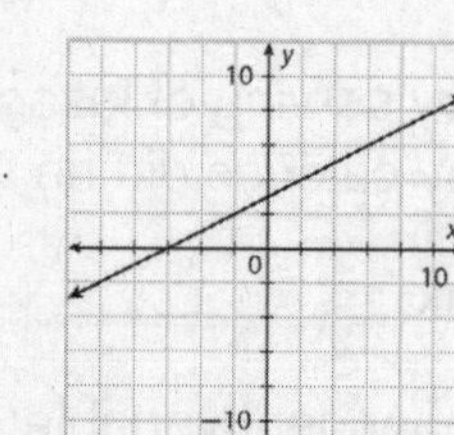

function? ______________

Name ______________________ Date ______________ Class ______________

LESSON 4-1

Identifying and Graphing Sequences

Reteach

A list of numbers in a specific order, or pattern, is called a **sequence**. Each number, or **term**, in the sequence corresponds with the position number that locates it in the list.

You can write a sequence as a function, where the **domain** is {1, 2, 3, 4,...} or the set of position numbers. The **range** is the set of the numbers, or terms, in the list.

Domain or position number: *n*	1	2	3	4	5
Range or term: *f*(*n*)	2	4	6	8	10

This sequence can be described by an **explicit rule** that defines each $f(n)$ in terms of n. The explicit rule is $f(n) = 2n$.

A sequence can be shown on a graph. Use the domain and range to make ordered pairs, $(n, f(n))$; then plot on a graph.

Example

Domain or position number: *n*	1	2	3	4
Range or term: *f*(*n*)	2	4	6	8

Ordered pairs: (1, 2) (2, 4), (3, 6), and (4, 8)

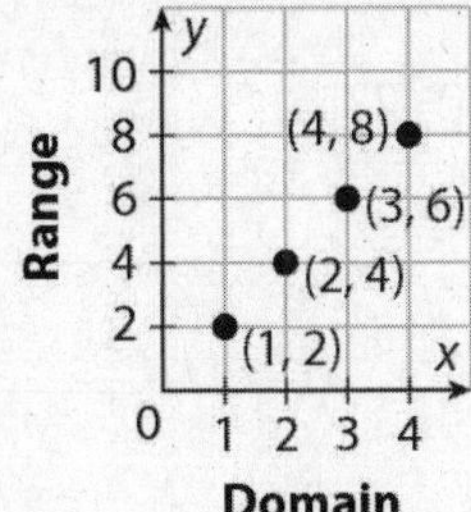

Complete each table for the given sequence. Then write the ordered pair.

1. $f(n) = 3n + 2$

n	1	2	3	4
***f*(*n*)**				

ordered pairs: ______________________

2. $f(n) = \frac{1}{2}n + 1$

n	1	2	3	4
***f*(*n*)**				

ordered pairs: ______________________

3. $f(n) = n - 1$

n	1	2	3	4
***f*(*n*)**				

ordered pairs: ______________________

Name ______________________ Date ______________ Class ______________

LESSON 4-2

Constructing Arithmetic Sequences

Reteach

An **arithmetic sequence** is a list of numbers (or **terms**) with a **common difference** between each number.

0, 6, 12, 18, …

+6 +6 +6

Find how much you add or subtract to move from term to term.

The difference between terms is constant.

In this example, $f(1) = 0$, $f(2) = 6$, $f(3) = 12$, $f(4) = 18$, ….
The common difference is 6.

Use the common difference, d, to write rules for an arithmetic sequence.

A **recursive** rule has this general form: Given $f(1)$, $f(n) = f(n - 1) + d$ for $n \geq 2$

Substitute $d = 6$: $f(n) = f(n - 1) + 6$ for $n \geq 2$

An **explicit** rule has this general form: $f(n) = f(1) + d(n - 1)$

Substitute $d = 6$ from the example: $f(n) = f(1) + 6(n - 1)$

Indicate whether each sequence is arithmetic. If so, find the common difference, and write an explicit rule for the sequence.

1. –1, 2, –3, 4, …

____

____

2. 14, 12, 10, 8, …

____

____

3. 3, 6, 9, 27, …

____

____

Write a recursive rule and an explicit rule for each sequence.

4. –5, 0, 5, 10, …

____

____

5. 7, 4, 1, –2, …

____

____

6. 4, 7, 10, 13, …

____

____

Use the explicit rule given to write the first three terms for each sequence.

7. $f(n) = 6 + 3(n - 1)$

____

8. $f(n) = 68 - 2(n - 1)$

____

9. $f(n) = f(n - 1) - 7$

____

Name ______________________ Date ______________ Class ______________

LESSON 4-3 Modeling with Arithmetic Sequences

Reteach

You can graph a function and use it to solve real-world problems.

A carnival game awards a prize if Karen can shoot a basket. The charge is $5.00 for the first shot, then $2.00 for each additional shot. Karen needed 6 shots to win a prize. What is the total amount Karen spent to win a prize?

Table ⟹ **Ordered Pairs** ⟹ **Graph**

Number of Shots	Cost ($)	Ordered Pairs
1	5	(1, 5)
2	7	(2, 7)
3	9	(3, 9)
4	11	(4, 11)
5	13	(5, 13)
6	15	(6, 15)

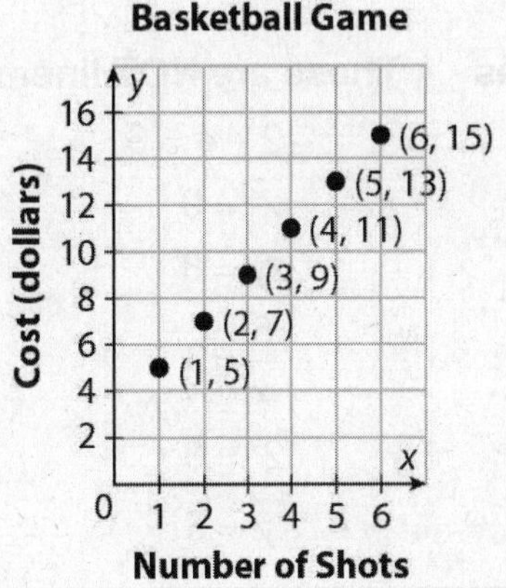

1. Anna buys 1 raffle ticket for $4. Each ticket after that costs $2. How many raffle tickets can she buy with $12? Complete the table and graph to solve.

Table ⟹ **Ordered Pairs** ⟹ **Graph**

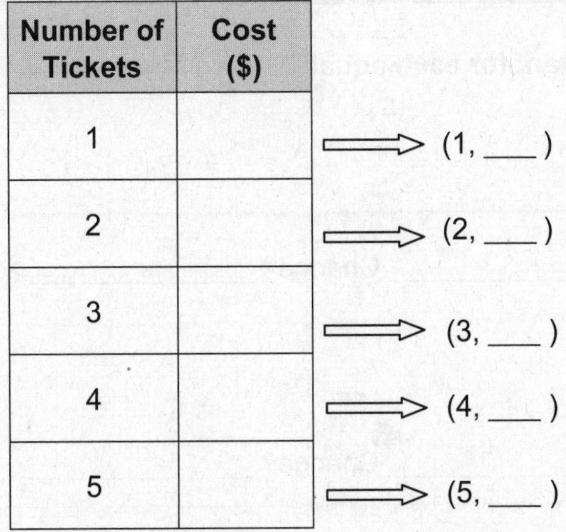

Number of Tickets	Cost ($)	Ordered Pairs
1		(1, ____)
2		(2, ____)
3		(3, ____)
4		(4, ____)
5		(5, ____)

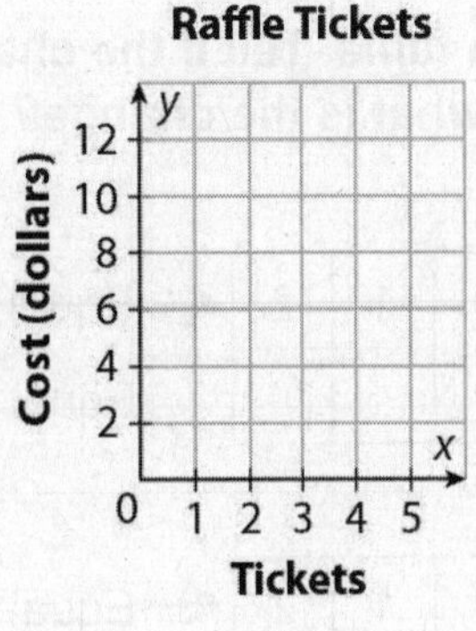

Name ______________________ Date ______________ Class ______________

LESSON 5-1

Understanding Linear Functions

Reteach

The graph of a **linear function** is a straight line.

$Ax + By + C = 0$ is the **standard form** for the equation of a linear function.

- *A*, *B*, and *C* are real numbers. *A* and *B* are not both zero.
- The variables *x* and *y*
  - have exponents of 1;
  - are not multiplied together;
  - are not in denominators, exponents or radical signs.

Examples **These are NOT linear functions:**

$2 + 4 = 6$	no variable
$x^2 = 9$	exponent on $x \geq 1$
$xy = 8$	*x* and *y* multiplied together
$\frac{6}{x} = 3$	*x* in denominator
$2^y = 8$	*y* in exponent
$\sqrt{y} = 5$	*y* in a square root

Tell whether each function is linear or not.

1. $14 = 2\sqrt{x}$ ______________

2. $3xy = 27$ ______________

3. $14 = \frac{28}{x}$ ______________

4. $6x^2 = 12$ ______________

One way to tell if a function is linear is to make a table of *x* and *y* values and see if there is a constant change for each equal interval.

Complete each table. Tell if the change is constant for each equal interval. If so, what is the change?

5. $y - 2 = 3x$

x	−1	0	1	2
y	−1	2		

← Equal interval

Equal change? ______________ Change? ______________

6. $x^2 + 2y = 5$

x	−1	0	1	2
y	2	$\frac{5}{2}$		

← Equal interval

Equal change? ______________ Change? ______________

Name ______________________ Date ______________ Class ______________

LESSON 5-2

Using Intercepts

Reteach

Doug has $12 to spend on popcorn and peanuts. The peanuts are $4 and popcorn is $2. If he spends all his money, the equation $4x + 2y = 12$ shows the amount of peanuts, *x*, and popcorn, *y*, he can buy. Here is the graph of $4x + 2y = 12$.

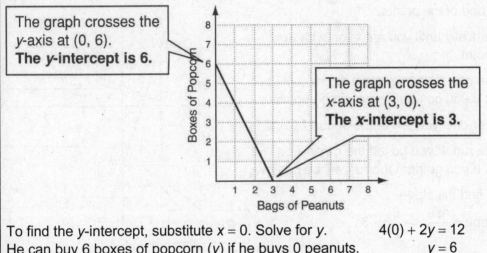

The graph crosses the *y*-axis at (0, 6).
The *y*-intercept is 6.

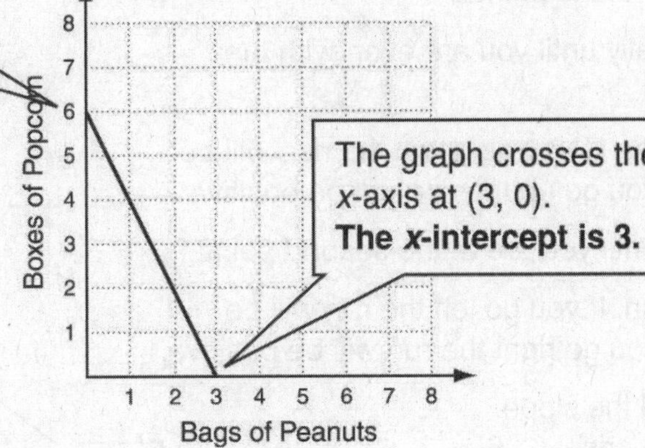

The graph crosses the *x*-axis at (3, 0).
The *x*-intercept is 3.

To find the *y*-intercept, substitute $x = 0$. Solve for *y*. $4(0) + 2y = 12$

He can buy 6 boxes of popcorn (*y*) if he buys 0 peanuts. $y = 6$

To find the *x*-intercept, substitute $y = 0$. Solve for *x*. $4x + 2(0) = 12$

He can buy 3 bags of peanuts (*x*) if he buys 0 popcorn. $x = 3$

Find each *x*- and *y*-intercept.

1.

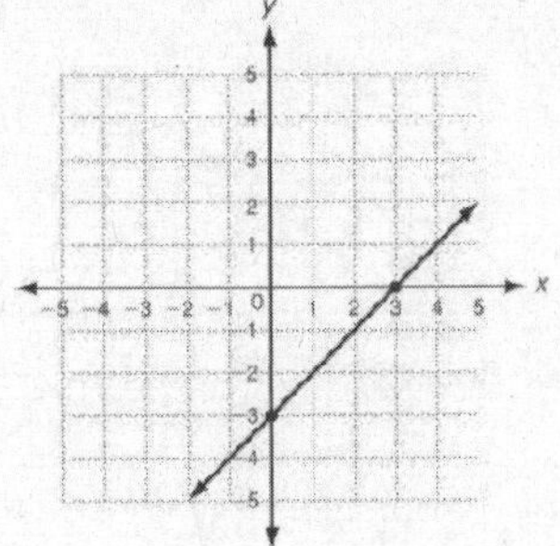

____

2.

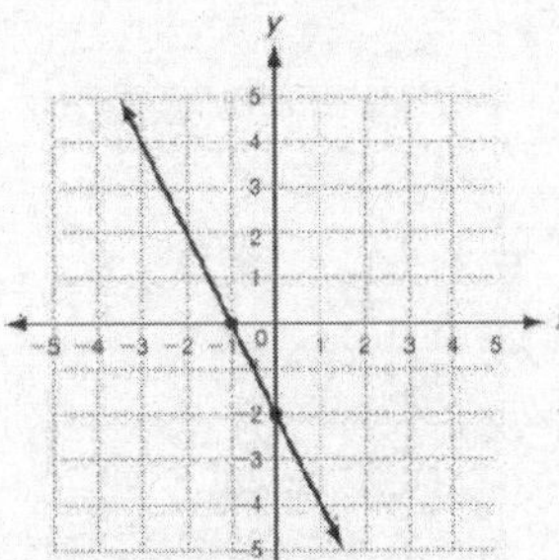

____

3.

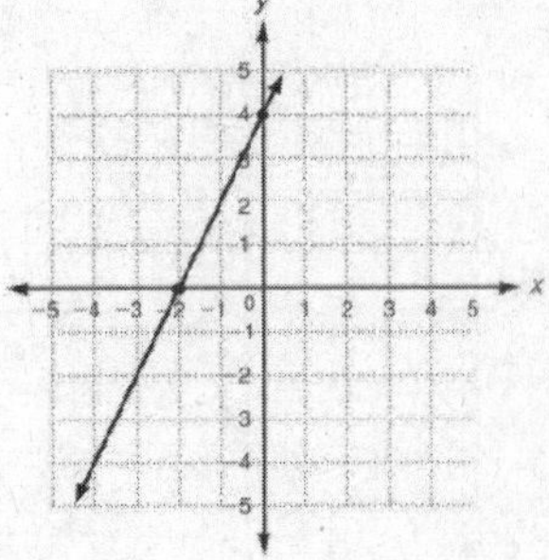

____

Find each intercept. Use these two points to graph each line.

4. $3x + 9y = 9$

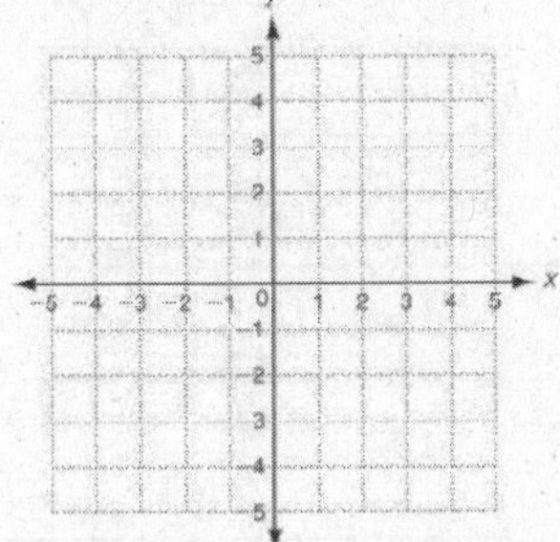

5. $4x + 6y = -12$

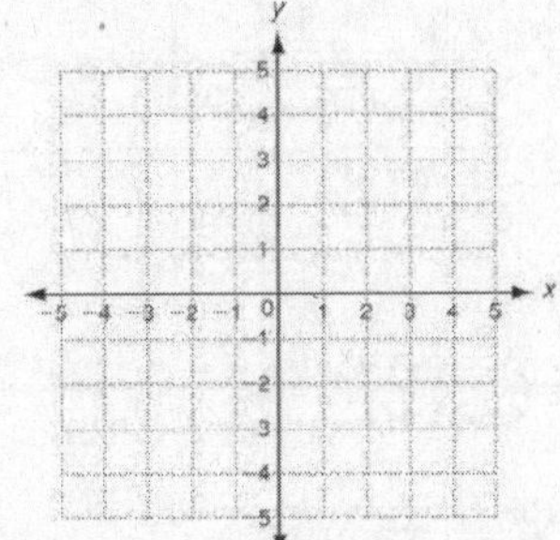

6. $2x - y = 4$

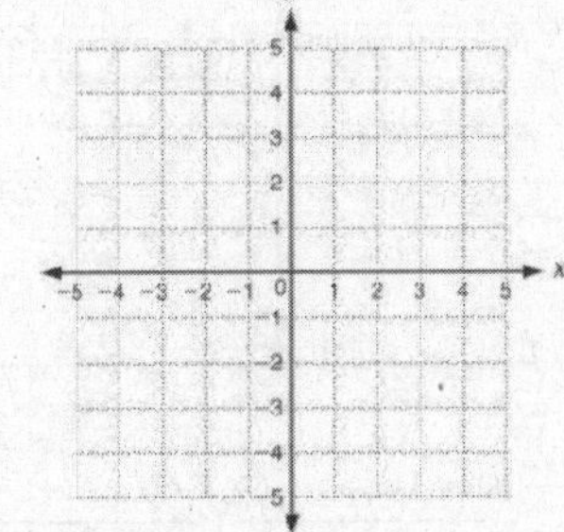

Name ______________________ Date ______________ Class ______________

LESSON 5-3

Interpreting Rate of Change and Slope

Reteach

Find the rate of change, or **slope**, for the graph of a straight line by finding $\frac{\text{change in } y}{\text{change in } x}$.

Step 1: First choose any two points on the line.

Step 2: Begin at one of the points.

Step 3: Count vertically until you are even with the second point.

This is the rise. If you go down the rise will be negative. If you go up the rise will be positive.

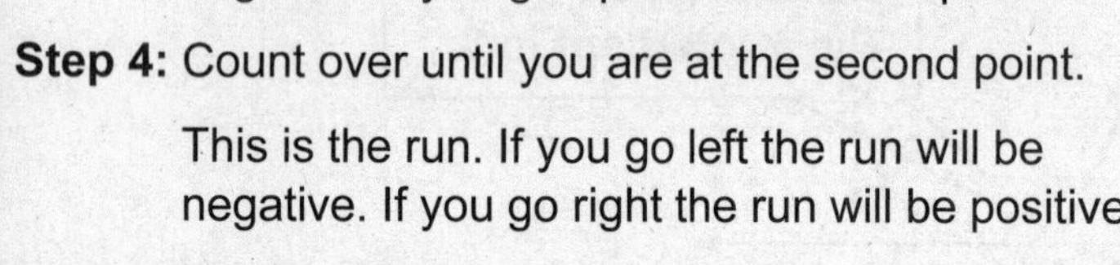

Step 4: Count over until you are at the second point.

This is the run. If you go left the run will be negative. If you go right the run will be positive.

Step 5: Divide to find the slope.

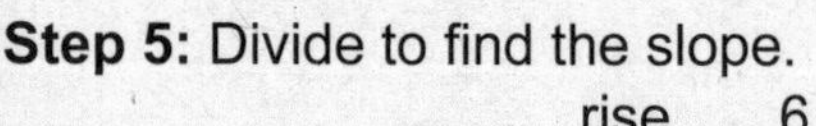

$$\text{slope} = \frac{\text{rise}}{\text{run}} = -\frac{6}{2} = -3$$

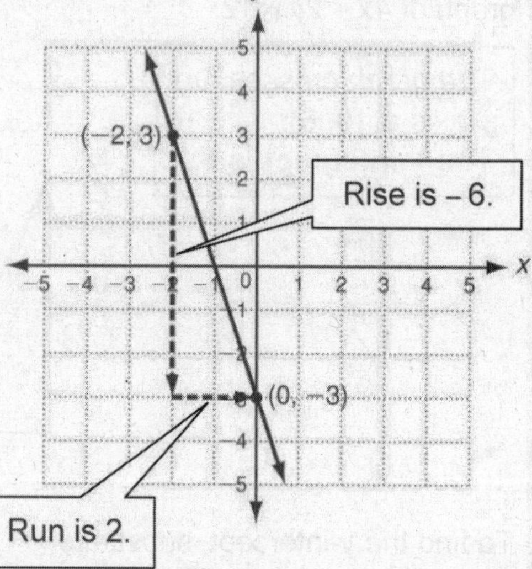

The **slope of a horizontal line is zero**. A horizontal line has no steepness at all.

The **slope of a vertical line is undefined**. A vertical line is infinitely steep.

Find the slope of each line.

1.

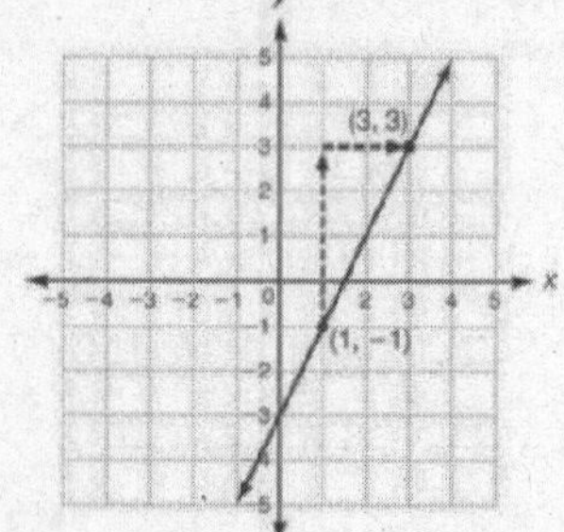

____

2.

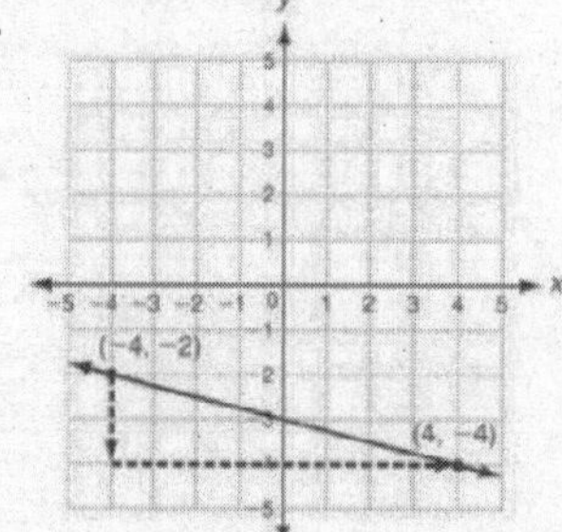

____

3.

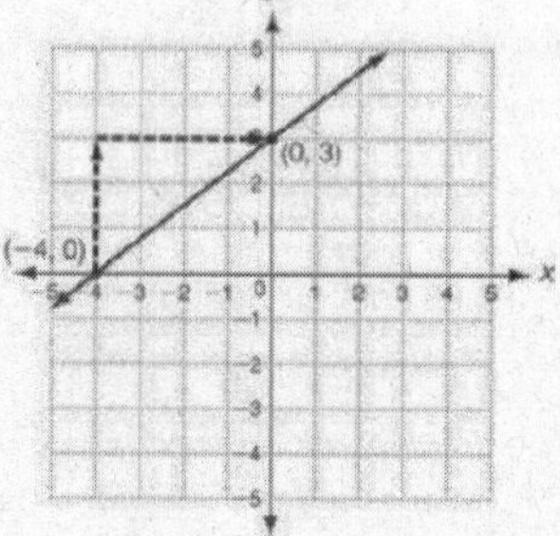

____

4.

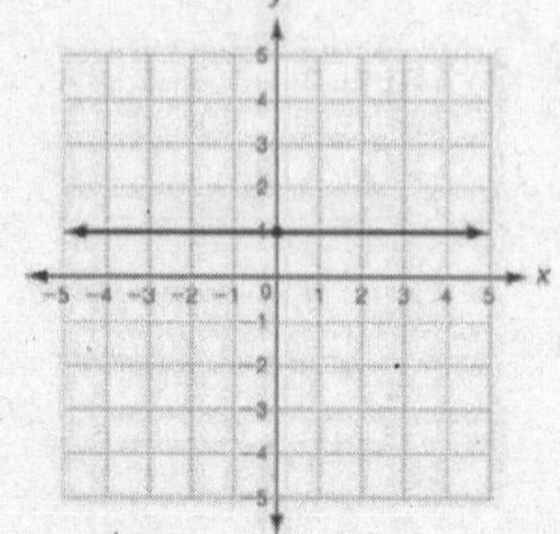

____

5.

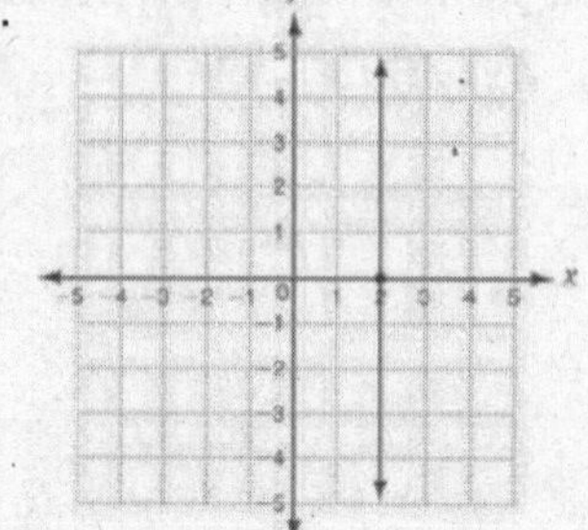

____

6.

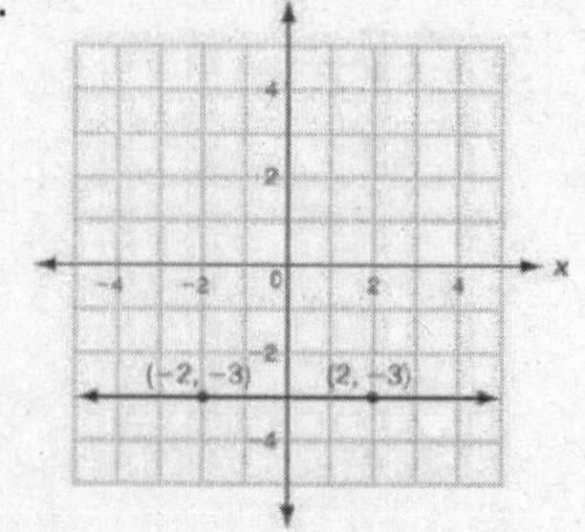

____

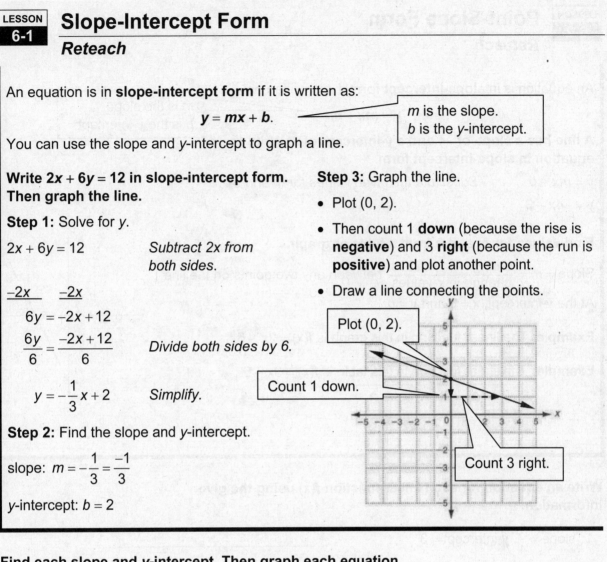

Name ______________________ Date ______________ Class ______________

LESSON 6-1

Slope-Intercept Form

Reteach

An equation is in **slope-intercept form** if it is written as:

$$\boldsymbol{y = mx + b}.$$

m is the slope.
b is the *y*-intercept.

You can use the slope and *y*-intercept to graph a line.

Write $2x + 6y = 12$ in slope-intercept form. Then graph the line.

Step 1: Solve for *y*.

$2x + 6y = 12$ *Subtract 2x from both sides.*

$\underline{-2x} \quad \underline{-2x}$

$6y = -2x + 12$

$\dfrac{6y}{6} = \dfrac{-2x+12}{6}$ *Divide both sides by 6.*

$y = -\dfrac{1}{3}x + 2$ *Simplify.*

Step 2: Find the slope and *y*-intercept.

slope: $m = -\dfrac{1}{3} = \dfrac{-1}{3}$

y-intercept: $b = 2$

Step 3: Graph the line.

- Plot (0, 2).
- Then count 1 **down** (because the rise is **negative**) and 3 **right** (because the run is **positive**) and plot another point.
- Draw a line connecting the points.

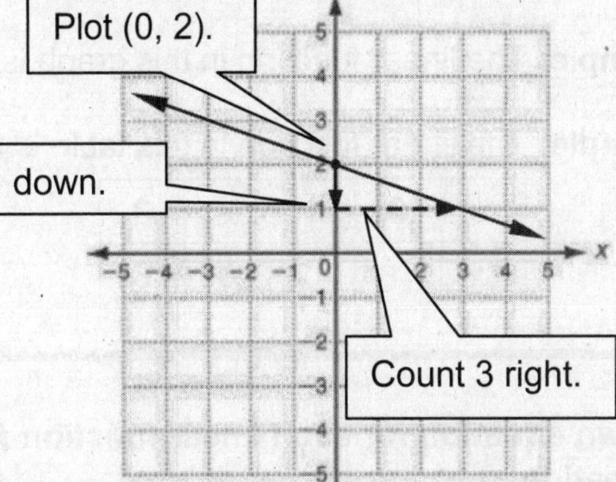

Plot (0, 2).
Count 1 down.
Count 3 right.
x
y

Find each slope and *y*-intercept. Then graph each equation.

1. $y = \dfrac{1}{2}x - 3$

slope: ______________

y-intercept: ______________

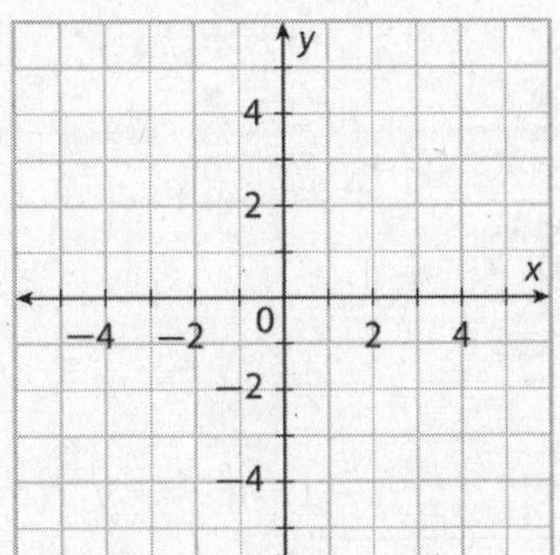

2. $3x + y = 2$

slope: ______________

y-intercept: ______________

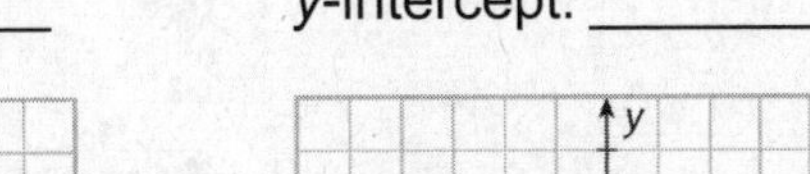

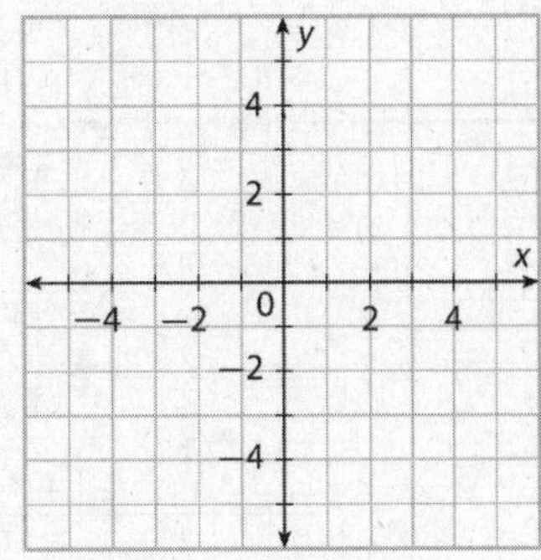

3. $2x - y = 3$

slope: ______________

y-intercept: ______________

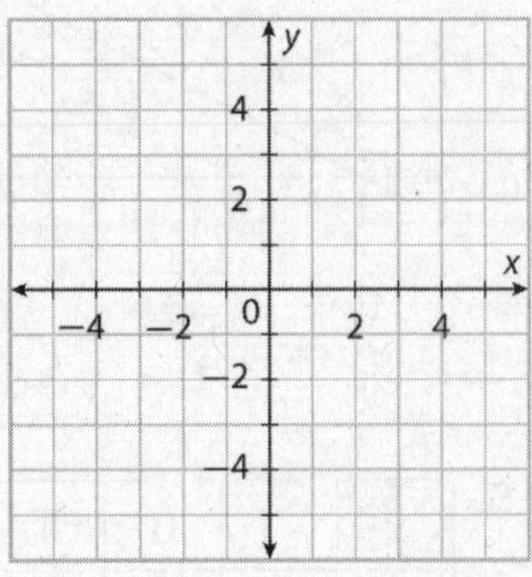

Name ____________________ Date ______________ Class ______________

LESSON 6-2

Point-Slope Form

Reteach

An equation is in **slope-intercept form** if it is written as:

$$y = mx + b.$$

m is the slope.
b is the *y*-intercept.

A line has a slope of –4 and a *y*-intercept of 3. Write the equation in slope-intercept form.

$y = mx + b$ *Substitute the given values for m and b.*

$y = -4x + 3$

Find values for *m* and *b* from a table or graph.

Slope $= m = \dfrac{\text{change in } y\text{-values}}{\text{change in } x\text{-values}}$ between any two points on the line.

At the *y*-intercept, $x = 0$ and $y = b$.

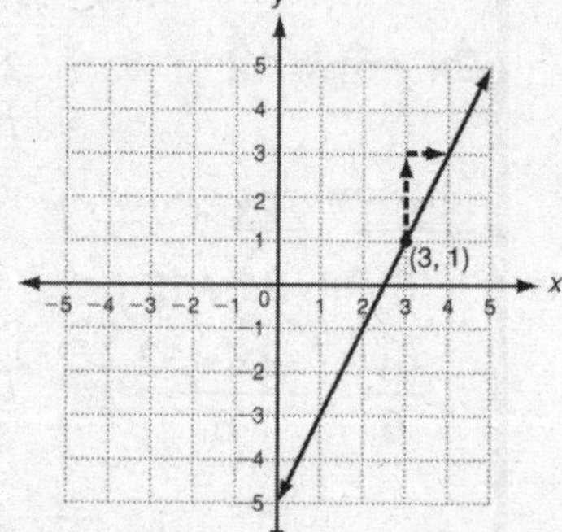

Example: The linear function in this graph is $f(x) = 2x - 5$.

Example: The linear function in this table is $f(x) = 3x - 6$.

x	0	1	2	3
f(*x*)	–6	–3	0	3

Write an equation for each linear function *f*(*x*) using the given information.

1. slope $= \frac{1}{4}$, *y*-intercept = 3 ____________________

2. slope = –5, *y*-intercept = 0 ____________________

3. slope = 7, *y*-intercept = –2 ____________________

4. ____________________

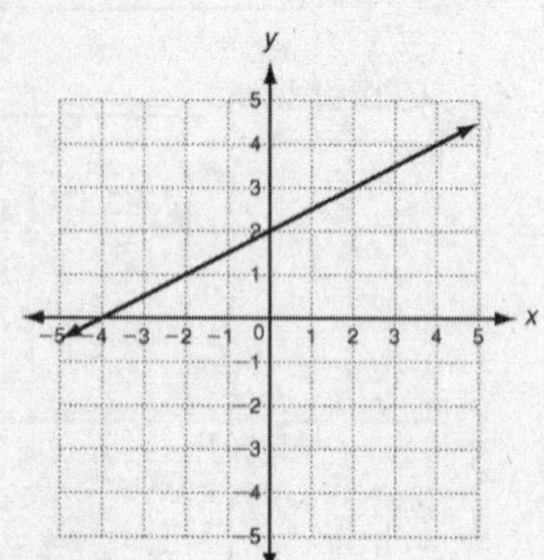

5. ____________________

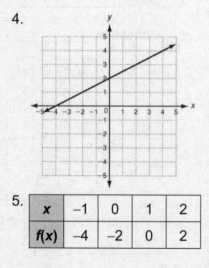

x	–1	0	1	2
f(*x*)	–4	–2	0	2

Name ______________________ Date ______________ Class ______________

LESSON 6-3

Standard Form

Reteach

The graph of a **linear function** is a straight line.

$Ax + By + C = 0$ is the **standard form** for the equation of a linear function.

- A, B, and C are real numbers. A and B are not both zero.
- The variables x and y:

  have exponents of 1.
  are not multiplied together.
  are not in denominators, exponents, or radical signs.

Examples **These are NOT linear functions:**

$2 + 4 = 6$	no variable	$\frac{6}{x} = 3$	x in denominator
$x^2 = 9$	exponent on $x \geq 1$	$2^y = 8$	y in exponent
$xy = 8$	x and y multiplied together	$\sqrt{y} = 5$	square root of y

Tell whether each function is linear or not.

1. $14 = 2\sqrt{x}$ ______
2. $3xy = 27$ ______
3. $14 = \frac{28}{x}$ ______
4. $6x^2 = 12$ ______

The graph of $y = C$ is always a **horizontal** line. The graph of $x = C$ is always a **vertical** line.

Examples

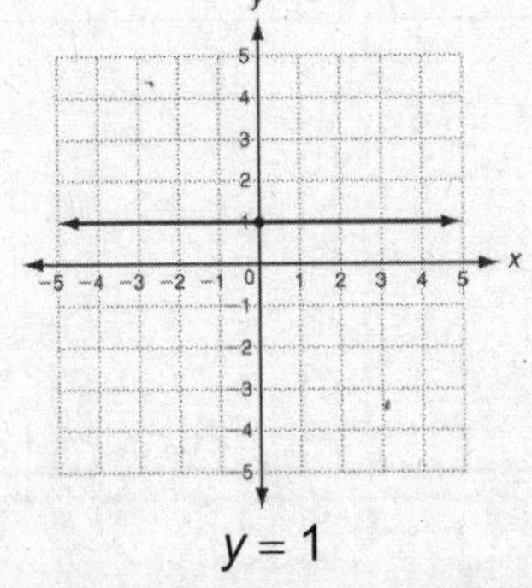

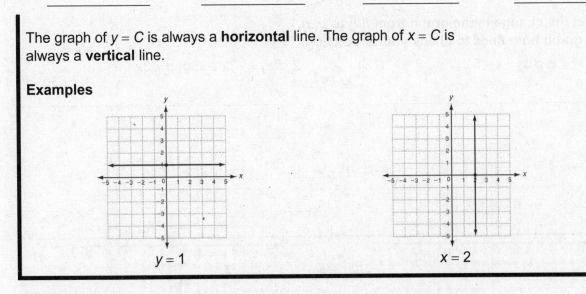

$y = 1$

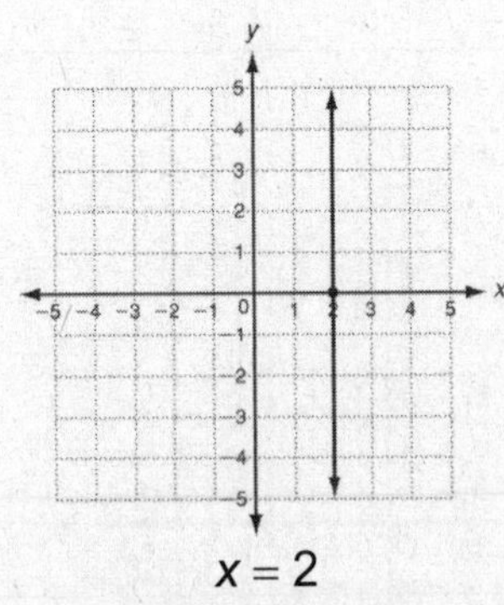

$x = 2$

Tell whether each equation represents a horizontal line, a vertical line, or neither.

5. $9y = 27$ ______
6. $6x + 7y = 10$ ______
7. $\frac{1}{2}x = 19$ ______
8. $x = 0$ ______

Name ______________________________ Date ______________ Class ______________

LESSON 6-4

Transforming Linear Functions

Reteach

For a linear function $f(x) = mx + b$, changing the value of b moves the graph up or down.

Description	Equation	y-intercept or b
Parent function	$f(x) = x$	0
Translate up 2	$g(x) = x + 2$	2
Translate down 4	$h(x) = x - 4$	−4

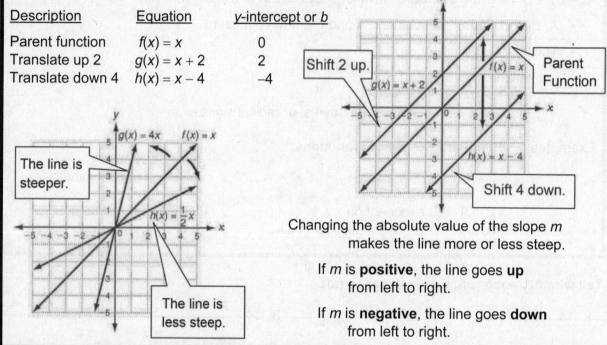

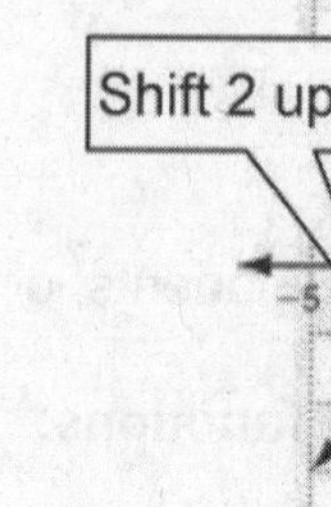

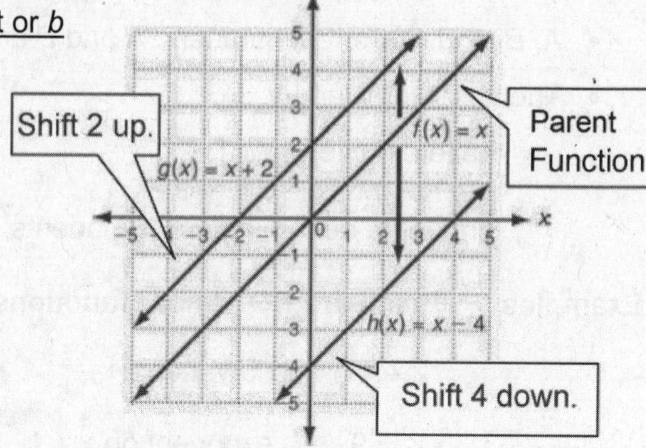

The line is steeper.

$g(x) = 4x$ $f(x) = x$ $h(x) = \frac{1}{2}x$

The line is less steep.

Changing the absolute value of the slope m makes the line more or less steep.

If m is **positive**, the line goes **up** from left to right.

If m is **negative**, the line goes **down** from left to right.

Predict the change in the graph from $f(x)$ to $g(x)$. Then graph both lines to check your prediction.

1. $f(x) = x$; $g(x) = x + 5$

____

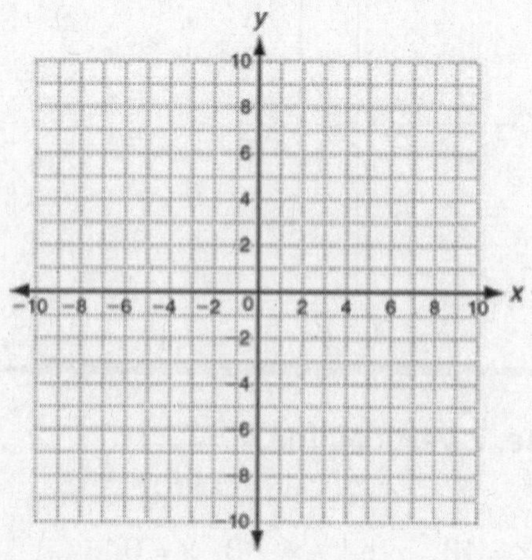

2. $f(x) = -3x + 1$; $g(x) = 3x + 1$

____

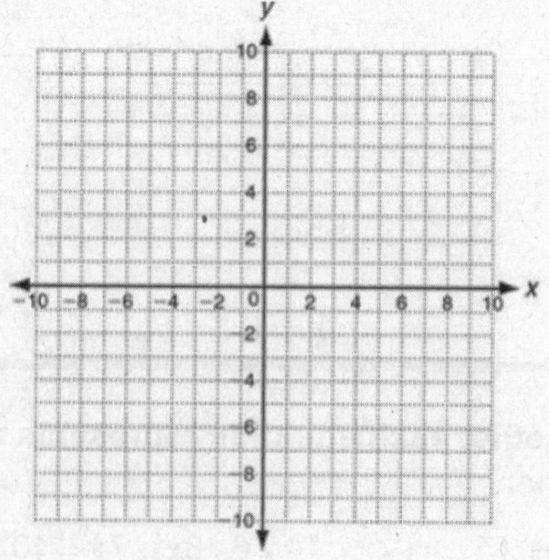

Name _______________ Date _______________ Class _______________

LESSON 6-5

Comparing Properties of Linear Functions

Reteach

You can describe a **linear function** with a table, a graph, or an equation.

The table shows $f(x)$.

x	−1	0	1	2	3	4
f(x)	5	4	3	2	1	0

The graph shows $g(x)$.

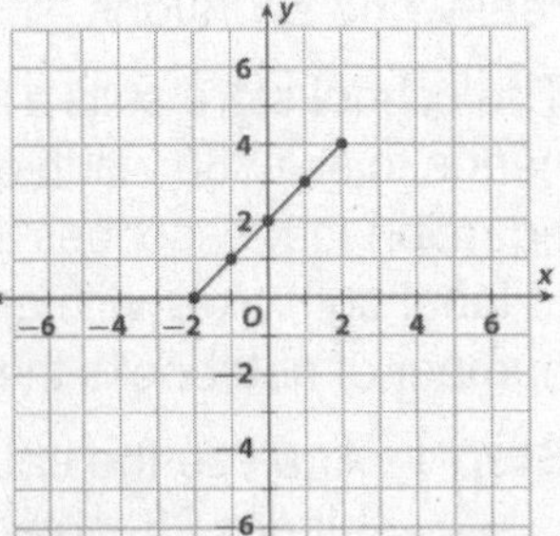

This chart compares $f(x)$ and $g(x)$.

	Domain	**Range**	**Initial (starting) value of f(x)**	***y*-intercept**	**Slope**
f(x)	from −1 to 4	from 5 to 0	5	4	−1
g(x)	from −2 to 2	from 0 to 4	0	2	1

Complete each chart. Assume that the domain of $f(x)$ includes all real numbers between the least and greatest values of x.

1.

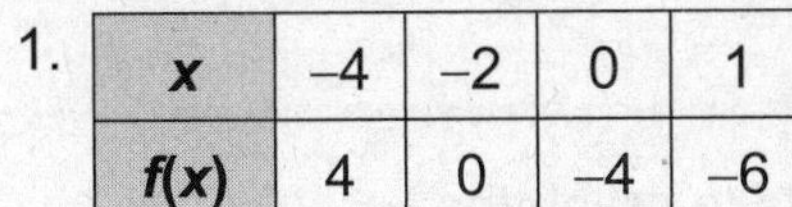

x	−4	−2	0	1
f(x)	4	0	−4	−6

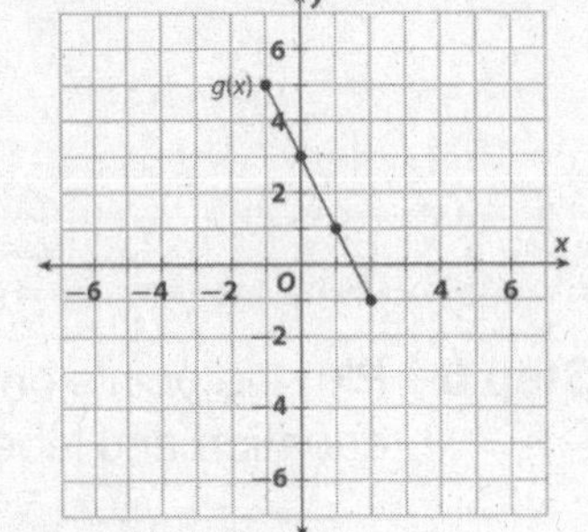

	Domain	**Range**	**Initial (starting) value of function**	***y*-intercept**	**Slope**
f(x)					
g(x)					

2.

x	−1	0	1	2	3	4
f(x)	−3	−2	−1	0	1	2

$h(x) = x + 1$, for $-2 \le x \le 2$

	Domain	**Range**	**Initial (starting) value of f(x)**	***y*-intercept**	**Slope**
f(x)					
h(x)					

Name ______________________ Date ______________ Class ______________

Modeling Linear Relationships

Reteach

Linear equations and their graphs can sometimes be used to model real-world situations.

The school store sells a binder for $5 and a notebook for $4. The store needs to sell $80 worth of these two items each week. Write a linear equation that describes the problem. Graph the linear equation, making sure to label both axes with appropriate titles. Use the graph to approximate the number of notebooks the store must sell if 12 binders are sold.

Step 1 Analyze the data.
binder $5, notebook $4, need to sell $80

Step 2 Make a plan.
Let *b* represent number of binders and *n* represent number of notebooks. Sales from binders = $5b$ and sales from notebooks = $4n$

Step 3 Write a linear equation to model the problem.
$5b + 4n = 80$

Step 4 Calculate three sets of values for binders and notebooks.

Binders	Notebooks
0	20
16	0
12	5

Step 5 Plot the points on a coordinate grid. Connect the points to graph the equation and label the axes.

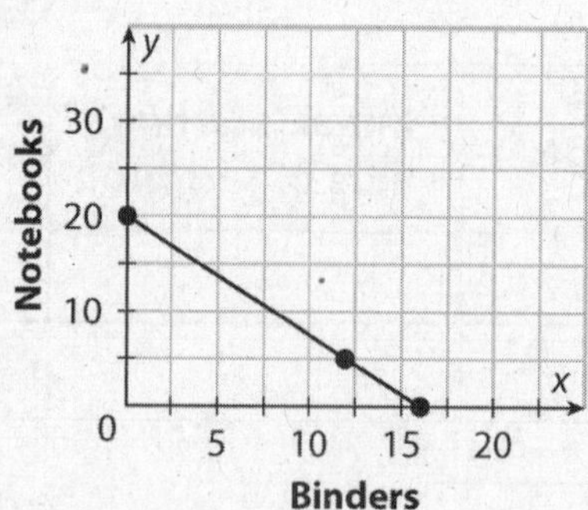

Step 6 Find the point on the line for 12 binders to find the number of notebooks needed to meet the goal.

Use the graph to answer the questions.

1. What does the point (0, 20) represent? ______________________

2. What does the point (16, 0) represent? ______________________

3. What is the approximate number of notebooks that need to be sold if 12 binders are sold? ______________________

Name ______________________ Date ______________ Class ______________

LESSON 7-2

Using Functions to Solve One-Variable Equations

Reteach

Having several methods to solve one-variable equations can help. Depending on the problem, often one method is easier than the others.

Algebraic Solution is often fastest and can handle decimals and fractions most easily.

$f(x) = 19 - 8x$ and $g(x) = -17 + 10x$

Solve using algebra.

Set $f(x) = g(x)$ and solve for x.

$$19 - 8x = -17 + 10x$$
$$36 = 18x$$
$$2 = x$$

Graphic Solution is often easier with graphing calculators and can give a visual understanding of a problem. This method also works well with decimals.

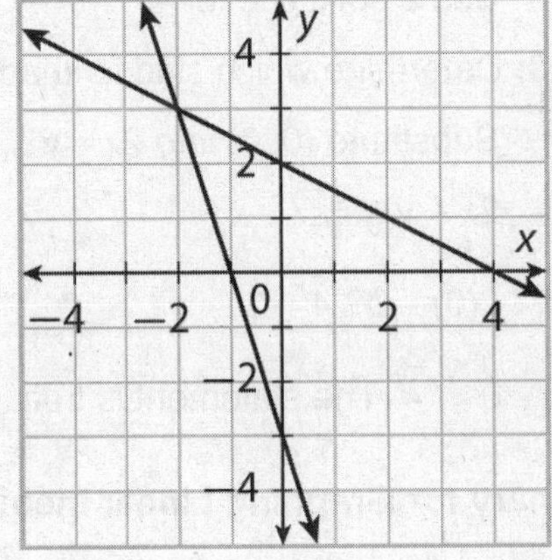

Solve using graphs.

$f(x) = -\frac{1}{2}x + 2$ and $g(x) = -3x - 3$

For $f(x)$

slope $= -\frac{1}{2}$ and y-intercept $= 2$

For $g(x)$

slope $= -3$ and y-intercept $= -3$

Plot $f(x)$ and $g(x)$ and find the intersection.

Tables work well with graphing calculators and are usually easiest for integers.

Solve with a table.

$f(x) = -3 + 2x$ and $g(x) = 12 - 3x$

x	**$f(x) = -3 + 2x$**	**$g(x) = 12 - 3x$**
0	−3	12
1	−1	9
2	1	6
3	**3**	**3**
4	5	0

1. In the algebraic example above, if $x = 2$, what does $f(x)$ equal? ____ What does $g(x)$ equal? ______

2. In the graphic example above, at what point do the lines for the equations intersect? ______

3. What does 3, 3 in the table indicate? ______________________________

Name ______________________ Date ______________ Class ______________

LESSON 7-3

Linear Inequalities in Two Variables

Reteach

To graph a linear inequality:

Step 1: Solve the inequality for *y*.

Step 2: Graph the boundary line. If $\le$ or $\ge$ use a solid line. If < or > use a dashed line.

Step 3: Determine which side to shade.

Graph the solutions of $2x + y \le 4$.

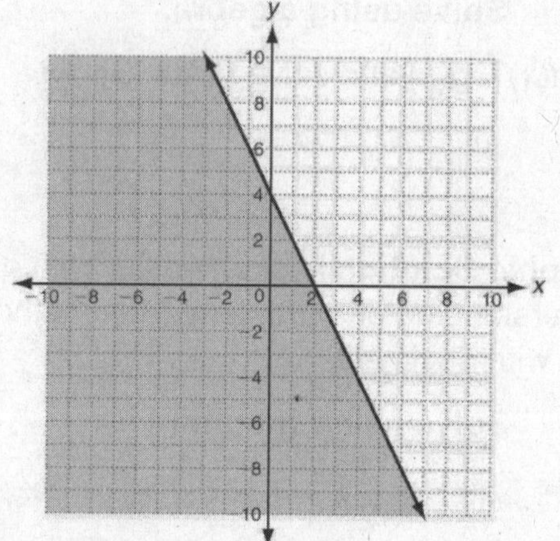

Step 1: Solve for *y*.

$$2x + y \le 4$$
$$-2x \qquad -2x$$
$$y \le -2x + 4$$

Step 2: Graph the boundary line.

Use a solid line for $\le$.

Step 3: Determine which side to shade.

Substitute (0, 0) into $2x + y \le 4$.

$2x + y \le 4$

$2(0) + 0 \overset{?}{\le} 4$

$0 \overset{?}{\le} 4$. The statement is true. Shade the side that contains the point (0, 0).

Summary for Graphing Linear Inequalities in Two Variables

- The boundary line is solid for $\le$ and $\ge$ and dashed for < and >.

When the inequality is written with *y* alone on the left, then:

- shade below and to the left of the line for < and $\le$,
- shade above and to the right of the line for > and $\ge$.

Graph the solutions of each linear inequality.
In the first one, the boundary line is already drawn.

1. $y < -2x - 9$

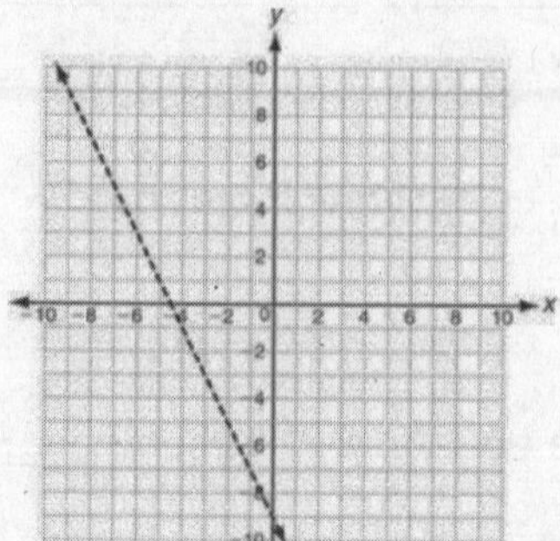

2. $y - x < 3$

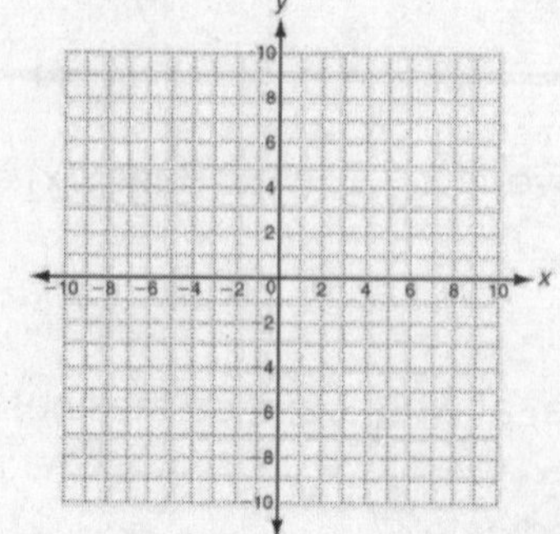

3. $x + y + 2 \ge 0$

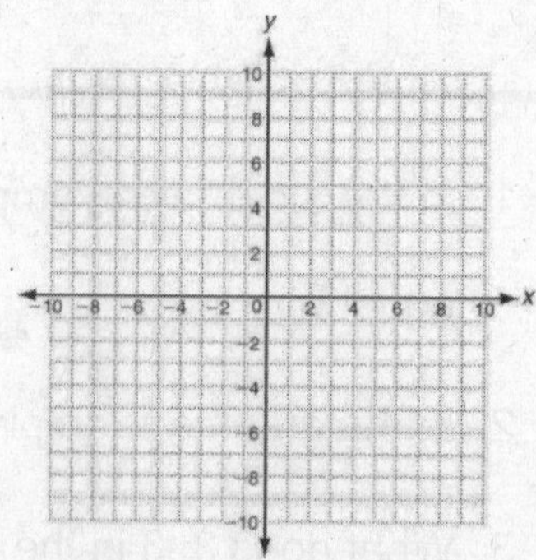

Name ____________________ Date ______________ Class ______________

LESSON 8-1

Two-Way Frequency Tables

Reteach

Students in grades 9 and 10 were asked if they favored or did not favor a change in the school mascot's outfit. To organize survey results, a two-way frequency table was used. There are two categories.

GRADE RESPONSE

Grades (**9 and 10**) → responses (**Yes or No**)

	Response	
Grade	**Yes**	**No**
9		
10		

There are four spaces for numbers. These numbers come from the survey.

Suppose Terry conducts a survey involving 110 randomly selected students from grade 9 and 90 students from grade 10. Now the two-way frequency table looks like this. Suppose that 68 ninth-graders want the uniform to change and 62 tenth graders do not want the change. The table at the left below shows the entries. Use subtraction to determine the number of ninth-graders who do not favor the change and the number of tenth graders who do favor the change.

	Response		
Grade	**Yes**	**No**	**Total**
9			110
10			90
Total			200

	Response		
Grade	**Yes**	**No**	**Total**
9	**68**		110
10		**62**	90
Total			200

110 − 68 = **42**   90 − 62 = **28**

	Response		
Grade	**Yes**	**No**	**Total**
9	68	**42**	110
10	**28**	62	90
Total	96	104	200

Complete the two-way frequency table.

1. A school administrator wanted to find out whether to have an assembly dealing with fire safety or community service. Fifty-six ninth-graders prefer community service and 53 tenth graders prefer fire safety.

	Assembly Preference		
Grade	**Fire Safety**	**Community Service**	**Total**
9			100
10			100
Total			200

Name ______________________ Date ______________ Class ______________

LESSON 8-2

Relative Frequency and Probability

Reteach

Shown at the right is the two-way frequency table about a survey that one school administrator conducted. The goal was to help determine the basis for class projects.

A student needs to use relative frequencies to interpret associations and trends between two categories in two-way frequency tables. How can such frequencies be calculated?

	Response		
Grade	**State Park**	**Train Station**	**Total**
9	64	56	120
10	54	66	120
Total	118	122	240

Marginal Relative Frequency

Compare, using a ratio, a column or row total to the grand total.

Train Station

The train station total is 122. → $\frac{122}{240}$ ✓

Joint Relative Frequency

Compare, using a ratio, a non-total frequency to the grand total.

Grade 9 and Train Station

56 is where Grade 9 and Train Station intersect. → $\frac{56}{240}$ ✓

Conditional Relative Frequency

Compare, using a ratio, a non-total frequency to a row total.

Condition: Grade 9. Use that **row**.

Given **Grade 9,** then Train Station

120 is the row total. → $\frac{56}{\mathbf{120}}$ ✓

Compare, using a ratio, a non-total frequency to a column total.

Condition: Train Station. Use that **column**.

Given **Train Station,** then Grade 9

122 is the column total. → $\frac{56}{\mathbf{122}}$ ✓

For this type of relative frequency, a condition is given first. This determines whether a row or column total is used as the denominator.

Determine each relative frequency. Leave answers in unsimplified fraction form.

1. that a student in either grade will prefer the state park ____________
2. grade 10 and the train station ____________
3. that a student will prefer the train station, given that the student is in grade 10 ____________
4. that a student is in grade 9 and prefers the state park ____________
5. grade 10 and the state park ____________
6. that a student will prefer the state park, given that the student is in grade 10 ____________

Name ____________________ Date ______________ Class ______________

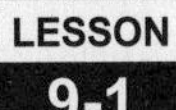

Measures of Center and Spread

Reteach

You can represent many values in a data set with just one central number. That **central number** may be the **mean** or the **median**.

Find the **mean** by adding the values and dividing by how many values are in the set. Find the **median** by arranging the values in order and finding the middle value.

Example

For the data set 6, 10, 8, 13, 20, 9, 5

Find the mean: $6 + 10 + 8 + 13 + 20 + 9 + 5 = 71$ and $71 \div 7 = 10.14$—the mean.

Find the median: 5, 6, 8, **9**, 10, 13, 20. The middle number is 9—the median.

If a data set has two middle numbers, the median is the average of those two numbers or the number that is halfway between them.

With a graphing calculator you can find several statistics about a data set.

Example

Find statistics about this data set: 13, 25, 9, 11, 23, 8, 7, 2, 18, 23.

Step 1: Use STAT and EDIT to enter the values into L_1. Check your entries for accuracy.

Step 2: Use STAT and CALC to see the 1-Var Stats by pressing ENTER twice.

$\bar{x} = 13.9$ — $\bar{x}$ is the symbol for the **mean**. The mean is 13.9.

$\sum X = 139$ — $\sum X$ is the symbol for the **sum of the values**. The sum is 139.

Skip down two to $\sigma x = 7.5$ (*rounded*). σx (say "sigma x") is the **standard deviation**.

- n = 10. n is the **number of values**. You entered 10 values.
- Min ***X*** = 2 tells you that the **minimum**, or lowest value, in the set is 2.
- Q1 = 8 tells you that the **first quartile** is 8. Quartiles divide the set into 4 quarters.
- Med = 12 tells you that the **median**, or **second quartile**, is 12.
- Q3 = 23 tells you that the **third quartile** is 23.
- max ***X*** = 25 tells you that the **maximum**, or highest value, in the set is 25.

To find the **range**, find maximum – minimum. The range in this set is $25 - 2 = 23$.
To find the **interquartile range**, find Q3–Q1. The interquartile range is $23 - 8 = 15$.

Range and standard deviation are measures of the **spread** of the data set.

Find each statistic for this data set: 5, 12, 22, 15, 17, 13, 25, 34, 7, 9.

1. mean ______________
2. median ______________
3. range ______________
4. first quartile ______________
5. interquartile range ______________
6. standard deviation ______________

Name _______________ Date __________ Class __________

LESSON 9-2

Data Distributions and Outliers

Reteach

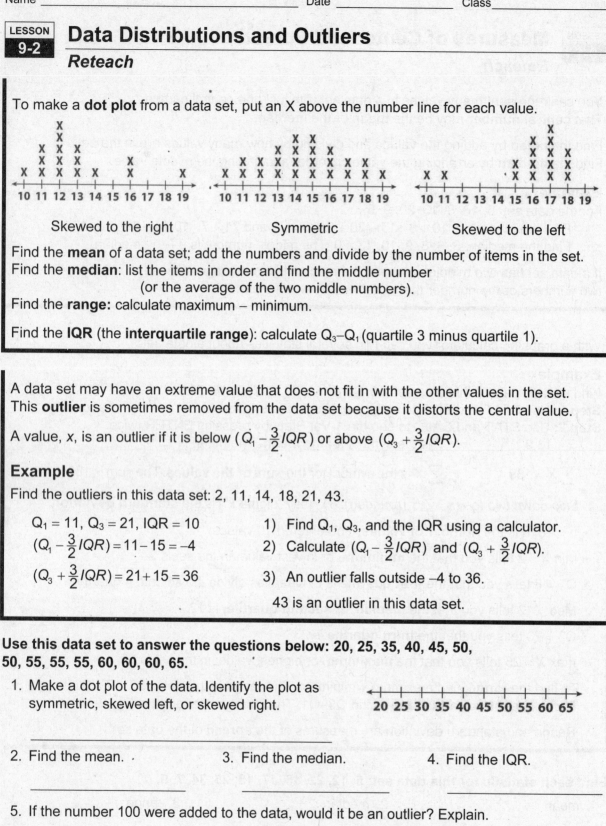

To make a **dot plot** from a data set, put an X above the number line for each value.

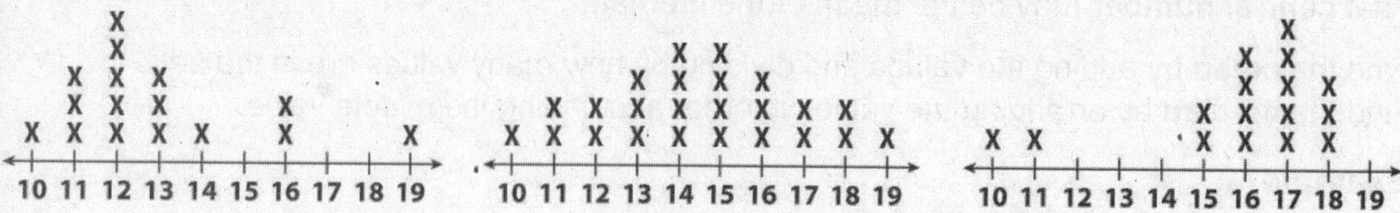

Skewed to the right | Symmetric | Skewed to the left

Find the **mean** of a data set; add the numbers and divide by the number of items in the set.
Find the **median**: list the items in order and find the middle number (or the average of the two middle numbers).
Find the **range:** calculate maximum – minimum.

Find the **IQR** (the **interquartile range**): calculate Q_3–Q_1 (quartile 3 minus quartile 1).

A data set may have an extreme value that does not fit in with the other values in the set. This **outlier** is sometimes removed from the data set because it distorts the central value.

A value, *x*, is an outlier if it is below $(Q_1 - \frac{3}{2}IQR)$ or above $(Q_3 + \frac{3}{2}IQR)$.

Example

Find the outliers in this data set: 2, 11, 14, 18, 21, 43.

$Q_1 = 11$, $Q_3 = 21$, $IQR = 10$

$(Q_1 - \frac{3}{2}IQR) = 11 - 15 = -4$

$(Q_3 + \frac{3}{2}IQR) = 21 + 15 = 36$

1) Find Q_1, Q_3, and the IQR using a calculator.
2) Calculate $(Q_1 - \frac{3}{2}IQR)$ and $(Q_3 + \frac{3}{2}IQR)$.
3) An outlier falls outside –4 to 36.

43 is an outlier in this data set.

Use this data set to answer the questions below: 20, 25, 35, 40, 45, 50, 50, 55, 55, 55, 60, 60, 60, 65.

1. Make a dot plot of the data. Identify the plot as symmetric, skewed left, or skewed right.

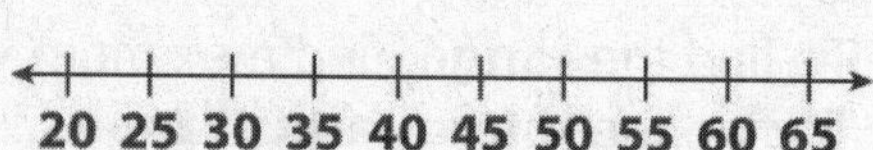

____

2. Find the mean. _______________

3. Find the median. _______________

4. Find the IQR. _______________

5. If the number 100 were added to the data, would it be an outlier? Explain.

____

6. Which of these would be changed by adding 90 to the data: mean, median, IQR? Explain.

____

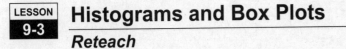

Name ______________________ Date ______________ Class ______________

LESSON 9-3

Histograms and Box Plots

Reteach

Make a Histogram

The estimated miles per gallon for selected cars are given: {26, 28, 32, 33, 26, 15, 21, 35, 17, 18, 25, 29, 30, 26, 27, 30, 24, 25, 24, 32, 25, 19, 22, 32, 25, 31, 28, 23, 27, 23, 24, 20, 38, 44, 18}.

Car Gas Mileage	
mi/gal	Frequency

Step 1: Find the difference between the greatest and least values. Try different widths for your intervals to determine the number of bars in the histogram. Use the difference to decide on intervals.

Step 2: Use the difference to decide on intervals. Try different widths for your intervals to determine the number of bars in the histogram.

Step 3: Create the frequency table.

Step 4: Use the frequency table to create the histogram. Draw each bar to the corresponding frequency.

1. Use the data set above to make a frequency table with intervals. Then make a histogram.

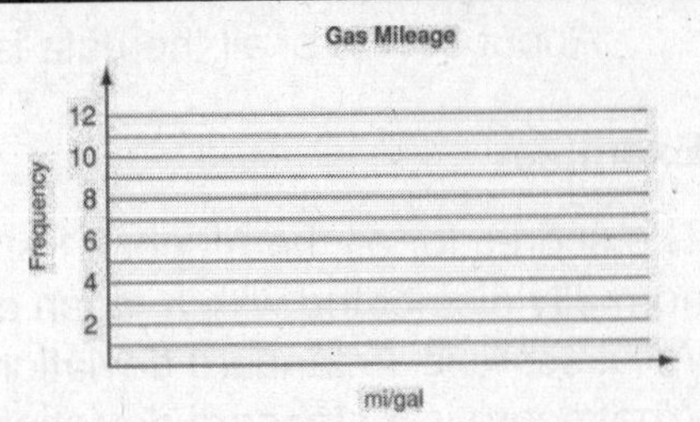

Box Plots

Consider the data set {3, 5, 6, 8, 8, 10, 11, 13, 14, 19, 20}.

Step 1: To make a **box plot**, first identify the five key numbers.

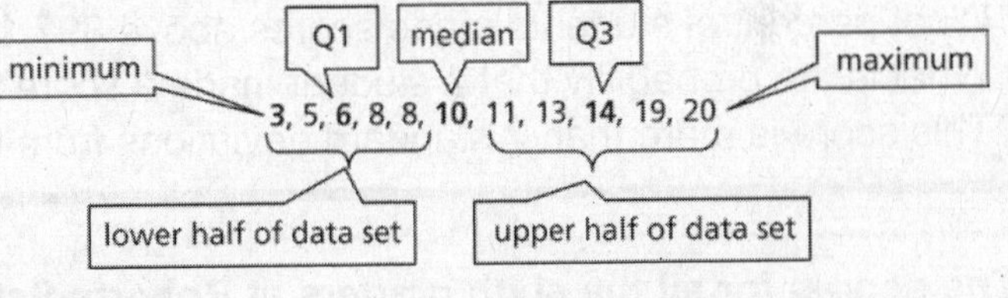

Step 2: Plot the five numbers above a number line. Draw a box so that the sides go through Q1 and Q3. Draw a line through the median. Connect the box to the minimum and maximum.

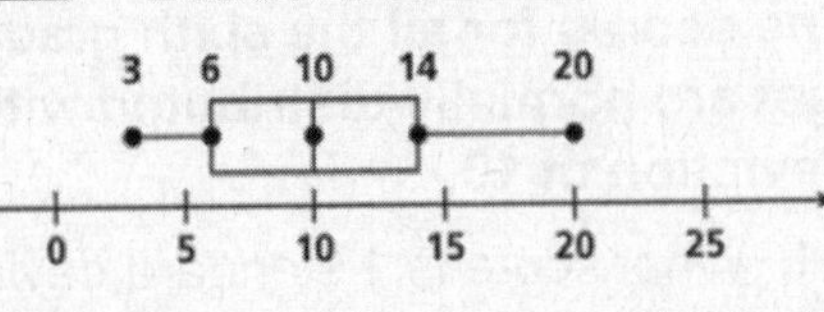

2. Write the following data in order: 9, 11, 18, 21, 18, 14, 5

____

3. Minimum: ______, Q1: ______, Median: ______, Q3: ______, Maximum: ______

4. Using the data set from Problem 2, draw the box plot.

Name ______________________ Date ______________ Class ______________

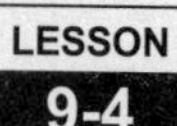

Normal Distributions

Reteach

You can take a table of relative frequencies showing measurement data and plot the frequencies as a histogram. When the intervals for the histogram are very small, the result is a special curve called a **normal curve**, or **bell curve**.

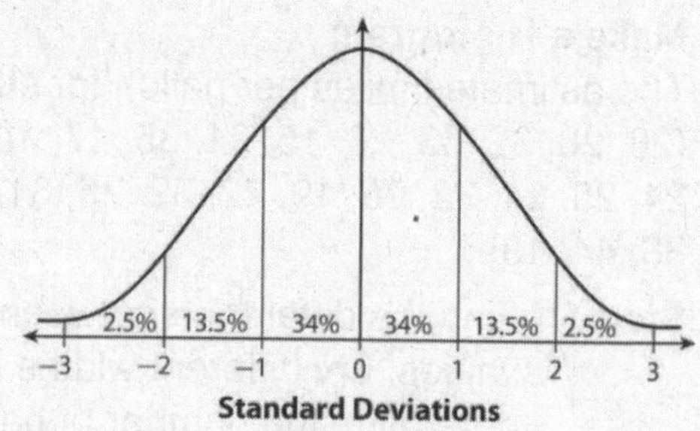

Data that fit this curve are called normally distributed.

When you know the **median** (the *y*-height at 0) and the **standard deviation** (marked as 1, 2, 3) of the data, you can use the curve to draw conclusions and make predictions about the data.

Here are some statements that are true about this special curve.

The mean and the median are the same—the center of the curve at its highest point.
The curve is symmetric. If you draw a vertical line at the median, the two sides match.
About 68% of all the data is within 1 standard deviation (−1 to +1) from the mean.
About 95% of all the data is within 2 standard deviations (−2 to +2) from the mean.
About 99.7% of all the data is within the 3 standard deviations (−3 to +3) from the mean.

Example

The scores for all the Algebra 1 students at Miller High on a test are normally distributed with a mean of 82 and a standard deviation of 7.
What score is 1 standard deviation above the mean? 82 + 7 = **89**
What score is 1 standard deviation below the mean? 82 − 7 = **75**
What percent of students made scores between 75 and 89? **68%**
What percent of students made scores above 89? 13.5% + 2.5% = **16%**
What is the probability that a student made a score above 96? 82 + 2(7) = **96**
This score is more than 2 standard deviations from the mean. The probability is **2.5%.**

The scores for all the sixth graders at Roberts School on a statewide test are normally distributed with a mean of 76 and a standard deviation of 10.

1. What score is 1 standard deviation above the mean?

____

2. What score is 2 standard deviations below the mean?

____

3. What percent of the scores were below 56?

____

4. What percent of the scores were above 86?

____

5. What is the probability that a student made a score between 66 and 86?

____

Name ______________________ Date ______________ Class ______________

LESSON 10-1

Scatter Plots and Trend Lines

Reteach

Correlation is one way to describe the relationship between two sets of data.

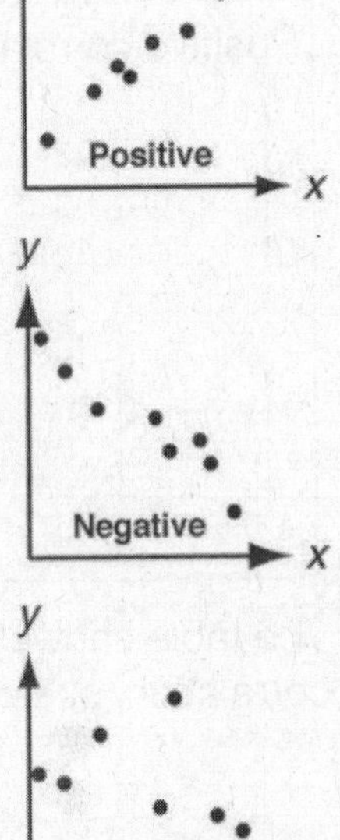

Positive Correlation

Data: As one set **increases,** the other set **increases.**

Graph: The graph **goes up** from left to right.

Negative Correlation

Data: As one set **increases,** the other set **decreases.**

Graph: The graph **goes down** from left to right.

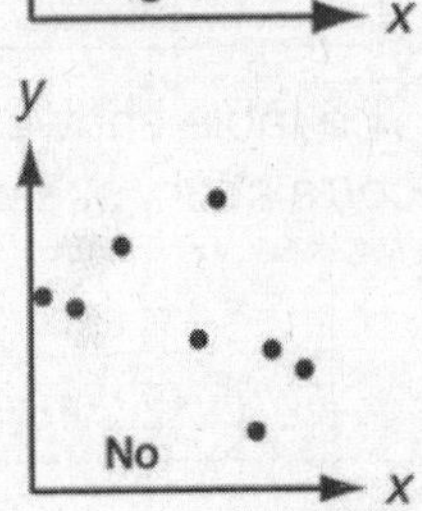

No Correlation

Data: There is **no relationship** between the sets.

Graph: The graph has **no pattern.**

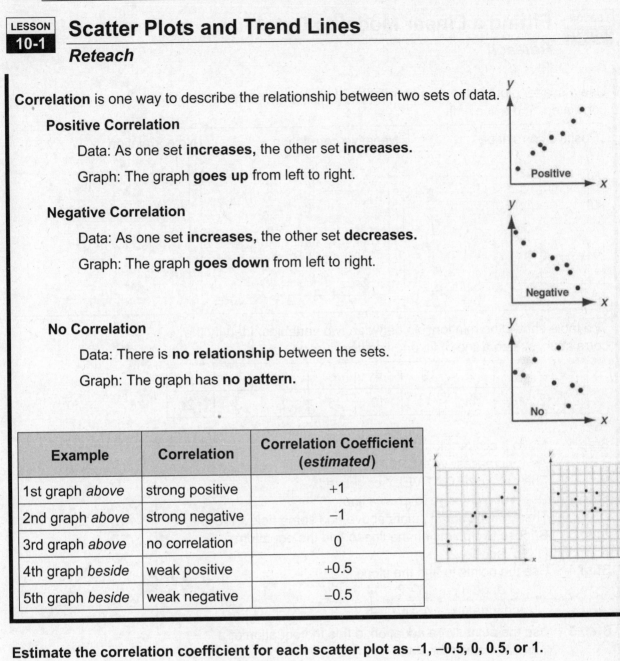

Example	Correlation	Correlation Coefficient (*estimated*)
1st graph *above*	strong positive	+1
2nd graph *above*	strong negative	–1
3rd graph *above*	no correlation	0
4th graph *beside*	weak positive	+0.5
5th graph *beside*	weak negative	–0.5

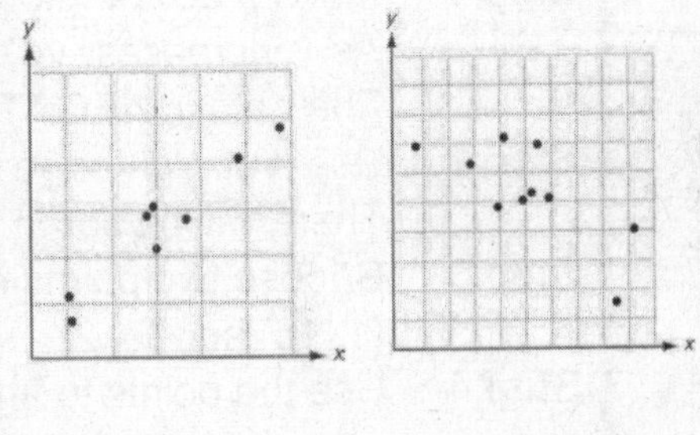

Estimate the correlation coefficient for each scatter plot as –1, –0.5, 0, 0.5, or 1.

1. 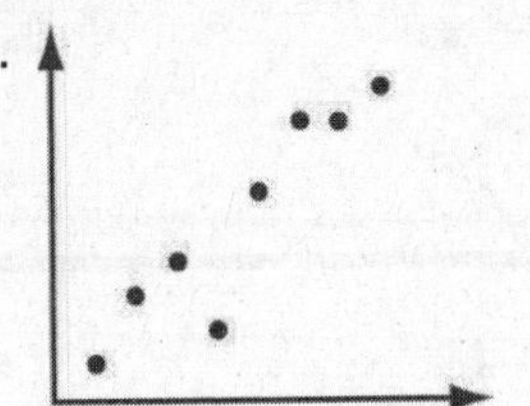

2. 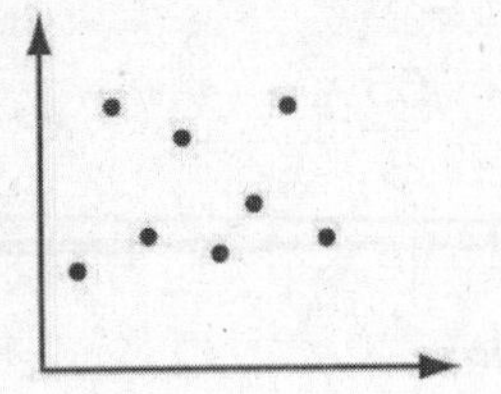

3. 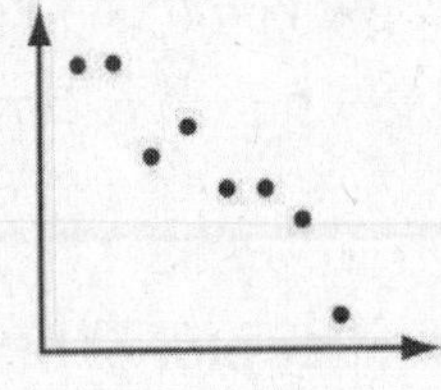

______________ ______________ ______________

Name ______________________ Date ______________ Class ______________

LESSON 10-2

Fitting a Linear Model to Data

Reteach

Use a scatter plot to identify a correlation. If the variables appear to be correlated, find a line of fit.

Positive correlation	Negative correlation	No correlation
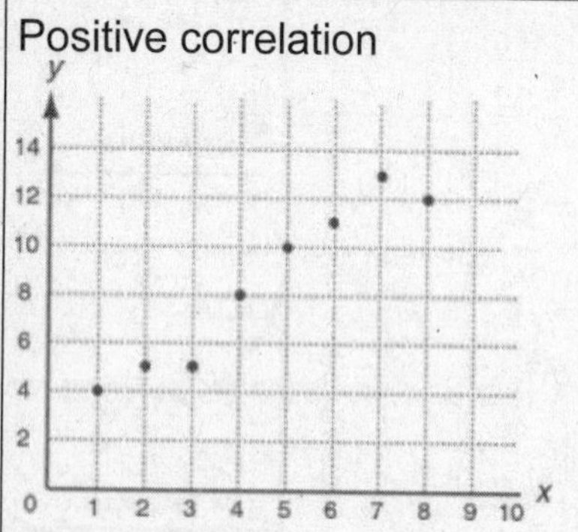	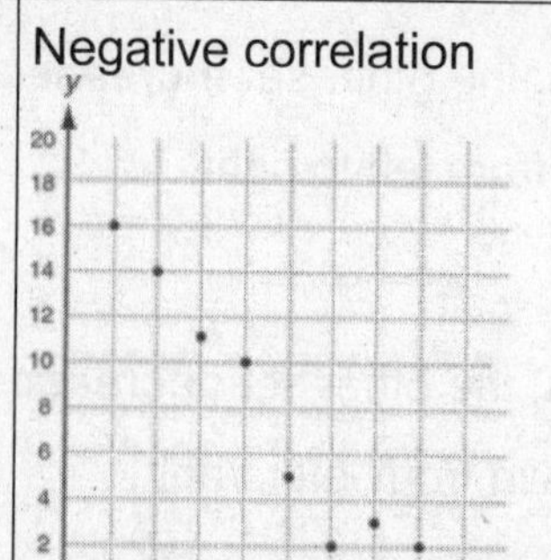	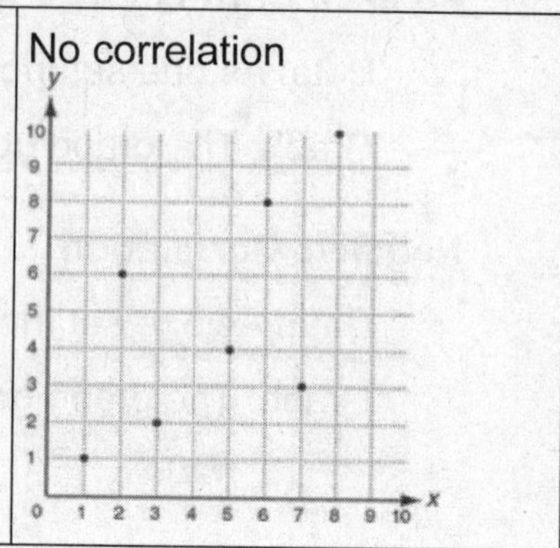

The table shows the relationship between two variables. Identify the correlation, sketch a line of fit, and find its equation.

x	1	2	3	4	5	6	7	8
y	16	14	11	10	5	2	3	2

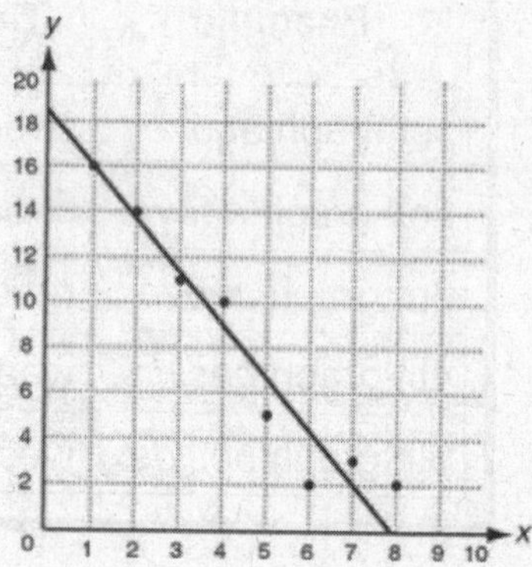

Step 1 Make a scatter plot of the data.
As x increases, y DECREASES.
The data is NEGATIVELY correlated.

Step 2 Use a straightedge to draw a line.
There will be some points above and some below the line.

Step 3 Choose two points on the line to find the equation:
(1, 16) and (7, 2).

Step 4 Use the points to find the slope:

$$m = \frac{\text{change in } y}{\text{change in } x} = \frac{16-2}{1-7} = \frac{14}{-6} = -\frac{7}{3}$$

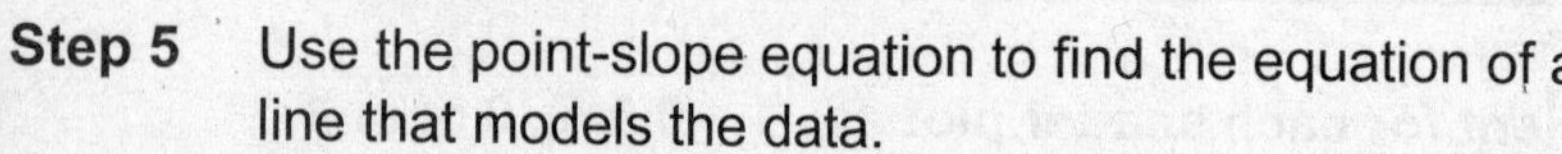

Step 5 Use the point-slope equation to find the equation of a line that models the data.

$y - y_1 = m(x - x_1)$

$y - 2 = -\frac{7}{3}(x - 7)$ or $y = -\frac{7}{3}x + \frac{55}{3}$

Use the scatter plot of the data to solve.

1. The correlation is ______________________.

2. Choose two points on the line and find the slope.

____

3. Find the equation of a line that models the data.

____

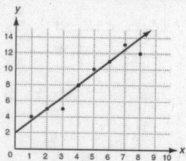

Name ______________________ Date ______________ Class ______________

LESSON 11-1

Solving Linear Systems by Graphing

Reteach

The solution to a system of linear equations can be found by graphing. Write both equations so that they are in slope-intercept form and draw their lines on a coordinate graph. The point of intersection is the solution. If the lines have the same slope but different *y*-intercepts they won't intersect and there is no solution. If the graphs are the same line then there are an infinite number of solutions.

Example

Solve the system. $4x + 2y = 4$, $-6x + 3y = -18$ Rewrite each equation in slope-intercept form.

$y = -2x + 2$

$y = 2x - 6$

Graph the lines and look for the point of intersection.

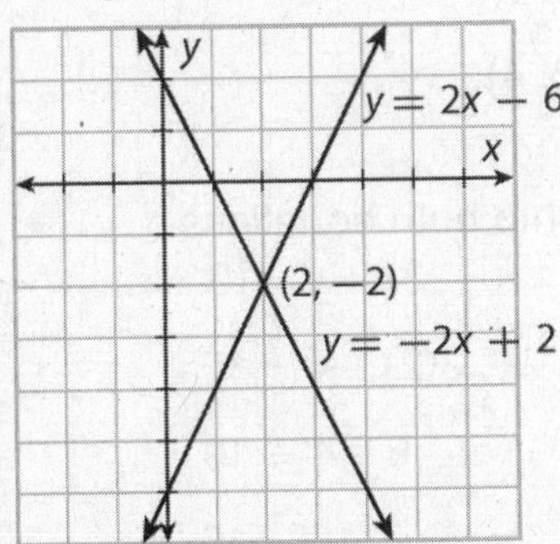

The lines intersect at (2, –2).

The solution to the system is (2, –2).

Solve each linear system of equations by graphing.

1. $\begin{cases} x + y = -1 \\ 4x - 2y = -16 \end{cases}$

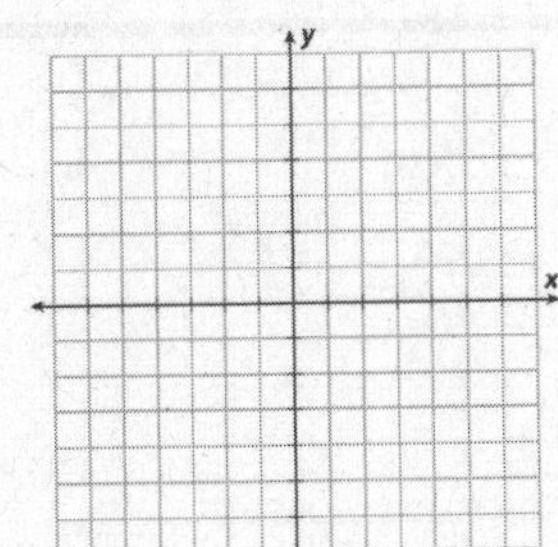

____

2. $\begin{cases} -3x + y = 10 \\ -2x + 4y = 0 \end{cases}$

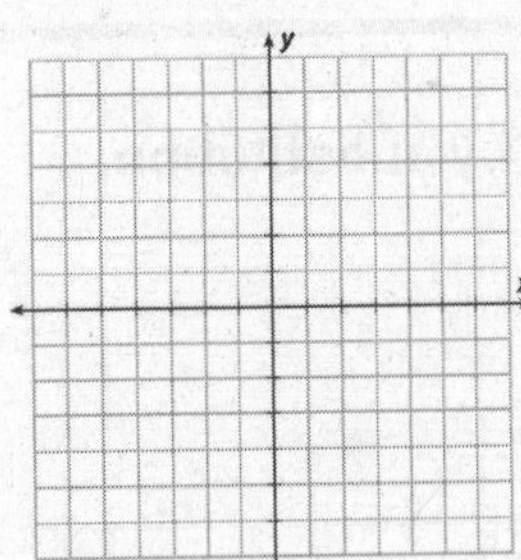

____

3. $\begin{cases} 2x + y = 4 \\ x - y = 2 \end{cases}$

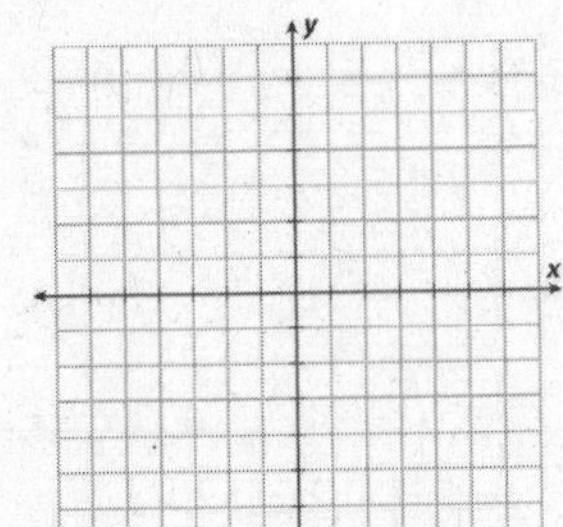

____

4. $\begin{cases} 6x - 3y = 12 \\ 2x + 2y = 10 \end{cases}$

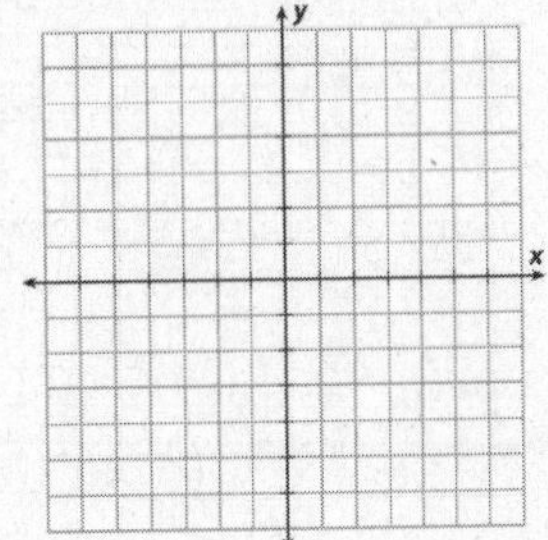

____

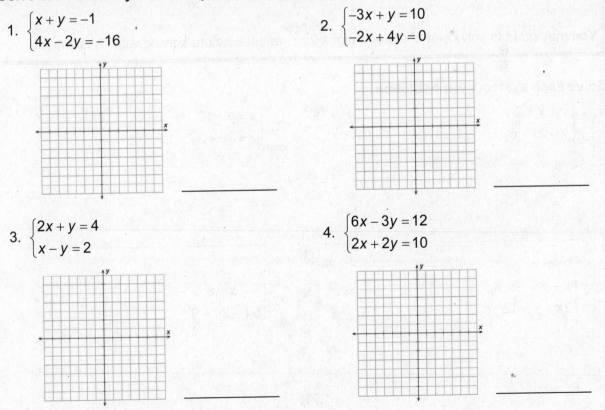

Name ______________________ Date ____________ Class ____________

LESSON 11-2

Solving Linear Systems by Substitution

Reteach

You can use substitution to solve a system of equations if one of the equations is already solved for a variable.

Solve $\begin{cases} y = x + 2 \\ 3x + y = 10 \end{cases}$

Step 1: Choose the equation to use as the substitute.

Use the first equation $y = x + 2$ because it is already solved for a variable.

Step 2: Solve by substitution.

$x + 2$

$$3x + y = 10$$
$$3x + (x + 2) = 10 \quad \textit{Substitute } x + 2 \textit{ for } y.$$
$$4x + 2 = 10 \quad \textit{Combine like terms.}$$
$$\underline{-2} = \underline{-2}$$
$$4x = 8$$
$$\frac{4x}{4} = \frac{8}{4}$$
$$x = 2$$

Step 3: Now substitute $x = 2$ back into one of the original equations to find the value of y.

$$y = x + 2$$
$$y = 2 + 2$$
$$y = 4$$

The solution is (2, 4).

Check:

Substitute (2, 4) into both equations.

$y = x + 2$	$3x + y = 10$
$4 \stackrel{?}{=} 2 + 2$	$3(2) + 4 \stackrel{?}{=} 10$
$4 \stackrel{?}{=} 4$ ✓	$6 + 4 \stackrel{?}{=} 10$
	$10 \stackrel{?}{=} 10$ ✓

You may need to solve one of the equations for a variable before solving with substitution.

Solve each system by substitution.

1. $\begin{cases} y = x + 2 \\ y = 2x - 5 \end{cases}$

____

2. $\begin{cases} x = y + 10 \\ x = 2y + 3 \end{cases}$

____

3. $\begin{cases} x - y = -3 \\ 2x + y = 12 \end{cases}$

____

4. $\begin{cases} y - x = 8 \\ 5x + 2y = 9 \end{cases}$

____

Name ______________________ Date ______________ Class ______________

LESSON 11-3

Solving Linear Systems by Adding or Subtracting

Reteach

To use the **elimination method** to solve a system of linear equations:

1. Add or subtract the equations to eliminate one variable.

2. Solve the resulting equation for the other variable.

3. Substitute the value for the known variable into one of the original equations.

4. Solve for the other variable.

5. Check the values in both equations.

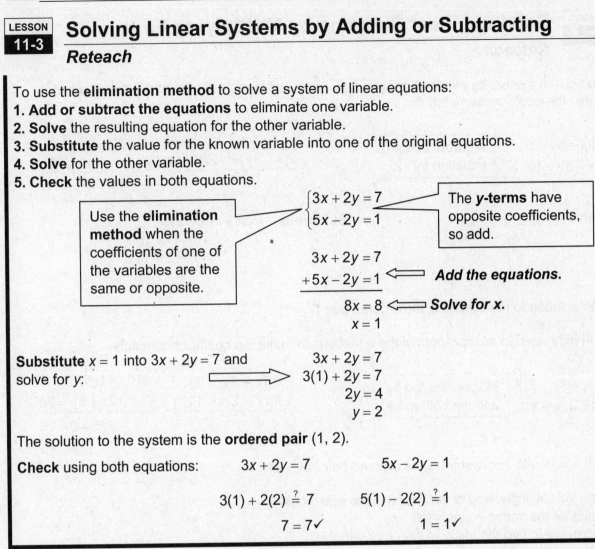

Use the **elimination method** when the coefficients of one of the variables are the same or opposite.

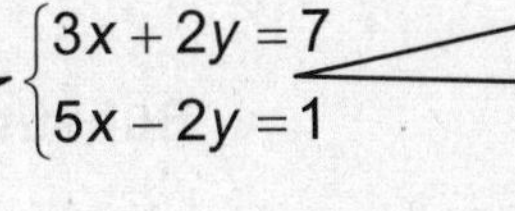

$$\begin{cases} 3x + 2y = 7 \\ 5x - 2y = 1 \end{cases}$$

The **y-terms** have opposite coefficients, so add.

$$\begin{array}{r} 3x + 2y = 7 \\ +5x - 2y = 1 \\ \hline 8x = 8 \\ x = 1 \end{array}$$

Add the equations.

Solve for x.

Substitute $x = 1$ into $3x + 2y = 7$ and solve for y:

$$\begin{array}{r} 3x + 2y = 7 \\ 3(1) + 2y = 7 \\ 2y = 4 \\ y = 2 \end{array}$$

The solution to the system is the **ordered pair** (1, 2).

Check using both equations:

$3x + 2y = 7$	$5x - 2y = 1$
$3(1) + 2(2) \overset{?}{=} 7$	$5(1) - 2(2) \overset{?}{=} 1$
$7 = 7$ ✓	$1 = 1$ ✓

Solve each system by adding or subtracting.

1. $\begin{cases} -2x - y = -5 \\ 3x + y = -1 \end{cases}$

____

2. $\begin{cases} 3x + 2y = 10 \\ 3x - 2y = 14 \end{cases}$

____

3. $\begin{cases} x + y = 12 \\ 2x + y = 6 \end{cases}$

____

4. $\begin{cases} 2x + y = 1 \\ -2x - 3y = 5 \end{cases}$

____

Name ______________________ Date ______________ Class ______________

LESSON 11-4

Solving Linear Systems by Multiplying First

Reteach

To solve a system by **elimination**, you may first need to multiply *one* of the equations to make the coefficients match.

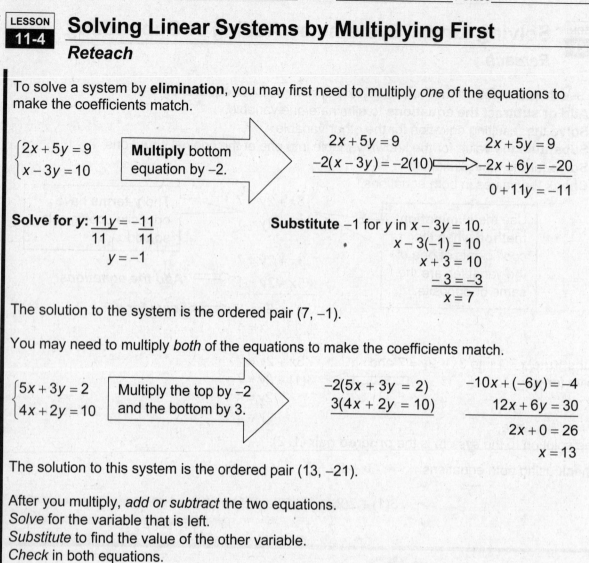

$$\begin{cases} 2x + 5y = 9 \\ x - 3y = 10 \end{cases}$$

Multiply bottom equation by –2.

$$\begin{aligned} 2x + 5y &= 9 \\ -2(x - 3y) &= -2(10) \end{aligned} \Rightarrow \begin{aligned} 2x + 5y &= 9 \\ -2x + 6y &= -20 \\ \hline 0 + 11y &= -11 \end{aligned}$$

Solve for *y*: $\frac{11y}{11} = \frac{-11}{11}$

$y = -1$

Substitute –1 for y in $x - 3y = 10$.

$$\begin{aligned} x - 3(-1) &= 10 \\ x + 3 &= 10 \\ -3 &= -3 \\ \hline x &= 7 \end{aligned}$$

The solution to the system is the ordered pair (7, –1).

You may need to multiply *both* of the equations to make the coefficients match.

$$\begin{cases} 5x + 3y = 2 \\ 4x + 2y = 10 \end{cases}$$

Multiply the top by –2 and the bottom by 3.

$$\begin{aligned} -2(5x + 3y &= 2) \\ 3(4x + 2y &= 10) \end{aligned} \qquad \begin{aligned} -10x + (-6y) &= -4 \\ 12x + 6y &= 30 \\ \hline 2x + 0 &= 26 \\ x &= 13 \end{aligned}$$

The solution to this system is the ordered pair (13, –21).

After you multiply, *add or subtract* the two equations.
Solve for the variable that is left.
Substitute to find the value of the other variable.
Check in both equations.

Solve each system by multiplying first. Check your answer.

1. $\begin{cases} 2x - 3y = 5 \\ x + 2y = -1 \end{cases}$

2. $\begin{cases} 3x - y = 2 \\ -8x + 2y = 4 \end{cases}$

______________________ ______________________

3. $\begin{cases} 2x + 5y = 22 \\ 10x + 3y = 22 \end{cases}$

4. $\begin{cases} 4x + 2y = 14 \\ 7x - 3y = -8 \end{cases}$

______________________ ______________________

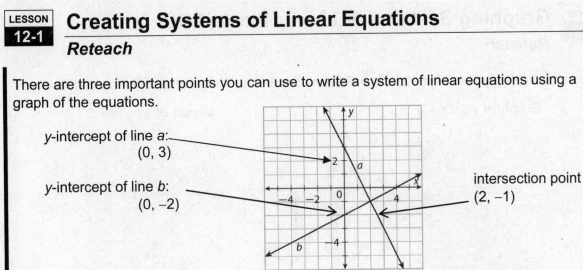

Name ______________________ Date ______________ Class ______________

LESSON 12-1

Creating Systems of Linear Equations

Reteach

There are three important points you can use to write a system of linear equations using a graph of the equations.

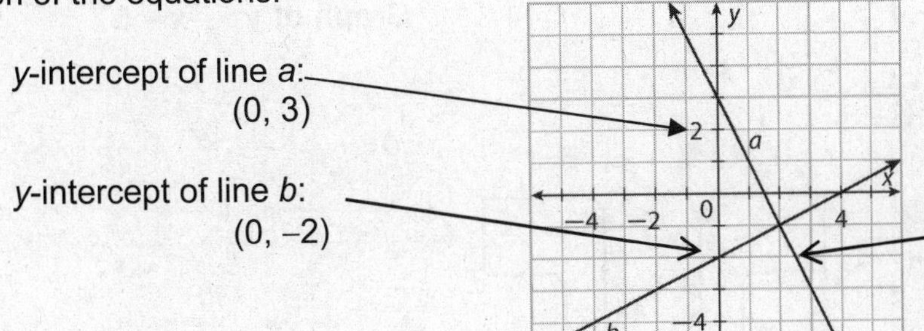

line *a*

$m = \frac{3-(-1)}{0-2} = -\frac{4}{-2} = -2$

$b = 3$

$y = -2x + 3$

line *b*

$m = \frac{-1-(-1)}{0-2} = \frac{-1}{-2} = \frac{1}{2}$

$b = -2$

$y = \frac{1}{2}x - 2$

Find the *y*-intercepts and intersection point for each graph. Then write a system of equations for each graph.

1.

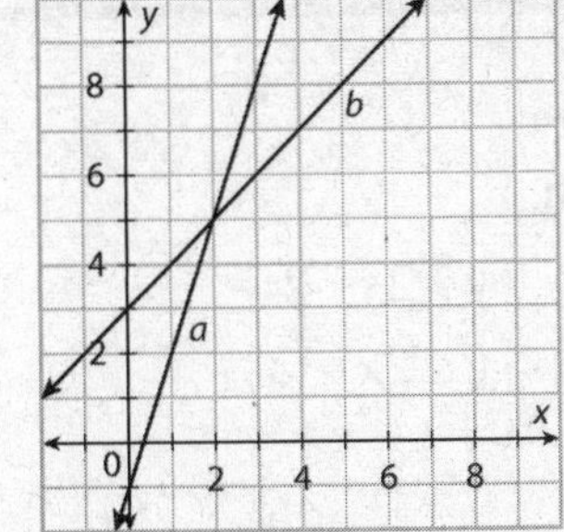

y-intercept of line *a*: ____

y-intercept of line *b*: ____

intersection: ________

____

2.

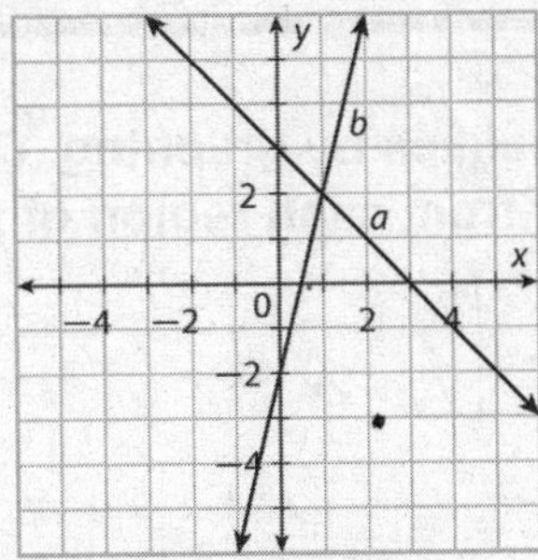

y-intercept of line *a*: ____

y-intercept of line *b*: ____

intersection: ________

____

3.

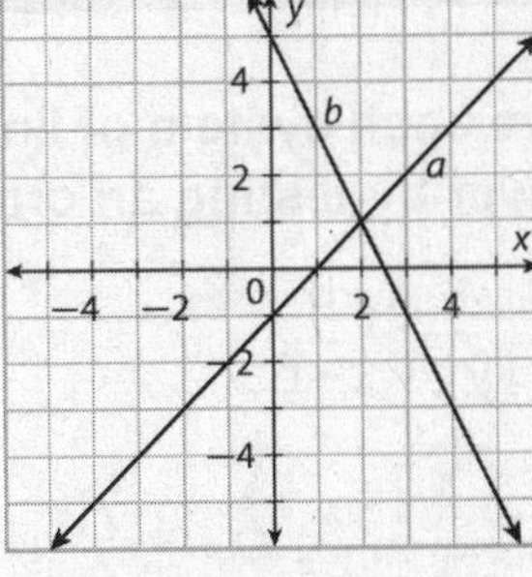

y-intercept of line *a*: ____

y-intercept of line *b*: ____

intersection: ________

____

Name ______________________________ Date ________________ Class ________________

LESSON 12-2

Graphing Systems of Linear Inequalities

Reteach

You can graph a system of linear inequalities by combining the graphs of the inequalities.

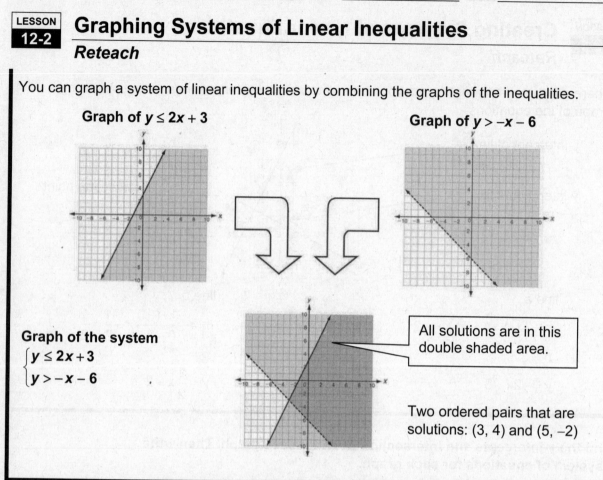

Graph of $y \le 2x + 3$

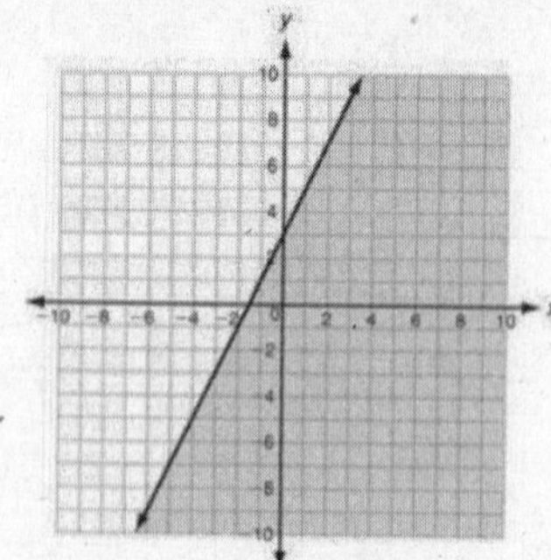

Graph of $y > -x - 6$

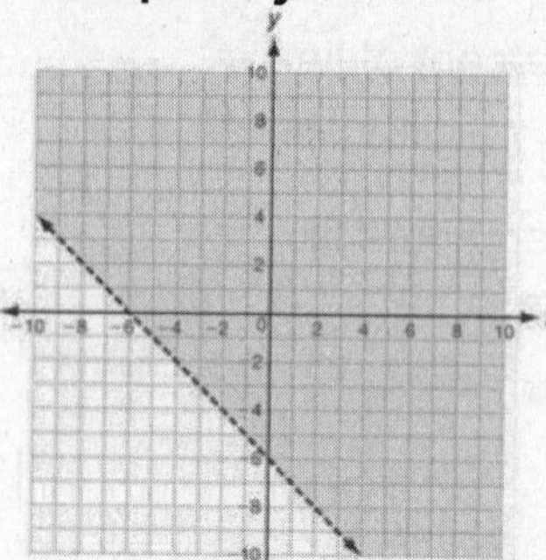

Graph of the system

$$\begin{cases} y \le 2x + 3 \\ y > -x - 6 \end{cases}$$

All solutions are in this double shaded area.

Two ordered pairs that are solutions: (3, 4) and (5, –2)

Solve each system of linear inequalities by graphing. Check your answer by testing an ordered pair from each region of your graph.

1. $\begin{cases} y > x - 3 \\ y \ge -x + 6 \end{cases}$

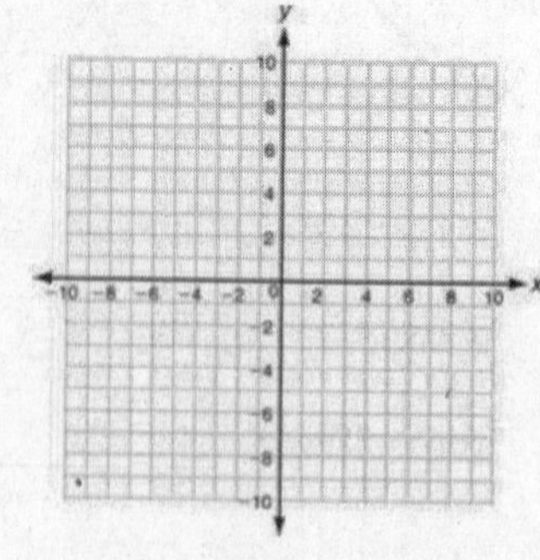

____

2. $\begin{cases} y < x \\ y > -2x + 1 \end{cases}$

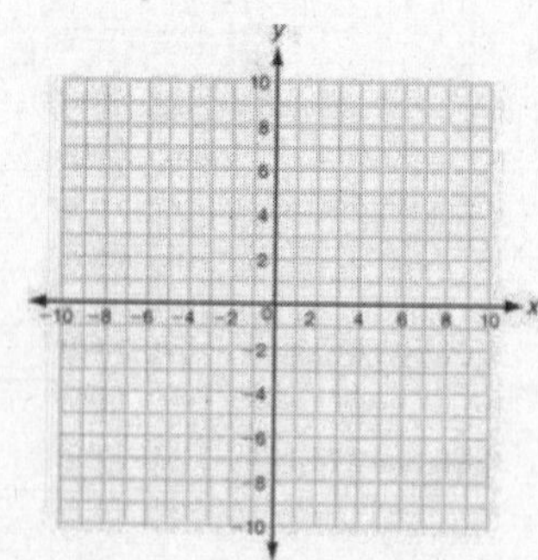

____

3. $\begin{cases} y > 2x - 2 \\ y \le 2x + 3 \end{cases}$

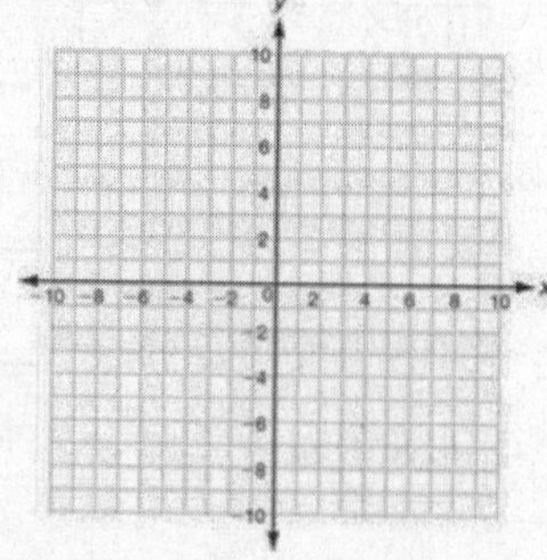

____

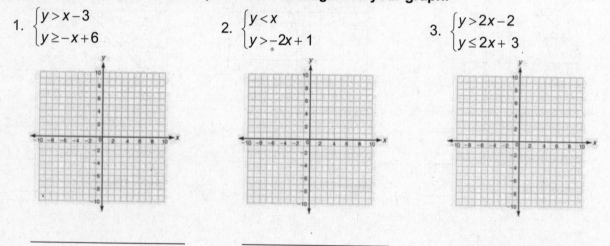

Name ____________________ Date ______________ Class ______________

LESSON 12-3

Modeling with Linear Systems

Reteach

Mrs. Hathaway bought a total of 12 items made up of some sticky notes and some pens. The sticky notes cost \$4 each and the pens cost \$2 each. She spent a total of \$40 on all items. How many pens and how many sticky notes did she buy?

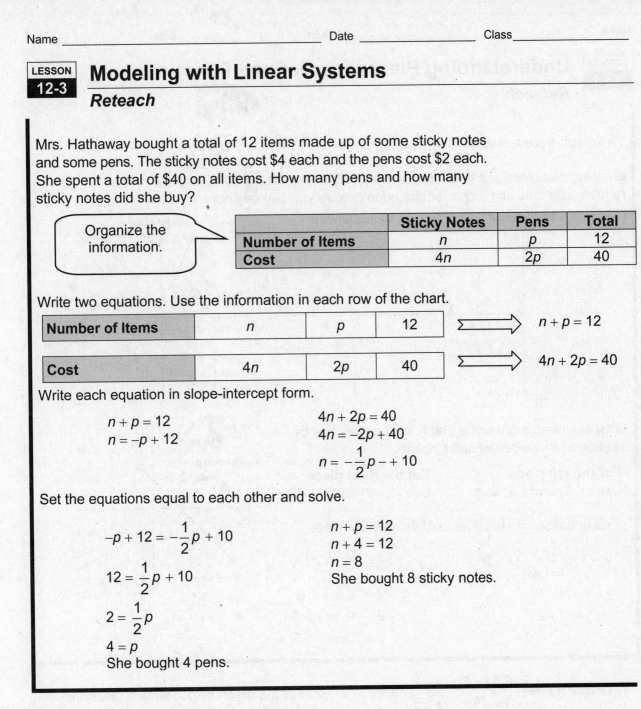

Organize the information.

	Sticky Notes	Pens	Total
Number of Items	n	p	12
Cost	$4n$	$2p$	40

Write two equations. Use the information in each row of the chart.

Number of Items	n	p	12	⇒ $n + p = 12$
Cost	$4n$	$2p$	40	⇒ $4n + 2p = 40$

Write each equation in slope-intercept form.

$n + p = 12$
$n = -p + 12$

$4n + 2p = 40$
$4n = -2p + 40$
$n = -\frac{1}{2}p - + 10$

Set the equations equal to each other and solve.

$-p + 12 = -\frac{1}{2}p + 10$

$12 = \frac{1}{2}p + 10$

$2 = \frac{1}{2}p$

$4 = p$

She bought 4 pens.

$n + p = 12$
$n + 4 = 12$
$n = 8$

She bought 8 sticky notes.

Solve.

1. Tia has 25 china figures in her collection. The horse figures cost \$2 each, and the cat figures cost \$1 each. She paid \$39 for all the figures in the collection. How many horses and how many cats does she have?

   Equations: ______________________

   Solution: ______________________

2. Mr. Wallace has 32 models of antique cars. The Hupmobile models cost \$5 each, and the Duesenberg models cost \$18 each. He paid a total of \$264 for all the models. How many Hupmobile models and how many Duesenberg models does he have?

   Equations: ______________________

   Solution: ______________________

Name ______________________ Date ______________ Class ______________

LESSON 13-1

Understanding Piecewise-Defined Functions

Reteach

You graph a piecewise function such as $f(x)=\begin{cases}-2x+1 & x\le 2\\ x+1 & x>2\end{cases}$ by graphing one piece at a time. Here are the steps. Remember that ≤ and ≥ require solid dots and < or > require open dots as you can see here.

First Interval

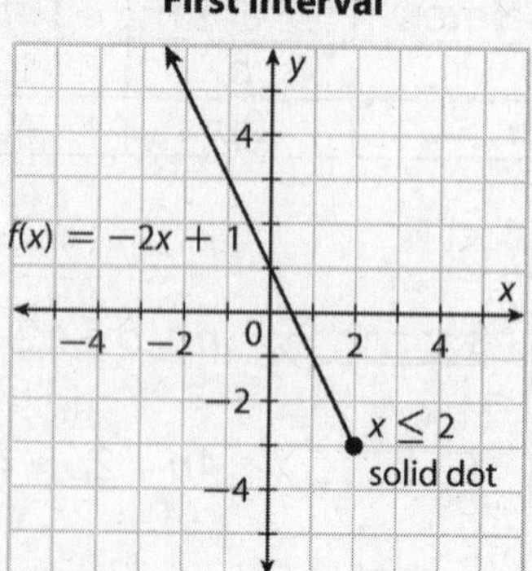

Second Interval

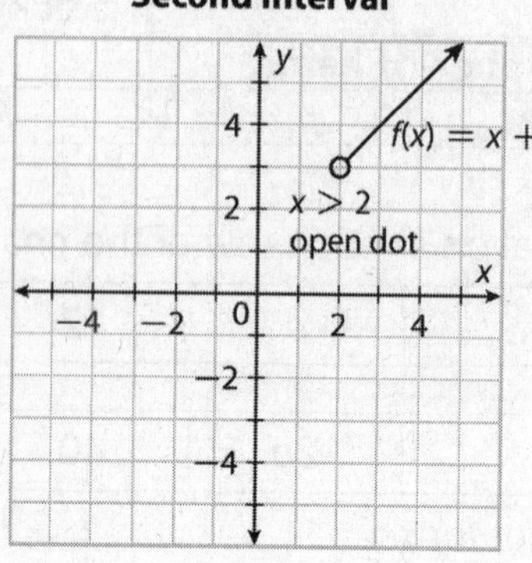

Both Intervals

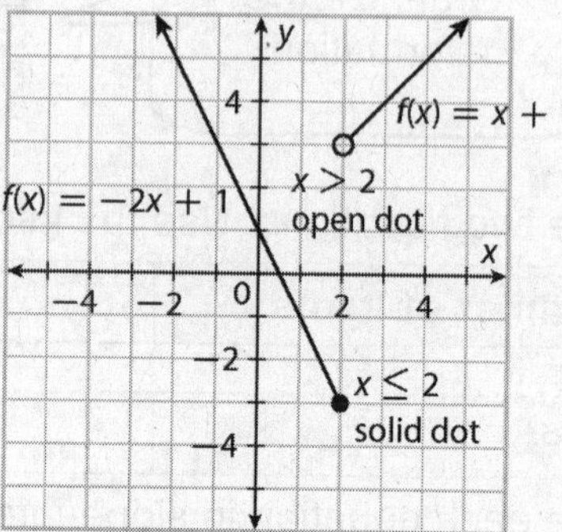

You can often represent a graph such as this one by writing a piecewise-defined function.

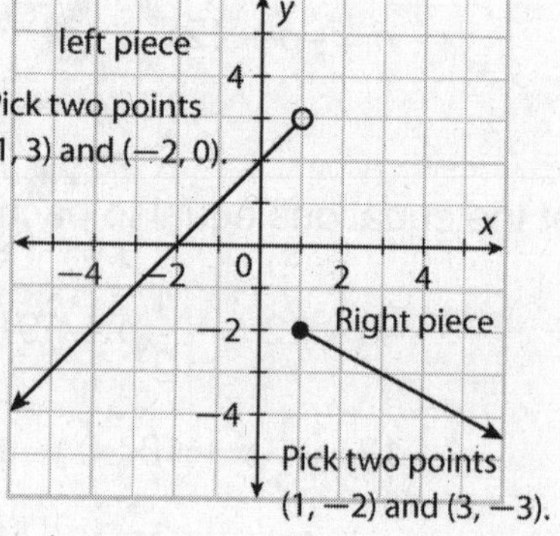

For the left piece
Use **(1, 3) and (−2, 0).**

For the right piece
Use **(1, −2) and (3, −3).**

Find equations for the lines containing these pairs.

$$y-3=\frac{3-0}{1-(-2)}(x-1)$$

$$y-3=x-1$$

$$y=x+2$$

$$y-(-2)=\frac{-2-(-3)}{1-3}(x-1)$$

$$y+2=-0.5(x-1)$$

$$y+2=-0.5x+0.5$$

$$y=-0.5x-1.5$$

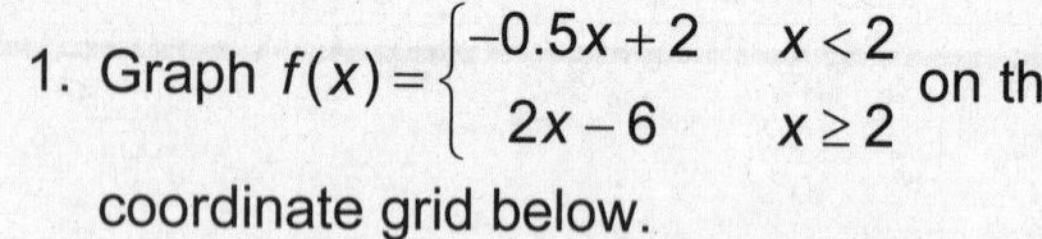

1. Graph $f(x)=\begin{cases}-0.5x+2 & x<2\\ 2x-6 & x\ge 2\end{cases}$ on the coordinate grid below.

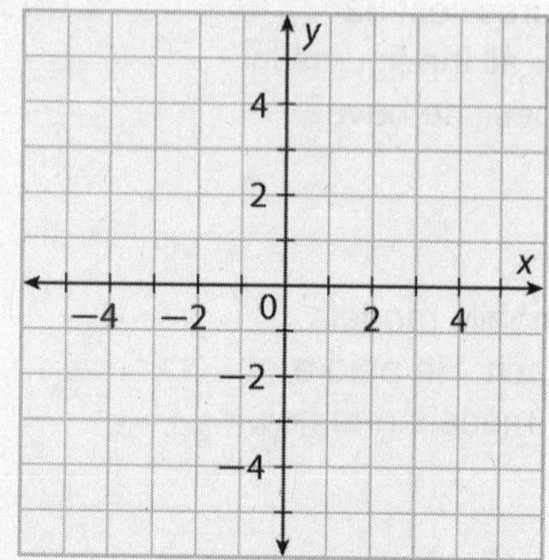

2. For the graph below, write a piecewise defined function to represent it.

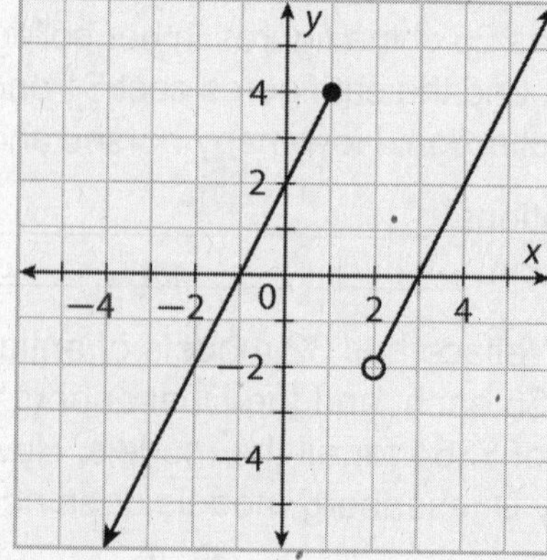

____

Name ______________________ Date ______________ Class ______________

LESSON 13-2

Absolute Value Functions and Transformations

Reteach

Transformations of an absolute value function start with understanding what the graph of $f(x) = |x|$ looks like. Let's start by making a table of values.

x	$f(x) = \|x\|$
–2	2
–1	1
0	0
1	1
2	2

Plot these points on a graph and connect the points.

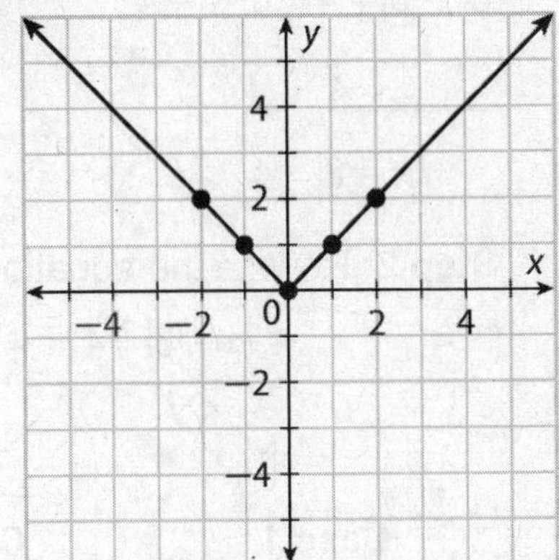

The graph of the absolute value function $f(x) = |x|$ is called the parent graph and is in the shape of a "V".

The general form of an absolute value function is $f(x) = a|x - h| + k$ where *a*, *h*, and *k* are real numbers. *h* and *k* affect the location of the vertex, and *a* affects the slope.

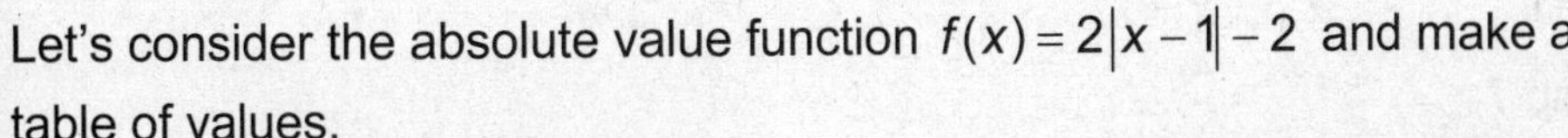

Let's consider the absolute value function $f(x) = 2|x - 1| - 2$ and make a table of values.

x	$f(x) = 2\|x - 1\| - 2$
–2	4
–1	2
0	0
1	–2
2	0
3	2

Plot these points on a graph and connect the points.

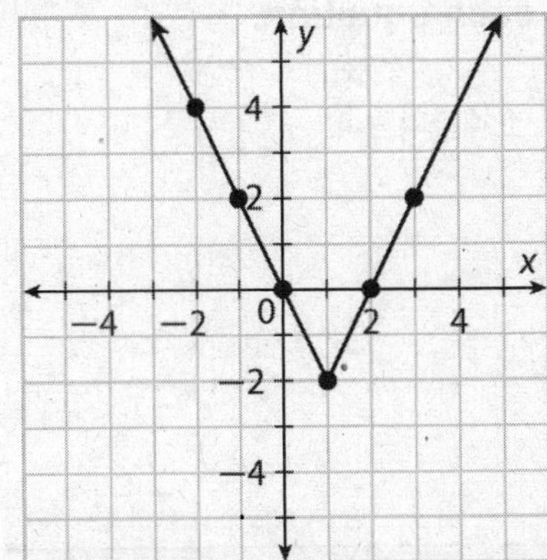

Compare this graph with the parent graph.

Use the graph to answer the questions.

1. What does the *k*-value (–2) do to the vertex? ______________________

2. What does the *h*-value (1) do to the vertex? ______________________

3. How did the *a*-value (2) affect the slope? ______________________

Name ______________________ Date ______________ Class ______________

LESSON 13-3

Solving Absolute-Value Equations

Reteach

There are three steps in solving an absolute-value equation.

Solve $|x - 3| + 4 = 8$.

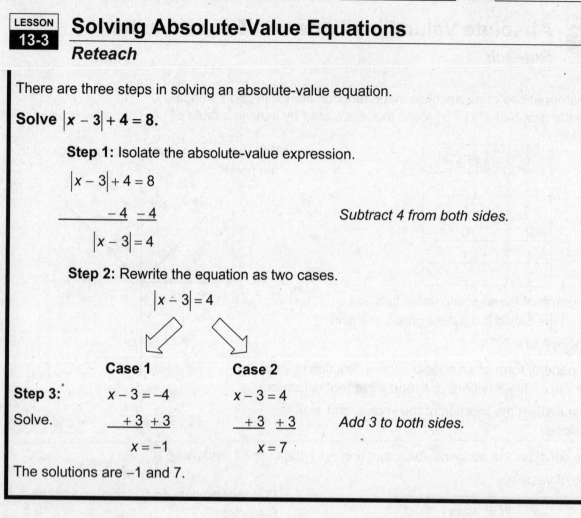

Step 1: Isolate the absolute-value expression.

$$\begin{aligned} |x - 3| + 4 &= 8 \\ -4 &\quad -4 \\ \hline |x - 3| &= 4 \end{aligned}$$

Subtract 4 from both sides.

Step 2: Rewrite the equation as two cases.

$|x - 3| = 4$

	Case 1	**Case 2**	
Step 3:	$x - 3 = -4$	$x - 3 = 4$	
Solve.	$+3 \quad +3$	$+3 \quad +3$	*Add 3 to both sides.*
	$x = -1$	$x = 7$	

The solutions are −1 and 7.

Solve each equation.

1. $|x - 2| - 3 = 5$

2. $|x + 7| + 2 = 10$

________________________ ________________________

3. $4|x - 5| = 20$

4. $|2x| + 1 = 7$

________________________ ________________________

Name ______________________ Date ______________ Class ______________

LESSON 13-4

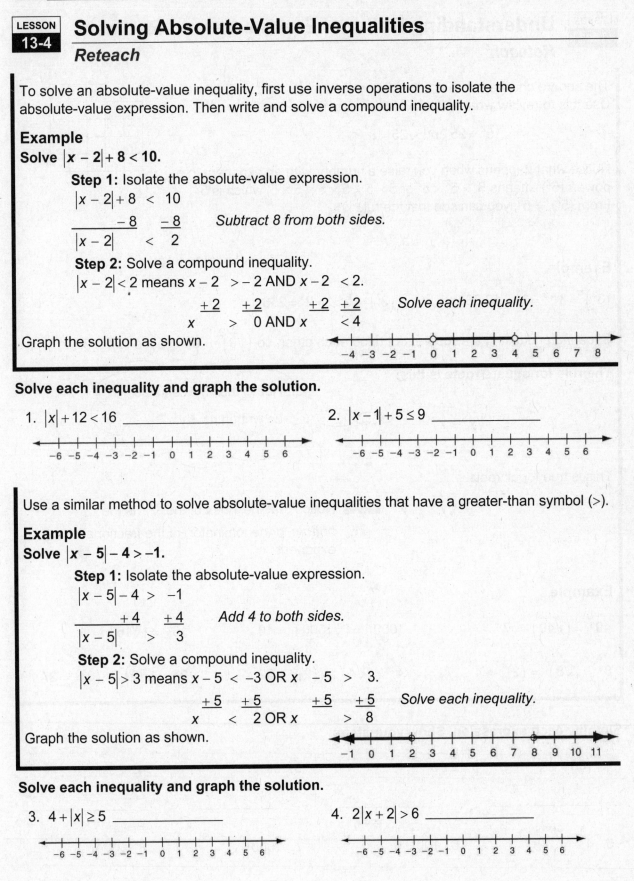

Solving Absolute-Value Inequalities

Reteach

To solve an absolute-value inequality, first use inverse operations to isolate the absolute-value expression. Then write and solve a compound inequality.

Example

Solve $|x-2|+8<10$.

Step 1: Isolate the absolute-value expression.

$$\begin{array}{rcl} |x-2|+8 & < & 10 \\ \underline{\quad -8} & & \underline{-8} \\ |x-2| & < & 2 \end{array}$$

Subtract 8 from both sides.

Step 2: Solve a compound inequality.

$|x-2|<2$ means $x-2>-2$ AND $x-2<2$.

$$\begin{array}{rcl} \underline{+2} \quad \underline{+2} & & \underline{+2} \quad \underline{+2} \\ x > 0 & \text{AND} & x < 4 \end{array}$$

Solve each inequality.

Graph the solution as shown.

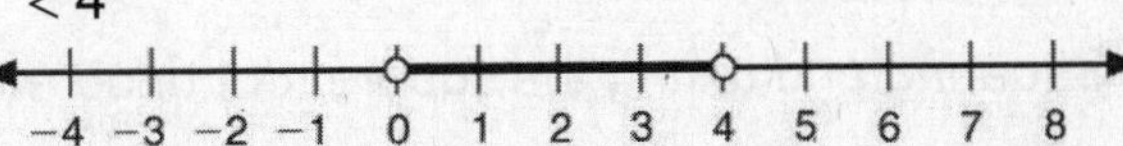

Solve each inequality and graph the solution.

1. $|x|+12<16$ ______________

2. $|x-1|+5\le 9$ ______________

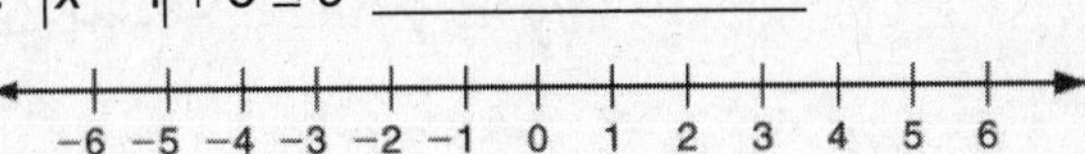

Use a similar method to solve absolute-value inequalities that have a greater-than symbol (>).

Example

Solve $|x-5|-4>-1$.

Step 1: Isolate the absolute-value expression.

$$\begin{array}{rcl} |x-5|-4 & > & -1 \\ \underline{\quad +4} & & \underline{+4} \\ |x-5| & > & 3 \end{array}$$

Add 4 to both sides.

Step 2: Solve a compound inequality.

$|x-5|>3$ means $x-5<-3$ OR $x-5>3$.

$$\begin{array}{rcl} \underline{+5} \quad \underline{+5} & & \underline{+5} \quad \underline{+5} \\ x < 2 & \text{OR} & x > 8 \end{array}$$

Solve each inequality.

Graph the solution as shown.

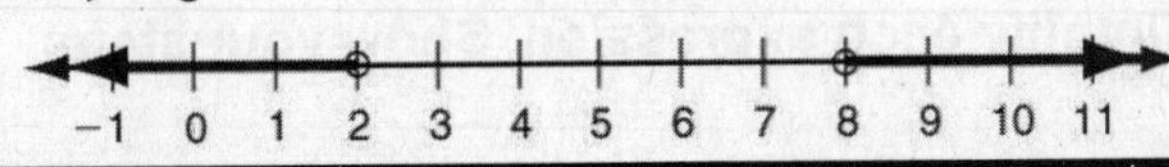

Solve each inequality and graph the solution.

3. $4+|x|\ge 5$ ______________

−6 −5 −4 −3 −2 −1 0 1 2 3 4 5 6

4. $2|x+2|>6$ ______________

−6 −5 −4 −3 −2 −1 0 1 2 3 4 5 6

Name ______________________ Date ______________ Class ______________

LESSON 14-1

Understanding Rational Exponents and Radicals

Reteach

The square checkerboard has 5 units on each side.
Use this to review what you know about exponents and roots.

$$5^2 = 25 \text{ and } \sqrt{25} = 5$$

Notice what happens when you raise a number with an exponent to a power: $(5^2)^3$ means $5^2 \times 5^2 \times 5^2$ or $5 \times 5 \times 5 \times 5 \times 5 \times 5$, which is 5^6.
From $(5^2)^3 = 5^6$, you can see that the rule is:

$$(a^m)^n = a^{mn}.$$

Example

$(3^3)^3 = 3^{3 \cdot 3} = 3^9 = 19{,}683$ $\qquad$ $(2^2)^4 = 2^{2 \cdot 4} = 2^8 = 256$

Squaring and taking the square root undo each other, so $\left(\sqrt{9}\right)^2 = 9$ because $(3)^2 = 9$.

The rule for square roots is this:

$$\sqrt[2]{y} = y^{\frac{1}{2}}$$

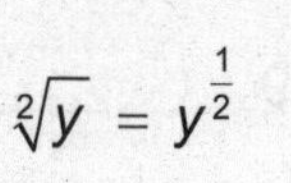

Recall that $\sqrt{y}$ can also be written as $\sqrt[2]{y^1}$.

This is true for all roots.

$$\sqrt[n]{y^m} = y^{\frac{m}{n}}$$

Notice that the index of the $\sqrt{}$ is the *bottom*, or denominator, of the fractional exponent.

Example

$49^{\frac{1}{2}} = \left(\sqrt[2]{49}\right)^1 = 7$ $\qquad$ $1000^{\frac{1}{3}} = \left(\sqrt[3]{1000}\right)^1 = 10$ $\qquad$ $16^{\frac{1}{2}} = \left(\sqrt[2]{16}\right)^1 = 4$

$8^{\frac{2}{3}} = \left(\sqrt[3]{8}\right)^2 = (2)^2 = 4$ $\qquad$ $4^{\frac{5}{2}} = \left(\sqrt[2]{4}\right)^5 = (2)^5 = 32$ $\qquad$ $9^{\frac{3}{2}} = \left(\sqrt[2]{9}\right)^3 = (3)^3 = 27$

Simplify each expression. Show your steps.

1. $100^{\frac{1}{2}}$ ________
2. $8^{\frac{1}{3}}$ ________
3. $9^{\frac{1}{2}}$ ________
4. $25^{\frac{1}{2}}$ ________
5. $4^{\frac{3}{2}}$ ________
6. $100^{\frac{5}{2}}$ ________
7. $1000^{\frac{2}{3}}$ ________
8. $27^{\frac{2}{3}}$ ________

Name ______________________ Date ______________ Class ______________

LESSON 14-2

Simplifying Expressions with Rational Exponents and Radicals

Reteach

Simplify $216^{\frac{1}{3}}$.

$216^{\frac{1}{3}} = \sqrt[3]{216} = 6$

What number, when taken as a factor 3 times, is equal to 216?

$6^3 = 6 \times 6 \times 6 = 216$

so $216^{\frac{1}{3}} = 6$

Simplify $125^{\frac{4}{3}}$.

$125^{\frac{4}{3}} = \left(\sqrt[3]{125}\right)^4 = (5)^4 = 625$

What number, when taken as a factor 3 times, is equal to 216?

$6^3 = 6 \times 6 \times 6 = 216$

so $216^{\frac{1}{3}} = 6$

Simplify $(x^{\frac{5}{3}})^7(y^{\frac{3}{2}})y^{\frac{1}{5}}$.

$(x^{\frac{5}{3}})^7(y^{\frac{3}{2}})y^{\frac{1}{5}} = (x^{\frac{35}{3}})(y^{\frac{3}{2}} \bullet y^{\frac{1}{5}})$ Multiply exponents in $(x^{\frac{5}{3}})^7$.

$= x^{\frac{35}{3}}(y^{\frac{3}{2}+\frac{1}{5}})$ Add exponents of powers with the same base.

$= x^{\frac{35}{3}}y^{\frac{17}{10}}$

Simplify each expression.

1. $64^{\frac{1}{2}}$ ____________
2. $100^{\frac{1}{2}}$ ____________
3. $25^{\frac{1}{2}}$ ____________
4. $8^{\frac{4}{3}}$ ____________
5. $128^{\frac{3}{7}}$ ____________
6. $256^{\frac{1}{4}}$ ____________
7. $8^{\frac{1}{3}} + 16^{\frac{1}{2}}$ ____________
8. $625^{\frac{1}{4}} - 0^{\frac{1}{2}}$ ____________
9. $81^{\frac{1}{4}} - 16^{\frac{1}{4}}$ ____________

Name ______________________ Date ______________ Class ______________

LESSON 15-1

Understanding Geometric Sequences

Reteach

It is important to understand the difference between arithmetic and geometric sequences.

Arithmetic sequences are based on adding a common difference, *d*.

Geometric sequences are based on multiplying a common ratio, *r*.

- If the first term of an arithmetic sequence, a_1, is 2 and the common difference is 3, the arithmetic sequence is: 2, 5, 8, 11, …
- If the first term of an arithmetic sequence, a_1, is 72 and the common difference is – 3, the arithmetic sequence is: 72, 69, 66, 63, …

- If the first term of a geometric sequence, a_1, is 2 and the common ratio is 3, the geometric sequence is: 2, 6, 18, 54, …
- If the first term of a geometric sequence, a_1, is 72 and the common ratio is $\frac{1}{3}$, the geometric sequence is: 72, 24, 8, $\frac{8}{3}$, …

Complete each table.

1. An arithmetic sequence has $a_1 = 4$ and $d = 3$:

a_n	a_1	a_2	a_3	a_4	a_5
Value					

2. A geometric sequence has $a_1 = 4$ and $r = 3$:

a_n	a_1	a_2	a_3	a_4	a_5
Value					

3. An arithmetic sequence has $a_1 = 96$ and $d = -4$:

a_n	a_1	a_2	a_3	a_4	a_5
Value					

4. A geometric sequence has $a_1 = 96$ and $r = \frac{1}{4}$:

a_n	a_1	a_2	a_3	a_4	a_5
Value					

Name ______________________ Date ______________ Class ______________

LESSON 15-2

Constructing Geometric Sequences

Reteach

In a **geometric sequence**, each term is *multiplied* by the same number to get to the next term. This number is called the **common ratio**.

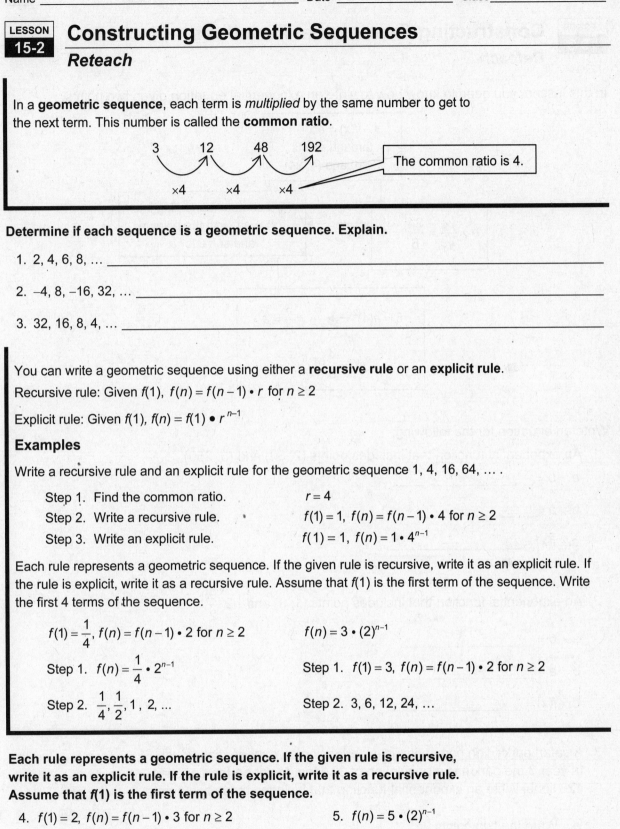

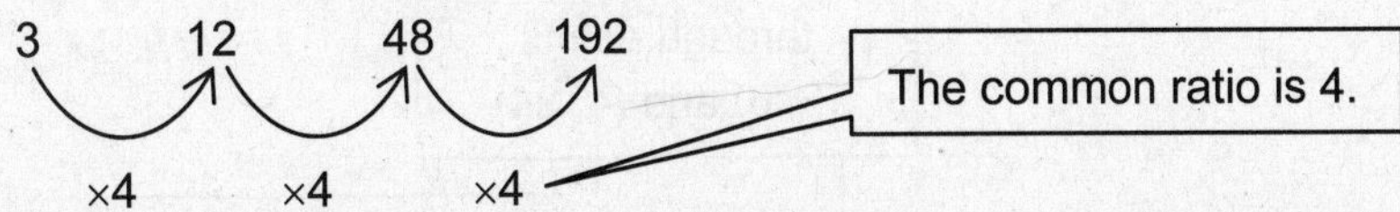

Determine if each sequence is a geometric sequence. Explain.

1. 2, 4, 6, 8, ... ______________________

2. –4, 8, –16, 32, ... ______________________

3. 32, 16, 8, 4, ... ______________________

You can write a geometric sequence using either a **recursive rule** or an **explicit rule**.

Recursive rule: Given $f(1)$, $f(n) = f(n-1) \cdot r$ for $n \geq 2$

Explicit rule: Given $f(1)$, $f(n) = f(1) \bullet r^{n-1}$

Examples

Write a recursive rule and an explicit rule for the geometric sequence 1, 4, 16, 64, ...

Step 1. Find the common ratio.	$r = 4$
Step 2. Write a recursive rule.	$f(1) = 1,\ f(n) = f(n-1) \cdot 4$ for $n \geq 2$
Step 3. Write an explicit rule.	$f(1) = 1,\ f(n) = 1 \cdot 4^{n-1}$

Each rule represents a geometric sequence. If the given rule is recursive, write it as an explicit rule. If the rule is explicit, write it as a recursive rule. Assume that $f(1)$ is the first term of the sequence. Write the first 4 terms of the sequence.

$f(1) = \frac{1}{4},\ f(n) = f(n-1) \cdot 2$ for $n \geq 2$	$f(n) = 3 \cdot (2)^{n-1}$
Step 1. $f(n) = \frac{1}{4} \cdot 2^{n-1}$	Step 1. $f(1) = 3,\ f(n) = f(n-1) \cdot 2$ for $n \geq 2$
Step 2. $\frac{1}{4}, \frac{1}{2}, 1, 2, \ldots$	Step 2. 3, 6, 12, 24, ...

Each rule represents a geometric sequence. If the given rule is recursive, write it as an explicit rule. If the rule is explicit, write it as a recursive rule. Assume that $f(1)$ is the first term of the sequence.

4. $f(1) = 2,\ f(n) = f(n-1) \cdot 3$ for $n \geq 2$

____

5. $f(n) = 5 \cdot (2)^{n-1}$

____

Name ______________________ Date ______________ Class ______________

LESSON 15-3

Constructing Exponential Functions

Reteach

In this lesson, you need to know how to write an exponential equation given two points.

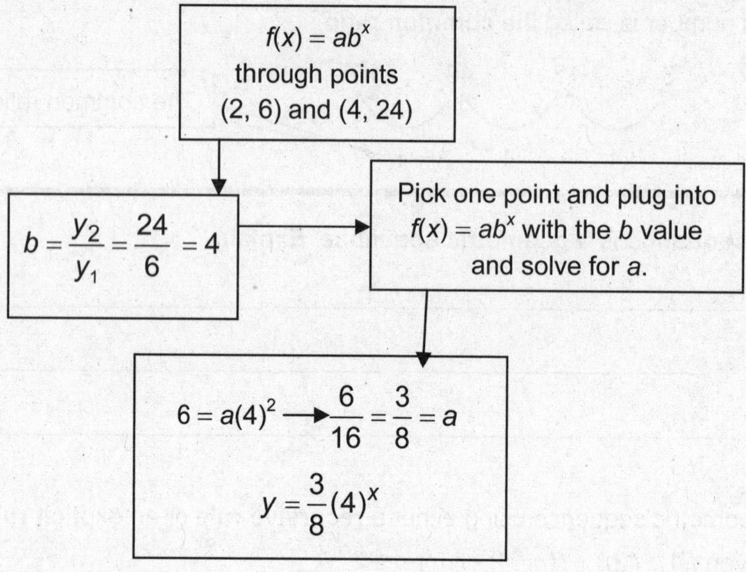

Write an equation for the following:

1. An exponential function that includes points (2, 50) and (3, 250)

   a. $b =$ ______________

   b. $a =$ ______________

   c. $f(x) =$ ______________

2. An exponential function that includes points (1, 3) and $\left(2, \frac{9}{2}\right)$

   a. $b =$ ______________

   b. $a =$ ______________

   c. $f(x) =$ ______________

3. A safari park's lion population is experiencing an exponential growth. In year 3 the park has a population of 32 lions. In year 4 the park has 128 lions. Write an exponential function that includes these two points.

   a. Write the two points. ______________

   b. Find b ______________. Find a ______________

   c. $f(x) =$ ______________

Name ______________________ Date ______________ Class ______________

LESSON 15-4

Graphing Exponential Functions

Reteach

An exponential function has the form $f(x) = ab^x$.
The independent variable is in an exponent.
The graph is always a curve in two quadrants.

$a \neq 0$
$b > 0$ and $\neq 1$
x is any real number

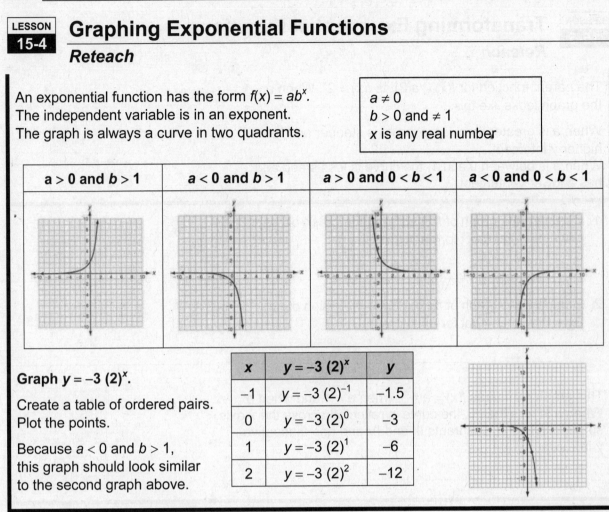

$a > 0$ and $b > 1$	$a < 0$ and $b > 1$	$a > 0$ and $0 < b < 1$	$a < 0$ and $0 < b < 1$

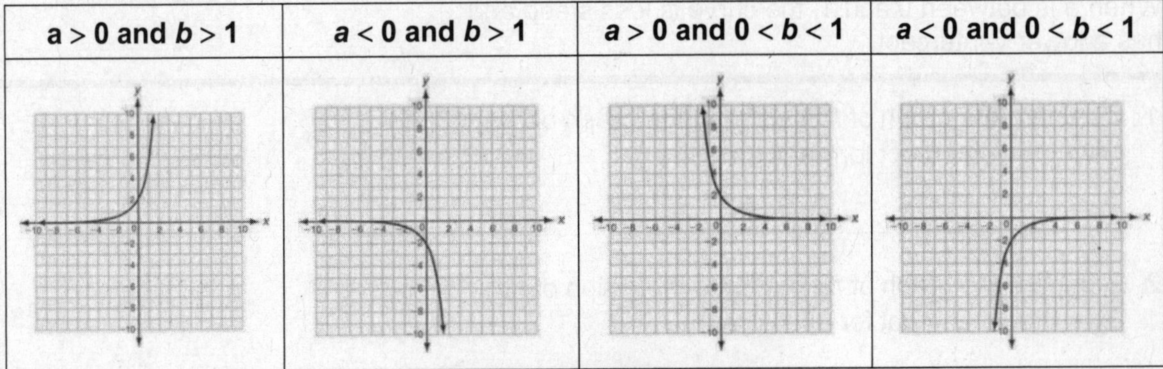

Graph $y = -3\,(2)^x$.

Create a table of ordered pairs.
Plot the points.

Because $a < 0$ and $b > 1$, this graph should look similar to the second graph above.

x	$y = -3\,(2)^x$	y
−1	$y = -3\,(2)^{-1}$	−1.5
0	$y = -3\,(2)^0$	−3
1	$y = -3\,(2)^1$	−6
2	$y = -3\,(2)^2$	−12

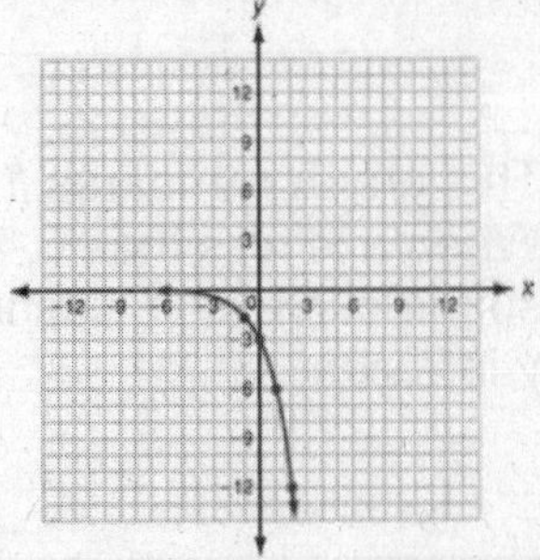

Graph each exponential function.

1. $y = -4\,(0.5)^x$

x	$y = -4\,(0.5)^x$	y
−2		
−1		
0		
1		

2. $y = 2\,(5)^x$

x	$y = 2\,(5)^x$	y
−1		
0		
1		
2		

3. $y = -1\,(2)^x$

x	$y = -1\,(2)^x$	y
−1		
0		
1		
2		

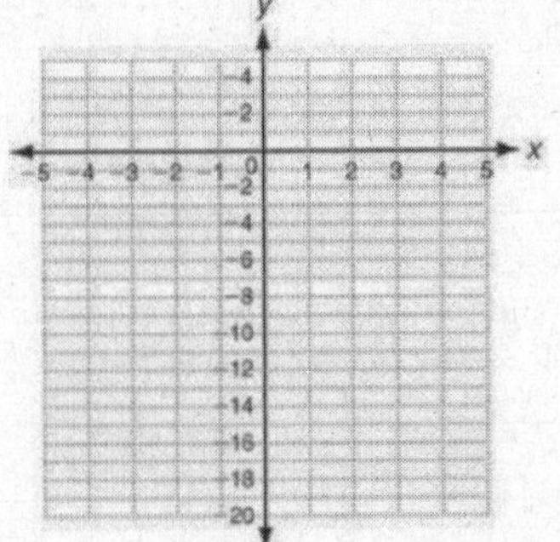

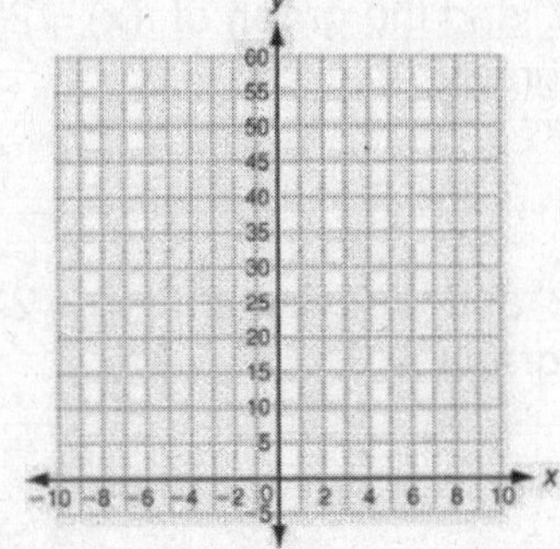

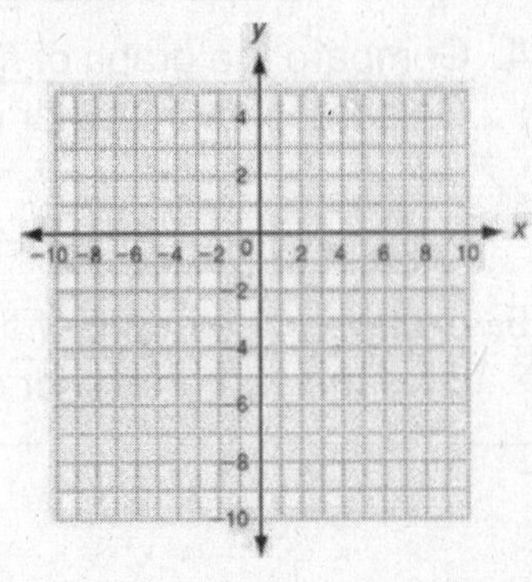

Name ______________________ Date ____________ Class ____________

LESSON 15-5

Transforming Exponential Functions

Reteach

The parent function for $f(x) = a(2)^x$ is $f(x) = 2^x$. When $a = 1$, the graph looks like this.

When a is greater than 1, the curve is steeper and has a higher y-intercept.
When a is between 0 and 1, the curve is less steep and has a lower y-intercept.

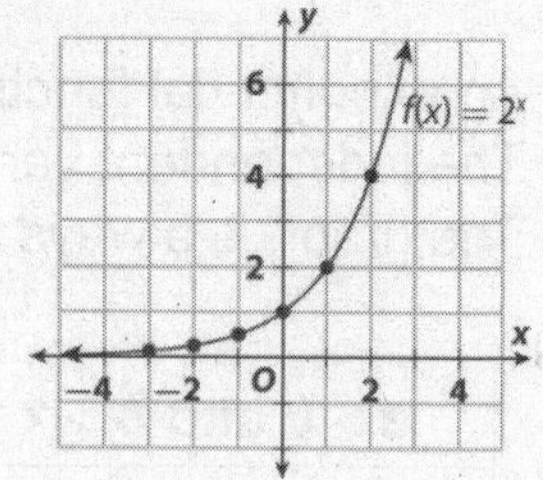

1. Compare the graph of $f(x) = 2^x$ and the graph of $f(x) = 3(2^x)$. Give the y-intercept for each graph.

____

2. Compare the graph of $f(x) = 2^x$ and the graph of $f(x) = 0.25(2^x)$. Give the y-intercept for each graph.

____

This graph compares $f(x) = a(4^x)$, when $a = 1$ and when $a = -1$. When a is less than 0, the curve is reflected across the x-axis, so the curve is in Quadrants III and IV and has a negative y-intercept.

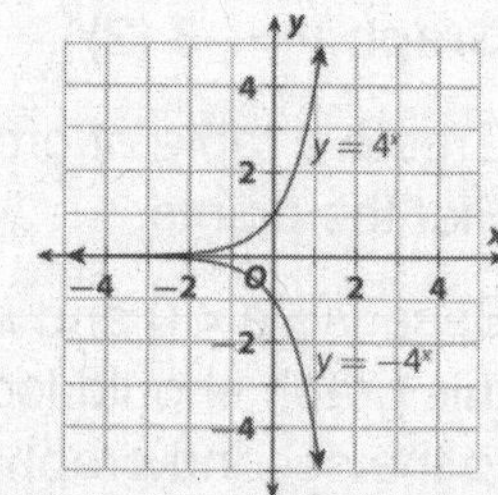

3. Compare the graph of $f(x) = 3(2^x)$ and the graph of $f(x) = -3(2^x)$. Give the y-intercept for each graph.

____

This graph compares $f(x) = 3^x$, $f(x) = 3^x + 5$, and $f(x) = 3^x - 5$.
For the function $f(x) = 3^x + c$, the curve has the same shape as for $f(x) = 3^x$ and is translated up or down the y-axis by c units.

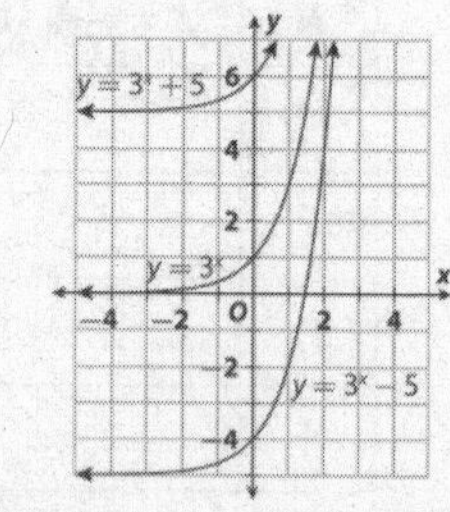

4. Compare the graph of $f(x) = 2^x$ and the graph of $f(x) = 2^x + 5$. Give the y-intercept for each graph.

____

5. Compare the graph of $f(x) = 2^x$ and the graph of $f(x) = 2^x - 3$. Give the y-intercept for each graph.

____

Name ______________________ Date ______________ Class ______________

LESSON 16-1

Using Graphs and Properties to Solve Equations with Exponents

Reteach

You can solve an equation with a variable exponent by writing both sides with the same base.

Example

Solve $25^3 = 5^x$.

$(5^2)^3 = 5^x$	Write 25 as a power of 5.
$5^6 = 5^x$	Use the properties of exponents to simplify.
$6 = x$	Since the bases are equal, the exponents are equal.

Solve each equation.

1. $4^x = 2^6$

   $x =$ ______________

2. $3^x = 27^4$

   $x =$ ______________

3. $2^x = \dfrac{1}{32}$

   $x =$ ______________

You can solve an equation with a variable exponent by graphing both sides of the equation as separate functions. The solution is the *x*-value at the point where the two graphs intersect.

You can use a calculator to find the point of intersection, or you can estimate from the graph. Check your estimate with a calculator.

Example

Solve $3 = 2^x$ by graphing.

Write two equations: $y = 3$ and $y = 2^x$.
Graph both of the equations.
Find the *x*-value for the intersection.
$x \approx 1.6$
Check: Is $2^{1.6} \approx 3$? Yes: $2^{1.6} = 3.0314\ldots$.

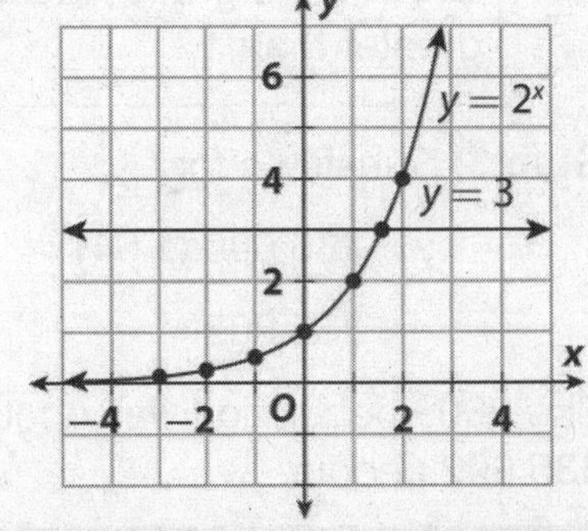

Solve each equation by graphing.

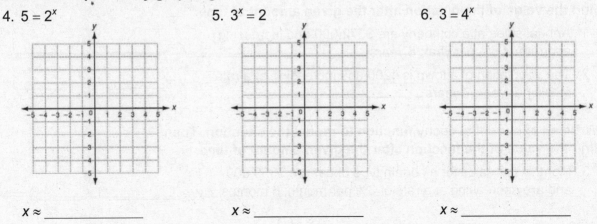

4. $5 = 2^x$

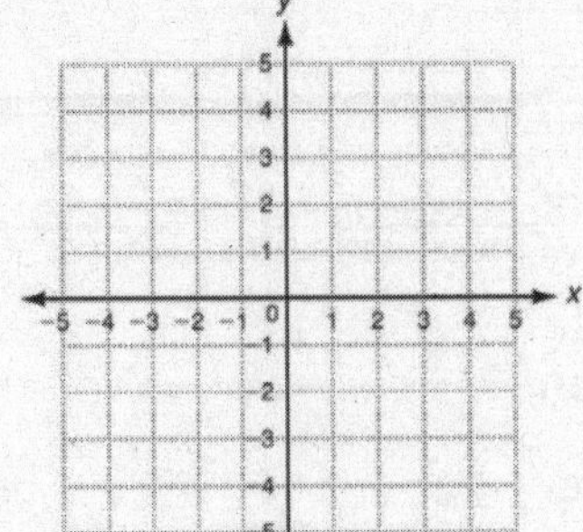

$x \approx$ ______________

5. $3^x = 2$

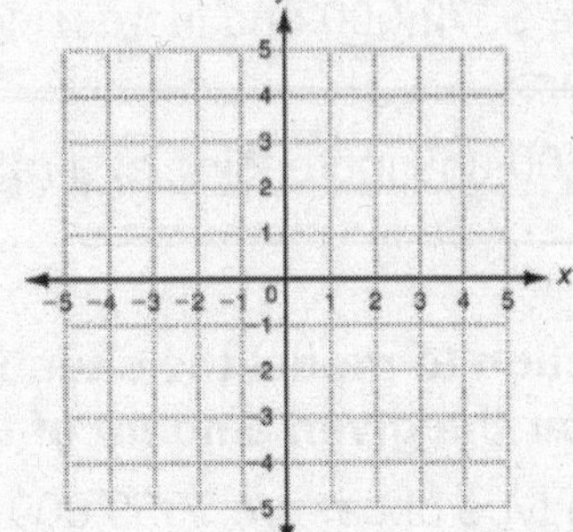

$x \approx$ ______________

6. $3 = 4^x$

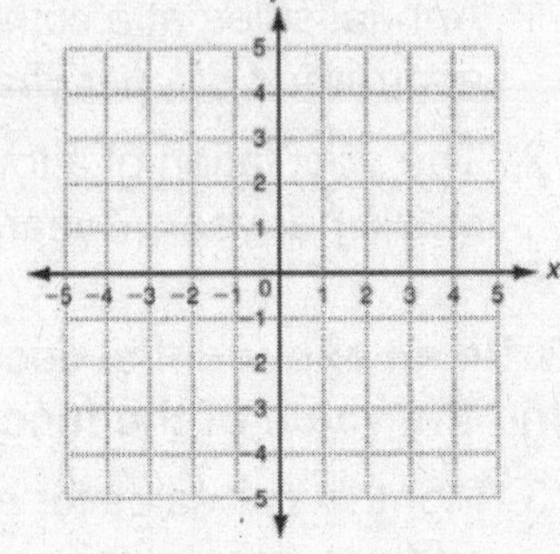

$x \approx$ ______________

Name ______________________ Date ______________ Class ______________

LESSON 16-2

Modeling Exponential Growth and Decay

Reteach

In the exponential growth and decay formulas, y = final amount, a = original amount, r = rate of growth or decay, and t = time.

Exponential growth: $y = a(1 + r)^t$

Exponential decay: $y = a(1 - r)^t$

The population of a city is increasing at a rate of 4% each year. In 2000, there were 236,000 people in the city. Write an exponential growth function to model this situation. Then find the population in 2009.

Step 1: Identify the variables.

$a = 236{,}000 \qquad r = 0.04$

Step 2: Substitute for a and r.

$y = a(1 + r)^t$

$y = 236{,}000(1 + 0.04)^t$

The exponential growth function is $y = 236{,}000(1.04)^t$.

Growth; the growth factor is greater than 1.

Step 3: Substitute for t.

$y = 236{,}000(1.04)^9$

$\approx 335{,}902$

The 2009 population was about 335,902 people.

The population of a city is decreasing at a rate of 6% each year. In 2000, there were 35,000 people in the city. Write an exponential decay function to model this situation. Then find the population in 2012.

Step 1: Identify the variables.

$a = 35{,}000 \qquad r = 0.06$

Step 2: Substitute for a and r.

$y = a(1 - r)^t$

$y = 35{,}000(1 - 0.06)^t$

The exponential decay function is $y = 35{,}000(0.94)^t$.

Decay; the growth factor is less than 1 and greater than 0.

Step 3: Substitute for t.

$y = 35{,}000(0.94)^{12}$

$\approx 16{,}657$

The 2009 population was about 16,657 people.

Write an exponential growth function to model each situation. Then find the value of the function after the given amount of time.

1. Annual sales at a company are $372,000 and increasing at a rate of 5% per year; 8 years ______________ $y =$ ________(1 + ______) —

2. The population of a town is 4200 and increasing at a rate of 3% per year; 7 years ______________ $y =$ ________(1 + ______) —

Write an exponential decay function to model the situation. Then find the value of the function after the given amount of time.

3. Monthly car sales for a certain type of car are $350,000 and are decreasing at a rate of 3% per month; 6 months $y =$ ________(1 + ______) —

____

Name ______________________ Date ______________ Class ______________

LESSON 16-3

Using Exponential Regression Models

Reteach

This table shows the number of computers sold at Computer Cave in the last six months.

Month	1	2	3	4	5	6
Number Sold	53	75	91	111	109	210

The owner wants to write a **regression equation** to model these sales. The owner will use the equation to predict future sales.

1. Enter the data in the table into your calculator, putting the month (x) in List 1 and the number sold (y) in List 2.

   Graph the data as a scatter plot. Sketch the graph of these points.

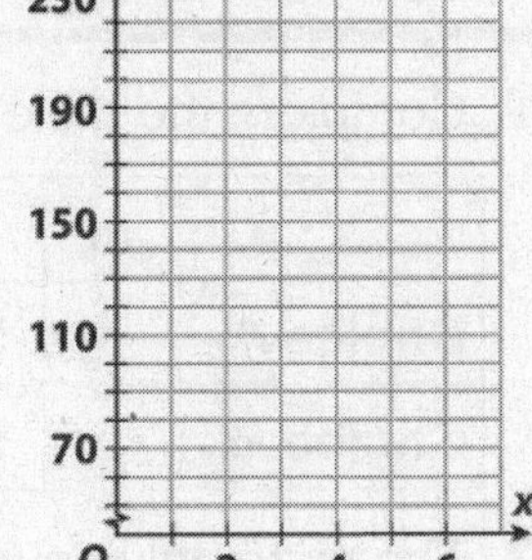

2. Are the points in a straight line? ______

When the data do not fit a linear model, an exponential model may fit.

To find the exponential regression equation, on the STAT menu select option 0 for exponential regression.

The computer screen shows you the values, a and b, for the exponential equation $y = ab^x$.

The screen also shows a value for r, the correlation coefficient. When the value of r is close to 1 or −1, the equation is a good fit.

Use the scatter plot of the data to solve.

3. Write the values of a, b, and r, rounded to the hundredth.

   $a =$ ______________ $b =$ ______________ $r =$ ______________

4. Use these values to write the exponential equation. ______________.

5. Does the value of r indicate that the equation is a good fit? In other words, can it predict future values fairly well? Explain.

   ____

6. According to the graph and the equation, are sales increasing or decreasing? Explain.

   ____

7. Use the equation (and a calculator) to predict the number of sales for Month 8.

   ____

Name ______________________ Date ______________ Class ______________

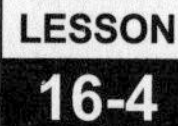

Comparing Linear and Exponential Models

Reteach

Suppose you won a contest and had your choice of one of these two prizes:

Choice A: $50 for the first month with the amount increasing by $10 each month

Choice B: $50 for the first month with the amount increasing by 10% each month

Which would be the better choice?

Let m = the number of months after the first month.

Let p = the amount paid in month m.

1. Complete the table.

	m	0	1	2	3	4	5	6
Choice A	p	50	$50 + 10(1) = 60$	$50 + 10(2) = 70$	80			
Choice B	p	50	$50 \times 1.10^1 = 55$	$50 \times 1.10^2 = 60.5$	66.55			

2. The prize only pays you for 6 months. Which is the better choice? Explain.

____

With Choice A, you *add* a *fixed* amount ($10) each month. This is a **constant change**. Choice A can be written as a **linear equation**.

With Choice B, you *multiply* by 10% each month—adding 10% of an *increasing* amount. This is a **constant percent change**. Choice B can be written as an **exponential equation**.

What happens if the prize pays you for longer than 6 months? Is Choice A still the better choice? To find out, compare the equations for the two choices.

3. Write Choice A and Choice B as equations using the variables m and p.

____

4. Use your equations to compare the amounts paid when $m = 11$.

Choice A: ______________ Choice B: ______________

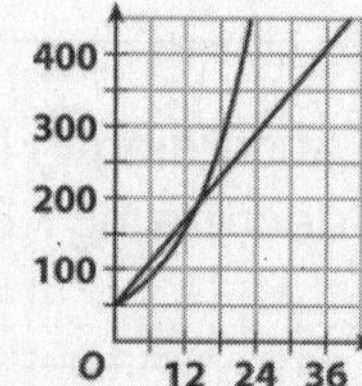

After a year, Choice A still pays more per month. To see if there is a month when Choice B will start to pay more each month, use the graph to find the intersection.

5. Use the graph to estimate the values of m and p after which Choice B starts to pay more each month than Choice A.

m = ______________ p = ______________

Name ______________________ Date ______________ Class ______________

LESSON 17-1

Understanding Polynomial Expressions

Reteach

Polynomials have special names based on the number of terms.

POLYNOMIALS				
No. of Terms	**1**	**2**	**3**	**4** or more
Name	**Mono**mial	**Bi**nomial	**Tri**nomial	**Poly**nomial

The degree of a monomial is the sum of the exponents in the monomial. The degree of a polynomial is the degree of the term with the greatest degree.

Examples

Find the degree of $8x^2y^3$.

$8x^2y^3$ *The exponents are 2 and 3.*

The degree of the monomial is $2 + 3 = 5$.

Find the degree of $4ab + 9a^3$.

$\underbrace{4ab}_{2} + \underbrace{9a^3}_{3}$

The degree of the binomial is 3.

Identify each polynomial. Write the degree of each expression.

1. $7m^3n^5$ ______________
2. $4x^2y^3 + y^4 + 7$ ______________
3. $x^5 - x^5y$ ______________

You can simplify polynomials by combining like terms.

The following are like terms: $4y$ and $7y$ $8x^2$ and $2x^2$ $7m^5$ and m^5

same variables raised to same power

The following are **not** like terms: $3x^2$ and $3x$ 47 and $7y$ $8m$ and m^5

same variable, different exponent

one with variable, one constant

same variable but different power

Examples

Add $3x^2 + 4x + 5x^2 + 6x$.

$3x^2 + 5x^2 + \underline{\underline{4x}} + \underline{\underline{6x}}$ *Identify and rearrange like terms so they are together.*

$8x^2 + 10x$ *Combine like terms.*

Simplify each expression.

4. $2y^2 + 3y + 7y + y^2$ ______________
5. $8m^4 + 3m - 4m^4$ ______________
6. $12x^5 + 10x^4 + 8x^4$ ______________

Name ______________________ Date ____________ Class ____________

LESSON 17-2

Adding Polynomial Expressions

Reteach

You can add polynomials by combining **like terms.**

These are examples of **like terms**: $4y$ and $7y$ $8x^2$ and $2x^2$ m^5 and $7m^5$

These are **like terms** because they have the same variables and same exponent.

These are not like terms: $3x^2$ and $3x$ $4y$ and 7 $8m$ and $8n$

- $3x^2$ and $3x$: same variable but different exponent
- $4y$ and 7: one with a variable, one is a constant
- $8m$ and $8n$: different variables

Add $(5y^2 + 7y + 2) + (4y^2 + y + 8)$.

$(\underline{5y^2} + \underline{\underline{7y}} + \underline{\underline{\underline{2}}}) + (\underline{4y^2} + \underline{\underline{y}} + \underline{\underline{\underline{8}}})$	*Identify like terms.*
$(\underline{5y^2} + \underline{4y^2}) + (\underline{\underline{7y}} + \underline{\underline{y}}) + (\underline{\underline{\underline{2}}} + \underline{\underline{\underline{8}}})$	*Rearrange terms so that like terms are together.*
$9y^2 + 8y + 10$	*Combine like terms.*

Add $(5y^2 + 7y + 2) + (4y^2 + y + 8)$.

$(\underline{5y^2} + \underline{\underline{7y}} + \underline{\underline{\underline{2}}}) + (\underline{4y^2} + \underline{\underline{y}} + \underline{\underline{\underline{8}}})$	*Identify like terms.*
$(\underline{5y^2} + \underline{4y^2}) + (\underline{\underline{7y}} + \underline{\underline{y}}) + (\underline{\underline{\underline{2}}} + \underline{\underline{\underline{8}}})$	*Rearrange terms so that like terms are together.*
$9y^2 + 8y + 10$	*Combine like terms.*

Add.

1. $(6x^2 + 3x) + (2x^2 + 6x)$ ____________________
2. $(m^2 - 10m + 5) + (8m + 2)$ ____________________
3. $(6x^3 + 5x) + (4x^3 + x^2 - 2x + 9)$ ____________________
4. $(2y^5 - 6y^3 + 1) + (y^5 + 8y^4 - 2y^3 - 1)$ ____________________

Name ______________________ Date ____________ Class ____________

LESSON 17-3

Subtracting Polynomial Expressions

Reteach

To subtract polynomials, you must remember to add the opposites.

Find the opposite of $(5m^3 - m + 4)$.

$(5m^3 - m + 4)$

$-(5m^3 - m + 4)$ *Write the opposite of the polynomial.*

$-5m^3 + m - 4$ *Write the opposite of each term in the polynomial.*

Subtract $(4x^3 + x^2 + 7) - (2x^3)$.

$(4x^3 + x^2 + 7) + (-2x^3)$ *Rewrite subtraction as addition of the opposite.*

$(4x^3 + x^2 + 7) + (-2x^3)$ *Identify like terms.*

$(4x^3 - 2x^3) + x^2 + 7$ *Rearrange terms so that like terms are together.*

$2x^3 + x^2 + 7$ *Combine like terms.*

Subtract $(6y^4 + 3y^2 - 7) - (2y^4 - y^2 + 5)$.

$(6y^4 + 3y^2 - 7) + (-2y^4 + y^2 - 5)$ *Rewrite subtraction as addition of the opposite.*

$(6y^4 + 3y^2 - 7) + (-2y^4 + y^2 - 5)$ *Identify like terms.*

$(6y^4 - 2y^4) + (3y^2 + y^2) + (-7 - 5)$ *Rearrange terms so that like terms are together.*

$4y^4 + 4y^2 - 12$ *Combine like terms.*

Subtract.

1. $(9x^3 - 5x) - (3x)$

____

2. $(6t^4 + 3) - (-2t^4 + 2)$

____

3. $(2x^3 + 4x - 2) - (4x^3 - 6)$

____

4. $(t^3 - 2t) - (t^2 + 2t + 6)$

____

5. $(4c^5 + 8c^2 - 2c - 2) - (c^3 - 2c + 5)$

____

Name ______________________ Date ______________ Class ______________

LESSON 18-1

Multiplying Polynomial Expressions by Monomials

Reteach

To multiply monomial expressions, multiply the constants, and then multiply variables with the same base.

Example

Multiply $(3a^2b)(4ab^3)$.

$(3a^2b)(4ab^3)$

$(3 \cdot 4)(a^2 \cdot a)(b \cdot b^3)$ — *Rearrange so that the constants and the variables with the same bases are together.*

$12a^3b^4$ — *Multiply.*

To multiply a polynomial expression by a monomial, distribute the monomial to each term in the polynomial.

Example

Multiply $2x(x^2 + 3x + 7)$.

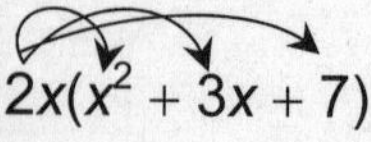

$2x(x^2 + 3x + 7)$

$(2x)x^2 + (2x)3x + (2x)7$ — *Distribute.*

$2x^3 + 6x^2 + 14x$ — *Multiply.*

Multiply.

1. $(-5x^2y^3)(2xy)$ ______________
2. $(2xyz)(-4x^2yz)$ ______________
3. $(3x)(x^2y^3)$ ______________

Fill in the blanks below. Then complete the multiplication.

4. $4(x - 5)$

   (____)x − (____)5

   ____
5. $3x(x + 8)$

   (____)x + (____)8

   ____
6. $2x(x^2 - 6x + 3)$

   (____)x^2 − (____)$6x$ + (____)3

   ____

Multiply.

7. $5(x + 9)$ ______________
8. $-4x(x^2 + 8)$ ______________
9. $3x^2(2x^2 + 5x + 4)$ ______________
10. $-3(5 - x^2 + 2)$ ______________
11. $(5a^3b)(2ab)$ ______________
12. $5y(-y^2 + 7y - 2)$ ______________

Name ______________________ Date ______________ Class ______________

LESSON 18-2

Multiplying Polynomial Expressions

Reteach

Use the Distributive Property to multiply binomial and polynomial expressions.

Examples

Multiply $(x + 3)(x - 7)$.

$(\mathbf{x} + \mathbf{3})(x - 7)$

$\mathbf{x}(x - 7) + \mathbf{3}(x - 7)$	*Distribute.*
$(x)x - (x)7 + (3)x - (3)7$	*Distribute again.*
$x^2 - \underline{7x} + \underline{3x} - 21$	*Multiply.*
$x^2 - 4x - 21$	*Combine like terms.*

Multiply $(x + 5)(x^2 + 3x + 4)$.

$(\mathbf{x} + \mathbf{5})(x^2 + 3x + 4)$

$\mathbf{x}(x^2 + 3x + 4) + \mathbf{5}(x^2 + 3x + 4)$	*Distribute.*
$(x)x^2 + (x)3x + (x)4 + (5)x^2 + (5)3x + (5)4$	*Distribute again.*
$x^3 + \underline{3x^2} + \underline{4x} + \underline{5x^2} + \underline{15x} + 20$	*Multiply.*
$x^3 + 8x^2 + 19x + 20$	*Combine like terms.*

Fill in the blanks below. Then finish multiplying.

1. $(x + 4)(x - 5)$

   __ $(x - 5)$ + __ $(x - 5)$

   ____

2. $(x - 2)(x + 8)$

   __ $(x + 8)$ − __ $(x + 8)$

   ____

3. $(x - 3)(x - 6)$

   __ $(x - 6)$ − __ $(x - 6)$

   ____

Multiply.

4. $(x - 2)(x - 3)$

   ____

5. $(x - 7)(x + 7)$

   ____

6. $(x + 2)(x + 1)$

   ____

Fill in the blanks below. Then finish multiplying.

7. $(x + 3)(2x^2 + 4x + 8)$

   __ $(2x^2 + 4x + 8)$ + __ $(2x^2 + 4x + 8)$

   ____

8. $(x + 2)(6x^2 + 4x + 5)$

   __ $(6x^2 + 4x + 5)$ + __ $(6x^2 + 4x + 5)$

   ____

Name ____________________ Date ____________ Class ____________

LESSON 18-3

Special Products of Binomials

Reteach

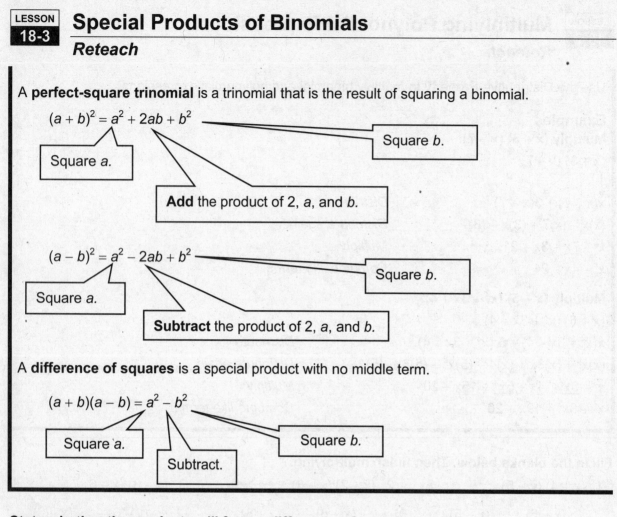

A **perfect-square trinomial** is a trinomial that is the result of squaring a binomial.

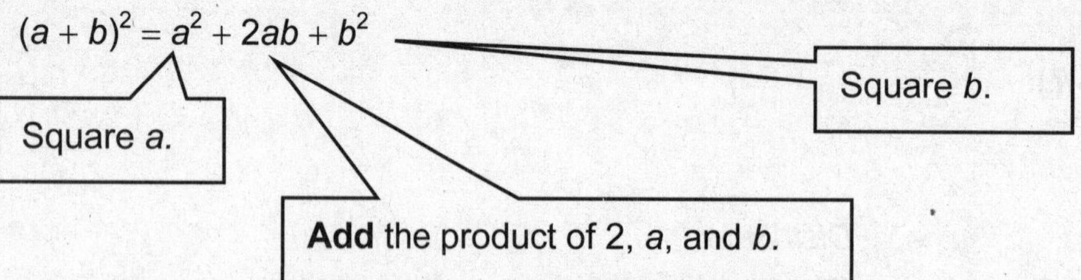
$(a+b)^2 = a^2 + 2ab + b^2$
Square *a*.
Square *b*.
Add the product of 2, *a*, and *b*.

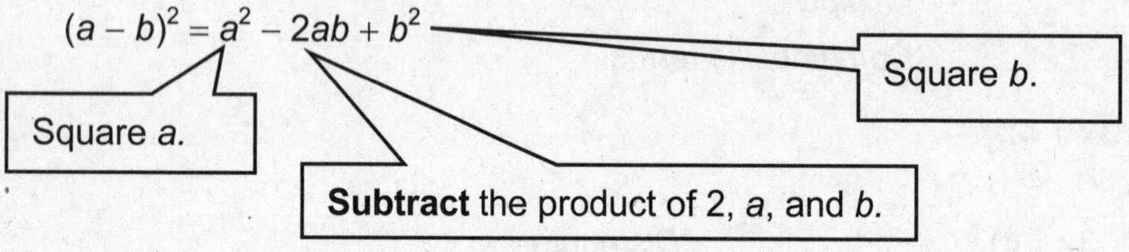
$(a-b)^2 = a^2 - 2ab + b^2$
Square *a*.
Square *b*.
Subtract the product of 2, *a*, and *b*.

A **difference of squares** is a special product with no middle term.

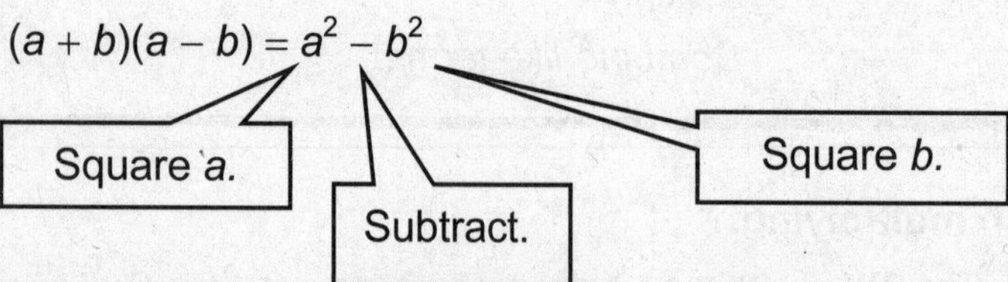
$(a+b)(a-b) = a^2 - b^2$
Square *a*.
Subtract.
Square *b*.

State whether the products will form a difference of squares or a perfect-square trinomial.

1. $(x+10)(x-10)$ ____________
2. $(y+6)(y+6)$ ____________
3. $(z-3)(z-3)$ ____________

Multiply.

4. $(x-8)^2$ ____________
5. $(x+2)^2$ ____________
6. $(7x-5)^2$ ____________
7. $(x+8)(x-8)$ ____________
8. $(10+x)(10-x)$ ____________
9. $(5x+2y)(5x-2y)$ ____________

Name ______________________ Date ______________ Class ______________

LESSON 19-1

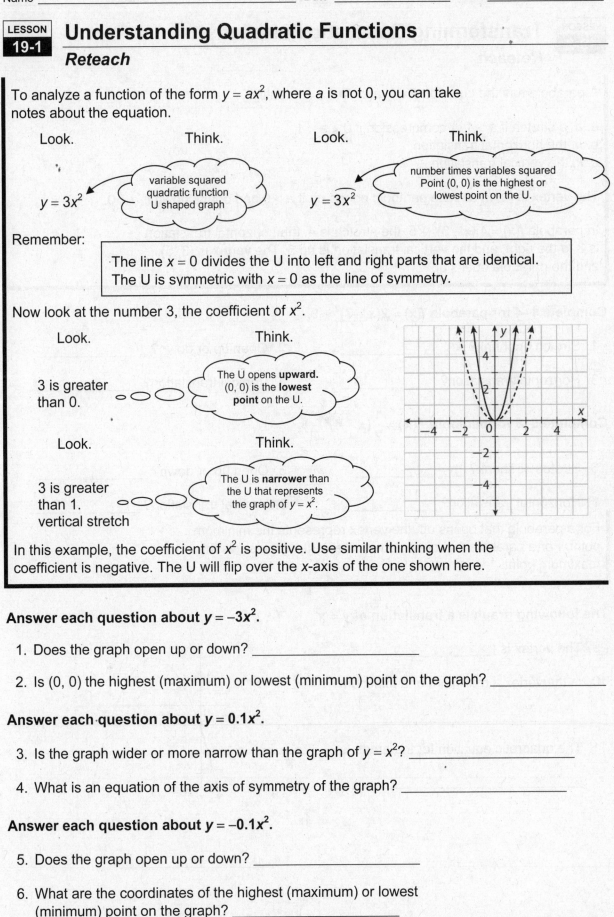

Understanding Quadratic Functions

Reteach

To analyze a function of the form $y = ax^2$, where a is not 0, you can take notes about the equation.

Look. Think. Look. Think.

$y = 3x^2$ — variable squared; quadratic function; U shaped graph

$y = 3x^2$ — number times variables squared; Point (0, 0) is the highest or lowest point on the U.

Remember:

The line $x = 0$ divides the U into left and right parts that are identical. The U is symmetric with $x = 0$ as the line of symmetry.

Now look at the number 3, the coefficient of x^2.

Look. Think.

3 is greater than 0. — The U opens **upward.** (0, 0) is the **lowest point** on the U.

Look. Think.

3 is greater than 1. vertical stretch — The U is **narrower** than the U that represents the graph of $y = x^2$.

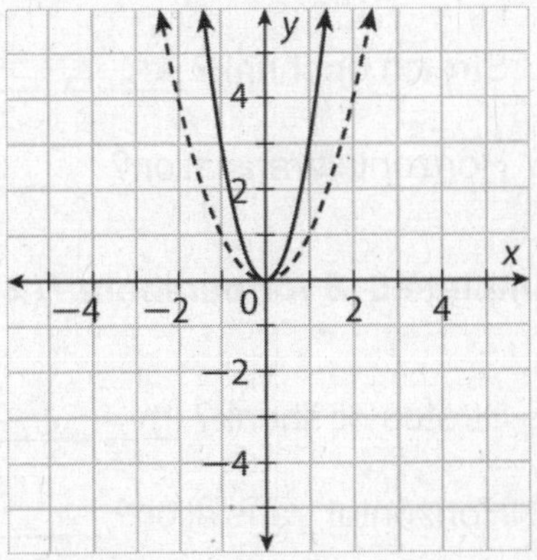

In this example, the coefficient of x^2 is positive. Use similar thinking when the coefficient is negative. The U will flip over the x-axis of the one shown here.

Answer each question about $y = -3x^2$.

1. Does the graph open up or down? ______________

2. Is (0, 0) the highest (maximum) or lowest (minimum) point on the graph? ______________

Answer each question about $y = 0.1x^2$.

3. Is the graph wider or more narrow than the graph of $y = x^2$? ______________

4. What is an equation of the axis of symmetry of the graph? ______________

Answer each question about $y = -0.1x^2$.

5. Does the graph open up or down? ______________

6. What are the coordinates of the highest (maximum) or lowest (minimum) point on the graph? ______________

Name ______________________ Date ____________ Class ____________

LESSON 19-2

Transforming Quadratic Functions

Reteach

A parabola has the equation $f(x) = a(x - h)^2 + k$. Identify:

a. a, a stretch if $a > 1$ or compression if $0 < a < 1$
b. h, the horizontal translation
c. k, the vertical translation

The vertex is (h, k) and the parabola opens up if $a > 0$ and opens down if $a < 0$.

In parabola $f(x) = 4(x - 3)^2 + 5$, the stretch is 4, the horizontal translation is 3 to the right, and the vertical translation is up 5. The vertex is (3, 5), and the parabola opens up.

Complete 1–4 for parabola $f(x) = 2(x + 7)^2 + 9$.

1. Stretch or shrink? ______________
2. Open up or down? ______________
3. Horizontal translation? ______________
4. Vertical translation? ______________

Complete 5–8 for parabola $f(x) = \frac{1}{2}(x - 4)^2 - 8$.

5. Stretch or shrink? ______________
6. Open up or down? ______________
7. Horizontal translation? ______________
8. Vertical translation? ______________

For a parabola that opens up, the vertex represents the minimum point. For a parabola that opens down, the vertex represents the maximum point.

The following graph is a translation of $y = x^2$.

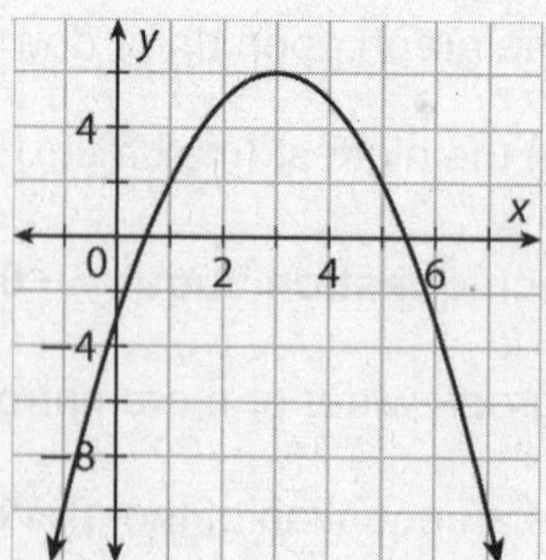

9. The vertex is (______, ______).

10. Is the vertex a maximum or a minimum?

____

11. The quadratic equation for the graph is

______________________________.

Name ______________________ Date ______________ Class ______________

LESSON 19-3

Interpreting Vertex Form and Standard Form

Reteach

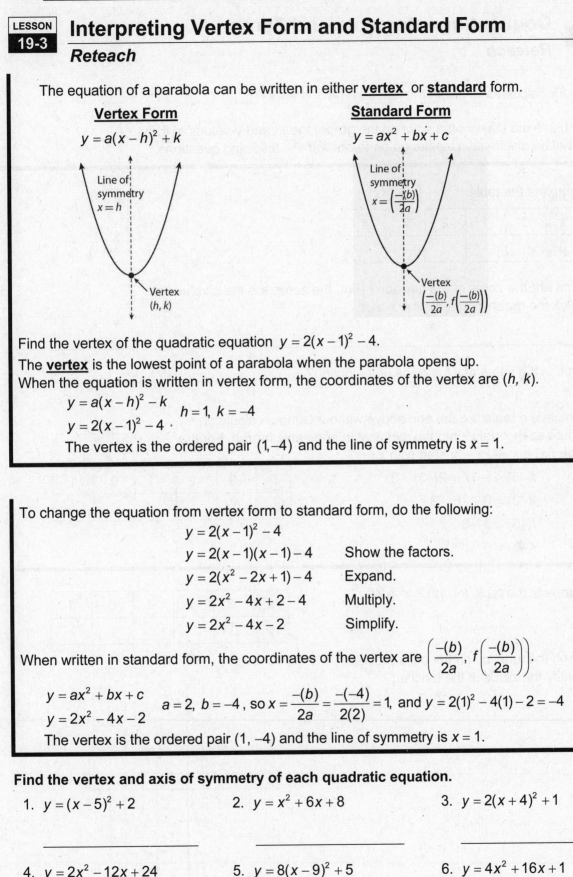

The equation of a parabola can be written in either **vertex** or **standard** form.

Vertex Form

$y = a(x-h)^2 + k$

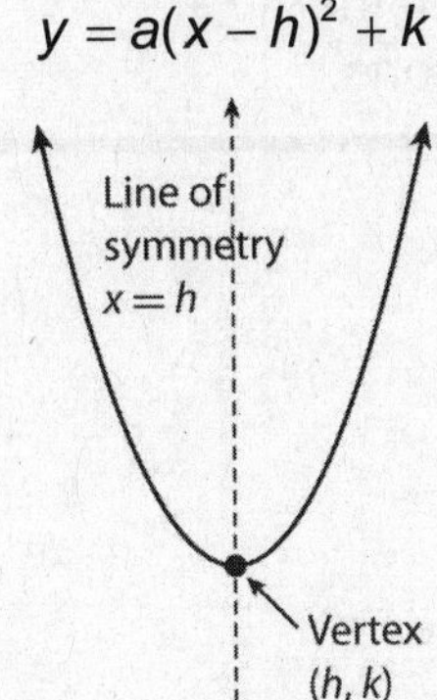

Standard Form

$y = ax^2 + bx + c$

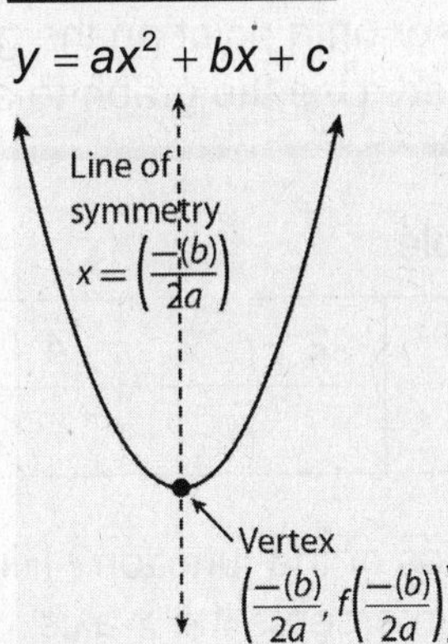

Find the vertex of the quadratic equation $y = 2(x-1)^2 - 4$.

The **vertex** is the lowest point of a parabola when the parabola opens up.
When the equation is written in vertex form, the coordinates of the vertex are (h, k).

$y = a(x-h)^2 - k$

$h = 1,\ k = -4$

$y = 2(x-1)^2 - 4$

The vertex is the ordered pair $(1,-4)$ and the line of symmetry is $x = 1$.

To change the equation from vertex form to standard form, do the following:

$y = 2(x-1)^2 - 4$	
$y = 2(x-1)(x-1) - 4$	Show the factors.
$y = 2(x^2 - 2x + 1) - 4$	Expand.
$y = 2x^2 - 4x + 2 - 4$	Multiply.
$y = 2x^2 - 4x - 2$	Simplify.

When written in standard form, the coordinates of the vertex are $\left(\frac{-(b)}{2a}, f\left(\frac{-(b)}{2a}\right)\right)$.

$y = ax^2 + bx + c$

$y = 2x^2 - 4x - 2$

$a = 2,\ b = -4$, so $x = \frac{-(b)}{2a} = \frac{-(-4)}{2(2)} = 1$, and $y = 2(1)^2 - 4(1) - 2 = -4$

The vertex is the ordered pair $(1, -4)$ and the line of symmetry is $x = 1$.

Find the vertex and axis of symmetry of each quadratic equation.

1. $y = (x-5)^2 + 2$ ______________
2. $y = x^2 + 6x + 8$ ______________
3. $y = 2(x+4)^2 + 1$ ______________
4. $y = 2x^2 - 12x + 24$ ______________
5. $y = 8(x-9)^2 + 5$ ______________
6. $y = 4x^2 + 16x + 1$ ______________

Name ______________________ Date ____________ Class ____________

LESSON 20-1

Connecting Intercepts and Zeros

Reteach

Use your calculator to graph the function $f(x) = x^2 - 4x - 5$.

If you place the cursor on a point on the graph, the *x*- and *y*-values of the point will be displayed. Use the graph to answer the following questions.

1. Complete the table.

x	0	1	2	3	4
y					

2. What are the zeros of the function? Hint: the zeros are the *x*-values at which the graph intercepts the *x*-axis.

____

3. What is the value of *y* for zeros of a function? ______________

To complete a table like the one above without using a calculator, substitute each *x*-value into the expression and solve for *f*(*x*). For the function $f(x) = x^2 + 2x - 3$, start with $x = -3$.

$f(-3) = (-3)^2 + 2(-3) - 3$

$f(-3) = 9 + -6 - 3$

$f(-3) = 3 - 3$

$f(-3) = 0$

x	−3	−2	−1	0	1
y	0				

4. Complete the table for $f(x) = x^2 + 2x - 3$.

x	−3	−2	−1	0	1
y	0				

5. Graph the function on the axes provided. Identify the zeros of the function.

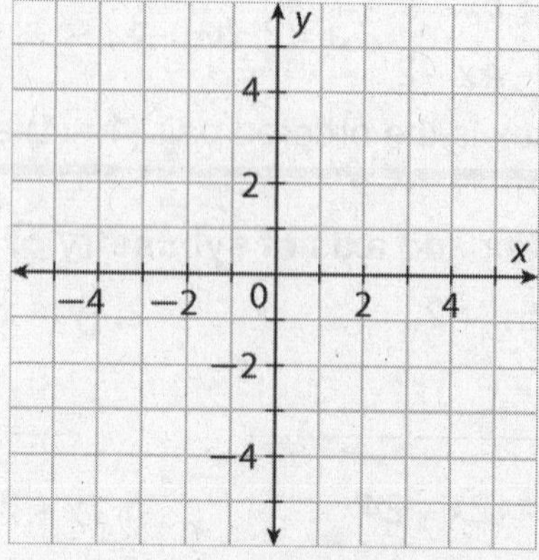

Name ______________________ Date ______________ Class ______________

LESSON 20-2

Connecting Intercepts and Linear Factors

Reteach

The *x*-intercepts of a quadratic function and the *x*-intercepts of its linear factors are the same. Graph the lines $y = x + 3$ and $y = x + 1$.

- The *x*-intercept of a line is where the line crosses the *x*-axis and *y* is equal to 0.
- Substitute 0 for *y* in each equation.

  $0 = x + 3,\ -3 = x$

  $0 = x + 1,\ -1 = x$

- Find the value that is halfway between the *x*-intercepts. $\dfrac{-3+(-1)}{2} = -2$

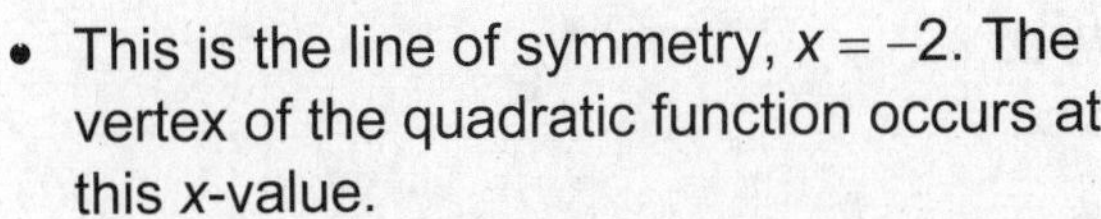

- This is the line of symmetry, $x = -2$. The vertex of the quadratic function occurs at this *x*-value.
- The quadratic function is the product of the two linear factors, $y = (x + 3)(x + 1)$.
- Substitute −2 for *x* to find the *y*-value of the vertex. $y = (-2 + 3)(-2 + 1)$
- The coordinates of the vertex are $(-2, -1)$.

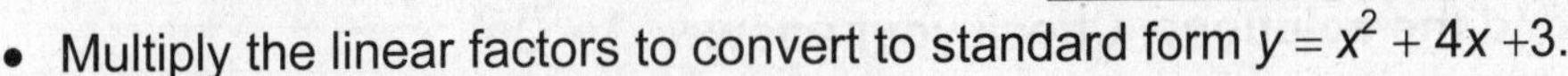

- Multiply the linear factors to convert to standard form $y = x^2 + 4x + 3$.
- Substitute 0 for *x* to find the *y*-intercept.
- Graph the quadratic equation.

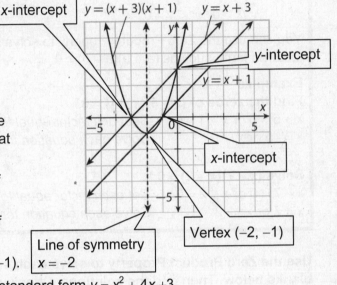

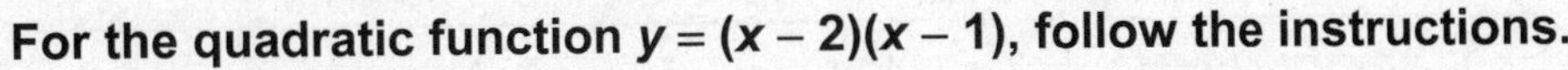

For the quadratic function $y = (x - 2)(x - 1)$, follow the instructions.

1. Graph the lines.
2. Plot points at the *x*-intercepts.
3. Draw the line of symmetry.
4. Find the coordinates of the vertex and plot the vertex point.
5. Write the quadratic equation in standard form.

   ____

6. Plot a point at the *y*-intercept.
7. Graph the quadratic function.

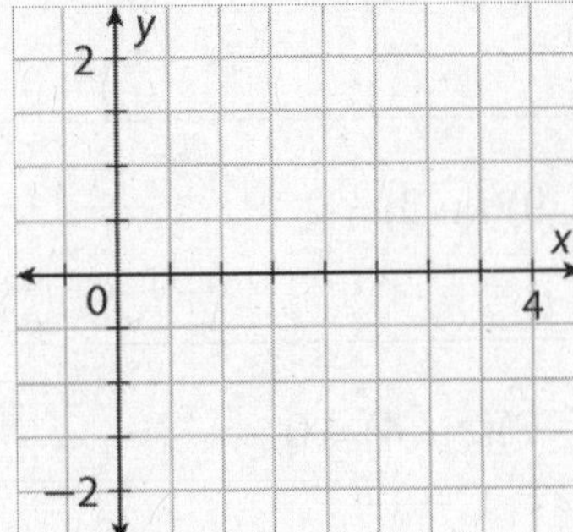

Name ______________________ Date ______________ Class ______________

LESSON 20-3

Applying the Zero Product Property to Solve Equations

Reteach

Quadratic equations in factored form can be solved by using the Zero Product Property.

If the product of two quantities equals zero, at least one of the quantities must equal zero.

If $(x)\,(y) = 0$, then $x = 0$ or $y = 0$

If $(x + 3)\,(x - 2) = 0$, then $x + 3 = 0$ or $x - 2 = 0$

You can use the Zero Product Property to solve any quadratic equation written in factored form, such as $(a + b)(a - b) = 0$.

Examples

Find the zeros of $(x + 5)(x - 1) = 0$.

$x + 5 = 0$ or $x - 1 = 0$ *Set each factor equal to 0.*

$x = -5$ or $x = 1$ *Solve each equation for x.*

Solve $(x - 7)(x + 2) = 0$.

$x - 7 = 0$ or $x + 2 = 0$ *Set each factor equal to 0.*

$x = 7$ or $x = -2$ *Solve each equation for x.*

Use the Zero Product Property to solve each equation by filling in the blanks below. Then find the solutions. Check your answer.

1. $(x - 6)\,(x - 3) = 0$

   $x =$ ________ or $x =$ ________

   ____

2. $(x + 8)\,(x - 5) = 0$

   $x =$ ________ or $x =$ ________

   ____

Use the Zero Product Property to solve each equation.

3. $(y - 7)(y - 3) = 0$ ____________________

4. $0 = (x + 6)(x - 3)$ ____________________

5. $(x + 4)(x + 3) = 0$ ____________________

6. $(t + 9)(t - 3) = 0$ ____________________

7. $(n - 5)(n + 3) = 0$ ____________________

8. $(a - 10)(a + 3) = 0$ ____________________

9. $(z - 6)(z + 4) = 0$ ____________________

10. $0 = (x + 4)(x - 2)$ ____________________

11. $0 = (g + 3)(g - 3)$ ____________________

Name ______________________ Date ____________ Class ____________

LESSON 21-1

Solving Equations by Factoring $x^2 + bx + c$

Reteach

To find the factors for a trinomial in the form $x^2 + bx + c$, answer these 2 questions.

1. What numbers have a product equal to c?
2. What numbers have a sum equal to b?

Find numbers for which the answer to both is yes.

Factor $x^2 + 5x + 6$.

What numbers have a product equal to c, 6?

1 and 6   −1 and −6   2 and 3   −2 and −3

What numbers have a sum equal to b, 5?

1 and 6   −1 and −6   (2 and 3)   −2 and −3

The factors of $x^2 + 5x + 6$ are $(x + 2)$ and $(x + 3)$.

Solve the trinomial by setting it equal to 0. Factor and use the Zero Product Property to solve.

Example
Solve $x^2 + 5x + 6 = 0$.

$x^2 + 5x + 6 = 0$

$(x + 2)(x + 3) = 0$ *Factor $x^2 + 5x + 6$.*

$x + 2 = 0$ or $x + 3 = 0$ *Set each factor equal to 0.*

$x = -2$ or $x = -3$ *Solve each equation for x.*

Complete the factoring.

1. $x^2 + x - 2$

   What numbers have a product equal to c, _____? ______________

   What numbers have a sum equal to b, _____? ______________

   Factors: ______________________________

Factor.

2. $x^2 + 4x + 4$ ______________

3. $x^2 - 4x + 3$ ______________

4. $x^2 + 3x - 10$ ______________

Solve.

5. $x^2 + 12x + 35 = 0$ ______________

6. $x^2 - 9x + 18 = 0$ ______________

7. $x^2 - x - 20 = 0$ ______________

Name ______________________ Date ______________ Class ______________

LESSON 21-2

Solving Equations by Factoring $ax^2 + bx + c$

Reteach

When a factorable quadratic expression is written in standard form, $ax^2 + bx + c = 0$, you can use the Zero Product Property to solve the equation.

To solve a quadratic equation, move all terms to the left side of the equation to get 0 on the right side.

Example

Solve $3x^2 + 4x = 8 - 6x$ by factoring.

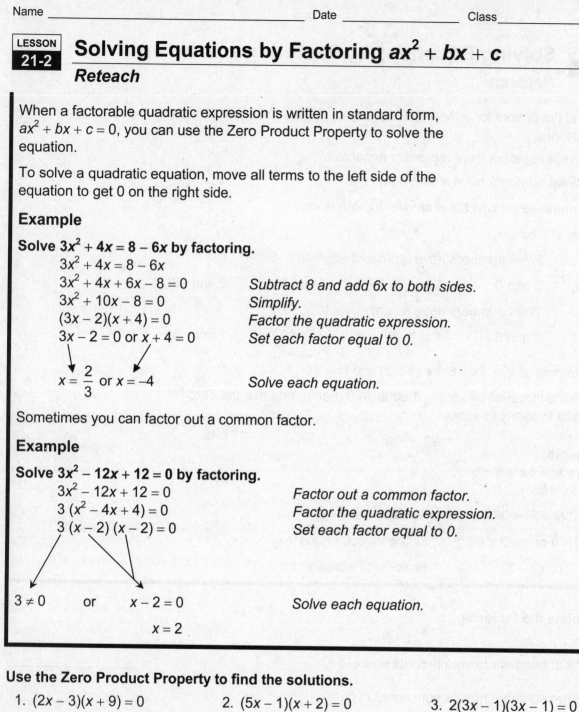

$3x^2 + 4x = 8 - 6x$	
$3x^2 + 4x + 6x - 8 = 0$	*Subtract 8 and add 6x to both sides.*
$3x^2 + 10x - 8 = 0$	*Simplify.*
$(3x - 2)(x + 4) = 0$	*Factor the quadratic expression.*
$3x - 2 = 0$ or $x + 4 = 0$	*Set each factor equal to 0.*
$x = \frac{2}{3}$ or $x = -4$	*Solve each equation.*

Sometimes you can factor out a common factor.

Example

Solve $3x^2 - 12x + 12 = 0$ by factoring.

$3x^2 - 12x + 12 = 0$	*Factor out a common factor.*
$3(x^2 - 4x + 4) = 0$	*Factor the quadratic expression.*
$3(x - 2)(x - 2) = 0$	*Set each factor equal to 0.*
$3 \neq 0$ or $x - 2 = 0$	*Solve each equation.*
$x = 2$	

Use the Zero Product Property to find the solutions.

1. $(2x - 3)(x + 9) = 0$ ____________
2. $(5x - 1)(x + 2) = 0$ ____________
3. $2(3x - 1)(3x - 1) = 0$ ____________

Solve the equations by factoring.

4. $2x^2 + 5x + 3 = -2x$ ____________
5. $6x^2 - 3x = 2 - 4x$ ____________
6. $7x^2 + 8x = -10x - 11$ ____________
7. $18x^2 + 24x + 8 = 0$ ____________
8. $10x^2 - 25x - 15 = 0$ ____________
9. $6x^2 = 96$ ____________

Name ______________________ Date __________ Class __________

LESSON 21-3

Using Special Factors to Solve Equations

Reteach

Use the difference of squares method or the perfect-square method to solve many projectile-motion word problems. The height of a projectile is often represented by one of these equations (where *h* is height in feet and *t* is time in seconds, and $-16t^2$ represents the force of gravity for all projectiles on Earth).

$h = -16t^2 + h_0$	$h = -16t^2 + v_0t + h_0$
Use when the initial velocity = 0 (the projectile is *dropped* from a height, h_0).	Use when the initial velocity ≠ 0 (the projectile is launched from a height, h_0, with an initial upward velocity of v_0).

Problem 1: $h = -16t^2 + 64$	**Problem 2: $h = -16t^2 + 24t - 9$**
✓ 64 represents the initial height of the projectile. ✓ To find when the projectile hits the ground set $h = 0$ and use the difference of squares to solve for *t*.	✓ 24 represents the initial velocity of the launched projectile. ✓ The −9 represents the initial height, in this case 9 feet under ground. ✓ Set $h = 0$ and use perfect-squares to solve for *t*.
1. Set $h = 0$. $h = -16t^2 + 64 = 0$ 2. Factor. $h = -16(t^2 - 4) = 0$ 3. $a = \sqrt{t^2} = t$ and $b = \sqrt{4} = 2$ 4. Use difference of squares to solve for *t*. $h = -16(t + 2)(t - 2) = 0$ $t = -2$ or 2 Pick positive *t*, so $t = 2$.	1. Set $h = 0$. $h = -16t^2 + 24t - 9 = 0$ 2. Factor. $h = -1(16t^2 - 24t + 9) = 0$ 3. $a = \sqrt{16t^2} = 4t$ and $b = \sqrt{9} = 3$ 4. Check middle term. $2ab = 24t$ 5. Use perfect-squares to solve for *t*. $h = -1(4t - 3)^2 = 0$, so $t = \frac{3}{4}$ seconds.

Find when each projectile below hits the ground.

1. $h = -16t^2 + 128$

   a. 128 represents __________.

   b. Set $h = 0$ and solve for *t*.

   $t =$ ________

2. $h = -16t^2 + 40t - 25$

   a. 40 represents __________.

   b. −25 represents __________.

   c. Set $h = 0$ and solve for *t*.

   $t =$ ________

Name ______________________ Date ______________ Class ______________

LESSON 22-1

Solving Equations by Taking Square Roots

Reteach

These equations have something in common. They have the same roots.

$2x^2 - 5 = 13$ $\qquad 2x^2 = 18$

This comes from adding 5 to each side of $2x^2 - 5 = 13$.

But $2x^2 = 18$ is easier to read and solve.

$2x^2 = 18$ $\qquad x^2 = 9$

This comes from dividing each side of $2x^2 = 18$ by 2.

Now $x^2 = 9$ is very easy to solve.

$x^2 = 9$ $\qquad x = \pm\sqrt{9}$ $\qquad x = \pm 3$

This comes from taking the square roots of 9.

Here is another example.

Given	Simpler	Simpler still	Done
$3x^2 + 7 = 13$	$3x^2 = 6$	$x^2 = 2$	$x = \pm\sqrt{2}$

Identify the reason for each step in the solution.

1. $4x^2 - 1 = 15 \rightarrow 4x^2 = 16 \rightarrow x^2 = 4 \rightarrow x = \pm 2$

   ____

2. $2x^2 + 3 = 9 \rightarrow 2x^2 = 6 \rightarrow x^2 = 3 \rightarrow x = \pm\sqrt{3}$

   ____

Solve using square roots.

3. $x^2 = 9$ ____________
4. $x^2 = 16$ ____________
5. $x^2 = 1$ ____________
6. $x^2 - 400 = 0$ ____________
7. $x^2 - 49 = 0$ ____________
8. $x^2 - 64 = 0$ ____________
9. $(x - 6)^2 = 144$ ____________
10. $(x + 5)^2 = 81$ ____________
11. $(x - 4)^2 = 100$ ____________
12. $(x + 3)^2 = 121$ ____________
13. $(x - 1)^2 = 36$ ____________
14. $(x + 2)^2 = 4$ ____________

Name ______________________ Date ______________ Class ______________

LESSON 22-2

Solving Equations by Completing the Square

Reteach

To solve a quadratic equation, complete the square. Here is an example.

Solve $x^2 + 10x = -24$.

Leave room for adding **a number** to each side of the equation.

$$x^2 + 10x + \underline{\quad\quad} = -24 + \underline{\quad\quad}$$

What number?

Answer: The square of one half of 10, the coefficient of *x* $\left(\frac{1}{2} \times 10\right)^2 = 5^2 = 25$

Now fill in the blanks with this number.

$$x^2 + 10x + \underline{\textbf{25}} = -24 + \underline{\textbf{25}}$$

$$x^2 + 10x + 25 = 1$$

$x^2 + 10x + 25$ is a perfect square trinomial. It equals $(x + 5)^2$.

Now you have a **simpler equation** to work with.

$$(x + 5)^2 = 1$$

$$\sqrt{(x + 5)^2} = \pm\sqrt{1}$$

$$x + 5 = \pm 1$$

Remember ±. There are two square roots.

Finish.

Two equations to solve.

$$x + 5 = 1 \qquad x + 5 = -1$$

$$x = -4 \qquad x = -6$$

The solutions are –4 and –6.

Solve by completing the square.

1. $x^2 - 6x = 7$ ______________
2. $x^2 + 8x = -12$ ______________
3. $x^2 - 2x = 63$ ______________
4. $x^2 + 4x = 32$ ______________
5. $x^2 - 14x = -24$ ______________
6. $x^2 + 6x = -9$ ______________
7. The product of two consecutive positive integers is 56. What are they?

____

Name ______________________ Date ______________ Class ______________

LESSON 22-3

Using the Quadratic Formula to Solve Equations

Reteach

Write the quadratic equation in standard form $ax^2 + bx + c = 0$. Use the quadratic formula.

$$x = \frac{-b \pm \sqrt{b^2 - 4ac}}{2a}$$

Solve $2x^2 - 5x - 12 = 0$ using the quadratic formula.

$2x^2 - 5x - 12 - 0$

Step 1: Identify *a*, *b*, and *c*.

$a = 2$
$b = -5$
$c = -12$

Step 2: Substitute into the quadratic formula.

$$x = \frac{-(-5) \pm \sqrt{(-5)^2 - 4(2)(-12)}}{2(2)}$$

Step 3: Simplify.

$$x = \frac{-(-5) \pm \sqrt{(-5)^2 - 4(2)(-12)}}{2(2)}$$

$$x = \frac{5 \pm \sqrt{25 - (-96)}}{4}$$

$$x = \frac{5 \pm \sqrt{121}}{4}$$

$$x = \frac{5 \pm 11}{4}$$

Step 4: Write two equations and solve.

$x = \frac{5+11}{4}$ or $x = \frac{5-11}{4}$

$x = 4$ or $x = -\frac{3}{2}$

Solve using the quadratic formula by filling in the blanks below.

1. $x^2 + 2x - 35 = 0$

   $a =$ ___; $b =$ ___; $c =$ ___

   $$x = \frac{-(\square) \pm \sqrt{(\square)^2 - 4(\square)(\square)}}{2\square}$$

   Simplify:

   ____

2. $3x^2 + 7x + 2 = 0$

   $a =$ ___; $b =$ ___; $c =$ ___

   $$x = \frac{-(\square) \pm \sqrt{(\square)^2 - 4(\square)(\square)}}{2\square}$$

   Simplify:

   ____

3. $x^2 + x - 20 = 0$

   $a =$ ___; $b =$ ___; $c =$ ___

   $$x = \frac{-(\square) \pm \sqrt{(\square)^2 - 4(\square)(\square)}}{2\square}$$

   Simplify:

   ____

4. $2x^2 - 9x - 5 = 0$

   $a =$ ___; $b =$ ___; $c =$ ___

   $$x = \frac{-(\square) \pm \sqrt{(\square)^2 - 4(\square)(\square)}}{2\square}$$

   Simplify:

   ____

Name ______________________ Date ______________ Class ______________

LESSON 22-4

Choosing a Method for Solving Quadratic Equations

Reteach

The method you choose to solve a quadratic equation depends on the form of the equation.

- If there are two terms and both have the same variable try factoring:

  $3x^2 + 6x = 0;\ 3x(x+2) = 0,\ x = 0$ of $x = -2$

- If there are two terms and one term is a constant try taking square roots:

  $x^2 - 25 = 0;\ x^2 = 25,\ \sqrt{x^2} = \pm\sqrt{25},\ x = 5$ of $x = -5$

- If there is a binomial squared equal to a constant try taking square roots:

  $(x+5)^2 = 9;\ \sqrt{(x+5)^2} = \pm\sqrt{9},\ x+5 = \pm 3,\ x = -2$ or $x = -8$

- If there are three terms try factoring into two binomials:

  $x^2 + 7x + 6 = 0;\ (x+1)(x+6) = 0,\ x = -1$ of $x = -6$

- If the equation does not seem to factor try writing the equation in standard form

  $ax^2 + bx + c = 0$ and use the quadratic formula $\dfrac{-b \pm \sqrt{b^2 - 4ac}}{2a}$:

  $$2x^2 - 5x - 6 = 0;\ \frac{-(-5) \pm \sqrt{(-5)^2 - 4(2)(-6)}}{2(2)} = \frac{5 \pm \sqrt{25+48}}{4} = \frac{5 \pm \sqrt{73}}{4}$$

Solve each quadratic equation by any means. Identify the method and explain why you chose it.

1. $4x^2 - 12x = 0$

____
____
____

2. $5x^2 + 30x = 0$

____
____
____

3. $x^2 - 49 = 0$

____
____
____

4. $4x^2 = 64$

____
____
____

5. $(2x-5)^2 = 49$

____
____
____

6. $(x+5)^2 = 81$

____
____
____

7. $x^2 + 14x + 49 = 0$

____
____
____

8. $2x^2 - 14x = -20$

____
____
____

9. $3x^2 - 4x = 20$

____
____
____

Name ______________________ Date ______________ Class ______________

LESSON 22-5

Solving Nonlinear Systems

Reteach

A *nonlinear system of equations* is a system in which at least one of the equations is nonlinear.

Possible Solutions for a Linear-Quadratic System

No Solutions	One Solution	Two Solutions

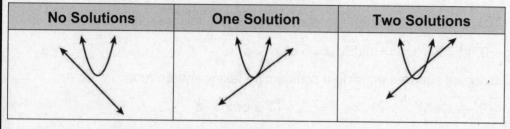

Solve the system by graphing. Check your answer.

$$\begin{cases} y = x^4 - 5x - 6 \\ y = -4x + 4 \end{cases}$$

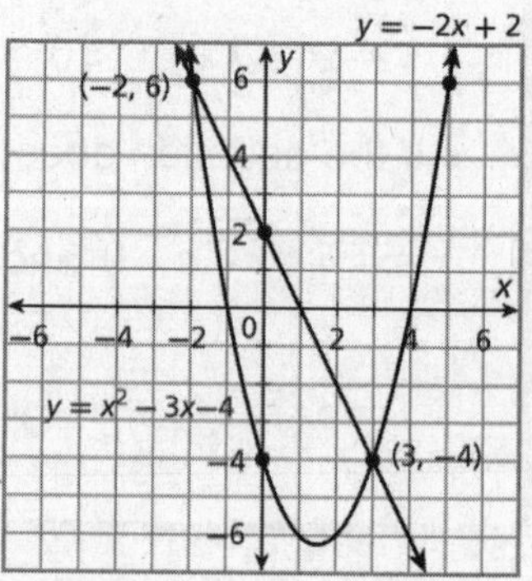

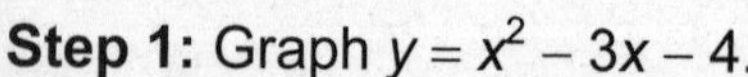

Step 1: Graph $y = x^2 - 3x - 4$.

Axis of symmetry: $x = 1.5$; vertex: $(1.5, -6.25)$

y-intercept: $(0, -4)$; another point $(-2, 6)$

Graph the points and reflect them across the axis of symmetry.

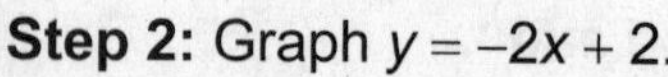

Step 2: Graph $y = -2x + 2$.

Slope: -2; y-intercept: 2

Step 3: Find the points of intersection: $(-2, 6)$ and $(3, -4)$.

Check: Substitute the solutions into each system.

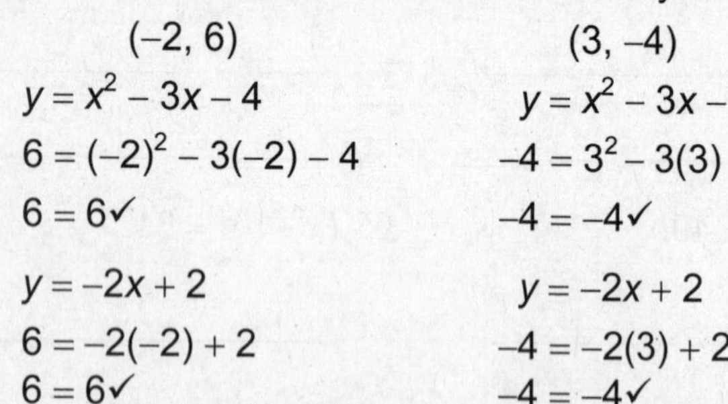

$(-2, 6)$	$(3, -4)$
$y = x^2 - 3x - 4$	$y = x^2 - 3x - 4$
$6 = (-2)^2 - 3(-2) - 4$	$-4 = 3^2 - 3(3) - 4$
$6 = 6$✓	$-4 = -4$✓
$y = -2x + 2$	$y = -2x + 2$
$6 = -2(-2) + 2$	$-4 = -2(3) + 2$
$6 = 6$✓	$-4 = -4$✓

Solve each system by graphing. Check your answers by solving algebraically.

1. $\begin{cases} y = x^4 + 5x - 6 \\ y = 6x - 6 \end{cases}$

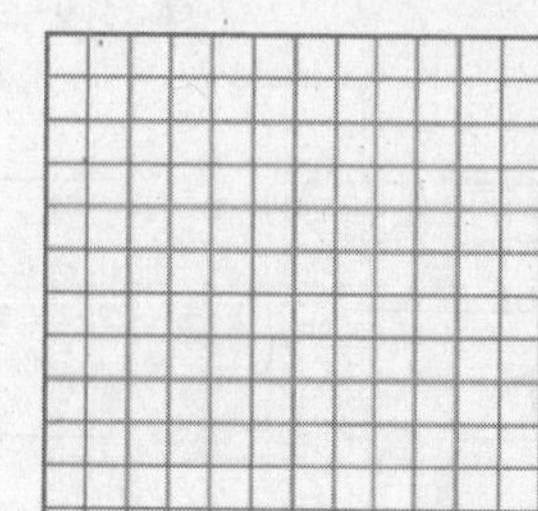

2. $\begin{cases} y = 5x^4 + 4x - 3 \\ y = 4x + 4 \end{cases}$

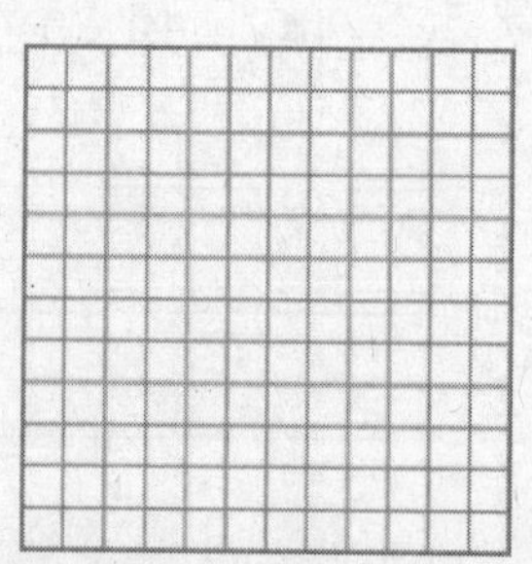

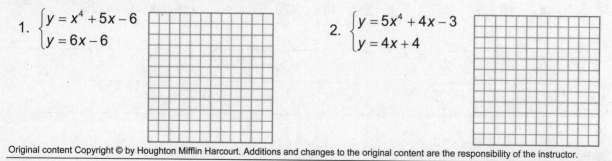

Name ______________________ Date ______________ Class ______________

LESSON 23-1

Modeling with Quadratic Functions

Reteach

The graph of $y = x^2 + 1$ below shows a **linear pattern in the values of *y*.**

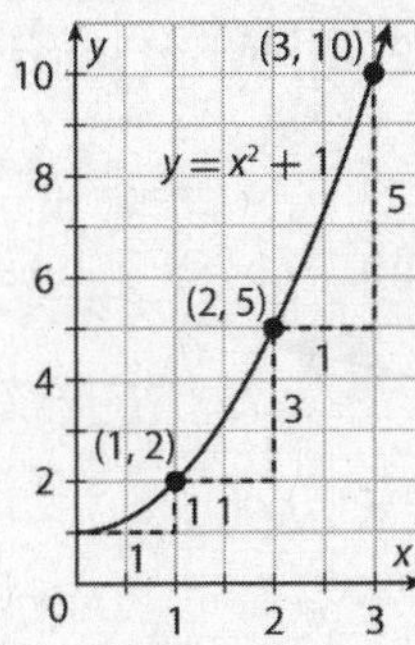

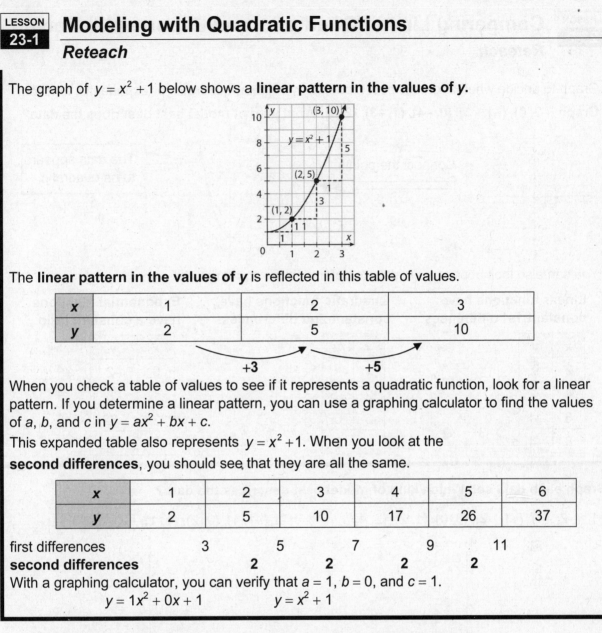

The **linear pattern in the values of *y*** is reflected in this table of values.

x	1	2	3
y	2	5	10

+3 +5

When you check a table of values to see if it represents a quadratic function, look for a linear pattern. If you determine a linear pattern, you can use a graphing calculator to find the values of *a*, *b*, and *c* in $y = ax^2 + bx + c$.

This expanded table also represents $y = x^2 + 1$. When you look at the **second differences**, you should see that they are all the same.

x	1	2	3	4	5	6
y	2	5	10	17	26	37

first differences 3 5 7 9 11

second differences **2** **2** **2** **2**

With a graphing calculator, you can verify that $a = 1$, $b = 0$, and $c = 1$.

$y = 1x^2 + 0x + 1$ $\qquad$ $y = x^2 + 1$

1. Verify that this table represents a quadratic function by finding the first and second differences.

x	1	2	3	4	5	6
y	–1	5	15	29	47	69

first differences ______ ______ ______ ______ ______

second differences ______ ______ ______ ______

2. Find the values of *a*, *b*, and *c* in $y = ax^2 + bx + c$ for this table of values. Write the equation.

x	1	2	3	4	5	6
y	3	8	15	24	35	48

____

Name ______________________ Date ______________ Class ______________

LESSON 23-2

Comparing Linear, Quadratic, and Exponential Models

Reteach

Graph to decide whether data is best modeled by a linear, quadratic, or exponential function.

Graph (–2, 0), (–1, –3), (0, –4), (1, –3), (2, 0). What kind of model best describes the data?

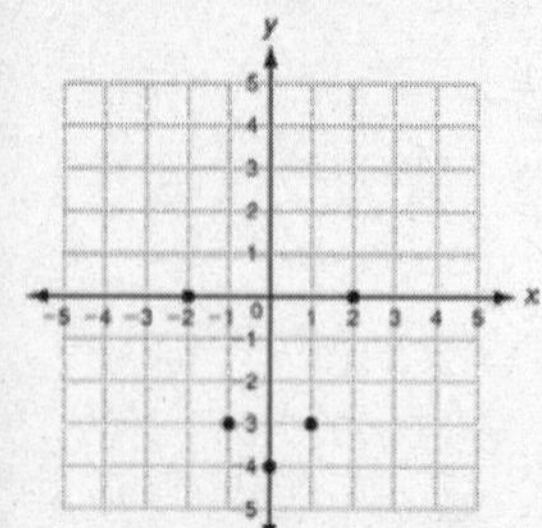

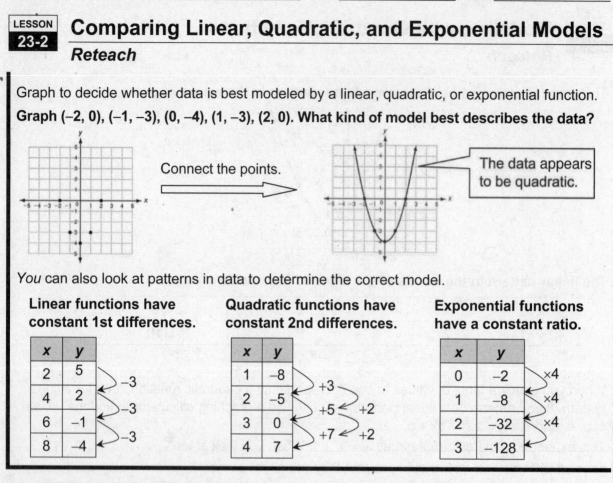

Connect the points.

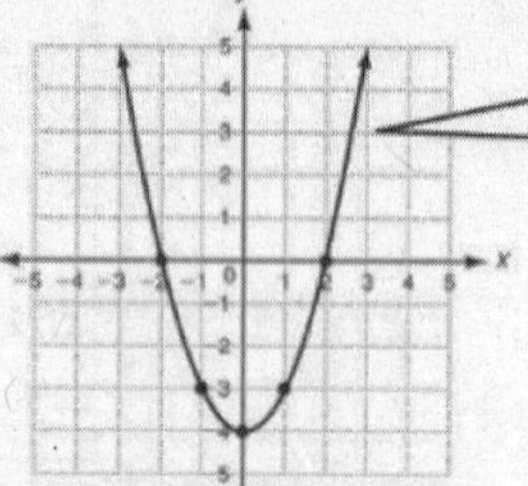

The data appears to be quadratic.

You can also look at patterns in data to determine the correct model.

Linear functions have constant 1st differences.

x	y
2	5
4	2
6	–1
8	–4

–3, –3, –3

Quadratic functions have constant 2nd differences.

x	y
1	–8
2	–5
3	0
4	7

+3, +5, +7; +2, +2

Exponential functions have a constant ratio.

x	y
0	–2
1	–8
2	–32
3	–128

×4, ×4, ×4

Graph each data set. Which kind of model best describes the data?

1. (–2, –4), (–1, –2), (0, 0), (1, 2), (2, 4)

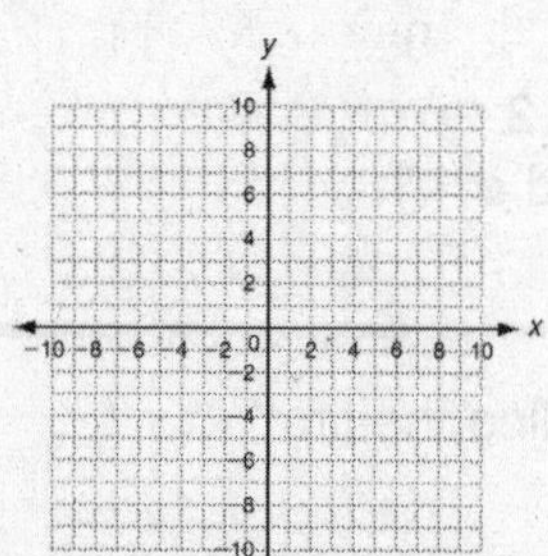

____

2. (–1, 4), (0, 2), (1, 1), $\left(2, \frac{1}{2}\right)$, $\left(3, \frac{1}{4}\right)$

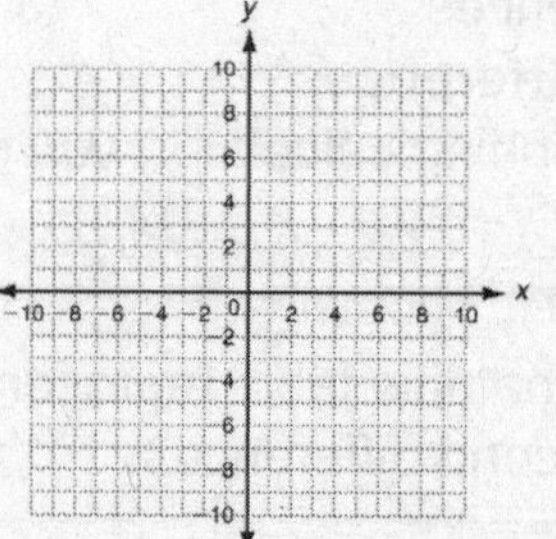

____

Look for a pattern in each data set. Determine which kind of model best describes the data.

3.

x	y
0	6
1	12
2	24
3	48

____

4.

x	y
0	10
1	18
2	28
3	40

____

5.

x	y
3	4
6	–2
9	–8
12	–14

____

Name ______________________ Date ______________ Class ______________

Graphing Polynomial Functions

Reteach

A polynomial function often has a graph that looks like a roller coaster with **ups** and **downs**. From a graph, you can use this table to tell the degree of the polynomial and whether its leading coefficient is positive or negative.

Odd Degree **1, 3, 5, . . .**		
leading coefficient	Left end behavior	Right end behavior
positive	down ↓	up ↑
negative	up ↑	down ↓

Even Degree **2, 4, . . .**		
leading coefficient	Left end behavior	Right end behavior
positive	up ↑	up ↑
negative	down ↓	down ↓

Symmetry in a graph can help you determine whether a function is even, odd, or neither.

Function	Symmetry
even	in the vertical axis
odd	in the origin

The graph and analysis below show how these facts are used.

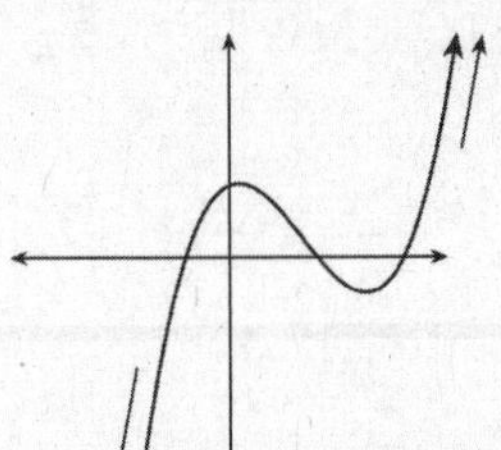

The graph goes down to the left and up to the right. The polynomial has odd degree and its leading coefficient is positive.

There is no symmetry in the vertical axis. The function is not even. There is no symmetry in the origin. The function is not odd. The function represented by the graph is neither.

Identify the degree of the function; whether the function is even, odd, or neither; and whether the leading coefficient is positive or negative.

1.

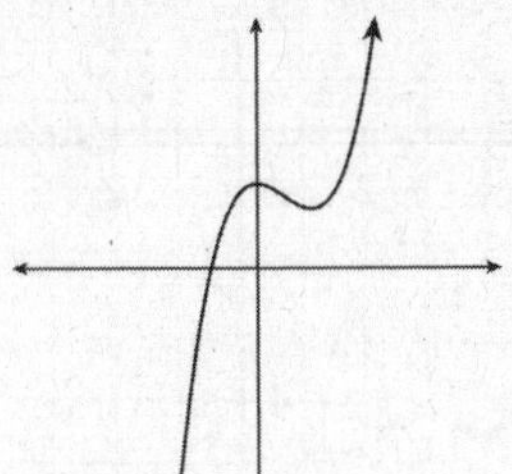

degree: ______________

function type: ______________

leading coefficient: ______________

2.

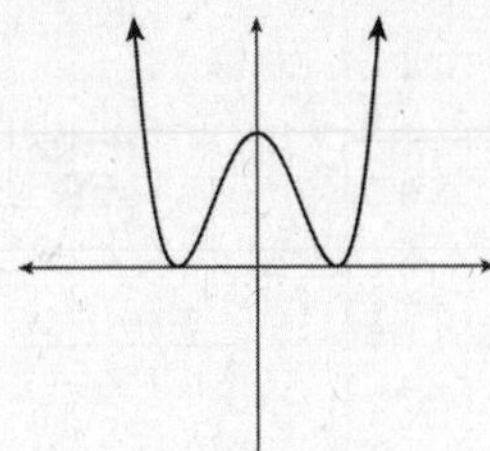

degree: ______________

function type: ______________

leading coefficient: ______________

Name ______________________ Date ______________ Class ______________

LESSON 24-2

Understanding Inverse Functions

Reteach

The inverse of a function is a reflection of the function across the line $y = x$.

Function: $f(x) = 3x + 1$

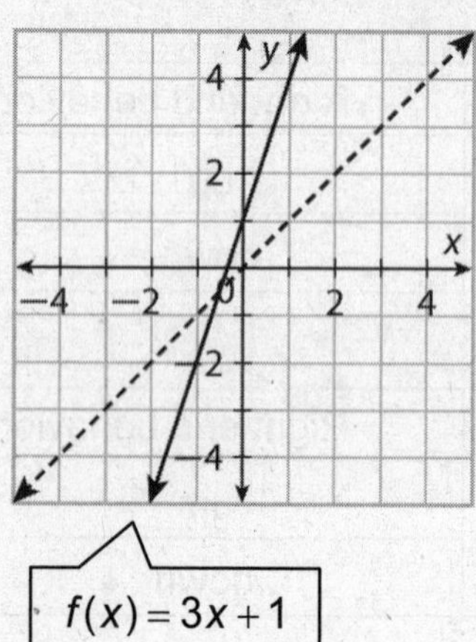

Inverse: $f^{-1}(x) = \dfrac{x-1}{3}$

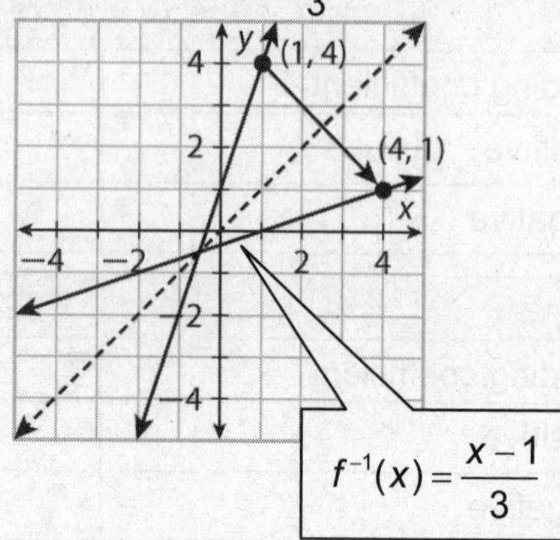

Notice that when the function is reflected over the line $y = x$, the *x* and *y* values of the coordinates change places: $(1, 4) \rightarrow (4, 1)$. This means that we can change the *x* and *y* in the original function and solve the equation for *y* to find the inverse function.

$f(x) = y = 3x + 1$	Start with the function.
$x = 3y + 1$	Exchange *x* and *y*.
$x - 1 = 3y$	Solve the equation for *y*.
$\dfrac{x-1}{3} = y = f^{-1}(x)$	You now have the inverse function.

Graph the function. Graph and write the inverse of the function.

1. $f(x) = 2x + 3$

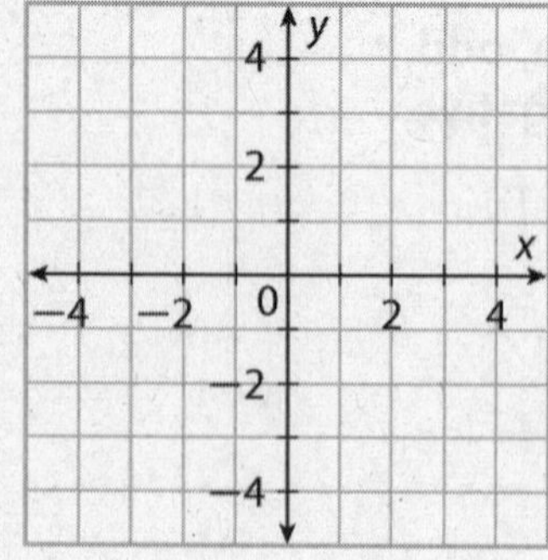

____

2. $f(x) = 3x - 2$

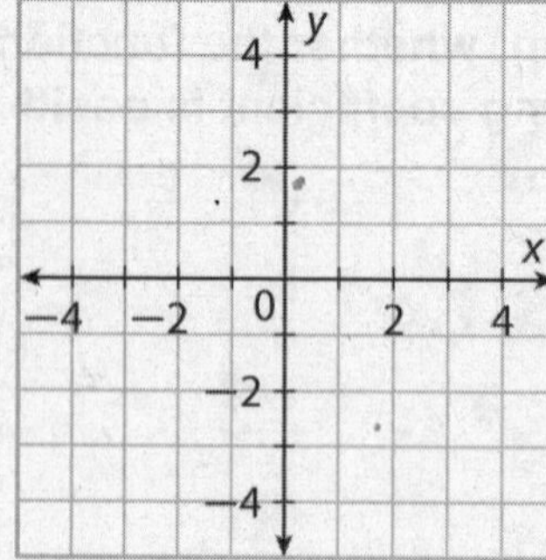

____

3. $f(x) = -2x + 3$

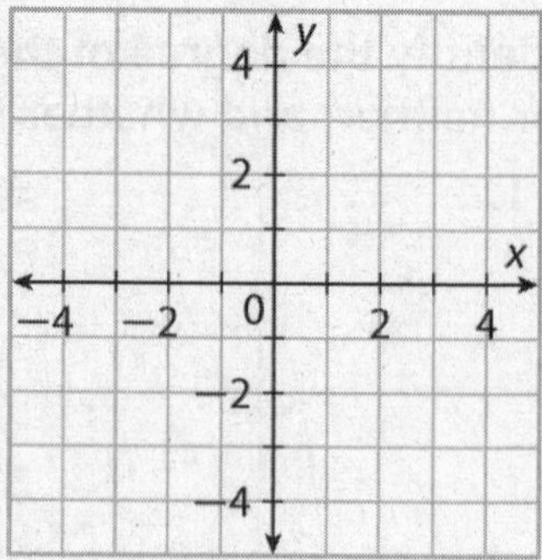

____

Name ________________ Date ________ Class ________

LESSON 24-3

Graphing Square Root Functions

Reteach

The inverse of $y = x^2$ is the parent square root function.

The parent square root function is $y = \sqrt{x}$ for $x \geq 0$.

The graph looks like this:

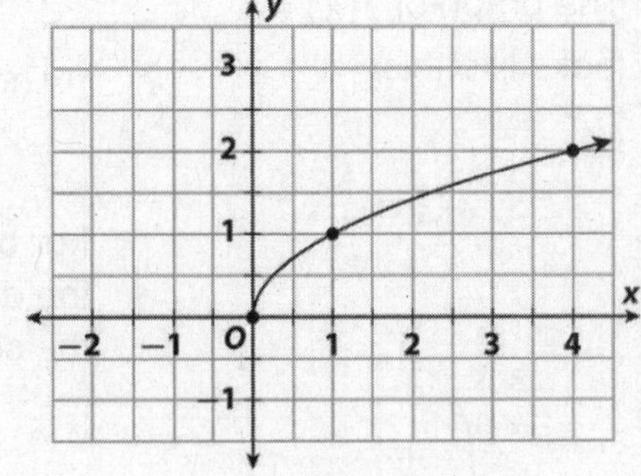

Notice that the graph is in Quadrant I only.

The domain is $x \geq 0$. The range is $y \geq 0$

because $y = \sqrt{x}$ is not defined for real numbers if $x < 0$.

Example

Find the domain of $y = \sqrt{2x+1} + 5$.

$2x + 1 \geq 0$	Look at possible values for what is under the square root sign.
$x \geq -\frac{1}{2}$	Solve the inequality.

The domain is the set of all real numbers greater than or equal to $-\dfrac{1}{2}$.

Find the range of $y = \sqrt{2x+1} + 5$.

$2x + 1 \geq 0$	Look at possible values for what is under the square root sign.
$y \geq 5$	Solve for *y* if the value for what is under the square root sign is 0.

The range is the set of all real numbers greater than or equal to 5.

Complete the table to find the domain and range of each square root equation. Then graph the function.

1. $y = \sqrt{x-1} - 2$

Domain: ________________

Range: ________________

x	$y = \sqrt{x-1} - 2$
1	$\sqrt{1-1} - 2 = -2$
5	
10	
17	

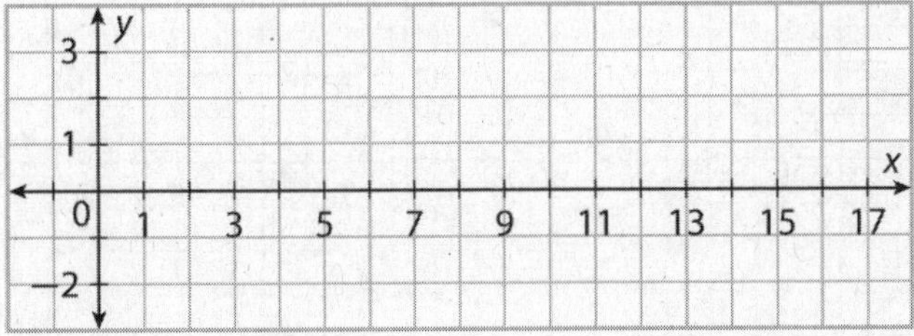

Name ______________________ Date ______________ Class ______________

LESSON 24-4

Graphing Cube Root Functions

Reteach

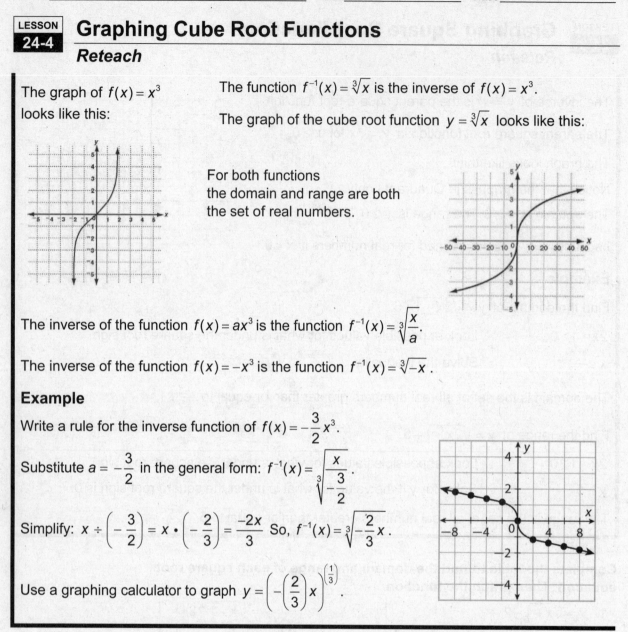

The graph of $f(x) = x^3$ looks like this:

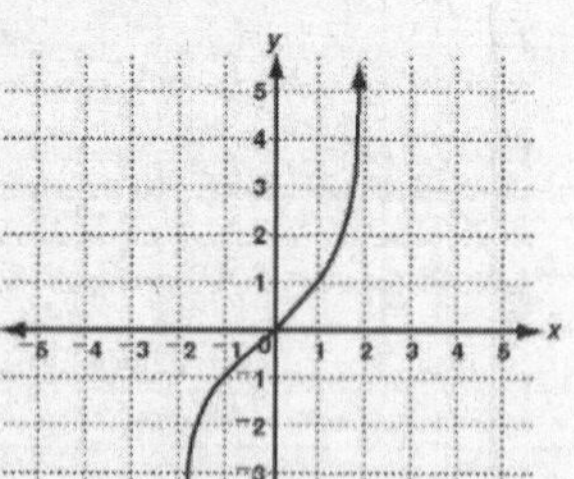

The function $f^{-1}(x) = \sqrt[3]{x}$ is the inverse of $f(x) = x^3$.

The graph of the cube root function $y = \sqrt[3]{x}$ looks like this:

For both functions the domain and range are both the set of real numbers.

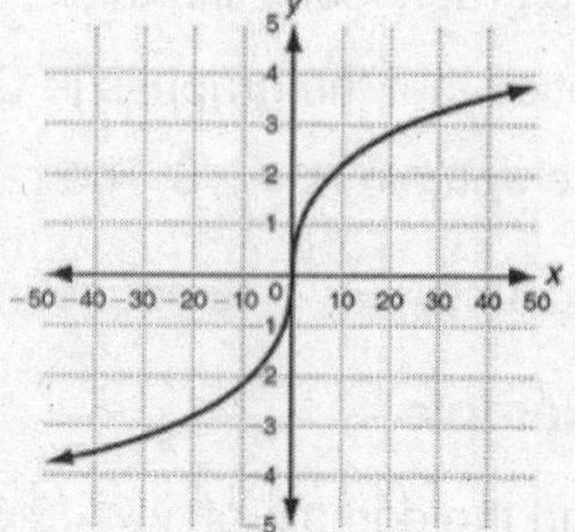

The inverse of the function $f(x) = ax^3$ is the function $f^{-1}(x) = \sqrt[3]{\frac{x}{a}}$.

The inverse of the function $f(x) = -x^3$ is the function $f^{-1}(x) = \sqrt[3]{-x}$.

Example

Write a rule for the inverse function of $f(x) = -\frac{3}{2}x^3$.

Substitute $a = -\frac{3}{2}$ in the general form: $f^{-1}(x) = \sqrt[3]{\frac{x}{-\frac{3}{2}}}$.

Simplify: $x \div \left(-\frac{3}{2}\right) = x \cdot \left(-\frac{2}{3}\right) = \frac{-2x}{3}$ So, $f^{-1}(x) = \sqrt[3]{-\frac{2}{3}x}$.

Use a graphing calculator to graph $y = \left(-\left(\frac{2}{3}\right)x\right)^{\left(\frac{1}{3}\right)}$.

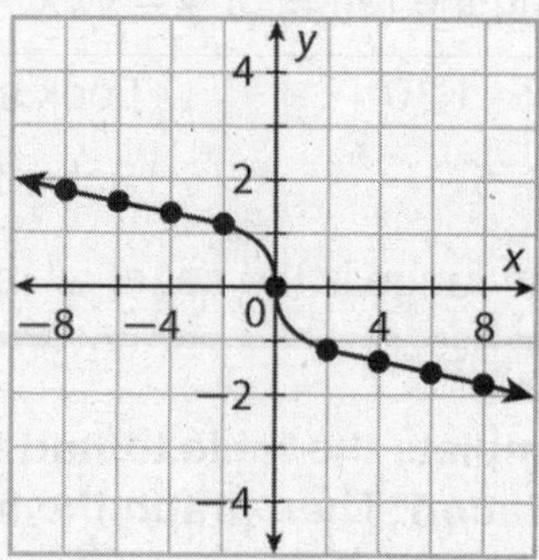

Write a rule for the inverse of each function and sketch the graph.

1. $f(x) = -3x^3$

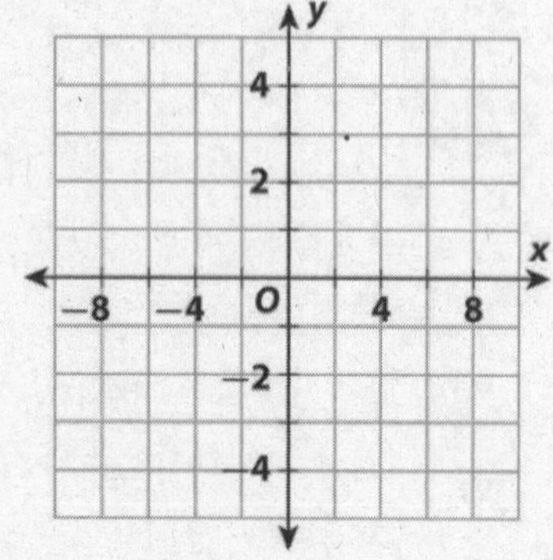

____

2. $f(x) = \frac{1}{2}x^3$

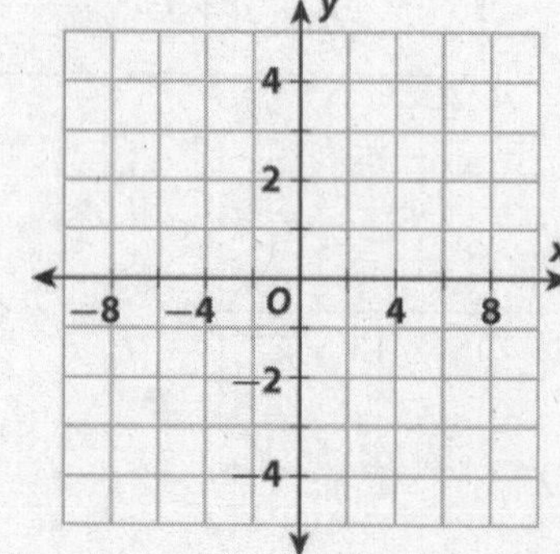

____

3. $f(x) = -\frac{2}{5}x^3$

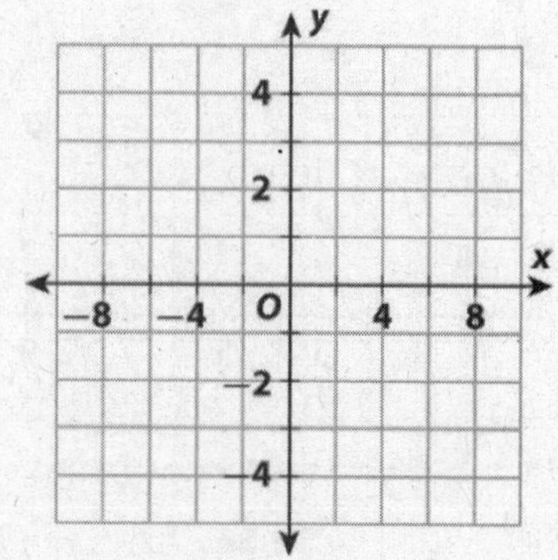

____

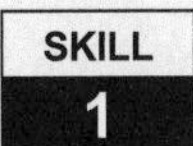

Add and Subtract Integers

KEY TEACHING POINTS

Example 1

Remind students that integers are the set of whole numbers and their opposites.

Say: The first addend is at 3 on the number line. The arrow shows the direction and distance to add 4 to 3.

Say: When you add a positive integer, you move right on a number line.

Check

Say: Adding positive integers is exactly the same as adding whole numbers.

Example 2

Point out that in this problem the addends are negative integers.

Say: The first addend is at –3 on the number line. The arrow shows the direction and distance to add –4 to –3. When you add a negative integer, you move to the left on a number line.

Check

Say: Adding two negative integers is like adding positive integers.

Ask: Is it possible for the sum of two negative integers to be a positive integer? **[No.]** Why? **[The sum must be less than either addend because you move left on a number line to add negative integers.]**

Example 3

Say: Absolute value is the distance a number is from 0 on a number line. Absolute values are always positive numbers.

Ask: What is the absolute value of –8? **[8]** What is the absolute value of –9? **[9]**

Say: Add the absolute values. The sign of the sum is the same as the sign of the addends. In this problem, the signs are negative.

Example 4

Ask: Why is there a point at –4? **[It is the first addend.]**

Say: Because 6 was added to –4, the arrow goes to the right 6 units.

Check

Have students draw number lines to help them find the sums.

Ask: Where do you place the point on the number line? **[At the point that represents the first addend]** When do you move to the right? **[When adding a positive integer]** To the left? **[When adding a negative integer]**

KEY TEACHING POINTS

Example 5

Remind students that absolute value is the distance a number is from 0 on a number line. Absolute values are always positive.

Ask: What is the absolute value of –7? **[7]** What is the absolute value of 5? **[5]** Which number has the greater absolute value? **[–7]** Will the sum be positive or negative? **[negative]**

Check

Ask: Is the sum of –8 + 6 positive or negative? **[negative]** How do you know? **[–8 has a greater absolute value than 6.]**

Ask: When adding a positive integer and a negative integer, how do you know if a sum is positive or negative? **[The sign used in the sum is the same as the sign of the integer with the greater absolute value.]**

Ask: How can a sum of a positive and a negative integer be 0? **[The sum is 0 if the two integers are opposites.]**

ALTERNATE STRATEGY

Strategy: Use two-color counters to add integers with different signs.

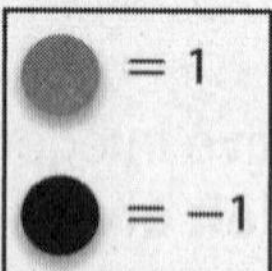

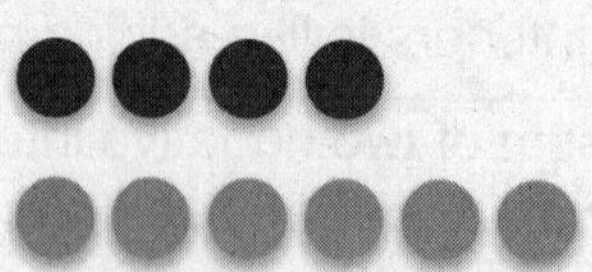

Show how to find the sum of –4 + 6 using the two-color counters.

1. Show 4 black counters to represent –4.
2. Show 6 gray counters to represent 6.
3. Make the zero pairs match, one black counter and one gray counter. The value of the zero pair is 0 because the sum of opposite integers is 0.
4. **Ask:** How many zero pairs are there? **[4]** When the zero pairs are removed what is left? **[2 gray counters]** What do they represent? **[2]**

COMMON MISCONCEPTION

Ask: What is the error in 19 + (–31) = 12?
Reason incorrect: –31 has a greater absolute value than 19. The sum is negative.

Solution: 19 + (–31) = –12

Say: Remember the sign of the sum is the same as the sign of the integer with the greater absolute value.

KEY TEACHING POINTS

Example 6

Explain that the subtrahend is the number being subtracted and the minuend is the number that the subtrahend is being subtracted from.

Say: 4 is shown on the number line. The arrow shows the direction and distance of subtracting 7 from 4.

Say: When you subtract a positive integer, you move to the left on a number line.

Check

Ask: When subtracting a positive integer from a positive integer, how do you know if the difference is positive or negative? **[If the subtrahend is less than the minuend, the difference is positive. If the subtrahend is greater, the difference will be negative.]**

Example 7

Say: –4 is shown on the number line. The arrow shows the direction and distance of subtracting –7 from –4.

Say: When you subtract a negative integer, you move right on a number line.

Example 8

Say: Subtracting a negative integer is like adding a positive integer.

Demonstrate how to rewrite a subtraction expression as an addition expression.
–8 – (–5) = –8 + 5

Say: –8 stays as is. Subtracting –5 is like adding 5.

Ask: How are –5 and 5 related? **[They are opposites.]**

Say: Subtracting a negative number is like adding its opposite.

Check

Ask: When subtracting a negative integer from a negative integer, how do you know if the difference is positive or negative? **[If the subtrahend is greater than the minuend, the difference is positive. If the subtrahend is less, the difference is negative.]**

Ask: What addition expression can you write for –4 – (–7)? **[–4 + 7]**

COMMON MISCONCEPTION

Ask: What is the error in 12 – (–8) = 4?

Reason incorrect: 12 – (–8) is rewritten as 12 + 8 not 12 + (–8) or 12 – 8.

Solution: 12 – (–8) = 12 + 8 = 20

Say: When subtracting a negative integer, rewrite the expression as an addition expression by adding the opposite of the subtrahend.

KEY TEACHING POINTS

Example 9

Say: In a word problem, look for a word or a phrase that tells which operations to use.

Ask: What do you know? **[Temperature at 8 A.M.: –6°C. Temperature at 12 P.M.: 3°C.]**

Ask: What do you need to find out? **[The change in temperature from –6°C to 3°C]**

Say: The change in the temperatures is a positive number.

Ask: What operation do you use to find the change in temperatures? **[Subtraction]**

Ask: What subtraction expression can you write? **[3 – (–6)]**

Ask: How can you rewrite the subtraction expression as an addition expression? **[3 + 6]**

Ask: What is the change in temperature, in degrees Celsius? **[9]**

Remind students to include the units in their answers.

Check

Say: Think about what you know and what you need to find out.

Ask: How do you know whether to add or subtract? **[Add when joining two groups and subtract when finding how many more or finding change.]**

ADDITIONAL ONLINE INTERVENTION RESOURCES

Use the following for students who have not mastered the concepts in Skill 1.

- Math on the Spot videos
- Personal Math Trainer with customized intervention
- Building Block worksheets (Skill 105: Understand Integers; Skill 107: Whole Number Operations)

Name ______________________ Date ______________ Class ______________

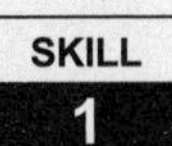

Add and Subtract Integers

Example 1

Use a number line to add positive **integers**.

Add: 3 + 4

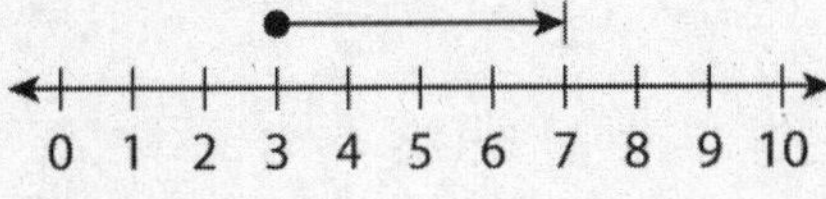

3 + 4 = 7

Vocabulary
- Integer
- Absolute value
- Opposite

Check

Find each sum.

1. 6 + 3 ________
2. 12 + 9 ________
3. 35 + 48 ________

Example 2

Use a number line to add negative integers.

Add: –3 + (–4)

–10 –9 –8 –7 –6 –5 –4 –3 –2 –1 0

–3 + (–4) = –7

Check

Find each sum.

4. –5 + (–2) ________
5. –15 + (–16) ________
6. –24 + (–49) ________

Example 3

To add negative integers, add the **absolute values** of the integers and use the sign of the integers for the sum.

Add: –8 + (–9)

Find the absolute values.	$\lvert -8 \rvert = 8$ and $\lvert -9 \rvert = 9$
Find the sum of the absolute values.	8 + 9 = 17
Use the sign of the integers for the sum.	–8 + (–9) = –17

Name ______________________ Date ______________ Class ______________

Check

Find each sum.

7. –5 + (–9) ________ 8. –27 + (–18) ________ 9. –32 + (–59) ________

Example 4

Use a number line to add positive and negative integers.

Add: –4 + 6

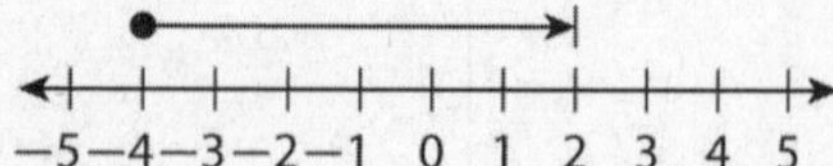

–4 + 6 = 2

Check

Find each sum.

10. –2 + 5 ________ 11. 4 + (–5) ________ 12. –3 + 3 ________

Example 5

To add positive and negative integers, subtract the lesser absolute value from the greater absolute value. Use the sign of the integer with the greater absolute value for the sum.

Add: –7 + 5

Find the absolute values. $|-7| = 7$ and $|5| = 5$

Subtract the lesser absolute value from the greater absolute value. 7 – 5 = 2

Use the sign of the integer for the greater absolute value for the sum. –7 + 5 = –2

Check

Find each sum.

13. –8 + 6 ________ 14. 12 + (–7) ________ 15. –16 + 31 ________

16. What's the Error? Explain the error. Find the correct solution.
19 + (–31) = 12

____

____

Name _______________ Date _______________ Class _______________

Example 6

Use a number line to subtract positive integers.

Subtract: 4 – 7

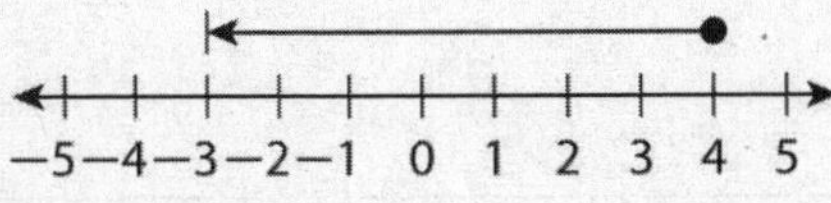

4 – 7 = –3

Check

Find each difference.

17. 5 – 2 ________ 18. 2 – 4 ________ 19. 5 – 9 ________

Example 7

Use a number line to subtract negative integers.

Subtract: –4 – (–7)

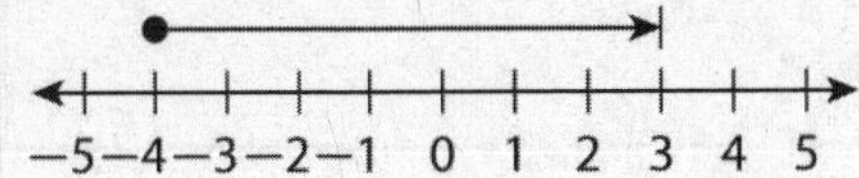

–4 – (–7) = 3

Check

Find each difference.

20. –3 – (–5) ________ 21. 2 – (–2) ________ 22. –5 – (–3) ________

Example 8

Subtracting a negative integer is like adding its opposite.
Subtract: –8 – (–5)

Rewrite as an addition expression. –8 + 5

Find the sum. –8 + 5 = –3

Name ______________________ Date ____________ Class ____________

Check

Find each difference.

23. –4 – (–7) ________ 24. –6 – (–6) ________ 25. 9 – (–7) ________

26. What's the Error? Explain the error. Find the correct solution.
12 – (–8) = 4

____

____

Example 9

The temperature at 8 A.M. was –6°C. By noon, the temperature was 3°C. Find the change in temperature.

Write a subtraction expression for the change.	3 – (–6)
Rewrite as an addition expression.	3 + 6
Find the sum.	3 + 6 = 9

The temperature changed by 9°C from 8 A.M. to noon.

Check

Write an expression. Then find the value of the expression.

27. Lisa played two rounds of miniature golf. Her score was –3 in the first round and +2 in the second round. What was Lisa's score after two rounds? ______________________

28. Craig carried the football two times for a total of –2 yards. He carried the football for 3 yards on his first carry. What is the number of yards that Craig carried the football on his second carry?

____

SKILL 1 ADD AND SUBTRACT INTEGERS

SKILL 2

Algebraic Expressions

KEY TEACHING POINTS

Example 1

Remind students that an algebraic expression contains at least one variable.

Say: To evaluate an algebraic expression, substitute a number for the variable.

Ask: To evaluate the expression $x + 4$ for $x = 6$, what number do you substitute for x? **[6]** What does the expression look like now? **[6 + 4]** What is 6 + 4? **[10]**

Ask: To evaluate the expression $x - 8$ for $x = 6$, what number do you substitute for x? **[6]** What does the expression look like now? **[6 – 8]** What is 6 – 8? **[–2]**

Check

Ask: What number will you substitute for *y* in the problems? **[8]**

Example 2

Say: The expression $7a$ means to multiply 7 times *a*.

Demonstrate the different ways to write 7 times *a*.

$7a$, $7 \times a$, $7 \cdot a$, $7(a)$, $(7)(a)$

Say: To evaluate a multiplication expression, multiply the number representing the variable by the coefficient.

Ask: In $7a$, what is the coefficient? **[7]** In $0.6a$ what is the coefficient? **[0.6]**

Ask: To evaluate the expression $7a$ for $a = 4$, what number do you substitute for *a*? **[4]** What does the expression look like now? **[7 × 4]** What is 7 × 4? **[28]**

Ask: In the expression $0.6a$ for $a = 4$, what number do you substitute for *a*? **[4]** What number sentence can you write? **[0.6 × 4]** What is 0.6 × 4? **[2.4]**

Check

Ask: What number will you substitute for *b* in the problems? **[7]**

Say: There are no operational symbols.

Ask: What operation will you use? **[multiplication]**

Example 3

Remind students that a fraction is another way to indicate division. A fraction means to divide the numerator by the denominator.

Say: The expression 12 over *c* means to divide 12 by *c*.

Ask: To evaluate the expression $c \div 2$ for $c = 2$, what number do you substitute for *c*? **[2]** What does the expression look like now? **[2 ÷ 2]** What is 2 ÷ 2? **[1]**

Check

Say: Notice that *d* can be the dividend or the divisor.

Ask: What is another way to write $\frac{18}{d}$? **[18 ÷ *d*]**

What number will you substitute for *d* in the problems? **[4]**

KEY TEACHING POINTS

Example 4

Review with students how to use the order of operations to evaluate multistep expressions. None of the problems will have parentheses or exponents, so the rules are as follows:

1. Substitute the values for the variables.
2. Multiply and divide from left to right.
3. Add and subtract from left to right.

Ask: When there is no operational symbol, what operation do you use? **[Multiplication]**

Ask: What number do you substitute for *e*? **[4]** What is the value of 3*e*? **[12]**

Ask: What number do you substitute for *f*? **[2]** What is the value of 2*f*? **[4]**

Demonstrate how to rewrite the expression.
$12 + 2 \times 2 - 6 \div 2$

Ask: In using the order of operations, what is the first step? **[Multiply $2 \times 2 = 4$]**

Ask: What is the second step? **[Divide $6 \div 2 = 3$]**

Say: The expression is now $12 + 4 - 3$.

Ask: What are the remaining steps? **[Add $12 + 4 = 16$ and subtract $16 - 3 = 13$]**

Check

Make sure students understand that they need to substitute 6 for *g* and 3 for *h* in each of the problems.

Example 5

Say: An algebraic expression is simplified or in its simplest form when it contains no like terms.

Say: Like terms are terms that have the same variable. Terms that do not have a variable are like terms.

Demonstrate how to simplify algebraic expressions by combining like terms.

- First identify the like terms.
- Then add or subtract the coefficients of each group of like terms.
- The variable remains as is.

Demonstrate how to reorder and group terms using the Commutative Property of Addition to reorder terms and then the Associative Property of Addition to group like terms.
$3x + 4y + 2x - 3y + 2 \rightarrow 3x + 2x + 4y - 3y + 2 \rightarrow (3x + 2x) + (4y - 3y) + 2$

Say: Add inside the parentheses to simplify the expression. $5x + y + 2$

ALTERNATE STRATEGY

Strategy: Use shapes to help you combine like terms.

1. Remind students that like terms have identical variables. Write $3x + 4y + 2x - 3y + 2$ on the board.
2. Circle the terms with *x* and draw a rectangle around the terms with *y*.
3. **Ask:** Can you add circles and rectangles and get a common term? **[No.]** Can you add constants and variables and get a common term? **[No.]** What is the sum of the terms in the circles? **[5*x*]** Simplify the terms with the rectangles. **[*y*]**
4. Use an expression in Example 5 Check and simplify using shapes.

KEY TEACHING POINTS

Example 6

Say: To simplify an expression, it may be necessary to use the Distributive Property.

Ask: What does $6(2x - 3)$ mean? **[Multiply 6 times 2*x* and multiply 6 times –3.]**

Say: It is not necessary to have like terms to multiply.

Ask: What is the product $6 \times 2x$? **[12*x*]** What is the product of $6 \times (-3)$? **[–18]** What is the product of $6(2x - 3)$? **[12*x* – 18]**

Say: The expression is now $12x - 18 + 4x$.

Ask: Are any of the terms like terms? **[Yes, 12*x* and 4*x* are like terms.]**

Check

Say: Each of these expressions requires the use of the Distributive Property.

Ask: Can you add or subtract inside the parentheses before multiplying? Why or why not? **[No, the terms inside the parentheses are not like terms.]**

Remind students that they can use the Commutative Property of Addition and the Associative Property of Addition to reorder and regroup the terms.

Example 7

Say: In solving word problems it is important to know how to write an expression. Knowing which operation to use is an important part of solving a word problem.

Say: Look for words that tell which operation to use. Sometimes the word that is the clue is naturally part of the operation like sum, difference, product, or quotient. Other times you may need to look at the context.

Make sure that students understand that multiplication joins equal groups and division shows how many are in equal groups or it gives the number of groups.

KEY TEACHING POINTS

Example 8

Ask: What do you know about the pencils? **[8 pencils cost *d* dollars each.]**

Ask: What do you know about the notebooks? **[3 notebooks cost $2 each.]**

Ask: What are you asked to do? **[Write an expression to represent the amount of money that Nadine spent in dollars.]**

Emphasize with students that when writing an expression involving money it is important to know if the currency is in dollars or cents.

Say: You can break the problem into two parts and then combine the parts.

Ask: How much money, in dollars, did Nadine spend on pencils? **[8*d*]** Can you be more specific? Why or why not? **[No, the value of *d* is unknown.]**

Ask: How much money, in dollars, did Nadine spend on the notebooks? **[$6]**

Say: Combine the two expressions to determine the amount of money Nadine spent at the school bookstore.

Ask: Can you add $8d + 6$? Why or why not? **[No, 8*d* and 6 are not like terms.]**

Check

Say: Think about what you know and what you need to find out.

Say: Break the problem into parts and then combine the expressions for each part.

COMMON MISCONCEPTION

Ask: What error did Emily make in writing the expression $8 + p + 3$? **[There are only two terms in the expression and Emily has three. Emily scored 8 points on 2-point field goals and *p* points on 3-point field goals.]**

Reason incorrect: Because Emily made any number of 3-point field goals, the points scored on 3-point field goals should be $3p$ not $p + 3$.

Solution: The expression $8 + 3p$ represents the number of points that Emily scored.

ADDITIONAL ONLINE INTERVENTION RESOURCES

Use the following for students who have not mastered the concepts in Skill 2.

- Math on the Spot videos
- Personal Math Trainer with customized intervention
- Building Block worksheets (Skill 19: Combine Like Terms; Skill 22: Connect Words and Algebra; Skill 23: Connect Words and Equations; Skill 24: Distributive Property; Skill 27: Evaluate Expressions; Skill 40: Function Tables; Skill 59: Multiplication Properties; Skill 81: Simplify Algebraic Expressions)

Name ______________________ Date ______________ Class ______________

SKILL 2

Algebraic Expressions

Vocabulary

Algebraic expression

Variable

Simplify

Order of operations

Like terms

Commutative Property of Addition

Associative Property of Addition

Distributive Property

Example 1

You can evaluate an algebraic expression involving addition or subtraction by substituting a number for the variable.

Evaluate each for $x = 6$.

$x + 4$

$6 + 4 = 10$

Substitute 6 for *x*.

$x - 8$

$6 - 8 = -2$

Check

Evaluate each expression for $y = 8$.

1. $12 + y =$ ______
2. $15 - y$ ______
3. $y - 12$ ______

Example 2

You can evaluate a multiplication algebraic expression by substituting a number for the variable.

Evaluate each for $a = 4$.

$7a$

$7 \times 4 = 28$

$7a = 7 \times a$

$0.6a$

$0.6 \times 4 = 2.4$

$0.6a = 0.6 \times a$

Check

Evaluate each expression for $b = 7$.

4. $6b$ ______
5. $0.5b$ ______
6. $\frac{3}{5}b$ ______

Example 3

You can evaluate a division algebraic expression by substituting a number for the variable.

Evaluate each for $c = 2$.

$c \div 2$

$2 \div 2 = 1$

$\frac{12}{c}$

$\frac{12}{2} = 6$

$\frac{12}{c} = 12 \div c$

Name ______________________ Date ____________ Class ____________

Check

Evaluate each expression for $d = 4$.

7. $32 \div d$ ________ 8. $d \div 20$ ________ 9. $\frac{18}{d}$ ________

Example 4

You can evaluate multistep algebraic expressions by using the order of operations.

Evaluate $3e + 2f - 6 \div 2$ for $e = 4$ and $f = 2$.

Substitute the values for the variables.	$3 \times 4 + 2 \times 2 - 6 \div 2$
Multiply and divide from left to right.	$12 + 2 \times 2 - 6 \div 2$
	$12 + 4 - 6 \div 2$
	$12 + 4 - 3$
Add and subtract from left to right.	$16 - 3$
	13

The value of $3e + 2f - 6 \div 2$ for $e = 4$ and $f = 2$ is 13.

Check

Evaluate each expression for $g = 6$ and $h = 3$.

10. $3g + 4h \div 2 + 3$ 11. $18 \div 2h + 3g - 4$ 12. $5g - 3h \times 4 \div 2$

________ ________ ________

Example 5

To simplify an expression, you can add like terms.

Simplify: $3x + 4y + 2x - 3y + 2$ Like terms have the same variable.

Identify like terms.	$\mathbf{3x} + \underline{4y} + \mathbf{2x} - \underline{3y} + 2$
Use the Commutative Property of Addition to reorder the terms.	$3x + 2x + 4y - 3y + 2$
Use the Associative Property of Addition to group the like terms.	$(3x + 2x) + (4y - 3y) + 2$
Add.	$5x + y + 2$

When simplified, $3x + 4y + 2x - 3y + 2$ is $5x + y + 2$.

Check

Simplify each expression.

13. $4a + 3b - 2a + 6 + 5b$ ________________

14. $6c - 3d + d + 2c - 7$ ________________

Name ______________________ Date ______________ Class ______________

Example 6

You can use the Distributive Property to simplify expressions.

Simplify: $6(2x - 3) + 4x$

Rename the expression. $(6 \times 2x) + (6 \times (-3)) + 4x$

Multiply. $12x + (-18) + 4x$

Add like terms. $16x + (-18)$

When simplified, $6(2x - 3) + 4x$ is $16x + (-18)$.

Check

Simplify each expression.

15. $3(4x + 5) + 2x - 6$ ______________

16. $0.75(8x + 4) - 3x + 2$ ______________

17. $\frac{2}{3}(9x - 6) + 4x - 3$ ______________

Example 7

Look for words that tell which operation to use in an expression.

Operation	Addition	Subtraction	Multiplication	Division
Words	plus sum more than	minus difference less than	times product groups of	quotient in each group in equal groups

The sum of a number plus 6 $n + 6$ or $6 + n$

8 less than a number $n - 8$

The product of a number and 5 $5n$

The quotient of a number and 6 $\frac{n}{6}$ or $n \div 6$

Check

Write an expression.

18. 12 more than *d* ______________

19. *e* less than 5 ______________

20. 16 split into *f* equal groups ______________

Name ______________________ Date ______________ Class ______________

Example 8

Write expressions to help solve problems.
Nadine bought 8 pencils and 3 notebooks from the school bookstore. Each pencil cost d dollars. Each notebook cost $2. Write an expression to represent the amount of money, in dollars, Nadine spent at the school bookstore.

Write an expression to represent the cost of the pencils.	$8d$
Write an expression to represent the cost of the notebooks.	3×2 or 6.
Combine the expressions.	$8d + 6$

The expression $8d + 6$ represents the amount of money Nadine spent.

Check

Write an expression to represent each situation.

21. Anna bought a computer game for $12 and two posters that each cost d dollars at the media store. How much money did Anna spend altogether?

____

22. Terrance picked 54 apples. He kept a apples for himself and gave each of 6 friends an equal number of apples. How many apples did each friend receive?

____

23. What's the Error? Emily scored 8 points on 2-point field goals and she made p 3-point field goals in the basketball game. She recorded the number of points she scored as $8 + p + 3$. Explain the error and write an expression that represents the number of points Emily scored.

____

____

SKILL 2 ALGEBRAIC EXPRESSIONS

SKILL 3

Algebraic Representations of Transformations

KEY TEACHING POINTS

Example 1

Remind students that an ordered pair names a point on the coordinate grid.

Say: A transformation is the movement of a figure. The preimage is the figure before it is transformed. The image is the figure after the transformation.

Say: The image is congruent to the preimage.

Ask: What does the image being congruent to the preimage mean? **[They are the same size and shape.]**

Draw a coordinate plane on the board.

Say: The *x*-axis is the number line that goes left to right. The *y*-axis is the number line that goes up and down.

Say: A translation is the same as a slide along a line. A translation can move a figure horizontally, which is left or right, or vertically, which is up or down. A translation can also move a figure both horizontally and vertically.

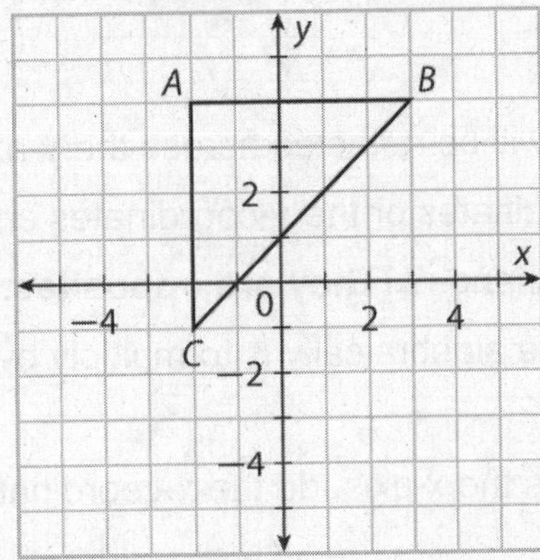

Say: The translation of triangle *ABC* moves it 2 units to the right and 3 units down.

Ask: What does it mean to move a figure 2 units to the right? **[Add 2 to the first coordinate in an ordered pair.]** How is adding 2 to the first coordinate in an ordered pair written algebraically? **[$x + 2$].**

Ask: What does it mean to move a figure 3 units down? **[Subtract 3 from the second coordinate in an ordered pair.]** How is subtracting 3 from the second coordinate in an ordered pair written algebraically? **[$y - 3$]**

Ask: To determine the coordinates of the image, what do you do to the coordinates of the preimage? **[Add 2 to each first coordinate and subtract 3 from each second coordinate.]**

Check

Encourage students to plot rectangle *DEFG* on a coordinate plane.

Ask: What does $(x - 2, y + 1)$ mean in a translation? **[Move 2 units left and 1 unit up.]**

KEY TEACHING POINTS

Example 2

Say: A reflection is a flip across a line. The image after a reflection forms a mirror image of the preimage. The image is congruent to the preimage.

Say: When a figure on a coordinate plane is reflected across the *x*-axis, the *x*-coordinate of the image remains the same as the preimage. The *y*-coordinate in the image becomes the opposite of the preimage.

Say: When a figure on a coordinate plane is reflected across the *y*-axis, the *y*-coordinate of the image remains the same as the preimage. The *x*-coordinate in the image becomes the opposite of the preimage.

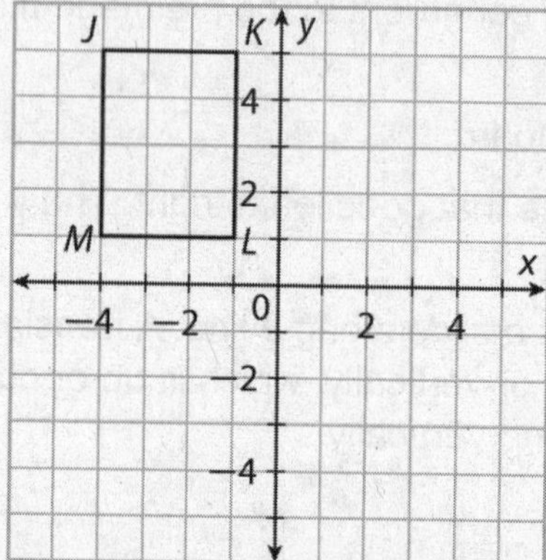

Say: Look at rectangle *JKLM*. It will be reflected across the *y*-axis.

Ask: In the image, do the *x*-coordinates or the *y*-coordinates change? **[*x*-coordinates]**

Ask: How do the *x*-coordinates change? **[They are opposites.]**

Say: The way to write an opposite algebraically is to multiply by –1.

Check

Ask: If a figure is reflected across the *x*-axis, do the *x*-coordinates or the *y*-coordinates change? **[*y*-coordinates]**

Ask: How do the *x*-coordinates change? **[They are opposites.]**

COMMON MISCONCEPTION

Ask: What error did Rosie make in reflecting triangle *BCD* across the *y*-axis? **[Rosie multiplied every coordinate by –1.]**

Reason incorrect: Rosie should have only multiplied the *x*-coordinates by –1. To reflect a figure across the *y*-axis, the *y*-coordinate of the image remains the same as the preimage and the *x*-coordinate in the image becomes the opposite of the preimage.

Solution: The vertices of triangle *B′C′D′* are *B′*(2, –4), *C′*(4, –5), and *D′*(3, –2).

KEY TEACHING POINTS

Example 3

Say: A 90° clockwise rotation is a quarter turn. Clockwise is the direction the hands of a clock move. A quarter turn moves the hands 3 hours forward.

Say: In a 90° clockwise rotation about the origin, switch the *x*- and *y*-coordinates. The opposite of the *x*-coordinate becomes the *y*-coordinate and the *y*-coordinate becomes the *x*-coordinate.

Say: A 90° counterclockwise rotation is a quarter turn. Counterclockwise is in the opposite direction from the hands of a clock. A quarter turn moves the hands 3 hours backward.

Say: A 90° counterclockwise rotation is also a 270° clockwise rotation.

Say: In a 90° counterclockwise rotation about the origin, switch the *x*- and *y*-coordinates. The opposite of the *y*-coordinate in the preimage becomes the *x*-coordinate of the image and the *x*-coordinate of the preimage becomes the *y*-coordinate of the image.

Say: A 180° rotation is a half turn. It does not matter if the turn is clockwise or counterclockwise.

Ask: Why does the direction not matter for a 180° rotation? **[The image will appear in the same location whether clockwise or counterclockwise.]**

Say: In a 180° rotation about the origin, find the opposites of the *x*- and *y*-coordinates. This means that you can multiply each coordinate by –1.

On the board, draw rectangle *JKLM* on a coordinate plane.

Say: Look at rectangle *JKLM*. It will be rotated 90° clockwise about the origin.

Ask: Before switching the coordinates, what do you do to each *x*-coordinate? **[Multiply it by –1.]** What do you to each *y*-coordinate? **[Nothing]**

ALTERNATE STRATEGY

Strategy: Use the quadrant names to help rotate figures about the origin.

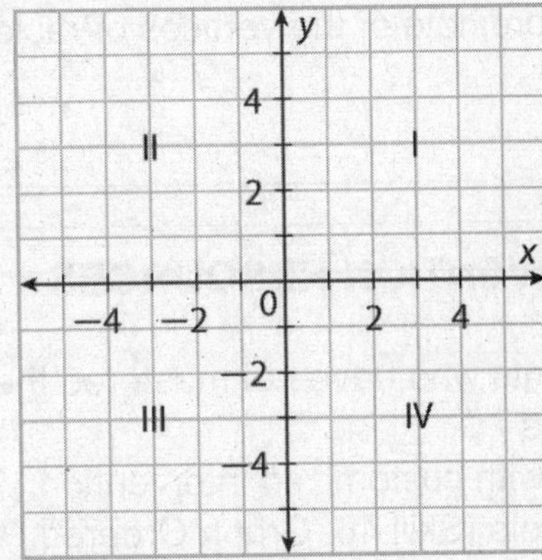

1. A 90° clockwise rotation about the origin moves the figure one quadrant in the direction of the hands of a clock. The order of the coordinates for an image is reversed from the preimage.

2. A 90° counterclockwise rotation about the origin moves the figure one quadrant in the opposite direction of the hands of a clock. The order of the coordinates for the image is reversed from the preimage.
3. A 180° rotation about the origin moves the figure two quadrants. The order of the coordinates for the image remains the same as the preimage.
4. Use this method for Example 3, if you were to rotate the figure 90° counterclockwise about the origin.

KEY TEACHING POINTS

Example 4

Say: A dilation changes the size of a figure, but not its shape. The image of a dilated figure is similar but not congruent to the preimage. A dilation that increases the size of a figure is called an enlargement. A dilation that decreases the size of a figure is called a reduction. Think of making a photocopy that is a different size than the original.

Say: The scale factor tells how to change every coordinate of the preimage to form the dilated figure. For the dilations on this page, the center of dilation is the origin.

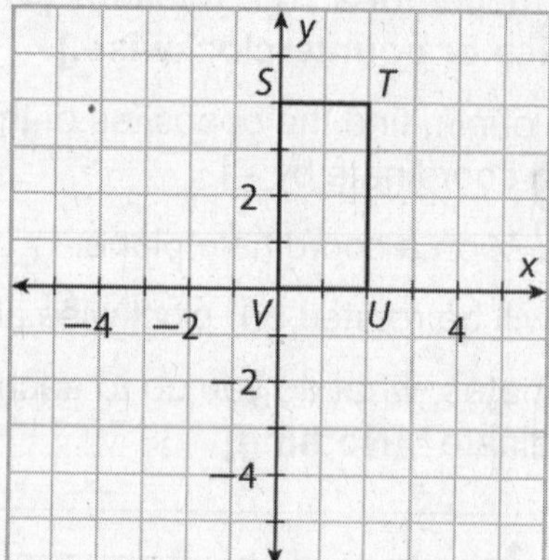

Say: Look at rectangle *STUV*. Rectangle *STUV* will be dilated with the origin as its center of dilation and a scale factor of $\frac{1}{2}$.

Ask: What do you do to each coordinate of the vertices of rectangle *STUV* to produce the dilated image? **[Multiply by $\frac{1}{2}$.]**

ADDITIONAL ONLINE INTERVENTION RESOURCES

Use the following for students who have not mastered the concepts in Skill 3.

- Math on the Spot videos
- Personal Math Trainer with customized intervention
- Building Block worksheets (Skill 46: Graph Ordered Pairs (First Quadrant); Skill 51: Integer Operations)

Name ______________________ Date ____________ Class ____________

SKILL 3

Algebraic Representations of Transformations

Example 1

The rules shown in the table describe how coordinates change when a figure is translated on the coordinate plane.

Right *a* units	Add *a* to the *x*-coordinate: $(x, y) \rightarrow (x + a, y)$
Left *a* units	Subtract *a* from the *x*-coordinate: $(x, y) \rightarrow (x - a, y)$
Up *b* units	Add *b* to the *y*-coordinate: $(x, y) \rightarrow (x, y + b)$
Down *b* units	Subtract *b* from the *y*-coordinate: $(x, y) \rightarrow (x, y - b)$

Find the vertices of triangle $A'B'C'$ after a translation of 2 units to the right and 3 units down.

Vertices of *ABC*	Rule: $(x + 2, y - 3)$	Vertices of $A'B'C'$
$A(-2, 4)$	$(-2 + 2, 4 - 3)$	$A'(0, 1)$
$B(3, 4)$	$(3 + 2, 4 - 3)$	$B'(5, 1)$
$C(-2, -1)$	$(-2 + 2, -1 - 3)$	$C'(0, -4)$

Preimage

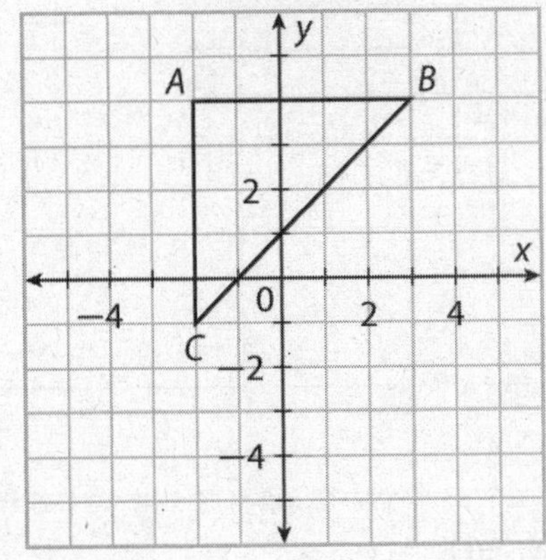

Image

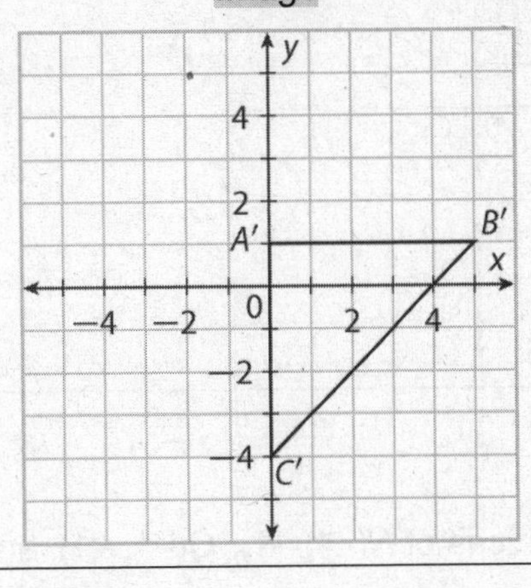

Vocabulary

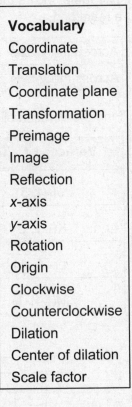

Coordinate
Translation
Coordinate plane
Transformation
Preimage
Image
Reflection
x-axis
y-axis
Rotation
Origin
Clockwise
Counterclockwise
Dilation
Center of dilation
Scale factor

Check

1. Rectangle *DEFG* has vertices of $D(-1, 2)$, $E(4, 2)$, $F(4, -2)$, and $G(-1, -2)$. Name the vertices of the image after a translation $(x, y) \rightarrow (x - 2, y + 1)$. Describe the translation.

____

Name ______________________ Date ______________ Class ______________

Example 2

The table shows the rules for changing the signs of the coordinates after a reflection.

Across the *x*-axis	Multiply each *y*-coordinate by −1: $(x, y) \rightarrow (x, -y)$
Across the *y*-axis	Multiply each *x*-coordinate by −1: $(x, y) \rightarrow (-x, y)$

Find the vertices of rectangle *J′K′L′M′* after a reflection across the *y*-axis.

Vertices of *JKLM*	Rule: $(-1 \cdot x, y)$	Vertices of *J′K′L′M′*
J(−4, 5)	((−1·−4), 5)	*J′*(4, 5)
K(−1, 5)	((−1·−1), 5)	*K′*(1, 5)
L(−1, 1)	((−1·−1), 1)	*L′*(1, 1)
M(−4, 1)	((−1·−4), 1)	*M′*(4, 1)

Preimage

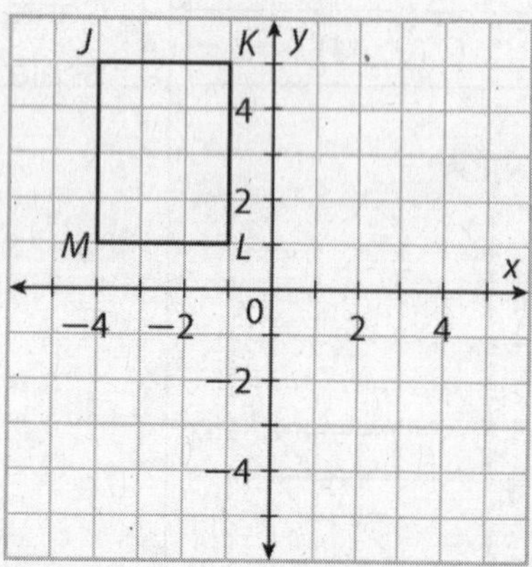

Image

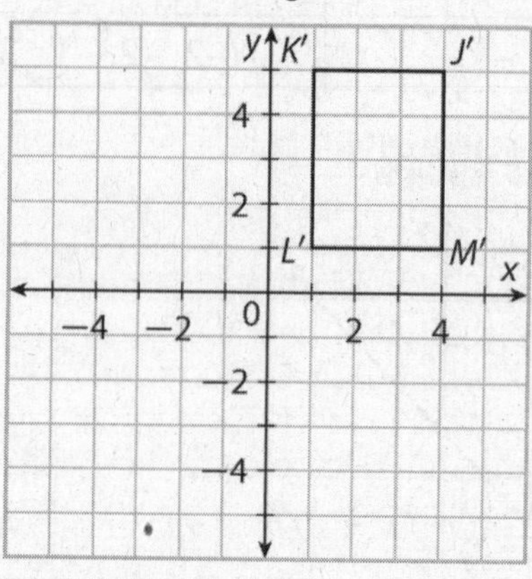

Check

2. Triangle *NOP* has vertices of *N*(−4, −1), *O*(−1, −1), and *P*(−2, −4). What are the vertices of the image after a reflection across the *x*-axis?

____

3. What's the Error? Triangle *BCD* has vertices of *B*(2, 4), *C*(4, 5), and *D*(3, 2). Rosie reflected triangle *BCD* across the *y*-axis. She said that the vertices of the image are *B′*(−2, −4), *C′*(−4, −5), and *D′*(−3, −2). Explain the error and name the correct vertices.

____

Name ______________________ Date ______________ Class ______________

Example 3

The table shows the rules to determine the coordinates of the image after a rotation about the origin (0, 0).

90° clockwise	Multiply each x-coordinate by –1; then switch the x- and y-coordinates: $(x, y) \rightarrow (y, -x)$
180°	Multiply both coordinates by –1: $(x, y) \rightarrow (-x, -y)$
90° counterclockwise	Multiply each y-coordinate by –1; then switch the x- and y-coordinates: $(x, y) \rightarrow (-y, x)$

Find the vertices of rectangle $J'K'L'M'$ after a 90° clockwise rotation about the origin.

Vertices of *JKLM*	Rule: $(y, -x)$	Vertices of $J'K'L'M'$
$J(-4, 5)$	$(5, -1\cdot(-4))$	$J'(5, 4)$
$K(-1, 5)$	$(5, -1\cdot(-1))$	$K'(5, 1)$
$L(-1, 1)$	$(1, -1\cdot(-1))$	$L'(1, 1)$
$M(-4, 1)$	$(1, -1\cdot(-4))$	$M'(1, 4)$

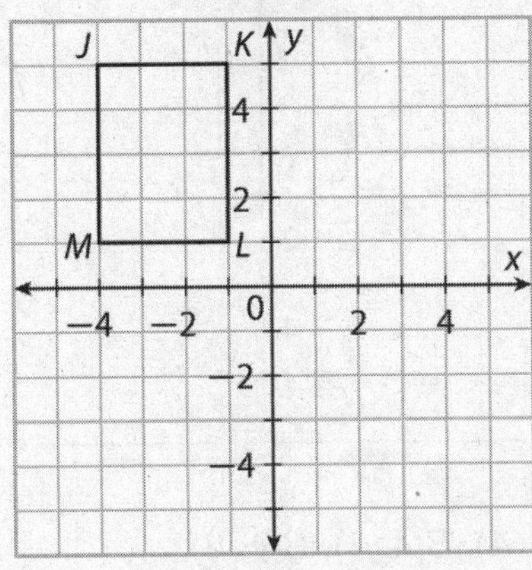

Image

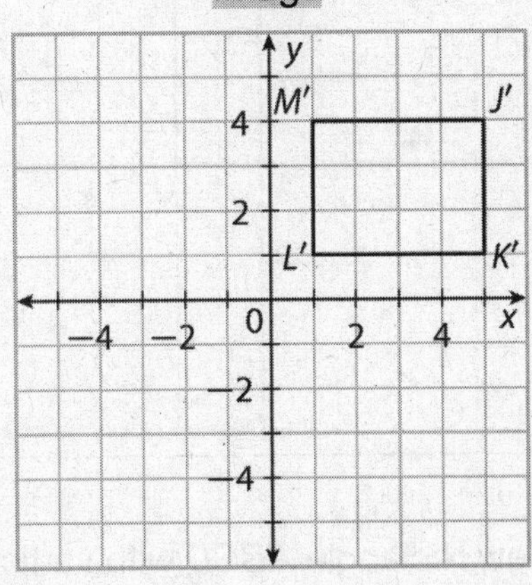

Check

4. Triangle *QRS* has vertices of $Q(1, -1)$, $R(4, -3)$, and $S(3, -5)$. What are the vertices of the image after a 180° rotation about the origin?

____

Name ______________________ Date ______________ Class ______________

Example 4

When a dilation in the coordinate plane has the origin as its center of dilation, you can find the coordinates of the dilated image by multiplying both coordinates of the preimage by the scale factor.

Find the vertices of rectangle $S'T'U'V'$ after a dilation with the origin as its center of dilation and a scale factor of $\frac{1}{2}$.

Vertices of *STUV*	Rule: $\left(\frac{1}{2}x, \frac{1}{2}y\right)$	Vertices of $S'T'U'V'$
$S(0, 4)$	$\left(\frac{1}{2}\cdot 0, \frac{1}{2}\cdot 4\right)$	$S'(0, 2)$
$T(2, 4)$	$\left(\frac{1}{2}\cdot 2, \frac{1}{2}\cdot 4\right)$	$T'(1, 2)$
$U(2, 0)$	$\left(\frac{1}{2}\cdot 2, \frac{1}{2}\cdot 0\right)$	$U'(1, 0)$
$V(0, 0)$	$\left(\frac{1}{2}\cdot 0, \frac{1}{2}\cdot 0\right)$	$V'(0, 0)$

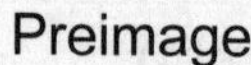

Preimage

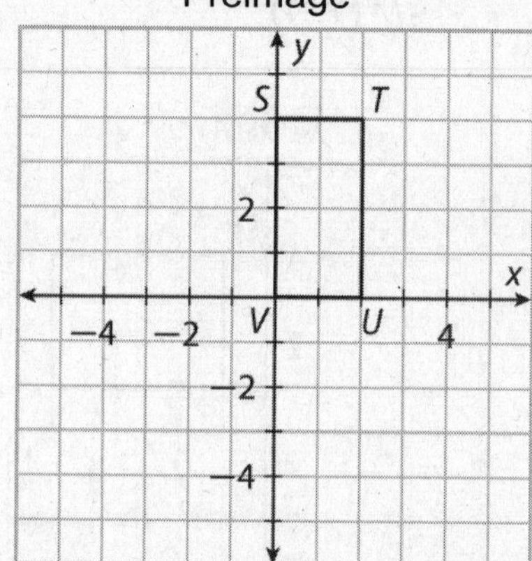

Dilated Image

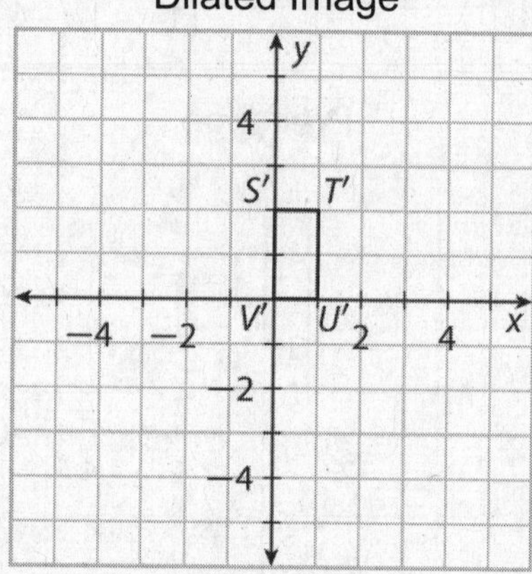

Check

5. Trevor drew rectangle *ABCD* with vertices at *A*(1, 4), *B*(4, 4), *C*(4, 2), and *D*(1, 2). Find the vertices of rectangle *A'B'C'D'* after a dilation with the origin as its center of dilation and a scale factor of 2.

____

____

SKILL 3 ALGEBRAIC REPRESENTATIONS OF TRANSFORMATIONS

SKILL 4

Constant Rate of Change

KEY TEACHING POINTS

Example 1
Review with students that a rate is a comparison by a ratio with two different types of units.

Say: The table shows that there are 36 players on 6 teams. Each team has the same number of players.

Ask: Why is it important to know that each team has the same number of players? **[If each team has the same number of players, the teams are divided into equal groups of players.]**

Say: The unit rate you are looking for is players per team.

Ask: How can you find the unit rate of players on each volleyball team? **[Divide 36 ÷ 6]** How many players are on each team? **[6]**

Say: Now that you know the unit rate, you can complete the table

Ask: What do you need to do to complete the table**? [Multiply the number of teams by the unit rate of 6 players per team.]**

Work with students to multiply each number of teams by 6 to complete the table. The completed table is shown.

Number of Teams	2	4	6	8	10	12
Number of Players	12	24	36	48	60	72

Check
Have students look at the first table and use it to answer questions 1 through 3.

Ask: Does a year always have the same number of months? **[Yes.]**

Ask: Without using a number, what is the unit rate that you are determining? **[Months per year]**

Ask: How can you find the unit rate? **[Divide 36 ÷ 3]**

Ask: Once you know the unit rate, what do you need to do to complete the table? **[Multiply the number of years by the unit rate of 12 months per year.]**

KEY TEACHING POINTS

Example 2

Explain to students that a proportion is a statement that two ratios are equivalent.

Say: 30 miles in 1 hour is proportional to 90 miles in 3 hours. Because $90 \div 3 = 30$, both ratios are 30 miles per hour.

Say: The fractions $\frac{5}{8}$ and $\frac{20}{32}$ are proportional. By dividing the numerator and denominator by the greatest common factor, 4, you have $\frac{20}{32} \div \frac{4}{4} = \frac{5}{8}$.

Say: 30 miles in 1 hour is not proportional to 45 miles in 2 hours. Because $45 \div 2 = 22.5$, the ratios are not equal. If the ratios are not equal, a proportion is not formed.

Say: The fractions $\frac{2}{3}$ and $\frac{5}{6}$ are not proportional. Because both fractions are written in simplest form, they have different values. You can also multiply $\frac{2}{3} \times \frac{2}{2} = \frac{4}{6}$ to find that $\frac{2}{3} \neq \frac{5}{6}$.

Check

Say: Check to see if the fractions or ratios can be written in simplest form.

ALTERNATE STRATEGY

Strategy: Find the cross products to determine if two ratios are proportional.

1. Write $\frac{12}{4}$ and $\frac{21}{7}$ on the board.
2. Draw an arrow from 12 to 7 and an arrow from 4 to 21.
3. **Say:** To find cross products, multiply the numerator of one fraction or ratio by the denominator of the other fraction or ratio.
4. **Ask:** What is the product of 12 times 7? **[84]** What is the product of 4 times 21? **[84]**
5. Write $84 = 84$.
6. **Say:** Because the cross products are equivalent, the ratios are proportional.

COMMON MISCONCEPTION

Ask: What is the error in saying that $\frac{\$42}{3 \text{ tickets}} = \frac{\$120}{8 \text{ tickets}}$?

Reason incorrect: The quotients are not equivalent.
Solution: If $42 for 3 tickets is correct, the cost for 8 tickets is $112.
If $120 for 8 tickets is correct, the cost for 3 tickets is $45.

Encourage students to either simplify fractions or use cross products to determine if two ratios are equivalent.

KEY TEACHING POINTS

Example 3

Make sure that students understand that the number that represents the unit rate and the constant rate of change are the same.

Say: The table shows the number of pencils and the cost, in dollars. In this table, the data is given. For this table, you can think of the rate of change is how the cost changes each time a pencil is added to the purchase.

Say: To find if there is a constant rate of change, divide the cost by the number of pencils.

Ask: How can you find the unit price per pencil? **[The cost of one pencil is given, so divide the cost by the number of pencils. If the quotients are equivalent, there is a constant rate of change.]**

Ask: What is the quotient of $0.70 ÷ 2? **[$0.35]** $1.05 ÷ 3? **[$0.35]** $1.40 ÷ 4? **[$0.35]** $1.75 ÷ 5? **[$0.35]**

Say: Because the quotients are all $0.35, the constant rate of change is $0.35.

Check

Say: For each table, divide each number in the bottom row by each corresponding number in the top row. If the quotients are always the same, there is a constant rate of change.

ALTERNATE STRATEGY

Strategy: Subtract to see if there is a constant rate of change.

1. **Say:** For Question 12 in the Check, you are given that the number of pages read in 1 day is 32. The number of days always increases by 1.
2. **Say:** See if the difference between numbers is always 32.
3. **Ask:** What does it mean if the difference between numbers is always 32? **[There is a constant rate of change.]**
4. **Say:** Look at the difference between the number of pages from day 1 to day 2.
5. **Ask:** What is the difference of 64 – 32? **[32]**
6. **Say:** Now, look at the difference between the number of pages from day 2 to day 3.
7. **Ask:** What is the difference of 106 – 64? **[42]**
8. **Ask:** Because 32 does not equal 42, is there a constant rate of change? **[No.]** Do the values in the table form a proportional relationship? **[No.]**

KEY TEACHING POINTS

Example 4

Make sure that students understand that a proportion can be written algebraically. Write $y = kx$ on the board.

Say: In the equation $y = kx$, the k represents the coefficient or the constant of proportionality. You can only write a value for k if there is a proportion formed.

Ask: How can you determine if the table shows a proportional relationship? **[Divide each value of *y* by each corresponding value of *x*.]**

Ask: What is the quotient of 27 ÷ 3? **[9]** 54 ÷ 6? **[9]** 81 ÷ 9? **[9]** 108 ÷ 12? **[9]** 135 ÷ 15? **[9]**

Ask: What is the constant of proportionality? **[9]**

Ask: What equation represents the table? **[$y = 9x$]**

Check

Say: For each table, divide each number in the bottom row by each corresponding number in the top row. If the quotients are always the same, there is a constant rate of change.

Say: What is the relationship between the quotient of $\frac{y}{x}$ and the constant of proportionality?

[They are the same.]

ADDITIONAL ONLINE INTERVENTION RESOURCES

Use the following for students who have not mastered the concepts in Skill 4.

- Math on the Spot videos
- Personal Math Trainer with customized intervention
- Building Block worksheets (Skill 5: Add and Subtract Like Fractions; Skill 63: Multiply Fractions; Skill 65: Multiply with Fractions and Decimals; Skill 68: Operations with Fractions)

Name ______________________ Date ______________ Class ______________

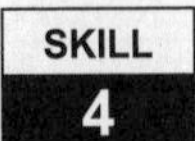

Constant Rate of Change

SKILL 4

Example 1

The table shows the number of volleyball players that are playing on each team for a fundraiser. Each team has the same number of players.

Number of Teams	2	4	6	8	10	12
Number of Players			36			

To determine the unit rate, divide the number of players by the number of teams: $36 \div 6 = 6$. The unit rate is 6 players per team. There are 6 players on each volleyball team.

Multiply the number of teams by 6 to complete the table.

Number of Teams	2	4	6	8	10	12
Number of Players	12	24	36	48	60	72

Vocabulary
Unit rate
Proportion
Rate of change
Constant of proportionality

Check

The table shows the relationship between the number of years and the number of months.

Number of Years	1	2	3	4	5
Number of Months			36		

1. What is the unit rate? ______________

2. Complete the table.

3. How many months are equal to 8 years? ______________

The table shows the relationship between the number of pounds and the number of ounces.

Number of Pounds	1	2	3	4	5
Number of Ounces				64	

4. What is the unit rate? ______________

5. Complete the table.

6. How many ounces are equal to 9 pounds? ______________

Name ______________________ Date ______________ Class ______________

Example 2

Proportions:	Not proportions:
$\frac{30\text{ mi}}{1\text{ h}} = \frac{90\text{ mi}}{3\text{ h}}$	$\frac{30\text{ mi}}{1\text{ h}} \neq \frac{45\text{ mi}}{2\text{ h}}$
$\frac{5}{8} = \frac{20}{32}$	$\frac{2}{3} \neq \frac{5}{6}$

Check

Determine if each pair of ratios forms a proportion. Explain why they are proportions or not proportions.

7. $\frac{12}{4}$ and $\frac{21}{7}$ ○ Proportional ○ Not Proportional

____

8. $\frac{100\text{ ft}}{6\text{ s}}$ and $\frac{75\text{ ft}}{4\text{ s}}$ ○ Proportional ○ Not Proportional

____

9. $\frac{\$90}{5\text{ shirts}}$ and $\frac{\$54}{3\text{ shirts}}$ ○ Proportional ○ Not Proportional

____

10. What's the Error? Explain what the error is. Write the correct proportion.

$$\frac{\$42}{3\text{ tickets}} = \frac{\$120}{8\text{ tickets}}$$

____

____

Name ______________________ Date ______________ Class ______________

Example 3

The table shows the cost of different numbers of pencils at the school bookstore.

Number of Pencils	1	2	3	4	5
Cost, in Dollars	0.35	0.70	1.05	1.40	1.75

Find if there is a constant rate of change.

$$\frac{\text{Cost, in dollars}}{\text{Number of pencils}} = \frac{\$0.35}{1\text{ pencil}}$$

$$\frac{\$0.70}{2\text{ pencils}} = \frac{\$0.35}{1\text{ pencil}}$$

$$\frac{\$1.05}{3\text{ pencils}} = \frac{\$0.35}{1\text{ pencil}}$$

$$\frac{\$1.40}{4\text{ pencils}} = \frac{\$0.35}{1\text{ pencil}}$$

$$\frac{\$1.75}{5\text{ pencils}} = \frac{\$0.35}{1\text{ pencil}}$$

When writing a proportion, make sure the units are aligned.

Number of Pencils	1	2	3	4	5
Cost, in Dollars	0.35	0.70	1.05	1.40	1.75
Rate of Change		0.35	0.35	0.35	0.35

The cost of the pencils is proportional. The constant rate of change is $0.35.

Check

Determine the constant rate of change. If there is not a constant rate of change, write *none*.

11.

Number of Hours	1	2	3	4	5
Number of Miles	45	90	135	180	225

Constant rate of change: ______________________

12.

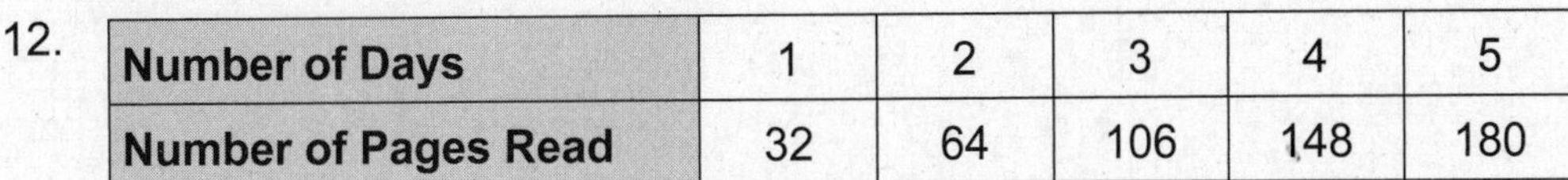

Number of Days	1	2	3	4	5
Number of Pages Read	32	64	106	148	180

Constant rate of change: ______________________

Name ______________________ Date ______________ Class ______________

Example 4

The table shows the relationship between x and y.

x	3	6	9	12	15
y	27	54	81	108	135

A proportional relationship between x and y can be described using the equation $y = kx$. The variable k is called the constant of proportionality.

Determine if the relationship is proportional.

$27 \div 3 = 9$
$54 \div 6 = 9$
$81 \div 9 = 9$
$108 \div 12 = 9$
$135 \div 15 = 9$

Divide $y \div x$.

Each quotient is 9. The relationship between x and y is proportional.

The constant of proportionality is 9. The equation is $y = 9x$.

Check

Find the constant of proportionality k. Then write an equation for the relationship between x and y.

13.

x	2	4	6	8
y	15	30	45	60

____

14.

x	4	8	12	16
y	2	4	6	8

____

SKILL 4 CONSTANT RATE OF CHANGE

SKILL 5

Exponents

KEY TEACHING POINTS

Example 1
Make sure students understand that the placement of the base and exponent matters.

Check
Ask: How can you write 4^3 as a multiplication expression? **[$4 \cdot 4 \cdot 4$]**

Ask: In 5^2, which number is the base? **[5]** Which number is the exponent? **[2]** In 2^5, which number is the base? **[2]** Which number is the exponent? **[5]**

COMMON MISCONCEPTION

The exponent tells how many times the base is used as a factor, not how many times the number is multiplied.

Ask: What is the error in the equation $9^4 = 9 \cdot 9 \cdot 9 \cdot 9 \cdot 9$?

Reason incorrect: 9 is used as a factor 5 times. It should only be used as a factor 4 times.

Solution: $9^4 = 9 \cdot 9 \cdot 9 \cdot 9$

KEY TEACHING POINTS

Example 2
Explain to students that a negative exponent does not result in a negative number. Instead, it means that the number is a unit fraction that has a denominator raised to the power of the exponent.

Say: 6^{-3} means $\frac{1}{6^3}$. A negative exponent results in numbers less than 1.

Ask: How can you write 6^{-3} as a multiplication expression? **[$\frac{1}{6} \cdot \frac{1}{6} \cdot \frac{1}{6}$]**

Say: To find the value of 6^{-3}, follow the same steps as finding 6^3. The value of 6^{-3} is the reciprocal of 6^3.

Example 3
Say: Any number except for 0 when it is raised to the zero power is equal to 1.

Check
Ask: Why is Question 8 not specific about a number? **[No matter what year, when that number is raised to the zero power, its value is 0.]**

KEY TEACHING POINTS

Example 4

Say: Numbers that are not written in exponential form are raised to the first power. The value of a base raised to the first power is equal to the base.

Say: So $5^1 = 5$ and $60^1 = 60$.

Check

Ask: How can you write a prime number in exponential form? **[Write the number as a base and raise it to the first power.]**

Example 5

Review with students how to add integers. Make sure students understand that the sum of two negative integers is a negative integer and that the sign of the sum of a positive integer and a negative integer depends on which integer has the greater absolute value.

Say: To multiply numbers in exponential form having the same base, add the exponents and keep the base the same. This is how the Product of Powers Property works.

Write $4^3 \cdot 4^5$ on the board.

Say: To find the value of $4^3 \cdot 4^5$, the base stays as 4 and the exponents are added.

Ask: What is 3 + 5? **[8]**

Say: In exponential form, $4^3 \cdot 4^5 = 4^8$.

Write $6^4 \cdot 6^{-8}$ on the board.

Say: To find the value of $6^4 \cdot 6^{-8}$ the base stays as 6 and the exponents are added.

Ask: What is 4 + (–8)? **[–4]**

Say: In exponential form, $6^4 \cdot 6^{-8} = 6^{-4}$.

Ask: How do you find the value of 6^{-4}? **[Write a unit fraction with 6^4 as the denominator.]**

COMMON MISCONCEPTION

Ask: What is the error in the equation $4^6 \cdot 4^3 = 4^{18}$?

Reason incorrect: The exponents were multiplied, not added.

Solution: $4^6 \cdot 4^3 = 4^9$

KEY TEACHING POINTS

Example 6
Review with students how to subtract integers. Make sure students understand that the difference of a positive integer from a negative integer is always negative, the difference of a negative integer from a positive integer is always positive, and the difference of two negative integers or two positive integers can be negative, 0, or positive.

Say: To divide numbers in exponential form having the same base, subtract the exponents and keep the base the same. This is how the Quotient of Powers Property works.

Write $\frac{3^7}{3^3}$ on the board.

Say: To find the value of $\frac{3^7}{3^3}$, the base stays as 3 and the exponents are subtracted.

Ask: What is 7 – 3? **[4]** In exponential form, what is $\frac{3^7}{3^3}$ equal to? $\left[\mathbf{3^4}\right]$

Write $\frac{8^3}{8^{-2}}$ on the board.

Say: To find the value of $\frac{8^3}{8^{-2}}$, the base stays as 8 and the exponents are subtracted.

Ask: What is 3 – (–2)? **[5]** In exponential form, what is $\frac{8^3}{8^{-2}}$ equal to? $\left[\mathbf{8^5}\right]$

COMMON MISCONCEPTION

Ask: What is the error in the equation $\frac{2^8}{2^{-2}} = 2^{-4}$?

Reason incorrect: The exponents were divided not subtracted.

Solution: $\frac{2^8}{2^{-2}} = 2^{10}$

KEY TEACHING POINTS

Example 7
Say: The Power of a Product Property states that the product of two factors being raised to a power is equivalent to the product of each factor being raised to that power.

Write $(4 \cdot 3)^4$ on the board.

Say: $(4 \cdot 3)^4 = 4^4 \cdot 3^4$. You can find the value of both and then multiply the values. The exponent for both bases is 4.

ALTERNATE STRATEGY

Strategy: Multiply inside the parentheses to simplify an expression.

1. Write $(6 \cdot 2)^{-3}$ on the board.
2. **Say:** You can use the Power of a Product Property or you can multiply inside the parentheses first.
3. **Ask:** What is $6 \cdot 2$? **[12]**? What is 12^{-3}? $\left[\frac{1}{1,728}\right]$
4. **Say:** This is the same value as multiplying 6^{-3} and 2^{-3}.

KEY TEACHING POINTS

Example 8

Write $(3^2)^4$ on the board.

Say: The Power of a Power Property states that a base raised to a power inside parentheses can be raised to a power outside the parentheses.

Say: In this case, the base stays as is and the exponents are multiplied.

Ask: What is $2 \cdot 4$? **[8]** In exponential form, what is $(3^2)^4$? $\left[\mathbf{3^8}\right]$

ALTERNATE STRATEGY

Strategy: Multiply inside the parentheses to simplify an expression.

1. Write $(2 \cdot 2)^{-3}$. on the board.
2. **Say:** Use the Power of a Power Property or you can multiply inside the parentheses first.
3. **Ask:** What is $2 \cdot 2$? **[4]** What is 4^{-3}? $\left[\frac{1}{64}\right]$
4. **Say:** This is the same value as simplifying 2^{-6}.

ADDITIONAL ONLINE INTERVENTION RESOURCES

Use the following for students who have not mastered the concepts in Skill 5.

- Math on the Spot videos
- Personal Math Trainer with customized intervention
- Building Block worksheets (Skill 24: Distributive Property; Skill 27: Evaluate Expressions; Skill 29: Evaluate Powers; Skill 30: Exponents; Skill 59: Multiplication Properties; Skill 69: Order of Operations; Skill 76: Reading and Writing Exponents; Skill 100: Squares and Square Roots.)

Name ______________________ Date ______________ Class ______________

SKILL 5

Exponents

Example 1

A number written in exponential form is written with a base and an exponent.

$7^4 = 7 \cdot 7 \cdot 7 \cdot 7 = 2{,}401$

The base is 7.

The exponent is 4.

Vocabulary

Exponential form

Base

Exponent

Negative Exponent Property

Zero Exponent Property

Product of Powers Property

Check

1. What is $3 \cdot 3 \cdot 3 \cdot 3 \cdot 3$ written in exponential form? ______________

2. What number is represented by 4^3? ______________

3. Do 5^2 and 2^5 represent the same number? Explain.

____

4. What's the Error? Explain the error and write the correct equation.

$9^4 = 9 \cdot 9 \cdot 9 \cdot 9 \cdot 9$

____

Example 2

The Negative Exponent Property states $a^{-n} = \frac{1}{a^n}$, $a \neq 0$, if n is an integer.

$6^{-3} = \frac{1}{6^3} = \frac{1}{216}$

Check

1. What multiplication expression means the same as 2^{-4}? ______________

2. What number is represented by 8^{-3}? ______________

Name ______________________ Date ______________ Class______________

Example 3

The **Zero Exponent Property** states $a^0 = 1,\ a \neq 0$.

$5^0 = 1$ $60^0 = 1$

Check

7. What number is represented by 675^0? ____________

8. Write the year that you were born. Raise it to the zero power.

   What is the value? ____________

Example 4

A base raised to the first power is equal to the base or $a^1 = a$.

$5^1 = 5$ $60^1 = 60$

Check

9. What number is represented by 55^1? ____________

10. Write 13 in exponential form. ____________

Example 5

You can multiply exponents having the same base by adding the exponents. The **Product of Powers Property** states $a^m \cdot a^n = a^{m+n}$.

$4^3 \cdot 4^5 = 4^{(3+5)} = 4^8 = 65,536$

$6^4 \cdot 6^{-8} = 6^{(4+(-8))} = 6^{-4} = \frac{1}{1,296}$

Name ______________________ Date ______________ Class ______________

Check

Simplify each expression.

11. $7^4 \cdot 7^2 =$ ________

12. $8^{-4} \cdot 8^{-3} =$ ________

13. $2^6 \cdot 2^{-3} =$ ________

14. $4^{-5} \cdot 4^2 =$ ________

15. What's the Error? Explain the error and write the correct equation.

$4^6 \cdot 4^3 = 4^{18}$

____

Example 6

You can divide numbers with exponents having the same base by subtracting the exponents. The Quotient of Powers Property states

$\frac{a^m}{a^n} = a^{m-n},\ a \neq 0.$

$\frac{3^7}{3^3} = 3^{(7-3)} = 3^4 = 81$

$\frac{8^3}{8^{-2}} = 8^{(3-(-2))} = 8^5 = 32{,}768$

Check

Simplify each expression.

16. $\frac{6^8}{6^4}$ ________

17. $\frac{9^{-3}}{9^{-5}}$ ________

18. $\frac{3^{-3}}{3^2}$ ________

19. $\frac{5^4}{5^{-2}}$ ________

20. What's the Error? Explain the error and write the correct equation.

$\frac{2^8}{2^{-2}} = 2^{-4}$

____

Name ______________________ Date ____________ Class ____________

Example 7

You can multiply the product of two or more numbers raised to a power.
The Power of a Product Property states $(a \cdot b)^n = a^n \cdot b^n$.

$(4 \cdot 3)^4 = 4^4 \cdot 3^4 = 256 \cdot 81 = 20{,}736$

$(6 \cdot 2)^{-3} = 6^{-3} \cdot 2^{-3} = \frac{1}{216} \cdot \frac{1}{8} = \frac{1}{1{,}728}$

Check

Simplify each expression.

21. $(7 \cdot 2)^3 =$ ________

22. $(3 \cdot 5)^3 =$ ________

23. $(4 \cdot 8)^{-2} =$ ________

24. $(9 \cdot 4)^{-4} =$ ________

Example 8

The Power of a Power Property states $(a^m)^n = a^{mn}$.

$(3^2)^4 = 3^{2 \cdot 4} = 3^8 = 6{,}561$

$(2^2)^{-3} = 2^{2 \cdot (-3)} = 2^{-6} = \frac{1}{64}$

Check

Simplify each expression.

25. $(6^3)^2 =$ ________

26. $(3^3)^4 =$ ________

27. $(4^{-2})^{-2} =$ ________

28. $(5^2)^{-3} =$ ________

SKILL 5 EXPONENTS

SKILL 6

Graphing Linear Nonproportional Relationships

KEY TEACHING POINTS

Example 1

Use contrasting examples to show the difference between nonproportional relationships and proportional relationships.

Say: A linear relationship when graphed will form a line. The line may be proportional or nonproportional. If the line of the graph of a linear relationship passes through the origin, the relationship is proportional.

Say: $y = mx + b$ is the slope-intercept form of the equation of a line. The *y*-intercept is the *y*-coordinate of the point where the graph intersects the *y*-axis, or when $x = 0$.

Say: Look at the equations. $y = 5x + 7$, $y = 0.3x - 2$, and $y = \frac{1}{3}x + 7$ are examples of nonproportional relationships. When 0 is substituted for *x*, the value of *y* is a number other than 0. So, the *y*-intercept is not the origin (0, 0).

Say: $y = 5x$, $y = 0.3x$, and $y = \frac{1}{3}x$ are proportional relationships because a straight line goes through the origin (0, 0). When you substitute 0 for *x*, then $y = 0$, too.

Check

Ask: How can you tell if an equation shows a nonproportional relationship? **[If the equation has a constant, it is a nonproportional relationship.]**

Check students' work and have them talk through their reasoning with you.

Example 2

Make sure students understand that the origin names (0, 0) on a coordinate plane and the *y*-intercept names the value of *y* when $x = 0$.

Ask: Why is the graph at left representative of a nonproportional relationship? **[The line does not pass through the origin.]**

Ask: Why is the graph at right representative of a proportional relationship? **[The line passes through the origin.]**

Check

Ask: Does the line in Question 5 show a linear relationship? **[Yes]**

Ask: What is the *y*-intercept? **[3]**

Ask: Does the line show a nonproportional relationship? **[Yes]**

KEY TEACHING POINTS

Example 3

Make sure students understand that real-world experiences can be displayed on a graph.

Ask: What is the meaning of the line segment on the graph? **[The line segment shows the cost of a taxicab ride during various distances.]**

Say: Let's fill the table. To find the points, substitute values for *x* in the equation to find values for *y*.

Write the following on the board. Have students give the answers.

$y = 0.5(0) + 1 = 1$

$y = 0.5(1) + 1 = 1.5$

$y = 0.5(2) + 1 = 2$

$y = 0.5(4) + 1 = 3$

$y = 0.5(6) + 1 = 4$

$y = 0.5(9) + 1 = 5.5$

Ask: What are the ordered pairs that we can determine from the table? **[(0, 1), (1, 1.5), (2, 2), (4, 3), (6, 4), (9, 5.5)]**

Ask: Does the graph show a nonproportional relationship? **[Yes]** Why? **[The line segment does not pass through the origin.]**

Check

Say: Remember that $y = mx + b$ is the slope-intercept form of the equation of a line.

Ask: What is the coefficient to the variable *x*? **[0.25]** What is the *y*-intercept? **[2]**

Ask: How can you find values for *y*? **[Substitute the values for *x* in the equation.]**

The following shows the equations that can be written for Question 7.

$y = 0.25(0) + 2 = 2$

$y = 0.25(1) + 2 = 2.25$

$y = 0.25(2) + 2 = 2.5$

$y = 0.25(4) + 2 = 3$

$y = 0.25(6) + 2 = 3.5$

$y = 0.25(8) + 2 = 4$

ALTERNATE STRATEGY

Strategy: Use a table to limit the number of points needed to draw the line of an equation.

1. **Say:** Because a linear relationship represents a line of a line segment, you can find 2 points and draw a line between them.
2. **Say:** The x-axis of the coordinate plane starts at 0 and the last number shown is 9. Substitute 0 and 9 for x.
3. Write the following on the board.

   $y = 0.5(0) + 1 = 1$

   $y = 0.5(9) + 1 = 5.5$
4. **Say:** The ordered pairs are (0, 1) and (9, 5.5). You can draw a line segment from (0, 1) to (9, 5.5). The remainder of the points can now be read.

COMMON MISCONCEPTION

Ask: What is the error to the answer that the line is a proportional relationship?

Reason incorrect: A proportional relationship and a nonproportional relationship will both be a straight line on a graph.

Solution: The line is a nonproportional relationship because it does not go through the origin.

Graph the line to help students correct this misconception.

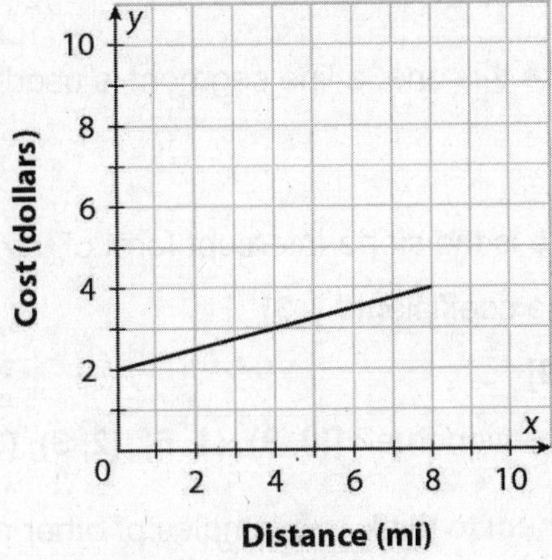

KEY TEACHING POINTS

Example 4

Say: The line segment shows the height of a candle that burns at a rate of 2 inches per hour. The candle was 8 inches high when it started to burn.

Ask: What is the *y*-intercept? **[8]** What does the *y*-intercept represent? **[The original height of the candle]**

Ask: What does the direction of the line segment mean? **[The line segment has a negative slope.]**

Remind students that all nonproportional relationships do not go through the origin (0, 0) when graphed.

Say: Let's fill the table. To find the points, substitute values for *x* in the equation to find values for *y*.

Write the following on the board. Have students give the answers.

$y = -2(0) + 8 = 8$

$y = -2(1) + 8 = 6$

$y = -2(2) + 8 = 4$

$y = -2(3) + 8 = 2$

$y = -2(4) + 8 = 0$

Ask: What are the ordered pairs that can be determined from the table? **[(0, 8), (1, 6), (2, 4), (3, 2), (4, 0)]**

Say: In a real-world situation like this one, a line segment is used because the candle cannot be less than 0 inches tall.

Check

Remind students that $y = mx + b$ is the slope-intercept form of the equation of a line.

Ask: In the equation, what is the coefficient? **[–3]**

Ask: What is the *y*-intercept? **[9]**

Ask: Which points make the equation true? **[(0, 9), (1, 6), (2, 3), (3, 0)]**

Check students work and ask them to think of examples of other real-world situations that can be nonproportional relationships.

ADDITIONAL ONLINE INTERVENTION RESOURCES

Use the following for students who have not mastered the concepts in Skill 6.

- Math on the Spot videos
- Personal Math Trainer with customized intervention
- Building Block worksheets (Skill 46: Graph Ordered Pairs (First Quadrant))

Name ________________ Date ____________ Class ____________

SKILL 6

Graphing Linear Nonproportional Relationships

Example 1

Nonproportional relationship:	Proportional relationship:
$y = 5x + 7$	$y = 5x$
$y = 0.3x - 2$	$y = 0.3x$
$y = \frac{1}{3}x + 7$	$y = \frac{1}{3}x$

Vocabulary
- Nonproportional relationship
- Proportional relationship
- *y*-intercept

Check

Determine if each shows a nonproportional relationship. Choose Yes or No.

1. $y = 2x$ ○ Yes ○ No
2. $y = 2x - 2$ ○ Yes ○ No
3. $y = 0.2x - 2$ ○ Yes ○ No
4. $y = \frac{1}{2}x - 2$ ○ Yes ○ No

Example 2

Nonproportional relationship:
$y = 4x + 1$

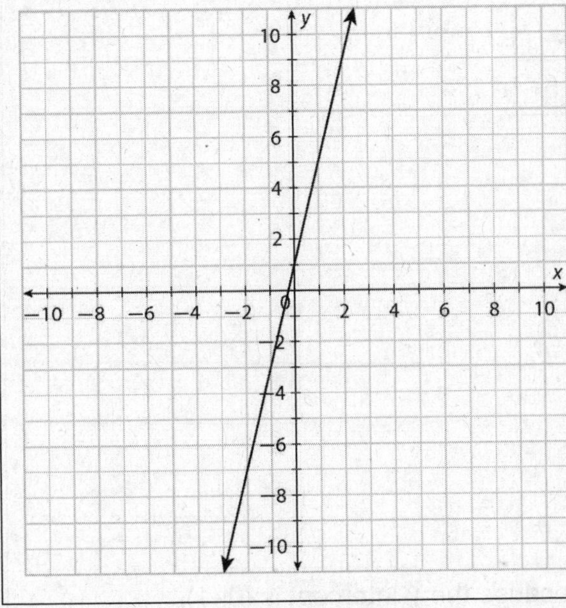

Proportional relationship:
$y = 4x$

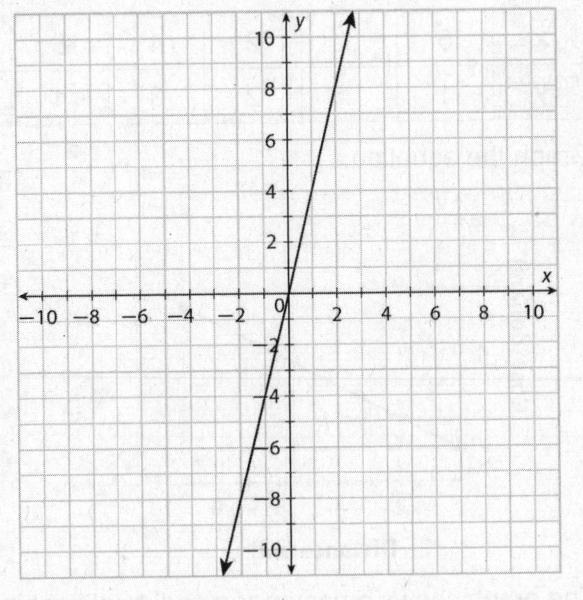

Name ______________________ Date ______________ Class ______________

Check

Determine if each shows a nonproportional relationship. Choose Yes or No.

5.

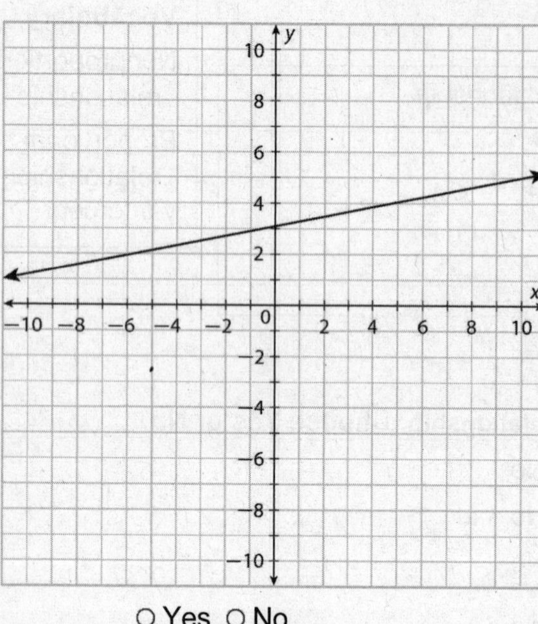

O Yes O No

6.

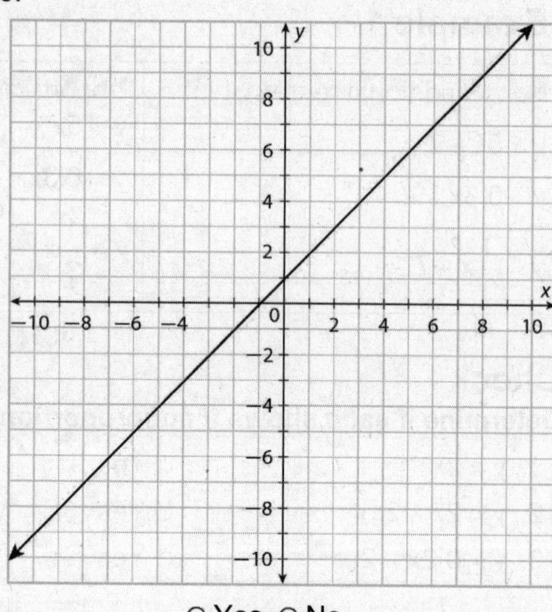

O Yes O No

Example 3

Tan's Taxi charges a fee of \$0.50 per mile traveled plus \$1.00. The equation $y = 0.5x + 1$ represents the cost of a ride, with x equal to the distance. To graph the equation, you can use a table to find the points to graph for the equation.

x	0	1	2	4	6	9
y	1	1.5	2	3	4	5.5

Graph the equation.

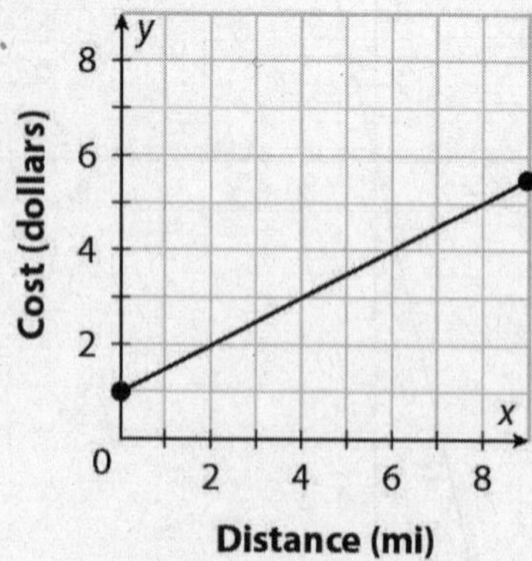

The graph shows a nonproportional relationship, because the y-intercept is (0, 1).

Name ______________________ Date ______________ Class ______________

Check

Carlton's Car Service charges a fee of $0.25 per mile traveled plus $2.00. The equation $y = 0.25x + 2$ represents the cost of a ride, with x equal to the distance.

7. Use the table to find the points to graph for the equation.

x	0	1	2	4	6	8
y						

8. Graph the equation.

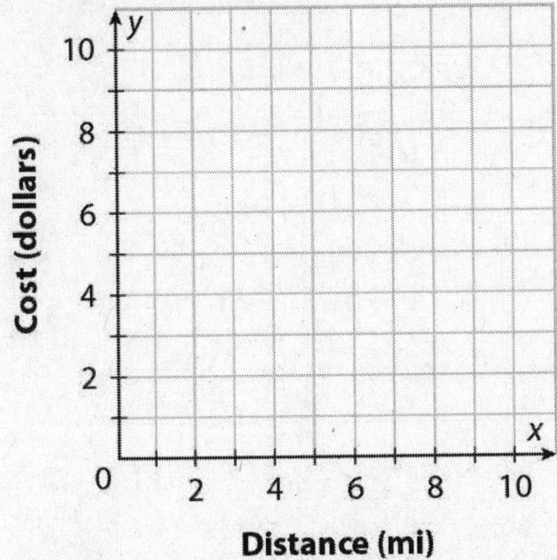

9. What's the Error? Bethany said the graph shows a proportional relationship because it is a straight line. Explain the error and name the correct relationship.

Example 4

An 8-inch candle burns at a rate of 2 inches per hour. The equation $y = -2x + 8$ represents the height of the burning candle over time. Use a table to find the points to graph for the equation.

x	0	1	2	3	4
y	8	6	4	2	0

Graph the equation.

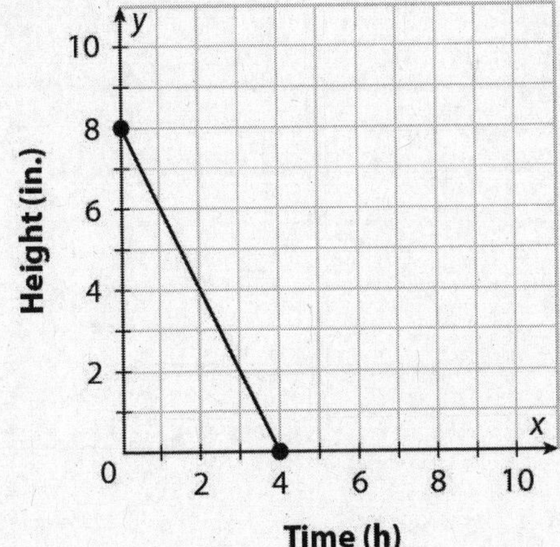

Name ______________________ Date ____________ Class ____________

Check

A 9-foot waxed wick burns at a rate of 3 feet per minute. The equation $y = -3x + 9$ represents the length of the wick over time.

10. Use the table to find the points to graph for the equation.

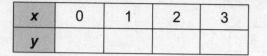

x	0	1	2	3
y				

11. Graph the equation.

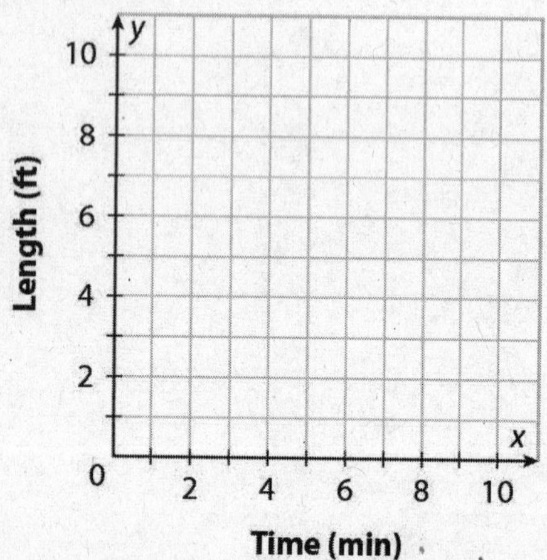

12. Is the equation a nonproportional relationship? ○ Yes ○ No

SKILL 6 GRAPHING LINEAR NONPROPORTIONAL RELATIONSHIPS

SKILL 7

Graphing Linear Proportional Relationships

KEY TEACHING POINTS

Example 1

Use contrasting examples to show the difference between proportional relationships and nonproportional relationships.

Say: A linear relationship when graphed will form a line. If the line of the graph of a linear relationship passes through the origin (0, 0), the relationship is proportional. If the line does not pass through the origin, it is nonproportional.

Say: $y = mx + b$ is the slope-intercept form of the equation of a line. The *y*-intercept is the *y*-coordinate of the point where the graph of the line intersects the *y*-axis, or when $x = 0$.

Say: Look at the equations at the left. $y = 2x$, $y = \frac{1}{3}x$, and $y = 13x$ are examples of proportional relationships. When 0 is substituted for *x*, the value of *y* is 0. So, the *y*-intercept is the origin (0, 0).

Say: The equations at the right are representative of nonproportional relationships, because when 0 is substituted for *x*, the value of *y* is a number other than 0. The *y*-intercept is not the origin.

Check

Ask: How can you tell if an equation shows a proportional relationship? **[When 0 is substituted for *x*, the value of *y* is 0, so the graph of the line passes through the origin.]**

Example 2

Make sure students understand that the origin names (0, 0) on a coordinate plane and the *y*-intercept names the value of *y* when $x = 0$.

Ask: Why is the graph at left representative of a proportional relationship? **[The line passes through the origin.]**

Ask: Why is the graph at right representative of a nonproportional relationship? **[The line does not pass through the origin.]**

Check

Say: Look at Question 5.

Ask: Does the line in Question 5 show a linear relationship? **[Yes]** Does the line pass through the origin? **[Yes]** Does the line show a proportional relationship? **[Yes]**

Say: Look at Question 6.

Ask: Does the line pass through the origin? **[Yes]** Does the line in Question 6 show a proportional relationship? **[Yes]**

KEY TEACHING POINTS

Example 3

Make sure students understand that real-world experiences can be displayed on a graph.

Ask: What is the meaning of the line segment on the graph? **[The line segment shows the cost of a delivery for various distances.]**

Say: Let's fill the table. To find the points, substitute values for *x* in the equation to find values for *y*.

Write the following on the board. Have students give the answers.

$y = 4(0) = 0$

$y = 4(1) = 4$

$y = 4(2) = 8$

$y = 4(3) = 12$

$y = 4(4) = 16$

$y = 4(5) = 20$

Ask: What are the ordered pairs that we can determine from the table? **[(0, 0), (1, 4), (2, 8), (3, 12), (4, 16), (5, 20)]**

Ask: Does the graph show a proportional relationship? **[Yes]** Why? **[The line segment passes through the origin.]**

Check

Say: Remember that $y = mx + b$ is the slope-intercept form of the equation of a line.

Ask: What is the coefficient to the variable *x*? **[1.5]**

Ask: How can you find values for *y*? **[Substitute the values for *x* in the equation.]**

The following shows the equations that can be written for Question 7.

$y = 1.5(0) = 0$

$y = 1.5(1) = 1.5$

$y = 1.5(2) = 3$

$y = 1.5(3) = 4.5$

$y = 1.5(4) = 6$

$y = 1.5(6) = 9$

$y = 1.5(8) = 12$

$y = 1.5(10) = 15$

ALTERNATE STRATEGY

Strategy: Use a table to limit the number of points needed to draw the line of an equation.

1. **Say:** Because a linear relationship represents a line or a line segment, you can find two points and draw a line connecting them.
2. **Say:** The *x*-axis of the coordinate plane starts at 0 and the middle number shown is 10. Substitute 0 and 10, respectively, for *x*.
3. Write the following on the board.

   $y = 1.5(0) = 0$

   $y = 1.5(10) = 15$
4. **Say:** The ordered pairs are (0, 0) and (10, 15). You can draw a line segment from (0, 0) to (10, 15). The remainder of the points can now be read.

COMMON MISCONCEPTION

Ask: What is the error to the answer that the line is a nonproportional relationship?

Reason incorrect: A proportional relationship and a nonproportional relationship will both be a straight line on a graph. The slope of either can be 1, less than 1, or greater than 1.

Solution: The line is a proportional relationship because it goes through the origin.

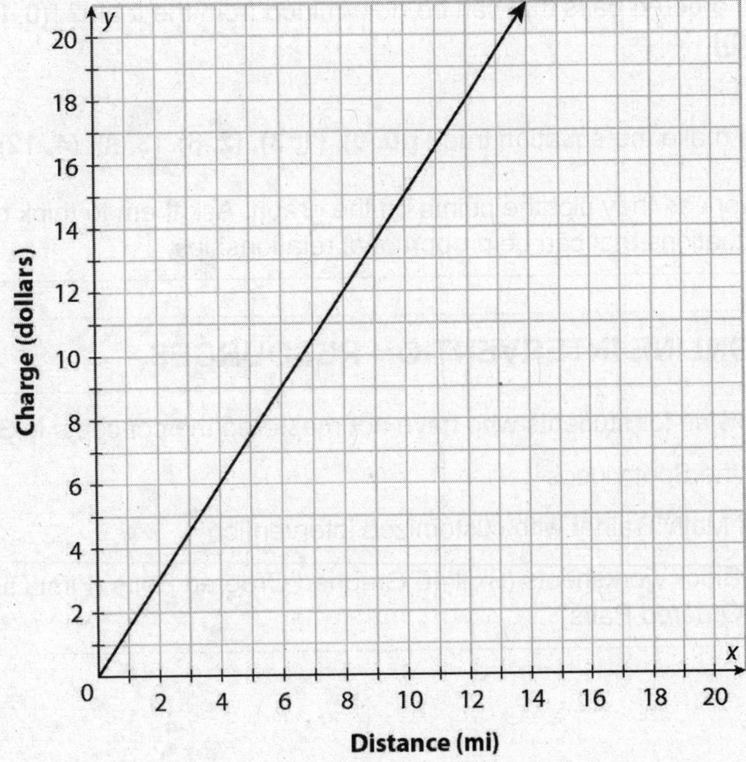

KEY TEACHING POINTS

Example 4
Make sure students understand that other real-world experiences can be shown on a graph.

Say: The line segment shows the height of water in a jug that fills at a rate of 2 inches per minute. The jug was empty when Len began to fill it.

Ask: Does the line go through the origin? **[Yes]** What does the origin represent? **[The empty jug.]**

Remind students that all proportional relationships go through the origin (0, 0) when graphed.

Say: Let's fill in the table. To find the points, substitute values for *x* in the equation to find values for *y*.

Write the following on the board. Have students give the answers.

$y = 2(0) = 0$

$y = 2(1) = 2$

$y = 2(2) = 4$

$y = 2(3) = 6$

$y = 2(4) = 8$

$y = 2(5) = 10$

Ask: What are the ordered pairs that can be determined from the table? **[(0, 0), (1, 2), (2, 4), (3, 6), (4, 8), (5, 10)]**

Check
Ask: Which points make the equation true? **[(0, 0), (1, 3), (2, 6), (3, 9), (4, 12)]**

Check students' work as they plot the points on the graph. Ask them to think of examples of other real-world situations that can be proportional relationships.

ADDITIONAL ONLINE INTERVENTION RESOURCES

Use the following for students who have not mastered the concepts in Skill 7.

- Math on the Spot videos
- Personal Math Trainer with customized intervention
- Building Block worksheets (Skill 46 Graphed Ordered Pairs (First Quadrant); Skill 70: Ordered Pairs)

Name ______________________ Date ______________ Class ______________

SKILL 7

Graphing Linear Proportional Relationships

Example 1

Proportional relationship:	Nonproportional relationship:
$y = 2x$	$y = 2x + 11$
$y = \frac{1}{3}x$	$y = \frac{1}{3}x + 7$
$y = 13x$	$y = 13x - 4$

Vocabulary
Proportional relationship
Nonproportional relationship
Origin
Slope

Check

Determine if each shows a proportional relationship. Choose Yes or No for each.

1. $y = 12x$ ○ Yes ○ No
2. $y = 12x - 12$ ○ Yes ○ No
3. $y = -1.2x$ ○ Yes ○ No
4. $y = \frac{1}{12}x$ ○ Yes ○ No

Example 2

Proportional relationship:

$y = \frac{2}{5}x$

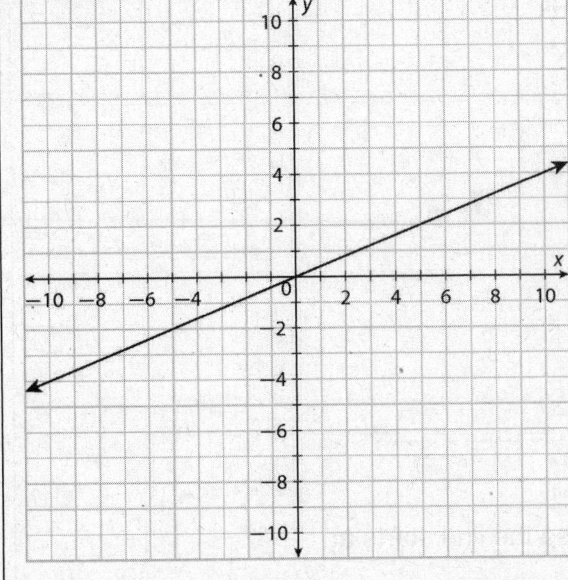

Nonproportional relationship:

$y = \frac{1}{5}x + 1$

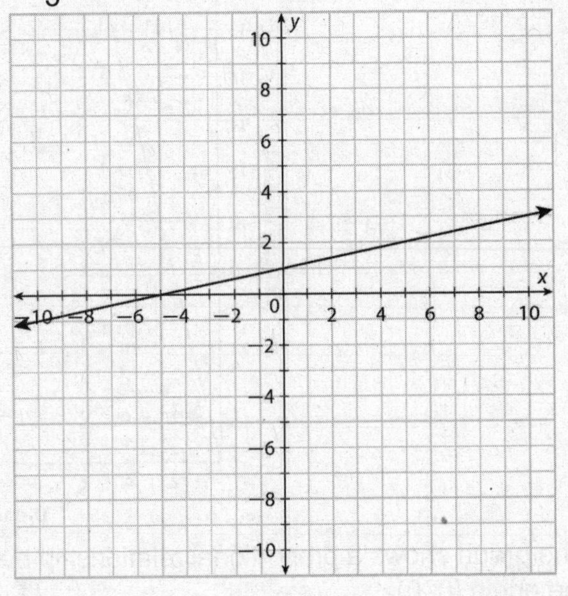

Name ______________________ Date ______________ Class ______________

Check

Determine if each shows a proportional relationship. Choose Yes or No for each.

5.

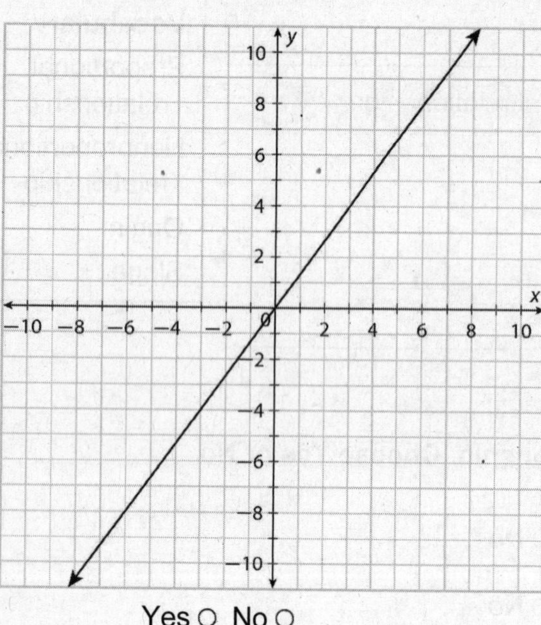

Yes ○ No ○

6.

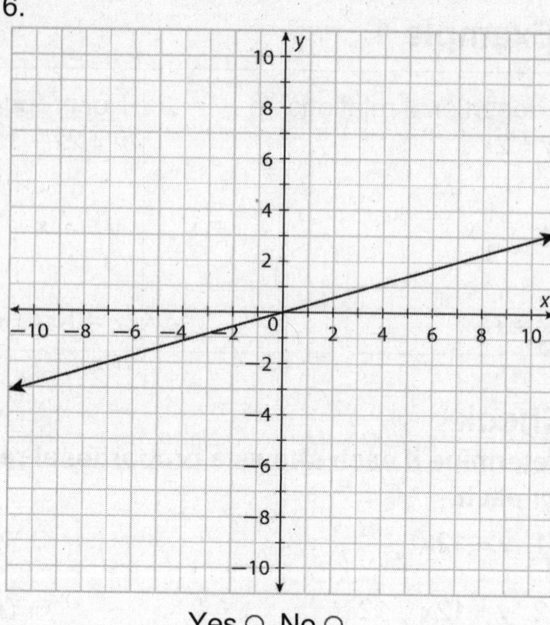

Yes ○ No ○

Example 3

D's Delivery Service charges \$4 per mile to a maximum of 5 miles per delivery. The equation $y = 4x$ represents the charge for a delivery. Use a table to find the points to graph the equation.

x	0	1	2	3	4	5
y	0	4	8	12	16	20

Graph the equation.

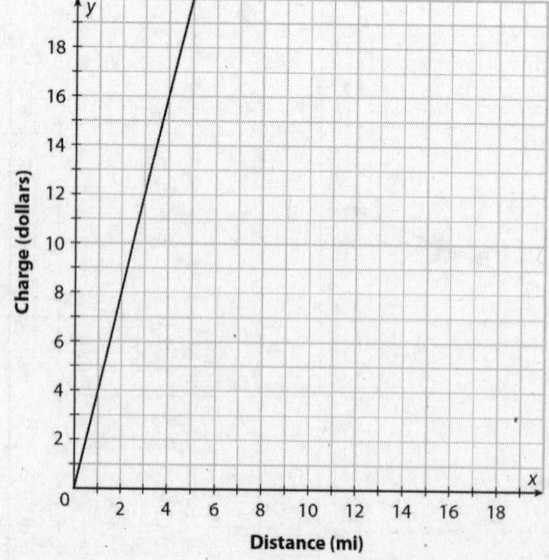

The graph shows a proportional relationship because the line starts at the origin (0, 0).

Name ________________________________ Date ________________ Class ________________

Bill's Used Bikes charges $1.50 per mile to rent a bike. The equation $y = 1.5x$ represents the cost to rent a bike.

7. Use the table to find the points to graph for the equation.

x	0	1	2	3	4	5	6	7	8	9	10
y											

8. Graph the equation.

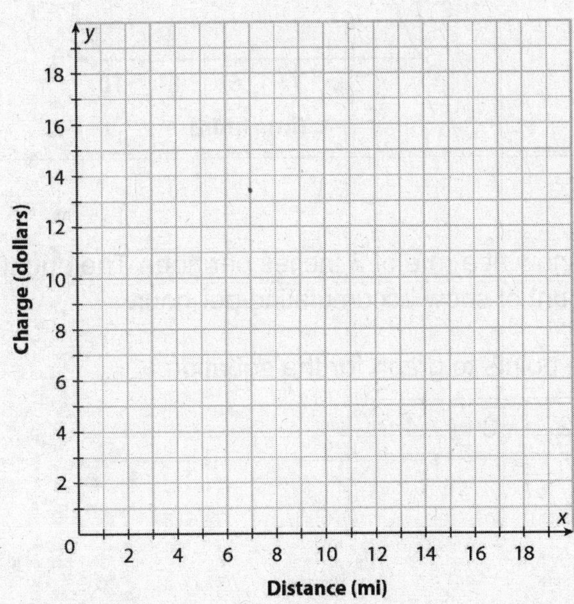

9. What's the Error? Thomas said the graph shows a nonproportional relationship because the slope of its line is greater than 1. Explain the error.

Example 4

Len fills his large jug with water at a rate of 2 inches per minute. The equation $y = 2x$ represents the height of the water in the jug over time. Use a table to find *x* and *y*.

x	0	1	2	3	4	5
y	0	2	4	6	8	10

Name ______________________ Date ______________ Class ______________

Graph the equation.

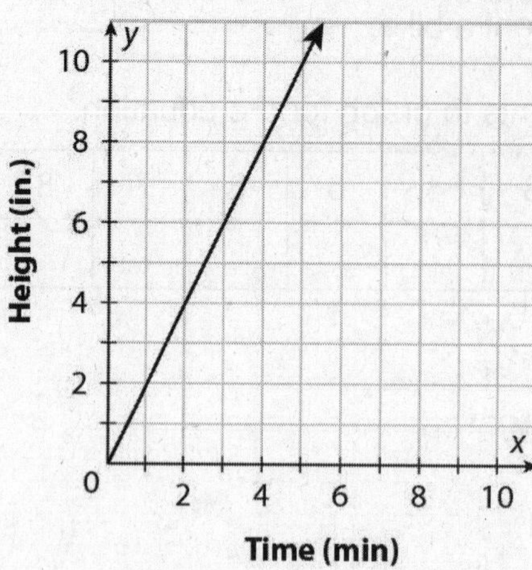

Check

A winter storm produces snow at a rate of 3 inches per hour. The equation $y = 3x$ represents the amount of snow accumulating per hour.

10. Use a table to find the points to graph for the equation.

x	0	1	2	3	4
y					

11. Graph the equation.

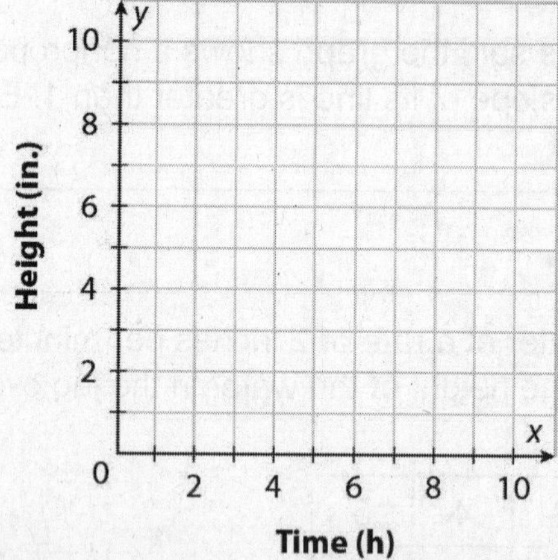

SKILL 7 GRAPHING LINEAR PROPORTIONAL RELATIONSHIPS

SKILL 8

Interpreting the Unit Rate as Slope

KEY TEACHING POINTS

Example 1

Say: A rate is a ratio comparing two different kinds of units. A unit rate is a ratio in which the denominator is 1 unit.

With students, brainstorm some other kinds of rates. Examples include cost per gallon, words per minute, teaspoons per serving, and so on.

Say: There are 3 unit rates given.

Ask: What do you notice that they have in common? **[The second unit is always 1.]**

Say: Look at the problem: 15 theater tickets were bought for $330.

Ask: Why would you want to know the unit rate? **[It is the cost for each ticket.]**

Say: When money is involved, a unit rate is called a unit price.

Check

Ask: What is the determining factor if the rate is a unit rate or a unit price? **[The second unit must be 1.]**

For the rate that is not the unit rate (125 words per 2 minutes), have students find the unit rate. (62.5 words per minute).

Example 2

Say: You can think of slope as a ramp. When going up the ramp, the steeper the ramp, the greater the slope. Slope measures rise over run.

Write the slope formula on the board: Slope $= \frac{(y_2 - y_1)}{(x_2 - x_1)}$.

Say: Pick two points on the line and use their coordinates to find the slope. y_2 means the second value of y and y_1 means the first value of y. It does not matter which value represents y_2, but you must be consistent between x and y. The same order you use for y, you must use for x.

Ask: What is the change in *y*? **[2]** What is the change in *x*? **[1]**

Say: The slope of the line is 2 because as the value of *x* increases by 1, the value of *y* increases by 2.

Check

Ask: In Question 4, does the line slant up or slant down? **[Down]**

Say: A line that slants down will have a negative slope.

Ask: What two ordered pairs can you use to find the slope? **[(0, 0) and (1, –3)]** What is the change in *y*? **[–3]** What is the change in *x*? **[1]** What is the slope? **[–3]**

KEY TEACHING POINTS

Example 3

Remind students that a proportional relationship is a line that passes through the origin on the coordinate plane.

Say: The coordinate plane shows the relationship between the time, in minutes, and the distance traveled in kilometers.

Ask: Does the coordinate plane show a proportional relationship? How do you know? **[The data starts at the origin.]**

Say: Because the line represents a proportional relationship, you can pick any two ordered pairs on the line to use to determine the slope.

Elicit from students that the best ordered pairs to use are the ones that have whole-number coordinates. For this line, those coordinates are (0, 0), (5, 3), (10, 6), (15, 9), and (20, 12).

Say: Let's use (0, 0) and (20, 12).

Ask: What is the rise? **[12]** What is the run? **[20]** If the rise is 12 and the run is 20, what is the slope? $\left[\frac{3}{5}\right]$

Say: The slope gives us the unit rate. We know that the distance traveled is 3 kilometers for every 5 minutes.

Ask: What do we need to do to find the unit rate? **[Find the number of kilometers traveled in 1 minute.]** How do we find the number of kilometers traveled in 1 minute? **[Use the slope.]**

Say: The slope is $\frac{3}{5}$, which describes the number of kilometers traveled each minute.

Check

Say: Find ordered pairs that have two whole number coordinates to find the slope.

Ask: What ordered pair can you use to find the slope of any proportional relationship? **[(0, 0)]**

KEY TEACHING POINTS

Example 4

Ask: What are the ordered pairs used to draw the line? **[(3, 10.5), (6, 21), (9, 31.5), and (12, 42)]**

Say: The relationship is proportional. If the data were graphed, the first ordered pair would be (0, 0).

Say: Let's use (6, 21) and (12, 42) to find the slope. They are the two ordered pairs that have whole numbers for coordinates.

Ask: What is the rise? **[21]** What is the run? **[6]**

Ask: If the rise over run is $\frac{21}{6}$, what is the slope? $\left[3\frac{1}{2}\right]$

Ask: How does the slope relate to the unit rate? **[They are the same.]**

Ask: What is the unit rate? **[It costs $3.50 per hour to rent a bicycle.]**

Check

Ask: Look at Question 8. Does the gas mileage represent a proportional relationship? **[Yes]**

Ask: What are the ordered pairs that would be plotted if the points were graphed? **[(3, 114), (6, 228), (9, 342), (12, 456)]**

Say: Pick two ordered pairs to find the slope.

Ask: How does the slope relate to the unit rate? **[They are the same.]**

ALTERNATE STRATEGY

Strategy: Divide to find if there is a proportional relationship.

1. Ask: How can you determine if the relationship between the time and cost is proportional? **[Divide the cost by the time. If the quotient is the same, the relationship is proportional.]**

2. Write the table on the board and then divide the cost by the time.

   $10.5 \div 3 = 3.5$

   $21 \div 6 = 3.5$

   $31.5 \div 9 = 3.5$

   $42 \div 12 = 3.5$

3. **Ask:** All of the quotients are 3.5—what does that mean? **[The slope is $3\frac{1}{2}$.]**

4. **Ask:** If the slope is $3\frac{1}{2}$, what is the unit rate? **[$3.50 per hour]**

5. **Say:** This method only works in a proportional relationship.

COMMON MISCONCEPTION

Ask: What is the error in Dan saying that the unit rate is 1 lap every 2.5 minutes?

Reason incorrect: A unit rate has 1 for the denominator, not the numerator.

Solution: By finding the slope of $\frac{2}{5}$, you can find the unit rate of $\frac{2}{5}$ lap per minute.

ADDITIONAL ONLINE INTERVENTION RESOURCES

Use the following for students who have not mastered the concepts in Skill 8.

- Math on the Spot videos
- Personal Math Trainer with customized intervention
- Building Block worksheets (Skill 111: Write Fractions as Decimals)

Name ______________________ Date ______________ Class ______________

SKILL 8

Interpreting the Unit Rate as Slope

Vocabulary
Unit rate
Slope
Proportional relationship

Example 1

Unit rates often use the word *per*.

18 points per game
24 miles per gallon
$15 per hour

A community group bought 15 theater tickets for $330. Each ticket cost the same amount of money. What was the unit price per ticket?

$330 ÷ 15 = $22
The unit price was $22 per ticket.

Check

Determine which are unit rates. Choose *Yes* or *No*.

1. 125 words per 2 minutes ○ Yes ○ No
2. 55 miles per hour ○ Yes ○ No
3. $2.25 for each slice of pizza ○ Yes ○ No

Example 2

Slope measures the ratio of $\frac{\text{rise}}{\text{run}}$ of a line, which can also be thought of as $\frac{\text{change in } y}{\text{change in } x}$.

Pick two points on the line.

Try (0, 0) and (1, 2).

$$\text{Slope} = \frac{(y_2 - y_1)}{(x_2 - x_1)}$$

$$= \frac{2-0}{1-0} = \frac{2}{1} = 2$$

The slope of the line is 2.

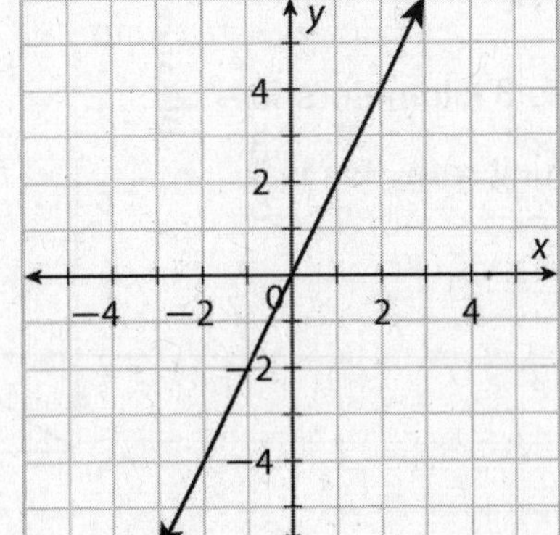

Name ______________________ Date ____________ Class ____________

Check

Determine the slope of each line.

4.

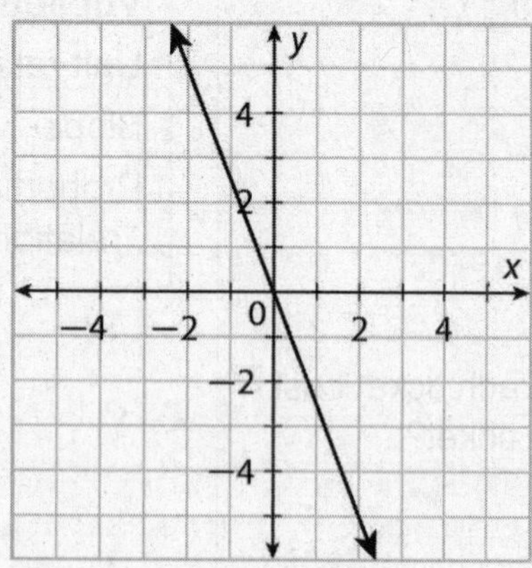

Slope = ________

5.

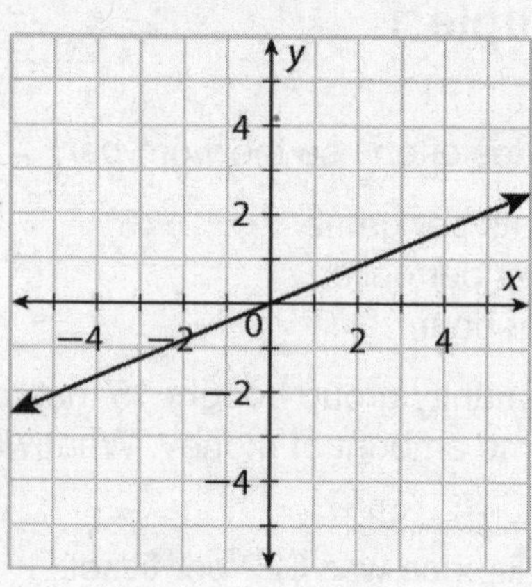

Slope = ________

Example 3

You can use the slope to find a unit rate of a proportional relationship. The slope is the unit rate.

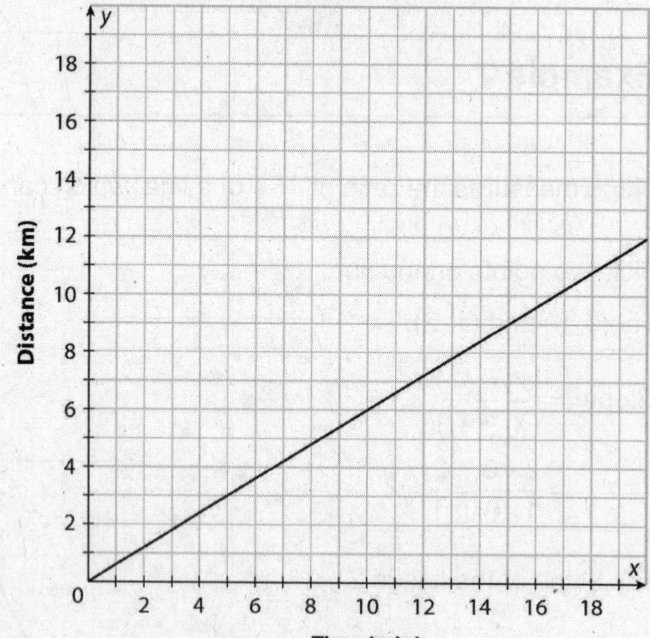

Pick two points on the line segment. Try (0, 0) and (20, 12).

$$\text{Slope} = \frac{(y_2 - y_1)}{(x_2 - x_1)}$$

$$= \frac{12 - 0}{20 - 0} = \frac{12}{20} = \frac{3}{5}$$

The distance traveled is 3 kilometers for every 5 minutes. As a unit rate, this is $\frac{3}{5}$ kilometer per minute.

Name ______________________ Date ______________ Class ______________

Check

Write the unit rate that the slope represents.

6. Unit rate = ______________

7. Unit rate = ______________

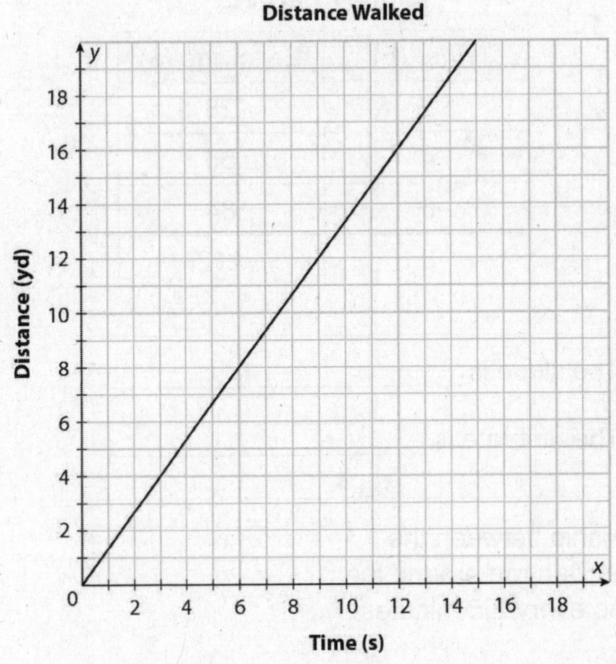

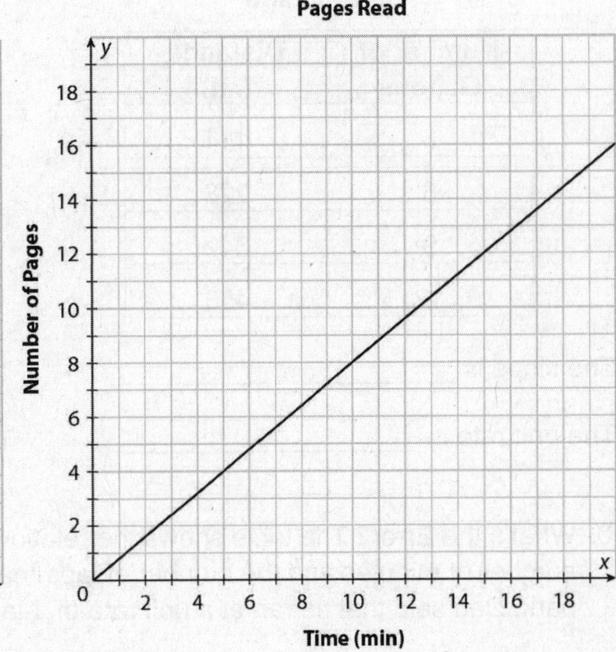

Example 4

You can use a table to determine the slope and the unit rate. The table shows the cost of renting a bicycle if the cost is prorated to the nearest minute.

Bike Rental

Time (h)	3	6	9	12
Cost ($)	10.5	21	31.5	42

Pick two points. Try (6, 21) and (12, 42).

$$\text{Slope } = \frac{42-21}{12-6} = \frac{21}{6} = \frac{7}{2} = 3\frac{1}{2}$$

The unit rate is $3.50 per hour to rent a bicycle.

Name ______________________ Date ______________ Class ______________

Check

Determine the slope and the unit rate from each table.

8.

Gas Mileage

Number of Gallons	Distance (mi)
3	114
6	228
9	342
12	456

The slope is ____________________.

The unit rate is ____________________.

9.

Money Earned

Time (h)	Earnings ($)
2	28
4	56
6	84
8	112

The slope is ____________________.

The unit rate is ____________________.

10. What's the Error? The table shows the relationship between the number of minutes and the number of laps that Dan ran around the park. Dan said that he ran at a unit rate of 1 lap every 2.5 minutes.

Laps Run

Time (min)	Laps Run
5	2
10	4
15	6
20	8

Explain Dan's error. What should be the unit rate?

____

SKILL 8 INTERPRETING THE UNIT RATE AS SLOPE

SKILL 9

Linear Associations

KEY TEACHING POINTS

Example 1

Use contrasting examples to show the difference between positive and negative associations and ones that exhibit linear or nonlinear associations.

Say: Data that exhibit a linear relationship, when graphed, will lie along a line.
Say: Look at the example on the left. As one data set increases, the other increases, too. This is a positive association.

Say: Look at the example in the middle. As one data set increases, the other decreases. This is a negative association.

Say: Look at the example on the right. The data are scattered and not along a line. There is no association between the data sets.

Check

Ask: How can you tell if data exhibit a linear association? **[When the data are graphed, they will lie along a line.]**

Example 2

Say: A trend line is the straight line on a scatter plot that helps show the correlation between data sets more clearly. In both scatter plots, the trend line goes through some of the data, but all of the data are close to the trend line.

Ask: Why is the scatter plot on the left representative of a positive association? **[When one data set increases, the other also increases.]**

Ask: Why is the scatter plot on the right representative of a negative association? **[When one data set increases, the other decreases.]**

Check

Say: Look at Question 4. There are three scatter plots that all represent the same data.

Ask: Does the trend line in the scatter plot on the left represent the correlation between the two sets? **[No]** Why not? **[The trend line is below all of the data.]**

Ask: Does the trend line in the middle scatter plot represent the correlation between the two sets? **[Yes]** Why? **[The trend line goes through some of the data, and all of the data are close to the trend line.]**

Ask: Does the trend line in the scatter plot on the right represent the correlation between the two sets? **[No]** Why not? **[The trend line is above all of the data.]**

KEY TEACHING POINTS

Example 3

Make sure students understand that real-world experiences can be displayed on a scatter plot with a trend line.

Ask: What is the meaning of the trend line on the graph? **[The trend line shows that profits increase as sales increase.]**

Say: Let's find the slope of the trend line.

Ask: What are two points through which the trend line passes? **[(6, 60) and (14, 140)]**

Say: Use the slope formula to find the slope using these two points.

Write the following on the board. Have students tell you each step.

$$m = \frac{(y_2 - y_1)}{(x_2 - x_1)}$$
$$= \frac{140 - 60}{14 - 6}$$
$$= \frac{80}{8}$$
$$= 10$$

Ask: Does the trend line pass through the origin? **[Yes]**

Say: Use the slope-intercept form $y = mx + b$ to write the equation of the trend line.

Ask: What is the equation of the trend line? **[$y = 10x$]**

Check

Say: Draw the trend line.

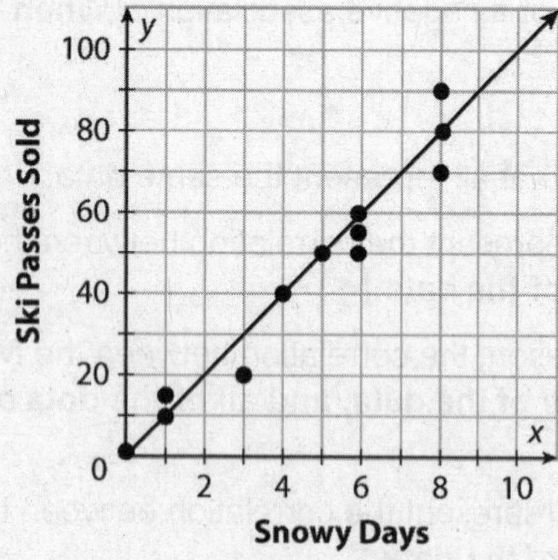

Say: Find the equation of the trend line, using the same steps we used in the example.

ALTERNATE STRATEGY

Strategy: Using the origin to find the slope.

Say: Because (0, 0) is a point on the trend line, use it as one of the two points to find the slope.

Say: Because (0, 0) is a point on the line, the slope formula can use a second point, (6, 60), to find the slope, by dividing 60 by 6. This will simplify the process of finding the slope.

COMMON MISCONCEPTION

Ask: What is the error in the answer that the scatter plot exhibits a nonlinear association?

Reason incorrect: The scatter plot exhibits a negative association, because as one data set increases, the other data set increases. A trend line shows most of the data along the line. If it had nonlinear or no association, the data would not lie along a line.

Solution: The trend line shows a linear association because most of the data are along the line.

Say: Look at the scatter plot.

Ask: What does the data represent? **[As the number of customers increases, the price decreases.]**

Say: Draw the trend line:

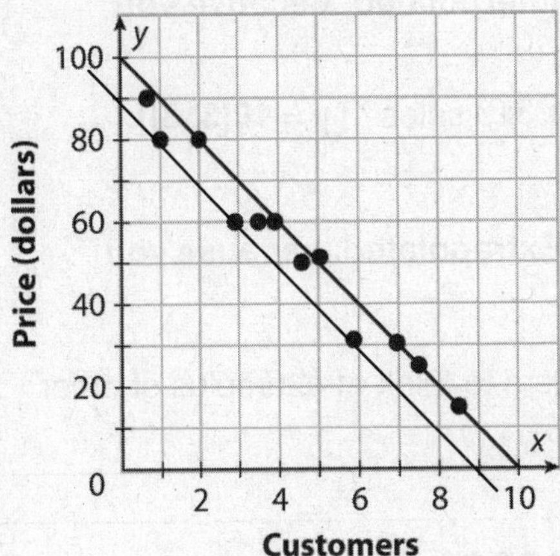

Ask: What type of association is shown? **[Negative association]**

KEY TEACHING POINTS

Example 4

Make sure students understand that other real-world experiences can be shown on a scatter plot.

Say: The scatter plot shows sales through 20. Let's predict what the profit of sales for 28 sales will be.

Ask: What is the equation of the trend line? **[$y = 10x$]** What does x represent? **[The number of sales]**

Say: Substitute 28 for x.

Write the following on the board. Have students give the answers.

$y = 10(28)$

$y = 280$

Ask: What does 280 represent? **[The profit predicted based on 28 sales]**

Say: Because this prediction uses data that are outside what is shown on the scatter plot, the predicted value is extrapolated.

Check

Ask: What is the formula on which to base the prediction for 17 sales? **[$y = 10(17)$]**

Ask: What is the prediction? **[170 profit]**

Ask: Is this prediction interpolated or extrapolated? Why? **[Interpolated, because you predict a value between points of data that are known]**

Ask: What is the formula on which to base the prediction for 313 sales? **[$y = 10(313)$]**

Ask: What is the prediction? **[3130 profit]**

Ask: Is this prediction interpolated or extrapolated? Why? **[Extrapolated, because you predict a value that is outside the known data]**

Check students' work as they make their predictions. Ask them to think of examples of other real-world situations that can be used in linear associations.

ADDITIONAL ONLINE INTERVENTION RESOURCES

Use the following for students who have not mastered the concepts in Skill 9.

- Math on the Spot videos
- Personal Math Trainer with customized intervention
- Building Block worksheets (Skill 42: Graph Equations; Skill 70: Ordered Pairs)

Name ____________________ Date ____________ Class ____________

SKILL 9

Linear Associations

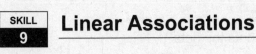

Example 1

- A positive association means that when one data set increases, the other data set increases.
- A negative association means that when one data set increases, the other decreases. Data that lie basically along a line exhibit a linear association.
- Data that do not lie basically along a line exhibit no association or a nonlinear association.

Vocabulary
Positive association
Negative association
Linear association
Nonlinear association
Trend line
Interpolate
Extrapolate

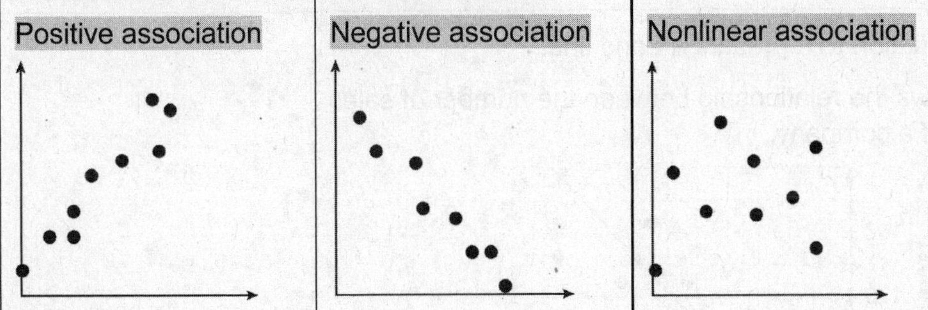

Check

Which of the following exhibit a linear association? Choose Yes or No.

1. 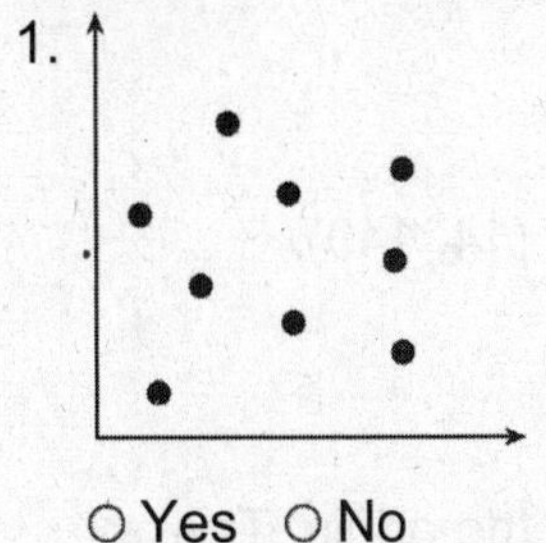

O Yes O No

2. 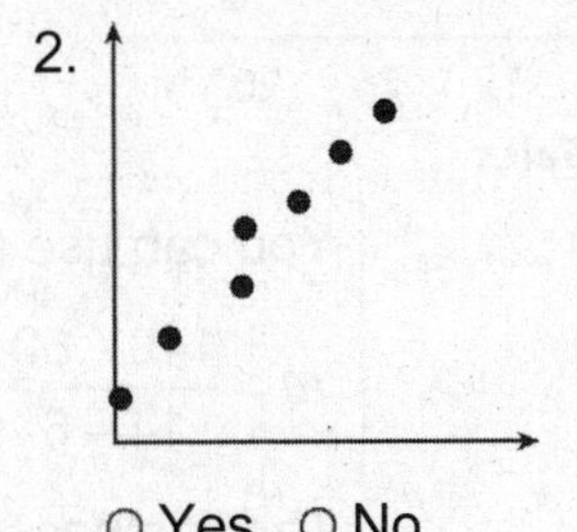

O Yes O No

3. 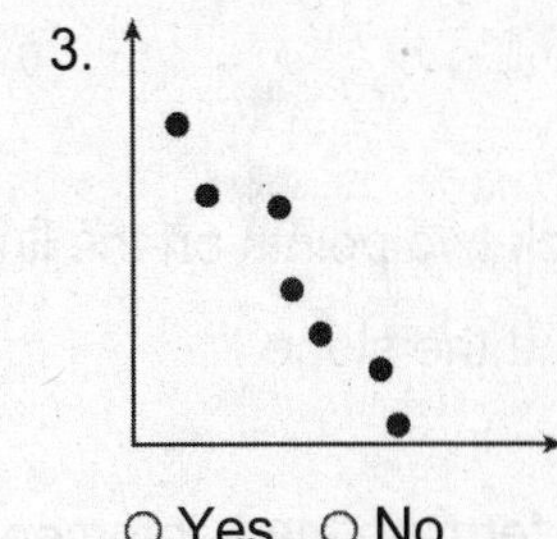

O Yes O No

Example 2

For data that exhibit a linear association, a trend line is the straight line that comes closest to the points on a scatter plot.

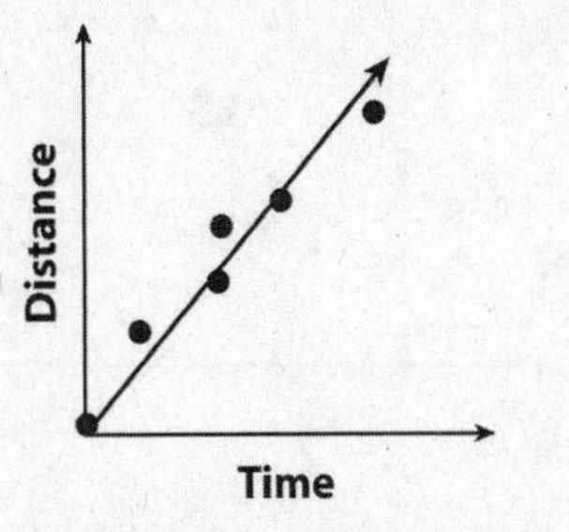

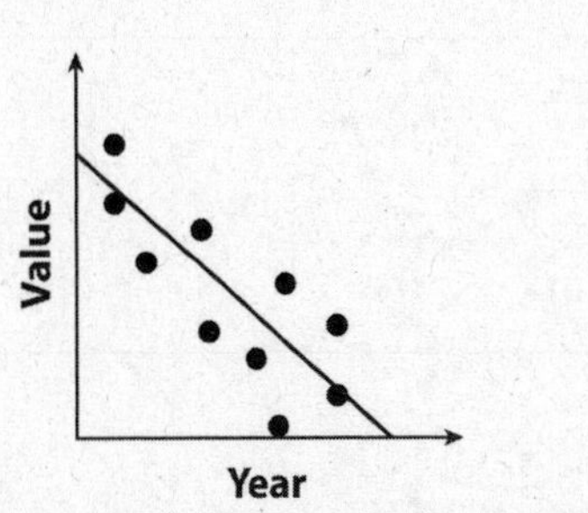

Name ________________ Date ________ Class ________

Check

4. Which scatter plot has a trend line that best represents the data?

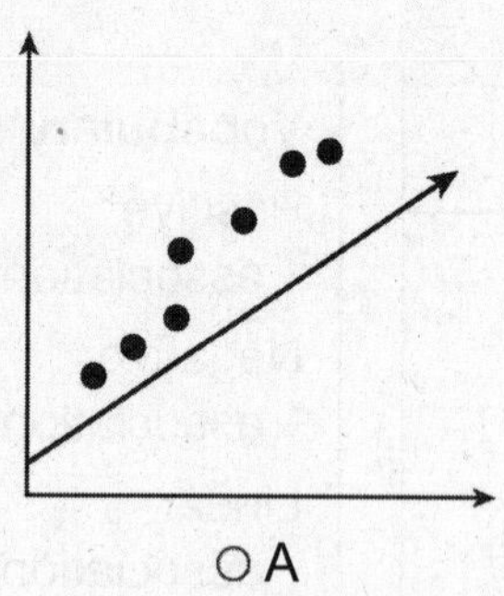

○ A

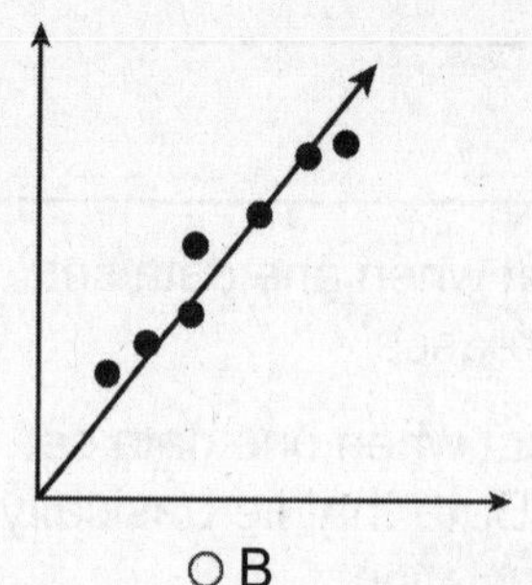

○ B

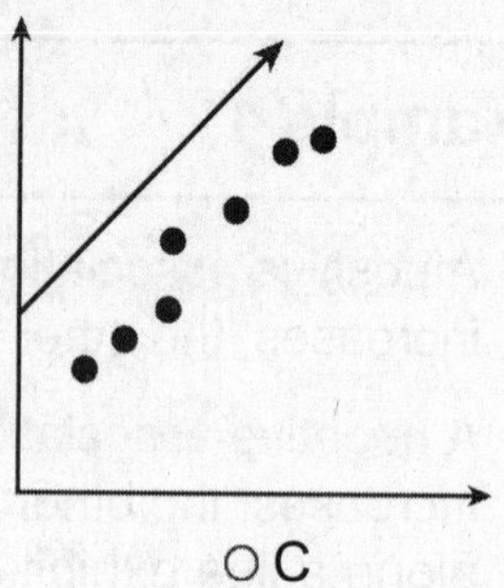

○ C

Example 3

You can write an equation to represent a trend line.

The scatter plot shows the relationship between the number of sales and the total profit of a company.

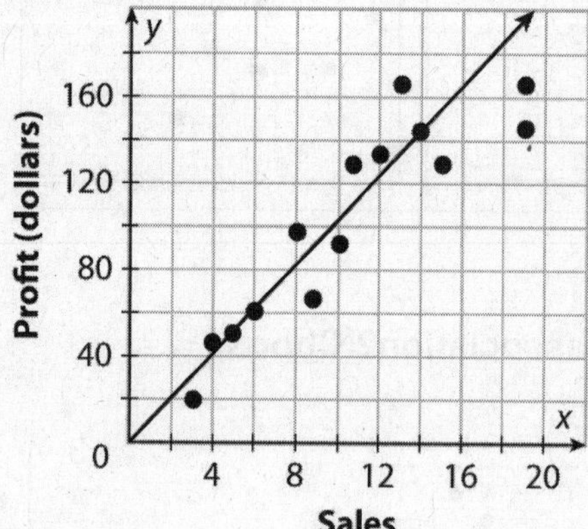

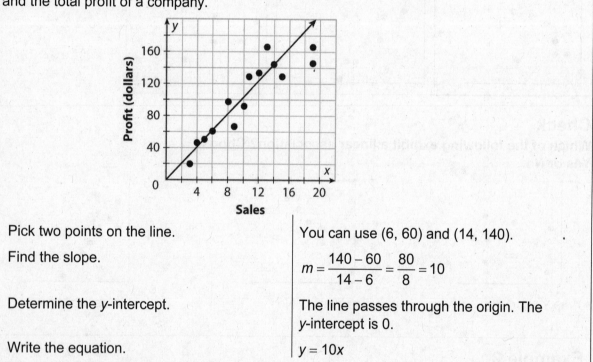

Pick two points on the line.	You can use (6, 60) and (14, 140).
Find the slope.	$m = \frac{140 - 60}{14 - 6} = \frac{80}{8} = 10$
Determine the y-intercept.	The line passes through the origin. The y-intercept is 0.
Write the equation.	$y = 10x$

Name ______________________ Date ______________ Class ______________

Check

The scatter plot shows the relationship between the number of snowy days in a month on a ski resort and the number of ski passes sold.

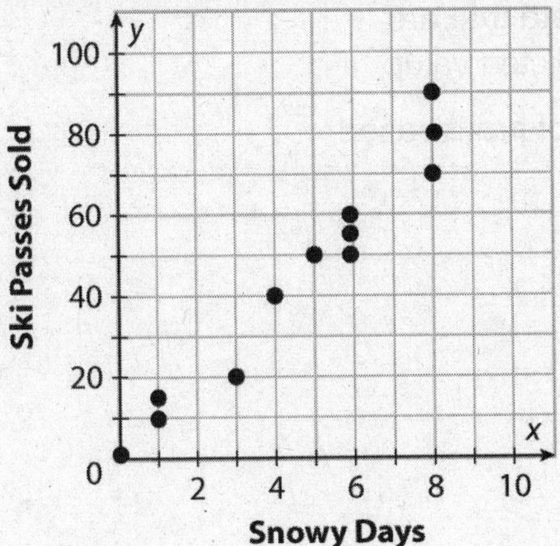

5. Draw the trend line.

6. What is the equation of the trend line? ______________

7. What's the Error? Caroline said the data on the scatter plot exhibit nonlinear association. Explain the error and name the correct association.

____

The scatter plot shows the relationship between the price of an item and the number of customers who bought the item.

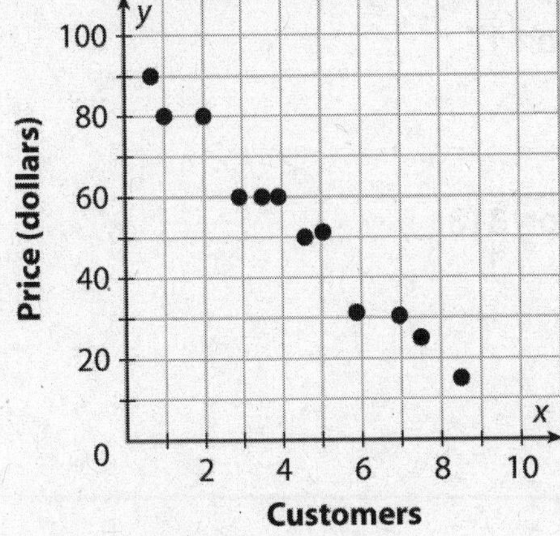

8. Draw the trend line.

9. What type of association is shown? ______________

Name ______________________ Date ______________ Class ______________

Example 4

To predict a value between data points that you already know, you interpolate the predicted value. When trying to predict data that are outside the data that you know, you extrapolate the predicted value.

Use the scatter plot in Example 3 to predict the amount of profit based on 28 sales.

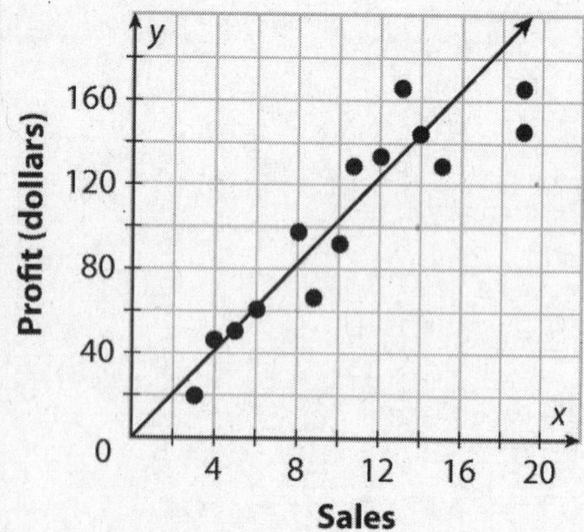

Write the equation of the trend line.	$y = 10x$
Substitute the number of sales, 28, for x.	$y = 10(28)$
	$y = 280$

The data are outside the scatter plot, so it was extrapolated.

Check

10. Using the trend line in Example 4, predict the profit based on 17 sales. ______________

11. Using the trend line in Example 4, predict the profit based on 313 sales. ______________

SKILL 9 LINEAR ASSOCIATIONS

SKILL 10

Linear Functions

KEY TEACHING POINTS

Example 1

Say: A function is a relationship that has exactly one output for each input.

Say: The relationship on the left is a function because each input has exactly one output. The ordered pairs would be (1, 3), (2, 9), (4, 7), and (5, 6). It is not necessary for a function to follow a rule.

Say: Look at the relationship on the right. Why is this not a function? **[The input 2 has two outputs.]**

Check

Have students match each input with its output.

Say: Check to see if any inputs have more than one output.

Ask: What is the difference between a function and a non-function? **[In a function, each input value has exactly one output. In a non-function, at least one input value has more than one output.]**

ALTERNATE STRATEGY

Strategy: Plot the relationship on a grid. See if any of the points share the same *x*-coordinate.

1. **Say:** Look at Question 1. Match the input with each output.
2. **Ask:** What are the matches as ordered pairs? **[(2, 4), (4, 5), (5, 8), (8, 6)]**
3. **Say:** Plot them on a coordinate plane.

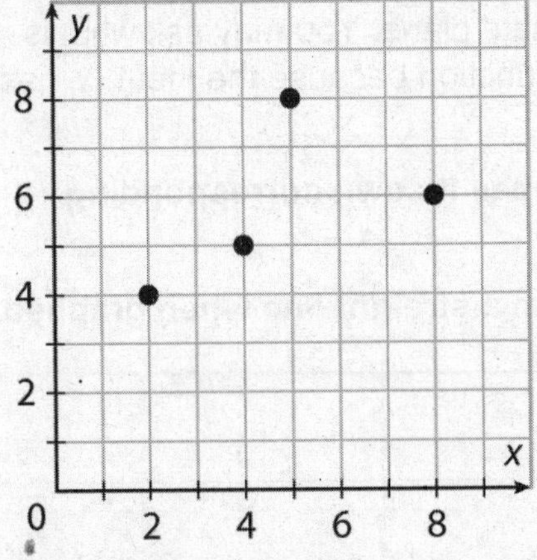

4. **Say:** Look to see if any of the plotted points share the same *x*-coordinate. Because they do not, it is a function.

KEY TEACHING POINTS

Example 2

Say: A table is another way to show a function. Look at values in the Input. If no input values repeat, it is a function.

Ask: In the left table, what are the input values? **[2, 3, 4]** Is it a function? **[Yes]**

Ask: In the right table, what are the input values? **[2, 2, 4]** Is it a function? **[No]** Why? **[The input of 2 repeats.]**

COMMON MISCONCEPTION

Ask: What is Abram's error in saying that the table is not a function?

Input	Output
3	2
5	2
7	2

Reason incorrect: Each input has a unique output.

Say: It does not matter that each input has the same output.

Solution: It is a function.

KEY TEACHING POINTS

Example 3

Say: A linear function is a function whose graph is a straight line. A linear equation is an equation whose solutions form a straight line on a coordinate plane. You may ask what is the difference. A linear equation such as $x = 3$ is not a linear function because the input, x, has more than one output, y.

Ask: Why is $y = x - 2$ a linear function? **[Each value of x has its own corresponding value of y.]**

Ask: Why is $y = x^3$ a nonlinear function? **[It does not form a straight line when graphed.]**

Check

Say: Determine if each graph forms a straight line.

KEY TEACHING POINTS

Example 4

Let students know that the graphs in Example 3 are examples of linear and nonlinear functions.

Say: The list on the left shows examples of linear functions. If each of these functions were drawn on a coordinate grid, the result would be a straight line.

Say: You can see that $y = \frac{x}{3}$ is a linear function and $y = \frac{3}{x}$ is a nonlinear function. Let's see why that is.

Make two function tables, one for each equation.

Function: $y = \frac{x}{3}$

x	y
1	$\frac{1}{3}$
2	$\frac{2}{3}$
3	1
4	$1\frac{1}{3}$

Function: $y = \frac{3}{x}$

x	y
1	3
2	1.5
3	1
4	0.75

Ask: What do you notice about how the value of *y* changes when *x* increases by 1 in $y = \frac{x}{3}$?

[The value of *y* increases by $\frac{1}{3}$.]

Ask: What do you notice about how the value of *y* changes when *x* increases by 1 in $y = \frac{3}{x}$?

[The change in *y* is 1.5, then 0.5, then 0.25.]

Say: When $y = \frac{3}{x}$ is graphed, it does not form a straight line. In fact, because you cannot divide by 0, two curves are formed when graphed.

Ask: Why is $y = 3x^2$ a nonlinear function? **[Only variables raised to the first power form lines.]** Why is $x = 3$ a nonlinear function? **[While $x = 3$ forms a line, it is not a function because each value of *x* has an infinite number of values for *y*.]**

Check

Have students use the examples in Example 4 to help them determine whether an equation forms a linear function or a nonlinear function.

KEY TEACHING POINTS

Example 5

Say: Linear functions can be represented in words, equations, tables, and graphs. In this real-world example, the function $y = 40x$ is represented as an equation, a table, and a graph.

Say: In the table, you can think of the time as x and the distance as y.

Write $y = 40x$ on the board. Go through how to find each value of y.

$40(0) = 0$

$40(1) = 40$

$40(2) = 80$

$40(3) = 120$

$40(4) = 160$

$40(5) = 200$

Ask: What ordered pairs do you plot on the graph? **[(0, 0), (1, 40), (2, 80), (3, 120), (4, 160), (5, 200)]**

Check

Make sure students know that the time represents x and the number of inches of snow represents y.

Ask: From where does the information to plot the points in the graph come? **[From the table]**

Ask: How do you find the number of inches of snow? **[Multiply the number of hours times 2.]** What ordered pairs will you plot? **[(0, 0), (1, 2), (2, 4), (3, 6), (4, 8), (5, 10)]**

ADDITIONAL ONLINE INTERVENTION RESOURCES

Use the following for students who have not mastered the concepts in Skill 10.

- Math on the Spot videos
- Personal Math Trainer with customized intervention
- Building Block worksheets (Skill 22: Connect Words and Algebra; Skill 23: Connect Words and Equations; Skill 27: Evaluate Expressions; Skill 40: Function Tables)

Name ______________________ Date ____________ Class ____________

SKILL 10

Linear Functions

Example 1

Function:

Input **Output**

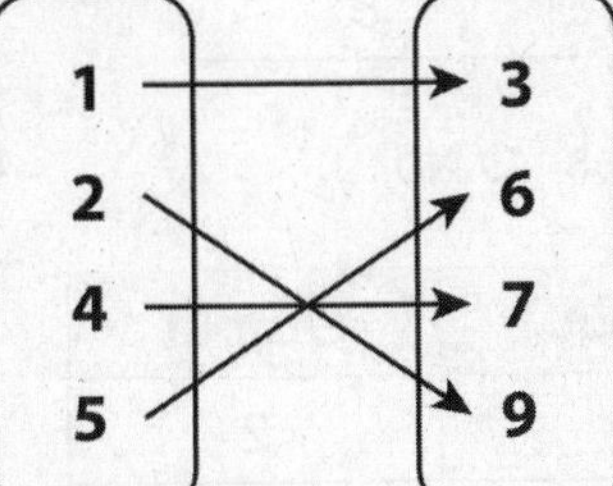

Each input value is paired with one output value.

Not a function:

Input **Output**

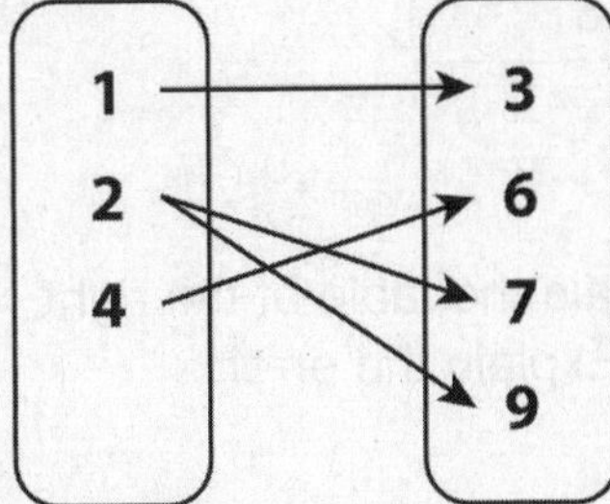

The input 2 has more than one output.

Vocabulary

Function

Linear function

Nonlinear function

Check

Determine if each relationship is a function.

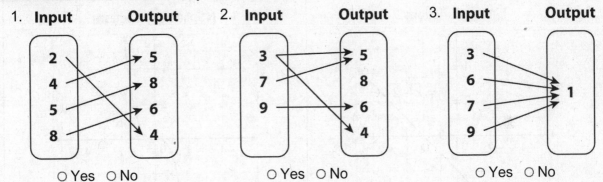

1. **Input** **Output**

2, 4, 5, 8 — 5, 8, 6, 4

○ Yes ○ No

2. **Input** **Output**

3, 7, 9 — 5, 8, 6, 4

○ Yes ○ No

3. **Input** **Output**

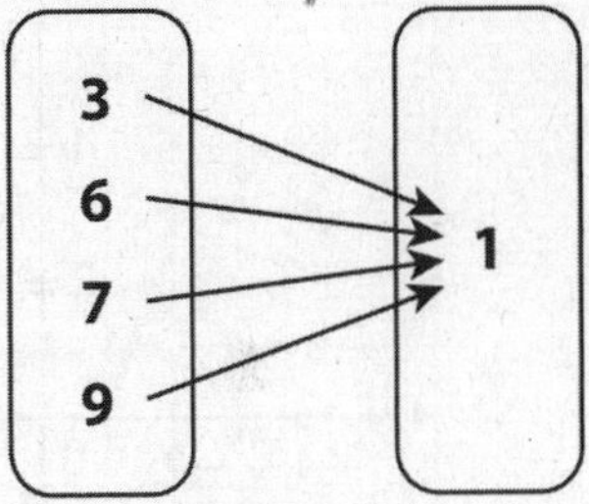

○ Yes ○ No

Example 2

Function:

Input	Output
2	5
3	8
4	6

Each input is unique.

Not a function:

Input	Output
2	5
2	8
4	6

Each input is not unique.

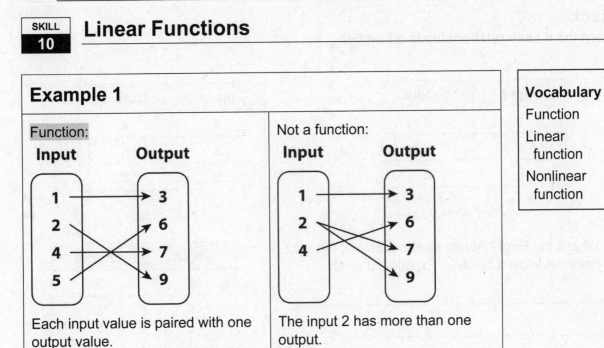

Name ______________________ Date ______________ Class ______________

Check

Determine if each relationship is a function.

4.

Input	Output
6	4
8	6
6	6

○ Yes ○ No

5.

Input	Output
4	4
2	6
8	8

○ Yes ○ No

6. What's the Error? Abram said the table at the right does not show a function. Explain the error.

Input	Output
3	2
5	2
7	2

____

____

Example 3

Linear Function:

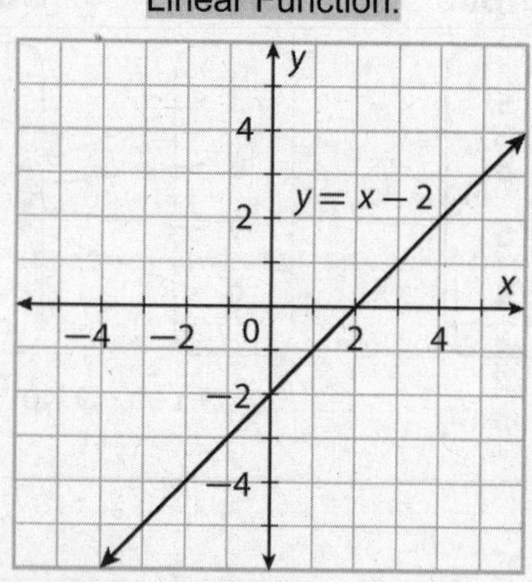

A straight line is formed.

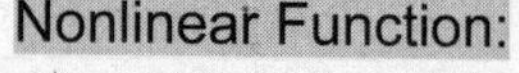
Nonlinear Function:

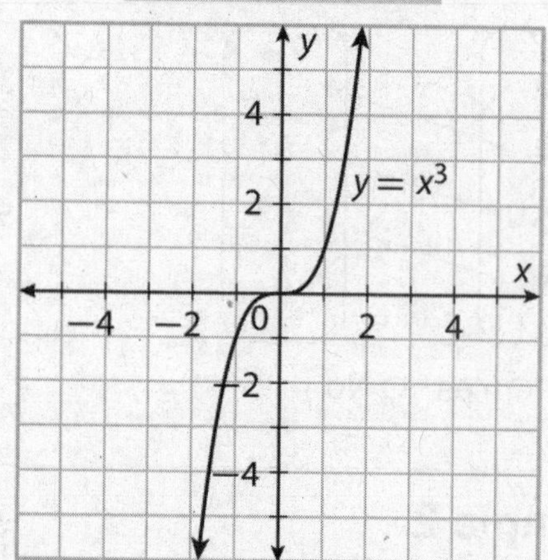

A straight line is not formed.

Name ______________________ Date ______________ Class ______________

Check

Determine if each graph represents a linear function.

7.

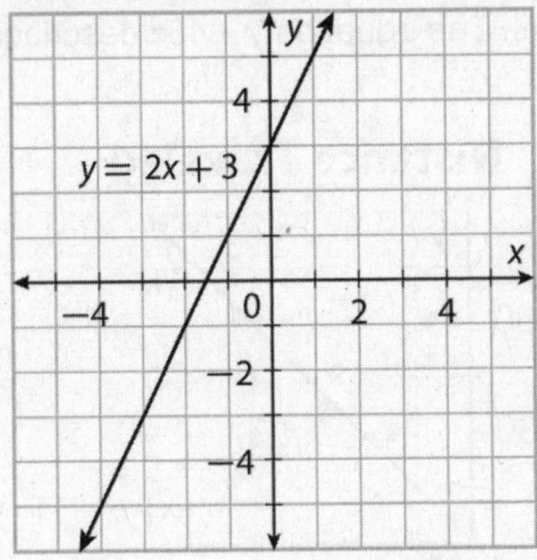

○ Yes ○ No

8.

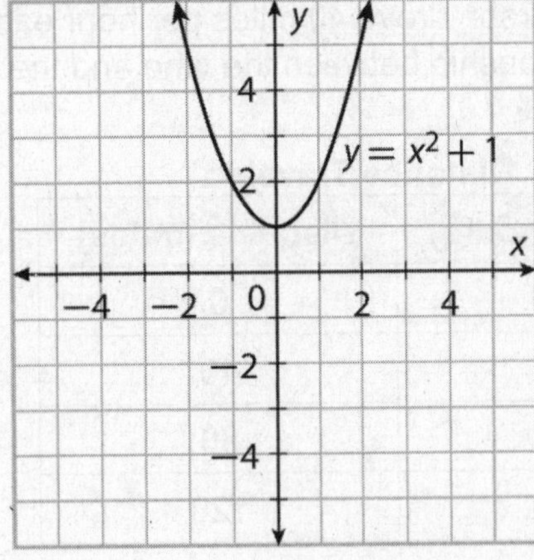

○ Yes ○ No

Example 4

Examples of Linear Functions:	Examples of Nonlinear Functions:
$y = x + 3$ $y = 3x$ $y = \frac{x}{3}$ $y = 3 - x$ $y = -3x$	$y = \frac{3}{x}$ $y = 3x^2$ $x = 3$

Check

Determine if each equation represents a linear function.

9. $y = -4x + 1$

○ Yes ○ No

10. $y = \frac{2}{3}x$

○ Yes ○ No

11. $y = x^2 + 4$

○ Yes ○ No

Name ______________________ Date ______________ Class ______________

Example 5

Mr. Anderson drove 40 miles per hour each hour for 5 hours. The equation $y = 40x$ describes the relationship between the time and the distance.

Distance Traveled

Time (hours)	Distance (miles)
0	0
1	40
2	80
3	120
4	160
5	200

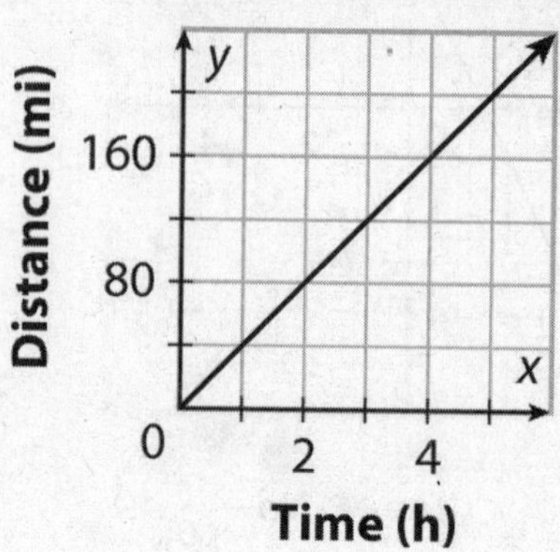

Check

The equation $y = 2x$ represents the total amount of snow that fell during a storm.

12. Complete the table.

Snowfall

Time (hours)	Amount of Snow (in.)
0	
1	
2	
3	
4	
5	

13. Complete the graph.

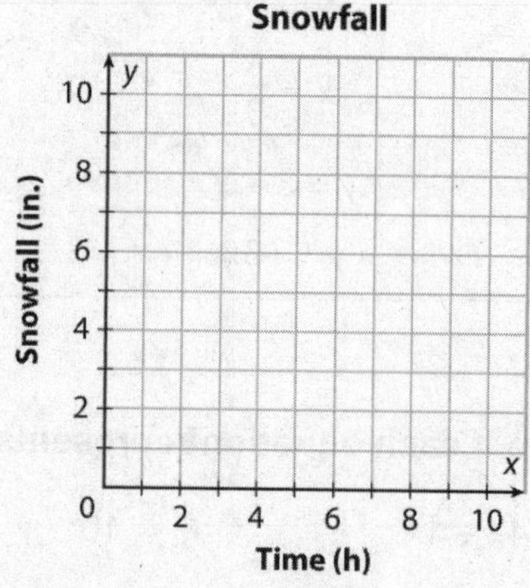

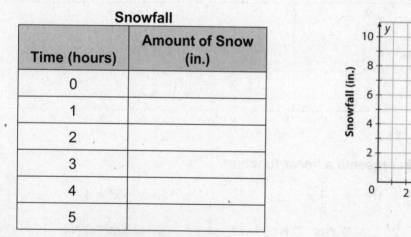

SKILL 10 LINEAR FUNCTIONS

SKILL 11 Multi-Step Equations

KEY TEACHING POINTS

Example 1

Say: Inverse operations are operations that undo each other. Addition and subtraction are inverse operations and multiplication and division are inverse operations.

Say: To solve an equation, use inverse operations to isolate the variable. What you do to one side of an equation, you must also do to the other side.

Write $4m + 6 = 18$ on the board.

Ask: What is the first step to finding the value of m? **[Subtract 6 from both sides of the equation.]** Why is 6 subtracted from both sides? **[To remove the constant]**

Say: After 6 is subtracted from both sides of the equation, we are left with $4m = 12$.

Ask: What is the next step? **[Divide both sides of the equation by 4.]** Why divide? **[To remove the coefficient and isolate the variable]**

Say: Check your solution by substituting 3 for m in the original equation: $4(3) = 12$ and $12 + 6 = 18$. The solution is correct.

Check

Say: Each of the first three equations are two-step equations.

Ask: For Question 1, what are the two steps needed to find the value of a? **[Subtract 4 from both sides of the equation and then divide by 2.]**

COMMON MISCONCEPTION

Ask: What is Gillian's error in her solution of $p = 1$ for the equation $3p - 9 = 12$?

Reason incorrect: The error is that Gillian subtracted 9 from both sides of the equation. She should have added 9 to both sides of the equation.

Solution: $3p - 9 + 9 = 12 + 9$

$$3p = 21$$

$$\frac{3p}{3} = \frac{21}{3}$$

$$p = 7$$

KEY TEACHING POINTS

Example 2

Review with students how to multiply and divide with integers and rational numbers. Remind them that if the signs are the same, the product or quotient is positive, and if the signs are different, the product or quotient is negative.

Say: Solve a two-step equation with negative numbers like you would solve a two-step equation with positive numbers.

Write $-3d - 5 = -7$ on the board.

Ask: What is the first step to finding the value of d? **[Add 5 to both sides of the equation.]**

Say: After 5 is added to both sides, we are left with $-3d = -2$.

Ask: What is the second step? **[Divide both sides by –3.]**

Say: The solution is $d = \frac{2}{3}$.

COMMON MISCONCEPTION

Ask: What is Patti's error in her solution of $j = -2$ for the equation $-5j - 2 = -12$?

Reason incorrect: The error is that Patti used the incorrect integer sign.

Solution:
$$\begin{aligned} -5j - 2 + 2 &= -12 + 2 \\ -5j &= -10 \\ \frac{-5j}{-5} &= \frac{-10}{-5} \\ j &= 2 \end{aligned}$$

KEY TEACHING POINTS

Example 3

Say: Coefficients that are fractions means that you may have to divide fractions to isolate the variable. To divide a fraction, multiply by the reciprocal of the divisor.

Write $\frac{2}{3}x - 4 = 6$ on the board.

Ask: What is the first step to finding the value of x? **[Add 4 to both sides of the equation.]**

What are we left with? $\left[\frac{2}{3}x = 10\right]$ What is the next step? **[Divide both sides of the equation by $\frac{2}{3}$.]**

Ask: Dividing by $\frac{2}{3}$ is like multiplying by what? $\left[\frac{3}{2}\right]$ What is the value of x? **[15]**

COMMON MISCONCEPTION

Ask: What is Eric's error in his solution of $v = 2\frac{2}{5}$ for the equation $\frac{2}{5}v - 2 = 4$?

Reason incorrect: The error is that Eric multiplied both sides of the equation by $\frac{2}{5}$. He should have multiplied both sides of the equation by $\frac{5}{2}$.

Solution: $\frac{2}{5}v - 2 + 2 = 4 + 2$

$$\frac{2}{5}v = 6$$

$$\frac{2}{5}v\left(\frac{5}{2}\right) = 6\left(\frac{5}{2}\right)$$

$$v = 15$$

ALTERNATE STRATEGY

Strategy: Convert fractions to decimals to solve equations.

1. **Say:** Sometimes it can be helpful to convert fractions to decimals. Look at Question 9.
2. **Ask:** What is $\frac{1}{2}$ written as a decimal? **[0.5]** What equivalent equation can you write using a decimal? **[$0.5r + 3 = 5$]**
3. **Say:** Now follow the steps for solving a two-step equation.
4. **Ask:** What are the two steps to isolate r? **[Subtract 3 from both sides of the equation and then divide by 0.5.]** What is the value of r? **[4]**

KEY TEACHING POINTS

Example 4

Say: The Distributive Property states that for all real numbers a, b, and c, $a(b + c) = ab + ac$, and $a(b - c) = ab - ac$.

Write $2(p - 4) = 6$ on the board.

Say: The first step to finding the value of p is to use the Distributive Property on the left side of the equation. Two is multiplied with p and then by -4.

Write $2p - 8 = 6$.

Say: Now we have a two-step equation. It is important to remember to multiply each term inside the parentheses by the number outside the parentheses.

COMMON MISCONCEPTION

Ask: What is Jeff's error in his solution of $f = 2$ for the equation $4(f - 2) = 6$?

Reason incorrect: The error is that Jeff did not use the Distributive Property. He multiplied $4(f)$, but did not multiply $4(-2)$.

Solution:

$$\begin{aligned} 4f - 8 &= 6 \\ 4f - 8 + 8 &= 6 + 8 \\ 4f &= 14 \\ f &= 3\frac{1}{2} \end{aligned}$$

KEY TEACHING POINTS

Example 5

Say: Sometimes there is a variable on both sides of the is-equal-to sign. In such a problem, use inverse operations to eliminate the variable from one of the sides.

Write $3x + 4 = 5x - 2$ on the board.

Ask: If we want to remove the variable from one of the sides of the equation, what is the first step? **[Subtract 3*x* from both sides of the equation.]**

Say: That leaves $4 = 2x - 2$. This is now a two-step equation.

COMMON MISCONCEPTION

Ask: What is Sixto's error in his solution of $x = \frac{2}{7}$ for the equation $2x - 4 = 5x + 2$?

Reason incorrect: The error is that Sixto added $2x$ to both sides of the equation. He should have subtracted $2x$ from both sides of the equation.

Solution:

$$\begin{aligned} 2x - 4 - 2x &= 5x - 2x + 2 \\ -4 &= 3x + 2 \\ -4 - 2 &= 3x + 2 - 2 \\ -6 &= 3x \\ -2 &= x \end{aligned}$$

ADDITIONAL ONLINE INTERVENTION RESOURCES

Use the following for students who have not mastered the concepts in Skill 11.

- Math on the Spot videos
- Personal Math Trainer with customized intervention
- Building Block worksheets (Skill 59: Multiplication Properties; Skill 98: Solve Two-Step Equations)

Name ______________________ Date ____________ Class ____________

SKILL 11

Multi-Step Equations

Example 1

You can use inverse operations to solve equations with more than one operation.

Solve: $4m + 6 = 18$

Subtract 6 from both sides of the equation.	$4m + 6 - 6 = 18 - 6$ $4m = 12$
Divide both sides of the equation by 4.	$\frac{4m}{4} = \frac{12}{4}$ $m = 3$

Vocabulary

Inverse operation

Equation

Coefficient

Reciprocal

Distributive Property

Variable

Check

Solve.

1. $2a + 4 = 8$ ____________

2. $3b - 4 = 11$ ____________

3. $4c + 3 = 7$ ____________

4. What's the Error? Gillian solved $3p - 9 = 12$ and found that $p = 1$. Explain the error and how to fix it. Include the correct solution in your explanation.

____

Example 2

You can solve equations with negative coefficients.

Solve: $-3d - 5 = -7$

Add 5 to both sides of the equation.	$-3d - 5 + 5 = -7 + 5$ $-3d = -2$
Divide both sides of the equation by -3.	$\frac{-3d}{-3} = \frac{-2}{-3}$ $d = \frac{2}{3}$

Name ______________________ Date ____________ Class ____________

Check

Solve.

5. $-2g + 4 = 6$

6. $-3j - 6 = -3$

7. $-4k + 2 = -6$

8. What's the Error? Patti solved $-5j - 2 = -12$ and found that $j = -2$. Explain the error. Give the correct solution.

Example 3

You can solve equations with fraction coefficients.

Solve: $\frac{2}{3}x - 4 = 6$

Add 4 to both sides of the equation.	$\frac{2}{3}x - 4 + 4 = 6 + 4$ $\frac{2}{3}x = 10$
Divide both sides of the equation by $\frac{2}{3}$.	$\frac{2}{3}x\left(\frac{3}{2}\right) = 10\left(\frac{3}{2}\right)$ $x = 15$

Divide by a fraction by multiplying by its reciprocal.

Check

Solve.

9. $\frac{1}{2}r + 3 = 5$

10. $\frac{3}{4}q - 2 = -4$

11. $-\frac{4}{5}s + 3 = 6$

12. What's the Error? Eric solved $\frac{2}{5}v - 2 = 4$ and found that $v = 2\frac{2}{5}$. Explain the error and how to fix it. Include the correct solution in your explanation.

Name ______________________ Date ______________ Class______________

Example 4

You can use the **Distributive Property** to solve equations.

Solve: $2(p - 4) = 6$

Use the Distributive Property.	$2(p) - 2(4) = 6$ $2p - 8 = 6$
Add 8 to both sides of the equation.	$2p - 8 + 8 = 6 + 8$ $2p = 14$
Divide both sides of the equation by 2.	$\frac{2p}{2} = \frac{14}{2}$ $p = 7$

Check

13. Explain how to use the Distributive Property to simplify the left side of the equation $4(a + 3) = 15$.

____

Solve.

14. $3(s - 2) = 12$

15. $4(y + 3) = 6$

16. $\frac{1}{2}(w - 4) = 5$

17. $\frac{3}{5}(a + 2) = 4$

18. $-3(b - 2) = 10$

19. $-2(v + 3) = -8$

20. What's the Error? Jeff solved $4(f - 2) = 6$ and found that $f = 2$. Explain the error and how to fix it. Include the correct solution in your explanation.

____

Name ______________________ Date ______________ Class ______________

Example 5

You can solve equations with the variable on both sides. Solve: $3x + 4 = 5x - 2$	
Subtract $3x$ from both sides of the equation.	$3x - 3x + 4 = 5x - 3x - 2$ $4 = 2x - 2$
Add 2 to both sides of the equation.	$4 + 2 = 2x - 2 + 2$ $6 = 2x$
Divide both sides of the equation by 2.	$\frac{6}{2} = \frac{2x}{2}$ $3 = x$

Solve.

21. $2x + 6 = 4x - 3$

22. $3z - 5 = z + 8$

23. $-2c - 2 = 3c + 6$

______________ ______________ ______________

24. What's the Error? Sixto solved $2x - 4 = 5x + 2$ and found that $x = \frac{2}{7}$.
Explain the error and how to fix it. Include the correct solution in your explanation.

____

____

SKILL 11 MULTI-STEP EQUATIONS

SKILL 12

Multiply and Divide Integers

KEY TEACHING POINTS

Example 1

Review with students that integers include the set of whole numbers and their opposites.

Say: Multiplication is a shortcut for repeated addition.

Ask: Why do the arrows on the number line face left? **[A negative number is being multiplied.]** Is the product greater than or less than the factors? **[Less than]**

Check

Ask: For Question 1, how can you use the number line to help you multiply a negative integer times a positive integer? **[I can subtract –3 two times to get –6.]**

Example 2

Explain to students that a yellow counter represents a positive integer and a red counter represents a negative integer.

Write the following on the board: (–4)(–2) = –4(–2).

Say: This equation shows that (–4)(–2) is like multiplying the opposite of 4(–2).

Say: The first model shows –8 using red counters because 4 times –2 is equal to –8.

Ask: What are opposites? **[Numbers that are the same distance, but on opposite sides of 0 on a number line]** What is the opposite of –8? **[8]**

Say: The second model shows 8, because 8 is the opposite of –8.

Check

Ask: How is multiplying two negative integers like multiplying two positive integers? **[It is the same.]**

ALTERNATE STRATEGY

Strategy: Use rules to multiply integers.

1. **Ask:** Is the product of two positive integers negative or positive? **[Positive]**
2. **Ask:** Is the product of a positive integer times a negative integer negative or positive? **[Negative]** Does the order of the factors matter? **[No]**
3. **Ask:** Is the product of two negative integers negative or positive? **[Positive]**
4. Write these rules on the board:

   +(+) = +

   +(–) or –(+) = –

   –(–) = +

KEY TEACHING POINTS

Example 3

Say: Knowing how to write expressions involving negative integers is important when solving a word problem.

Ask: What do you know? **[Jim was sacked 3 times. The team lost 7 yards each time he was sacked.]** What do you need to find? **[The total number of yards lost because of the sacks]**

Say: You need to multiply the number of times Jim was sacked by the number of yards of each sack.

Ask: What number represents the number of times Jim was sacked? **[3]** What number represents the number of yards of each sack? **[–7]**

Say: Absolute value is the distance of a number from 0 on a number line. Absolute value is a positive number.

Say: To find the total number of yards, multiply 3(–7).

Ask: What is 3(–7)? **[–21]**

Say: The total number of yards from the sacks was –21.

Check

Ask: What do you know? **[Lydia played 4 games. She scored –3 each time.]** What do you need to find? **[Lydia's total score]**

Ask: What expression can you use to find Lydia's total score? **[4(–3)]** What was Lydia's total score? **[–12]**

Example 4

Say: Division is a shortcut for repeated subtraction.

Ask: Why do the arrows on the number line face right? **[The divisor is a positive number.]** What is the purpose of the number line? **[To show how many are in each of two moves to get from –8 to 0]**

Check

Ask: For Question 10, how can you use the number line to help you divide a negative integer by a positive integer? **[I can subtract –2 three times to get from –6 to 0.]**

Example 5

Say: In a division expression, look at the sign of the dividend and the divisor.

Say: In 12 ÷ (–4), there is one positive integer and one negative integer. The quotient is negative because the signs in the expression are different.

Check

Ask: Is the quotient of a positive integer divided by a negative integer positive or negative? **[Negative]**

KEY TEACHING POINTS

Example 6
Say: Look at the sign of the dividend and the divisor.

Say: In –18 ÷ (–6), there are two negative integers. Divide as you would with whole numbers. The quotient is positive because the signs in the expression are the same.

COMMON MISCONCEPTION

Ask: What is the error in the equation –42 ÷ (–6) = –7?

Reason incorrect: The quotient of two negative integers is positive.

Solution: –42 ÷ (–6) = 7

ALTERNATE STRATEGY

Strategy: Relate division of integers to multiplication of integers.

1. **Say:** The rules for dividing integers are the same as for multiplying two integers.
2. **Ask:** When multiplying, if the signs are the same, is the product negative or positive? **[Positive]** If the signs are different, is the product negative or positive? **[Negative]**
3. **Say:** Now let's relate division to multiplication.
4. **Ask:** When dividing, if the signs are the same, is the quotient negative or positive? **[Positive]** If the signs are different, is the quotient negative or positive? **[Negative]**
5. Write these rules on the board:

   + ÷ + = +

   + ÷ (–) or – ÷ + = –

   – ÷ (–) = +

KEY TEACHING POINTS

Example 7
Say: In a division expression, look at the sign of the dividend and the divisor.

Say: In 12 ÷ (–4), there is one positive integer and one negative integer. The quotient is negative because the signs in the expression are different.

Ask: If the signs are the same, what sign is the quotient? **[Positive]** If the signs are different, what sign is the quotient? **[Negative]**

Check
Ask: Is the quotient of a positive integer divided by a negative integer positive or negative? **[Negative]**

ALTERNATE STRATEGY

Strategy: Write a fraction to show division.

1. **Say:** Look at $\frac{-36}{9}$. The numerator is negative and the denominator is positive.
2. **Ask:** How can you rewrite $\frac{-36}{9}$? **[−36 ÷ 9]**
3. **Ask:** What is −36 ÷ 9? **[−4]**

KEY TEACHING POINTS

Example 8
Say: Knowing how to write expressions involving negative integers is important when solving a word problem.

Ask: What do you know? **[The temperature was −10°C at 2 A.M. The temperature changed by −2°C each hour from when the temperature was 0°C.]** What do you need to find? **[What time was the temperature 0°C?]**

Say: You need to find the change in temperature. The temperature was −10°C at 2 A.M. and 0° from the starting point. Subtract −10 −°0 = −10. The change is −10°C.

Ask: How can you find the number of hours? **[Divide −10 ÷ (−2).]** What is −10 ÷ (−2)? **[5]**

Say: Count back 5 hours from 2 A.M.

Ask: When was the starting time? **[9 P.M.]**

Say: It was 0°C at 9 P.M.

Check
Check that students correctly write division expressions to represent each situation.

ADDITIONAL ONLINE INTERVENTION RESOURCES

Use the following for students who have not mastered the concepts in Skill 12.

- Math on the Spot videos
- Personal Math Trainer with customized intervention
- Building Block worksheets (Skill 26: Division Facts; Skill 58: Multiplication Facts)

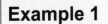

Name ______________________ Date ______________ Class ______________

SKILL 12

Multiply and Divide Integers

Example 1

You can use a number line to multiply a negative integer times a positive integer.

Multiply: –4(2)

+ (–4) + (–4)

–10 –8 –6 –4 –2 0

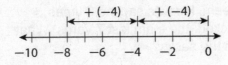

–4(2) = –8

Vocabulary
Integer
Opposite
Absolute value

Check

Find each product.

1. –3(2) ____________ 2. –2(5) ____________ 3. –3(3) ____________

4. What sign will the product of a negative integer times a positive integer have?

____

Example 2

You can use two-color counters to model multiplying two negative integers.

Multiply: (–4)(–2)

Write –4(–2), which means the opposite of 4(–2).

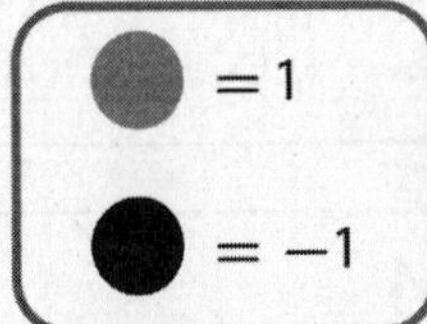

2 groups of –4

Use the same model to show the opposite of 4(–2).

The opposite of 2 groups of –4

(–4)(–2) = 8

Name ______________________ Date ____________ Class ____________

Check

Find each product.

5. (–5)(–4) ____________ 6. (–3)(–6) ____________ 7. (–5)(–6) ____________

8. What sign will the product of two negative integers have?

____

Example 3

Jim is the quarterback on his football team. He was sacked 3 times during the game. Each time he was sacked, the team lost 7 yards. What was the total number of yards lost from the sacks?

Multiply: 3(–7)

Determine the absolute value of each factor. $|3| = 3$ and $|-7| = 7$

Multiply the absolute values. $3(7) = 21$

Assign the correct sign. $3(-7) = -21$

The total number of yards from the sacks was –21.

Check

Write a multiplication expression for the problem. Then find the value of the expression.

9. Lydia played miniature golf 4 times last week. Each time she shot 3 strokes under par (–3). What was Lydia's total score?

____

Example 4

You can use a number line to divide a negative integer by a positive integer.

Divide: –8 ÷ 2

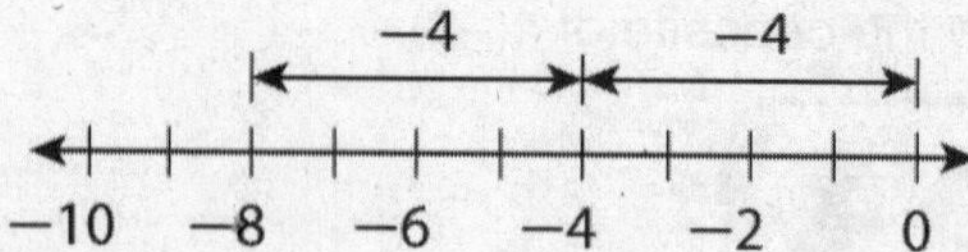

–8 ÷ 2 = –4

Name ________________ Date ________ Class ________

Check

Find each quotient.

10. –6 ÷ 3 ________ 11. –10 ÷ 5 ________ 12. –9 ÷ 3 ________

13. What sign will the quotient of a negative integer divided by a positive integer have?

____

Example 5

Divide: 12 ÷ (–4)

Determine the sign of the quotient.

12 is positive.
–4 is negative.
The sign of the quotient will be negative.

Divide: 12 ÷ (–4) = –3

Check

Find each quotient.

14. 21 ÷ (–3) ________ 15. 35 ÷ (–7) ________ 16. 56 ÷ (–8) ________

17. What sign will the quotient of a positive integer divided by a negative integer have?

____

Example 6

Divide: –18 ÷ (–6)

Determine the sign of the quotient.

–18 is negative.
–6 is negative.
The sign of the quotient will be positive.

Divide: –18 ÷ (–6) = 3

Check

Find each quotient.

18. –24 ÷ (–4) ________ 19. –64 ÷ (–8) ________ 20. –72 ÷ (–9) ________

21. What's the Error? Explain the error. Find the correct solution.

–42 ÷ (–6) = –7

____

Name ______________________ Date ______________ Class ______________

Example 7

Fractions are another way to show division.

$\frac{-15}{5} = -3$ $\frac{18}{-2} = -9$ $\frac{-24}{-3} = 8$

Find each quotient.

22. $\frac{-36}{9}$ ________

23. $\frac{49}{-7}$ ________

24. $\frac{-54}{-6}$ ________

Example 8

The temperature at 2 A.M. was –10°C. At an earlier time the temperature was 0°C. It changed by –2°C each hour until 2 A.M. At what earlier time was the temperature 0°C?

Subtract –10 – 0 to find the change in temperature.	–10 – 0 = –10
Divide –10 ÷ (–2) to find the number of hours.	–10 ÷ (–2) = 5
Subtract 5 hours from 2 A.M. to find the time the temperature was 0°C.	The time was 9 P.M.

The temperature was 0°C at 9 P.M.

Check

Write a division expression for each problem. Then find the value of the expression.

25. Jerome's game score changed by –20 points because of penalties that were worth –5 points each. How many times was Jerome penalized?

____

26. Cassie took 2 quizzes last week. She scored the same in each quiz. Her score was –12 from being perfect. What was the difference between Cassie's score and a perfect score on each quiz?

____

SKILL 12 MULTIPLY AND DIVIDE INTEGERS

SKILL 13

One-Step Equations

KEY TEACHING POINTS

Example 1

Review with students the difference between an expression and an equation. An expression does not contain an equal sign but an equation does.

Say: An equation states that two expressions are equal. An equation may or may not contain a variable. For example, $2 + 2 = 4$ is an equation and $2 + x = 4$ is also an equation.

Say: Look for a word or phrase that gives a clue as to which operation to use when writing an equation.

Ask: In the statement, "The sum of a number and 8 is equal to 14," what words tell you that it is an equation and not an expression? **[is equal to]** What word tells you to add? **[sum]**

COMMON MISCONCEPTION

Ask: What is Jimmy's error in thinking that the equation for "8 equal groups with 48 members" can only be written as $8g = 48$?

Reason incorrect: A multiplication equation can also be written as a related division equation.

Solution: Jimmy could also write $48 \div g = 8$ or $48 \div 8 = g$.

KEY TEACHING POINTS

Example 2

Say: Writing an equation is part of the problem-solving process.

Ask: What do you know? **[Maria bought a sweater for $24 and a pair of leggings. The total cost was $40.]**

Ask: What do you need to find? **[An equation that represents the situation]**

Say: Two groups are being joined, the $24 sweater and the leggings, so the equation will use addition. Let l represent the cost of the leggings. So, $24 + l = 40$ represents the situation.

Check

Say: For Problems 6 and 7, it does not matter what you name the variable. What does matter is that you explain what the variable represents.

KEY TEACHING POINTS

Example 3

Review with students that inverse operations are operations that undo each other.

Write the following on the board: $3 + b = 9$.

Say: You can use inverse operations to find the value of *b*.

Ask: What is the inverse operation of addition? **[Subtraction]** What do you do to both sides of the equation? **[Subtract 3]**

Show the work on the board.

Say: The solution is $b = 6$. It is the same result as using a related fact $9 - 3 = 6$. It is good to use inverse operations with numbers that take more effort to compute.

ALTERNATE STRATEGY

Strategy: Use algebra tiles to solve an equation.

1. Write $x + 8 = 14$ on the board.
2. Draw the following:

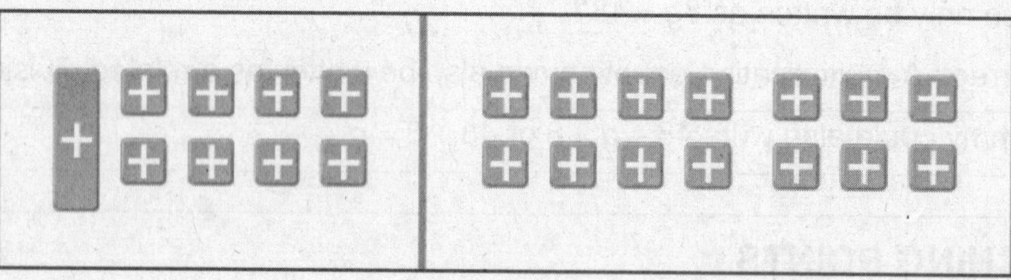

3. **Say:** On the left is an *x* tile and eight 1 tiles. On the right are fourteen 1 tiles. You can remove 1 tile from the left and right until there are no 1 tiles on the left.
4. **Ask:** How many 1 tiles can be removed from both sides? **[8]**
5. Erase 8 tiles from each side.
6. **Say:** On the left is the *x* tile, and on the right are still six 1 tiles. So $x = 6$.

KEY TEACHING POINTS

Example 4

Say: To solve a subtraction equation, add to remove the constant.

Write the following on the board: $k - 7 = 12$.

Say: You can use inverse operations to find the value of *k*.

Ask: What is the inverse operation of subtraction? **[Addition]** What do you do to both sides of the equation? **[Add 7]**

Show the work on the board.

Say: The solution is $k = 19$. It is the same result as using the related fact $12 + 7 = 19$.

KEY TEACHING POINTS

Example 5

Write the following on the board: $4q = 20$.

Say: There is no operation symbol between the 4, the coefficient, and *q*, the variable. When there is no operation symbol, it means to multiply. To solve a multiplication equation, you can divide by the coefficient.

Ask: What is the inverse operation of multiplication? **[Division]** What do you do to both sides of the equation? **[Divide by 4]**

Show the work on the board.

Say: The solution is $q = 5$. It is the same result as using the related fact $20 \div 4 = 5$.

Write $-4r = 24$ on the board.

Say: This problem involves a negative integer, but the step is the same.

Ask: What do you need to do to isolate the variable? **[Divide by –4]**

Show the work on the board.

Say: There is one negative factor, and the product is positive.

Ask: Will the unknown factor be positive or negative? **[Negative]** Why? **[Two negative factors result in a positive factor.]**

Example 6

Write $\frac{2}{3}v = 12$ on the board.

Ask: What do you need to do to isolate the variable? **[Divide both sides by $\frac{2}{3}$.]** How do you divide by a fraction? **[Multiply by the reciprocal of the divisor.]**

Say: When solving a multiplication equation involving a fraction coefficient, multiply both sides of the equation by the reciprocal of the coefficient.

Ask: What is the reciprocal of $\frac{2}{3}$? **[$\frac{3}{2}$]**

Show the work on the board and give the solution $v = 18$.

Write $0.3w = 2.4$ on the board.

Say: To find the value of *w*, you can divide both sides by 0.3. This gives $2.4 \div 0.3$ on the right side of the equation. To divide decimals, it is helpful to multiply the dividend and divisor by a power of 10 that makes the divisor a whole number.

Ask: The divisor is in tenths, so what power of 10 should you multiply both the divisor and dividend by? **[10]** What is the equivalent equation after multiplying by 10? **[$3w = 24$]**

Say: The solution is $w = 8$.

KEY TEACHING POINTS

Example 7
Review with students that a fraction is another way to express division.

Write $\frac{a}{4} = 3$ on the board.

Ask: What is the inverse operation of division? **[Multiplication]** How do you isolate the variable? **[Multiply by the reciprocal of the fraction.]**

Say: After multiplying both sides by 4, the solution for *a* is 12.

Write $\frac{b}{-9} = 4$ on the board.

Say: There is a negative denominator and a positive quotient.

Ask: Is the numerator, *b*, positive or negative? **[Negative]** Why? **[To have a positive quotient, the dividend and divisor or numerator and denominator must have the same sign.]**

Check
Check to see if students notice that they multiply the denominator of the fraction times the integer on the other side of the equation to find the value of the variable.

Example 8
Say: Let's put writing and solving an equation together to solve a word problem.

Ask: What do you know? **[Sophie buys 5 identical packages of balloons. There are a total of 375 balloons.]**

Ask: What do you need to find? **[How many balloons are in each package?]**

Say: Let *b* represent the number of balloons in each package.

Ask: What equation can you write? **[5*b* = 375]** What do you need to do to isolate the variable? **[Divide both sides by 5.]** How many balloons are in each package? **[75]**

ADDITIONAL ONLINE INTERVENTION RESOURCES

Use the following for students who have not mastered the concepts in Skill 13.

- Math on the Spot videos
- Personal Math Trainer with customized intervention
- Building Block worksheets (Skill 19: Combine Like Terms; Skill 22: Connect Words and Algebra; Skill 23: Connect Words and Equations; Skill 27: Evaluate Expressions; Skill 81: Simplify Algebraic Expressions; Skill 92: Solve Multiplication Equations; Skill 93: Solve One-Step Equations)

Name ______________________ Date ______________ Class ______________

SKILL 13

One-Step Equations

Example 1

You can write an equation to represent a situation.

The sum of a number and 8 is equal to 14.

$n + 8 = 14$

The difference of 16 and a number is equal to 7.

$16 - n = 7$

Eight equal groups have 48 members.

$8g = 48$

Six is equal to the quotient of 12 and a number.

$6 = 12 \div n$

Vocabulary
Equation
Inverse operations
Solution
Constant
Coefficient
Reciprocal
Power of 10

Check

Write an equation to represent each situation.

1. A number and 9 is equal to 13. ______________

2. The product of 7 and a number is equal to 35. ______________

3. Four is equal to a number split into 8 equal parts. ______________

4. Nine less than a number is equal to 5. ______________

5. What's the Error? Jimmy said that the only way to write an equation for "Eight equal groups have 48 members" is as the multiplication equation $8g = 48$. What is the error in Jimmy's thinking?

____

Example 2

Equations represent real-world situations, too.
Maria bought a sweater for \$24 and a pair of leggings. The total cost was \$40. Write an equation to represent the cost of the leggings.

Let l represent the cost of the leggings.

Addition is used to join groups. $24 + l = 40$

The equation $24 + l = 40$ represents the situation.

Name ______________________ Date ______________ Class ______________

Check

Write an equation to represent each situation. Tell what your variable represents.

6. There are 5 players on each basketball team. There are 40 players in all. How many teams are there?

____

7. A jacket regularly costs \$72. Today it is on sale for \$12 less. What is the sale price of the jacket?

____

Example 3

Addition and subtraction are inverse operations. Use subtraction to find the solution to an addition equation.

$3 + b = 9$

$3 - 3 + b = 9 - 3$

$b = 6$

Subtract the constant from both sides of the equation.

$c + 0.8 = 2.4$

$c + 0.8 - 0.8 = 2.4 - 0.8$

$c = 1.6$

Check

Solve each equation.

8. $d + 8 = 14$ ____________

9. $0.75 + e = 1.4$ ____________

10. $\frac{3}{5} + f = 1\frac{2}{5}$ ____________

Example 4

Use addition to find the solution to a subtraction equation.

$k - 7 = 12$

$k - 7 + 7 = 12 + 7$

$k = 19$

Add the constant to both sides of the equation.

$l - \frac{5}{8} = 1\frac{7}{8}$

$l - \frac{5}{8} + \frac{5}{8} = 1\frac{7}{8} + \frac{5}{8}$

$l = 1\frac{12}{8} = 2\frac{1}{2}$

Name ______________________ Date ____________ Class ____________

Check

Solve each equation.

11. $m - 5 = 8$ ______________

12. $n - 0.7 = 1.4$ ______________

13. $p - \frac{3}{8} = \frac{1}{2}$ ______________

Example 5

Use division to find the solution to a multiplication equation.

$$4q = 20$$
$$\frac{4q}{4} = \frac{20}{4}$$
$$q = 5$$

Divide both sides of the equation by the coefficient.

$$-4r = 24$$
$$\frac{-4r}{-4} = \frac{24}{-4}$$
$$r = -6$$

Check the integer signs.

Check

Solve each equation.

14. $5s = 45$ ______________

15. $12t = 180$ ______________

16. $-7u = -49$ ______________

Example 6

You can solve multiplication equations involving fractions and decimals.

$$\frac{2}{3}v = 12$$
$$\frac{2}{3}v \div \frac{2}{3} = 12 \div \frac{2}{3}$$
$$\frac{2}{3}v\left(\frac{3}{2}\right) = 12\left(\frac{3}{2}\right)$$
$$v = 18$$

Divide a fraction by multiplying by its reciprocal.

$$0.3w = 2.4$$
$$0.3w(10) = 2.4(10)$$
$$3w = 24$$
$$\frac{3w}{3} = \frac{24}{3}$$
$$w = 8$$

Multiply both sides of the equation by an appropriate power of 10.

Check

Solve each equation.

17. $0.6x = 4.2$ ______________

18. $\frac{5}{8}y = 16$ ______________

19. $\frac{3}{4}z = \frac{2}{5}$ ______________

Name ______________________ Date ____________ Class ____________

Example 7

Use multiplication to find the solution to a division equation.

$\frac{a}{4} = 3$

$\frac{a}{4}(4) = 3(4)$

$a = 12$

Divide a fraction by multiplying the reciprocal of the divisor.

$\frac{b}{-9} = 4$

$\frac{b}{-9}(-9) = 4(-9)$

$b = -36$

Check

Solve each equation.

20. $\frac{c}{5} = 6$ ____________
21. $\frac{d}{-4} = 2$ ____________
22. $\frac{e}{-3} = -5$ ____________

Example 8

You can solve real-world problems by writing and solving an equation.
Sophie buys 5 identical packages of balloons. There are a total of 375 balloons. What is the number of balloons in each package?

Write an equation. $5b = 375$
Let b represent the number of balloons in each package.

Solve. $\frac{5b}{5} = \frac{375}{5}$

$b = 75$

There are 75 balloons in each package.

Write an equation and solve.

23. The Terriers and Wolves scored 92 points in all. The Terriers scored 56 points. How many points did the Wolves score?

____

24. There are 48 students participating in a debating tournament. Each team has 3 students. How many debating teams are there?

____

SKILL 13 ONE-STEP EQUATIONS

SKILL 14

One-Step Inequalities

KEY TEACHING POINTS

Example 1

Say: An inequality is a mathematical statement that shows that two quantities are not equal.

Write the symbols $>$ and $<$ on the board.

Say: The phrase less than means to use $<$. The phrase greater than means to use $>$.

Write the symbols $\geq$ and $\leq$ on the board.

Say: The symbol $\geq$ means is greater than or equal to. This means the number is part of the solution set. For example in $3n \geq 21$, the value that we solve for n is part of the solution set.

Say: The symbol $\leq$ means is less than or equal to. This also means that the number is part of the solution set. For example in $\frac{n}{4} \leq 6$, the value that we solve for n is part of the solution set.

Check

Ask students to name the word that tells which operation to use in each of the problems.

Example 2

Review with students that inverse operations are operations that undo each other. Addition and subtraction are inverse operations. Multiplication and division are inverse operations.

Write $8 + x \leq 14$ on the board.

Say: You can use inverse operations to find the value of x.

Ask: What is the inverse operation of addition? **[Subtraction]** What do you do to both sides of the inequality? **[Subtract 8]**

Show the work on the board.

Say: The solution set is $x \leq 6$, which includes 6 and every number less than 6.

ALTERNATE STRATEGY

Strategy: Solve an inequality like an equation by using an is-equal-to symbol.

1. Write $a + 9 > 17$ and $a + 9 = 17$ on the board.
2. **Say:** Solving an inequality and solving an equation involve the same steps, so let's turn this inequality to an equation.
3. **Ask:** What is the first step to solving this equation? **[Subtract 9]** What is the first step to solving this inequality? **[Subtract 9]**
4. **Ask:** In the equation, what is the value of a? **[8]** In the inequality, what is the solution set for a? **[any number greater than 8]**
5. **Say:** As you can see, the only difference is the inequality symbol instead of =.

KEY TEACHING POINTS

Example 3

Say: To solve a subtraction inequality, add to remove the constant.

Write $x - 7 \geq 5$ on the board.

Say: You can use inverse operations to find the value of x.

Ask: What is the inverse operation of subtraction? **[Addition]** What do you do to both sides of the equation? **[Add 7]**

Show the work on the board.

Say: The solution is $x \geq 12$.

COMMON MISCONCEPTION

Ask: What is Colin's error in solving the inequality $x - 4.2 \geq 5.5$ as $x \geq 1.3$?

Reason incorrect: Colin did not use inverse operations. He subtracted 4.2 from both sides of the inequality instead of adding 4.2.

Solution: $x \geq 9.7$

KEY TEACHING POINTS

Example 4

Write the following on the board: $3x \geq 15$.

Say: There is no operation symbol between 3, the coefficient, and x, the variable. When there is no operational symbol, it means to multiply. To solve a multiplication inequality, you can divide by the coefficient.

Ask: What is the inverse operation of multiplication? **[Division]** What do you do to both sides of the inequality? **[Divide by 3]**

Show the work on the board.

Say: The solution set is $x \geq 5$. The inequality symbol remains the same.

Write $0.4x \geq 12$ on the board.

Say: In a multiplication inequality involving a decimal, multiply both sides of the inequality by a power of 10, so the coefficient is a whole number.

Ask: Which power of 10 can we multiply so the coefficient is a whole number? **[10]**

Show the work on the board.

Say: Now we have the inequality $4x \geq 120$.

Ask: What is the step needed to find the solution set? **[Divide both sides by 4]** What is the solution set? **[$x \geq 30$]**

KEY TEACHING POINTS

Example 5

Write $\frac{x}{4} < 2$ on the board.

Ask: What is the inverse operation of division? **[Multiplication]** How do you isolate the variable? **[Multiply by the reciprocal of the fraction]**

Show the work on the board and give the solution $x < 8$.

Write $\frac{x}{6} \geq -3$ on the board.

Say: There is a negative integer on one side of the inequality. If the negative number is on the opposite side of the inequality than the variable, proceed as if there were no negative numbers.

Ask: How do you isolate the variable? **[Multiply by the reciprocal of the fraction]**

Show the work on the board and give the solution $x \geq -18$.

Check

Encourage students to check their solution sets by putting their solution into the original inequality.

Example 6

Write $-3x < 12$ on the board.

Say: There is a negative coefficient. This will come into play later.

Ask: What is the first step to isolating the variable? **[Divide both sides by −3.]**

Say: When both sides are divided by −3, we find that $x < -4$. Let's check to see if that is true. If x is less than −4, let's try −5.

Ask: What is −3 times −5? **[15]** Is 15 less than 12? **[No]**

Say: When you multiply or divide both sides by a negative number in an inequality, it is necessary to reverse the inequality symbol in the solution.

Write $x > -4$ on the board.

Say: Now let's check to see if that is true. If x is greater than −4, let's try −3.

Ask: What is −3 times −3? **[9]** Is 9 less than 12? **[Yes]**

Check

Make sure students understand that they need to reverse the inequality symbol in the solution when the negative sign is on the side of the inequality with the variable. Also note in Problem 17 that $\frac{p}{-3} < 5$ can also be written as $-\frac{p}{3} < 5$.

KEY TEACHING POINTS

Example 7
Say: Let's put together writing and solving an inequality to solve a word problem.

Ask: What do you know? **[Anna needs to score at least 275 points in all. She has already scored 128 points.]**

Ask: What do you need to find? **[The least number of points she needs to score in the second game]**

Say: Let p represent the least number of points that Anna needs to score in the second game.

Ask: What inequality can you write? **[$128 + p \geq 275$]** What made you choose greater than or equal to? **[Anna needs to score at least 275 points. She can score more than 275 points.]** What do you need to do to isolate the variable? **[Subtract 128 from both sides.]** What are the least number of points Anna can score to win the tournament? **[147]**

Check
Encourage students to look for a word or phrase that tells them which operation to use.

Example 8
Say: A number line can be used to represent the solution set of an inequality.

Say: Look at the number lines for $x > 3$ and $x < 3$. An open circle is used to show that the number is not part of the solution set.

Ask: For greater than, which way does the ray point? **[right]** Why? **[Because every number to the right of 3 is greater than 3.]** For less than, which way does the ray point? **[left]** Why **[Because every number to the left of 3 is less than 3.]**

Say: Look at the number lines for $x \geq 3$ and $x \leq 3$. A closed circle is used to show that the number is part of the solution set.

Ask: If you were to graph the solution to $x + 4 \leq 2$, would you use an open circle or a closed circle on the number line? **[closed circle]** Why? **[2 is part of the solution set.]**

Check
Make sure students understand when to use an open circle and when to use a closed circle.

ADDITIONAL ONLINE INTERVENTION RESOURCES

Use the following for students who have not mastered the concepts in Skill 14.

- Math on the Spot videos
- Personal Math Trainer with customized intervention
- Building Block worksheets (Skill 52: Inverse Operations)

Name ______________________ Date ______________ Class ______________

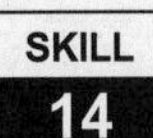

One-Step Inequalities

SKILL 14

Example 1

You can write a one-step **inequality** to represent a situation.

A number and 5 is less than 9. $n + 5 < 9$	6 less than a number is greater than 10. $n - 6 > 10$
3 times a number is greater than or equal to 21. $3n \geq 21$	A number split into 4 equal parts is less than or equal to 6. $\frac{n}{4} \leq 6$

Vocabulary
- Inequality
- Inverse operations
- Solution set
- Constant
- Coefficient
- Power of 10
- Reciprocal

Check

Write an inequality to represent each situation.

1. A number and 7 is greater than 12. ______________

2. A number split into 2 equal parts is less than 4. ______________

Example 2

Addition and subtraction are **inverse operations**. Use subtraction to find the **solution set** to an addition inequality.

$$8 + x \leq 14$$
$$8 - 8 + x \leq 14 - 8$$
$$x \leq 6$$

Subtract the **constant** from both sides of the inequality.

$$0.9 + x > 2.7$$
$$0.9 - 0.9 + x > 2.7 - 0.9$$
$$x > 1.8$$

Solve an inequality like you would an equation.

Check

Solve each inequality.

3. $a + 9 > 17$ ______________

4. $-3 + b < -9$ ______________

5. $\frac{3}{4} + c \leq 1\frac{2}{5}$ ______________

Name ______________________ Date ____________ Class ____________

Example 3

Use addition to find the solution to a subtraction inequality.

$x - 7 \geq 5$ $x - 7 + 7 \geq 5 + 7$ $x \geq 12$	Add the constant to both sides of the inequality.	$x - \frac{1}{3} < \frac{3}{4}$ $x - \frac{1}{3} + \frac{1}{3} < \frac{3}{4} + \frac{1}{3}$ $x < 1\frac{1}{12}$

Check

Solve each inequality.

6. $d - 4 > 6$ ______________

7. $e - 0.28 < 0.75$ ______________

8. $f - \frac{4}{5} \geq \frac{3}{10}$ ______________

9. What's the Error? Colin was given the inequality $x - 4.2 \geq 5.5$ to solve. He said the solution set was $x \geq 1.3$. Describe Colin's error and give the correct solution set in your explanation.

____

Example 4

Use division to find the solution to a multiplication inequality.

$3x \geq 15$ $\frac{3x}{3} \geq \frac{15}{3}$ $x \geq 5$	Divide both sides of the inequality by the coefficient.	$0.4x \geq 12$ $4x \geq 120$ $\frac{4x}{4} \geq \frac{120}{4}$ $x \geq 30$	Multiply both sides of the inequality by an appropriate power of 10.

Check

Solve each inequality.

10. $3g > 36$ ______________

11. $0.5h < 24$ ______________

12. $4j \geq -12$ ______________

Name ______________________ Date ______________ Class______________

Example 5

Use multiplication to find the solution to a division equation.

$\frac{x}{4} < 2$

$\frac{x}{4}(4) < 2(4)$

$x < 8$

Divide by a fraction by multiplying by its reciprocal.

$\frac{x}{6} \geq -3$

$\frac{x}{6}(6) \geq -3(6)$

$x \geq -18$

Check

Solve each inequality.

13. $\frac{k}{3} \geq 4$ ______________

14. $\frac{l}{6} < 0.2$ ______________

15. $\frac{m}{5} > -6$ ______________

Example 6

If the variable in a multiplication or division inequality is negative, it is necessary to reverse the inequality symbol in the solution.

$-3x < 12$

$\frac{-3x}{-3} < \frac{12}{-3}$

$x > -4$

The inequality symbol reverses.

$\frac{x}{-2} \geq -4$

$\frac{x}{-2}(-2) \geq -4(-2)$

$x \leq -8$

The inequality symbol reverses.

Check

Solve each inequality.

16. $-4n \geq 20$ ______________

17. $\frac{p}{-3} < 5$ ______________

18. $-\frac{q}{8} > -4$ ______________

Example 7

Anna is in a tournament. She needs to score at least 275 points in her two rounds to win. She scored 128 points in her first round. What is the least number of points she needs to score to win the tournament?

Write an inequality. $128 + p \geq 275$

Solve. $128 - 128 + p \geq 275 - 128$

$p \geq 147$

Anna needs to score at least 147 points to win the tournament.

Name ______________________ Date ______________ Class ______________

Check

Write an inequality to represent each situation. Then solve your inequality.

19. Mark had 8 models. He bought some additional models and now he has more than 15 models. How many models did Mark buy?

____

20. The temperature dropped at least 10 °F. The temperature dropped 2 °F each hour. How many hours did the temperature drop?

____

Example 8

You can graph the solution set to an inequality.

$x > 3$

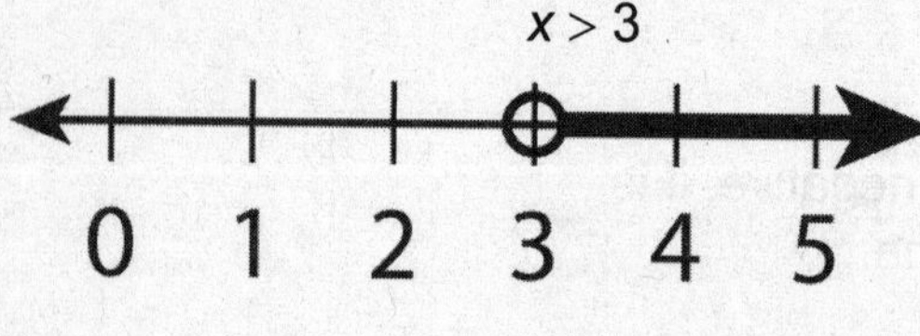

$x < 3$

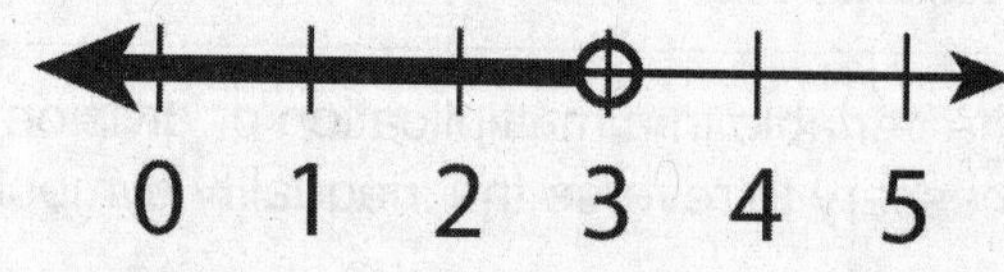

$x \geq 3$

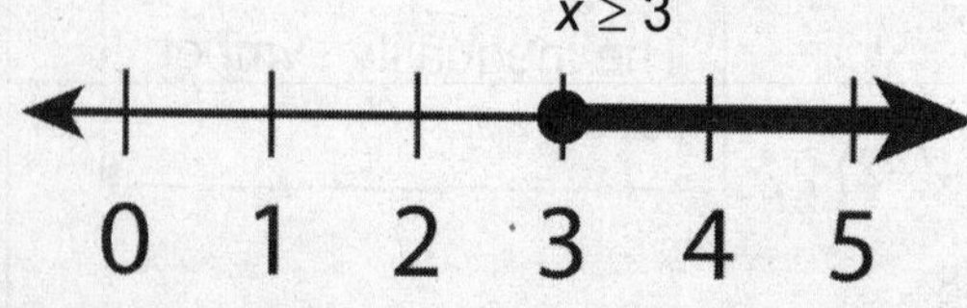

$x \leq 3$

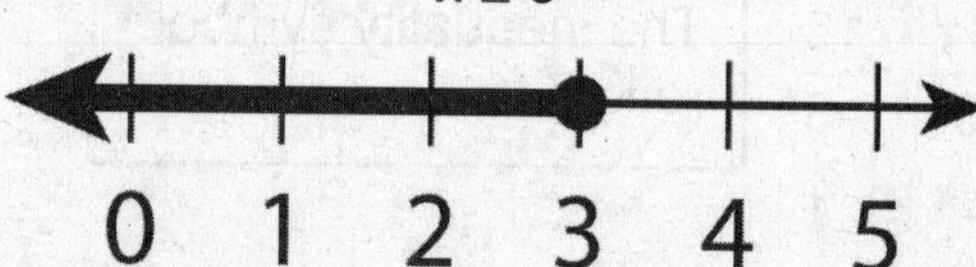

Solve each inequality. Graph the solution.

21. $-2 + r \geq 2$ ______________

−5 −4 −3 −2 −1 0 1 2 3 4 5

22. $2s < -8$ ______________

−5 −4 −3 −2 −1 0 1 2 3 4 5

SKILL 14 ONE-STEP INEQUALITIES

SKILL 15

Percent

KEY TEACHING POINTS

Example 1

Say: Sales tax is a percent of the cost of an item that is charged by a government—usually state or city—to raise money. Cities, counties, and states often charge sales taxes.

Say: When solving application problems with percents, you have to rename the percent. Most of the time, it is helpful to rename the percent as a decimal, but there are other times when renaming the percent as a fraction is more helpful. It is most helpful to rename the percent as a fraction if the percent is equivalent to a unit fraction.

Ask: To find the total cost of the movie ticket, what do you need to do? **[Find the sales tax and add it to the cost of the ticket.]**

Say: Seven percent is equivalent to the decimal 0.07.

Ask: What do you need to do to find the sales tax? **[Multiply $12(0.07)]** What is $12(0.07)? **[$0.84]** What is the total cost of the movie ticket? **[$12.84]**

Example 2

Say: You have probably bought items that were on sale. Sometimes the discount is a flat amount like $5 off and other times it is a percent of the cost of the item.

Ask: Why do people want to buy items that are on sale? **[They are less expensive.]**

Say: The sale price is the cost of an item after the discount has been applied.

Say: The dress Este wants to buy normally costs $60. It is on sale for 30% off.

Ask: Will Este spend more or less than $60? **[less than]** How much less money will Este pay for the dress? **[$18]** How much will Este pay for the dress? **[$42]**

ALTERNATE STRATEGY

Strategy: Find a sale price by finding the percent of the cost that someone will pay.

1. **Say:** Look at Problem 3.
2. **Ask:** If you receive a 15% discount, what percent of the item will you pay? **[85%]** Why 85%? **[The full cost is 100%.]**
3. **Ask:** How can you find the sale price? **[Multiply $90(0.85)]** What is the sale price? **[$76.50]**

KEY TEACHING POINTS

Example 3

Say: The percent decrease is the percent of the sale or a markdown. To find the percent decrease, divide the difference of the markdown price from the original price by the original price. This also works for numbers not involving money.

Write on the board: Percent decrease $= \frac{\text{original amount} - \text{new amount}}{\text{original amount}}$

Ask: How much money did Dave save on the sneakers? **[$15]** How can you find the percent decrease once you know the difference between the costs? **[Divide the difference of the costs by the original cost]** What do we divide? **[15 ÷ 75]**

Ask: What is 15 ÷ 75? **[$\frac{1}{5}$ or 0.2]** What percent is equivalent to $\frac{1}{5}$? **[20%]**

Say: The percent discount on the sneakers is 20%.

Example 4

Say: Businesses earn money by producing items that cost one price and then selling those items for a greater price. This is a markup or percent increase. This also works for numbers that do not involve money.

Say: To find the percent increase, divide the difference of the original amount from the new amount by the original amount.

Write on the board: Percent increase $= \frac{\text{new amount} - \text{original amount}}{\text{original amount}}$

Ask: What is the original cost to Teo's per T-shirt? **[$4]** How much does Teo's sell each T-shirt? **[$12]** What is the difference between the price that Teo's sells its T-shirts for and the amount it costs Teo's to produce the T-shirt? **[$8]**

Ask: What is the markup? **[200%]**

Say: You may notice the price that Teo's sells its T-shirts for is 3 times the cost, but the markup is 2 times.

COMMON MISCONCEPTION

Ask: What is Tonya's error in saying that the percent increase from 25 to 40 is 37.5%?

Reason incorrect: Tonya used the new amount for the denominator in the fraction instead of the original amount.

Solution: Percent increase $= \frac{40 - 25}{25} = \frac{15}{25} = 60\%$

KEY TEACHING POINTS

Example 5

Say: Simple interest is a percent that is added to the principal. Principal could be money that is deposited into an account or the amount that is owed in a loan.

Write $I = prt$ on the board.

Say: The formula $I = prt$ is used to find simple interest. I represents the simple interest, p represents the principal, r represents the rate of interest, and t represents the time in years. It is particularly important to pay attention to the time that is given.

Ask: What is Nikki's principal? **[$800]** What is the interest rate? **[2.5% annually]** What is the time? **[18 months]**

Say: We can substitute $800 for p.

Ask: What do we substitute for r? **[0.025]** What do we substitute for t? **[1.5]** Why is 1.5 used instead of 18? **[18 months = 1.5 years]**

Say: Because the simple interest is annually, the time needs to be in years. There are 12 months in a year and 18 ÷ 12 = 1.5.

Substitute the numbers into the formula. Show the work on the board.

Say: Nikki will earn $30 in simple interest in 18 months.

Check

Make sure students understand that the rate should be written as a decimal and the time should be written in terms of years not months.

COMMON MISCONCEPTION

Ask: What is Mary's error in saying that she will earn $120 in simple interest with an account that has $500 earning 4% annual simple interest in 6 months?

Reason incorrect: The interest is annual simple interest. Mary used 6 instead of 0.5 to represent 6 months for the time.

Solution: Mary earned $10 in simple interest.

Simple interest = $500(0.04)(0.5) = $10

KEY TEACHING POINTS

Example 6

Discuss with students that items that are on sale have a percent off the normal price, but then sales tax also needs to be added to the sale price. Another example is eating at a restaurant where sales tax is added to the bill and then it is up to the customer whether to include the sales tax in computing the tip.

Ask: What do you know? **[The MP3 player normally costs $250. It is on sale for 30% off. The sales tax is 6%.]** What do you need to find out? **[The cost after the discount and sales price have been applied]**

Say: Let's find the discount first.

Ask: If the MP3 player is 30% off, what percent of the price will Frank have to pay? **[70%]**

Ask: What is $250(0.7)? **[$175]**

Say: The sale price is $175. The sales tax will be applied on a cost of $175.

Ask: What is $175(0.06)? **[$10.50]** How do you find the total cost of the MP3 player? **[Add the sales tax to the sale price.]** What is the cost to Frank? **[$185.50]**

Check

Students should know that they pay the sales tax on the sale price. Make sure that students do not add the percent of the sales tax to the percent of the discount.

ALTERNATE STRATEGY

Strategy: Streamline finding sales tax by adding before multiplying.

1. **Say:** Sales tax is computed after the cost has been determined whether it is the normal price or the sale price. You can add the percent of sales tax to 100% and then multiply saving a step.
2. **Ask:** If you know the cost with a 6% sales tax, by what number do you multiply to compute the total cost? **[1.06]**
3. **Say:** Look at Problem 14.
4. **Ask:** Once you determine the sale price, by what number can you multiply to find the total cost? **[1.08]**

ADDITIONAL ONLINE INTERVENTION RESOURCES

Use the following for students who have not mastered the concepts in Skill 15.

- Math on the Spot videos
- Personal Math Trainer with customized intervention
- Building Block worksheets (Skill 37: Find the Percent of a Number; Skill 39: Fractions, Decimals, and Percents; Skill 72: Percents and Decimals)

Name ______________________ Date ______________ Class______________

SKILL 15

Percent

Example 1

Sales tax is a percent added to the cost of an item.

A movie ticket costs $12 with 7% sales tax added on. What is the total cost of the movie ticket?

Rename 7% as a decimal.	7% = 0.07
Multiply to find the sales tax.	$12(0.07) = $0.84
Add the sales tax to the cost.	$12 + $0.84 = $12.84

100% = 1

The total cost of the movie ticket was $12.84.

Vocabulary
- Sales tax
- Percent
- Discount
- Sale price
- Percent decrease
- Retail price
- Markup
- Percent increase
- Simple interest
- Principal

Check

Find the cost after the sales tax is applied.

1. Cost: $80; Sales Tax: 6% ______________________

2. Cost: $250; Sales Tax: 8% ______________________

Example 2

Shoppers often look for discounts. The sale price is the actual cost after the discount has been applied.

The dress that Este wants to buy normally costs $60. The dress is discounted at 30% off. What is the sale price of the dress?

Rename 30% as a decimal.	30% = 0.3
Multiply to find the discount.	$60(0.3) = $18
Subtract to find the sale price.	$60 – $18 = $42

30% off is the same as paying for 70% of the cost.

The sale price of the dress is $42.

Check

Find the sale price.

3. Cost: $90; Discount: 15% ______________________

4. Cost: $150; Discount: 40% ______________________

Name ______________________ Date ______________ Class ______________

Example 3

To find the discount or percent decrease, use the following formula:

$$\text{Percent decrease} = \frac{\text{original amount} - \text{new amount}}{\text{original amount}}$$

Dave bought a pair of sneakers for a sale price of $60. The price tag on the box of the sneakers was $75. What was the discount?

Substitute the numbers into the formula. $\frac{75-60}{75} = \frac{15}{75} = \frac{1}{5}$

Rename as a percent. $\frac{1}{5} = 20\%$

The discount is 20%.

Check

Find the percent decrease.

5. Original Price: $40; Sale Price: $30

____

6. Original Price: $90; Sale Price: $58.50

____

Example 4

Businesses buy or produce products at one price and sell them for a greater price, the retail price. This is known as a markup or a percent increase.

$$\text{Percent increase} = \frac{\text{new amount} - \text{original amount}}{\text{original amount}}$$

It costs Teo's Tees $4 for each T-shirt it produces. Teo's sells the T-shirts for $12 each. What is the percent increase?

Substitute the numbers into the formula. $\frac{12-4}{4} = \frac{8}{4} = 2$

Rename as a percent. $2 = 200\%$

The percent increase is 200%.

Name ______________________ Date ____________ Class ____________

Check

Find the percent of increase.

7. Original Price: $60; Retail Price: $84

____

8. Original Price: $135; Retail Price: $162

____

9. What's the Error? Tonya said the percent increase from 25 to 40 is 37.5%. Describe Tonya's error and give the correct percent increase.

____

Example 5

Simple interest is a percent that is added to the principal. Use the formula $I = prt$, where p represents principal, r represents the rate, and t represents the time to find simple interest.

Nikki deposits $800 into a savings account that earns 2.5% annual simple interest. If she does not make any deposits or withdrawals for 18 months, how much simple interest will she earn?

Convert 18 months to years.	18 months = 1.5 years
Rename 2.5% as a decimal.	2.5% = 0.025
Substitute the values into the formula.	$I = 800(0.025)(1.5) = 30$

Nikki will earn $30 simple interest.

Check

Find the simple interest earned.

10. Principal: $450; Rate: 3% annual simple interest; Time: 2 years

____

11. Principal: $1200; Rate: 15% annual simple interest; Time: 9 months

____

12. What's the Error? Mary has an account with $500. She earns a rate of 4% annual simple interest. She has the money in the account for 6 months without making any deposits or withdrawals. Mary said she would earn $120 in simple interest. Describe Mary's error and give the correct amount of simple interest that she actually earned.

____

Name ______________________ Date ______________ Class ______________

Example 6

Shoppers often have two percents to compute: a sale price and the sales tax. To find the sale price and sales tax combination, follow these steps:

1. Find the sale price.
2. Compute the sales tax from the sale price.

The MP3 player that Frank wants to buy costs \$250. It is on sale at 30% off. The sales tax is 6%. How much will Frank pay for the MP3 player?

Find the percent that Frank will pay.	100% − 30% = 70%
Find the sale price.	\$250(0.7) = \$175
Find the sales tax.	\$175(0.06) = \$10.50
Add the sales tax to the sale price.	\$175 + \$10.50 = \$185.50

100% = original cost

Frank will pay \$185.50 for the MP3 player.

Check

Find the actual cost.

13. Original Cost: \$50; Discount: 40%; Sales Tax 6%

____

14. Original Cost: \$120; Discount: 35%; Sales Tax 8%

____

SKILL 15 PERCENT

SKILL 16

Real Numbers

KEY TEACHING POINTS

Example 1

Say: A number that can be written in the form of $\frac{a}{b}$, where a and b are integers and $b \neq 0$ is a rational number.

Write $\frac{0}{3}$ and $\frac{3}{0}$ on the board.

Say: The fraction $\frac{0}{3}$ is a rational number because the denominator is not 0. The fraction $\frac{3}{0}$ is not a rational number because the denominator is 0. Remember, you cannot divide by 0.

Say: Any rational number can be written as a decimal. To express a fraction as a decimal, you can divide the numerator by the denominator. The decimal for $\frac{4}{5}$ will terminate. The decimal for $\frac{1}{3}$ will repeat.

Check

Make sure students divide the numerator by the denominator or find an equivalent fraction using a power of 10 as the denominator.

ALTERNATE STRATEGY

Strategy: Write an equivalent fraction to express a fraction as a decimal.

1. **Say:** Look at Problem 1.
2. **Ask:** Is 4 a factor of 10? **[No]** Is 4 a factor of 100? **[Yes]** What number times 4 is equal to 100? **[25]**
3. **Say:** If we multiply the denominator by 25, we also multiply the numerator by 25. So $\frac{3}{4} = \frac{75}{100}$. Because $\frac{75}{100}$ is read seventy-five hundredths like 0.75, $\frac{75}{100} = 0.75$.
4. Have students look for the other denominator in the set that is a factor of 100. **[20]**

KEY TEACHING POINTS

Example 2

Say: Use the least decimal place to determine the denominator when expressing a decimal as a fraction. For 0.775, the least decimal place is thousandths, so then write the decimal 775 as the numerator and 1000 as the denominator.

Ask: To write $\frac{775}{1000}$ in simplest form, what number can you divide the numerator and denominator by? **[25]**

Say: We can divide by 25, which is the greatest common factor of 775 and 1000 to get $\frac{31}{40}$.

Say: Expressing a repeating decimal as a fraction is a little more challenging. To write $0.\overline{7}$ as a fraction, write an equation $x = 0.\overline{7}$. The next step is to make the value of the nonvariable side of the equation a number greater than 1. We can multiply both sides by 10 to get $10x = 7.\overline{7}$.

Say: Because $x = 0.\overline{7}$, we can now subtract x from one side of the equation and $0.\overline{7}$ from the other side of the equation. This results in $10x - x = 9x$ and $7.\overline{7} - 0.\overline{7} = 7$ or $9x = 7$.

Ask: What is the value of x? $\left[\frac{7}{9}\right]$ What fraction is equivalent to $0.\overline{7}$? $\left[\frac{7}{9}\right]$

Check

Make sure students understand that to express a repeating decimal as a fraction, they need to multiply by the power of 10 that is the reciprocal of the least place in the decimal before it repeats.

COMMON MISCONCEPTION

Ask: What is George's error in saying that $0.8\overline{3} = \frac{83}{100}$?

Reason incorrect: George did not account for the decimal repeating.

Solution:

$$\begin{aligned} x &= 0.8\overline{3} \\ 100x &= 83.\overline{3} \\ 99x &= 82.5 \\ 198x &= 165 \\ x &= \frac{165}{198} \\ x &= \frac{5}{6} \end{aligned}$$

KEY TEACHING POINTS

Example 3

Say: A square root of a positive number *p* is *x* if $x^2 = p$. For example, 8 is the square root of 64 because $8^2 = 64$. Each positive number has two square roots because a negative number times itself is equal to a positive number. So, $(-8)^2 = 64$.

Say: The product of an integer times itself is called a perfect square. So, 64 is a perfect square.

Ask: What are some other perfect squares? **[Answers include 1, 4, 9, 16 and so on.]**

Write $\sqrt{64}$ on the board.

Say: When the radical is written with a square root, it implies the primary square root and the positive square root.

Check

Tell students that to find the square root of a fraction, find the square root of the numerator and then the square root of the denominator.

Example 4

Say: A cube root of a positive number *p* is *x* if $x^3 = p$. For example, 5 is the cube root of 125 because $5^3 = 125$. The product of an integer times itself twice is called a perfect cube. So, 125 is a perfect cube.

Ask: What are some other perfect cubes? **[Answers include 1, 8, 27, 64 and so on]**

Say: To find the cube root of a fraction, find the cube root of the numerator and then the cube root of the denominator.

Check

Tell students that it may be necessary to write the equation in simplest form.

Example 5

Say: Irrational numbers are numbers that cannot be written in the form $\frac{a}{b}$, where *a* and *b* are integers and $b \neq 0$. This set includes most square roots and cube roots.

Say: A square root can be approximated without the use of a calculator by placing the square root between two perfect squares. For example, $\sqrt{5}$ is between perfect squares 4 and 9, which are equivalent to 2 and 3. So, $\sqrt{5}$ is between 2 and 3.

Ask: Is 5 closer to 4 or 9? **[4]** What decimals to tenths do you think $\sqrt{5}$ is between? **[2.2 and 2.3]**

Say: We can multiply $2.2^2 = 4.84$ and $2.3^2 = 5.29$ to determine that $\sqrt{5}$ is between 2.2 and 2.3 and is closer to 2.2.

KEY TEACHING POINTS

Example 6

Say: The set of real numbers includes the sets of rational numbers and irrational numbers. A number cannot be both a rational number and an irrational number.

Ask: Are all whole numbers integers? **[Yes]** Are all integers whole numbers? **[No]** Why? **[Integers include whole numbers and their opposites, so the negative integers are not whole numbers.]** Are all integers rational numbers? **[Yes]**

Ask: Are there numbers that are not integers that are rational numbers? **[Decimals that repeat or terminate are also rational numbers.]** Why? **[Repeating and terminating decimals can be written as fractions with a denominator that is an integer that is not 0.]**

Write $\sqrt{4}$ and $\sqrt{5}$ on the board.

Ask: Is $\sqrt{4}$ a rational number or an irrational number? **[rational]** Why? **[$\sqrt{4} = 2$]** If $\sqrt{4} = 2$, is $\sqrt{4}$ an integer? **[Yes]** Is $\sqrt{4}$ a whole number? **[Yes]**

Ask: Is $\sqrt{5}$ a rational number or an irrational number? **[irrational]** Why? **[It cannot be written in the form $\frac{a}{b}$, where *a* and *b* are integers and $b \neq 0$.]**

Example 7

Say: To compare and order real numbers, write or approximate each number in the same form. Decimals usually work best.

Write 3.25, $\frac{11}{4}$, π, $\sqrt{8}$ on the board.

Ask: What mixed number is $\frac{11}{4}$ equivalent to? $\left[2\frac{3}{4}\right]$ What decimal is equivalent to $2\frac{3}{4}$? **[2.75]** What is the approximation for π? **[3.14]**

Ask: What perfect squares is $\sqrt{8}$ between? **[4 and 9]** What is the best approximation to one decimal place for $\sqrt{8}$? **[2.8]**

Say: All of the numbers have now been expressed as decimals. Order from least to greatest.

Ask: What is the order from least to greatest? **[$\frac{11}{4}$, $\sqrt{8}$, π, 3.25]**

ADDITIONAL ONLINE INTERVENTION RESOURCES

Use the following for students who have not mastered the concepts in Skill 16.

- Math on the Spot videos
- Personal Math Trainer with customized intervention
- Building Block worksheets (Skill 30: Exponents; Skill 38: Find the Square of a Number; Skill 76: Reading and Writing Exponents; Skill 109: Write a Mixed Number as an Improper Fraction)

Name ____________________ Date ____________ Class ____________

SKILL 16

Real Numbers

Example 1

A rational number is any number that can be written as a ratio in the form $\frac{a}{b}$, where a and b are integers and $b \neq 0$.

To express a fraction as a decimal, divide the numerator by the denominator.
The resulting decimal can be a terminating decimal or a repeating decimal.

Terminating Decimal	Repeating Decimal
$\frac{4}{5} = 0.8$ $5\overline{)4.0}$ quotient 0.8; -40; 0 The decimal terminates.	$\frac{1}{3} = 0.\overline{3}$ $3\overline{)1.0}$ quotient 0.3; -9; 1 The bar indicates the digit or digits that repeat.

Vocabulary

- Rational numbers
- Terminating decimals
- Repeating decimals
- Square roots
- Perfect squares
- Integers
- Cube roots
- Perfect cubes
- Irrational numbers
- Real numbers

Check

Write each fraction as a decimal.

1. $\frac{3}{4}$ __________ 2. $\frac{1}{6}$ __________ 3. $\frac{7}{15}$ __________ 4. $\frac{13}{20}$ __________

Example 2

Terminating and repeating decimals can be expressed as fractions.

0.775

$$\frac{775}{1000} \div \frac{25}{25} = \frac{31}{40}$$

$0.\overline{7}$

$$x = 0.\overline{7}$$
$$(10)x = (10)0.\overline{7}$$
$$10x = 7.\overline{7}$$
$$10x - x = 7.\overline{7} - 0.\overline{7}$$
$$9x = 7$$
$$x = \frac{7}{9}$$

Because $x = 0.\overline{7}$, you can subtract x from one side and $0.\overline{7}$ from the other.

Name ______________________ Date ______________ Class ______________

Check

Write each decimal as a fraction in simplest form.

5. 0.35 ________

6. $0.2\overline{6}$ ________

7. 0.425 ________

8. $0.\overline{63}$ ________

9. What's the Error? George said that $0.8\overline{3}$ is written as $\frac{83}{100}$ in simplest form.

Describe the error that George made and write $0.8\overline{3}$ as a fraction in simplest form.

____

Example 3

The **square root** of a positive number p is x if $x^2 = p$. Each positive number has two square roots. A number that is a **perfect square** has square roots that are **integers**.

$\sqrt{64} = 8$ The square root of 64 is also –8 because $(-8)^2 = 64$. The square root of 64 is ±8.	64 is a perfect square. $8^2 = 64$ and $(-8)^2 = 64$

Check

Solve each equation for *x*.

10. $x^2 = 49$ ________

11. $x^2 = 100$ ________

12. $x^2 = \frac{4}{25}$ ________

13. $x^2 = \frac{16}{81}$ ________

Example 4

The **cube root** of a positive number p is x if $x^3 = p$. A number that is a **perfect cube** has cube roots that are integers.

$\sqrt[3]{125} = 5$	$\sqrt[3]{\frac{1}{8}} = \frac{1}{2}$

Check

Solve each equation for *x*.

14. $x^3 = 64$ ________

15. $x^3 = 729$ ________

16. $x^3 = \frac{27}{1000}$ ________

17. $x^3 = \frac{216}{512}$ ________

Name ______________________ Date ______________ Class ______________

Example 5

Irrational numbers cannot be written in the form $\frac{a}{b}$, where a and b are integers and $b \neq 0$.

They can be estimated.

Estimate the value of $\sqrt{5}$.

Find the consecutive perfect squares that $\sqrt{5}$ is between.	$\sqrt{4} = 2$ and $\sqrt{9} = 3$
Use guess-and-test to find a better estimate.	$2.2^2 = 4.84$ and $2.3^2 = 5.29$ $\sqrt{5} \approx 2.2$ ≈ means approximate

Because 4.84 is closer than 5.29 to 5, you can estimate $\sqrt{5}$ as close to 2.2.

Check

Approximate each irrational number to one decimal place without a calculator.

18. $\sqrt{12}$ ______
19. $\sqrt{20}$ ______
20. $\sqrt{30}$ ______
21. $\sqrt{40}$ ______

Example 6

The set of real numbers includes rational numbers and irrational numbers.

Rational Numbers	Irrational numbers include:
fractions and mixed numbers repeating decimals terminating decimals whole numbers integers	square roots that result in nonterminating, nonrepeating decimals cube roots that result in nonterminating, nonrepeating decimals π

Check

Write all the names that apply to each number. Use *real number*, *rational number*, *integer*, *whole number*, and *irrational number*.

22. –6 ______

23. 3.125 ______

24. $\frac{5}{8}$ ______

25. $\sqrt{10}$ ______

Name ______________________ Date ______________ Class ______________

Example 7

You can order real numbers. Rename the numbers into the same form and then compare.

Order from least to greatest: 3.25, $\frac{11}{4}$, π, $\sqrt{8}$.

Rename the improper fraction as a decimal.	$\frac{11}{4} = 2.75$
Approximate π.	$\pi \approx 3.14$
Approximate $\sqrt{8}$.	$\sqrt{8} \approx 2.8$
Order the decimals from least to greatest.	2.75, 2.8, 3.14, 3.25

Then order from least to greatest is $\frac{11}{4}$, $\sqrt{8}$, π, 3.25.

Order the numbers from least to greatest.

26. $1\frac{1}{2}$, $\sqrt{2}$, 1.48

____

27. 7.25, $7\frac{1}{5}$, $\sqrt{50}$

____

SKILL 16 REAL NUMBERS

SKILL 17

Scale Factor and Scale Drawings

KEY TEACHING POINTS

Example 1
Describe the elements of a scale drawing. Explain the meaning of the scale and how it is helpful in our everyday lives, such as for finding distances on a map.

Say: A map is a scale drawing that people use every day. A scale drawing uses a scale, which is the ratio between two sets of measurements.

Say: Look at the map in the example. The two points represent the distance between the university and the post office.

Say: Look at the scale below the drawing.

Ask: What does the scale tell you? **[What each unit on the map represents in real life]** How many miles is 1 inch equal to? **[1 inch is equal to 5 miles.]**

Say: Because 3 is 3 times 1, multiply 5(3) = 15 to find that the distance between the university and the post office is 15 miles.

Check
Ask: What is the scale of the map? **[1 inch is equal to 9 miles.]**

Ask: How does a scale help you? **[It helps to tell you what the actual distance is between the towns.]**

Ask: Why do you have to use a proportion? **[We know the distance on the map, and we know the scale, so a proportion will tell us what the actual distance is.]**

Ask: How would you find the distance between Glanville and Jackson? **[First find the distance on the map between the two points. Then set up a proportion to find the actual distance.]**

Example 2
Say: A blueprint is like a map; a map shows where things like towns are located, and a blueprint shows where objects, such as rooms, are located.

Say: Look at the different measurements on the blueprint.

Ask: What is the scale? **[1 inch is equal to 18 feet.]**

Say: Look at the table in the example.

Ask: How is a table useful to find the real measurements? **[You can set up proportions for all the given measurements in the blueprint and find the actual measurements.]**

Check
Say: Look at Problem 3.

Ask: What is the scale? **[2 inches is equal to 5 feet.]**

KEY TEACHING POINTS

Example 3

Make sure students understand that a dilation of a shape means that only the size changes, but the shape remains the same. The scale factor describes how the shape's size changes.

Say: Look at the example on the left with the triangles.

Ask: Is triangle $A'B'C'$ larger or smaller than triangle ABC? **[Larger]**

Say: Let's set up a proportion to see how much larger the new figure is.

Ask: What is the length of side AB? **[2 units]** What is the length of side BC? **[2 units]**

Ask: What is the length of side $A'B'$? **[6 units]** What is the length of side $B'C'$? **[6 units]**

Say: Set up a proportion to find the scale factor of the dilation.

Ask: How can you find the scale factor? **[Divide the lengths of the image by the lengths of the pre-image.]** What is the scale factor? **[3]**

Say: Now look at the example on the right with the rectangles.

Say: Let's set up a proportion to see how much smaller the new figure is.

Ask: What is the length of side AB? **[2 units]** What is the length of side AD? **[4 units]**

Ask: What is the length of side $A'B'$? **[1 unit]** What is the length of side $A'D'$? **[2 units]**

Say: Set up a proportion to find the scale factor of the dilation.

Ask: How can you find the scale factor? **[Divide the lengths of the image by the lengths of the pre-image.]** What is the scale factor? $\left[\frac{1}{2}\right]$

Check

Say: Look at Problem 5.

Ask: What is the length of each side square $ABCD$? **[2 units]**

Ask: What is the length of each side of square $A'B'C'D'$? **[3 units]**

Say: Set up a proportion to find the scale factor of the dilation.

Ask: How can you find the scale factor? **[Divide the lengths of the image by the lengths of the pre-image.]** What is the scale factor? $\left[1\frac{1}{2}\right]$

ALTERNATE STRATEGY

Strategy: Calculate the perimeter of each figure to find the scale factor.

Say: Because the size of each figure changes but the shape stays the same in a dilation, you can calculate the perimeter of each figure and set up a proportion to find the scale factor.

Say: Look at squares *ABCD* and *A′B′C′D′* in the Check.

Say: The perimeter of a figure is the sum of the lengths of its sides.

Ask: What is the perimeter of square *ABCD*? **[8 units]** What is the perimeter of square *A′B′C′D′*? **[12 units]**

Say: Because the dilation is an enlargement, set up the equation: $12 \div 8 = 1.5$. The scale factor of the dilation is 1.5.

KEY TEACHING POINTS

Example 4

Make sure students understand that real-world experiences can be displayed using a scale drawing.

Say: Look at the scale drawing.

Ask: What do the two squares represent? **[The smaller square is Martin's current garden and the larger one is his proposed new garden.]**

Ask: What is the scale factor? **[6]** What information are you trying to find? **[The difference in area between the larger square and the smaller square]**

Ask: The scale factor of the new figure is 6. Is the area also a scale factor of 6? **[No.]**

Ask: How do you calculate the area of a square? **[Square the side length.]** What is the area of the pre-image? **[4 square units]** What is the area of the image? **[144 square units]**

Ask: How many times greater is the area of the larger figure compared to the smaller figure? **[144 square units compared to 4 square units, or 36 times greater]**

Ask: What can you say about the relationship between the scale factor and area of two figures? **[If you square the scale factor, that will tell you how many times as many the area of the new figure is compared to the area of the original figure.]**

Check

Ask: What does the scale drawing show? **[Two rectangles, with the new one exhibiting a reduction]**

Ask: What are the corresponding sides? **[*AB* corresponds to *A′B′*; *BC* corresponds to *B′C′*; *CD* corresponds to *C′D′*; and *DA* corresponds to *D′A′*.]**

Ask: How does the scale factor between the two rectangles compare to the area between the two rectangles? **[While the scale factor is $\frac{1}{4}$, the area of the reduction is proportionally $\frac{1}{16}$ smaller.]**

COMMON MISCONCEPTION

Ask: What is the error in the answer that Donald gave about the relation of the scale factor to the area?

Reason incorrect: Donald's error was to assume the scale factor applied to area, too. He did not realize that the scale factor shows how corresponding sides relate to each other, not how the area as a whole relates to each other. If he had squared the scale factor, it would have told him how much larger or smaller the area of the new figure is compared to the area of the original figure.

Solution: The scale factor is $\frac{1}{4}$, which means each side of the new figure is $\frac{1}{4}$ the length of the original figure. Area is found by multiplying length by the width, so the area of the new figure is $\left(\frac{1}{4}\right)^2 = \frac{1}{16}$ the area of the original figure. The equation for the area of the new figure is $32\left(\frac{1}{16}\right) = 2$.

ADDITIONAL ONLINE INTERVENTION RESOURCES

 Use the following for students who have not mastered the concepts in Skill 17.

- Math on the Spot videos
- Personal Math Trainer with customized intervention
- Building Block worksheets (Skill 13: Change Units; Skill 95: Solve Proportions)

Name ______________________ Date ______________ Class ______________

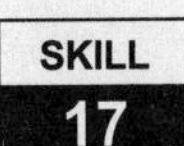

Scale Factor and Scale Drawings

Example 1

A scale drawing is a drawing that is proportional to an actual object. A scale is the ratio between two sets of measurements.

Look at the map.

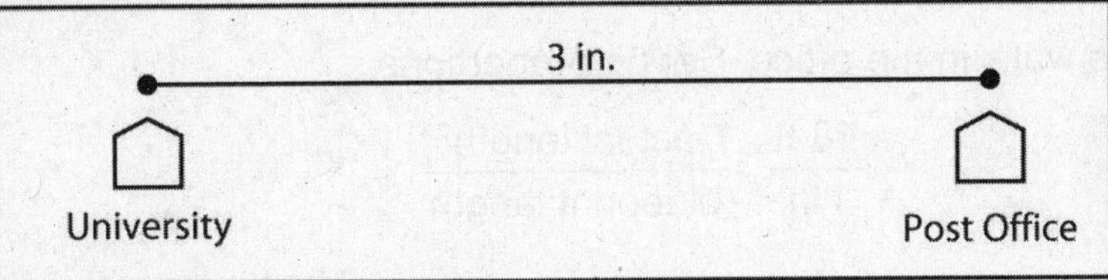

Scale: 1 in. = 5 mi

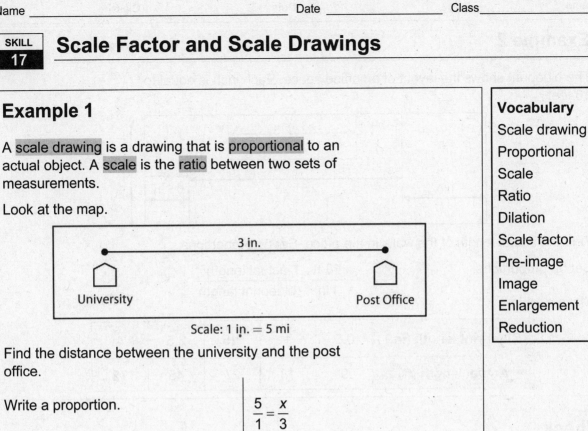

Find the distance between the university and the post office.

Write a proportion. $\frac{5}{1} = \frac{x}{3}$

Solve for x. $x = 15$

The distance between the university and the post office is 15 miles.

Vocabulary
- Scale drawing
- Proportional
- Scale
- Ratio
- Dilation
- Scale factor
- Pre-image
- Image
- Enlargement
- Reduction

Check

Write a proportion to find each distance.

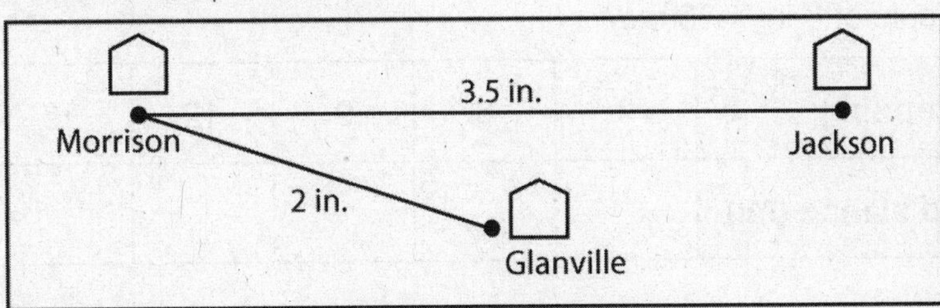

Scale: 1 in. = 9 mi

1. Find the actual distance between Morrison and Jackson.

____

2. Find the actual distance between Glanville and Morrison.

____

Name ____________________ Date ____________ Class ____________

Example 2

The blueprint shows the layout of an office space. Each inch is equal to 18 feet.

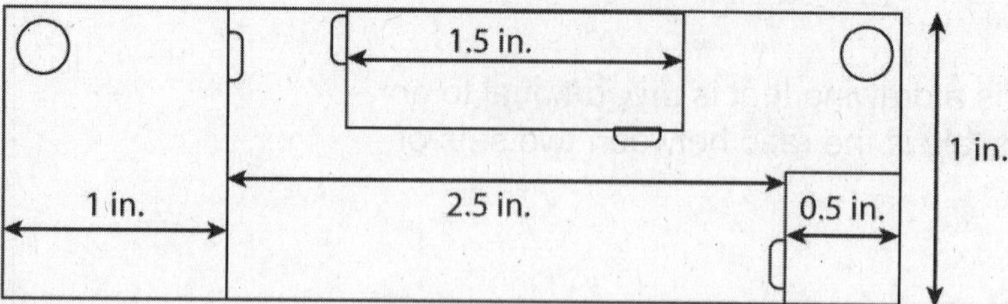

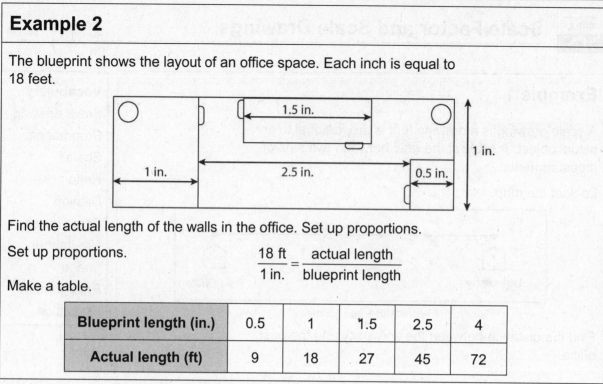

Find the actual length of the walls in the office. Set up proportions.

Set up proportions. $\frac{18 \text{ ft}}{1 \text{ in.}} = \frac{\text{actual length}}{\text{blueprint length}}$

Make a table.

Blueprint length (in.)	0.5	1	1.5	2.5	4
Actual length (ft)	9	18	27	45	72

Check

Complete each table.

3. A set of blueprints has a scale of 2 in. = 5 ft.

Blueprint length (in.)	1	2	4	5	7
Actual length (ft)					

4. A map has a scale of 3 in. = 25 mi.

Map (in.)	3	6	9	12	15
Actual distance (mi)					

Name ______________________ Date ______________ Class ______________

Example 3

A **dilation** changes the size of a figure but not its shape. The **scale factor** is the ratio between the **pre-image** and the **image**.

Find the lengths of the sides.

Triangle ABC: $AB = 2$ $BC = 2$
Triangle $A'B'C'$: $A'B' = 6$ $B'C' = 6$

Find the ratio of corresponding sides.

$$\frac{A'B'}{AB} = \frac{6}{2} = 3 \quad \frac{B'C'}{BC} = \frac{6}{2} = 3$$

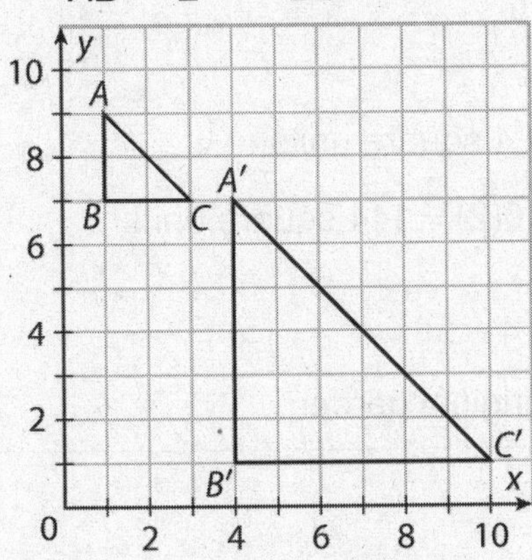

The scale factor of the dilation is 3. Triangle $A'B'C'$ is an **enlargement**.

Find the lengths of the sides.

Rectangle $ABCD$: $AB = 4$ $AD = 2$
Rectangle $A'B'C'D'$: $A'B' = 2$ $A'D' = 1$

Find the ratio of corresponding sides.

$$\frac{A'D'}{AD} = \frac{2}{4} = \frac{1}{2} \quad \frac{A'B'}{AB} = \frac{1}{2}$$

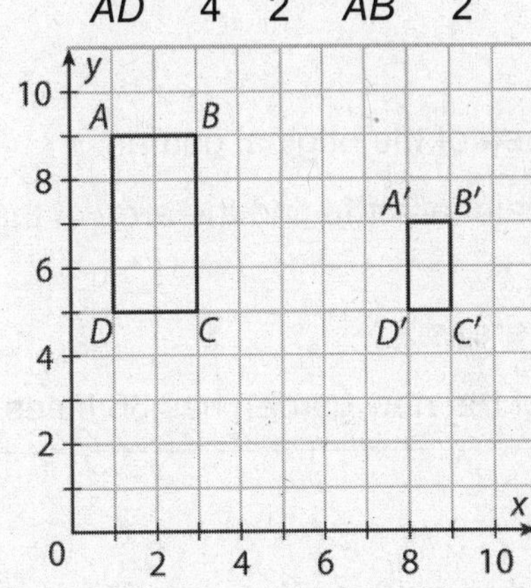

The scale factor of the dilation is $\frac{1}{2}$. Rectangle $A'B'C'D'$ is a **reduction**.

Check

Determine the scale factor for each dilation.

5. $ABCD$ to $A'B'C'D'$

____

6. $RSTU$ to $R'S'T'U'$

____

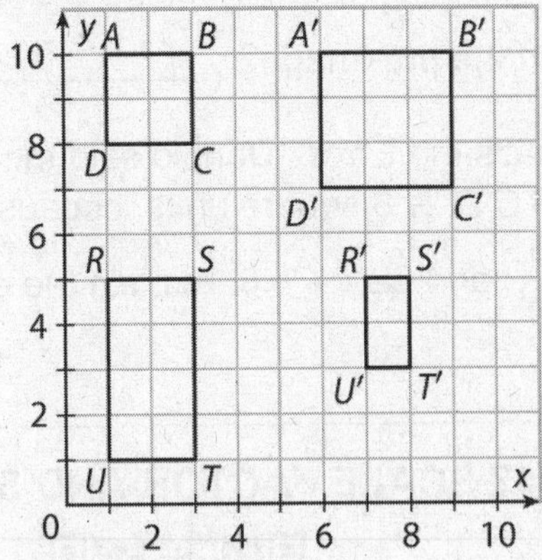

Name ______________________ Date ______________ Class______________

Example 4

Martin is increasing the size of his garden by a scale factor of 6. He wants to know how much more area his new garden will have. His plans are shown on the right.

Find how many times as many the area of the new garden is than the original garden.

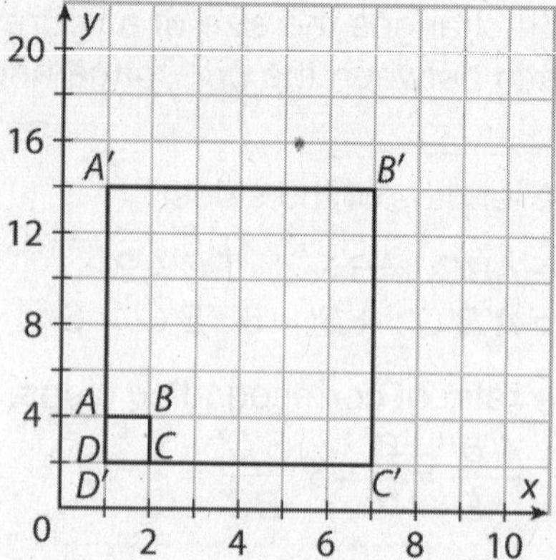

Find the area of the original garden.	$2(2) = 4$ square units
Use the scale factor to find the area of the new garden.	$6(2) \cdot 6(2) = 144$ square units
Divide the areas.	$144 \div 4 = 36$

The area of the new garden has 36 times the area as the original garden.

Check

Use the grid to answer the questions.

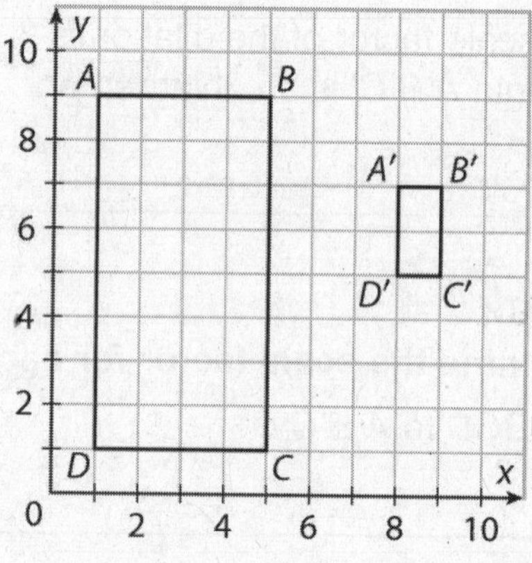

7. What is the scale factor? ______________

8. How many times as many is the area of the image than the pre-image? ______________

9. What's the Error? Donald said the area of rectangle $A'B'C'D'$ is 8 square units, because the scale factor is $\frac{1}{4}$, and $32 \div 4 = 8$. Explain the error.

____

SKILL 17 SCALE FACTOR AND SCALE DRAWINGS

SKILL 18

Scatter Plots

KEY TEACHING POINTS

Example 1

Describe the elements of a scatter plot. Explain what an outlier and a cluster are and how to identify them.

Say: A scatter plot is a graph that shows the correlation between two sets of data.

Say: Look at the example on the left. The plotted points represent data on a scatter plot.

Say: Look at the example in the middle. While most of the data lie along a line, one point is far away from the other data.

Say: Look at the example on the right. The data are grouped together in two bunches or clusters.

Check

Ask: How can you tell if data are in a cluster? **[The data are grouped around a point or along a line.]**

Ask: What is the meaning of an outlier in a data set? **[It is a data point that is very different from the rest of the data set.]**

Example 2

Use contrasting examples to show the difference among positive association, negative association, and no association.

Say: Data that exhibit a linear relationship will lie along a line when graphed.

Say: Look at the example on the left. As one data set increases, the other increases, too. These data exhibit a positive association.

Say: Look at the example in the middle. As one data set increases, the other decreases. This is a negative association.

Say: Look at the example on the right. The data are scattered and not along a line. There is no association between the data sets.

Check

Ask: How can you tell if data exhibit a linear association? **[When the data are graphed, they lie along a line.]**

KEY TEACHING POINTS

Example 3

Make sure students understand that real-world experiences can be displayed in a table and on a scatter plot.

Ask: What is the meaning of the data in the table? **[The data show the association between the Hours Worked and Tips in dollars.]**

Say: Let's compare the data in the table with what is plotted on the graph.

Ask: How many points are on the scatter plot? **[12]**

Ask: How do these points correspond to the data in the table? **[Each data point shows the number of Hours Worked on the *x*-axis and the amount of Tips in dollars on the *y*-axis.]**

Ask: Do the data exhibit linear association? **[Yes]**

Ask: What is the meaning of point (7, 52)? **[It is an outlier.]**

Ask: Is there a cluster among the data points? **[Other than the outlier (7, 52), the data are clustered in an upward pattern along a line.]**

Check

Say: Plot the data points in the table onto the graph.

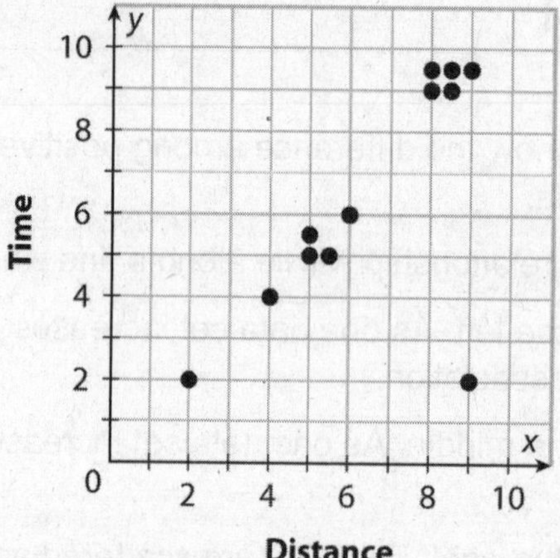

Ask: What type of association do the data exhibit?

ALTERNATE STRATEGY

Strategy: Analyze the data in the table for the Check to identify the outlier without making a scatter plot.

Say: A quick look at the data shows four points with matching *x*- and *y*-coordinates: (2, 2), (4, 4), (5, 5), (6, 6).

Say: Plotting these four points shows that the data set runs along a straight line that goes through the origin (0, 0).

Say: Look at the remaining data.

Say: Points (9.5, 9), (5, 5.5), (8, 9.5), (8,9), (5.5, 5), (8.5, 9), and (8.5, 9.5) have an *x*-coordinate and a *y*-coordinate that are close to each other and therefore will be close to the line from the origin.

Ask: What point is not close to the others, in terms of having a matching *x*- and *y*-coordinate?

Say: Point (9, 2) is different from the others and is the outlier.

Say: Check your work by plotting the points.

COMMON MISCONCEPTION

Ask: What is the error in the answer that William gave, which was that the outlier is (2, 2) because it is closer to the origin than any other data point?

Reason incorrect: An outlier is a data point that is very different from the data set. The scatter plot exhibits a positive association; as one data set increases, the other data set increases. Point (2, 2) is part of the positive association. An outlier is very different than the rest of the data, so it would not be (2, 2).

Solution: The line along which the data lie goes from the origin, through points (2,2) and (5, 5), and in an upward direction through the rest of the data. The outlier is (9, 2) because it lies far outside the line.

KEY TEACHING POINTS

Example 4
Make sure students understand the concept of a trend line in relation to the data on a scatter plot. Show them that other real-world experiences can be displayed on a scatter plot.

Say: Look at the scatter plot with the labels Time Studying (hours) and Test Scores.

Ask: What do the data represent? **[As the time studying increases, the test scores increase, too.]**

Say: Look at the trend line.

Ask: What do you notice about the trend line? **[Most of the data points run along the line.]**

Say: The trend line is a helpful way to analyze the data and their association.

Say: A trend line can also help you more easily identify clusters and outliers, as well as make predictions about the data set.

Ask: What type of association is shown? **[Positive association]**

Ask: Is there an outlier? **[No]**

Ask: Is there a cluster? **[The data are grouped along a line in an upward direction in a positive association.]**

Check

Ask: What do the data exhibit? **[The relationship between the amount of time and the points scored]**

Ask: What type of association is shown? **[Positive association]**

Say: Draw the trend line.

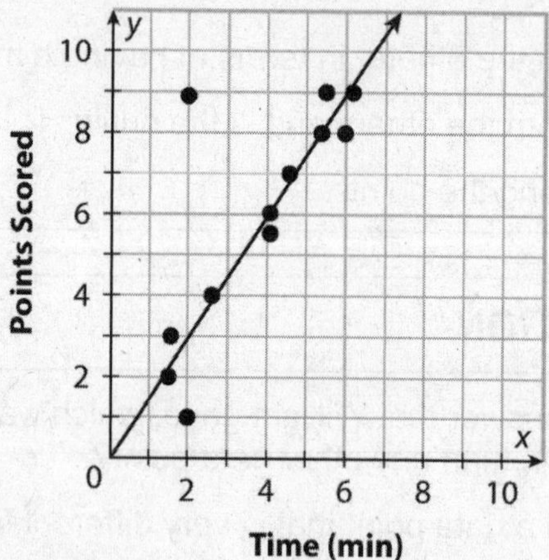

Ask: Is there an outlier? **[Yes, at (2, 9)]**

Ask: What is the prediction? **[It will take 3.5 minutes to score 5 points, and you can score 10 points in 7 minutes.]**

Check students' work as they make their predictions. Ask them to think of examples of other real-world situations that can be used in linear associations.

ADDITIONAL ONLINE INTERVENTION RESOURCES

Use the following for students who have not mastered the concepts in Skill 18.

- Math on the Spot videos
- Personal Math Trainer with customized intervention
- Building Block worksheets (Skill 46: Graph Ordered Pairs (First Quadrant); Skill 70: Ordered Pairs)

Name ______________________ Date ______________ Class______________

SKILL 18

Scatter Plots

Example 1

A scatter plot is a graph with plotted points that show the correlation between two sets of data.

An outlier is a data point that is very distant from the other data in a set.

A cluster is a set of closely grouped data points around a point or along a line.

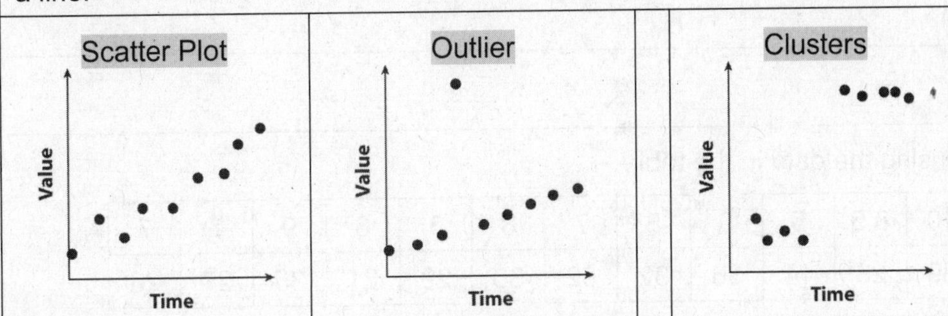

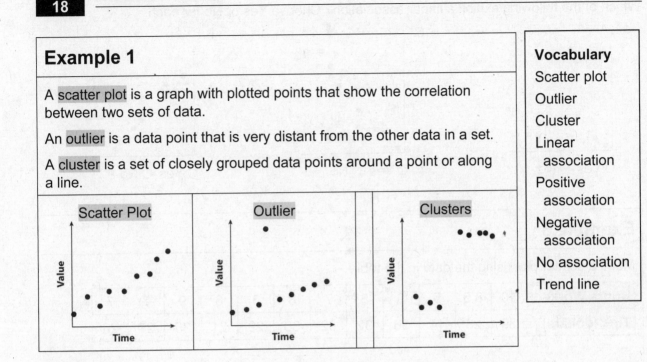

Vocabulary

Scatter plot

Outlier

Cluster

Linear association

Positive association

Negative association

No association

Trend line

Check

Which of the following apply to each scatter plot: cluster, outlier, or neither?

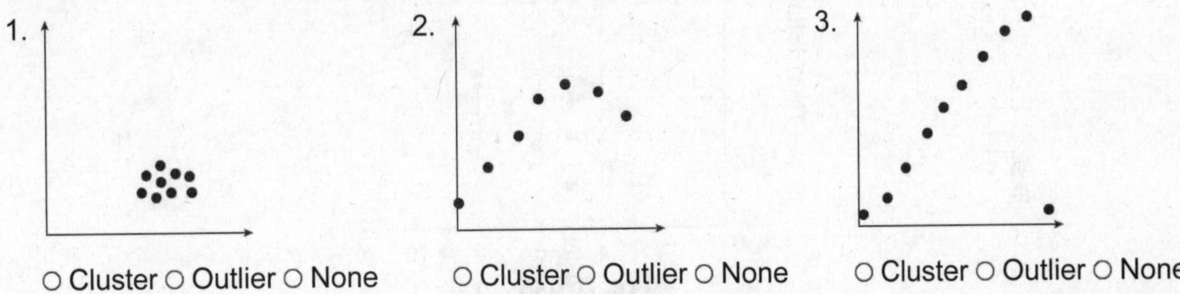

1. ○ Cluster ○ Outlier ○ None

2. ○ Cluster ○ Outlier ○ None

3. ○ Cluster ○ Outlier ○ None

Example 2

Data that lie along a line in a scatter plot exhibit a linear association.

A scatter plot can have:

- positive association: one data set increases, the other data set increases
- negative association: one data set increases, the other decreases
- no association: data do not lie along a line

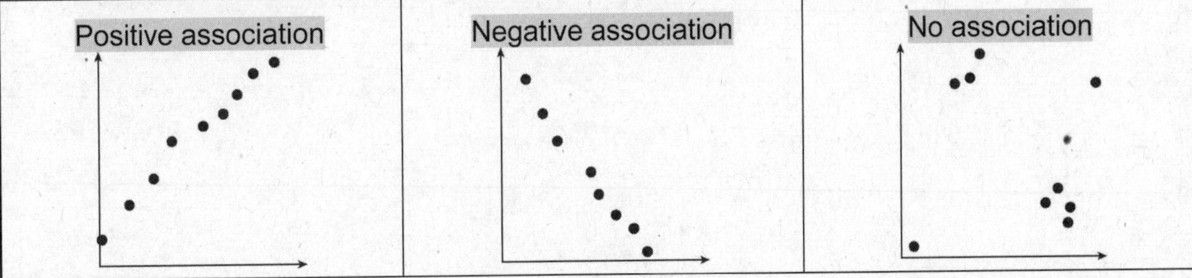

Name ______________________ Date ______________ Class ______________

Check

Which of the following exhibit a linear association? Choose Yes or No for each.

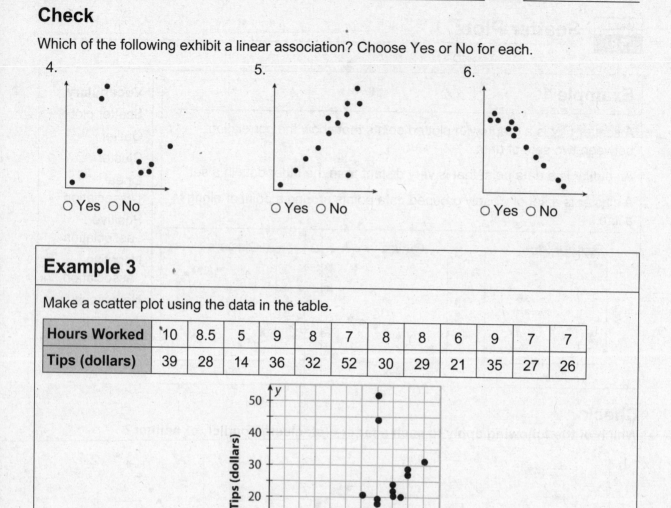

4.

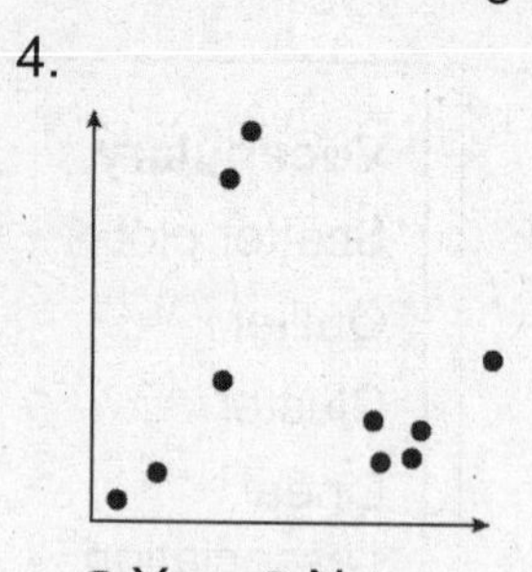

○ Yes ○ No

5.

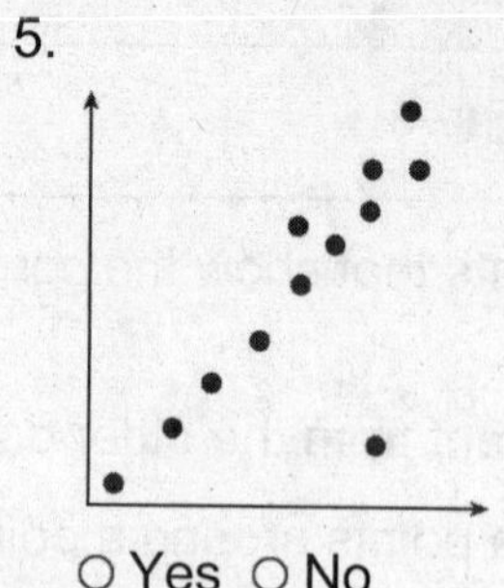

○ Yes ○ No

6.

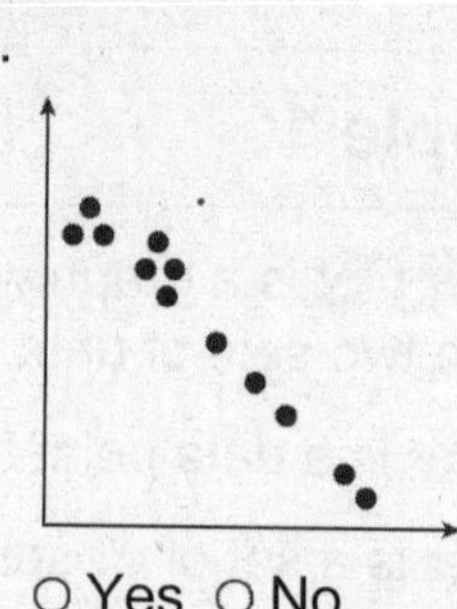

○ Yes ○ No

Example 3

Make a scatter plot using the data in the table.

Hours Worked	10	8.5	5	9	8	7	8	8	6	9	7	7
Tips (dollars)	39	28	14	36	32	52	30	29	21	35	27	26

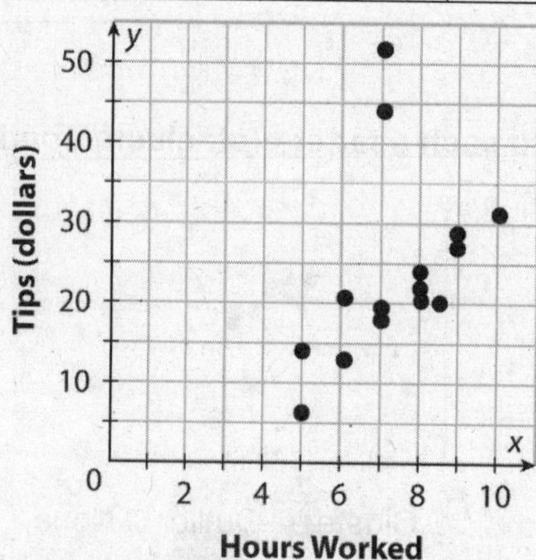

The data show a positive association between the number of hours worked and the amount of tips. As the number of hours worked increases, the tips increase, too. Two outliers exist at (7, 52) and (7, 57).

Name ______________________ Date ______________ Class ______________

Check

Make a scatter plot using the data in the table.

Distance (mi)	9	5	4	9.5	2	5	8	8	5.5	8.5	6	8.5
Time (h)	2	5	4	9	2	5.5	9.5	9	5	9	6	9.5

7.

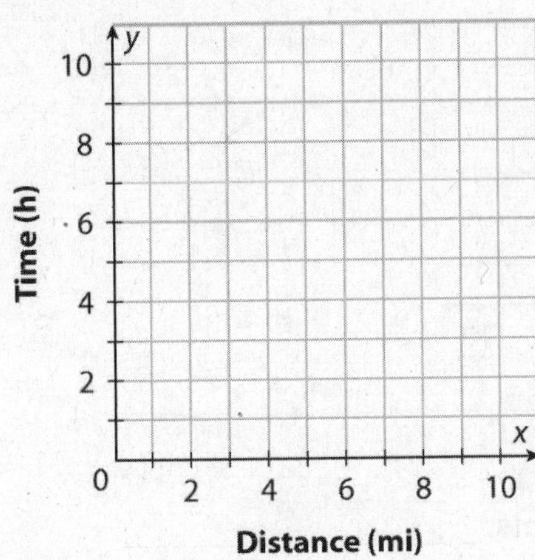

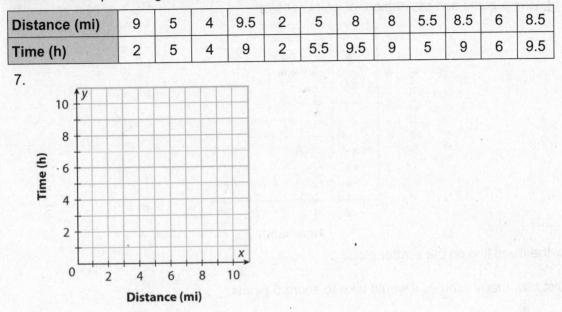

8. Are there any outliers in the scatter plot? Explain. ______________________

9. Describe any clusters present in the scatter plot. ______________________

10. What's the Error? William said the outlier is at (2, 2) because it is closer to the origin (0, 0) than any other point in the data. Explain the error and identify the outlier.

____

Example 4

A trend line is the straight line closest to the points in data that exhibit a linear association.

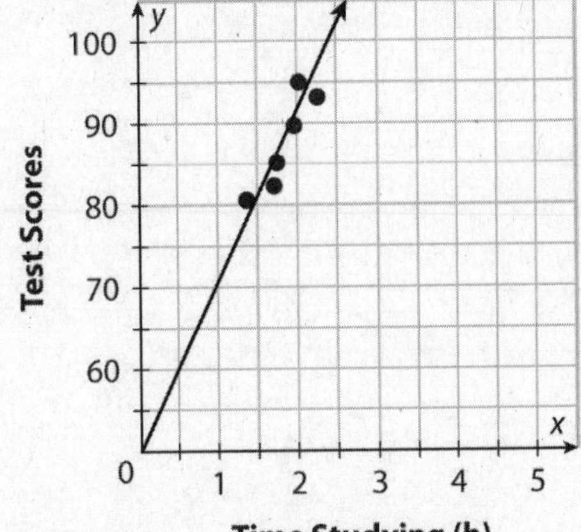

The trend line shows as time studying increases, test scores also increase. Make predictions based on the trend line. For example, studying 2.5 hours will produce a test score of 100.

Name ______________________________ Date ______________ Class ______________

Check

The data in the scatter plot shows the relationship between the number of minutes playing a game and the number of points scored.

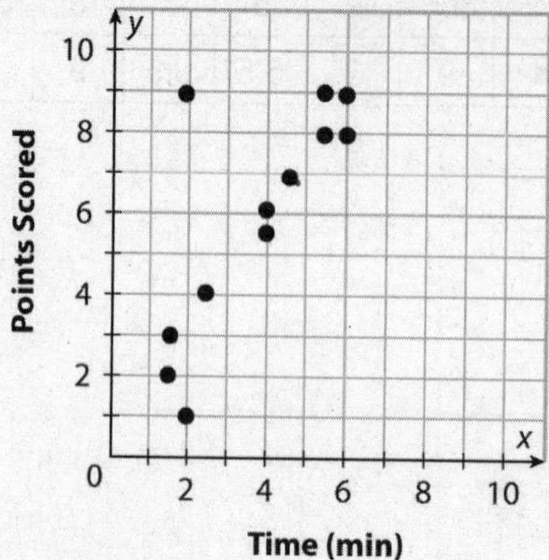

11. Draw the trend line on the scatter plot.

12. Predict how many minutes it would take to score 5 points. ______________

13. Predict how many points will be scored in 7 minutes. ______________

SKILL 18 SCATTER PLOTS

SKILL 19

Significant Digits

KEY TEACHING POINTS

Example 1

Say: Precision is tied to the unit of measure used to determine the measurement. For example, if you were replacing a door, measuring to the nearest inch is more precise than measuring to the nearest foot. If you measure to the nearest foot, you may choose a door that is too large or too small.

Write 2.75 and 2.7 on the board.

Say: These measures are in liters, so we can compare the numbers.

Say: The decimal 2.75 has a digit in the hundredths place. The decimal 2.7 does not. This makes 2.75 liters the more precise measurement.

ALTERNATE STRATEGY

Strategy: Write the measures in the same units.

1. **Say:** Look at Problem 3. We can rename 4.21 meters as centimeters or 5.7 centimeters as meters. Let's rename 4.21 as centimeters.
2. **Ask:** How many centimeters are equal to 1 meter? **[100]** How many centimeters are equal to 4.21 meters? **[421]** Which is more precise, 421 centimeters or 5.7 centimeters? **[5.7 cm]** Why? **[A tenth of a centimeter is more precise than a centimeter.]**

KEY TEACHING POINTS

Example 2

Say: Significant digits are used to indicate how precise a measurement is. Look at the table.

Say: The first row states that all nonzero digits are significant. The two examples show numbers that do not have any zeros. So, all of the digits in 287 and 42.952 are significant.

Say: The second row states that zeros between two other significant digits are significant. The 0 in the hundreds place of 9025 is significant and the zeros in the tenths and hundredths places of 2.004 are also significant.

Say: The third row states that zeros at the end of a number to the right of a decimal point are significant. So, 2.3000 has 5 significant digits.

Ask: How many significant digits does 2.300 have? **[4]**, 2.30? **[3]**

Say: The fourth row states that zeros to the left of the first nonzero digit in the decimal are not significant. So, 0.006 has 1 significant digit.

Ask: How many significant digits does 0.0006 have? **[1]**

Say: The bottom row states that zeros at the end of a number without a decimal point are not significant. So, 275 has the same number of significant digits as 275,000. **[3]**

COMMON MISCONCEPTION

Ask: What is Gina's error in saying that 0.0306 has 2 significant digits?

Reason incorrect: The zero in the thousandths place is between significant digits, so it too is significant.

Solution: There are 3 significant digits: 0.0**306**

KEY TEACHING POINTS

Example 3

Say: You can compute using significant digits. The number of significant digits in the solution may differ from the number of significant digits in the original measurements.

Say: Let's use significant digits to find the perimeter of a rectangle that has a length of 8.4 inches and a width of 6 inches.

Ask: How many significant digits does 8.4 have? **[2]** How many significant digits does 6 have? **[1]**

Say: The rule for addition is that the sum must be rounded to the same place value as the least significant digit in the least precise measurement.

Ask: Which is less precise: 8.4 inches or 6 inches? **[6 inches]** What is the perimeter of the rectangle? **[28.8 inches]** To which place do you round? **[ones]**

Say: Using significant digits, the perimeter is 29 inches.

Example 4

Say: For multiplication and division, the product or quotient must have no more significant digits than the least precise measurement.

Ask: If the length is 8.4 inches and the width is 6 inches, how many significant digits will the area have? **[1]**

Ask: What is the area of the rectangle? **[50.4 square inches]** If there is 1 significant digit, to which place is the area rounded? **[tens]**

Say: Using significant digits, the area is 50 square inches.

ADDITIONAL ONLINE INTERVENTION RESOURCES

Use the following for students who have not mastered the concepts in Skill 19.

- Math on the Spot videos
- Personal Math Trainer with customized intervention
- Building Block worksheets (Skill 57: Measure with Customary and Metric Units; Skill 77: Round Decimals; Skill 78: Round Whole Numbers; Skill 79: Rounding and Estimation)

Name ______________________ Date ______________ Class ______________

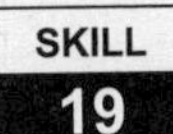

Significant Digits

Vocabulary
Precision
Significant digits

Example 1

The precision of a measurement is related to the unit of measure used. The smaller the unit of measure, the more precise it is. For example, a measure of 2.75 liters is more precise than a measure of 2.7 liters because a hundredth of a liter is a smaller unit of measure than a tenth of a liter. A foot is more precise than a yard because it is a smaller unit of measure.

Check

Choose the more precise measurement in each pair.

1. 3 ft; 34 in. ______________
2. 45 oz; 4 lb ______________
3. 4.21 m; 5.7 cm ______________
4. 1 h; 45 min ______________

Example 2

Significant digits are a way to carry meaning about the precision of a measurement. To identify significant digits, follow these rules:

Rule	Examples
All nonzero digits are significant.	**287** has 3 significant digits.
Zeros between two other significant digits are significant.	**9025** has 4 significant digits. **2.004** has 4 significant digits.
Zeros at the end of a number to the right of a decimal point are significant.	**2.3000** has 5 significant digits.
Zeros to the left of the first nonzero digit in the decimal are not significant.	0.00**6** has 1 significant digit. 0.0**7025** has 4 significant digits.
Zeros at the end of a number without a decimal point are not significant.	**275**,000 has 3 significant digits. **5,250**,000 has 4 significant digits.

Check

Identify the number of significant digits in each measurement.

5. 225 lb ______________
6. 0.075 L ______________
7. 880 yd ______________

8. What's the Error? Gina said that 0.0306 has 2 significant digits. Describe Gina's error and give the correct number of significant digits.

____

Name ______________________ Date ____________ Class ____________

Example 3

The number of significant digits in the solution may differ from the number of significant digits in the original measurement. When adding and subtracting, the sum or difference must be rounded to the same place value as the least significant digit in the least precise measurement.

Find the perimeter of a rectangle that has a length of 8.4 inches and a width of 6 inches using the correct number of significant digits.

Find the perimeter.	8.4 in. + 8.4 in. + 6 in. + 6 in. = 28.8 in.
Identify the least precise measurement.	The least precise measurement is 6 in., which is in the ones place.
Round to the least precise measurement.	The perimeter is 29 in.

Check

Use the correct number of significant digits to write the measure.

9. Jason jogged 3.8 miles on Monday, 4.25 miles on Tuesday, and 5.1 miles on Wednesday. Find the total number of miles Jason jogged.

____

Example 4

When multiplying or dividing, the product or quotient must have no more significant digits than the least precise measurement.

Find the area of a rectangle that has a length of 8.4 inches and a width of 6 inches using the correct number of significant digits.

Find the area.	8.4 in. • 6 in. = 50.4 in^2
Identify the number of significant digits in the least precise measurement.	6 in. has 1 significant digit.
Round to 1 significant digit.	The area is 50 in^2.

Use the correct number of significant digits to write the measure.

10. Find the area of a rectangle that has a length of 15 inches and a width of 7.5 inches. _______________

SKILL 19 SIGNIFICANT DIGITS

SKILL 20

Slope

KEY TEACHING POINTS

Example 1

Say: Slope is the measure of the ratio of rise over run. You can think of a ramp. The slope is based on how high it goes, the rise, and based on how long it is, the run.

Say: Slope is how a line changes as it goes from left to right. There are four types of slopes.

Have students look at the four types of slopes. Ask them to pay attention to how the line changes as it goes from left to right.

Ask: What do you notice about the positive slope? **[It slants up as it goes from left to right.]** What do you notice about the negative slope? **[It slants down as it goes from left to right.]**

Say: The other two types of slope are zero, which is a horizontal line, and undefined, which is a vertical line. Because there is no change in the run, the denominator of the rise over run fraction is 0. It is not possible to divide by 0, so the slope is undefined.

ALTERNATE STRATEGY

Strategy: Use a right triangle to model slope.

1. **Say:** You can use a right triangle on a grid to model slope.
2. Draw a 3-4-5 right triangle on a grid with vertices at $A(1, 1)$, $B(4, 1)$, and $C(4, 5)$.
3. **Ask:** How could you find the slope of the line hypotenuse $\overline{AC}$ lies on? **[Find the lengths of $\overline{AB}$ and $\overline{BC}$.]**
4. **Ask:** What are the lengths? **[$\overline{AB} = 3$, $\overline{BC} = 4$]**
5. Point out that by using $\frac{\text{rise}}{\text{run}}$, you can find the slope to be $\frac{4}{3}$.

KEY TEACHING POINTS

Example 2

Say: The other two types of slope are zero, which is a horizontal line, and undefined, which is a vertical line. Because there is no change in the run, the denominator of the rise over run fraction is 0. It is not possible to divide by 0, so the slope is undefined.

Ask: For a horizontal line, what is the change in the *y*-coordinate? **[There is no change, 0.]**

Say: There is no or zero rise, so the $\frac{\text{rise}}{\text{run}} = 0$.

Ask: For a vertical line, what is the change in the *x*-coordinate? **[There is no change or 0.]**

Ask: Can you divide by zero? **[No, it is undefined.]**

COMMON MISCONCEPTION

Ask: What is Steve's error in saying that a line of $x = 4$ has a slope of 0?
Reason incorrect: The equation $x = 4$ forms a vertical line when it is graphed.
Solution: A vertical line has an undefined slope.

KEY TEACHING POINTS

Example 3

Write $m = \frac{(y_2 - y_1)}{(x_2 - x_1)}$ on the board.

Say: The slope formula shows how to find the change in *y* over the change in *x*. It does not matter which order you subtract the values of *y* and *x*, but the order must be consistent.

Say: The numbers in the formula are used to name different points. When we choose two ordered pairs, one value of *y* is y_1 and the other value of *y* is y_2.

Ask: By looking at the line on the coordinate plane, is the slope positive or negative? **[Positive]** How do you know? **[The line slants up as it goes from left to right.]**

Say: To find the slope, we can pick any two points on the line. Let's try (–1, 0) and (0, 2).

Say: The first step is to find the change in *y*. We can subtract 2 – 0 or 0 – 2. Let's subtract 2 – 0 = 2. The change in *y* is 2.

Ask: Because we used 2 for the value of y_2, what value of *x* do you have to use for x_2? **[0]** What do we subtract to find the change in *x*? **[0 – (–1) = 1]**

Say: The rise or change in *y* is 2. The run or change in *x* is 1.

Ask: What is the slope? **[2]**

ALTERNATE STRATEGY

Strategy: Make a table to find the slope.

1. **Say:** You can use the slope formula to find the slope. Another way is to make a table.
2. Make a table showing the integer values for *x*.

x	–4	–3	–2	–1	0	1	2
y							

3. Fill in the values for *y*.

x	–4	–3	–2	–1	0	1	2
y	–6	–4	–2	0	2	4	6

4. **Ask:** How does the value of *y* change when *x* increases by 1? **[The value of *y* increases by 2.]** What is the slope? **[2]**
5. Point out to students that while this method works with integers, it is not as effective as using the slope formula.

KEY TEACHING POINTS

Example 4

Say: Two ordered pairs of a line are all that are needed to find the slope of that line. From those two ordered pairs, we will have enough information to find the change in *y* and the change in *x*.

Say: We know that a line passes through (–3, 5) and (1, 13).

Ask: Will the slope be positive or negative? **[Positive]** How do you know? **[When graphed, it will rise as it goes from left to right.]**

Ask: What is the change in *y*? **[8]** What is the change in *x*? **[4]**

Say: The rise is 8 and the run is 4.

Ask: What is the slope? **[2]**

Check

Have students compare the values for *x* and *y*. If the value of *x* is greater in the second ordered pair, then you can tell whether the slope is positive or negative by determining which value of *y* is greater. If the value of *y* in the second ordered pair is greater, the slope is positive. If the value of *y* in the first ordered pair is greater, the slope is negative.

KEY TEACHING POINTS

Example 5

Write $y = mx + b$ on the board.

Say: In slope-intercept form $y = mx + b$, m represents the slope and b represents the y-intercept. The y-intercept is the value of y when the line crosses the y-axis or when $x = 0$.

Write $y = 4x + 3$ on the board.

Ask: In $y = 4x + 3$, what is the slope? **[4]** What is the y-intercept? **[3]** What ordered pair represents the y-intercept if it is 3? **[(0, 3)]**

Have students look at the table.

Say: Let's pick two ordered pairs. Let's try (1, 5) and (2, 8).

Ask: How do we find the change in y? **[Subtract 8 – 5 = 3.]** How do we find the change in x? **[Subtract 2 – 1 = 1.]** What is the slope? **[3]**

Say: We can use the slope to find the y-intercept. We know that as the value of x increases by 1, the value of y increases by 3.

Ask: If we decrease the value of x by 1, what happens to the value of y? **[It decreases by 3.]** What is the value of y if $x = 0$? **[2]**

Say: The y-intercept is 2. Now let's write the equation. The slope is 3 and the y-intercept is 2.

Ask: What equation represents the data in the table? **[$y = 3x + 2$]**

Check

Make sure students understand that slope measures the change in the value of y when the value of x increases by 1.

ADDITIONAL ONLINE INTERVENTION RESOURCES

Use the following for students who have not mastered the concepts in Skill 20.

- Math on the Spot videos
- Personal Math Trainer with customized intervention
- Building Block worksheets (Skill 51: Integer Operations; Skill 95: Solve Proportions; Skill 98: Solve Two-Step Equations)

Name ______________________ Date ______________ Class ______________

SKILL 20

Slope

Example 1

Slope measures the ratio of $\frac{\text{rise}}{\text{run}}$ of a line.

- For a positive slope, the line slants up from left to right.
- For a negative slope, the line slants down from left to right.

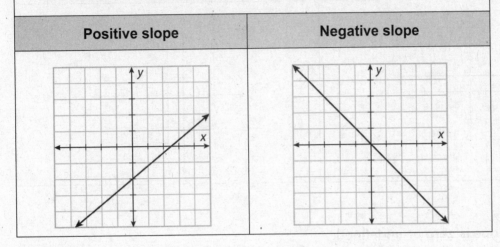

Positive slope	Negative slope

Vocabulary
Slope
Slope-intercept form
y-intercept

Check

Tell whether the slope is positive or negative.

1.

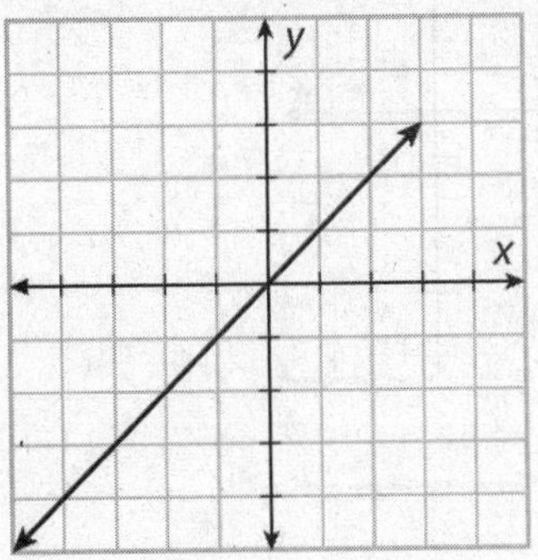

____

2.

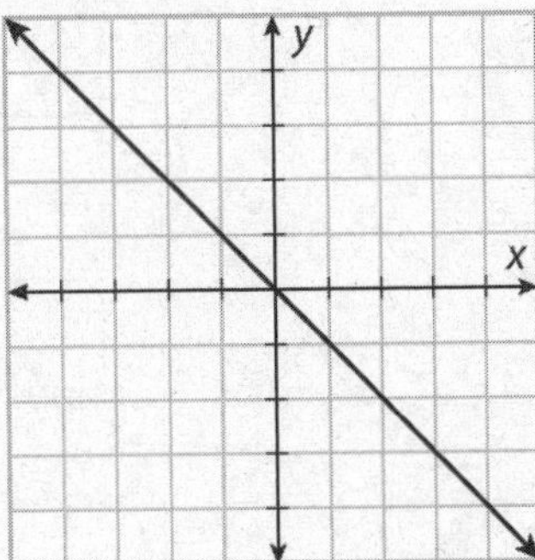

____

3.

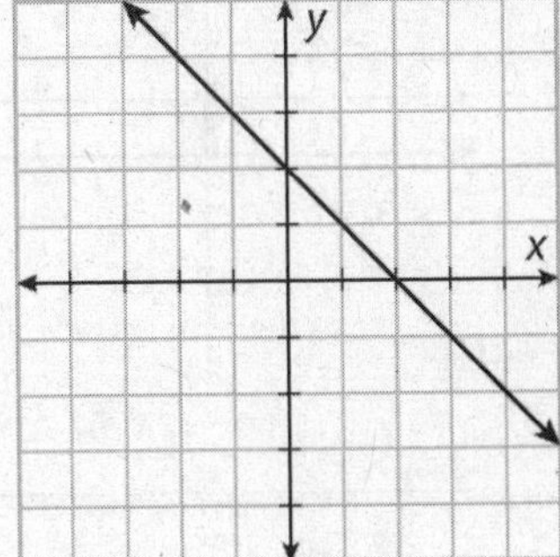

____

4. For a positive slope, as *x* increases, *y* ______________.

5. For a negative slope, as *x* increases, *y* ______________.

6. Does it matter when finding if a slope is positive or negative if the line goes through the origin?

____

____

Name ______________________ Date ____________ Class ____________

Example 2

Horizontal and vertical lines have special slopes.

- A horizontal line has a slope of 0.
- A vertical line has an undefined slope because it is not possible to divide by 0.

Zero slope	Undefined slope

Check

Tell whether the slope is zero or undefined.

7. 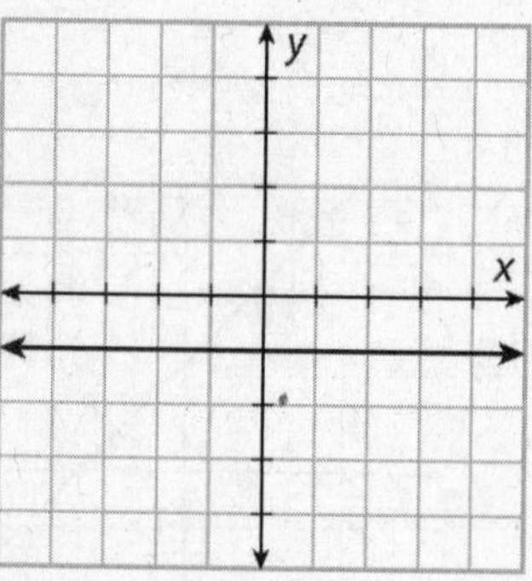

____

8. 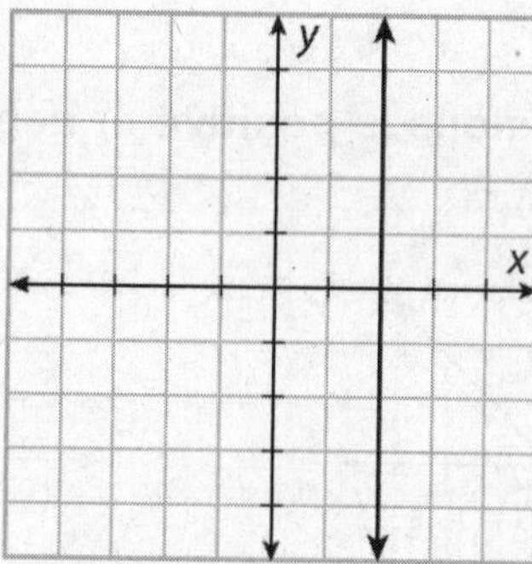

____

9. What is the slope of the *x*-axis, the line where $y = 0$? ______________

10. What is the slope of the *y*-axis, the line where $x = 0$? ______________

11. What's the Error? Steve said that the line for $x = 4$ has a slope of 0. Describe Steve's error and give the correct slope.

____

Name ______________________ Date ______________ Class ______________

Example 3

The slope formula is $m = \frac{(y_2 - y_1)}{(x_2 - x_1)}$, where m is the slope.

Find the slope of the line on the grid.

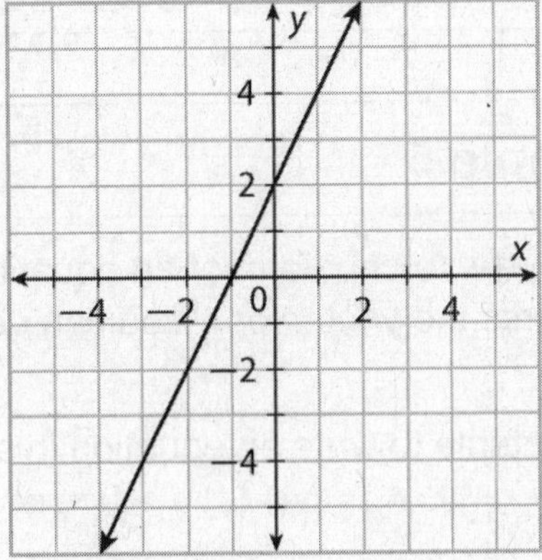

Pick two points.	Try (–1, 0) and (0, 2).
Find the change in y.	$2 - 0 = 2$
Find the change in x.	$0 - (-1) = 1$
Remember, $\frac{\text{change in } y}{\text{change in } x} = \frac{\text{rise}}{\text{run}}$.	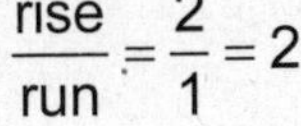 $\frac{\text{rise}}{\text{run}} = \frac{2}{1} = 2$
Find the slope.	

The slope is 2.

Check

Determine the slope of each line.

12.

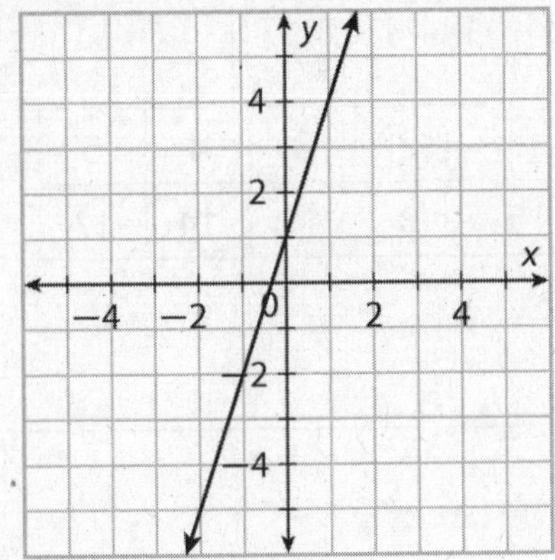

Slope = ______________

13.

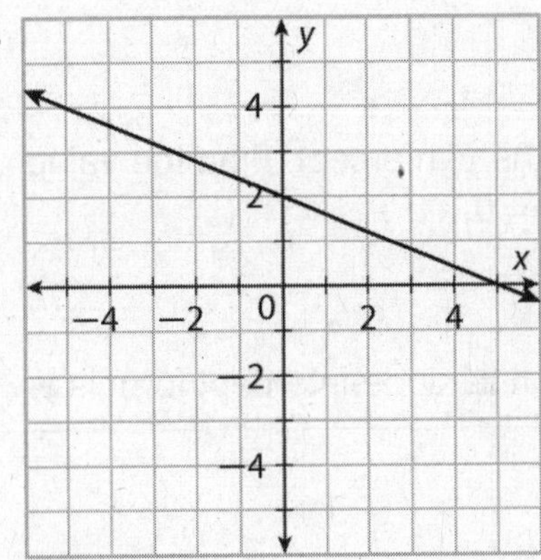

Slope = ______________

Example 4

You can find the slope if given two ordered pairs of a line.

A line passes through (–3, 5) and (1, 13). Find the slope.

Find the change in y.	$13 - 5 = 8$
Find the change in x.	$1 - (-3) = 4$
Find the slope.	$\frac{8}{4} = 2$

The slope is 2.

Name ______________________ Date ______________ Class ______________

Check

Find the slope using the two points of a line given.

14. (–3, 6) and (5, 10)

____

15. (–4, 8) and (2, –6)

____

Example 5

The slope-intercept form of an equation is $y = mx + b$, where m represents the slope and b represents the y-intercept. You can determine the slope-intercept form of an equation from a table.

Use the table to write an equation in slope-intercept form.

x	1	2	3	4	5
y	5	8	11	14	17

Pick two points.

Try (1, 5) and (2, 8).

Use the slope formula.

$$m = \frac{(y_2 - y_1)}{(x_2 - x_1)}$$

$$= \frac{8 - 5}{2 - 1} = \frac{3}{1} = 3$$

Determine the y-intercept. Find the value of y when $x = 0$.

x	**0**	1	2	3	4	5
y	**2**	5	8	11	14	17

When $x = 0$, $y = 2$.

The equation in slope-intercept form is $y = 3x + 2$.

Check

Use the table to write an equation in slope-intercept form.

16.

x	1	2	3	4	5
y	6	8	10	12	14

____

17.

x	2	4	6	8	10
y	12	9	6	3	0

____

SKILL 20 SLOPE

SKILL 21

Two-Step Equations

KEY TEACHING POINTS

Example 1
Review with students that an equation is a mathematical statement that two quantities are equal.

Say: We know that Matt bought 3 notebooks, each the same price, and an $8 calculator.

Ask: What operation does the word "and" indicate in an equation? **[Addition]**

Say: On one side of the equation is $3n + 8$. On the other side is 20. So the equation $3n + 8 = 20$ can be used to find the cost of the notebooks.

Check
For Problem 1, have students determine what they know and what they need to find out. If necessary, they can break the problem into expressions and then combine those expressions to form an equation.

COMMON MISCONCEPTION

Ask: What is Tamara's error in writing the equation $6t + 5 = 55$ to represent the cost of each movie ticket?

Reason incorrect: A coupon reduces the total cost. It does not add to the total cost.

Solution: The correct equation is $6t - 5 = 55$.

KEY TEACHING POINTS

Example 2
Write $4x + 2 = 22$ on the board.

Say: We are now going to describe a situation that can be represented by $4x + 2 = 22$. There are countless situations we can write.

Ask: What does $4x + 2 = 22$ mean in words? **[4 times a number plus 2 is equal to 22.]**

Say: Look at the situation that involves a number of people playing a game in teams.

Ask: In the problem, how many teams are there? **[4]** How many people are on each team? **[*x*]** How many people are on the 4 teams in all? **[4*x*]**

Say: There are 2 people waiting to play.

Ask: Are the 2 people on one of the teams? **[No]** Are they part of $4x$? **[No]**

Say: These 2 people are added to $4x$. There are 4 teams with x number of players on each team. This is represented by $4x$. There are 2 people waiting to play. The number of people is represented by $4x + 2$. The value of $4x + 2$ is 22, so $4x + 2 = 22$.

Have volunteers come up with their own situations for $4x + 2 = 22$.

KEY TEACHING POINTS

Example 3

Review with students that inverse operations are operations that undo each other. Addition and subtraction are inverse operations. Multiplication and division are inverse operations.

Write $2x - 6 = 12$ on the board.

Say: You can use inverse operations to find the value of x. We want to isolate x on one side of the equation.

Ask: What is the first step in isolating x? **[Remove the constant, 6.]** How do we remove the 6? **[Add 6 to both sides of the equation.]**

Say: Adding 6 to both sides of the equation results in $2x = 18$.

Ask: What is the second step in isolating x? **[Remove the coefficient, 2.]** How do we remove the 2? **[Divide both sides of the equation by 2.]**

Say: Dividing both sides by 2 results in $x = 9$.

Show the work on the board.

Say: We can check our answer by substituting 9 for x.

Show that $2(9) = 18$ and $18 - 6 = 12$.

Check

Make sure students understand that the first step is to remove the constant and the second step is to remove the coefficient. It may sometimes work to divide first, but because it will usually result in fractions, it is not recommended.

ALTERNATE STRATEGY

Strategy: Use algebra tiles to solve an equation.

1. Write $2x + 4 = 10$ on the board.
2. Draw the following:

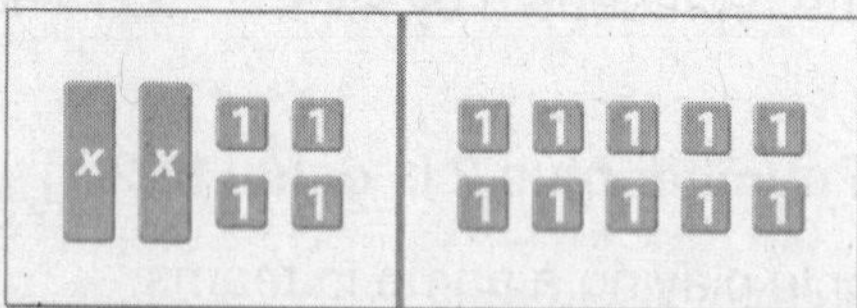

3. **Say:** On the left side are two x tiles and four 1 tiles. On the right side are ten 1 tiles. You can remove one 1 tile from each side until there are no 1 tiles remaining on the left.
4. **Ask:** How many 1 tiles can be removed from each side? **[4]**
5. Erase four 1 tiles from each side.
6. **Ask:** What is left? **[two *x* tiles on one side and six 1 tiles on the other]**
7. **Say:** Now we divide each part into two equal groups.
8. **Ask:** How many 1 tiles are left? **[3]** What is the value of x? **[3]**

KEY TEACHING POINTS

Example 4

Say: Solving a two-step equation with decimals uses the same steps as solving a two-step equation with whole numbers.

Write $0.7x + 1.5 = 1.85$ on the board.

Ask: What is the first step to isolating the variable? **[Subtract 1.5 from both sides of the equation.]**

Say: Subtracting 1.5 from both sides of the equation results in $0.7x = 0.35$.

Ask: What is the second step in isolating *x*? **[Remove the coefficient, 0.7.]** How do we remove the 0.7? **[Divide both sides of the equation by 0.7.]**

Say: One way to divide both sides by 0.7 is to first multiply both sides of the equation by 10, so the coefficient is a whole number. This results in $7x = 3.5$. Now we can divide both sides by 7.

Ask: Why did we multiply both sides by 10? **[It is easier to divide by a whole number than by a decimal.]** What is the value of *x*? **[0.5]**

Say: We can check our answer by substituting 0.5 for *x*.

Check the solution by showing that $0.7(0.5) = 0.35$ and $0.35 + 1.5 = 1.85$.

Example 5

Say: Solving a two-step equation with fractions uses the same steps as solving a two-step equation with whole numbers.

Write $\frac{2}{3}x - 9 = 6$ on the board.

Ask: What is the first step to isolating the variable? **[Add 9 to both sides of the equation.]**

Say: Adding 9 to both sides of the equation results in $\frac{2}{3}x = 15$.

Ask: What is the second step in isolating *x*? **[Remove the coefficient, $\frac{2}{3}$.]** How do we remove the $\frac{2}{3}$? **[Divide both sides of the equation by $\frac{2}{3}$.]**

Ask: How do you divide by a fraction? **[Multiply by the reciprocal.]** What is the reciprocal of $\frac{2}{3}$? $\left[\frac{3}{2}\right]$

Say: We can multiply both sides by $\frac{3}{2}$, which will isolate the variable.

Ask: What is the value of *x*? $\left[22\frac{1}{2}\right]$

Check the solution by showing that $\frac{2}{3}\left(22\frac{1}{2}\right) - 9 = \frac{2}{3}\left(\frac{45}{2}\right) - 9 = \frac{90}{6} - 9 = 15 - 9 = 6$.

KEY TEACHING POINTS

Example 6

Make sure students understand that when dividing integers, if the signs of the dividend and divisor are the same, the quotient is positive, and if the signs are different, the quotient is negative.

Write $-5x - 8 = 12$ on the board.

Ask: What is the first step to isolating the variable? **[Add 8 to both sides of the equation.]**

Say: Adding 8 to both sides of the equation results in $-5x = 20$.

Ask: What is the second step in isolating x? **[Remove the coefficient, –5.]** How do we remove the –5? **[Divide both sides of the equation by –5.]**

Ask: Is the quotient of a positive number divided by a negative number positive or negative? **[negative]** What is the value of x? **[–4]**

Example 7

Say: We are now going to write and solve an equation to find the solution to a real-world problem.

Ask: What do you know? **[A group of people each spent $8 on an entrance fee. They spent a total of $20 on skate rentals. They spent $60 in all.]**

Ask: What do you need to find? **[the number of people in the group]**

Say: Let p represent the number of people in the group. One side of the equation is 60.

Ask: What represents the entrance fee per person? **[8*p*]** What is on the opposite side from 60? **[$8p + 20$]**

Say: To find the number of people, solve the equation $8p + 20 = 60$.

Ask: What is the first step in isolating the variable? **[Subtract 20 from both sides of the equation.]**

Say: Subtracting 20 from both sides of the equation results in $8p = 40$.

Ask: What is the second step in isolating the variable? **[Divide both sides by 8.]** What is the value of p? **[5]** How many people are in the group? **[5]**

ADDITIONAL ONLINE INTERVENTION RESOURCES

Use the following for students who have not mastered the concepts in Skill 21.

- Math on the Spot videos
- Personal Math Trainer with customized intervention
- Building Block worksheets (Skill 22: Connect Words and Algebra; Skill 23: Connect Words and Equations; Skill 98: Solve Two-Step Equations)

Name ____________________ Date ____________ Class ____________

SKILL 21

Two-Step Equations

Vocabulary
Equation
Inverse operations
Constant
Coefficient
Power of 10
Reciprocal

Example 1

You can write a two-step equation to represent a real-world situation.

Matt bought 3 notebooks and a calculator. The calculator cost \$8 and Matt spent \$20 in all. Each notebook cost the same amount. Write an equation that can be used to find the cost of each notebook.

What do you know?	Matt bought 3 notebooks. Matt bought a calculator that cost \$8. The total cost was \$20.
What do you need to find? Use a variable to represent what you are trying to find.	Let n be the cost of each notebook.
Write an expression to represent the cost of the notebooks.	$3n$
Write an expression to represent the cost of the notebooks and the calculator.	$3n + 8$
Write an equation to represent the situation.	$3n + 8 = 20$

The equation $3n + 8 = 20$ can be used to find the cost of the notebooks.

Check

1. Max studies the same amount of time each day for 5 days for a social studies test. He also studies 45 minutes for a math quiz. He studied for a total of 300 minutes. Write an equation that can be used to find the total number of minutes each day that Max studied for his social studies test.

____

2. What's the Error? A group of 6 friends went to the movies. They had a coupon for \$5 off the cost of one movie ticket. After using the coupon, the total cost of the movie tickets was \$55. Tamara said the equation $6t + 5 = 55$ can be used to find the amount that each ticket cost. Describe Tamara's error and give the correct equation.

____

Name ______________________ Date __________ Class __________

Example 2

You can write a situation that can be represented by a two-step equation. Write a situation for $4x + 2 = 22$.

Break the equation in parts.

- x is the solution of the problem or the quantity you are looking for.
- $4x$ means the quantity you are looking for has been multiplied by 4.
- $+ 2$ means that 2 is added to $4x$.
- $= 22$ means that after adding 2 to $4x$, the result is 22.

Below is one situation that can be described by $4x + 2 = 22$.

There are 4 teams with x number of people playing on each team. There are 2 people waiting to play. Altogether there are 22 people. How many players are on each team?	• 4 represents the number of teams. • x represents the number of people on each team. • 2 represents the number of people not on a team. • 22 represents the total number of people.

Check

3. Write a situation that can be represented by $3x + 5 = 14$.

____

Example 3

To solve a two-step equation, use inverse operations to isolate the variable. The first step is to remove the constant. The second step is to use inverse operations to remove the coefficient. At that point, the variable will be isolated.

Solve for x: $2x - 6 = 12$.

Add 6 to both sides of the equation to remove the constant.	$2x - 6 + 6 = 12 + 6$ $2x = 18$
Divide both sides of the equation by 2 to remove the coefficient.	$\frac{2x}{2} = \frac{18}{2}$ $x = 9$

Check

Solve each equation.

4. $2a + 4 = 10$ ______________

5. $4b - 3 = 17$ ______________

6. $3c + 5 = 11$ ______________

Name ______________________ Date ____________ Class ____________

Example 4

Solve for x: $0.7x + 1.5 = 1.85$.

Subtract 1.5 from both sides of the equation to remove the constant.	$0.7x + 1.5 - 1.5 = 1.85 - 1.5$ $0.7x = 0.35$
Divide both sides of the equation by 0.7 to remove the coefficient.	$\frac{0.7x}{0.7} = \frac{0.35}{0.7}$ $10\left(\frac{0.7x}{0.7}\right) = 10\left(\frac{0.35}{0.7}\right)$ $\frac{7x}{7} = \frac{3.5}{7}$ $x = 0.5$ Multiply both sides by a power of 10, so the denominator is a whole number.

Check

Solve each equation.

7. $0.25d + 4 = 7$ ____________

8. $2.4e - 1.8 = 10.2$ ____________

9. $6.4f + 3.6 = 18.8$ ____________

Example 5

Solve for x: $\frac{2}{3}x - 9 = 6$.

Add 9 to both sides of the equation to remove the constant.	$\frac{2}{3}x - 9 + 9 = 6 + 9$ $\frac{2}{3}x = 15$
Divide both sides of the equation by $\frac{2}{3}$ to remove the coefficient.	$\frac{2}{3}x\left(\frac{3}{2}\right) = 15\left(\frac{3}{2}\right)$ $x = \frac{45}{2} = 22\frac{1}{2}$ Divide by a fraction by multiplying its reciprocal.

Check

Solve each equation.

10. $\frac{1}{4}g - 2 = 5$ ____________

11. $\frac{3}{5}h + \frac{7}{10} = 2\frac{1}{5}$ ____________

12. $\frac{5}{8}j - \frac{3}{4} = \frac{1}{2}$ ____________

Name ______________________ Date ______________ Class ______________

Example 6

Coefficients can be negative numbers. Solve for x: $-5x - 8 = 12$.

Add 8 to both sides of the equation to remove the constant.	$-5x - 8 + 8 = 12 + 8$ $-5x = 20$
Divide both sides by –5 to remove the coefficient.	$\frac{-5x}{-5} = \frac{20}{-5}$ $x = -4$

Use rules for dividing integers.

Check

Solve each equation.

13. $-2k + 4 = 6$ ______________

14. $-3l - 5 = 7$ ______________

15. $-\frac{1}{2}m - 4 = -6$ ______________

Example 7

The entrance fee is \$8 to go roller skating at a rink. A group of people spent a total of \$20 on skate rentals. They spent \$60 in all. How many people were in the group?

Write an equation. Let p represent the people.	$8p + 20 = 60$
Solve.	$8p + 20 - 20 = 60 - 20$ $8p = 40$ $\frac{8p}{8} = \frac{40}{8}$ $p = 5$

There were 5 people in the group.

Check

Write an equation and solve.

16. From Sunday to Friday, Desiree jogged the same number of miles. On Saturday, she jogged 12 miles. She jogged 54 miles last week. How many miles did Desiree jog each day from Sunday to Friday?

____

SKILL 21 TWO-STEP EQUATIONS

SKILL 22

Two-Step Inequalities

KEY TEACHING POINTS

Example 1

Review with students that an inequality is a mathematical statement that two quantities are not necessarily equal. Make sure students know that > means "is greater than," < means "is less than," ≥ means "is greater than or equal to," and ≤ means "is less than or equal to."

Say: We know that Janet is reading a 275-page book. We know that she read 35 pages the first day and she wants to finish the rest of the book within no more than 6 days.

Say: On one side of the inequality is the number of pages that Janet has left to read and the pages she has already read.

Ask: What expression represents the pages she has left to read and the pages read? **[$6p + 35$]**

Say: 275 is on the other side of the inequality.

Ask: Which inequality symbol should be used? **[≥]** Why? **[Janet could finish the book in less than 6 days.]** If Janet finishes the book in less than 6 days, what does it do to the average number of pages per day? **[It increases.]**

Check

For Problem 1, have students determine what they know and what they need to find out. If necessary, they can break the problem into expressions and then combine those expressions to form an inequality.

COMMON MISCONCEPTION

Ask: What is Cindy's error in writing the inequality $4l + 5 < 40$ to represent the cost of each lunch?

Reason incorrect: The symbol < means "is less than." The lunch will be at least $40, so the correct symbol to use is ≥.

Solution: The correct inequality is $4l + 5 \geq 40$.

KEY TEACHING POINTS

Example 2

Write $6x - 10 \leq 50$ on the board.

Say: We are now going to describe a situation that can be represented by $6x - 10 \leq 50$. There are countless situations we can write.

Ask: What does $6x - 10 \leq 50$ mean in words? **[10 less than 6 times a number is less than or equal to 50.]**

Say: Look at the situation involving Bianca.

Ask: In the problem, how many books did she buy? **[6]** What was the cost of each book? **[x]** What does the coupon do? **[It reduces the total cost by $10.]**

Say: On one side of the inequality, we have Bianca buying 6 books that cost the same amount and she used a $10 off coupon.

Ask: What does 50 represent? **[The maximum total cost after the coupon was applied.]** What words tell us about the cost? **[She spent no more than $50.]** Could Bianca have spent exactly $50? **[Yes]**

Say: The situation can be represented by $6x - 10 \leq 50$.
Have volunteers come up with their own situations for $6x - 10 \leq 50$.

Example 3

Review with students that inverse operations are operations that undo each other. Addition and subtraction are inverse operations. Multiplication and division are inverse operations.
Write $3x - 4 > 17$ on the board.

Say: Solving an inequality involving positive numbers is like solving an equation. The same steps are used.

Ask: What is the first step in isolating x? **[Remove the constant, 4.]** How do we remove the 4? **[Add 4 to both sides of the inequality.]**

Say: Adding 4 to both sides of the inequality results in $3x > 21$.

Ask: What is the second step in isolating x? **[Remove the coefficient, 3.]** How do we remove the 3? **[Divide both sides of the inequality by 3.]** What is the solution set for x? **[$x > 7$]**

Check

Make sure students understand that the first step is to remove the constant and the second step is to remove the coefficient. It may sometimes work to divide first, but because it will usually result in fractions, it is not recommended.

ALTERNATE STRATEGY

Strategy: Solve an inequality like an equation by using an is-equal-to symbol.

1. Write $2a - 8 \leq 6$ and $2a - 8 = 6$ on the board.
2. **Say:** Solving an inequality and solving an equation involve the same steps, so let's turn this inequality into an equation.
3. **Ask:** What is the first step to solving this equation? **[Add 8.]** What is the result of adding 8 to both sides of the equation? **[$2a = 14$]**
4. **Ask:** What is the second step to solving this equation? **[Divide by 2.]** What is the value of a? **[$a = 7$]**
5. **Ask:** Let's turn the equation back into an inequality. What is the first step to solving this inequality? **[Add 8.]** What is the result of adding 8 to both sides of the equation? **[$2a \leq 14$]**
6. **Ask:** What is the second step to solving this inequality? **[Divide by 2.]** What is the solution set for a? **[$a \leq 7$]**
7. **Say:** As you can see, the only difference is using the inequality symbol instead of the equal symbol.

KEY TEACHING POINTS

Example 4

Say: Solving a two-step inequality with fractions uses the same steps as solving a two-step equation with fractions.

Write $\frac{3}{5}x+2<8$ on the board.

Ask: What is the first step to isolating the variable? **[Subtract 2 from both sides of the inequality.]** What is the result of subtracting 2 from both sides of the inequality? **[$\frac{3}{5}x<6$]**

Ask: What is the second step in isolating x? **[Remove the coefficient, $\frac{3}{5}$.]** How do we remove the $\frac{3}{5}$? **[Divide both sides of the inequality by $\frac{3}{5}$.]**

Ask: How do you divide by a fraction? **[Multiply by the reciprocal.]** What is the reciprocal of $\frac{3}{5}$? $\left[\frac{5}{3}\right]$ What is the solution set for x? **[10]** What is the inequality? **[$x<10$]**

Example 5

Make sure students understand that when dividing integers, if the signs are the same, the quotient is positive, and if the signs are different, the quotient is negative.

Write $-4x-2>14$ on the board.

Ask: What is the first step to isolating the variable? **[Add 2 to both sides of the inequality.]**

Say: Adding 2 to both sides of the inequality results in $-4x>16$.

Ask: What is the second step in isolating x? **[Remove the coefficient, –4.]** How do we remove the –4? **[Divide both sides of the equation by –4.]**

Ask: What is $16\div-4$? **[–4]**

Say: Let's see if $x>-4$. Let's try –3.

Ask: What is –3(–4)? **[12]** What is 12 – 2? **[10]** Is 10 > 14? **[No]**

Say: When you multiply or divide both sides by a negative number in an inequality, it is necessary to reverse the inequality symbol in the solution.

Write $x<-4$ on the board.

Say: Now let's check to see if this solution set is true. If x is less than –4, let's try –5.

Ask: What is –5(–4)? **[20]** What is 20 – 2? **[18]** Is 18 > 14? **[Yes]**

Check

Make sure students understand that they need to reverse the inequality symbol in the solution when the negative sign is on the side of the inequality with the variable.

COMMON MISCONCEPTION

Ask: What is Drew's error in writing the solution set of $k \leq 3$ for the inequality $-5k + 2 \leq 17$?

Reason incorrect: Drew did not reverse the inequality symbol.

Solution: The correct solution set is $k \geq 3$.

KEY TEACHING POINTS

Example 6

Ask: What do you know? **[Ezra earns $5 for each dog he walks. He has $150 in his savings account. He wants to have at least $225 in that account.]**

Ask: What do you need to find? **[The number of dogs he has to walk]**

Say: Let *d* represent the number of dogs that Ezra has to walk. On one side of the inequality is 225.

Ask: What represents the number of dogs that Ezra has to walk? **[5*d*]** What is on the opposite side from 225? **[5*d* + 150]**

Say: To find the number of dogs, solve the inequality $5d = 150 \leq 225$.

Ask: What are the two steps needed to solve the inequality? **[Subtract 150 from both sides and then divide both sides by 5.]** How many dogs does Ezra have to walk? **[at least 15]**

Example 7

Say: A number line can be used to represent the solution set to an inequality.

Say: Look at the number lines for $2x - 2 > 4$ and $2x - 2 < 4$. An open circle is used to show that the number is not part of the solution set.

Ask: For greater than, which way does the ray point? **[right]** Why? **[Because every number to the right of 3 is greater than 3.]** For less than, which way does the ray point? **[left]** Why? **[Because every number to the left of 3 is less than 3.]**

Say: Look at the number lines for $2x - 2 \geq 4$ and $2x - 2 \leq 4$. A closed circle is used to show that the number is part of the solution set.

Ask: If you were to graph the solution to $3x + 1 < 7$, would you use an open circle or a closed circle on the number line? **[open circle]** Why? **[The symbol < means that the solution is not part of the set.]**

ADDITIONAL ONLINE INTERVENTION RESOURCES

Use the following for students who have not mastered the concepts in Skill 22.

- Math on the Spot videos
- Personal Math Trainer with customized intervention
- Building Block worksheets (Skill 52: Inverse Operations; Skill 54: Locate Points on a Number Line; Skill 88: Solve and Graph Inequalities; Skill 110: Write an Inequality for a Graph)

Name ______________________ Date ______________ Class ______________

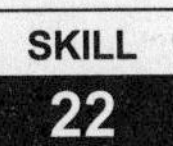

Two-Step Inequalities

Example 1

You can write a two-step **inequality** to represent a real-world situation.

Janet is reading a 275-page book. She read 35 pages the first day. She wants to finish the book within no more than 6 days. Write an inequality to find the average number of pages she will need to read each day to reach her goal.

What do you know?	Janet's book is 275 pages. She read 35 pages the first day. She wants to finish the rest of the book within 6 days.
What do you need to find? Use a variable to represent what you are trying to find.	Let p represent the number of pages she will average.
Write an expression to represent the number of pages that she has to read.	$6p$
Write an expression to represent the number of pages she has to read and the number of pages she has already read.	$6p + 35$
Write an inequality to represent the situation.	$6p + 35 \geq 275$

Write an inequality because it may take Janet less than 6 days to finish the book.

The inequality $6p + 35 \geq 275$ can be used to find the number of pages that Janet needs to read to reach her goal.

Vocabulary

Inequality
Inverse operations
Constant
Coefficient
Power of 10
Reciprocal

Check

1. Brittany has budgeted no more than $90 for guitar lessons. Lessons cost $15 each. She has already spent $30 on lessons. Write an inequality that can be used to find the total number of guitar lessons that Brittany can still have.

____

2. What's the Error? Four friends are having lunch at Dan's Diner. Cindy's parents are treating for the lunch. They each ordered Dan's lunch special and shared a $5 pitcher of lemonade. The total cost of the bill was at least $40. Cindy said the inequality $4l + 5 < 40$ can be used to find the cost of each lunch special. Describe Cindy's error and give the correct inequality.

____

Name ______________________ Date ______________ Class ______________

Example 2

You can write a situation that can be represented by a two-step inequality. Write a situation involving $6x - 10 \leq 50$.

Break the inequality into parts.

- x is the solution of the problem or the quantity you are looking for.
- $6x$ means the quantity you are looking for has been multiplied by 6.
- -10 means that 10 is subtracted from $6x$.
- ≤ 50 means that after subtracting 10 from $6x$, the solution is less than or equal to 50.

Below is one situation that can be described by $6x - 10 \leq 50$.

Bianca bought 6 books that each cost x dollars. She had a \$10 off coupon. After applying the coupon, Bianca spent no more than \$50. What is the cost of each of the books before the coupon was applied?	• 6 represents the number of books. • x represents the cost of each book before the coupon was applied. • -10 represents the change in cost with the coupon. • ≤ 50 represents that the total cost was less than or equal to \$50.

Check

3. Write a situation that can be represented by $2x + 6 > 20$.

____

Example 3

To solve a two-step inequality, use inverse operations to isolate the variable. The first step is to use inverse operations to remove the constant. The second step is to use inverse operations to remove the coefficient. At that point, the variable will be isolated.

Solve for x: $3x - 4 > 17$.

Add 4 to both sides of the inequality to remove the constant.	$3x - 4 + 4 > 17 + 4$ $3x > 21$
Divide both sides of the inequality by 3 to remove the coefficient.	$\frac{3x}{3} > \frac{21}{3}$ $x > 7$

Solve an inequality as you would an equation.

Check

Solve each inequality.

4. $2a - 8 \leq 6$ ____________

5. $3b + 6 \geq 15$ ____________

6. $0.4c + 2 > 8$ ____________

Name ______________________ Date ______________ Class ______________

Example 4

Solve for x: $\frac{3}{5}x + 2 < 8$.

Subtract 2 from both sides of the inequality.	$\frac{3}{5}x + 2 - 2 < 8 - 2$ $\frac{3}{5}x < 6$
Divide both sides of the inequality by $\frac{3}{5}$ to remove the coefficient.	$\frac{3}{5}x\left(\frac{5}{3}\right) < 6\left(\frac{5}{3}\right)$ $x < \frac{30}{3}$ $x < 10$

Divide by a fraction by multiplying by its reciprocal.

Check

Solve each inequality.

7. $\frac{1}{2}d + 3 > 7$

8. $\frac{2}{3}e + \frac{1}{6} < \frac{7}{12}$

9. $\frac{4}{5}f - \frac{1}{2} \geq 2\frac{1}{10}$

______________ ______________ ______________

Example 5

Solve for x: $-4x - 2 > 14$

Add 2 to both sides of the equation to remove the constant.	$-4x - 2 + 2 > 14 + 2$ $-4x > 16$
Divide both sides by -4 to remove the coefficient.	$\frac{-4x}{-4} > \frac{16}{-4}$
Reverse the inequality symbol.	$x < -4$

Reverse the inequality symbol when multiplying or dividing both sides by a negative number.

Check

Solve each inequality.

10. $-3g + 8 \geq 14$

11. $-0.6h - 0.5 < 2.5$

12. $-\frac{3}{4}j + 2 > -4$

______________ ______________ ______________

13. What's the Error? Drew said the solution set for $-5k + 2 \leq 17$ is $k \leq -3$. Describe the error and give the correct solution set for the inequality.

____

Name ______________________ Date ______________ Class ______________

Example 6

Ezra earns $5 for each dog he walks. He has $150 in his savings account. He wants to have at least $225 in his savings account. How many dogs does he have to walk? Write and solve an inequality to represent this situation.

Write an inequality. Let *d* represent the dogs.	$5d + 150 \geq 225$
Solve.	$5d + 150 - 150 \geq 225 - 150$ $5d \geq 75$ $\frac{5d}{5} \geq \frac{75}{5}$ $d \geq 15$

Ezra has to walk at least 15 dogs to reach his goal.

14. Len has $25 to bowl and to buy a snack. Each game costs $4 and the snack Len wants to buy costs $3. What is the greatest number of games that Len can bowl? Write an inequality and solve.

____

Example 7

You can graph the solution set to an inequality.

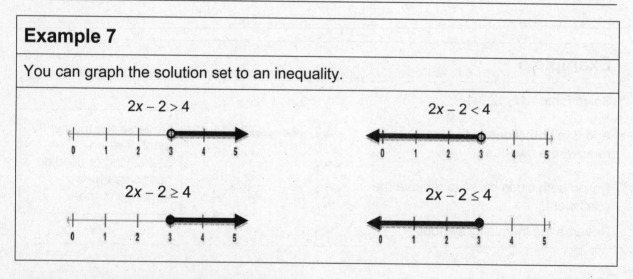

$2x - 2 > 4$

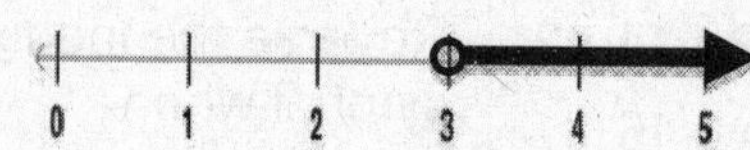

$2x - 2 < 4$

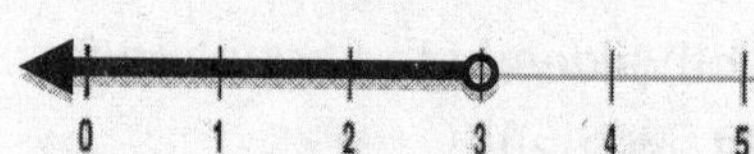

$2x - 2 \geq 4$

0 1 2 3 4 5

$2x - 2 \leq 4$

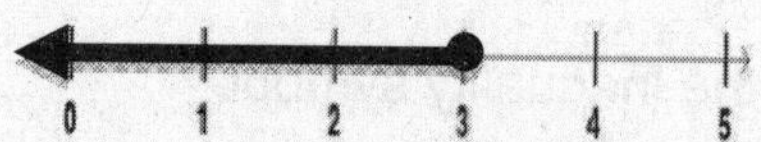

Solve each inequality. Graph the solution.

15. $3x + 1 > 7$ ______________

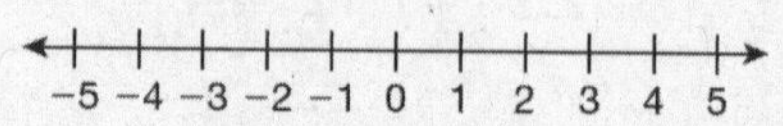

16. $-2s + 3 \leq -5$ ______________

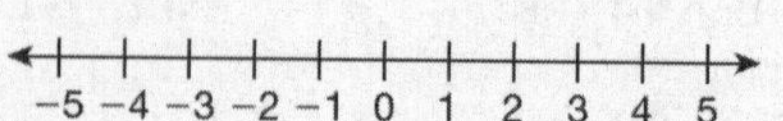

SKILL 22 TWO-STEP INEQUALITIES

SKILL 23

Unit Rates

KEY TEACHING POINTS

Example 1

Review with students that a rate is a comparison of two quantities with different units.

Say: A unit rate can be written as a fraction with 1 as the denominator.

Write $\frac{18 \text{ points}}{1 \text{ game}}$, $\frac{24 \text{ miles}}{1 \text{ gallon}}$, $\frac{\$15}{1 \text{ hour}}$, and $\frac{\frac{1}{2} \text{ page}}{1 \text{ minute}}$ on the board.

Ask: What do all of the unit rates have in common? **[Each has 1 unit as the denominator.]**

Say: The word *per* means for each. Rates will often use the word *per*. Look at the rates that are not unit rates.

Ask: What do you notice about this list? **[The second quantity has numbers other than 1.]**

Example 2

Say: A unit price is a unit rate with money. When you go to the food store, many of the items will be unit priced. Items may be in price per pound, price per ounce, or price per unit.

Say: Three packages of paper cost \$15.75. We want to find the cost for 1 package of paper.

Ask: How is the unit price determined? **[Divide the price by the number of units.]**

Say: The price is \$15.75. There are 3 units.

Ask: What is the unit price? **[\$5.25]**

Check

Each question tells what the second unit should be. Remind students that the unit rate can be a number less than 1.

Example 3

Using a unit rate to solve a problem is a longer version of using a proportion. The result is the same as using a proportion and for many this will be a preferable method.

Ask: What do you know? **[320 people saw 2 performances of a play. There are 7 performances of the play.]** What does "at that rate" mean? **[The number of people per performance will remain the same.]**

Say: To find the unit rate, divide the number of people by the number of performances.

Ask: What is 320 ÷ 2? **[160]**

Say: So, an average of 160 people saw each performance of the play. We can now use that number to find how many people would see 7 performances.

Ask: What do we do to find the number of people that would see 7 performances? **[Multiply 160(7).]** What is 160(7)? **[1120]**

ALTERNATE STRATEGY

Strategy: Use the units to find an equivalent rate.

1. Write $\frac{320}{2} = \frac{x}{7}$ on the board.
2. **Say:** The equation shows 320 people saw 2 performances and a number of people that could see 7 performances. We know what both denominators are and we know one of the numerators.
3. **Say:** We can find the number of people that could see 7 performances by finding what factor times 2 is equal to 7. Then we can use that number to multiply times 320.
4. **Ask:** What is $7 \div 2$? **[3.5]**
5. **Say:** We can multiply 320(3.5) to find the number of people that could see 7 performances.
6. **Ask:** What is 320(3.5)? **[1120]**

Explain to students that you did not find a unit rate, but the result is the same. This is a particularly good method to use when one denominator is a factor of the other denominator.

COMMON MISCONCEPTION

Ask: What is Grant's error in saying that the cost for 9 nights is $1485?

Reason incorrect: Grant multiplied the 3-night rate by 9 instead of finding the unit rate.

Solution: Follow these steps:

1. Divide the cost by the number of nights to find the unit rate: $\frac{\$165}{3} \div \frac{3}{3} = \frac{\$55}{1}$.
2. Multiply the unit rate times the extended number of nights: $\frac{\$55}{1} \cdot \frac{9}{9} = \frac{\$495}{9}$.

The actual cost for 9 nights is $495.

KEY TEACHING POINTS

Example 4

Say: There are 84 books on 2 shelves.

Ask: What is the unit rate of books per shelf? **[42]**

Write $\frac{42}{1} = \frac{504}{x}$ on the board.

Say: This time we need to find the value of the denominator, which is the number of shelves.

Ask: How can we find the number of shelves? **[Divide 504 ÷ 42.]** What is 504 ÷ 42? **[12]**

Say: It will take 12 shelves for 504 books.

KEY TEACHING POINTS

Example 5

Explain to students that a complex fraction is a fraction that contains a fraction in its numerator, its denominator, or both.

Show that a complex fraction is another way to divide: $\dfrac{\frac{1}{2}}{3} = \dfrac{1}{2} \div 3$, $\dfrac{4}{\frac{2}{3}} = 4 \div \dfrac{2}{3}$, $\dfrac{\frac{2}{5}}{\frac{1}{4}} = \dfrac{2}{5} \div \dfrac{1}{4}$.

Ask: Read the problem. What do you know? **[A train travels 20 miles in $\frac{1}{4}$ hour.]** What is the unit rate? **[The distance traveled in 1 hour]**

Say: In this problem, 1 is greater than the unit you have been given.

Ask: How can you find the distance traveled in 1 hour? **[Multiply by the reciprocal of the fraction.]** What is the reciprocal of $\frac{1}{4}$? **[4]**

Say: You can multiply 20(4) = 80 to find the distance traveled in 1 hour.

Check

Point out to students that dividing by a unit fraction is the same as multiplying by the denominator.

Example 6

Say: Everybody loves a bargain and no one likes to spend money they don't have to. Knowing which items provide the better buy is one way to save money.

Say: The table shows that a 32-fluid-ounce bottle of water costs $0.96 and a 48-fluid-ounce bottle of water costs $1.36. We want to know which is the better buy.

Ask: How can we tell which is the better buy? **[The size with the lesser unit price is the better buy.]**

Ask: What is $0.96 ÷ 32? **[$0.03]** What is $1.36 ÷ 48? **[approximately $0.0283]**

Say: Because we are comparing unit prices, we could have stopped once we found out that the 48-fluid-ounce bottle cost less than $0.03 per fluid ounce. The 48-fluid-ounce bottle is the better buy.

Check

Point out to students that the larger size is often, but not always, the better buy. Problem 15 is an example of when the smaller size is the better buy.

Discuss Problem 16 with students, asking when a smaller size that has a more expensive unit price might be what is needed.

ALTERNATE STRATEGY

Strategy: Use factors to compare rates.

1. Have students look at Problem 14.
2. **Say:** You can use a common factor to compare rates.
3. **Ask:** What are the factors of 12? **[1, 2, 3, 4, 6, and 12]** What are the common factors of 16? **[1, 2, 4, 8, and 16]** What is the greatest common factor? **[4]**
4. **Say:** You can find which is the better buy for 4 ounces. Divide the cost by the number that will give 4 ounces. Divide by 3 for the 12 ounce size and by 4 for the 16 ounce size.
5. **Ask:** What is $2.88 ÷ 3? **[$0.96]** What is $3.52 ÷ 4? **[$0.88]**
6. **Say:** Which is the better buy? **[16 ounces for $3.52]**

Explain to students that you did not find a unit rate, but the result is the same. This is a particularly good method to use when one denominator is a factor of the other denominator.

ADDITIONAL ONLINE INTERVENTION RESOURCES

Use the following for students who have not mastered the concepts in Skill 23.

- Math on the Spot videos
- Personal Math Trainer with customized intervention
- Building Block worksheets (Skill 5: Add and Subtract Like Fractions; Skill 63: Multiply Fractions; Skill 65: Multiply with Fractions and Decimals; Skill 68: Operations with Fractions)

Name ____________________ Date ______________ Class ______________

SKILL 23

Unit Rates

Example 1

A unit rate is a rate in which the second quantity is one unit. When the unit rate is an amount of money, it is called the unit price or unit cost.

Unit Rates	Not Unit Rates
18 points per game	45 points in 3 games
24 miles per gallon	120 miles per 5 gallons
$15 per hour	$60 for 4 hours
$\frac{1}{2}$ page per minute	1 page per $\frac{1}{2}$ minute

Vocabulary
Unit rate
Unit price
Unit cost
Complex fraction
Reciprocal

Check

Determine if each is a unit rate.

1. 20 miles per hour
   ○ Yes ○ No

2. 6 quarts per 1.5 gallons
   ○ Yes ○ No

3. 0.75 mile per minute
   ○ Yes ○ No

Example 2

Three packages of paper cost $15.75. What is the unit price of the paper?

Divide the cost by the number of packages: $\frac{\$15.75}{3} = \$5.25$.

The unit price per package is $5.25.

Check

Find the unit rate or unit price.

4. A 512-page book has 16 chapters that each has an equal number of pages. How many pages are there per chapter?

   ____

5. Mr. Hernandez drives 30 miles in 40 minutes. How many miles does he drive per minute?

   ____

6. Jody typed 1200 words in 15 minutes. How many words can he type per minute?

   ____

Name ______________________ Date ____________ Class ____________

Example 3

You can use a unit rate to solve problems by using an equivalent rate.

A total of 320 people saw 2 performances of a play. At that rate, how many people can see 7 performances of the play?

Find the unit rate. $\frac{320}{2} \div \frac{2}{2} = \frac{160}{1}$

Use equivalent rates. $\frac{160}{1} \bullet \frac{7}{7} = \frac{1{,}120}{7}$

Multiply by the unit rate.

A total of 1120 people can see the 7 performances of the play.

Check

Solve.

7. A box of 6 pencils costs $2.10. At that rate, what is the cost for 15 pencils?

____

8. What's the Error? It costs customers $165 to spend 3 nights at the Econo Motel. Grant said that it costs $1485 to spend 9 nights at the Econo Motel. Describe Grant's error and give the correct cost for 9 nights.

____

Example 4

You can use a unit rate to solve problems to find the number of units.

There are 84 books on 2 shelves. At that rate, how many shelves are needed for 504 books?

Find the unit rate. $\frac{84}{2} \div \frac{2}{2} = \frac{42}{1}$

Use equivalent rates. $\frac{42}{1} \bullet \frac{12}{12} = \frac{504}{12}$

Multiply by the unit rate.

A total of 12 shelves are needed for 504 books.

Name _______________ Date _______________ Class _______________

Check

Solve.

9. It cost \$18 to buy a box of 24 golf balls. At that rate, how many golf balls can be bought for \$108?

____

10. A group of hikers hiked 4.5 miles in 2 hours. At that rate, how many hours will it take the group to hike 7.65 miles?

____

Example 5

A unit rate may contain a complex fraction.

A train travels 20 miles in $\frac{1}{4}$ hour. What is the train's speed in miles per hour?

Write an equation.

$$\frac{20\text{ mi}}{\frac{1}{4}\text{h}} = \frac{x\text{ mi}}{1\text{ h}}$$

Find the unit rate.

$$\frac{20\text{ mi}}{\frac{1}{4}\text{h}} \cdot \frac{4}{4} = \frac{80\text{ mi}}{1\text{ h}}$$

Divide by a fraction by multiplying by its reciprocal.

The train's speed is 80 miles per hour.

Check

Solve.

11. Evan read 18 pages in $\frac{1}{2}$ hour. What is Evan's rate of pages per hour?

____

12. Mr. Ryder drove 30 miles in $\frac{2}{3}$ hour. What is Mr. Ryder's average speed in miles per hour?

____

13. A recipe calls for $\frac{1}{3}$ cup of water for each $\frac{1}{4}$ cup of soy sauce. How many cups of water are needed for 1 cup of soy sauce?

____

Name ______________________ Date ______________ Class ______________

Example 6

You can compare unit prices to find the better buy. The lower the unit price, the better the bargain.

The table shows the costs of two sizes of bottled water. Which is the better buy?

Size (fl oz)	Price ($)
32	$0.96
48	$1.36

Find the unit price for the 32 fl oz bottle. $\frac{\$0.96}{32} \div \frac{32}{32} = \frac{\$0.03}{1}$

Find the unit price for the 48 fl oz bottle. $\frac{\$1.36}{48} \div \frac{48}{48} = \frac{\$0.028\overline{3}}{1}$

Compare the unit prices. $\$0.03 > \$0.028\overline{3}$

The 48 fluid ounce bottle is the better buy.

Check

Choose the better buy.

14. 12 oz for $2.88
    16 oz for $3.52

    ____

15. 46 fl oz for $5.52
    128 fl oz for $16.64

    ____

16. Is there ever any reason to buy a size of product that is not the better or best buy?

    ____

SKILL 23 UNIT RATES

SKILL 24

Writing Linear Equations

KEY TEACHING POINTS

Example 1

Write $y = mx + b$ on the board.

Say: This is the form for an equation that is in slope-intercept form. The variable *m* represents the slope and *b* represents the *y*-intercept.

Ask: What is slope? **[The ratio of rise over run]** What is the *y*-intercept? **[The point where a line crosses the *y*-axis]** What is the value of *x* for any *y*-intercept? **[0]**

Say: Look at the problem. In the problem, $4x$ represents the cost per person and 8 represents the one-time cost for parking. In slope-intercept form, *x* represents the independent variable. In this situation, *x* can be any whole number. *y* represents the dependent variable. The value of *y* depends on the value of *x*.

Ask: For example, if $x = 3$, what is the value of *y*? **[20]** If $x = 5$, what is the value of *y*? **[28]**

Check

Make sure students understand that the coefficient in the problem is the number that is multiplied by the variable. The constant is the stand-alone number.

Example 2

Say: To write an equation in slope-intercept form using data from a graph, you need to find the slope and the *y*-intercept. Let's find the slope first.

Say: We can pick any two ordered pairs. When possible, it is best to pick ordered pairs that are integers. Let's try (0, 5) and (4, 10).

Write $m = \frac{y_2 - y_1}{x_2 - x_1}$ on the board.

Say: To find the slope, we subtract one value of *y* from the other value of *y* and then we subtract one value of *x* from the other value of *x*. It does not matter in which order we subtract as long as the order for *y* and *x* are the same.

Say: Let's find the change in *y*.

Ask: What is 10 – 5? **[5]**

Say: Let's find the change in *x*.

Ask: What is 4 – 0? **[4]** What is the slope? $\left[\frac{5}{4}\right]$

Say: Now let's find the *y*-intercept, which can be read from the graph.

Ask: What is the *y*-intercept? **[5]** What is the equation of the data? $\left[y = \frac{5}{4}x + 5\right]$

KEY TEACHING POINTS

Example 3

Say: To write an equation in slope-intercept form using data from a graph, you need to find the slope and the *y*-intercept. Let's find the slope first.

Ask: What two ordered pairs can we use? **[(16, 24) and (24, 33)]** What is the change in *y*? **[9]** What is the change in *x*? **[8]** What is the slope? $\left[\frac{9}{8}\right]$

Write $y = mx + b$ on the board.

Say: Here is the equation in slope-intercept form.

Ask: What is the value of *m*? $\left[\frac{9}{8}\right]$

Say: We can choose the values for *x* and *y* from either ordered pair. Let's try 24 for *x* and 33 for *y*. Let's substitute the values in for the variables.

Ask: What is $\frac{9}{8} \cdot 24$? **[27]**

Say: Now we have $33 = 27 + b$.

Ask: What is the value of *b*? **[6]**

Say: The equation $y = \frac{9}{8}x + 6$ represents the cost of the juice.

COMMON MISCONCEPTION

Ask: What is Jim's error in writing the equation $y = 150x + 100$?

Reason incorrect: Jim owes less money with each month he makes a payment, which indicates a negative slope. The *y*-intercept is also incorrect because the amount would be greater than $1000.

Solution: Follow these steps:

1. Write two ordered pairs to represent the situation: (3, 1000) and (6, 550).
2. Find the slope: $m = \frac{1000 - 550}{3 - 6} = \frac{450}{-3} = -150$.
3. Use the slope to find the *y*-intercept. Pick one ordered pair to use. Try (3, 1000).

$$1000 = -150 \cdot 3 + b$$
$$1000 = -450 + b$$
$$1000 + 450 = -450 + 450 + b$$
$$1450 = b$$

The correct equation is $y = -150x + 1450$.

KEY TEACHING POINTS

Example 4

Say: Writing an equation from a table is much easier than from a description because the ordered pairs are essentially given. Pick any two ordered pairs. Let's try (1, 35) and (2, 50).

Ask: What is the change in *y*? **[15]** What is the change in *x*? **[1]** What is the slope? **[15]**

Say: We can use the slope to find the *y*-intercept. Pick one ordered pair to use. Try (1, 35).

Write $35 = 15(1) + b$ on the board.

Ask: What is 15(1)? **[15]**

Say: We now have $35 = 15 + b$.

Ask: What is the value of *b*? **[20]** What is the *y*-intercept? **[20]** What is the equation represented by the table? **[$y = 15x + 20$].**

ALTERNATE STRATEGY

Strategy: Draw a graph to represent the data in the table.

1. Draw a graph as shown.

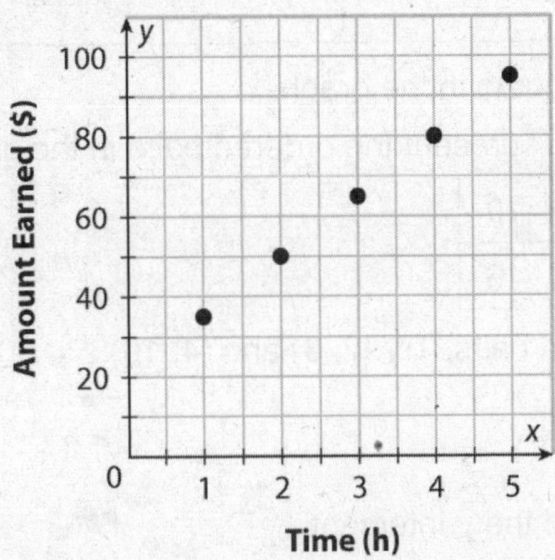

2. **Ask:** What is the change in *y* when *x* increases by 1? **[15]** What is the slope? **[15]**
3. **Say:** You can subtract 15 from (1, 35) to find the *y*-intercept.
4. **Ask:** What is 35 – 15? **[20]**
5. **Ask:** What is the equation represented by the table? **[$y = 15x + 20$]**

KEY TEACHING POINTS

Example 5

This graph shows related data and has a line showing the data is linear. The steps are the same as the graph problem in Example 2.

Say: The data is linear as the line shows. To write an equation in slope-intercept form using data from a graph, you need to find the slope and the *y*-intercept. Let's find the slope first.

Say: We can pick any two ordered pairs. Let's try (10, 150) and (20, 250).

Ask: What is the change in *y*? **[100]** What is the change in *x*? **[10]** What is the slope? **[10]**

Say: We can read the *y*-intercept from the graph.

Ask: What is the *y*-intercept? **[50]** What equation represents the amount of money the lawyer charges? **[$y = 10x + 50$]**

Check

Neither of the graphs in Problems 9 and 10 have the *y*-intercept displayed. Make sure students know that they can use the slope to determine the *y*-intercept.

ALTERNATE STRATEGY

Strategy: Make a table to represent the data in the graph.

1. Look at Problem 9. Make a table to represent the ordered pairs in the graph.

x	0	2	4	6	8	10
y		8	10	12	14	16

2. Find the slope. Pick any two ordered pairs. Try (2, 8) and (4, 10).

$$m = \frac{y_2 - y_1}{x_2 - x_1} = \frac{10 - 8}{4 - 2} = \frac{2}{2} = 1$$

3. Use the slope and point (2, 8) to find the *y*-intercept.

$$8 = 1 \cdot 2 + b$$
$$8 = 2 + b$$
$$8 - 2 = 2 - 2 + b$$
$$6 = b$$

4. The equation is $y = x + 6$.

ADDITIONAL ONLINE INTERVENTION RESOURCES

Use the following for students who have not mastered the concepts in Skill 24.

- Math on the Spot videos
- Personal Math Trainer with customized intervention
- Building Block worksheets (Skill 52: Inverse Operations; Skill 111: Write Fractions as Decimals)

Name ______________________ Date ______________ Class ______________

SKILL 24

Writing Linear Equations

Example 1

An equation in slope-intercept form is written in the form of $y = mx + b$, where m represents the slope and b represents the y-intercept.

It costs $4 per person to get a beach badge and $8 to park at the Shore town beach. Write an equation in slope-intercept form to represent the situation.

Break the description into parts.

- Let y represent the total cost.
- $4x$ represents the cost for each person to go on the beach.
- 8 represents the cost to park for the group.

The equation $y = 4x + 8$ represents the situation.

Vocabulary
Slope-intercept form
Slope
y-intercept

Check

1. A gym charges $60 per month and a $50 enrollment fee at the beginning of the membership. Write an equation in slope-intercept form to represent the situation.

____

2. A handyman charges a $20 per home visit and $45 per hour for his work. Write an equation in slope-intercept form to represent the situation.

____

Example 2

You can use data from a graph to write an equation in slope-intercept form.

Choose two points to find the slope.

Try (0, 5) and (4, 10).

$$m = \frac{y_2 - y_1}{x_2 - x_1}$$

$$m = \frac{10 - 5}{4 - 0} = \frac{5}{4}$$

Read the y-intercept from the graph.

The y-intercept is 5.

The equation is $y = \frac{5}{4}x + 5$.

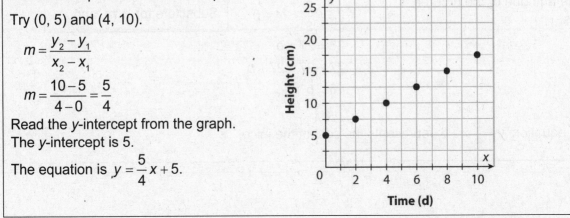

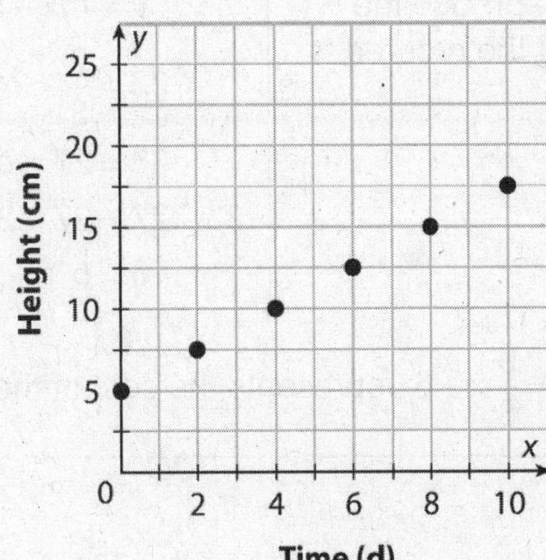

Name ______________________ Date __________ Class __________

Check

Write an equation in slope-intercept form for each graph.

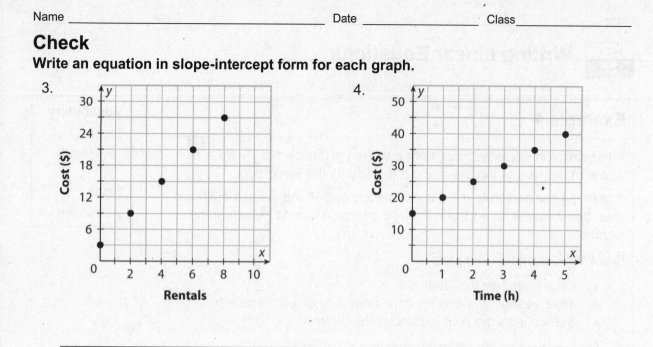

3.

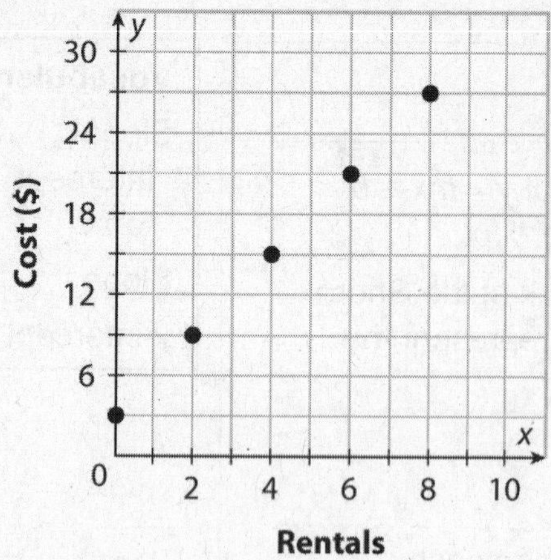

4.

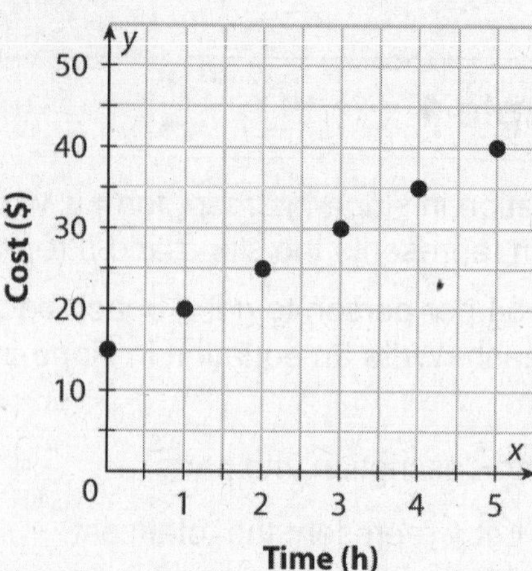

______________________ ______________________

Example 3

You can use information from a description of a linear relationship to find the slope and the *y*-intercept. Then you can write an equation to represent the situation.

A 16-ounce portion of juice costs $24.
A 24-ounce portion of juice costs $33.

Write an equation in slope-intercept form to describe the cost of the snapper.

Write two ordered pairs from the information given.	Use (16, 24) and (24, 33).
Find the slope.	$m = \frac{y_2 - y_1}{x_2 - x_1} = \frac{33 - 24}{24 - 16} = \frac{9}{8}$
Find the *y*-intercept. Use the slope and one of the ordered pairs.	$y = mx + b$ $33 = \frac{9}{8} \cdot 24 + b$ Substitute for *y*, *m*, and *x*. $33 = 27 + b$ $33 - 27 = 27 - 27 + b$ $6 = b$

The equation $y = \frac{9}{8}x + 6$ represents the cost of the juice.

Name ______________________ Date ____________ Class____________

Check

Write an equation in slope-intercept form that represents each situation.

5. Mr. Carson earns $880 for 40 hours of work and $1210 for 50 hours of work within the same month.

____

6. What's the Error? Three months after buying a computer, Jim owed $1000. Six months after buying the computer, Jim owed $550. Jim said the equation $y = 150x + 100$ represents the situation. Describe Jim's error and write the correct equation.

____

Example 4

You can use information from a table to write an equation in slope-intercept form.

Time (h)	1	2	3	4	5
Amount Earned ($)	35	50	65	80	95

Pick two ordered pairs from the table. — Try (1, 35) and (2, 50).

Find the slope.

$$m = \frac{y_2 - y_1}{x_2 - x_1} = \frac{50-35}{2-1} = \frac{15}{1} = 15$$

Find the y-intercept.

$$y = mx + b$$
$$35 = 15.1 + b$$
$$35 - 15 = 15 - 15 + b$$
$$20 = b$$

Substitute for y, m, and x.

The equation $y = 15x + 20$ represents the situation.

Check

Write an equation in slope-intercept form from the information in the table.

7.

Time (w)	0	1	2	3	4
Height (in.)	20	35	50	65	80

____

8.

Time (mo)	2	4	6	8	10
Amount Owed ($)	950	800	650	500	350

____

Name ______________________ Date ______________ Class ______________

Example 5

You can use the points on a graph of a linear relationship to write an equation for the relationship.

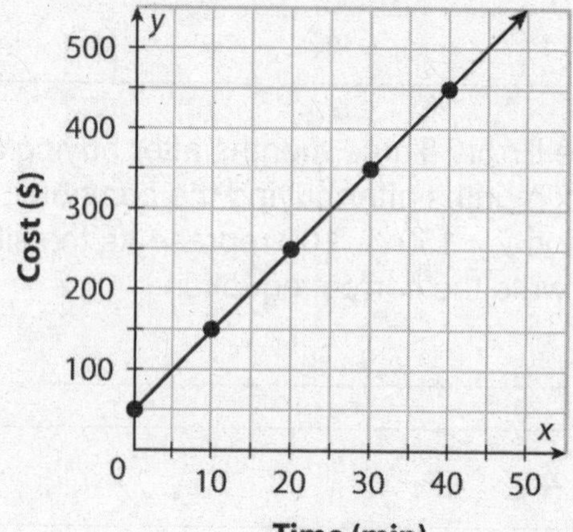

The graph shows the relationship between the number of minutes and the amount of money a lawyer charges for her services.

Choose two points.
Try (10, 150) and (20, 250).

Find the slope.

$$m = \frac{y_2 - y_1}{x_2 - x_1} = \frac{250 - 150}{20 - 10} = \frac{100}{10} = 10$$

Find the *y*-intercept from the graph.
The *y*-intercept is 50.

The equation that represents the amount the lawyer charges is $y = 10x + 50$.

Check

Write the equation of the line that connects each set of data points.

9\.

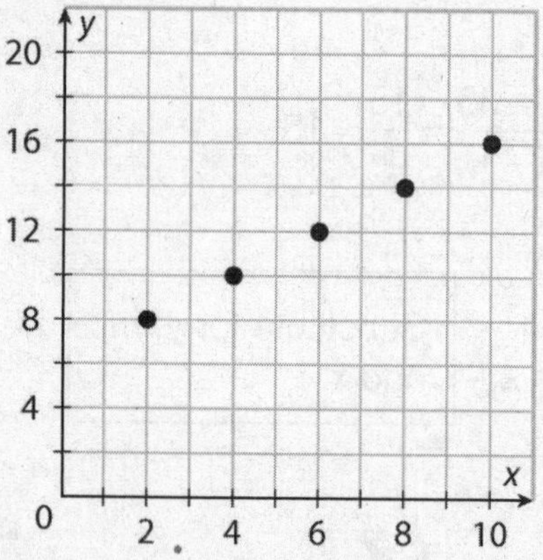

10\.

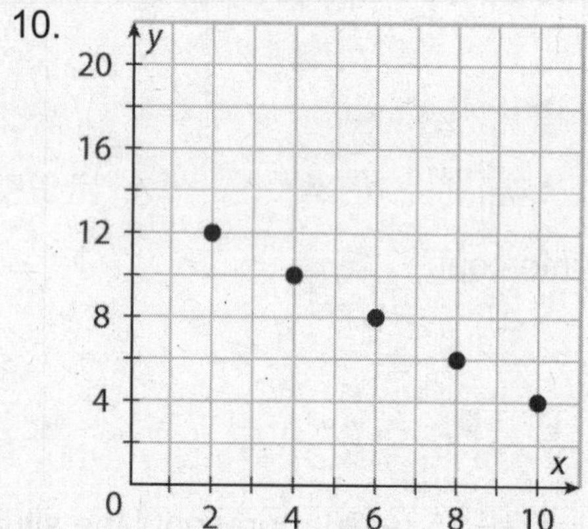

______________________ ______________________

SKILL 24 WRITING LINEAR EQUATIONS

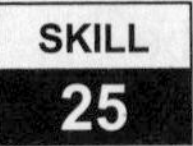

Two-Way Frequency Tables

KEY TEACHING POINTS

Example 1

Say: Frequency is the number of times an event occurs. A two-way table shows the frequencies of data that are categorized in two ways. The rows indicate one category and the columns indicate another.

Draw the two-way table on the board.

	≤2 Miles	>2 Miles	TOTAL
Walk			
Do Not Walk			
TOTAL			

Ask: What data is being categorized by the rows? **[whether a ninth-grader walks to school or not]** What data is being categorized by the columns? **[whether a ninth-grader lives 2 miles or less from school or more than 2 miles from school]**

Say: To fill in the table, use the information given. Your goal is to fill in the table with the numbers for each category. You are given one of the nine numbers, which is 160, the number of ninth-graders at Fillmore High School.

Fill in 160 in the bottom right cell.

Say: You can evaluate the percents to fill in the other cells. Let's start with the right column.

Ask: How many ninth-graders are there? **[160]** What percent of the ninth-graders walk to school? **[35%]** How can we find the number of ninth-graders who walk to school? **[Multiply the number of ninth-graders by the percent who walk to school.]** What is 160 × 35%? **[56]**

Fill in 56 in the upper-right cell.

Ask: How can you find the number of ninth-graders who do not walk to school? **[Subtract the number of ninth-graders who walk to school from the total number of ninth-graders.]** How many ninth-graders do not walk to school? **[104]**

Fill in 104 in the middle right cell.

Say: Now you can evaluate the percents to fill the top row. You know the total must be 56. You know that 87.5% of the ninth-graders who walk to school live 2 miles or less from school.

Ask: What is 56 × 87.5%? **[49]**

Fill in 49 in the top left cell.

Ask: How can you find the number of ninth-graders who walk to school and live more than 2 miles from school? **[Subtract the number of ninth-graders who walk to school who live 2 miles or less from school from the total number of ninth-graders who walk to school.]** How many ninth-graders walk more than 2 miles to school? **[7]**

Fill in the top middle cell.

Say: Now you can evaluate the percents to fill the middle row. You know the total must be 104. You know that 75% of the ninth-graders who do not walk to school live more than 2 miles from school.

Ask: What is $104 \times 75\%$? **[78]**

Fill in 78 in the middle cell in the middle row.

Ask: How can you find the number of ninth-graders who do walk to school and live 2 miles or less from school? **[Subtract the number of ninth-graders who do not walk to school who live more than 2 miles from school from the total number of ninth-graders who do not walk to school]** How many ninth-graders do not walk to school but live 2 miles or less from school? **[26]**

Fill in 26 in the left cell of the middle row.

Say: To fill in the bottom row is to add the columns.

Ask: How many students live 2 miles or less from school? **[75]** How many students live more than 2 miles from school? **[85]**

Say: Add the rows and the columns to make sure the sums are correct. Let's check: $49 + 7 = 56$, $26 + 78 = 104$, $75 + 85 = 160$, $49 + 26 = 75$, $7 + 78 = 85$, and $56 + 104 = 160$. The two-way table is filled in correctly.

ALTERNATE STRATEGY

Strategy: Write an equation for each cell of a two-way table.

1. Write the two-way table for Problem 1.

	Like Sports	Do Not Like Sports	TOTAL
Like Talk Radio			
Do Not Like Talk Radio			
TOTAL			

2. **Ask:** Which cell can you fill without having to compute? **[bottom right]** With what number? **[200]**
3. **Ask:** What equation can you write to find the number of people that like talk radio? **[$x = (0.8)(200)$]** How many people like talk radio? **[160]** What equation can you write to find the number of people who do not like talk radio? **[$200 - 160 = 40$]**
4. **Ask:** What equation can you write to find the number of people who like talk radio and who are also sports fans? **[$x = (0.6)(160)$]** How many people who like talk radio are also sports fans? **[96]** What equation can you write to find the number of people who like talk radio and who are not also sports fans? **[$160 - 96 = 64$]**
5. **Ask:** What equation can you write to find the number of people who do not like talk radio and are also not sports fans? **[$x = (0.3)(40)$]** How many people dislike talk radio and sports? **[12]** What equation can you write to find the number of people who do not like talk but are sports fans? **[$40 - 12 = 28$]**
6. **Say:** You can add the columns to fill the bottom row.

KEY TEACHING POINTS

Example 2

Say: You are asked to determine if there is an association between a college student being satisfied with his or her grades and having a job. To determine if there is an association, you must find and then compare the relative frequencies.

If the relative frequencies are equal or close, there is no association. If the relative frequencies are very different, then there is an association.

Say: Let's find the relative frequency of students being satisfied with their grades.

Ask: What ratio do you use to find the relative frequency of a college student being satisfied with his or her grades? **[the number of students who are satisfied with their grades to the total number of students]** What is the relative frequency of a college student being satisfied with his or her grades? **[59%]**

Say: Let's find the relative frequency of having a job and being satisfied with his or her grades.

Ask: What ratio do you use to find the relative frequency of a college student with a job being satisfied with his or her grades? **[the number of students who have a job and are satisfied to the total number of students who have a job]** What is the relative frequency of a college student who has a job being satisfied with his or her grades? **[80%]**

Say: Now let's compare the relative frequencies. The relative frequency of a student who has a job being satisfied with his or her grades is 80%. The relative frequency of a student being satisfied with his or her grades is 59%.

Ask: Is there a correlation between a college student being satisfied with his or her grades and having a job? **[Yes]** Why? **[the relative frequency of a student being satisfied with his or her grades is greater for those students who have a job than those who do not have a job.]**

Say: To check, you can find the relative frequency of a student being satisfied with his or her grades who does not have a job. Of the 70 students who do not have a job, only 35 are satisfied, which is 50%. This is less than the general population.

	Satisfied	Not Satisfied	TOTAL
Job	24 (80%)	6 (20%)	30
No Job	35 (50%)	35 (50%)	70
TOTAL	59 (59%)	41 (41%)	100

Check

Make sure students are aware that if the relative frequencies of the bottom row are equal to the relative frequencies of one of the rows, then the relative frequency of the bottom row is also equal to the other row's relative frequencies. If the relative frequencies are equal, then there is no association.

In the first table (Problem 6), there is an association, and in the second table (Problem 10), there is no association.

COMMON MISCONCEPTION

Ask: What is Sarah's error in determining that the relative frequency of a boy liking modern art is 60%?

Reason incorrect: Sarah found the ratio of a boy liking modern art to a boy not liking modern art. Sarah should have found the ratio of a boy liking modern art to the total number of boys.

Solution: Follow these steps:

1. Write the ratio of a boy liking modern art to the total number of boys: $\frac{45}{120}$
2. Find the relative frequency: $\frac{45}{120} = 37.5\%$

The relative frequency of a boy liking modern art is 37.5%.

ADDITIONAL ONLINE INTERVENTION RESOURCES

Use the following for students who have not mastered the concepts in Skill 25.

- Math on the Spot videos
- Personal Math Trainer with customized intervention
- Building Block worksheets (Skill 6: Analyze Data; Skill 72: Percents and Decimals; Skill 114: Read a Table)

Name ______________________ Date ______________ Class ______________

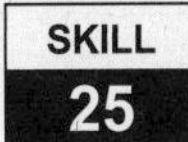

Two-Way Frequency Tables

Example 1

A two-way table shows the frequencies of data that are categorized in two ways.

Of the 160 ninth-graders at Fillmore High School, 35% walk to school. Of those students that walk to school, 87.5% live 2 or fewer miles from school. Of those students who do not walk to school, 75% live more than 2 miles away.

Set up a two-way table.

	≤2 Miles	>2 Miles	TOTAL
Walk			
Do Not Walk			
TOTAL			

Start in the bottom right cell of the table. Enter the total number of students in the ninth-grade class. There are 160 students in the ninth-grade class.

	≤2 Miles	>2 Miles	TOTAL
Walk			
Do Not Walk			
TOTAL			160

Fill in the right column. Because $160 \times 35\% = 56$, there are 56 ninth-graders who walk to school. Because $160 - 56 = 104$, there are 104 ninth-graders who do not walk to school.

	≤2 Miles	>2 Miles	TOTAL
Walk			56
Do Not Walk			104
TOTAL			160

Fill in the top row. Because $56 \times 87.5\% = 49$, there are 49 ninth-graders who live 2 or fewer miles from and walk to school. Because $56 - 49 = 7$, there are 7 ninth-graders who walk more than 2 miles to school.

	≤2 Miles	>2 Miles	TOTAL
Walk	49	7	56
Do Not Walk			104
TOTAL			160

Fill in the second row. Of those students who do not walk to school, 75% live more than 2 miles away. Because $104 \times 75\% = 78$, there are 78 ninth-graders who do not walk to school and live more than 2 miles away. Because $104 - 78 = 26$, there are 26 ninth-graders who do not walk to school and live 2 or fewer miles from school.

Vocabulary

- Two-way table
- Frequency
- Relative frequency

Name _________________________________ Date _______________ Class _______________

	≤2 Miles	>2 Miles	TOTAL
Walk	49	7	56
Do Not Walk	26	78	104
TOTAL			160

Fill in the bottom row. Add the numbers in each column to give the totals.

	≤2 Miles	>2 Miles	TOTAL
Walk	49	7	56
Do Not Walk	26	78	104
TOTAL	75	85	160

Check

1. A poll of 200 radio listeners found that 80% like to listen to talk radio. Of those who like talk radio, 60% are sports fans. Of those who do not like talk radio, 30% are not sports fans. Complete the two-way table.

	Like Sports	Do Not Like Sports	TOTAL
Like Talk Radio			
Do Not Like Talk Radio			
TOTAL			

2. There are 100 shoppers who are involved in a taste test of fruit cups. Of the taste testers, 60% are adults. Of the students, 45% disliked the fruit cups. Of the adults, 85% liked the fruit cups. Complete the two-way table.

	Like	Dislike	TOTAL
Students			
Adults			
TOTAL			

3. In a survey of 75 students, 60% said they own a personal computer. Of the students who own a personal computer, 40% also own an e-reader. Of the students who do not own a personal computer, 80% own an e-reader. Complete the two-way table.

	Own E-Reader	Do Not Own E-Reader	TOTAL
Own Computer			
Do Not Own Computer			
TOTAL			

Name ______________________ Date ____________ Class ____________

Example 2

Relative frequency can be used to determine if there is an association between two variables or events.

$$\text{Relative frequency} = \frac{\text{number of times an event occurs}}{\text{total number of events}}$$

A total of 100 college students were surveyed about whether they had jobs and whether they were satisfied with their grades. The two-way table shows the results.

	Satisfied	Not Satisfied	TOTAL
Job	24	6	30
No Job	35	35	70
TOTAL	59	41	100

Is there an association between being satisfied with one's grades and having a job?

Find the relative frequency of being satisfied with one's grades.

$$\frac{59}{100} = 59\%$$

Find the relative frequency of being satisfied with one's grades among those who have a job.

$$\frac{24}{30} = \frac{8}{10} = 80\%$$

Compare the relative frequencies.

College students who have a job are more likely to be satisfied with their grades than those who do not have a job. Those with a job are 80% satisfied with their grades compared to the general population, which is 59% satisfied.

Check

Use the two-way table.

A total of 100 students were surveyed about whether they have ever been outside of the United States. The two-way table shows the results.

	Have Been Outside U.S.	Have Not Been Outside U.S.	TOTAL
Elementary School	12	48	60
Middle School	12	28	40
TOTAL	30	70	100

Name ______________________ Date ____________ Class ____________

4. What is the relative frequency of an elementary school student having been outside the United States?

____

5. What is the relative frequency of a middle school student having been outside the United States?

____

6. Is there an association between the age of a student and he or she having been outside of the United States? Explain.

____

____

Use the two-way table to find the relative frequency.

A total of 280 high school students were surveyed about whether they like modern art. The two-way table shows the results.

	Like Modern Art	**Do Not Like Modern Art**	**TOTAL**
Boys	45	75	120
Girls	60	100	160
TOTAL	105	175	280

7. What's the Error? Sarah said that the relative frequency of a boy liking modern art is 60%. Describe Sarah's error and give the correct relative frequency of a boy liking modern art.

____

____

8. What is the relative frequency of a boy not liking modern art?

____

9. What is the relative frequency of a girl not liking modern art?

____

10. Is there an association between gender and liking modern art? Explain.

____

____

SKILL 25 TWO-WAY FREQUENCY TABLES

SKILL 26

Two-Way Relative Frequency Tables

KEY TEACHING POINTS

Example 1

Say: Frequency is the number of times an event occurs. Relative frequency is the frequency of a specific data value divided by the total number of data values in the set.

Draw this table on the board.

Sport Played	Track	Softball	Soccer	TOTAL
Frequency	36	20	24	80

Ask: To find the relative frequency, by what number will you divide each number of players in each sport? **[80]**

Divide each number in the table by 80.

Ask: How do you rename a decimal as a percent? **[Multiply by 100 and annex a percent symbol.]**

Say: Notice that when written as decimals, the sum of the relative frequencies is equal to 1. When written as percents, the sum of the relative frequencies is equal to 100%.

Say: A frequency table has categorical data. The category is sports played, and there are three possible data values: Track, Softball, and Soccer. You can split the categories into sophomores and juniors.

Draw this two-way frequency table on the board.

	Track	Softball	Soccer	TOTAL
Sophomores	9	6	6	
Juniors	27	14	18	
TOTAL				

Ask students to find the total of each row and then each column. Fill in the table as students answer.

Ask: What do you notice about the bottom row of the two-way frequency table when compared to the frequency table? **[The data is the same.]**

Say: Now you can make a two-way relative frequency table. You can find joint relative frequency and marginal relative frequency.

Say: Joint relative frequency is the ratio of the frequency in a particular category divided by the total number of data values. So, divide each data by the grand total, 80.

Say: Marginal relative frequency is the sum of the joint relative frequencies in a row or column of a two-way table.

Have students compute each joint relative frequency and marginal relative frequency.

	Track	Softball	Soccer	TOTAL
Sophomores	0.1125	0.075	0.075	0.2625
Juniors	0.3375	0.175	0.225	0.7375
TOTAL	0.45	0.25	0.3	1

Ask: Is 0.2625 a joint relative frequency or a marginal relative frequency? **[marginal relative frequency]** Is 0.175 a joint relative frequency or a marginal relative frequency? **[joint relative frequency]**

Check

For Problems 3–5, it is necessary to complete Problem 3. All of the necessary data is given for students to determine the unknown numbers. Once students complete Problem 3, the solutions to Problems 4 and 5 are found by computing.

ALTERNATE STRATEGY

Strategy: Rename fractions before renaming as a decimal.

1. Write the two-way table for Problem 1.

Music	Rock	Country	Rap	TOTAL
Frequency	18	8	14	40

2. Rewrite the numbers in the table using fractions.

Music	Rock	Country	Rap	TOTAL
Frequency	$\frac{18}{40}$	$\frac{8}{40}$	$\frac{14}{40}$	$\frac{40}{40}$

3. **Say:** Can you rename the fractions so the denominator is a factor of 100? **[Yes]**
4. **Ask:** What are the fractions for each type of music? $\left[\mathbf{\frac{18}{40}=\frac{9}{20}, \frac{8}{40}=\frac{2}{10}, \frac{14}{40}=\frac{7}{20}}\right]$
5. **Ask:** What number times 20 is equal to 100? **[5]** What number times 10 is equal to 100? **[10]**
6. Have students complete the table using decimals.

Music	Rock	Country	Rap	TOTAL
Frequency	0.45	0.2	0.35	1

KEY TEACHING POINTS

Example 2

Say: Conditional relative frequency is found by dividing a frequency that is not in the Total row or Total column by the frequency's row total or column total. Do not use the grand total as the denominator when determining conditional relative frequency.

Say: The same data that was in Example 1 is now in Example 2.

Ask: To find the conditional relative frequency for the sophomores, by what number do you divide? **[21]** Why 21? **[This is the number of sophomores who play varsity sports.]**

Say: When you divide, you find that you have repeating decimals. You can either use a bar to name the digits that repeat or you can approximate to a certain decimal place. Usually hundredths is appropriate. When written as a decimal, the sum of the conditional relative frequencies is 1.

Say: You can also find the conditional relative frequency for each sport for sophomores and juniors. Notice that you will only add the columns. Once again the sums are all 1.

Check

For Problems 6 and 7, it is necessary to complete Problem 6 first. All of the necessary data are given for students to determine the unknown numbers. Once students complete Problem 6, the solution to Problem 7 is found by computing.

COMMON MISCONCEPTION

Ask: What is Nick's error in saying that the conditional relative frequency for a junior varsity athlete being involved in track is 75%?

Reason incorrect: Nick divided the number of junior varsity track athletes by the total number of varsity track athletes instead of the number of junior athletes. In other words, he divided by 36 instead of 59.

Solution: Follow these steps:

1. Write the ratio of the number of junior track athletes to the number of junior athletes: $\frac{27}{59}$
2. Find the relative frequency: $\frac{27}{59} \approx 46\%$

The conditional relative frequency for a junior varsity athlete being involved in track is approximately 46%.

KEY TEACHING POINTS

Example 3

Say: You are asked to determine if there is an association between variables. Another way of looking at this is to answer the question "Is there a sport for which it is significantly harder or easier for a sophomore to make the varsity?"

Say: The same data that was in Example 1 is now in Example 3.

Say: You want to know the percent of varsity athletes that are sophomores. You can use the marginal relative frequency of $\frac{21}{80} = 26.25\%$. So, 26.25% of the varsity athletes are sophomores.

Ask: To find the conditional relative frequency of each sport in terms of the sophomores, what do you divide for track? **[9 ÷ 36]** What percent of the track athletes are sophomores? **[25%]** Is there an association between an athlete being on the track team and being a sophomore? **[No]** Why? **[because 25% is very close to 26.25%]**

Ask: To find the conditional relative frequency of each sport in terms of the sophomores, what do you divide for softball? **[6 ÷ 20]** What percent of the softball athletes are sophomores? **[30%]** Is there an association between an athlete being on the softball team and being a sophomore? **[No]** Why? **[because 30% is very close to 26.25%]**

Ask: To find the conditional relative frequency of each sport in terms of the sophomores, what do you divide for soccer? **[6 ÷ 24]** What percent of the soccer athletes are sophomores? **[25%]** Is there an association between an athlete being on the soccer team and being a sophomore? **[No]** Why? **[because 25% is very close to 26.25%]**

Check

Use the data from Problems 6 and 7 to answer Problem 9. Point out to students that they can use either grade for the comparison. If using seventh grade, for example, and the conditional relative frequencies are close to 40% (the percent of seventh-grade students surveyed), then there is no association. If the conditional relative frequencies are very different from 40%, there is an association.

ADDITIONAL ONLINE INTERVENTION RESOURCES

Use the following for students who have not mastered the concepts in Skill 26.

- Math on the Spot videos
- Personal Math Trainer with customized intervention
- Building Block worksheets (Skill 6: Analyze Data; Skill 72: Percents and Decimals; Skill 114: Read a Table)

Name ______________________ Date ______________ Class ______________

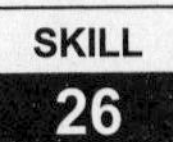

Two-Way Relative Frequency Tables

Example 1

You can use the data in a frequency table to convert it into a relative frequency table. The table shows the number of students who are on the varsity of different spring teams.

Sport Played	Track	Softball	Soccer	TOTAL
Frequency	36	20	24	80

To convert the frequency table to a relative frequency table, divide the number from each team by the total number of students. Write the quotient as a decimal.

Sport Played	Track	Softball	Soccer	TOTAL
Frequency	$\frac{36}{80} = 0.45$	$\frac{20}{80} = 0.25$	$\frac{24}{80} = 0.3$	$\frac{80}{80} = 1$

You can also write the relative frequency as a percent.

Sport Played	Track	Softball	Soccer	TOTAL
Frequency	0.45 = 45%	0.25 = 25%	0.3 = 30%	100%

The categorical variable was sport played, and the variable had three possible data values: Track, Softball, and Soccer. The categorical data can have paired values and then be listed in a two-way frequency table. Complete the table.

	Track	Softball	Soccer	TOTAL
Sophomores	9	6	6	
Juniors	27	14	18	
TOTAL				

Add the frequencies of each row.

Sophomores: $9 + 6 + 6 = 21$
Juniors: $27 + 14 + 18 = 59$

Add the frequencies of each column.

Track: $9 + 27 = 36$
Softball: $6 + 14 = 20$
Soccer: $6 + 18 = 24$

	Track	Softball	Soccer	TOTAL
Sophomores	9	6	6	21
Juniors	27	14	18	59
TOTAL	36	20	24	80

Vocabulary

Frequency table
Relative frequency table
Two-way frequency table
Two-way relative frequency table
Joint relative frequency
Marginal relative frequency
Conditional relative frequency

Name ________________________ Date ____________ Class ____________

The two-way frequency table can now be converted into a two-way relative frequency table. Find the joint relative frequency by dividing each data by the grand total. Find the marginal relative frequency by dividing a row or column total by the grand total.

	Track	Softball	Soccer	TOTAL
Sophomores	$\frac{9}{80}=0.1125$	$\frac{6}{80}=0.075$	$\frac{6}{80}=0.075$	$\frac{21}{80}=0.2625$
Juniors	$\frac{27}{80}=0.3375$	$\frac{14}{80}=0.175$	$\frac{18}{80}=0.225$	$\frac{59}{80}=0.7375$
TOTAL	$\frac{36}{80}=0.45$	$\frac{20}{80}=0.25$	$\frac{24}{80}=0.3$	$\frac{80}{80}=1$

Check

Convert the frequency table to a relative frequency table.

Music	Rock	Country	Rap	TOTAL
Frequency	18	8	14	40

1. Use decimals.

Music	Rock	Country	Rap	TOTAL
Frequency				

2. Use percents.

Music	Rock	Country	Rap	TOTAL
Frequency				

3. Complete the two-way frequency table.

	Peach	Pear	Strawberry	TOTAL
Students		21		80
Adults	32		24	
TOTAL	78	45		160

4. Convert the table to a two-way relative frequency table. Use decimals.

	Peach	Pear	Strawberry	TOTAL
Students				
Adults				
TOTAL				

5. Convert the table to a two-way relative frequency table. Use percents.

	Peach	Pear	Strawberry	TOTAL
Students				
Adults				
TOTAL				

Name ______________________ Date ______________ Class ______________

Example 2

Conditional relative frequency is found by dividing a frequency of a category (row or column) by the frequency's row total or column total.

	Track	Softball	Soccer	TOTAL
Sophomores	9	6	6	21
Juniors	27	14	18	59
TOTAL	36	20	24	80

Find the conditional relative frequency for the sophomores for each sport.

	Track	Softball	Soccer	TOTAL
Sophomores	$\frac{9}{21} = 0.428571$	$\frac{6}{21} = 0.285714$	$\frac{6}{21} = 0.285714$	$\frac{21}{21} = 1$

Find the conditional relative frequency for each sport per grade.

	Track	Softball	Soccer
Sophomores	0.25	0.3	0.25
Juniors	0.75	0.7	0.75
TOTAL	1	1	1

Check

6. The table shows the type of numbers that seventh- and eighth-grade students prefer to use to calculate. Complete the two-way frequency table.

	Fractions	Decimals	Percents	TOTAL
Seventh Grade		20		40
Eighth Grade	15		20	
TOTAL	25	45	30	100

7. Find the conditional relative frequency for each type of math per grade. Use decimals.

	Fractions	Decimals	Percents
Seventh Grade			
Eighth Grade			
TOTAL			

8. What's the Error? Using the data in Example 2, Nick said that the conditional relative frequency for a junior athlete being involved in track is 75%. Describe the error and give the correct conditional relative frequency.

____

____

Name ______________________ Date ______________ Class ______________

Example 3

You can use the conditional relative frequency to determine if there is an association between variables. Is there an association between sport and whether a student is a sophomore or a junior? Use the sophomores to decide if there is an association.

	Track	Softball	Soccer	TOTAL
Sophomores	9	6	6	21
Juniors	27	14	18	59
TOTAL	36	20	24	80

Identify the percent of sophomores who are on teams: $\frac{21}{80} = 26.25\%$

Identify the percent of sophomores who are members of each varsity team. This is the conditional relative frequency.

	Track	Softball	Soccer
Sophomores	$\frac{9}{36} = 25\%$	$\frac{6}{20} = 30\%$	$\frac{6}{24} = 25\%$

Compare the conditional relative frequencies to 26.25%. Because each conditional relative frequency is close to 26.25%, there is no association between sport and whether a student is a sophomore or a junior for any of the sports.

Check

9. Using the data in Problems 6 and 7, determine if there is an association between the type of numbers used and grade. Explain your answer.

____

____

SKILL 26 TWO-WAY RELATIVE FREQUENCY TABLES

SKILL 27

Absolute Value

KEY TEACHING POINTS

Example 1

Say: The absolute value of an integer is positive. It is the integer's distance from 0 on a number line.

On the board, draw a number line from –10 to 10 and place a point at 4.

Say: I have placed a point at 4 on the number line.

Ask: What is the value of the point? **[4]** What is the distance from 0 to 4? **[4]**

Say: Because 4 is 4 units from 0, the absolute value of 4 is 4.

Write $|4| = 4$ on the board.

Check

Have students complete Problems 1–3.

Ask: Do you notice a pattern between the value of a positive integer and its absolute value? **[They are the same number.]**

Example 2

Say: As with positive integers, the absolute value of a negative integer is the integer's distance from 0 on a number line.

On the board, draw a number line from –10 to 10 and place a point at –4.

Say: I have placed a point at –4 on the number line.

Ask: What is the value of the point? **[–4]** What is the distance from –4 to 0? **[4]**

Say: Because –4 is 4 units from 0, the absolute value of –4 is 4.

Write $|-4| = 4$ on the board.

Say: The absolute value of a negative integer is positive. It counts the distance from 0, which is always a positive number.

Check

Have students complete Problems 4–6.

Ask: Do you notice a pattern between the value of a negative integer and its absolute value? **[The absolute value is the opposite of a negative integer.]**

KEY TEACHING POINTS

Example 3

Read the problem in Example 3 to students.

Ask: What do you know? **[Melissa has $30. She buys a book for $12.]**

Ask: What do you need to find? **[what negative integer and what absolute value represents the change in the amount of money Melissa has]**

Say: Because you are interested only in the change in the amount of money, you do not have to compute.

Ask: What integer represents the change in Melissa's money? **[–$12]** Why? **[Melissa will have $12 less after paying for the book.]**

Say: The integer –12 represents the change in dollars.

Draw a number line from –12 to 0 on the board.

Ask: What is the absolute value of –12? **[12]** Why 12? **[The distance from –12 to 0 is 12 units.]**

Check

For Problem 7, the absolute value represents the change in elevation from 0 feet to –20 feet. Remind students that when answering questions involving units, it is important to identify the units.

ALTERNATE STRATEGY

Strategy: Draw a number line.

1. Draw a number line from –20 to 0.

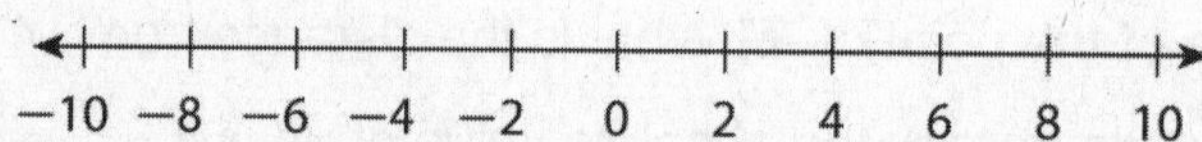

2. **Ask:** What is the distance from –20 to 0 on the number line? **[20]**
3. **Ask:** What is the absolute value of –20? **[20]**

COMMON MISCONCEPTION

Ask: What is Lynn's error in saying that the absolute value of –7 is –7?

Reason incorrect: Lynn did not realize that absolute value is the distance from a number to 0 on the number line. Distance is a positive number. The distance from –7 to 0 is 7.

The absolute value of –7 is 7 or $|-7| = 7$.

KEY TEACHING POINTS

Example 4

Say: Like integers, absolute values can be compared. Unlike integers, where a positive number is always greater than a negative number, you can ignore the signs when determining the greater absolute value.

On the board, draw a number line from –5 to 5 and place points at –5 and 3.

Ask: Which point is farther from 0: –5 or 3? **[–5]** What is the absolute value of –5? **[5]** What is the absolute value of 3? **[3]** Which is greater: $|-5|$ or $|3|$? **[$|-5|$]**

Check

Ask: Why does ignoring the integer signs when comparing absolute values work? **[The greater absolute value is the number that is farther from 0 on a number line.]**

Example 5

Read the problem in Example 5 to students.

On the board, draw a number line from –10 to 10.

Ask: What does less than 8 feet below sea level mean in terms of 0? **[less than 8 feet from 0]** How many feet in elevation must someone who is less than 8 feet below sea level climb to get to 0 feet? **[less than 8 feet]**

Check

For Problem 13, ask what the temperature being greater than –6 °C means. Students should know that the temperature could be any positive number of degrees or any negative number greater than –6.

Example 6

Say: Rational numbers are numbers that can be written in the form of $\frac{a}{b}$, where *a* and *b* are integers and *b* does not equal 0. Finding the absolute value of a rational number that is not an integer is the same as finding the absolute value of an integer.

Ask: How are the steps for finding the absolute value of a non-integer rational number like finding the absolute value of an integer? **[The steps are the same.]**

Check

For Problem 18, ask students how the digits of $|-3.6|$ change. Students will note that the digits do not change, only the sign of the rational number changes.

COMMON MISCONCEPTION

Ask: What is Eric's error in saying $\left|-3\frac{3}{4}\right| < \left|3\frac{3}{4}\right|$?

Reason incorrect: Absolute values of opposites have the same value. Remind students that opposites are two numbers whose sum is 0. Since $-3\frac{3}{4}+3\frac{3}{4}=0$, $-3\frac{3}{4}$ and $3\frac{3}{4}$ are opposites.

Solution:

1. $\left|-3\frac{3}{4}\right| = 3\frac{3}{4}$
2. $\left|3\frac{3}{4}\right| = 3\frac{3}{4}$

So, $\left|-3\frac{3}{4}\right| = \left|3\frac{3}{4}\right|$.

ADDITIONAL ONLINE INTERVENTION RESOURCES

 Use the following for students who have not mastered the concepts in Skill 27.

- Math on the Spot videos
- Personal Math Trainer with customized intervention
- Building Block worksheets (Skill 1: Absolute Value; Skill 4: Add and Subtract Integers; Skill 54: Locate Points on a Number Line)

Name ______________________ Date ______________ Class ______________

SKILL 27

Absolute Value

Example 1

The absolute value of an integer is the integer's distance from 0 on a number line.

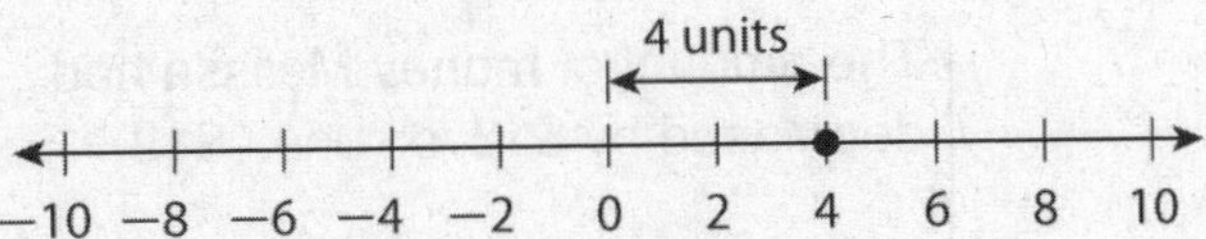

The absolute value of 4 is 4 because 4 is 4 units from 0.
The absolute value of 4 is written $|4|$.

Vocabulary
Absolute value
Integer
Rational number

Check

Find the absolute value of each number.

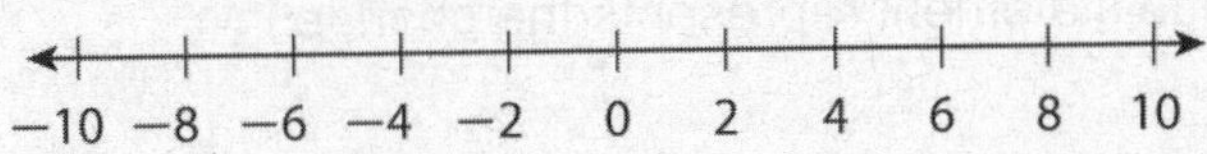

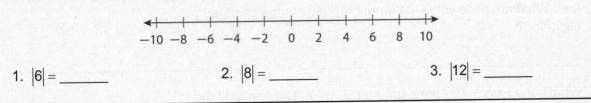

1. $|6| =$ ______
2. $|8| =$ ______
3. $|12| =$ ______

Example 2

The absolute value of a negative is the integer's distance from 0 on a number line. It is also positive.

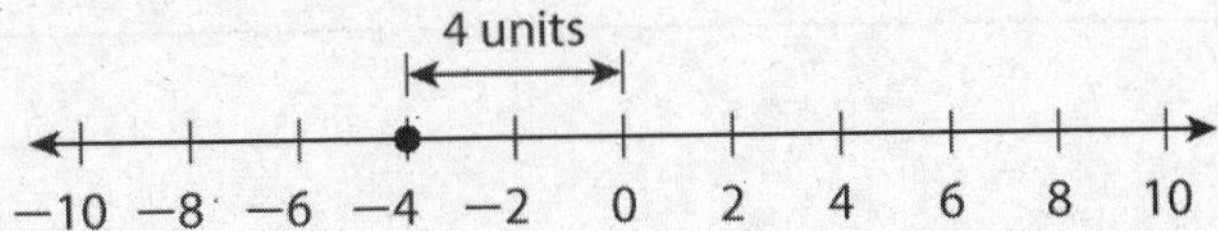

The absolute value of –4 is 4 because –4 is 4 units from 0.

So, $|-4| = 4$.

Check

Find the absolute value of each number.

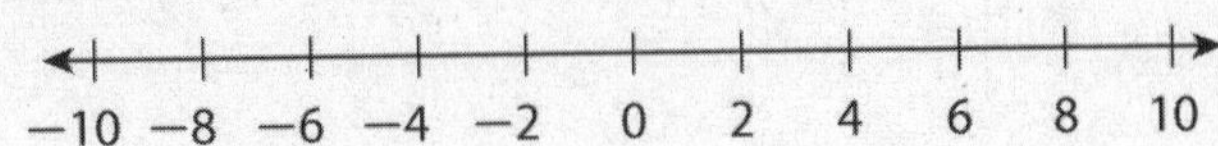

4. $|-8| =$ ______
5. $|-5| =$ ______
6. $|-9| =$ ______

Name ______________________ Date ____________ Class ____________

Example 3

In real-world problems, you may describe values using either negative numbers or absolute values of those numbers.

Melissa has $30 in her purse. She buys a book for $12. What negative integer and what absolute value represent the change in the amount of money Melissa has?

Find the negative integer.	The amount of money Melissa had decreased by $12, so use –$12.
Find the absolute value of –$12.	$\lvert -12 \rvert = 12$

The amount of money Melissa had decreased by $12.

Check

7. A diver is at an elevation of 0 feet. She dives to an elevation of –20 feet. What absolute value statement represents the change in elevation?

____

8. What's the Error? The temperature fell to –7 °C. Lynn said the absolute value of –7 is equal to –7. Describe the error Lynn made. Then write the correct absolute value statement.

____

____

Example 4

Absolute values can be compared.

Compare: $\lvert -5 \rvert$ ______ $\lvert 3 \rvert$

Find $\lvert -5 \rvert$.	$\lvert -5 \rvert = 5$
Find $\lvert 3 \rvert$.	$\lvert 3 \rvert = 3$
Compare 5 ______ 3.	$5 > 3$

So, $\lvert -5 \rvert > \lvert 3 \rvert$.

Name ______________________ Date ______________ Class ______________

Check

Compare. Use >, <, or =.

−10 −8 −6 −4 −2 0 2 4 6 8 10

9. |8|_____|3|

10. |7|_____|−4|

11. |−4|_____|−6|

12. |−3|_____|6|

Example 5

You can use words to determine if an absolute value applies to a problem.

A person is digging a ditch that is less than 8 feet below sea level. He drops a rock to the bottom of the ditch. Is the rock more than 8 feet or less than 8 feet from the surface elevation of 0 feet?

Think about what less than 8 feet below sea level means. Because the rock's elevation is less than −8 feet, the rock is less than 8 feet from the surface elevation of 0 feet.

Check

13. The temperature is greater than −6 °C. Does the temperature need to increase by more than 6 °C or less than 6 °C to get back to 0 °C? Explain your answer.

____

____

14. Greg's game score is less than −10. Does he need to score more than 10 points or fewer than 10 points to get his score back to 0? Explain your answer.

____

____

Name ______________________ Date ____________ Class ____________

Example 6

You can find the absolute value of a rational number the same way you find the absolute value of an integer.

$|6.38| = 6.38$ $\left|4\frac{1}{2}\right| = 4\frac{1}{2}$

$|-2.7| = 2.7$ $\left|-3\frac{3}{8}\right| = 3\frac{3}{8}$

Check

Find the absolute value of each number.

15. $|4.2| =$ ______
16. $\left|6\frac{2}{3}\right| =$ ______
17. $|0.72| =$ ______
18. $|-3.6| =$ ______
19. $\left|-2\frac{1}{2}\right| =$ ______
20. $\left|-\frac{5}{7}\right| =$ ______
21. What's the Error? Eric said $\left|-3\frac{3}{4}\right| < \left|3\frac{3}{4}\right|$. Explain why Eric's statement is incorrect and give the correct symbol to compare the two absolute values.

____

____

SKILL 27 ABSOLUTE VALUE

SKILL 28

Measures of Center

KEY TEACHING POINTS

Example 1
Say: A measure of center is a number that is used to describe a typical value from the data set. Measures of center include mean, median, and mode.

Say: Let's discuss the mode first.

Ask: What is the mode? **[The number or numbers that occur most often in a data set]**

Say: If all of the numbers occur just once, there is no mode. If two or more numbers occur most often, there can be more than one mode.

Say: Look at the data. You can make a tally table, line plot, dot plot, stem-and-leaf plot, or some other organized way to see which number occurs most often.

Make the tally chart, going through each value with students.

Number of Dogs	Tally
0	|||
1	||||
2	~~||||~~ |||
3	||
4	|

Ask: Which number occurs most often? **[2]** What is the mode? **[2]**

Check
Encourage students to use some sort of organized way to arrange the data. Remind students that there may be more than one mode.

ALTERNATE STRATEGY

Strategy: Make a stem-and-leaf plot to find the mode.

1. **Say:** Look at Problem 1. Let's make a stem-and-leaf plot to organize the data.
2. **Ask:** What are the stems? **[7, 8, and 9]**
3. **Ask:** What leaves go with 7? **[2, 2, 6]** With 8? **[0, 4, 4]** With 9? **[2, 2, 2, 6]**
4. **Ask:** Which number occurs most often? **[92]**
5. **Say:** Because 92 is the number that occurs most often, it is the mode.

COMMON MISCONCEPTION

Ask: What is Annemarie's error is saying that the mode is 12 because it occurs three times?

Reason incorrect: There are two modes because 12 is not the only number that occurs three times.

Solution:

Number	Tally
8	||
9	||
10	|||
12	|||

Because 10 also occurs three times, the modes are 10 and 12.

KEY TEACHING POINTS

Example 2

Say: When people refer to an average, it is usually assumed that they are talking about the mean.

Ask: What is the mean? **[The sum of the values of a data set divided by the number of data values in the data set.]**

Say: Averages are used in sports. One average is points per game in basketball, which you will find for Kira.

Say: The first step is to find the sum of Kira's points.

Ask: How many points has Kira scored? **[112]** How do you find the mean? **[Divide the number of points by the number of games played, 8.]** What is 112 ÷ 8? **[14]**

Say: The mean is 14 points per game.

Example 3

Say: The median is the middle value in an ordered data set with an odd number of values.

Ask: To find the median, does it matter whether you order the numbers from least to greatest or greatest to least? **[No; the middle number will still be in the same position.]**

Say: Order the temperatures. Let's go from least to greatest.

Ask: What is the order? **[52, 54, 55, 56, 58, 60, 62]**

Say: There are 7 numbers. The middle number is the fourth number, which is 56.

Ask: What is the median? **[56 °F]**

Make sure students understand that they should include units when dealing with measures. Saying the median is 56 is an incomplete answer.

Check

Have students check whether there are an even number or an odd number of data when finding the median. In this set, all of the sets have 7 data.

ALTERNATE STRATEGY

Strategy: Cross out numbers to find the median.

1. **Say:** Because the median is the middle number, you can cross out numbers.
2. For Problem 7, order the numbers from least to greatest: 51, 53, 64, 68, 69, 72, 74.
3. **Say:** Cross out the leftmost number and the rightmost number until only one number remains.
4. **Ask:** What is the median? **[68]**

COMMON MISCONCEPTION

Ask: What is Curtis's error in saying that the median is 28?

Reason incorrect: Curtis did not order the data from least to greatest. He chose the middle number.

Follow these steps:

1. Determine if there are an odd number or an even number of data. There are 7 data, which is an odd number.
2. Order the data from least to greatest: 21, 27, 28, 32, 39, 43, 54.
3. Identify the middle number: 21, 27, 28, **32**, 39, 43, 54.

The median of Curtis's data is 32.

KEY TEACHING POINTS

Example 4

Say: With an even number of data, there will be two middle numbers. The median is the mean of those two numbers.

Say: Let's order Kira's points from least to greatest.

Ask: What is the order? **[10, 12, 12, 12, 14, 16, 16, 20]**

Ask: What are the two middle numbers? **[12 and 14]** What is the mean of 12 and 14? **[13]**

Say: The median of Kira's points is 13.

Check

Have students check whether there are an even number or an odd number of data when finding the median. In this set, all of the sets have an even number of data.

KEY TEACHING POINTS

Example 5

Say: An outlier is a number that is very different from the rest of the data in a set. Each data set will have a least and greatest value. Being the least or greatest value does not automatically make a number an outlier.

Say: Let's look at Daisy's scores.

Ask: By sight, do you see an outlier? **[Yes, 428 is much greater than the other numbers.]**

Say: Let's see if 428 greatly affects the data. Let's find the mean.

Ask: What is Daisy's total score? **[1848]** How many games did Daisy play? **[6]** What is Daisy's mean score? **[308]**

Say: Let's compare 308 to the other scores.

Ask: How does 308 compare to the scores other than 428? **[It is greater than all of the other scores.]**

Say: Let's find the median to see if that is a better choice.

Ask: What are the two middle numbers when ordered? **[286 and 292]** What is the median? **[289]**

Say: Because 289 is greater than 3 of the scores and less than 3 of the scores, it represents the data well. The score of 428 greatly skews the data.

Point out to students that without the outlier of 428, the mean falls from 308 to 284 and the median falls from 289 to 286.

Say: An outlier will affect the mean much more than the median or mode. When there is no outlier, either the mean or median can be used to represent the data set well.

Check

Students should determine that Problem 12 does not contain an outlier. The least and greatest values of 84 and 100 are not very different from the remainder of the data.

ADDITIONAL ONLINE INTERVENTION RESOURCES

Use the following for students who have not mastered the concepts in Skill 28.

- Math on the Spot videos
- Personal Math Trainer with customized intervention
- Building Block worksheets (Skill 2: Add and Subtract Decimals; Skill 6: Analyze Data; Skill 26: Division Facts; Skill 115: Find Range; Skill 116: Find Median and Mode; Skill 117: Find Mean)

Name ______________________ Date ______________ Class ______________

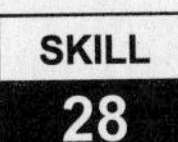

Measures of Center

Example 1

A measure of center is a single number used to describe a typical value from the data set. One measure is the mode, which is the number or numbers that occur most often.

The data set shows the number of dogs that students in Mr. Masse's class own.

2, 1, 0, 2, 1, 2, 2, 1, 0, 2, 4, 3, 1, 2, 3, 2, 0, 2

Make a tally table.

Number of Dogs	Tally
0	|||
1	||||
2	~~||||~~ |||
3	||
4	|

There can be more than one mode if two or more numbers occur most.

Because 2 occurs most often, 2 is the mode.

Vocabulary
Measure of center
Mode
Mean
Median
Outlier

Check

Find the mode(s) of each data set.

1. 76, 84, 92, 84, 92, 72, 80, 96, 92, 72 ______________

2. 28, 40, 52, 36, 44, 48, 52, 20, 56, 32 ______________

3. 36, 48, 42, 36, 48, 24, 28, 32, 52, 40 ______________

4. What's the Error? Annemarie was given this data set:

   12, 10, 9, 12, 10, 9, 8, 12, 10, 8

   Annemarie said that the mode is 12 because it occurs three times. What is Annemarie's error? Give the correct mode.

   ____

Name ______________________ Date ____________ Class ____________

Example 2

The mean is also known as the average. The mean is the sum of the data values divided by the number of data values in the set.

The table shows the number of points Kira scored in her first eight basketball games.

Game	1	2	3	4	5	6	7	8
Points	12	16	10	14	20	12	16	12

Find Kira's mean or average points per game.

Find the sum of the data.	$12 + 16 + 10 + 14 + 20 + 12 + 16 + 12 = 112$
Divide the sum by the number of data.	$112 \div 8 = 14$

Kira has scored a mean of 14 points per game.

Check

Find the mean of each data set.

5. 53, 68, 72, 69, 74

____

6. 72, 48, 54, 60, 78, 72

____

Example 3

The median is another measure of center. The median represents the middle value in an ordered data set with an odd number of values.

Phil recorded the high temperature each day last week. The high temperatures are shown in the table.

Day	S	M	T	W	T	F	S
High Temp. (°F)	56	62	54	60	58	52	55

Find the median high temperature.

Order the temperatures from least to greatest.	52, 54, 55, 56, 58, 60, 62
Identify the middle number. That is the median.	52, 54, 55, **56**, 58, 60, 62

The median high temperature was 56 °F.

Name ______________________ Date ____________ Class ____________

Check

Find the median of each data set.

7. 53, 68, 72, 69, 74, 64, 51

8. 72, 48, 54, 60, 78, 48, 75

______________________ ______________________

9. What's the Error? Curtis was given this data set:

27, 21, 32, 28, 43, 54, 39

Curtis said that the median is 28 because it is the middle number. What error did Curtis make? Give the correct median.

____

Example 4

With an even number of data, the median is the mean of the two middle values.

The table shows the number of points Kira scored in her first eight basketball games.

Game	1	2	3	4	5	6	7	8
Points	12	16	10	14	20	12	16	12

Find the median number of points Kira scored.

Order the data from least to greatest.	10, 12, 12, 12, 14, 16, 16, 20
Identify the two middle numbers.	10, 12, 12, **12, 14**, 16, 16, 20
Find the mean of the two middle numbers.	$\frac{12+14}{2} = \frac{26}{2} = 13$

The median number of points Kira scored is 13.

Check

Find the median of each data set.

10. 82, 68, 90, 54, 72, 66

11. 38, 52, 42, 64, 32, 70, 78, 42

______________________ ______________________

Name ______________________ Date ______________ Class______________

Example 5

An outlier is a number that is very different from the rest of the data in a set. When there is an outlier, the median may be better than the mean to use as measure of center. Without an outlier, either measure may be used.

The number of points Daisy scored in a board game is shown.

Game	1	2	3	4	5	6
Points	302	286	428	268	292	272

Does the mean or median better describe the measure of center of Daisy's scores?

Find the mean.	$302 + 286 + 428 + 268 + 292 + 272 = 1848$ $1848 \div 6 = 308$
Order the data from least to greatest.	268, 272, 286, 292, 302, 428
Determine if there is an outlier.	The mean of 308 is greater than all but one value, 428. So, 428 is an outlier.
Find the median.	268, 272, **286, 292**, 302, 428 $\frac{286 + 292}{2} = \frac{578}{2} = 289$

The median better represents the data than the mean.

Check

12. Does the median or mean better describe the data set below? Explain your reasoning.

    92, 84, 90, 86, 100, 88

    ____

    ____

SKILL 28 MEASURES OF CENTER

SKILL 29

Box Plots

KEY TEACHING POINTS

Example 1

Say: A box plot shows how the values in a data set are distributed.

Ask: In the box plot, what is the least value? **[24]** What is the greatest value? **[36]**

Say: The left vertical segment in the box represents the lower quartile. The lower quartile is the median of the lower half of the data, that is, the values that are less than the median.

Ask: What is the value of the lower quartile? **[26]**

Say: The vertical segment inside the box represents the median. The median is the middle number of the data set.

Say: The right vertical segment in the box represents the upper quartile. The upper quartile is the median of the upper half of the data, that is, the values that are greater than the median.

Ask: What is the value of the upper quartile? **[34]**

Check

Have students refer to the box plot in Example 1 to help them determine the values in Problems 1–5.

Example 2

Say: Making a box plot requires knowledge of how to determine the median.

Ask: How do you determine the median of a data set with an odd number of data? **[Order the data from least to greatest. The median is the middle number.]**

Have students order the data from least to greatest: 13, 14, 14, 17, 20, 21, 24

Ask: What is the least value? **[13]** What is the greatest value? **[24]**

Draw a number line from 10 to 30 on the board. Place the points for 13 and 24 to start the box plot.

Ask: When ordered, what is the middle number? **[17]**

Say: The median is 17.

Ask: Which values are less than the median? **[13, 14, 14]** Why do we include 14 twice? **[The Terriers scored 14 points twice.]** What is the median of these three values? **[14]**

Ask: Which values are greater than the median? **[20, 21, 24]** What is the median of these three values? **[21]**

Check

For Problem 6, students will make a box plot on their own.

There are 11 data values, so there will be an odd number of data on each side of the median. Remind students that with an odd number of data, the median, or quartile, is the middle value.

KEY TEACHING POINTS

Example 3

Say: Now you are going to make a box plot from an even number of data. This time the data is already ordered from least to greatest.

Draw a number line from 34 to 58 by twos on the board. Make marks for the odd integers.

Ask: What is the least value? **[36]** What is the greatest value? **[56]**

Draw dots at 36 and 56.

Ask: How do you find the median of an even numbered data set? **[Find the mean of the two middle values.]** What are the two middle values? **[42 and 44]** How do you find the mean of the two middle values? **[Find the sum and then divide by 2.]** What is the median? **[43]**

Place a vertical line segment at 43.

Say: For an even number of data values in a set, you include every number when finding the quartiles.

Ask: What is the lower half of the data? **[36, 38, 40, 42]**

Say: There are four data values in this set.

Ask: How do you find the lower quartile with four data values? **[Find the mean of the two middle values.]** What are the two middle values? **[38 and 40]** What is the lower quartile? **[39]**

Place a vertical line segment at 39.

Say: You can follow the same steps for the upper quartile.

Ask: What is the upper half of the data? **[44, 48, 54, 56]** What are the two middle values? **[48 and 54]** What is the sum of 48 and 54? **[102]** What is 102 ÷ 2? **[51]**

Place a vertical line segment at 51 and complete the box.

Check

In Problem 7, there are ten data values. There will be five data values on each side of the median, so there will be no computation necessary to find the quartiles.

ALTERNATE STRATEGY

Strategy: Cross out numbers to find the quartiles.

1. **Say:** You can think of the quartiles as medians. This means you can cross out numbers.
2. For Problem 7, order the numbers from least to greatest:
   72, 72, 76, 78, 80, 84, 88, 90, 90, 92
3. **Say:** Divide the data into halves.
4. **Ask:** Which numbers are in the lower half? **[72, 72, 76, 78, 80]**
5. **Say:** Cross out the least and greatest numbers until only the middle number remains.
6. **Ask:** What is the lower quartile? **[76]**
7. **Ask:** Which numbers are in the upper half? **[84, 88, 90, 90, 92]**
8. **Say:** Cross out the least and greatest numbers until only the middle number remains.
9. **Ask:** What is the upper quartile? **[90]**

KEY TEACHING POINTS

Example 4

Say: A measure of spread is a single number that describes the spread of a data set. One measure is the range. The range is the difference between the greatest and least values in a data set.

Say: Look at the box plot.

Ask: What is the least value? **[24]** What is the greatest value? **[36]** How do you find the range? **[Subtract 36 – 24.]** What is the range? **[12]**

Say: Another measure of spread is the interquartile range. This gives the spread of the middle 50 percent of a data set. It is less susceptible to outliers than the range.

Say: Interquartile range or IQR is the difference between the upper quartile and the lower quartile.

Say: Look at the box plot again.

Ask: What is the lower quartile? **[26]** What is the upper quartile? **[34]** How do you find the interquartile range? **[Subtract 34 – 26.]** What is the interquartile range? **[8]**

COMMON MISCONCEPTION

Ask: What is Caleb's error in saying that the range is 42 and the IQR is 22?

Reason incorrect: The range is correct, but Caleb subtracted the median from the greatest value instead of subtracting the lower quartile from the upper quartile.

Solution: Follow these steps:

1. Write the numbers in the set: 54, 62, 70, 74, 82, 88, 96
2. Identify the number of values. There are 7 values, which is an odd number.
3. Identify the median, which is 74.
4. Identify the lower half of the data. The lower half is 54, 62, and 70.
5. Identify the lower quartile, which is 62.
6. Identify the upper half of the data. The upper half is 82, 88, and 96.
7. Identify the upper quartile, which is 88.
8. Subtract the lower quartile from the upper quartile: 88 – 62 = 26.

The IQR is 26.

ADDITIONAL ONLINE INTERVENTION RESOURCES

Use the following for students who have not mastered the concepts in Skill 29.

- Math on the Spot videos
- Personal Math Trainer with customized intervention
- Building Block worksheets (Skill 6: Analyze Data; Skill 47: Graph Points on a Number Line; Skill 54: Locate Points on a Number Line)

Name ________________ Date ________________ Class ________________

SKILL 29

Box Plots

Example 1

A **box plot** shows how data can be displayed. It shows five pieces of data: the least value, the **lower quartile**, the **median**, the **upper quartile**, and the greatest value.

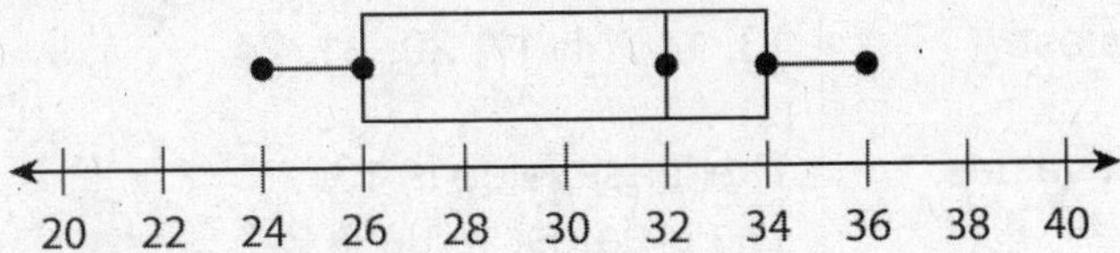

- The least value is 24.
- The lower quartile, or the median of the values less than the median, is 26.
- The median, or the middle value, is 32.
- The upper quartile, or the median of the values greater than the median, is 34.
- The greatest value is 36.

Vocabulary

Box plot
Lower quartile
Median
Upper quartile
Mean
Measures of spread
Range
Interquartile range

Check

Use the box plot to give the values. All values are integers.

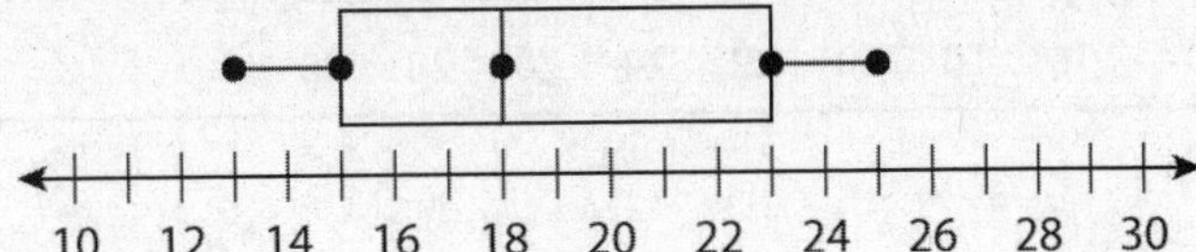

1. Greatest value ____________
2. Median ____________
3. Lower quartile ____________
4. Least value ____________
5. Upper quartile ____________

Name ______________________ Date ____________ Class ____________

Example 2

You can make a box plot.

The number of points the Terriers scored in each of their first seven games is shown in the table.

Game	1	2	3	4	5	6	7
Points	14	21	17	24	13	14	20

Order the data from least to greatest.	13, 14, 14, 17, 20, 21, 24
Determine the least and greatest values.	The least value is 13. The greatest value is 24.
Determine the median.	13, 14, 14, **17**, 20, 21, 24 The median is the middle number, 17.
Determine the lower quartile, the median of the values less than the median.	13, **14**, 14, | 17 |, 20, 21, 24 The lower quartile is 14.
Determine the upper quartile, the median of the values greater than the median.	13, 14, 14, | 17 |, 20, **21**, 24 The upper quartile is 21.

Make the box plot to represent the data.

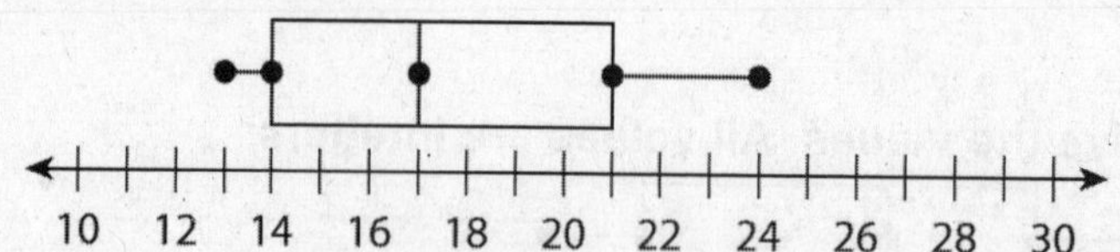

Check

6. Make a box plot for the set of values.
80, 96, 88, 92, 100, 88, 90, 82, 90, 85, 94

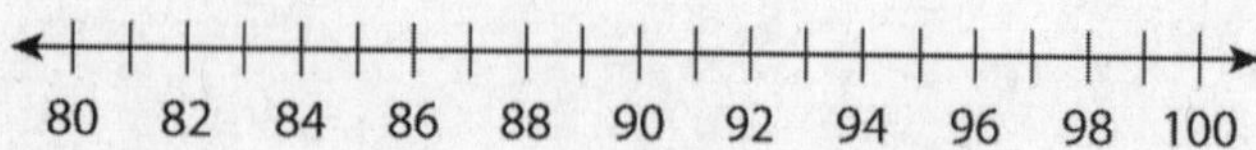

Name ______________________ Date ______________ Class ______________

Example 3

If there are an even number of data values in a set, the mean of the two middle numbers is the median.

A set of data is shown from least to greatest:
36, 38, 40, 42, 44, 48, 54, 56

There are 8 data values, an even number of data.

Determine the least and greatest values.	The least value is 36. The greatest value is 56.
Determine the median.	36, 38, 40, **42, 44**, 48, 54, 56 The median is the mean of 42 and 44, which is 43.
Determine the lower quartile.	36, **38, 40**, 42 | 44, 48, 54, 56 The lower quartile is the mean of 38 and 40, which is 39.
Determine the upper quartile.	36, 38, 40, 42 | 44, **48, 54**, 56 The upper quartile is the mean of 48 and 54, which is 51.

Make the box plot.

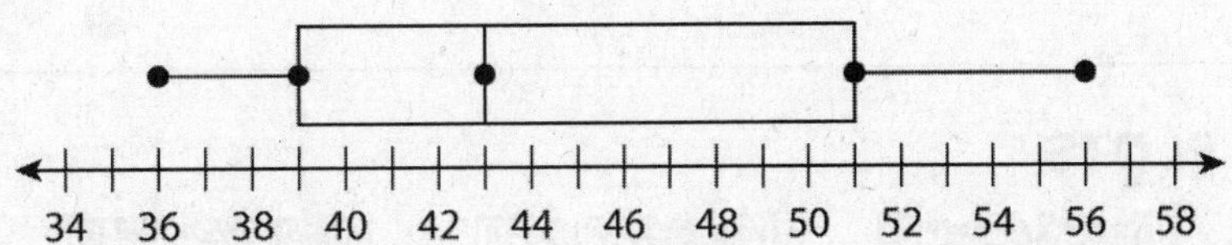

Check

7. Make a box plot for the set of values:
72, 80, 78, 76, 92, 84, 90, 88, 72, 90

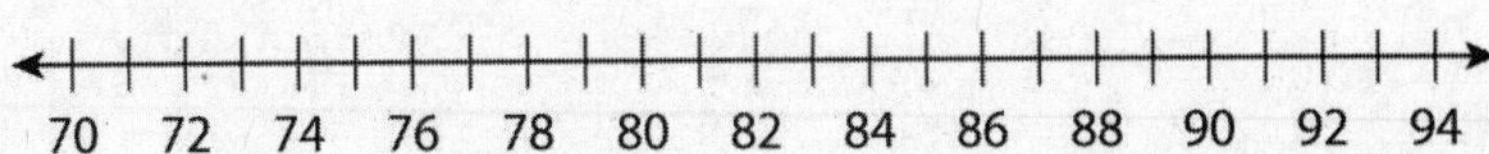

Name ______________________ Date ______________ Class ______________

Example 4

There are two measures of spread that can be determined from a box plot. One measure of spread is the range and the other is the interquartile range (IQR).

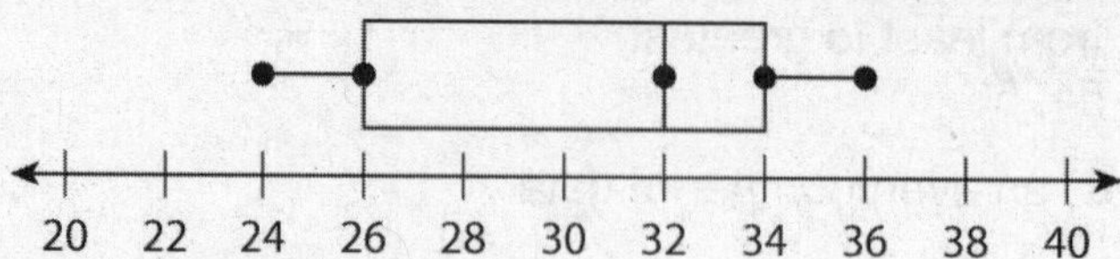

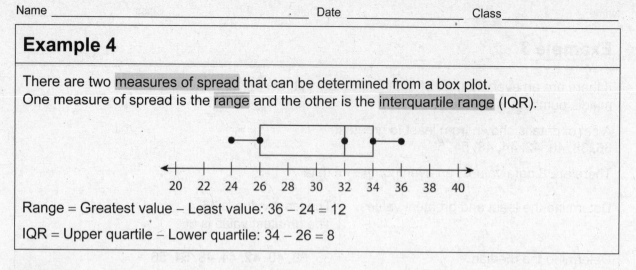

Range = Greatest value – Least value: 36 – 24 = 12

IQR = Upper quartile – Lower quartile: 34 – 26 = 8

Check

Use the box plot to find each value. All values are integers.

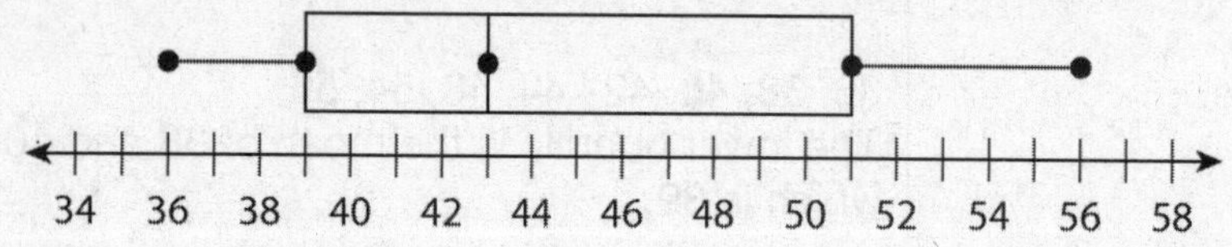

8. Range = __________ 9. IQR = __________

10. What's the Error? Caleb was given this data set: 54, 62, 70, 74, 82, 88, 96. He said the range is 42 and the IQR is 22. What error did Caleb make? Correct Caleb's error.

____

SKILL 29 BOX PLOTS

SKILL 30

Histograms

KEY TEACHING POINTS

Example 1

Say: A histogram is a type of bar graph that uses frequencies within equal intervals. Unless the frequency of an interval is 0, there is no space between the bars of a histogram.

Say: You have been given the number of pages that students in a class read. You can make a tally table to find the frequency of our intervals. With two-digit numbers, it is common to use intervals of 10.

Draw the outline of a tally table on the board.

Interval	Frequency
10–19	
20–29	
30–39	
40–49	
50–59	

Say: The intervals are equal. Go through each interval and mark each tally as appropriate.

Ask: What should the intervals for the histogram be? **[the same as for the tally table]**

Draw the histogram.

Say: Place the intervals on the horizontal axis of your histogram.

ALTERNATE STRATEGY

Strategy: Use a stem-and-leaf plot to organize the data for a histogram.

1. **Say:** If you know that your intervals will be tens, you can use a stem-and-leaf plot to organize the data.
2. **Ask:** What intervals should you use for Josie's data? **[30–39, 40–49, 50–59, 60–69, 70–79]**
3. **Say:** In a stem-and-leaf plot with two-digit numbers, the tens are the stems and the ones are the leaves. Because we are using stem-and-leaf plot to count frequency, the leaves do not need to be ordered.
4. **Ask:** What are the stems? **[3, 4, 5, 6, and 7].** What are the leaves for 3? **[8]** What are the leaves for 4? **[2, 7]** What are the leaves for 5? **[4, 0, 8, 8, 5]** What are the leaves for 6? **[2, 6, 0, 5, 6]** What are the leaves for 7? **[2, 6, 5]**
5. **Say:** You now have all you need to make the histogram.
6. Have students compare this method to using a tally table to organize data.

KEY TEACHING POINTS

Example 2

Say: A histogram has strengths and weaknesses as a tool to represent data. Histograms make it possible to show many data. Histograms also make it possible to approximate mean, median, and range.

Ask: What is a weakness of a histogram? **[You can only approximate measures of center and range because each data point is not given.]**

Say: From a histogram, you can make a table to show the frequencies.

Make a table to show the frequencies of the intervals in the histogram.

Check

To answer Problems 2 and 3, it is necessary for students to count the number of data. This is accomplished by adding the value of the bars.

Ask: How many quiz scores are there? **[20]**

COMMON MISCONCEPTION

Ask: What mistake did Christina make in saying that the median of the histogram in Example 2 could be 78?

Reason incorrect: There are 20 data values. The median of a set with 20 data values is the mean of the tenth and eleventh values when ordered. There were only 8 students that scored less than 81, so the median must be greater than 78.

Solution: Because the median is the mean of the tenth and eleventh values when ordered, the median must be greater than or equal to 81 and less than or equal to 90.

ADDITIONAL ONLINE INTERVENTION RESOURCES

Use the following for students who have not mastered the concepts in Skill 30.

- Math on the Spot videos
- Personal Math Trainer with customized intervention
- Building Block worksheets (Skill 6: Analyze Data; Skill 47: Graph Points on a Number Line; Skill 118: Read Bar Graphs)

Name ______________________ Date ______________ Class ______________

SKILL 30

Histograms

Example 1

The number of pages that each student read yesterday is shown.

36, 28, 42, 54, 32, 18, 25, 40, 52, 48, 22,
16, 42, 38, 55, 37, 44, 12, 31, 44, 28

The data can be represented in a **histogram**. Organize the data in **intervals**. One way to do this is to create a tally table.

Interval	Frequency
10–19	|||
20–29	||||
30–39	𝍸
40–49	𝍸 |
50–59	|||

Each interval is 10.

Make the histogram. Remember to label the axes and give the histogram a title.

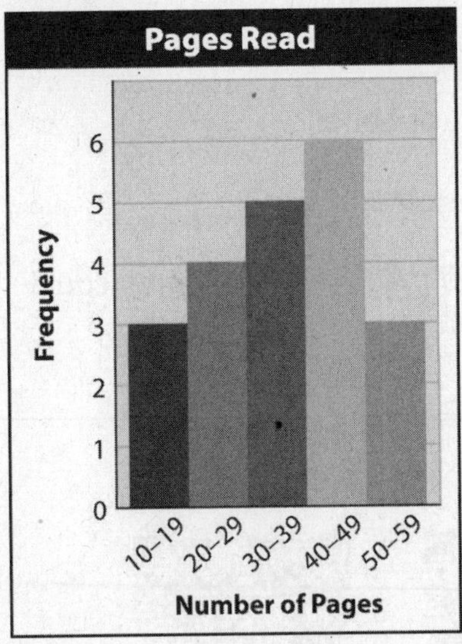

Vocabulary
Histogram
Intervals

Check

1. The number of kilometers Josie rode her bicycle each week for 16 weeks is shown below.

   54, 62, 50, 66, 72, 60, 42, 58, 76, 65, 58, 38, 47, 55, 75, 66

   Make a histogram on a separate piece of paper to represent the data.

Name ______________________ Date ____________ Class ____________

Example 2

The histogram represents the quiz scores in Ms. Alvarez's math class.

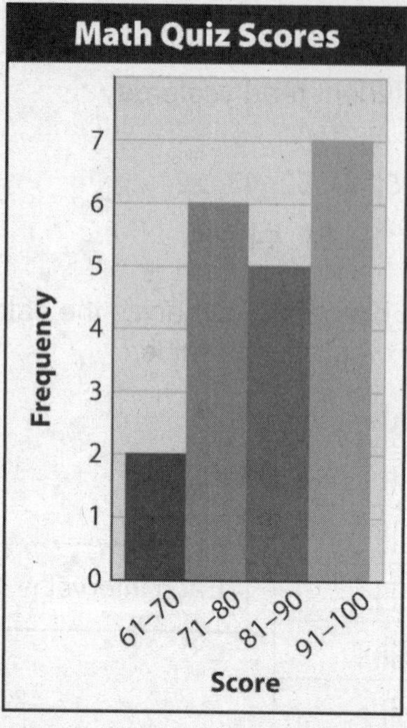

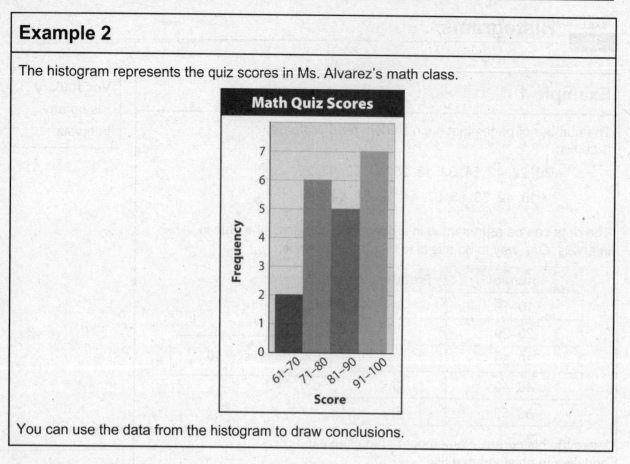

You can use the data from the histogram to draw conclusions.

Check

Use the histogram in Example 2.

2. What percent of the students scored 81 or better? ____________

3. What percent of the students scored less than 91? ____________

4. What's the Error? Christina said that the median of the scores could be 78. Explain why Christina is incorrect.

____

SKILL 30 HISTOGRAMS

SKILL 31

Squares and Square Roots

KEY TEACHING POINTS

Example 1

Say: 4^2 is written in exponential form. The 4 is the base and the exponent is 2. When a base has an exponent of 2, it is said to be squared.

Say: A square is a number that is multiplied by itself. For example $4^2 = 16$ because $4 \times 4 = 16$. It does not matter if the base is a whole number, decimal, or fraction.

Ask: How do you square a fraction? **[Multiply the numerator by itself and then multiply the denominator by itself.]**

Example 2

Say: The square root of a positive number p is x if $x^2 = p$. The square root is a number that is equal to a square when it is multiplied by itself.

Ask: Why does every positive number have two square roots? **[Because two negative factors form a positive product]**

Say: So, 16 has two square roots because $4 \times 4 = 16$ and $-4 \times (-4) = 16$.

Say: The decimal 0.25 has two decimal places.

Ask: How many decimal places will the square root of 0.25 have? **[1]** How do you know? **[The number of decimal places in a product is equal to the sum of the decimal places in the factors.]**

Ask: How do you find the square root of a fraction? **[Find the square root of the numerator and then find the square root of the denominator.]**

COMMON MISCONCEPTION

Write the equation as you ask the following question.

Ask: What is Jonah's error in saying that $\sqrt{100} = \pm 10$?

Reason incorrect: If a radical is used, the square root must be positive.

Solution: $\sqrt{100} = 10$

KEY TEACHING POINTS

Example 3

Say: A perfect square has square roots that are integers. So, 16 is a perfect square because $4 \times 4 = 16$ and $-4 \times (-4) = 16$.

Ask: Is 1 a perfect square? Why or why not? **[Yes, because $1 \times 1 = 1$ and $-1 \times (-1) = 1$.]**

Ask: Is 0.09 a perfect square because $0.3 \times 0.3 = 0.09$? Why or why not? **[No, because 0.3 is a decimal.]**

KEY TEACHING POINTS

Example 4

Review with students that irrational numbers are numbers that cannot be written in the form of $\frac{a}{b}$, where a and b are both integers and $b \neq 0$. Square roots can be rational or irrational.

Say: If a square root is irrational, it can be approximated. You can approximate a square root with a calculator or you can use guess-and-test. Let's approximate $\sqrt{8}$.

Ask: Between which two perfect squares does 8 fall? **[4 and 9]** Between which two consecutive integers does $\sqrt{8}$ fall? **[2 and 3]**

Say: Because $2^2 = 4$ and $3^2 = 9$, we know that $\sqrt{8}$ is between 2 and 3. Now let's find the square root of the greatest decimal to one place that is less than 8 and the least decimal to one place that is greater than 8. Let's try 2.8 and 2.9.

Ask: What is 2.8^2? **[7.84]** What is 2.9^2? **[8.41]** Which is closer to 8? **[7.84]** Which decimal to one place is the best approximation for $\sqrt{8}$? **[2.8]**

ALTERNATE STRATEGY

Strategy: Use perfect squares and fractions to approximate a square root.

1. **Ask:** Between what two perfect squares does 18 fall? **[16 and 25]**
2. **Ask:** Between which two consecutive integers does $\sqrt{18}$ fall? **[4 and 5]**
3. **Ask:** What is 4^2? **[16]** What is 5^2? **[25]**
4. **Say:** We know that $\sqrt{18}$ is between 4 and 5. To write the fraction, subtract 18 – 16 for the numerator and the difference between the perfect squares for the denominator.
5. **Ask:** What is 18 – 16? **[2]** What is 25 – 16? **[9]**
6. **Say:** The mixed number $4\frac{2}{9}$ is a good approximation for $\sqrt{18}$.
7. **Ask:** What is $4\frac{2}{9}$ written as a decimal to the nearest tenth? **[4.2]**
8. Have students compare this method to the guess-and-test method.

ADDITIONAL ONLINE INTERVENTION RESOURCES

Use the following for students who have not mastered the concepts in Skill 31.

- Math on the Spot videos
- Personal Math Trainer with customized intervention
- Building Block worksheets (Skill 29: Evaluate Powers; Skill 30: Exponents; Skill 38: Find the Square of a Number; Skill 100: Squares and Square Roots)

Name ______________________ Date ______________ Class ______________

SKILL 31

Squares and Square Roots

Example 1

A square is a number raised to the second power.

A square number can be written in exponential form with a base that has an exponent of 2.

Integer	Decimal	Fraction
$4^2 = 4 \cdot 4 = 16$	$0.7^2 = 0.7 \cdot 0.7 = 0.49$	$\left(\frac{3}{5}\right)^2 = \frac{3}{5} \cdot \frac{3}{5} = \frac{9}{25}$

Vocabulary

Square
Exponential form
Base
Exponent
Square root
Principal square root
Perfect square
Integer

Check

Evaluate.

1. $3^2 =$ ____
2. $5^2 =$ ____
3. $0.8^2 =$ ____
4. $0.2^2 =$ ____
5. $\left(\frac{4}{9}\right)^2 =$ ____
6. $\left(\frac{2}{7}\right)^2 =$ ____

Example 2

The square root of a positive number p is x if $x^2 = p$.

There are two squares roots for every positive number. The square roots of 16 are 4 and –4 because $4^2 = 16$ and $(-4)^2 = 16$. The symbol $\sqrt{\ }$ indicates the positive, or principal square root.

$x^2 = 16$
$x = \pm\sqrt{16}$
$x = \pm 4$

$x^2 = 0.25$
$x = \pm\sqrt{0.25}$
$x = \pm 0.5$

$x^2 = \frac{1}{9}$
$x = \pm\sqrt{\frac{1}{9}}$
$x = \pm\frac{1}{3}$

Check

Solve each equation for *x*.

7. $x^2 = 81$

$x =$ ________

8. $x^2 = 0.36$

$x =$ ________

9. $x^2 = \frac{25}{64}$

$x =$ ________

Name ______________________ Date ______________ Class ______________

10. What's the Error? Jonah said that $\sqrt{100} = \pm 10$. What error did Jonah make? Give the correct answer.

____

Example 3

A number that is a perfect square has square roots that are integers.
Because the square roots of 16 are 4 and −4, 16 is a perfect square.

Check

Determine if each number is a perfect square. Write Yes or No.

11. 36 ________ 12. 50 ________ 13. 121 ________

Example 4

You can approximate or estimate square roots.
Estimate the value of $\sqrt{8}$.

Find two consecutive perfect squares such that $\sqrt{8}$ is between their consecutive square roots.	Perfect squares: 4 and 9 $\sqrt{4} = 2$ and $\sqrt{9} = 3$
Use guess-and-test to find a better estimate.	$2.8^2 = 7.84$ and $2.9^2 = 8.41$ $\sqrt{8} \approx 2.8$

≈ means approximate

Because 7.84 is closer than 8.41 is to 8, you can estimate $\sqrt{8}$ as about 2.8.

Check

Approximate each irrational number to one decimal place without a calculator.

14. $\sqrt{18}$ 15. $\sqrt{32}$ 16. $\sqrt{50}$ 17. $\sqrt{76}$

________ ________ ________ ________

SKILL 31 SQUARES AND SQUARE ROOTS

SKILL 32

Cubes and Cube Roots

KEY TEACHING POINTS

Example 1

Say: 4^3 is written in exponential form. The 4 is the base and the exponent is 3. When a base has an exponent of 3, it is said to be cubed.

Say: A cube is a number that is multiplied by itself two times. For example $4^3 = 64$ because $4 \times 4 \times 4 = 64$. It does not matter if the base is a whole number, decimal, or fraction.

Ask: How do you cube a fraction? **[Multiply the numerator by itself two times and then multiply the denominator by itself two times.]**

Check

Say: Look at Problem 1. What expression is equal to 2^3? **[2 × 2 × 2]**

Example 2

Say: The cube root of a positive number *p* is *x* if $x^3 = p$. For example, the cube root of 64 is 4 because $4^3 = 64$.

Ask: Why does a positive number only have one cube root? **[Because three negative factors form a negative product]**

Say: The decimal 0.125 has three decimal places.

Ask: How many decimal places will the cube root of 0.125 have? **[1]** How do you know? **[The number of decimal places in a product is equal to the sum of the decimal places in the factors.]**

Ask: How do you find the cube root of a fraction? **[Find the cube root of the numerator and then find the cube root of the denominator.]**

Example 3

Say: A perfect cube has a cube root that is an integer. So, 64 is a perfect cube because $4 \times 4 \times 4 = 64$.

Check

Ask: How can you tell if a number is a perfect cube? **[If it is an integer and has a root that can be multiplied by itself two times.]**

Students can use guess-and-test if necessary to determine perfect cubes.

COMMON MISCONCEPTION

Ask: What is Nate's error in saying that 64 is the only number less than 100 that is both a perfect square and a perfect cube?

Reason incorrect: 1 raised to any positive integer power is equal to 1.

Solution: 1

ALTERNATE STRATEGY

Strategy: Make a list of perfect cubes to use for reference.

1. Multiply each integer from 1–10 by itself two times to make a list of perfect cubes.
2. **Ask:** What are the first ten perfect cubes? **[1, 8, 27, 64, 125, 216, 343, 512, 729, 1000]**

KEY TEACHING POINTS

Example 4

Review with students that a cube is a solid figure that has 6 square faces. The three dimensions of a cube are equal.

Say: The volume of a cube is 729 cubic inches.

Ask: What does that statement mean? **[The product of the length, width, and height is 729. The factors are equal.]**

Ask: How can you find the length of the edges? **[Find the cube root of 729.]** What is the cube root of 729? **[9]** What are the edge lengths? **[9 inches]**

Remind students that when measures are given, it is necessary to give the units.

ADDITIONAL ONLINE INTERVENTION RESOURCES

Use the following for students who have not mastered the concepts in Skill 32.

- Math on the Spot videos
- Personal Math Trainer with customized intervention
- Building Block worksheets (Skill 29: Evaluate Powers; Skill 30: Exponents)

Name ______________________ Date ______________ Class ______________

SKILL 32

Cubes and Cube Roots

Example 1

A number that is cubed is raised to the third power.

Numbers that are cubed can be written in exponential form with a base that has an exponent of 3.

Integer	Decimal	Fraction
$4^3 = 4 \cdot 4 \cdot 4 = 64$	$0.7^3 = 0.7 \cdot 0.7 \cdot 0.7 = 0.343$	$\left(\frac{3}{5}\right)^3 = \frac{3}{5} \cdot \frac{3}{5} \cdot \frac{3}{5} = \frac{27}{125}$

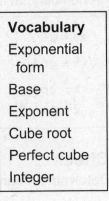

Vocabulary
Exponential form
Base
Exponent
Cube root
Perfect cube
Integer

Check

Evaluate.

1. $2^3 =$ ____
2. $8^3 =$ ____
3. $0.6^3 =$ ____
4. $0.3^3 =$ ____
5. $\left(\frac{1}{9}\right)^3 =$ ____
6. $\left(\frac{3}{10}\right)^3 =$ ____

Example 2

The cube root of a positive number p is x if $x^3 = p$. There is one cube root for every positive number. The symbol $\sqrt[3]{}$ indicates the cube root.

$$x^3 = 64$$
$$\sqrt[3]{x^3} = \sqrt[3]{64}$$
$$x = \sqrt[3]{64}$$
$$x = 4$$

$$x^3 = 0.125$$
$$\sqrt[3]{x^3} = \sqrt[3]{0.125}$$
$$x = \sqrt[3]{0.125}$$
$$x = 0.5$$

$$x^3 = \frac{27}{343}$$
$$\sqrt[3]{x^3} = \sqrt[3]{\frac{27}{343}}$$
$$x = \sqrt[3]{\frac{27}{343}}$$
$$x = \frac{3}{7}$$

Check

Solve each equation for *x*.

7. $x^3 = 216$

$x =$ ________

8. $x^3 = 0.008$

$x =$ ________

9. $x^3 = \frac{64}{729}$

$x =$ ________

Name ______________________ Date ______________ Class______________

Example 3

A number that is a perfect cube has a cube root that is an integer.

$x^3 = 64$ $\sqrt[3]{x^3} = \sqrt[3]{64}$ $x = \sqrt[3]{64}$ $x = 4$	$x^3 = 125$ $\sqrt[3]{x^3} = \sqrt[3]{125}$ $x = \sqrt[3]{125}$ $x = 5$

Check

Determine if each number is a perfect cube. Write Yes or No.

10. 16 __________ 11. 27 __________ 12. 216 __________

13. What's the Error? Nate said that 64 is the only positive number less than 100 that is both a perfect square and perfect cube. Explain why Nate is incorrect. Give any other numbers less than 100 that are both perfect squares and perfect cubes.

____

____

Example 4

A cube has a volume of 729 in^3. What is the length of each edge of the cube?

Write an equation.	$e = \sqrt[3]{729}$
Solve for e.	$\sqrt[3]{x^3} = \sqrt[3]{729}$ $x = \sqrt[3]{729}$ $x = 9$

The edges have a length of 9 inches.

Check

Find the length of the edges of each cube.

14. $V = 125$ cm^3: $e =$ __________ 15. $V = 343$ in^3: $e =$ __________

SKILL 32 CUBES AND CUBE ROOTS

Answer Key

Pre-Test 1: Quantitative Reasoning

1. 6.2
2. $s = \frac{-10}{3}$
3. 17 h
4. 42 ft
5. 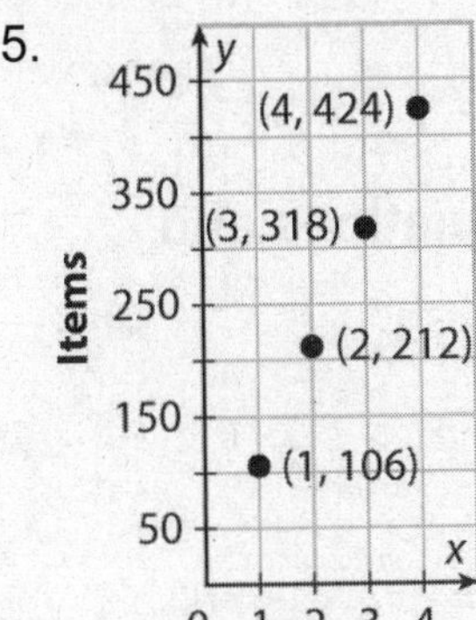

6. A
7. m = –4.75
8. A = 5 ft × s ft
9. 27 ft
10. C
11. A. No, B. Yes, C. No, D. No

Pre-Test 2: Algebraic Models

1. 6
2. 23 °F
3. $8w + 3$
4. \$23.13
5. $\frac{x}{5} - 4$
6. $m = \frac{19}{3}$ or $6\frac{1}{3}$
7. $m = 4$
8. $m = 28$
9. $m = 3.6$
10. 60°
11. $x \geq \frac{7}{2}$
12. $x < 7$
13. $x \leq 7.7$
14. $x < -20$
15. $3x \leq 20; x \leq 6.66$
16. $x = 4$
17. $x = 2$
18. $x = 3.125$
19. $x \geq \frac{12}{5}$ or $2\frac{2}{5}$
20. $x \leq 42$
21. $x < 11.11$ or $11\frac{1}{9}$
22. 4 h
23. $h \geq \frac{43}{12}$ or $h \geq 3\frac{7}{12}$

Pre-Test 3: Functions and Models

1. The graph of a linear function forms a straight line.
2.

x	–2	–1	0	1	2
y	–3	–1	1	3	5

3. Yes. The line does not go through the origin. The line of a proportional relationship must go through the origin.
4. A No, B Yes, C Yes, D No
5. After 3 hours the weather balloon is 7.5 miles above the surface.
6.

x	1	2	3	4	5
y	9.5	14	18.5	23	27.5

Pre-Test 4: Patterns and Sequences

1. Variables will vary: $2n - 8$
2. Variables will vary: $-7n$
3. 5
4. –10
5. negative
6. –6
7. Variables will vary: $15 \div n$
8. $12 - (-4) = 16$
9. –72

9. –72

10. 6

11. 8.16

12. 13

13. $14x + 36$

14. $6 + 9$

15. –16

16. Variables will vary: $7n + 4$

17. 8

18. left

Pre-Test 5: Linear Functions

1. 5

2. $y = 5x$

3.

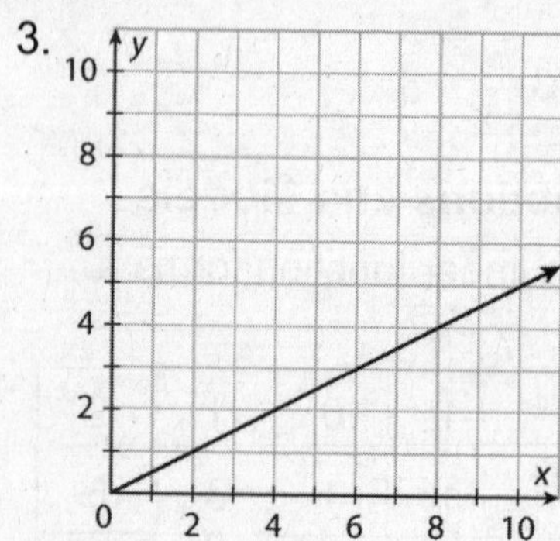

4. Yes

5. $a = 6$

6. $b = 1$

7. 1.5 miles per minute

8. It is the same.

9. 2

10. $y = 6x - 1$

11. $4.60

12. 54 miles per hour

Pre-Test 6: Forms of Linear Equations

1.

T-Shirt Costs	
Number of T-Shirts	Cost (dollars)
1	13
2	26
3	39
4	52
5	65

2. $y = 13x$

3. Yes

4. A. Yes, B. No, C. Yes

5. positive

6. $y = -2x + 11$

7. 1

8. $k = 7$

9. $m = 2.3$

10. 15 toy cars per minute

11. $1\frac{1}{2}$ c

Pre-Test 7: Linear Equations and Inequalities

1. –1.5

2. $2.1s - 8.4t - 8.7$

3. $5m + 60$

4. No

5. Yes

6.

x	y
0	25
2	23
4	21
6	19
8	17

7. Variables may vary. $y = 40x + 30$

8. $y = 3x + 2$

Pre-Test 8: Multi-Variable Categorical Data

1. $77.04

2. 30%

3. $1236

4.

	Boys	Girls	TOTAL
Enjoy Challenges of School	52	78	130
Do Not Enjoy Challenges of School	49	21	70
TOTAL	101	99	200

5.

	Prefer Rain	Prefer Snow	TOTAL
Adults	29	16	45
Students	22	53	75
TOTAL	51	69	120

6.

	Comedy	Drama	Musical
Boys	0.59	0.46	0.35
Girls	0.41	0.54	0.65
TOTAL	1	1	1

Pre-Test 9: One-Variable Data Distributions

1. 91
2. 92
3. 87
4. 130
5. 10
6. 6
7. 15
8.

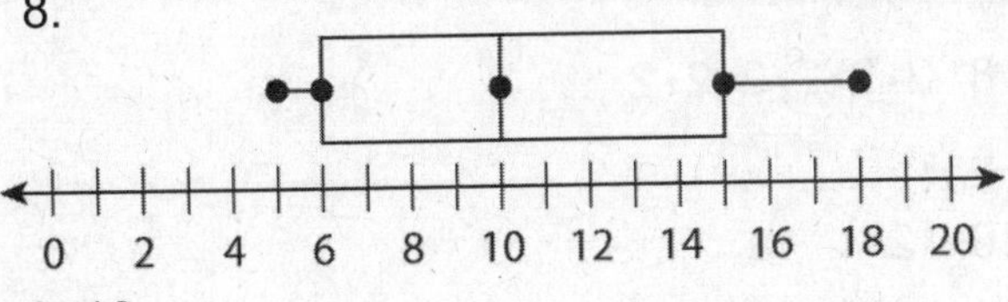

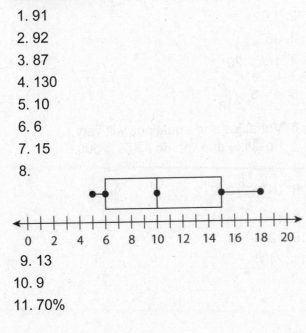

9. 13
10. 9
11. 70%

Pre-Test 10: Linear Modeling and Regression

1. Yes
2. Trends lines may vary. Possible trend line is shown.

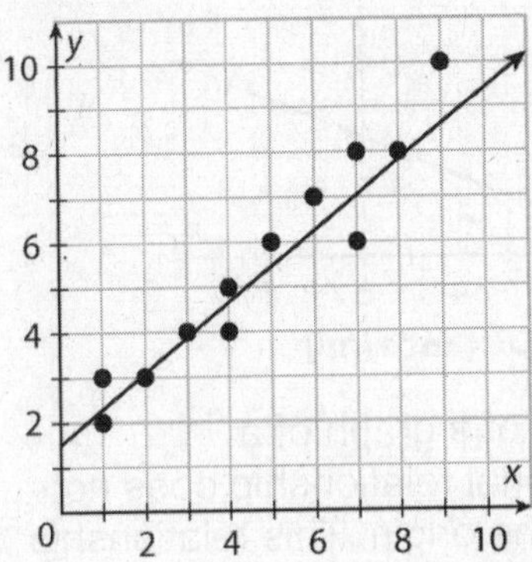

3. Yes
4. No
5. No
6. Yes
7. No
8. Cluster
9. $y = 37.5x - 500$
10. $y = 2x + 8$

Pre-Test 11: Solving Systems of Linear Equations

1. 12
2. $b \div 6$
3. −17
4. Variables will vary: $5f - 2$
5.

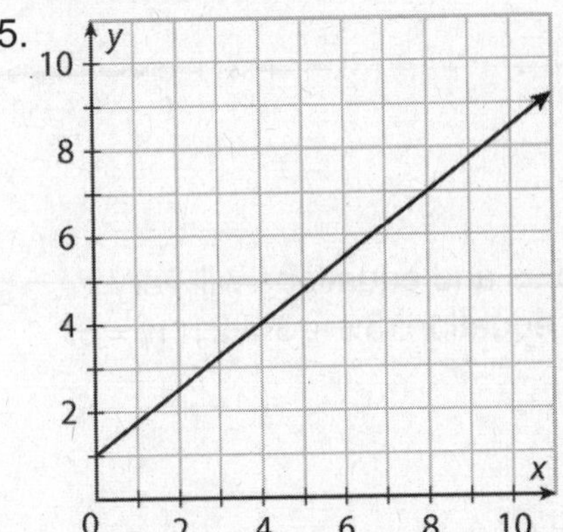

6. No. For the line of a graph to represent a proportional relationship, the line must go through the origin.

7.

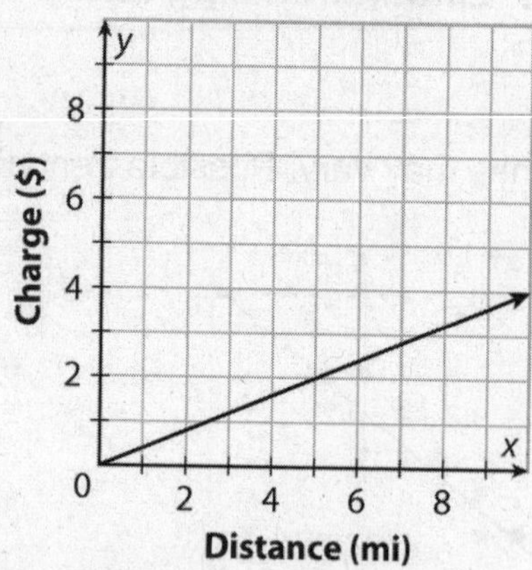

8 No. The line of a graph of a nonproportional relationship does not go through the origin. This relationship does go through the origin.

9. Yes

Pre-Test 12: Modeling with Linear Systems

1. $12e - 17$
2. Variables will vary: $n - 15$
3. –99
4. Yes
5. Yes
6. No
7. Yes
8. $a > 4$
9. $b \leq 35$
10. $c > 15$
11.

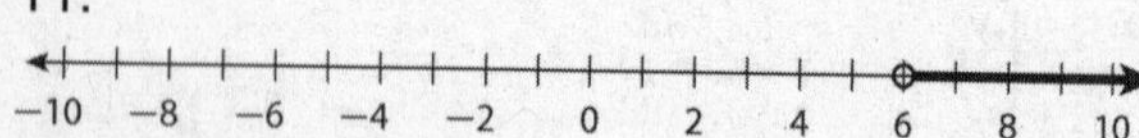

12. $e = 3$
13. $f = 7$
14. 6; Variables and equations will vary. Possible equation: $3w + 3 = 21$; $w = 6$.
15. $g \geq 6$
16. $h > 8$
17. $x \leq 1$

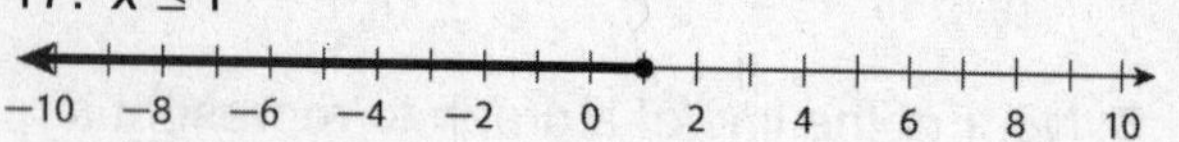

Pre-Test 13: Piecewise-Defined Functions

1. Yes
2. A. Yes, B. No, C. No, D. Yes
3. $a = 7$
4. $b = -1$
5. $c = -7.5$ or $c = -7\frac{1}{2}$
6. $d = 12$
7. $e = \frac{3}{4}$
8. Variables will vary: $6m + 4 > 46$ or $6m > 42$
9. $f \geq 9$
10. $g > -3$
11. –4 –2 0 2 4
12. 2.4
13. 5
14. Dave needs to score more than 12 points because 12 added to a number less than –12 gives a negative sum.

Pre-Test 14: Rational Exponents and Radicals

1. A. No, B. Yes, C. No, D. Yes
2. 1.62
3. 38
4. $16k - 20$
5. $n \div 6$ or $\frac{n}{6}$
6. Variables and equations will vary. Possible answer: $8c - 150 = 600$.
7. 7^5
8. 2•2•2•2•2•2
9. 1
10. 12
11. 2401

12. $\frac{1}{36}$

13. $\frac{1}{32}$

14. 16

15. 32,768

16. 0.65

17. $\frac{8}{9}$

18. $x = \pm 9$

19. $x = \pm\frac{2}{11}$

20. $x = 8$

21. 6.7

Pre-Test 15: Geometric Sequences and Exponential Functions

1. Variables will vary: $6n$
2. Possible answers $10n$, $10 \times n$, $n \times 10$, $10 \cdot n$, $n \cdot 10$
3. 6
4. $1.3q + 1.17$
5. Variables will vary: $3b + 2$
6. $\frac{1}{6} \cdot \frac{1}{6} \cdot \frac{1}{6} \cdot \frac{1}{6}$
7. 10,000 people
8. 1
9. 7
10. 243
11. 15,625
12. $\frac{1}{81}$
13. 1728
14. 1296
15. $\frac{1}{32,768}$
16. $r = 5$
17. $s = 4$
18. $t = -7\frac{1}{5}$
19. $u = -6$
20. $v = 5$
21. $w = 4$

Pre-Test 16: Exponential Equations and Models

1. A. Yes, B. No, C. No, D. Yes
2. 8
3. $y = 8x$
4. 1024
5. $\frac{1}{343}$
6. \$48.60
7. 40%
8. \$22.50
9.

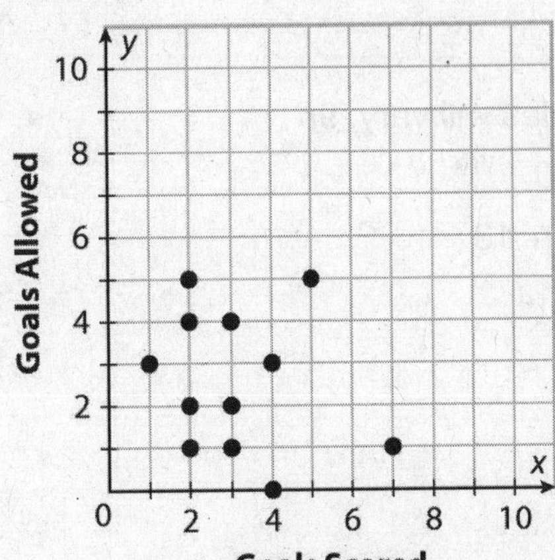

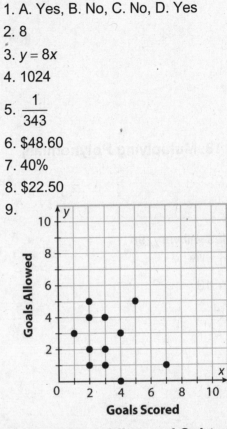

Pre-Test 17: Adding and Subtracting Polynomials

1. –3
2. 5
3. –11
4. –2
5. right
6. –9 °C
7. 3 + 7
8. 6.9
9. 12
10. Variables will vary: $18 - n$
11. $16c - 41$
12. $d - 2e + 10$
13. –45
14. 3^6

15. $\left(\frac{1}{6}\right)^5$

16. 4096

17. 729

18. 12

19. 6^7

20. 5^{12}

21. 3^8

22. 20^3

23. 5^{-5}

Pre-Test 18: Multiplying Polynomials

1. 0.288
2. 3.45
3. 7.13
4. Variables will vary: $9n$
5. $2d + 20$
6. $-a + b + 13$
7. $25g - 14$
8. 9^7
9. 4^{-6}
10. 1
11. 3
12. 625
13. 5^8
14. 4^6
15. 7^{12}
16. 6^4
17. 6^9
18. 8^{-6}
19. –28
20. –40
21. 54
22. –55 ft
23. –9
24. 3
25. –4
26. –4 °C

Pre-Test 19: Graphing Quadratic Functions

1. $8x - 5y - 4$
2. $16a + 10$
3. A' (0, 2) B' (2, 0) C' (–2, 0)
4. A' (3, 2) B' (5, 4) C' (1, 4)
5. A' (–3, –2) B' (–5, –4) C' (–1, –4)
6. A' (–2, –3) B' (–4, –5) C' (–4, –1)
7. A' (2, 3) B' (4, 5) C' (4, 1)
8. A' (–3, 2) B' (–5, 4) C' (–1, 4)
9. D' (8, 8) E' (8, 2) F' (0, 2)
10. D' (2, 2) E' (2, 0.5) F' (0, 0.5)
11. 729
12. $\frac{1}{512}$
13. Yes

Pre-Test 20: Connecting Intercepts, Zeros, and Factors

1. $a \div 4$
2. A Yes, B No, C No, D Yes
3. –22
4. 54
5. 1024
6. $\frac{1}{81}$
7. 256
8. $\frac{1}{729}$
9. 6561
10. Yes
11. A Yes, B No, C No, D Yes
12.

Number of Slices, x	Cost in Dollars, y
3	14
5	20
7	26
9	32

Pre-Test 21: Using Factors to Solve Quadratic Equations

1. Variables will vary: $2n + 6$
2. Variables will vary: $\frac{n-4}{3}$
3. Variables will vary: $40h + 35d$
4. –6
5. 512
6. 16,384
7. $\frac{1}{81}$
8. 390,625
9. 8^4
10. 343
11. $b = 6.5$
12. $c = -5$
13. $d = 30$
14. $e = 1$
15. $f = -1.8$
16. $g = -2$
17. 8; Variables and equations will vary: $12h + 30 = 126$, $h = 8$
18. 12; Variables and equations will vary: $8r - 32 = 128$, $r = 20$

Pre-Test 22: Using Square Roots to Solve Quadratic Equations

1. –9
2. 6.5
3. –6
4. Variables will vary: $20 - n$
5. Variables will vary: $6n + 4$
6. 1
7. 16
8. $\frac{1}{59{,}049}$
9. 2,401
10. 46,656
11. $\frac{1}{65{,}536}$
12. $b = 5$
13. $c = -6$
14. $d = 48$
15. $e = 4$
16. $f = -5.5$
17. $g = 7$
18. $h = -7$
19. $j = 1.75$

Pre-Test 23: Linear, Exponential, and Quadratic Models

1. 3.5
2. $y = 3.5x$
3. 3. 70
4.

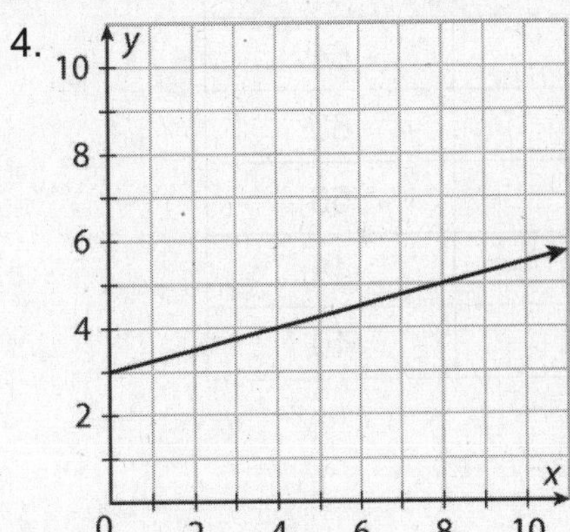

5. A Yes, B No, C No, D Yes
6.

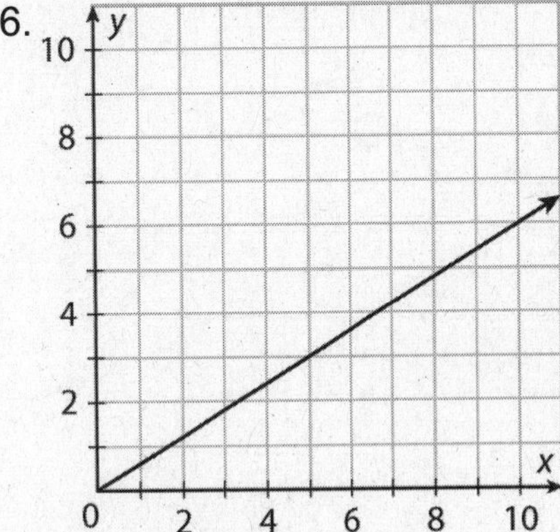

7. A No, B Yes, C Yes, D No
8.

x	y
0	10
2	26
4	42
6	58
8	74

Pre-Test 24: Functions and Inverses

1. 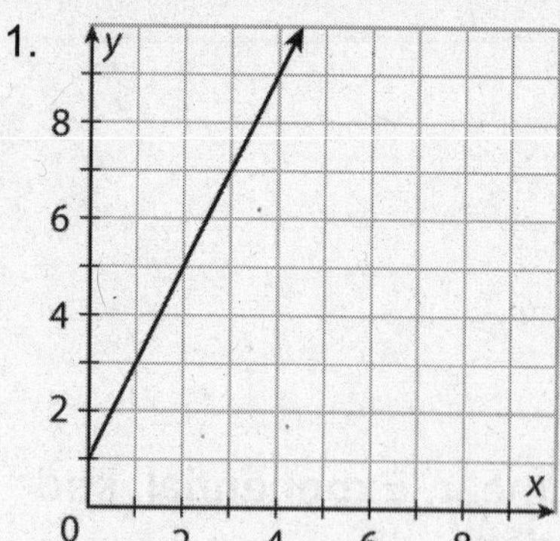

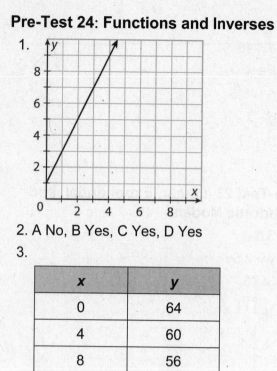

2. A No, B Yes, C Yes, D Yes

3.

x	*y*
0	64
4	60
8	56
16	48
24	40

4. 36

5. $\frac{9}{64}$ and $\frac{27}{512}$

6. $x = \pm 10$

7. $x = \pm\frac{4}{5}$

8. 7 and 8

9. 4.7

10. $x = 6$

11. $x = \frac{5}{9}$

12. 8 cm

Answer Key

Skill 1: Add and Subtract Integers

Post-Test

1. –14
2. –4
3. 4
4. 6
5. –3
6. B
7. –3°C
8. right
9. 2 – 5
10. 13 ft
11. –3
12. –12
13. 4 + 8
14. right
15. 0
16. –7
17. A. False, B. True, C. False, D. True

Skill 2: Algebraic Expressions

Post-Test

1. 3
2. –4
3. 3.2
4. $d \div 8$
5. 8
6. 56
7. A. No, B. Yes, C. Yes, D. No
8. $-2n + 6p - 6$
9. $4s + 12$
10. $15u - 14$
11. $-0.3v + 5.1$
12. $10 - n$
13. $n \div 8$ or $\frac{n}{8}$
14. $n + 3$ or $3 + n$
15. 18
16. $6r - 9s + 8$
17. Possible answers include: $8m$, $8 \times m$, $8 \cdot m$
18. $6d + 20$

Skill 3: Constant Rate of Change

Post-Test

1. $A'(0, 1)$ $B'(4, 1)$ $C'(4, -1)$ $D'(0, -1)$
2. $A'(-5, 2)$ $B'(-1, 2)$ $C'(-1, 4)$ $D'(-5, 4)$
3. $A'(5, -2)$ $B'(1, -2)$ $C'(1, -4)$ $D'(5, -4)$
4. $A'(-2, 5)$ $B'(-2, 1)$ $C'(-4, 1)$ $D'(-4, 5)$
5. $A'(2, -5)$ $B'(2, -1)$ $C'(4, -1)$ $D'(4, -5)$
6. $A'(5, 2)$ $B'(1, 2)$ $C'(1, 4)$ $D'(5, 4)$
7. No, the transformations move rectangle *ABCD* but they do not change its size.
8. $L'(4, 8)$ $M'(8, 2)$ $N'(2, 2)$
9. $L'(0.5, 1)$ $M'(1, 0.25)$ $N'(0.25, 0.25)$ or $L'\left(\frac{1}{2},1\right)M'\left(1,\frac{1}{4}\right)N'\left(\frac{1}{4},\frac{1}{4}\right)$
10. $L'(3, 6)$ $M'(6, 1.5)$ $N'(1.5, 1.5)$ or $L'(3,6)M'\left(6,1\frac{1}{2}\right)N'\left(1\frac{1}{2},1\frac{1}{2}\right)$
11. Yes, the dilations with a scale factor greater than 1 enlarge the triangle. Those with a scale less than 1 reduce the size of the triangle.

Skill 4: Exponents

Post-Test

1. \$25 per ticket
2.

Number of Tickets	Cost, in Dollars
1	25
2	50
3	75
4	100
5	125

3. $25
4. $300
5. 4 tickets with $10 left over
6. A Yes, B No, C Yes, D No
7. $16 per hour
8. 16
9. $y = 16x$
10. $40
11. 2.75
12. $y = 2.75x$

Skill 5: Exponents

Post-Test

1. 8^6
2. 729
3. $\frac{1}{3^5}$
4. $\frac{1}{128}$
5. 1
6. 15
7. 3^{-4}
8. $8^2 \cdot 8^3 = 8^5 = 32{,}768$
9. $6^{-2} \cdot 6^{-3} = 6^{-5} = \frac{1}{7776}$
10. $4^{-5} \cdot 4^3 = 4^{-2} = \frac{1}{16}$
11. $9^2 \cdot 9^{-5} = 9^{-3} = \frac{1}{729}$
12. $\frac{5^6}{5^3} = 5^3 = 125$
13. $\frac{2^3}{2^{-3}} = 2^6 = 64$
14. $\frac{7^{-2}}{7^{-3}} = 7^1 = 7$
15. 13,824 people
16. $(5 \cdot 2)^6 = 5^6 \cdot 2^6 = 15{,}625 \cdot 64 = 1{,}000{,}000$
17. $(7^2)^3 = 7^6 = 117{,}649$
18. $(4^{-3})^{-4} = 4^{12} = 16{,}777{,}216$
19. $(3^{-3})^3 = 3^{-9} = \frac{1}{19{,}683}$
20. $(6^2)^{-4} = 6^{-8} = \frac{1}{1{,}679{,}616}$

Skill 6: Graphing Linear Nonproportional Relationships

Post-Test

1. A No; B Yes; C Yes; D Yes
2. A Yes; B No; C Yes, D Yes
3.

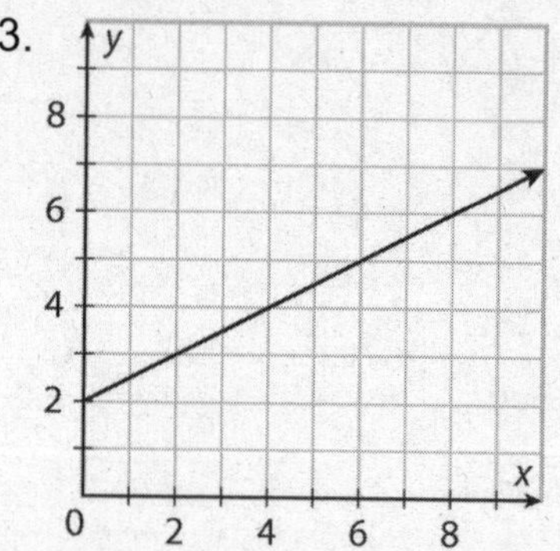

4.

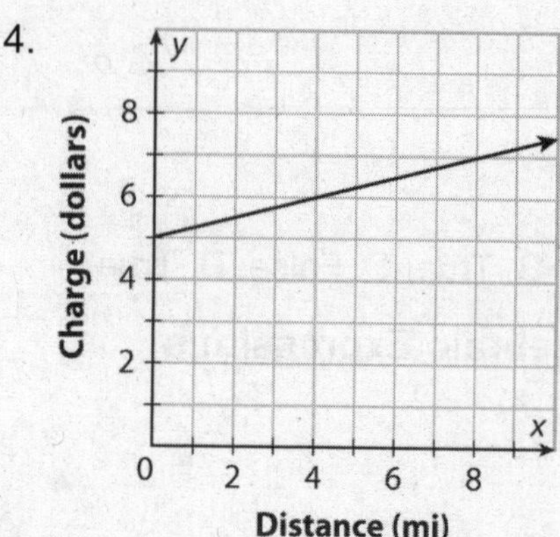

5. Yes

Skill 7: Graphing Linear Proportional Relationships

Post-Test

1. A No; B Yes; C Yes; D Yes
2. A Yes; B Yes; C No; D Yes
3.

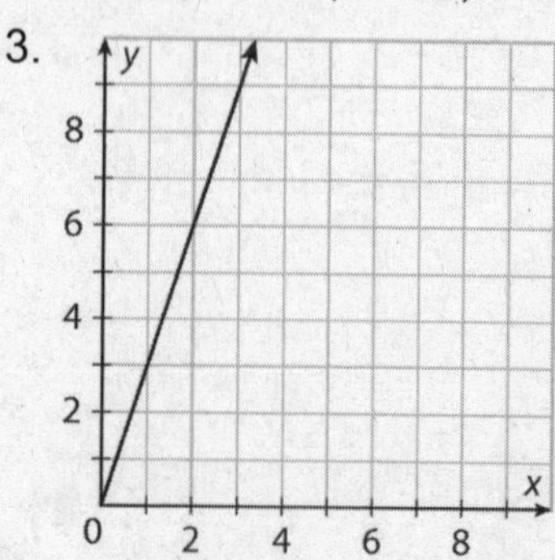

4. 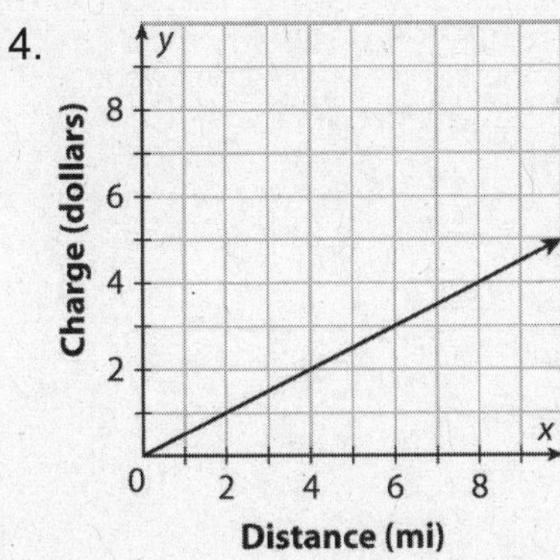

5. Yes

Skill 8: Interpreting the Unit Rate as Slope

Post-Test

1. A. No; B. Yes; C. Yes; D. Yes
2. 7 miles per day
3. $12 per baseball hat
4. $\frac{2}{3}$
5. 1.25 gallons per second
6. 0.75 mile per minute

Skill 9: Linear Associations

Post-Test

1. A. No; B. Yes; C. Yes
2. A. No; B. Yes
3. 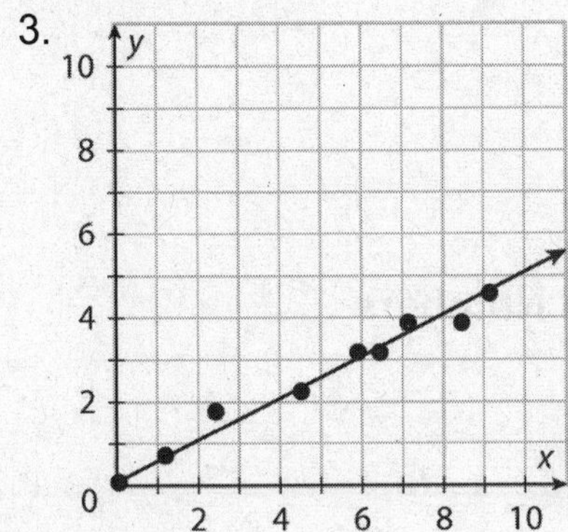

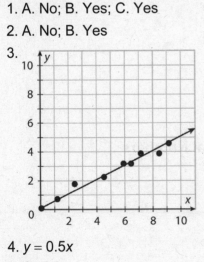

4. $y = 0.5x$
5. $18

Skill 10: Linear Functions

Post-Test

1. No
2. Yes
3. Yes
4. Each input has exactly one output.
5. Yes
6. A. Yes; B. No; C. Yes; D. No
7.

x	y
0	8
2	6
4	4
6	2
8	0

Skill 11: Multi-Step Equations

Post-Test

1. subtraction
2. multiplication
3. $a = 3$
4. $b = 3$
5. $c = -2$
6. $d = 1$
7. $e = 11\frac{2}{3}$
8. $f = 3$
9. $g = 4\frac{2}{3}$
10. $h = 8$
11. $j = 44$
12. $k = 2\frac{2}{3}$
13. $m = 5$
14. $n = 4$
15. $p = 1$

Skill 12: Multiply and Divide Integers

Post-Test

1. –15
2. –12
3. –30
4. –28
5. negative
6. 27
7. 40

8. positive
9. −8(4) or 4(−8)
10. −32
11. −4
12. −7
13. −8
14. −9
15. positive
16. negative
17. 6
18. 4
19. −2
20. 8
21. $-9 \div 3$

Skill 13: One-Step Equations

Post-Test

1. Variables will vary: $8n = 56$
2. Variables will vary: $n - 15 = 12$
3. Variables and equations will vary. Possible equation: $12b = 72$
4. Variables and equations will vary. Possible equation: $175 + g = 411$
5. $a = 0.69$
6. $b = \frac{3}{8}$
7. $c = 42$
8. $d = -12$
9. $e = 32$
10. $f = \frac{5}{6}$
11. $g = 28$
12. $h = -18$
13. Variables and equations will vary. Possible equation: $5d = 85$; $d = 17$

Skill 14: One-Step Inequalities

Post-Test

1. Variables will vary: $16 + n < 28$
2. Variables will vary: $9n \geq 36$
3. $a < 3.9$
4. $b \geq \frac{2}{3}$
5. $c > 4.2$
6. $d < \frac{1}{2}$
7. $e < 14$
8. $f \geq -12$
9. $g > 63$
10. $h < 48$
11. Variables and inequalities will vary. Possible equation: $37.5 + p \leq 50$
12. Variables will vary. $p \leq 12.5$
13. 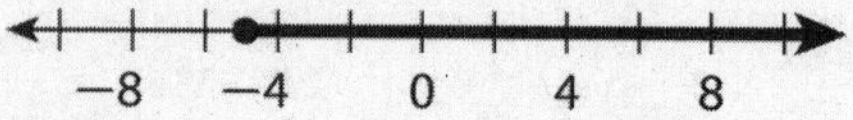 −8 −4 0 4 8
14. 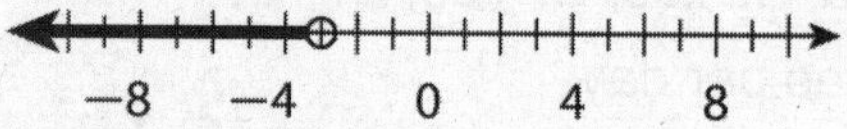 −8 −4 0 4 8

Skill 15: Percent

Post-Test

1. $1.20
2. $42.80
3. $36
4. $272
5. 40%
6. 25%
7. 1500%
8. 35%
9. $22.50
10. $270
11. $6.30

Skill 16: Real Numbers

Post-Test

1. 0.48
2. $0.91\overline{6}$
3. $\frac{17}{25}$
4. $\frac{11}{18}$
5. $x = \pm 12$
6. $x = \pm\frac{5}{11}$

7. $x = 7$

8. $x = \frac{2}{5}$

9. 8.4

10. 9.5

11. real number, rational number, integer

12. real number, rational number, integer, whole number

13. real number, irrational number

14. $\sqrt{21}$, 4.65, $4\frac{3}{4}$

Skill 17: Scale Factor and Scale Drawings

Post-Test

1. A. No, B. No, C. Yes, D. Yes

2.

Blueprint Length (in.)	Actual length (ft)
0.5	1.75
1	3.5
1.5	5.25
2	7
5	17.5
7	24.5
10	35

3. 3

4. 36 square units

Skill 18: Scatter Plots

Post-Test

1. A. Cluster, B. None, C. Outlier

2. A. No, B. Yes

3.

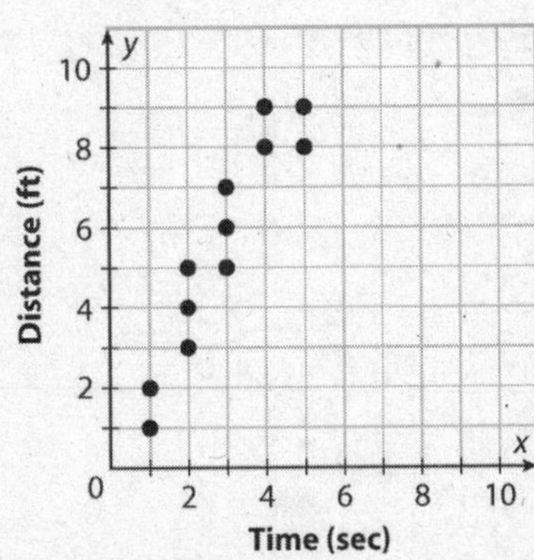

4.

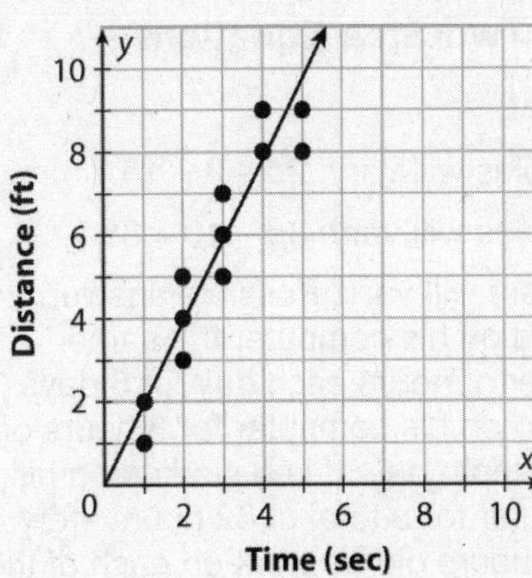

5. 10 ft

6. 7 sec

Skill 19: Significant Digits

Post-Test

1. 60 g

2. 40 oz

3. 3.82 ft

4. 4.3 mg

5. 5

6. 4

7. 1

8. 3

9. 4

10. 38 cm

11. 82 cm^2

12. 300 yd

13. 4000 yd^2

Skill 20: Slope

Post-Test

1. negative

2. zero

3. 1

4. vertical

5. $-\frac{3}{5}$

6. 3

7. −2

8. $y = 2x + 1$

9. $y = -2x + 21$

Skill 21: Two-Step Equations

Post-Test

1. Variables will vary: $2p + 3 = 15$
2. Variables will vary: $3p - 10 = 35$
3. Answers will vary. Possible answer: Leo worked on his computer the same number of hours each day for 6 days. He worked on his computer for 8 hours on the seventh day. If Leo worked on his computer for a total of 32 hours, how many hours did he work on each of the first 6 days?
4. $a = 7$
5. $b = 1$
6. $c = 5.6$
7. $d = 1.5$
8. $e = 12\frac{1}{2}$
9. $f = 44$
10. $g = -1$
11. $h = -2$
12. 19; Variables and equations will vary: $5s + 22 = 117$, $s = 19$
13. \$50; Variables and equations will vary: $0.7s + 40 = 75$, $s = 50$

Skill 22: Two-Step Inequalities

Post-Test

1. Variables will vary: $0.25q + 0.15 \geq 1.65$
2. Variables will vary: $6k + 15 \leq 75$
3. Answers will vary. Possible answer: Jill scored 9 points on free throws and the rest of her points on 3-point field goals. She scored less than 24 points in the game. How many 3-point field goals did Jill make?
4. $j > 3$
5. $k \leq 9$
6. $l \geq 3.4$
7. $m > 4\frac{1}{2}$
8. $n \leq 32$
9. $p \leq 2$
10. $q > -1$
11. \$9; Variables and inequalities will vary: $6d + 8 < 62$
12. 22.5 min; Variables and inequalities will vary: $6m + 45 > 180$
13. 0 1 2 3 4 5

Skill 23: Unit Rates

Post-Test

1. A. Yes; B. No; C. Yes
2. 24 cookies
3. 9 mpm
4. 5.8 mi per day
5. \$2.88
6. \$4.80
7. 16 days
8. 18 calls
9. 50 mph
10. $1\frac{1}{8}$ c
11. 250 sheets for \$1.25
12. 150 sheets for \$0.90

Skill 24: Writing Linear Functions

Post-Test

1. $y = 125x + 50$
2. $y = 80x + 15$
3. $y = 4x + 4$
4. $y = 32x - 280$
5. $y = -5x + 375$
6. $y = 5x + 10$
7. $y = -4x + 68$
8. $y = 2x + 2$

Skill 25: Two-Way Frequency Tables

Post-Test

1.

	Will Buy Hybrid	Will Not Buy Hybrid	TOTAL
Own Hybrid	16	4	20
Do Not Own Hybrid	42	63	105
TOTAL	58	67	125

2.

	Prefer Basketball	Prefer Volleyball	TOTAL
Boys	18	32	50
Girls	24	36	60
TOTAL	42	68	110

3. 45%
4. 54%
5. Yes; Possible explanation: Because a greater percentage of girls than boys prefer science to social studies, there is an association between preferring science and gender.

Skill 26: Two-Way Relative Frequency Tables

Post-Test

1.

Color	Red	Blue	Green	TOTAL
Frequency	0.48	0.32	0.2	1

2.

	Cats	Dogs	Birds	TOTAL
Boys	8	13	3	24
Girls	10	12	2	24
TOTAL	18	25	5	48

3.

	Cats	Dogs	Birds	TOTAL
Boys	0.17	0.27	0.06	0.5
Girls	0.21	0.25	0.04	0.5
TOTAL	0.38	0.52	0.1	1

4. The joint relative frequency is the ratio of the frequency of a particular category divided by the total number of data values.
5. The marginal relative frequency is the sum of the joint relative frequencies in a row or column of a two-way table.

6.

	Alg. 1	World History	Sci.
Boys	0.56	0.75	0.43
Girls	0.44	0.25	0.57
TOTAL	1	1	1

7. Yes. Possible explanation: Boys make up 60% of the population. Boys were 75% of those who chose world history, so there is an association between boys and world history.

Skill 27: Absolute Value

Post-Test

1. 4
2. 9
3. 3
4. 7
5. The distance of a number from 0 on a number line.
6. −10
7. $|-10|$
8. <
9. >
10. >
11. <
12. Fewer than 15 points; Possible explanation: Adding 15 to a number greater than −15 gives a positive sum.

13. More than 9°C; Possible explanation: Adding 9 to a number less than −9 gives a negative sum.
14. 3.4
15. $5\frac{1}{3}$
16. 2.09
17. $6\frac{4}{5}$
18. =
19. <
20. <
21. >

Skill 28: Measures of Center

Post-Test

1. 36
2. 72
3. 42 and 97
4. 64.8
5. 83
6. 97
7. 77
8. 82
9. 32
10. No outlier
11. Median; Possible explanation: An outlier greatly affects the mean, but does not greatly affect the median.
12. 15
13. 13.5
14. 13

Skill 29: Box Plots

Post-Test

1. 78
2. 63
3. 64
4. 70
5. 76
6. 48
7. 30
8. 40
9. 32
10. 42
11.

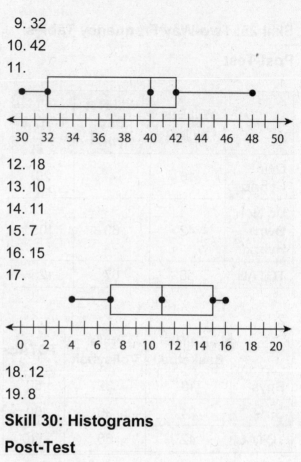

30 32 34 36 38 40 42 44 46 48 50

12. 18
13. 10
14. 11
15. 7
16. 15
17.

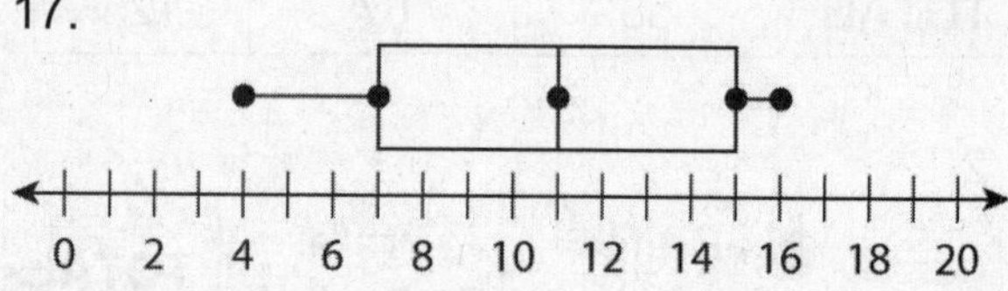

18. 12
19. 8

Skill 30: Histograms

Post-Test

1. 16
2. 68.75%
3. 62.5%
4. Yes. The median with a set of 16 data is the mean of the eighth and ninth ordered values. Because the eighth and ninth ordered values are from 6 to 8, the median could be 7.
5. Possible answer: 7–10, 11–14, 15–18, 19–22. Possible explanation: Using intervals of 4 starting with 7 covers all of Kevin's point totals.
6. Histograms will vary. Possible histogram based on the sample answer in Problem 5 is shown.

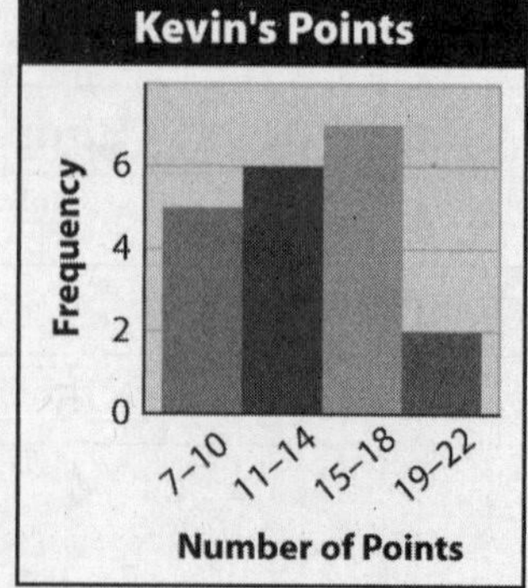

Skill 31: Squares and Square Roots

Post-Test

1. 81
2. 49
3. 0.01
4. 0.36
5. $\frac{4}{9}$
6. $\frac{1}{16}$
7. 225 in.^{2}
8. $x = \pm 5$
9. $x = \pm 8$
10. $x = \pm 0.9$
11. $x = \pm 0.2$
12. $x = \pm\frac{1}{7}$
13. $x = \pm\frac{3}{10}$
14. 9 in.
15. A. No; B. Yes; C. Yes; D. No
16. 9, 16; 3, 4
17. 36, 49; 6, 7
18. 64, 81; 8, 9
19. 3.5
20. 6.7
21. 8.5
22. 9.5
23. 12.2 ft

Skill 32: Cubes and Cube Roots

Post-Test

1. 1
2. 125
3. 0.064
4. 0.512
5. $\frac{8}{27}$
6. $\frac{1}{64}$
7. 1728 in.^{3}
8. $x = 5$
9. $x = 8$
10. $x = 0.3$
11. $x = 0.9$
12. $x = \frac{1}{6}$
13. $x = \frac{8}{9}$
14. 7 cm
15. A. No; B. Yes; C. Yes; D. No
16. 1; Possible explanation: Because the product of three negative numbers is negative.
17. Its cube root is an integer.
18. 2 in.

Answer Key

LESSON 1-1 Reteach

1. $x + (-7) = 12$; $x = 19$
2. $y + 1 = -5$; $y = -6$
3. $-4 = p + (-2)$; $p = (-2)$
4. $-7 = 4 + (-a)$; $a = 11$
5. $k = -16$
6. $g = -6$
7. $h = -3$
8. $d = 19$

LESSON 1-2 Reteach

1. $\frac{3\text{ ft}}{1\text{ yd}}$
2. $\frac{1\text{ m}}{100\text{ cm}}$
3. $\frac{8\text{ fl oz}}{1\text{ c}}$
4. $\frac{1000\text{ m}}{1\text{ km}}$; $\frac{3{,}391{,}100\text{ m}}{83.5\text{ h}}$; $40612\ \frac{\text{m}}{\text{h}}$
5. $320\ \frac{\text{c}}{\text{min}}$

LESSON 1-3 Reteach

1. 180 min
2. 7.65 g
3. 2.50 in.
4. 7.203 qt
5. 3 c
6. 35.4 yd
7. 4.9 oz
8. 42 mi

LESSON 2-1 Reteach

1. $2b + 7$
2. $3b + 4p$
3. $1 + 2m$

LESSON 2-2 Reteach

1. $m + 2m = 18$; Mako runs 6 miles.
2. $18 + 0.15m = 29.25$; 75 min
3. $\frac{e + (3e - 20)}{2} = 50$; Eric collected \$30, and Charlotte collected \$70.

LESSON 2-3 Reteach

1. $b = \frac{2A}{h}$
2. $l = \frac{A}{w}$
3. $s = \frac{2R + 6t - 5}{2}$
4. $c = P - a - b$
5. $t = \frac{2I}{pr}$
6. $H = \frac{GK}{J}$
7. $n = 360 - m - p - q$
8. $s = \frac{t}{(r + 1)}$
9. $a = \frac{bc}{d}$

LESSON 2-4 Reteach

1. $-3e - 10 \le -4$

   $-3e - 10 + 10 \le -4 + 10$

   $-3e \le 6$

   $\frac{-3e}{-3} \le \frac{6}{-3}$

   $e \ge -2$

2. $\frac{c}{2}+8>11$

$\frac{c}{2}+8-8>11-8$

$\frac{c}{2}>3$

$2\left(\frac{c}{2}\right)>3 \cdot 2$

$c>6$

3. $s \leq -3$

4. $j>4$

5. $c>-4$

6. $x<\frac{3}{2}$

7. $a>15$

8. $t<30$

LESSON 2-5 Reteach

1. $x<1$; $x>4$

2. OR

3. 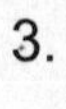

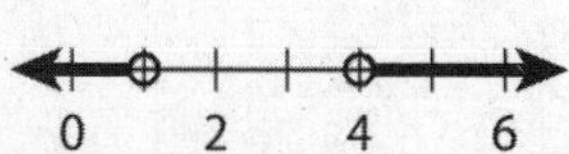

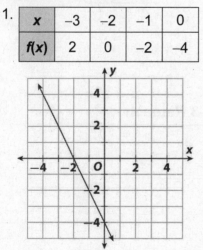

4. either; includes

LESSON 3-1 Reteach

1. Graph A

2. Graph A

LESSON 3-2 Reteach

1.

x	–3	–2	–1	0
f(x)	2	0	–2	–4

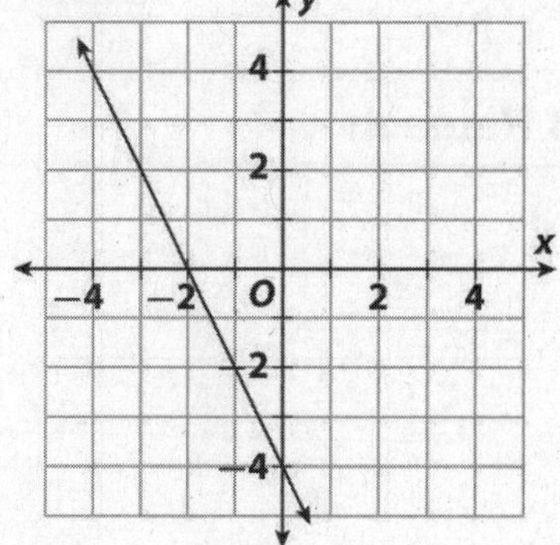

2. $f(x) = -x$; yes; D = {0, 1, 2, 3}; R = {0, –1, –2, –3}

3. No, because there are two different values for y that correspond to an x-value of 1.

4. $f(x) = x + 1$; yes; D = {0, 1, 2, 3}; R = {1, 2, 3, 4}

LESSON 3-3 Reteach

1. Think: 7 hours; total amount earned; independent variable: hours worked; dependent variable: total earned

2. Think: 103 minutes; total cost; independent variable: number of minutes used; dependent variable: total cost

3. Think: 3 servings; total calories; independent variable: number of servings; dependent variable: total calories

LESSON 3-4 Reteach

1.

x	y
1	5
2	8
3	11
4	14

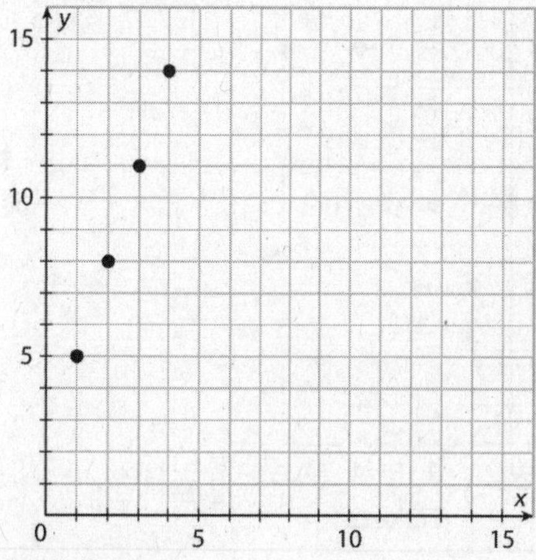

Function? Yes

2. Yes

3. No

4. Yes

LESSON 4-1 Reteach

1. 5, 8, 11, 14; ordered pairs: (1, 5), (2, 8), (3, 11), (4, 14)

2. 1.5, 2, 2.5, 3; ordered pairs: (1, 1.5), (2, 2), (3, 2.5), (4, 3)
3. 0, 1, 2, 3; ordered pairs: (1, 0), (2, 1), (3, 2), (4, 3)

LESSON 4-2 Reteach

1. No
2. Yes; $d = -2$; $f(n) = 14 + (-2)(n - 1)$
3. No
4. $f(1) = -5$, $f(n) = f(n - 1) + 5$, for $n \geq 2$; $f(n) = -5 + 5(n - 1)$
5. $f(1) = 7$, $f(n) = f(n - 1) + (-3)$, for $n \geq 2$; $f(n) = 7 + (-3)(n - 1)$
6. $f(1) = 4$, $f(n) = f(n - 1) + 3$, for $n \geq 2$; $f(n) = 4 + 3(n - 1)$
7. 6, 9, 12
8. 68, 66, 64
9. −7, −6, −5

LESSON 4-3 Reteach

1. Cost: 4; 6, 8, 10, 12; Ordered Pairs (1, 4), (2, 6), (3, 8), (4, 10), (5,12)

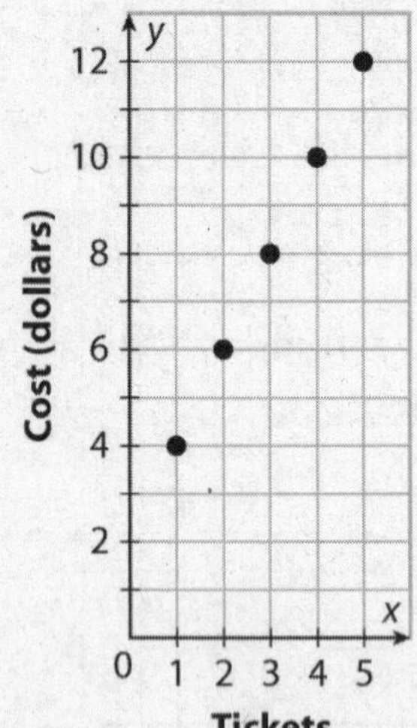

LESSON 5-1 Reteach

1. no
2. no
3. no
4. no
5. 5, 8; yes; 3
6. 2, $\frac{1}{2}$; no

LESSON 5-2 Reteach

1. x-int: 3; y-int: −3
2. x-int: −1; y-int: −2
3. x-int: −2; y-int: 4
4.

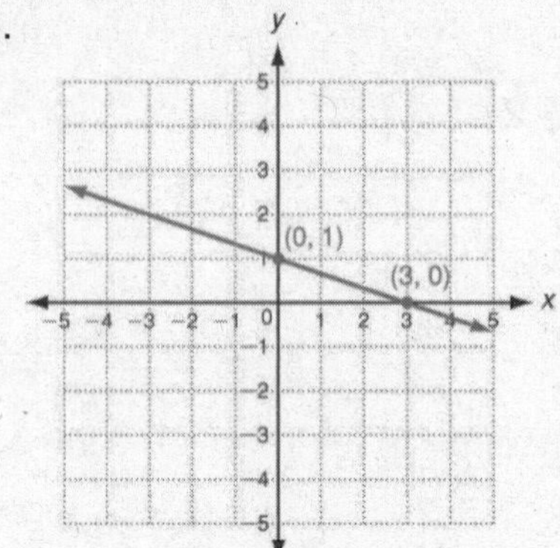

5.

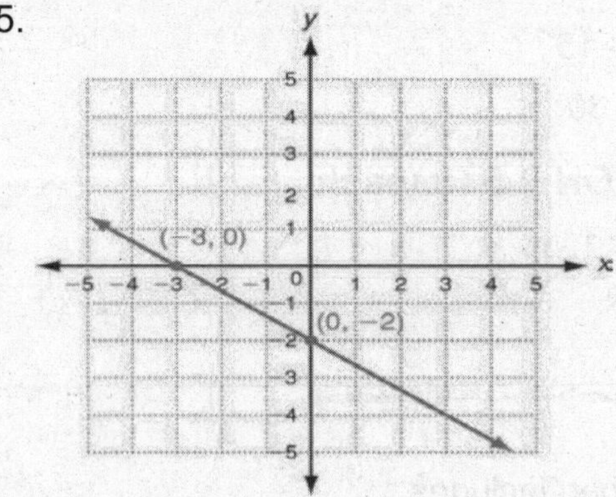

6.

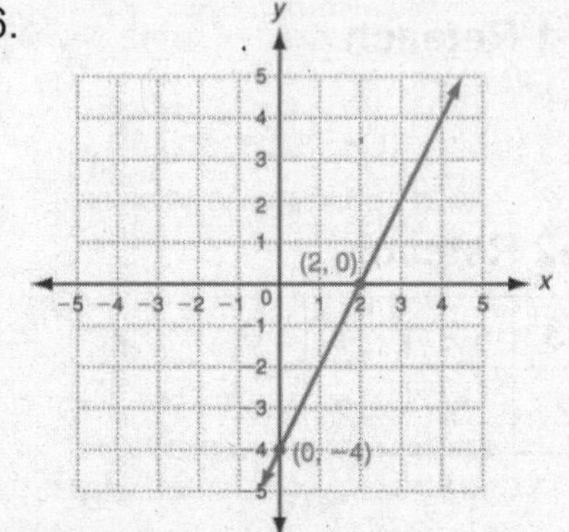

LESSON 5-3 Reteach

1. 2
2. $-\frac{1}{4}$
3. $\frac{3}{4}$
4. zero
5. undefined
6. zero

LESSON 6-1 Reteach

1. $m = \frac{1}{2}$; $b = -3$

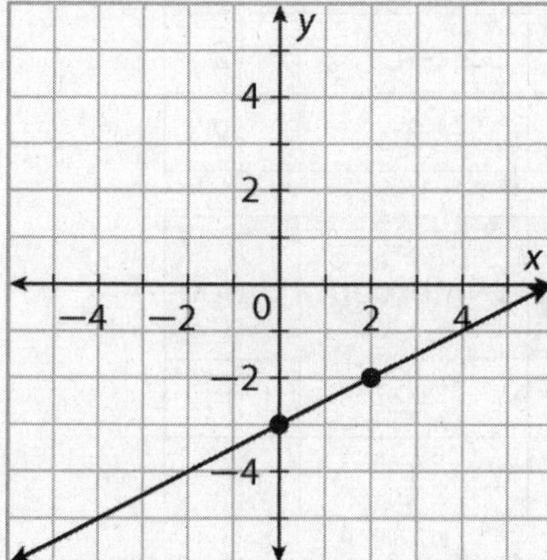

2. $m = -3$; $b = 2$

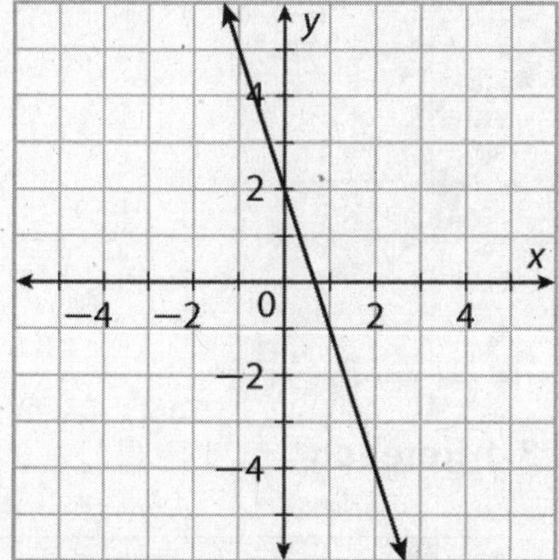

3. $m = 2$; $b = -3$

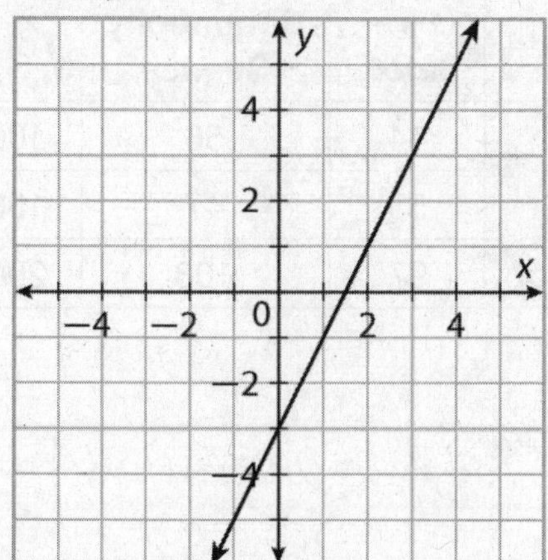

LESSON 6-2 Reteach

1. $f(x) = \frac{1}{4}x + 3$

2. $f(x) = -5x$

3. $f(x) = 7x - 2$

4. $f(x) = \frac{1}{2}x + 2$

5. $f(x) = 2x - 2$

LESSON 6-3 Reteach

1. no
2. no
3. no
4. no
5. horizontal
6. neither
7. vertical
8. vertical

LESSON 6-4 Reteach

1. Slopes are the same; shift $f(x)$ up 5 to make $g(x)$.

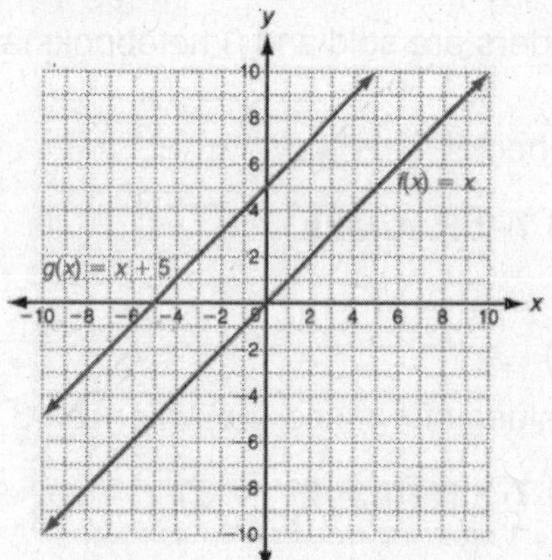

2. y-intercepts are the same; steepness is the same but $f(x)$ falls from left to right; $g(x)$ rises from left to right.

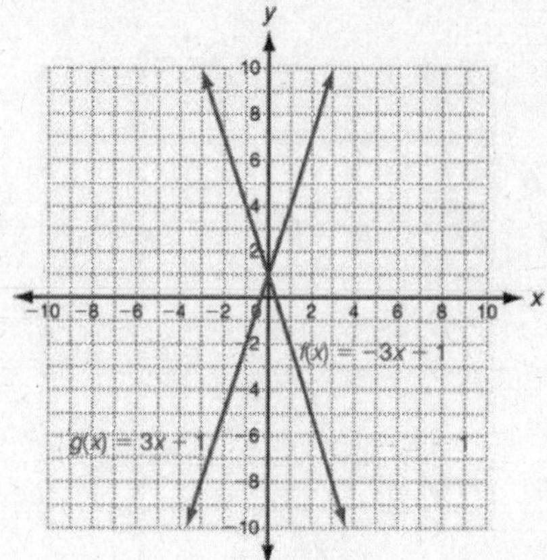

LESSON 6-5 Reteach

1.

	Domain	Range	Initial (starting) value of $f(x)$	y-intercept	Slope
$f(x)$	from –4 to 1	from 4 to –6	4	–4	–2
$g(x)$	from –1 to 2	from 5 to –1	5	3	–2

2.

	Domain	Range	Initial (starting) value of $f(x)$	y-intercept	Slope
$f(x)$	from –1 to 4	from –3 to 2	–3	–2	1
$g(x)$	from –2 to 2	from –1 to 3	–1	1	1

LESSON 7-1 Reteach

1. 20 notebooks are sold and 0 binders are sold.
2. 16 binders are sold and 0 notebooks are sold.
3. 5 notebooks

LESSON 7-2 Reteach

1. 3, 3
2. (–2, 3)
3. The values of $f(x)$ and $g(x)$ when $x = 3$

LESSON 7-3 Reteach

1.

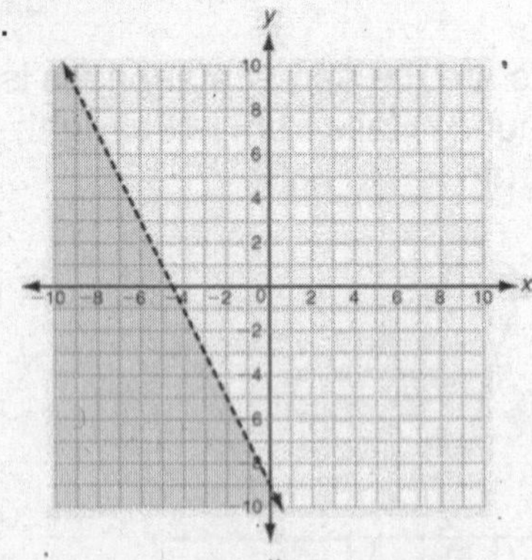

2.

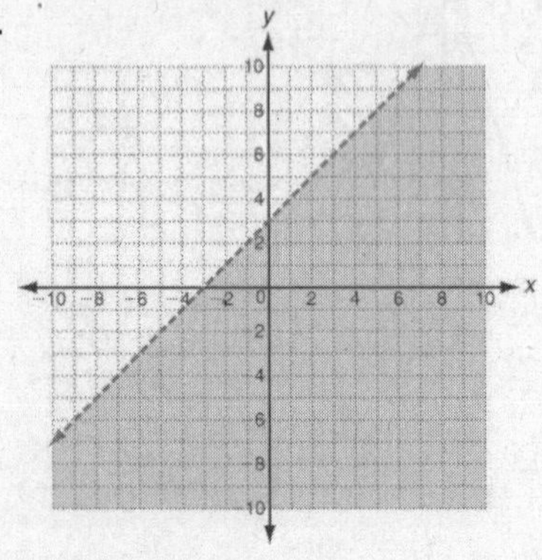

3.

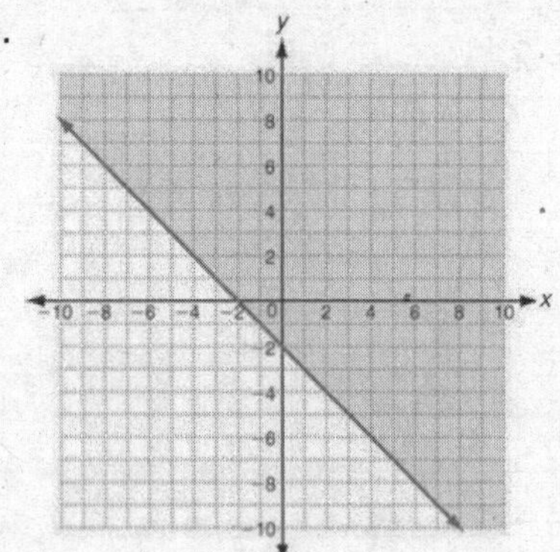

LESSON 8-1 Reteach

1.

	Assembly Preference		
Grade	Fire Safety	Community Service	Total
9	44	56	100
10	53	47	100
Total	97	103	200

LESSON 8-2 Reteach

1. $\frac{118}{240}$
2. $\frac{66}{240}$
3. $\frac{66}{120}$
4. $\frac{64}{240}$
5. $\frac{54}{240}$
6. $\frac{54}{120}$

LESSON 9-1 Reteach

1. 15.9
2. 14
3. 29
4. 9
5. 13
6. 8.5

LESSON 9-2 Reteach

1. skewed left

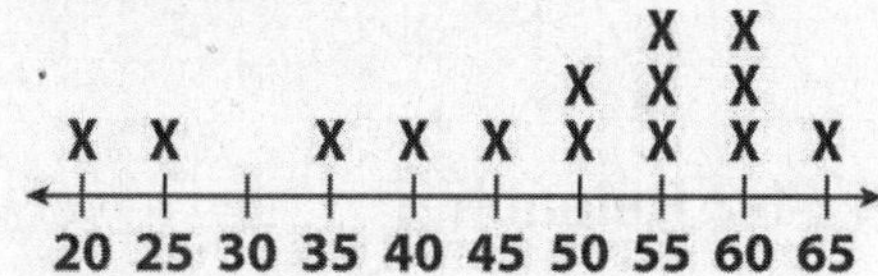

2. 48.2
3. 52.5
4. 20
5. Yes, because 100 > 60 + (1.5)(60 − 40)
6. The mean would increase to 51, and the median would increase to 55. The IQR is unchanged.

LESSON 9-3 Reteach

1.

Car Gas Mileage	
Mi/gal	Frequency
15–19	5
20–24	8
25–29	12
30–34	7
35–39	2
40–44	1

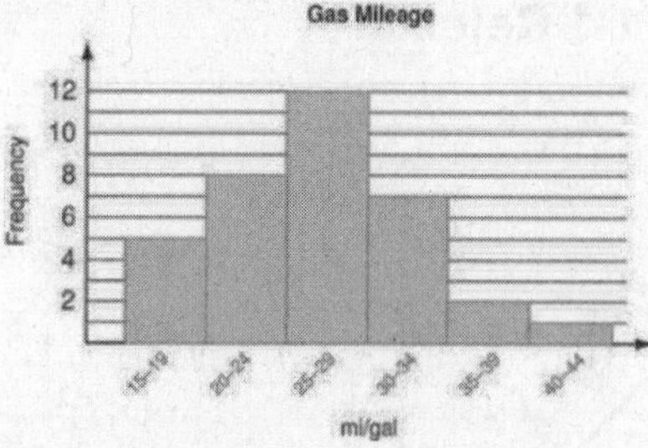

2. 5, 9, 11, 14, 18, 18, 21
3. 5, 9, 14, 18, 21
4.

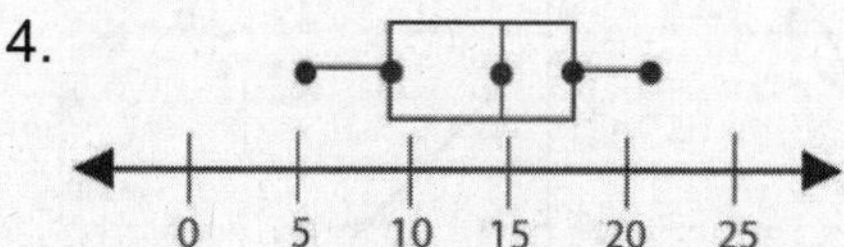

LESSON 9-4 Reteach

1. 86
2. 56
3. 2.5%
4. 16%
5. 68%

LESSON 10-1 Reteach

1. 1
2. 0
3. –1

LESSON 10-2 Reteach

1. Positive
2. Possible answer: (4, 8) and (6, 11); $m = \frac{3}{2}$
3. $y = \frac{3}{2}x + 2$

LESSON 11-1 Reteach

1. (–3, 2)

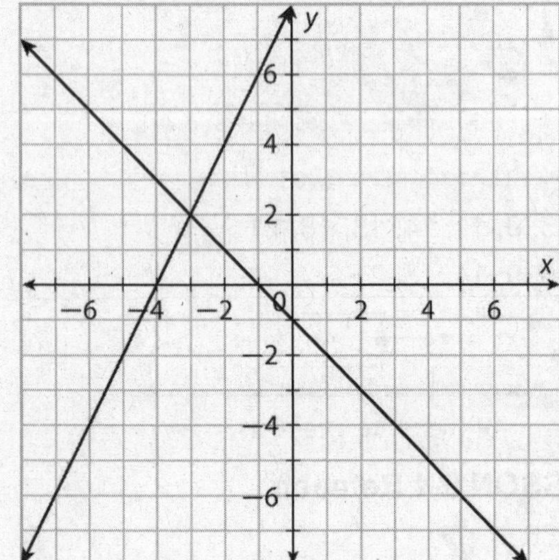

2. (–4, –2)

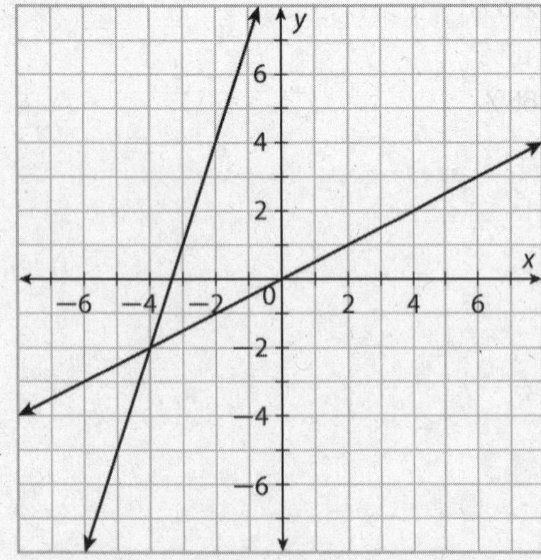

3. (2, 0)

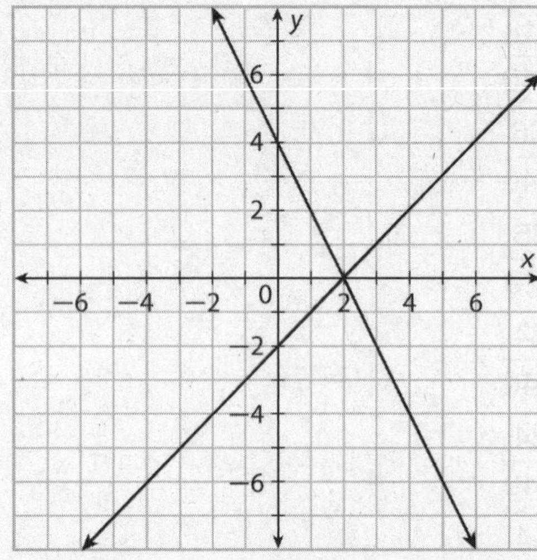

4. (3, 2)

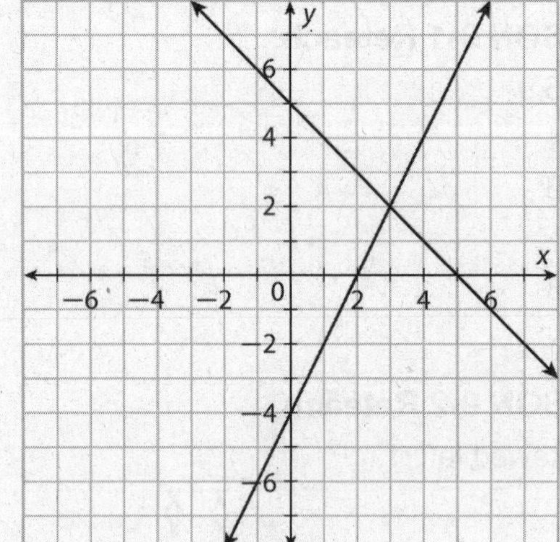

LESSON 11-2 Reteach

1. (7, 9)
2. (17, 7)
3. (3, 6)
4. (–1, 7)

LESSON 11-3 Reteach

1. (–6, 17)
2. (4, –1)
3. (–6, 18)
4. (2, –3)

LESSON 11-4 Reteach

1. (1, –1)
2. (–4, –14)
3. (1, 4)
4. (1, 5)

LESSON 12-1 Reteach

1. (0, –1); (0, 3); (2, 5); $\begin{cases} y = x + 3 \\ y = 3x - 1 \end{cases}$

2. (0, 3); (0, –2); (1, 2) $\begin{cases} y = 4x - 2 \\ y = -x + 3 \end{cases}$

3. (0, –1); (0, 5); (2, 1) $\begin{cases} y = x - 1 \\ y = -2x + 5 \end{cases}$

LESSON 12-2 Reteach

1.

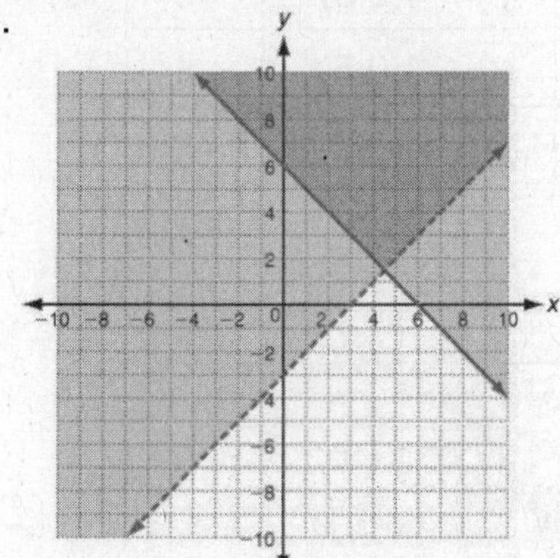

2.

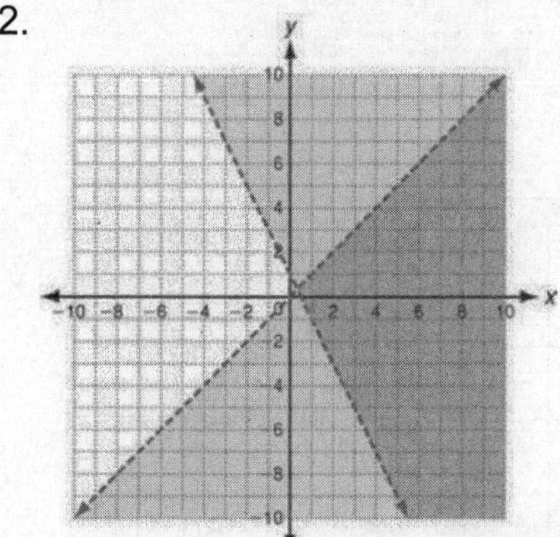

3.

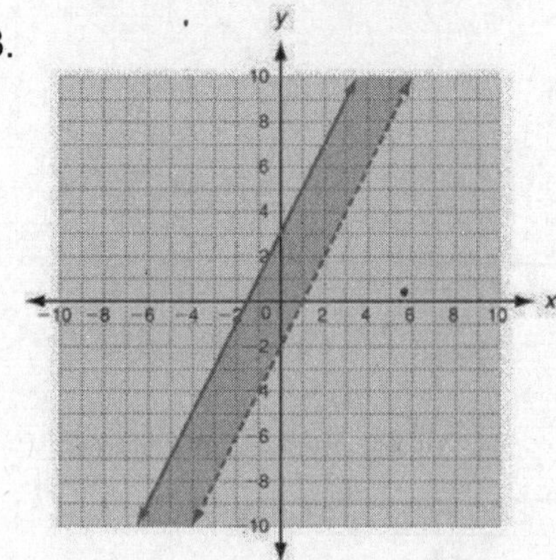

LESSON 12-3 Reteach

1. $h + c = 25$; $2h + c = 39$; 14 horses, 11 cats
2. $h + d = 32$; $5h + 18d = 264$; 24 Hupmobiles, 8 Duesenbergs

LESSON 13-1 Reteach

1.

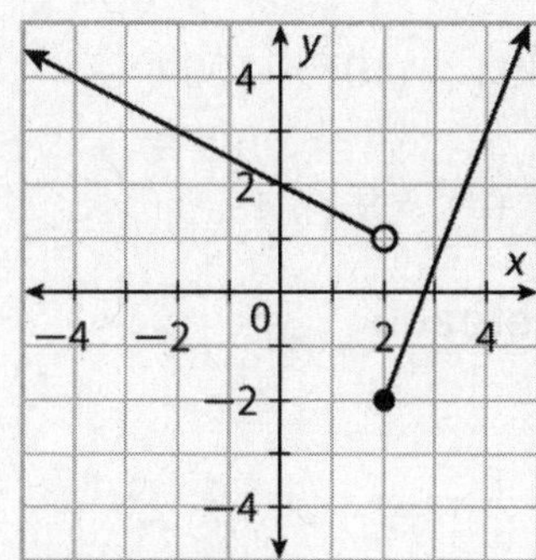

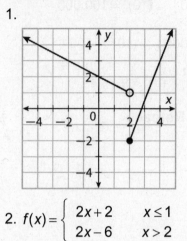

2. $f(x) = \begin{cases} 2x + 2 & x \le 1 \\ 2x - 6 & x > 2 \end{cases}$

LESSON 13-2 Reteach

1. *k* moves the vertex down 2.
2. *h* moves the vertex right 1.
3. *a* makes the slope twice as steep.

LESSON 13-3 Reteach

1. $x = -6$ or $x = 10$
2. $x = -15$ or $x = 1$
3. $x = 0$ or $x = 10$
4. $x = -3$ or $x = 3$

LESSON 13-4 Reteach

1. $x > -4$ AND $x < 4$

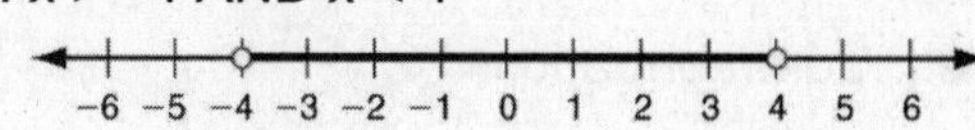

2. $x \ge -3$ AND $x \le 5$

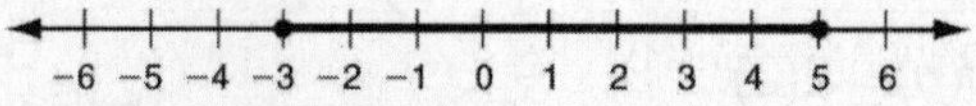

3. $x \le -1$ OR $x \ge 1$

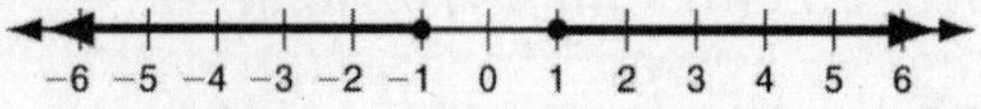

4. $x < -5$ OR $x > 1$

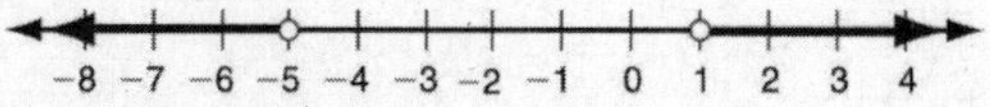

LESSON 14-1 Reteach

1. $100^{\frac{1}{2}} = \sqrt{100} = 10$
2. $8^{\frac{1}{3}} = \sqrt[3]{8} = 2$

3. $9^{\frac{1}{2}} = \sqrt{9} = 3$

4. $25^{\frac{1}{2}} = \sqrt{25} = 5$

5. $4^{\frac{3}{2}} = \left(\sqrt{4}\right)^3 = (2)^3 = 8$

6. $100^{\frac{5}{2}} = \left(\sqrt{100}\right)^5 = (10)^5 = 100{,}000$

7. $1000^{\frac{2}{3}} = \left(\sqrt[3]{1000}\right)^2 = (10)^2 = 100$

8. $27^{\frac{2}{3}} = \left(\sqrt[3]{27}\right)^2 = (3)^2 = 9$

LESSON 14-2 Reteach

1. 8
2. 10
3. 5
4. 16
5. 8
6. 4
7. 6
8. 5
9. 1

LESSON 15-1 Reteach

1. 4, 7, 10, 13, 16
2. 4, 12, 36, 108, 324
3. 96, 92, 88, 84, 80
4. 96, 24, 6, 1.5, 0.375

LESSON 15-2 Reteach

1. No. The terms are not common multiples of each other.
2. Yes. Common ratio is –2
3. Yes. Common ratio is $\frac{1}{2}$.
4. $f(n) = 2(3)^{(n-1)}$
5. $f(1) = 5$; $f(n) = f(n-1) \cdot 2$ for $n \geq 2$

LESSON 15-3 Reteach

1. a. 5

   b. 2

   c. $2(5)^x$

2. a. 1.5

   b. 2

   c. $2(1.5)^x$

3. a. (3, 32) and (4, 128)

   b. 4, $\frac{1}{2}$

   c. $\frac{1}{2}(4)^x$

LESSON 15-4 Reteach

1.

x	$y = -4(0.5)^x$	y
–2	$y = -4(0.5)^{-2}$	–16
–1	$y = -4(0.5)^{-1}$	–8
0	$y = -4(0.5)^0$	–4
1	$y = -4(0.5)^1$	–2

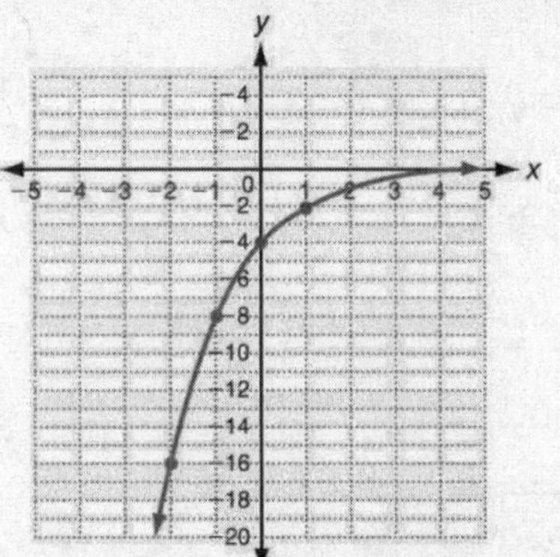

2.

x	$y = 2(5)^x$	y
–1	$y = 2(5)^{-1}$	0.4
0	$y = 2(5)^0$	2
1	$y = 2(5)^1$	10
2	$y = 2(5)^2$	50

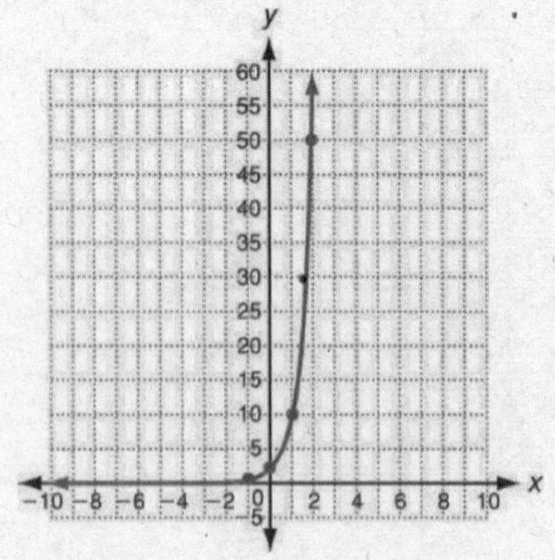

3.

x	$y = -1(2)^x$	y
–1	$y = -1(2)^{-1}$	–0.5
0	$y = -1(2)^0$	–1
1	$y = -1(2)^1$	–2
2	$y = -1(2)^2$	–4

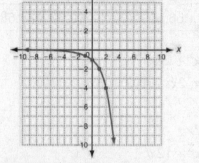

LESSON 15-5 Reteach

1. The graph of $f(x) = 3(2^x)$ is steeper and has an intercept of $y = 3$; the intercept for $f(x) = 2^x$ is $y = 1$.
2. The graph of $f(x) = 0.25(2^x)$ is less steep and has an intercept of $y = 0.25$; the intercept for $f(x) = 2^x$ is $y = 1$.
3. The graph of $f(x) = 3(2^x)$ has an intercept of $y = 3$; the graph of $f(x) = -3(2^x)$ is the graph of $f(x) = 3(2^x)$ reflected over the x-axis and has an intercept of $y = -3$.
4. The graph of $f(x) = 2^x$ has an intercept of $y = 1$; the graph of $f(x) = 2^x + 5$ has an intercept of $y = 6$ and is the same shape as the graph of $f(x) = 2^x$ but moved up the y-axis by 5 units.
5. The graph of $f(x) = 2^x$ has an intercept of $y = 1$; the graph of $f(x) = 2^x - 3$ has an intercept of $y = -2$ and is the same shape as the graph of $f(x) = 2^x$ but moved down the y-axis by 3 units.

LESSON 16-1 Reteach

1. 3
2. 12
3. –5

4. $x \approx 2.3$

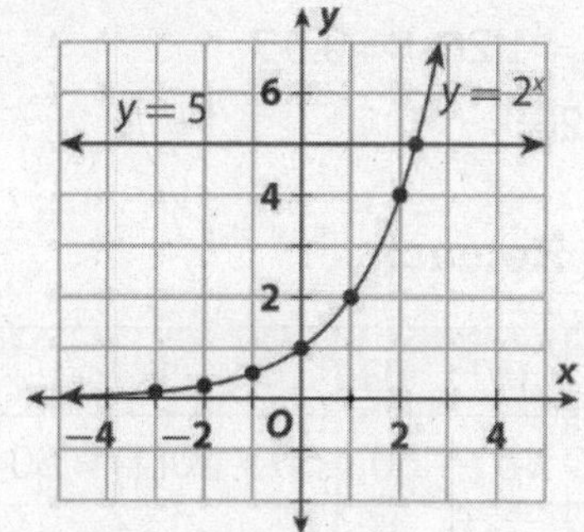

5. $x \approx 0.6$

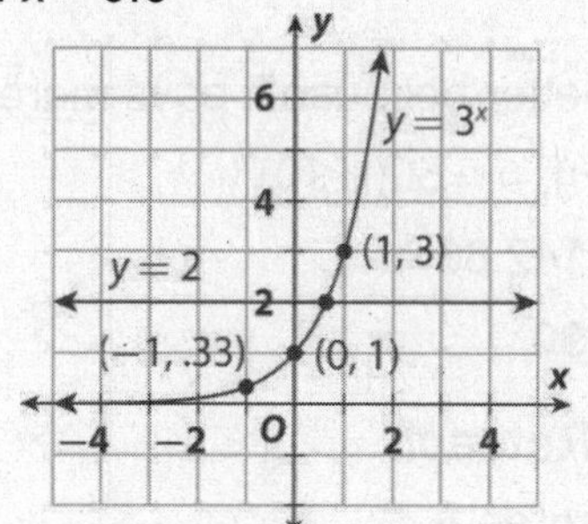

6. $x \approx 0.8$

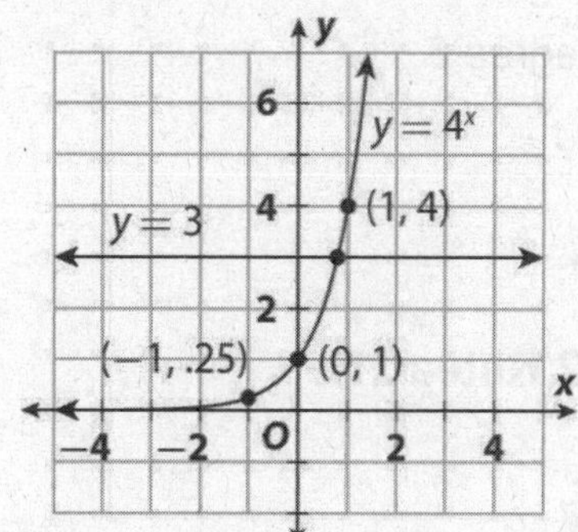

LESSON 16-2 Reteach

1. $y = 372{,}000(1 + 0.05)^t$; ≈ \$549,613
2. $y = 4200(1.03)^t$; ≈ 5165 people
3. $y = 350{,}000(1 - 0.03)^t$; ≈ \$291,540

LESSON 16-3 Reteach

1.

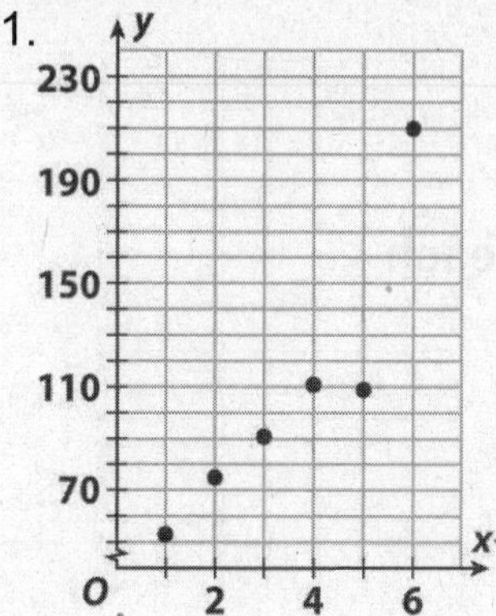

2. No.

3. $a = 43.41$, $b = 1.26$; $r = 0.95$

4. $y = 43.41(1.26)^x$

5. Yes, 0.95 is close to a 1.

6. Increasing; the graph is rising and the value of b is $1 + 0.26$.

7. 276

LESSON 16-4 Reteach

1.

	m	0	1	2	3	4	5	6
Choice A	p	50	$50 + 10(1) = 60$	$50 + 10(2) = 70$	80	90	100	110
Choice B	p	50	$50 \times 1.10^1 = 55$	$50 \times 1.10^2 = 60.5$	66.55	73.21	80.53	88.58

2. Choice A is better because it pays more.

3. $p = 50 + 10(m)$; $p = 50(1.10)^m$

4. A: \$160; B: \$142.66

5. $m = 14$; $p = 190$

LESSON 17-1 Reteach

1. monomial; degree 8
2. trinomial; degree 5
3. binomial; degree 6
4. $3y^2 + 10y$
5. $4m^4 + 3m$
6. $12x^5 + 18x^4$

LESSON 17-2 Reteach

1. $8x^2 + 9x$
2. $m^2 - 2m + 7$
3. $10x^3 + x^2 + 3x + 9$
4. $3y^5 + 8y^4 - 8y^3$

LESSON 17-3 Reteach

1. $9x^3 - 8x$
2. $8t^4 + 1$
3. $-2x^3 + 4x + 4$
4. $t^3 - t^2 - 4t - 6$
5. $4c^5 - c^3 + 8c^2 - 7$

LESSON 18-1 Reteach

1. $-10x^3y^4$
2. $-8x^3y^2z^2$
3. $3x^3y^3$
4. 4; 4; $4x - 20$
5. $3x$; $3x$; $3x^2 + 24x$
6. $2x$; $2x$; $2x$; $2x^3 - 12x^2 + 6x$
7. $5x + 45$
8. $-4x^3 - 32x$
9. $6x^4 + 15x^3 + 12x^2$
10. $3x^2 - 21$
11. $10a^4b^2$
12. $-5y^3 + 35y^2 - 10y$

LESSON 18-2 Reteach

1. x; 4; $x^2 - x - 20$
2. x; 2; $x^2 + 6x - 16$
3. x; 3; $x^2 - 9x + 18$
4. $x^2 - 5x + 6$
5. $x^2 - 49$
6. $x^2 + 3x + 2$
7. x, 3; $2x^3 + 10x^2 + 20x + 24$
8. x, 2; $6x^3 + 16x^2 + 13x + 10$

LESSON 18-3 Reteach

1. difference of squares
2. perfect-square trinomial
3. perfect-square trinomial
4. $x^2 - 16x + 64$
5. $x^2 + 4x + 4$
6. $49x^2 - 70x + 25$
7. $x^2 - 64$
8. $100 - x^2$
9. $25x^2 - 4y^2$

LESSON 19-1 Reteach

1. down
2. highest
3. wider
4. $x = 0$
5. down
6. (0, 0)

LESSON 19-2 Reteach

1. stretch
2. up
3. left 7
4. up 9
5. shrink
6. up
7. right 4
8. down 8
9. (3, 6)
10. maximum
11. $y = -(x - 3)^2 + 6$

LESSON 19-3 Reteach

1. Vertex (5, 2), axis of symmetry $x = 5$
2. Vertex (–3, –1), axis of symmetry $x = -3$
3. Vertex (–4, 1), axis of symmetry $x = -4$
4. Vertex (3, 6), axis of symmetry $x = 3$
5. Vertex (9, 5), axis of symmetry $x = 9$
6. Vertex (–2, –15), axis of symmetry $x = -2$

LESSON 20-1 Reteach

1.

x	0	1	2	3	4
y	–5	–8	–9	–8	–5

2. $x = -1$ and $x = 5$
3. 0
4.

x	–3	–2	–1	0	1
y	0	–3	–4	–3	0

5. $x = -3$ and $x = 1$

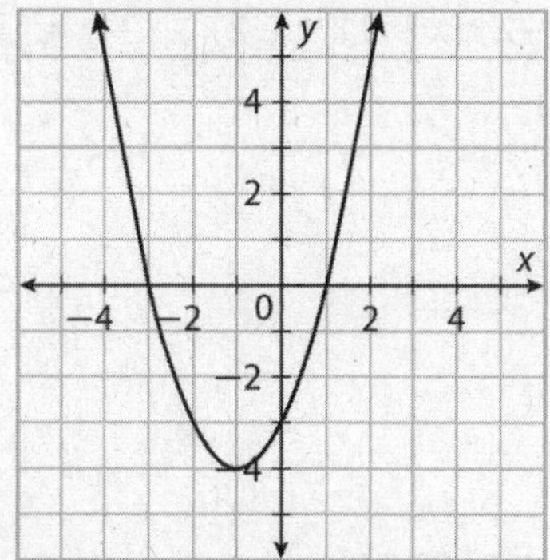

LESSON 20-2 Reteach

$y = x^2 - 3x + 2$

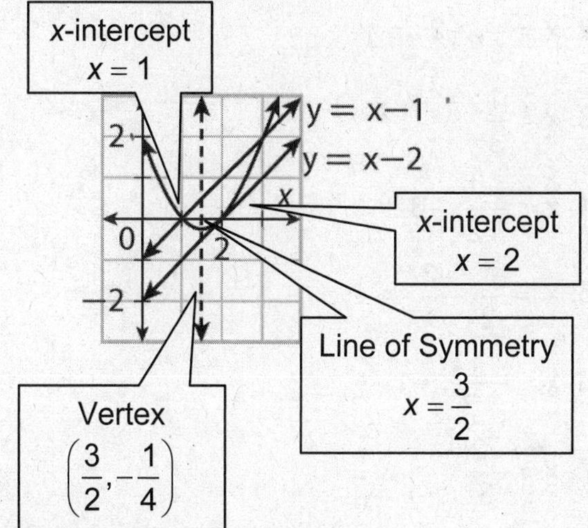

LESSON 20-3 Reteach

1. $x = 6, x = 3$
2. $x = -8, x = 5$
3. $y = 7, y = 3$
4. $x = -6, x = 3$
5. $x = -4, x = -3$
6. $t = -9, t = 3$
7. $n = 5, n = -3$
8. $a = 10, a = -3$
9. $z = 6, z = -4$
10. $x = -4, x = 2$
11. $g = -3, g = 3$

LESSON 21-1 Reteach

1. –2; –1, 2; 1, –2; $(x-1)(x+2)$
2. $(x+2)(x+2)$
3. $(x-3)(x-1)$
4. $(x-2)(x+5)$
5. –7, –5
6. 6, 3
7. 5, –4

LESSON 21-2 Reteach

1. $x = \frac{3}{2}, -9$
2. $x = \frac{1}{5}, -2$
3. $x = \frac{1}{3}$
4. $x = -\frac{1}{2}, -3$
5. $x = \frac{1}{2}, \frac{-2}{3}$
6. $x = -\frac{11}{7}, -1$
7. $x = \frac{-2}{3}$
8. $x = -\frac{1}{2}, 3$
9. $x = -4, 4$

LESSON 21-3 Reteach

1. a) initial height, b) $2\sqrt{2}$
2. a) initial velocity, b) initial height, c) $\frac{5}{4}$

LESSON 22-1 Reteach

1. Add 1 to each side. Divide each side by 4. Take the square roots of each side.
2. Subtract 3 from each side. Divide each side by 2. Take the square roots of each side.
3. $x = 3$ and $x = -3$
4. $x = 4$ and $x = -4$
5. $x = 1$ and $x = -1$
6. $x = 20$ and $x = -20$
7. $x = 7$ and $x = -7$
8. $x = 8$ and $x = -8$
9. $x = 18$ and $x = -6$
10. $x = 4$ and $x = -14$
11. $x = 14$ and $x = -6$
12. $x = 8$ and $x = -14$
13. $x = 7$ and $x = -5$
14. $x = -4$ and $x = 0$

LESSON 22-2 Reteach

1. $x = -1$ or $x = 7$
2. $x = -6$ or $x = -2$
3. $x = -7$ or $x = 9$
4. $x = -8$ or $x = 4$
5. $x = 2$ or $x = 12$
6. $x = -3$
7. 7 and 8

LESSON 22-3 Reteach

1. $a = 1$; $b = 2$; $c = -35$;
   $x = \frac{-2 \pm \sqrt{(2)^2 - 4(1)(-35)}}{2(1)}$; 5 and –7
2. $a = 3$; $b = 7$; $c = 2$;
   $x = \frac{-7 \pm \sqrt{(7)^2 - 4(3)(2)}}{2(3)}$; $-\frac{1}{3}$ and –2
3. $a = 1$; $b = 1$; $c = -20$;
   $x = \frac{-1 \pm \sqrt{(1)^2 - 4(1)(-20)}}{2(1)}$; 4 and –5
4. $a = 2$; $b = -9$; $c = -5$;
   $x = \frac{-(-9) \pm \sqrt{(-9)^2 - 4(2)(-5)}}{2(2)}$; 5 and $-\frac{1}{2}$

LESSON 22-4 Reteach

1. $x = 0$ or $x = 3$; factoring because $c = 0$
2. $x = 0$ or $x = -6$ factoring because $c = 0$
3. $x = 7$ or $x = -7$; taking the square roots because $b = 0$
4. $x = 4$ or $x = -4$; taking the square roots because $b = 0$
5. $x = 6$ or $x = -1$; taking the square roots because binomial is squared
6. $x = 4$ or $x = -14$; taking the square roots because $b = 0$

7. $x = -7$; factoring because not too many factors to check
8. $x = 5$ or $x = 2$; factoring because not too many factors to check
9. $x = \frac{10}{3}$ or $x = -2$; factoring or quadratic formula

LESSON 22-5 Reteach

1. (0, –6), (1, 0)
2. Answer may vary due to rounding. Possible answer: (–1.088, –0.35), (1.088, 8.35)

LESSON 23-1 Reteach

1. first differences: 6, 10, 14, 18, 22
   second differences: 4
2. $y = x^2 + 2x$

LESSON 23-2 Reteach

1. linear

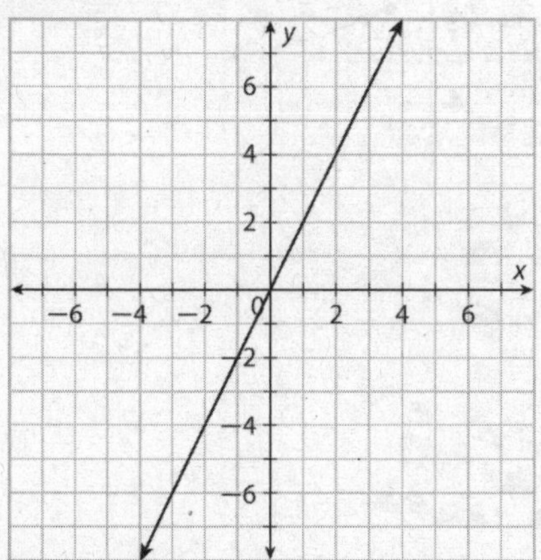

2. exponential

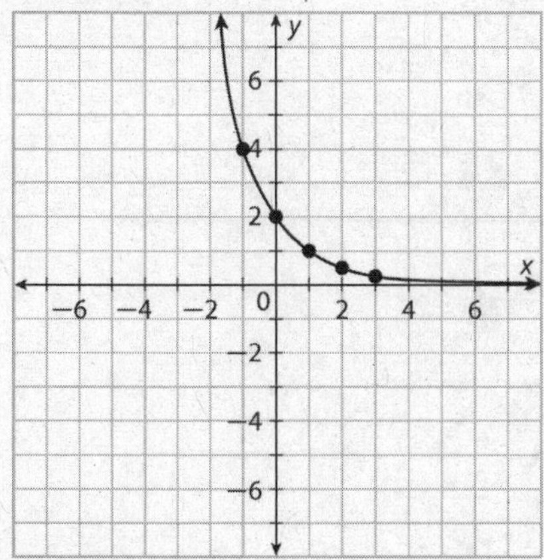

3. exponential
4. quadratic
5. linear

LESSON 24-1 Reteach

1. 3; neither even nor odd, positive
2. 4; even; positive

LESSON 24-2 Reteach

1. $f^{-1}(x) = \frac{x-3}{2}$

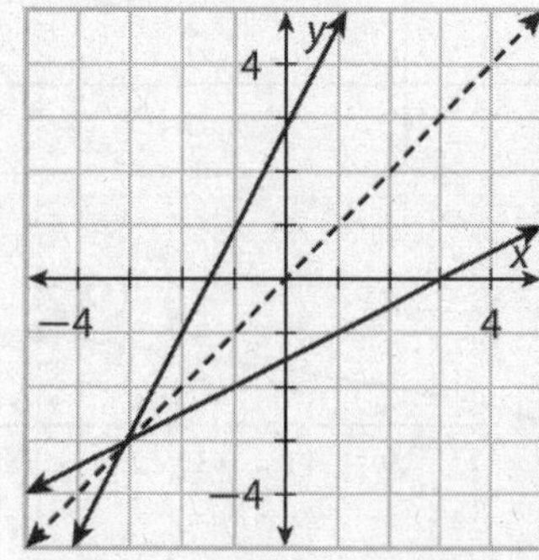

2. $f^{-1}(x) = \frac{x+2}{3}$

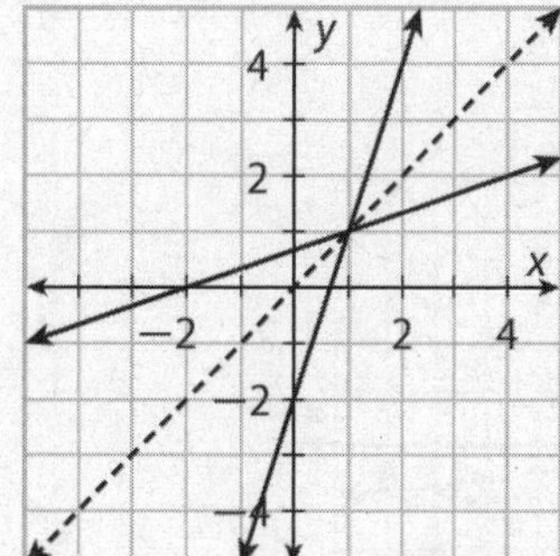

3. $f^{-1}(x) = \frac{-x+3}{2}$

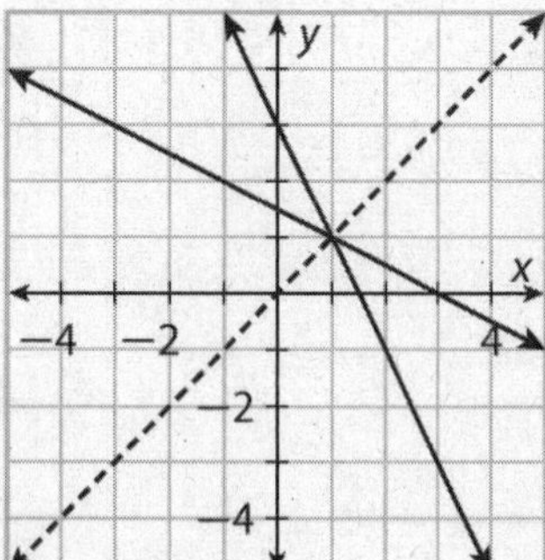

LESSON 24-3 Reteach

1. Domain: $x \geq 1$, Range: $y \geq -2$

x	$y = \sqrt{x-1} - 2$
1	$\sqrt{1-1} - 2$
5	0
10	1
17	2

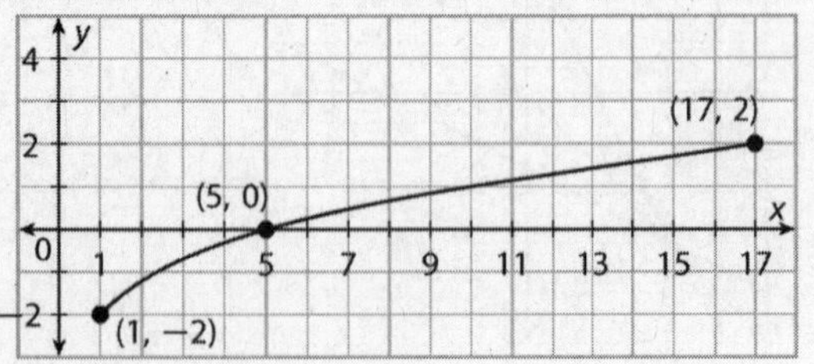

LESSON 24-4 Reteach

1. $f^{-1}(x) = \sqrt[3]{-\frac{1}{3}x}$

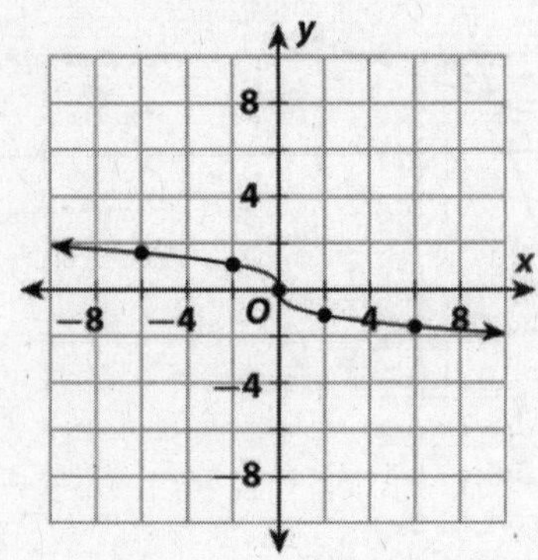

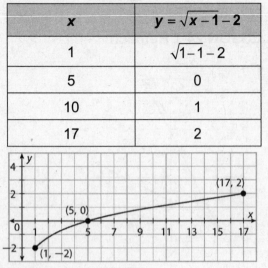

2. $f^{-1}(x) = \sqrt[3]{2x}$

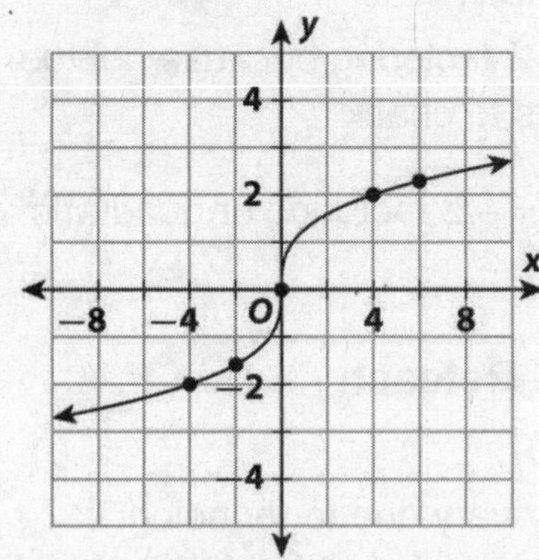

3. $f^{-1}(x) = \sqrt[3]{-\frac{5}{2}x}$

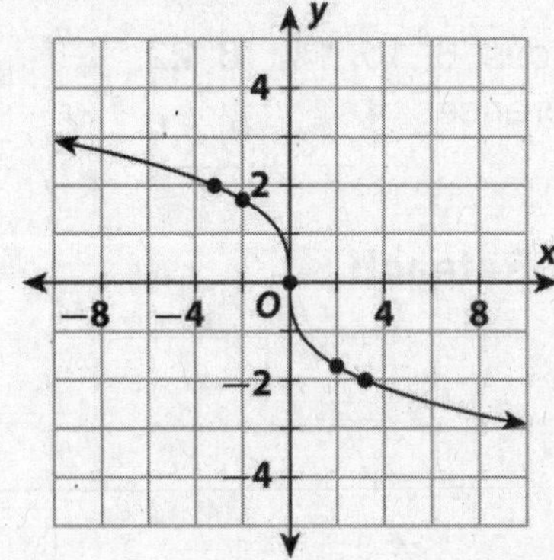

Answer Key

Skill 1: Add and Subtract Integers

1. 9
2. 21
3. 83
4. –7
5. –31
6. –73
7. –14
8. –45
9. –91
10. 3
11. –1
12. 0
13. –2
14. 5
15. 15
16. The wrong sign was used in the sum. The negative integer has the greater absolute value. The sum is –12.
17. 3
18. –2
19. –4
20. 2
21. 4
22. –2
23. 3
24. 0
25. 16
26. Subtracting a negative number is like adding a positive number; $12 - (-8) = 12 + 8 = 20$.
27. $-3 + 2$; $-3 + 2 = -1$
28. $-2 - 3$; $-2 - 3 = -5$ yd

Skill 2: Algebraic Expressions

1. 20
2. 7
3. –4
4. 42
5. 3.5
6. $4\frac{1}{5}$
7. 8
8. 0.2 or $\frac{1}{5}$
9. $4\frac{1}{2}$ or 4.5
10. 27
11. 17
12. 12
13. $2a + 8b + 6$
14. $8c - 2d - 7$
15. $14x + 9$
16. $3x + 5$
17. $10x - 7$
18. $d + 12$ or $12 + d$
19. $5 - e$
20. $16 \div f$ or $\frac{16}{f}$
21. $12 + 2d$ or $2d + 12$
22. $(54 - a) \div 6$ or $\frac{54 - a}{6}$
23. The error is that 3 is the coefficient for the variable p. The expression should be $8 + 3p$.

Skill 3: Algebraic Representations of Transformations

1. $D'(-3, 3)$, $E'(2, 3)$, $F'(2, -1)$, $G'(-3, -1)$; 2 units to the left and 1 unit up
2. $N'(-4, 1)$, $O'(-1, 1)$, $P'(-2, 4)$
3. Both coordinates were multiplied by –1 instead of just the x-coordinates; $B'(-2, 4)$, $C'(-4, 5)$, $D'(-3, 2)$.
4. $Q'(-1, 1)$, $R'(-4, 3)$, $S'(-3, 5)$
5. $A'(2, 8)$, $B'(8, 8)$, $C'(8, 4)$, $D'(2, 4)$

Skill 4: Constant Rate of Change

1. 12 months per year
2.

Number of Years	1	2	3	4	5
Number of Months	12	24	36	48	60

3. 96
4. 16 ounces per pound
5.

Number of Pounds	1	2	3	4	5
Number of Ounces	16	32	48	64	80

6. 144
7. Proportional; both expressions are equal to 3
8. Not proportional; the expressions are not equivalent
9. Proportional; each shirt costs $18
10. Possible answer: $\$42 \div 3 = 14$ and $\$120 \div 8 = 15$, so the ratios are not proportional. The cost for 8 tickets should be $112.
11. 45 miles each hour
12. none
13. $k = 7.5$; $y = 7.5x$
14. $k = 0.5$; $y = 0.5x$

Skill 5: Exponents

1. 3^5
2. 64
3. No, $5^2 = 5 \cdot 5 = 25$ and $2^5 = 2 \cdot 2 \cdot 2 \cdot 2 \cdot 2 = 32$
4. Because the exponent is 4, the base 9 should be used as a factor 4 times, not 5 times. $9^4 = 9 \cdot 9 \cdot 9 \cdot 9$
5. $\frac{1}{2^4}$ or $\frac{1}{2} \cdot \frac{1}{2} \cdot \frac{1}{2} \cdot \frac{1}{2}$
6. $\frac{1}{512}$
7. 1
8. 1
9. 55
10. 13^1
11. 117,649
12. $\frac{1}{2,097,152}$
13. 8
14. $\frac{1}{64}$
15. The exponents were multiplied. To multiply numbers with exponents having the same base, add the exponents. The correct equation is $4^6 \cdot 4^3 = 4^9$.
16. 1296
17. 81
18. $\frac{1}{243}$
19. 15625
20. The exponents were divided. To divide exponents with the same base, subtract the exponents. The correct equation is $\frac{2^8}{2^{-2}} = 2^{(8-(-2))} = 2^{(8+2)} = 2^{10}$.
21. 2744
22. 3375
23. $\frac{1}{1024}$
24. $\frac{1}{1,679,616}$
25. 46,656
26. 531,441
27. 256
28. $\frac{1}{15,625}$

Skill 6: Graphing Linear Nonproportional Relationships

1. No
2. Yes
3. Yes
4. Yes
5. Yes
6. Yes

7.

x	0	1	2	4	6	8
y	2	2.25	2.5	3	3.5	4

8.

Cost (dollars)

Distance (mi)

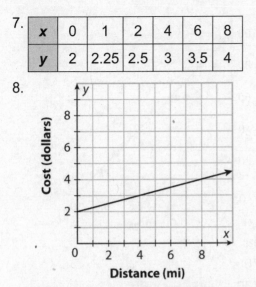

9. The line of a proportional relationship goes through the origin. It is a straight line, but a nonproportional relationship is a straight line, too. However, a nonproportional relationship does not go through the origin. The graph shows a nonproportional relationship.

10. Use the table to find the points to graph for the equation.

x	0	1	2	3
y	9	6	3	0

11.

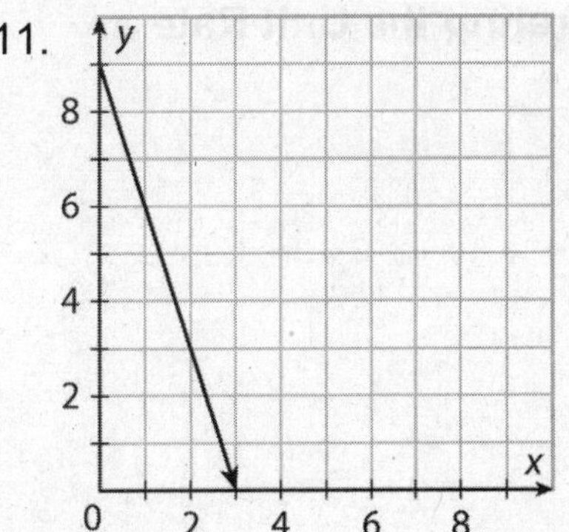

12. Yes

Skill 7: Graphing Linear Proportional Relationships

1. Yes
2. No
3. Yes
4. Yes
5. Yes
6. Yes

7.

x	0	1	2	3	4	5	6	7	8	9	10
Y	0	1.5	3	4.5	6	7.5	9	10.5	12	13.5	15

8.

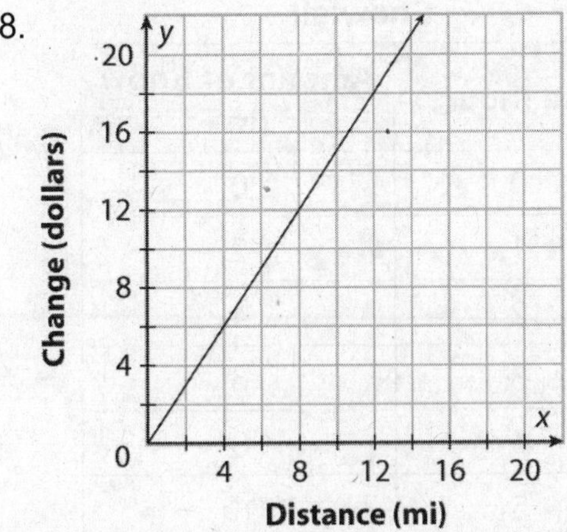

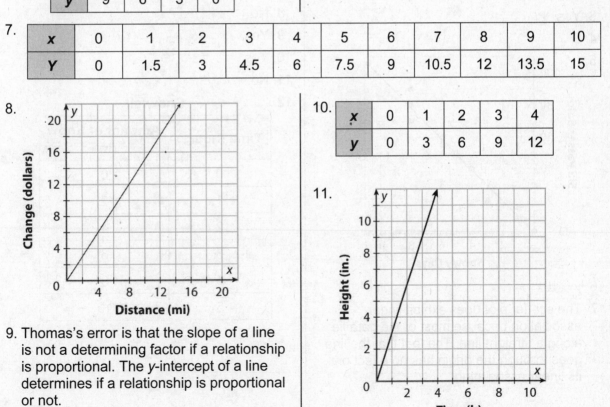

9. Thomas's error is that the slope of a line is not a determining factor if a relationship is proportional. The y-intercept of a line determines if a relationship is proportional or not.

10.

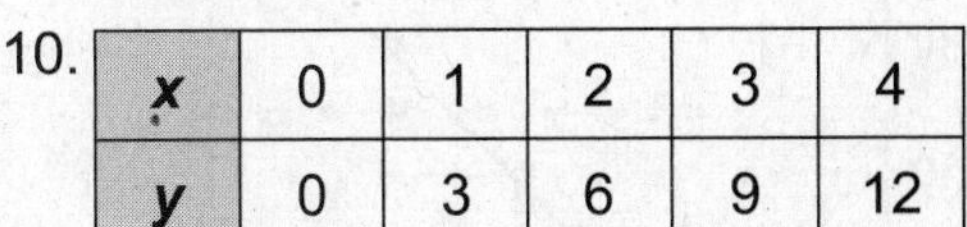

x	0	1	2	3	4
y	0	3	6	9	12

11.

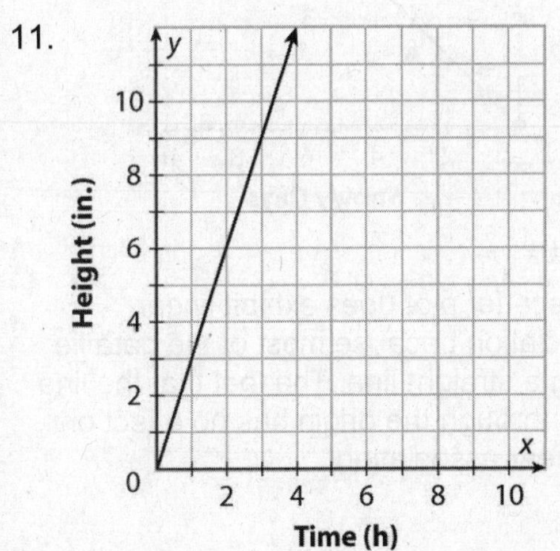

Skill 8: Interpreting the Unit Rate as Slope

1. No
2. Yes
3. Yes
4. $-\frac{5}{2}$ or -2.5
5. $\frac{5}{12}$
6. $\frac{4}{3}$ yards walked per second
7. $\frac{4}{5}$ page read per minute
8. 38; 38 miles per gallon
9. 14; $14 per hour
10. Possible answer: Dan's error is that he had 1 as the first unit. In a unit rate, 1 is the number of units for the second unit.

    The unit rate is $\frac{2}{5}$ lap run per minute.

Skill 9: Linear Associations

1. No
2. Yes
3. Yes
4. B
5. 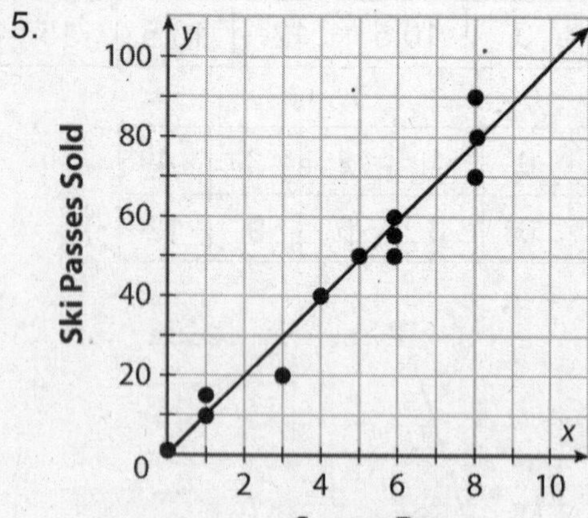

6. $y = 10x$
7. The scatter plot does exhibit linear association because most of the data lie along a straight line. The fact that the line goes through the origin has no effect on its linear association.
8. 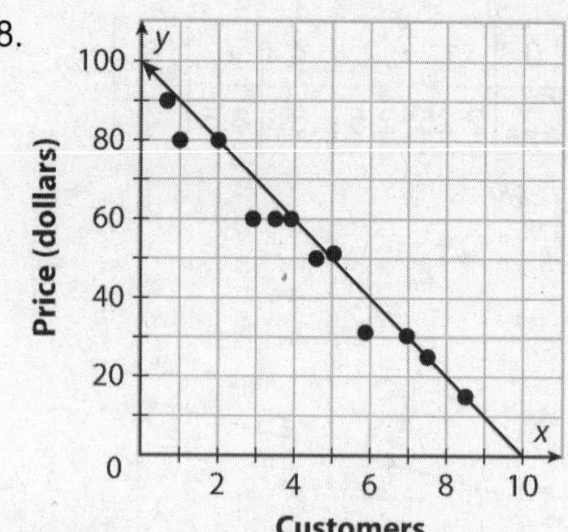

9. linear
10. $170
11. $3130

Skill 10: Linear Functions

1. Yes
2. No
3. Yes
4. No
5. Yes
6. It is a function because each input has a unique output.
7. Yes
8. No
9. Yes
10. Yes
11. No
12. **Snowfall**

Time (hours)	Amount of Snow (in.)
0	0
1	2
2	4
3	6
4	8
5	10

13.

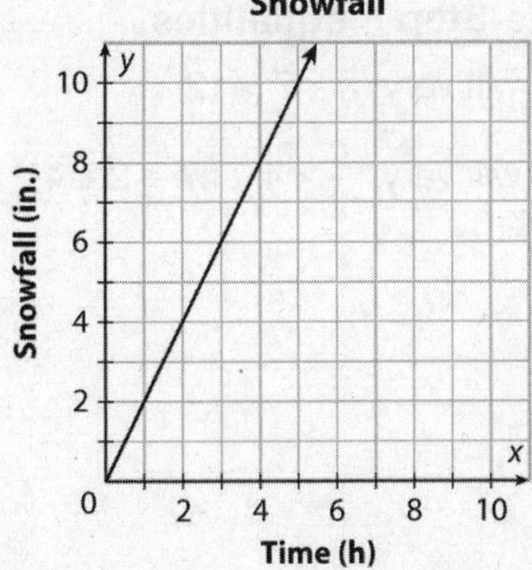

Skill 11: Multi-Step Equations

1. $a = 2$
2. $b = 5$
3. $c = 1$
4. The error is that Gillian subtracted 9 from both sides of the equation. She should have added 9 to both sides of the equation. The correct solution is $p = 7$.
5. $g = -1$
6. $j = -1$
7. $k = 2$
8. The error is that Patti used the incorrect integer sign. The correct solution is $j = 2$.
9. $r = 4$
10. $q = -\frac{8}{3}$
11. $s = -\frac{15}{4}$
12. Eric multiplied both sides of the equation by $\frac{2}{5}$. He should have multiplied both sides of the equation by $\frac{5}{2}$. The correct solution is $v = 15$.
13. Multiply the number outside the parentheses by each term inside the parentheses: $4(a) + 4(3) = 4a + 12$.
14. $s = 6$
15. $y = -\frac{3}{2}$
16. $w = 14$
17. $a = 4\frac{2}{3}$ or $a = \frac{14}{3}$
18. $b = -1\frac{1}{3}$
19. $v = 1$
20. The error is that Jeff did not correctly use the Distributive Property. He did not multiply $4(-2)$ and instead used -2. The correct solution is $f = 3\frac{1}{2}$ or $f = \frac{7}{2}$
21. $x = 4\frac{1}{2}$ or $x = \frac{9}{2}$
22. $z = 6\frac{1}{2}$ or $z = \frac{13}{2}$
23. $c = -1\frac{3}{5}$ or $c = -\frac{8}{5}$
24. The error is that Sixto added $2x$ to both sides of the equation. He should have subtracted $2x$ from both sides of the equation. The correct solution is $x = -2$.

Skill 12: Multiply and Divide Integers

1. –6
2. –10
3. –9
4. negative
5. 20
6. 18
7. 30
8. positive
9. $4(-3)$ or $-3(4)$; -12
10. –2
11. –2
12. –3
13. negative
14. –7
15. –5
16. –7
17. negative
18. 6
19. 8
20. 8
21. The quotient should be a positive number; $-42 \div (-6) = 7$
22. –4

23. −7

24. 9

25. −20 ÷ (−5); 4

26. −12 ÷ 2; −6

Skill 13: One-Step Equations

1. Variables will vary: $n + 9 = 13$
2. Variables will vary: $7n = 35$
3. Variables will vary: $4 = \frac{n}{8}$ or $4 = n \div 8$
4. Variables will vary: $n - 9 = 5$
5. Jimmy could have also written $48 \div 8 = g$ or $48 \div g = 8$.
6. Variables and equations will vary. Possible answer: $5t = 40$; t represents the number of teams
7. Variables and equations will vary. Possible answer: $j + 12 = 72$; j represents the sale price of the jacket
8. $d = 6$
9. $e = 0.65$
10. $f = \frac{4}{5}$
11. $m = 13$
12. $n = 2.1$
13. $p = \frac{7}{8}$
14. $s = 9$
15. $t = 15$
16. $u = 7$
17. $x = 7$
18. $y = 25\frac{3}{5}$
19. $z = \frac{8}{15}$
20. $c = 30$
21. $d = -8$
22. $e = 15$
23. Variables and equations will vary. Possible answer: $56 + w = 92$; $w = 36$ points
24. Variables and equations will vary. Possible answer: $3t = 48$; $t = 16$ teams

Skill 14: One-Step Inequalities

1. Variables will vary: $n + 7 > 12$
2. Variables will vary: $\frac{n}{2} < 4$ or $n \div 2 < 4$
3. $a > 8$
4. $b < -6$
5. $c \le \frac{13}{20}$
6. $d > 10$
7. $e < 1.03$
8. $f \ge 1\frac{1}{10}$
9. Colin did not use inverse operations. He subtracted 4.2 from both sides of the inequality instead of adding 4.2. The correct solution is $x \ge 9.7$.
10. $g > 12$
11. $h < 48$
12. $j \ge -3$
13. $k \ge 12$
14. $l \le 1.2$
15. $m > -30$
16. $n \le -5$
17. $p > -15$
18. $q < 32$
19. Variables and inequalities will vary. Possible answer: $8 + m > 15$; $m > 7$
20. Variables and inequalities will vary.
21. $r \ge 4$

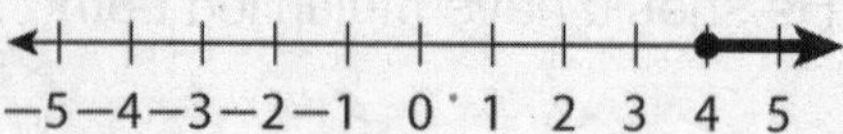

22. $s < -4$;

−5 −4 −3 −2 −1 0 1 2 3 4 5

Skill 15: Percent

1. $84.80
2. $270
3. $76.50
4. $90
5. 25%
6. 35%

7. 40%
8. 20%
9. Tonya used 40 as the original amount. She should have used 25. The percent increase is 60%.
10. \$27
11. \$135
12. Mary calculated 4% for each month, so she used 6 as the time. She should have used 0.5 because 6 months is 0.5 year. Mary actually earned \$10 in simple interest.
13. \$31.80
14. \$84.24

Skill 16: Real Numbers

1. 0.75
2. $0.1\overline{6}$
3. $0.4\overline{6}$
4. 0.65
5. $\frac{7}{20}$
6. $\frac{4}{15}$
7. $\frac{17}{40}$
8. $\frac{7}{11}$
9. George ignored the bar over the 3, which means that the 3 repeats. The correct fraction in simplest form is $\frac{5}{6}$.
10. $x = \pm 7$
11. $x = \pm 10$
12. $x = \pm\frac{2}{5}$
13. $x = \pm\frac{4}{9}$
14. $x = 4$
15. $x = 9$
16. $x = \frac{3}{10}$
17. $x = \frac{3}{4}$
18. 3.5
19. 4.5
20. 5.5
21. 6.3
22. integer, rational number, real number
23. rational number, real number
24. rational number, real number
25. irrational number, real number
26. $\sqrt{2}$, 1.48, $1\frac{1}{2}$
27. $\sqrt{50}$, $7\frac{1}{5}$, 7.25

Skill 17: Scale Factor and Scale Drawings

1. 31.5 mi
2. 18 mi
3.

Blueprint length (in.)	1	2	4	5	7
Actual length (ft)	2.5	5	10	12.5	17.5

4.

Map (in.)	3	6	9	12	15
Actual distance (mi)	25	50	75	100	125

5. 1.5
6. 0.5
7. $\frac{1}{4}$
8. 16
9. Donald did not take into account that there are two dimensions. Because the scale factor is 4, multiply 4(4) = 16 to find how many times larger one area is than the other. The area of *A'B'C'D'* is 2 units because 32 ÷ 16 = 2.

Skill 18: Scatter Plots

1. Cluster
2. None

3. Outlier
4. No
5. Yes
6. Yes
7.

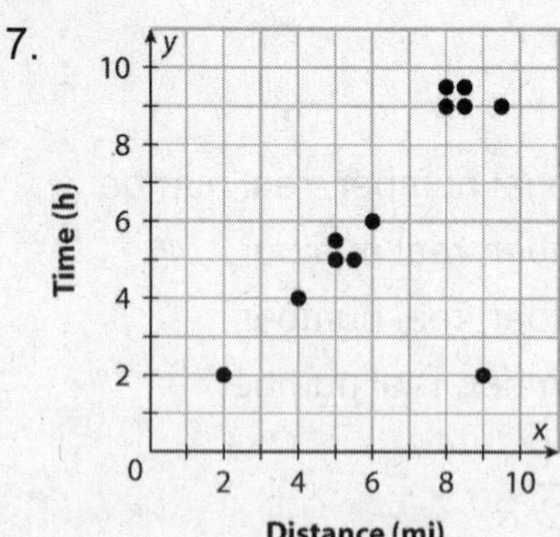

8. Yes, (9, 2) is an outlier because it is distant from the other data and does not lie along a line with the rest of the data.
9. There is a cluster with five of the plotted points: (8, 9), (8, 9.5), (8.5, 9), (8.5, 9.5), (9, 9.5).
10. (2, 2) is not an outlier to the data, because the data exhibits a positive linear association. The outlier is (9, 2) because it is very different from the rest of the data.
11.

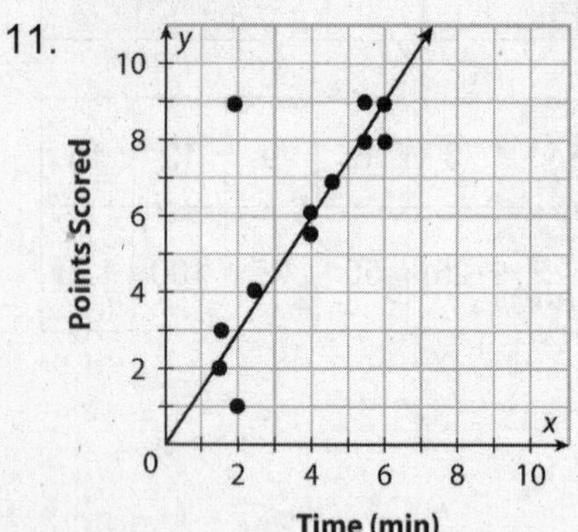

12. 3.5 min
13. 10 points

Skill 19: Significant Digits

1. 34 in.
2. 45 oz
3. 5.7 cm
4. 45 min
5. 3
6. 2
7. 2
8. The 0 in the thousandths place is also significant. There are 3 significant digits.
9. 13.2 mi
10. 113 in.^{2}

Skill 20: Slope

1. positive
2. negative
3. negative
4. increases
5. decreases
6. No, the line can go through (0, 0), but it doesn't need to. Whether it is positive or negative depends on whether the slant goes up or down from left to right.
7. 0
8. undefined
9. 0
10. undefined
11. Steve's error is that $x = 4$ forms a vertical line when graphed. A vertical line has an undefined slope.
12. 3
13. $-\frac{2}{5}$
14. $\frac{1}{2}$
15. $-\frac{7}{3}$
16. $y = 2x + 4$
17. $y = -\frac{3}{2}x + 15$

Skill 21: Two-Step Equations

1. Variables will vary: $5m + 45 = 300$
2. Tamara added coupon to the cost when she should have subtracted the value of the coupon. The correct equation is $6t - 5 = 55$.
3. Answers will vary. Possible answer: A used car salesman sold x number of cars for 3 days and then 5 cars on the fourth day. How many cars did the salesman sell each of the first 3 days if he sold 14 cars in all?

4. $a = 3$
5. $b = 5$
6. $c = 2$
7. $d = 12$
8. $e = 5$
9. $f = 2.375$
10. $g = 28$
11. $h = 2\frac{1}{2}$ or $\frac{5}{2}$
12. $j = 2$
13. $k = -1$
14. $l = -4$
15. $m = 4$
16. 7 mi; Possible equation: $6d + 12 = 54$

Skill 22: Two-Step Inequalities

1. Variables will vary: $15l + 30 \leq 90$
2. Cindy used an incorrect inequality symbol. She should have used $\geq$ because the cost of the lunch would be \$40 or more. The correct inequality is $4l + 5 \geq 40$
3. Answers will vary. Possible answer: Zoe bought 2 movie tickets and a popcorn that cost \$6. The total cost was more than \$20. How much did each movie ticket cost?
4. $a \leq 7$
5. $b \geq 3$
6. $c > 15$
7. $d > 8$
8. $e < \frac{5}{8}$
9. $f \geq 3\frac{1}{4}$ or $\frac{13}{4}$
10. $g \leq -2$
11. $h > -5$
12. $j < 8$
13. Drew forgot to reverse the inequality symbol. The correct solution is $k \geq -3$.
14. 5 games; Variables will vary: $4g + 3 \leq 25$
15. $x > 2$;

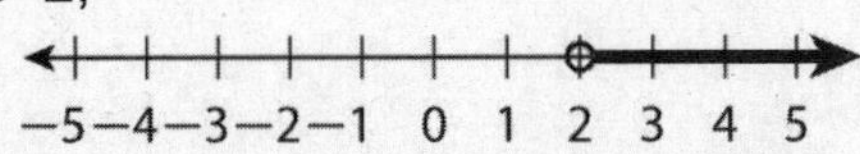

16. $s \geq 4$;

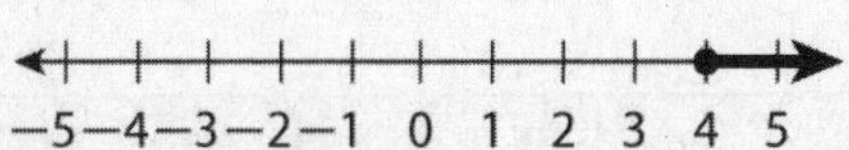

Skill 23: Unit Rates

1. Yes
2. No
3. Yes
4. 32 pages
5. $\frac{3}{4}$ mi
6. 80 words
7. \$5.25
8. The error is that Grant multiplied the 3-day rate by 9. He should have multiplied the unit rate by 9. The correct cost is \$495 for 9 nights.
9. 144 golf balls
10. 3.4 h
11. 36 pages per hour
12. 45 mph
13. $1\frac{1}{3}$ c
14. 16 oz for \$3.52
15. 46 fl oz for \$5.52
16. Yes; the size may be more convenient; the smaller amount may be all you need.

Skill 24: Writing Linear Equations

1. $y = 60x + 50$
2. $y = 45x + 20$
3. $y = 3x + 3$
4. $y = 5x + 15$
5. $y = 33x - 440$
6. The error is that Jim used a positive slope and found the amount he would owe once the \$150 were over. The correct equation is $y = -150x + 1{,}450$.
7. $y = 15x + 20$
8. $y = -75x + 1100$
9. $y = x + 6$
10. $y = -x + 14$

Skill 25: Two-Way Frequency Tables

1.

	Like Sports	Do Not Like Sports	TOTAL
Like Talk Radio	96	64	160
Do Not Like Talk Radio	28	12	40
TOTAL	124	76	200

2.

	Like	Dislike	TOTAL
Students	22	18	40
Adults	51	9	60
TOTAL	73	27	100

3.

	Own E-Reader	Do Not Own E-Reader	TOTAL
Own Computer	18	27	45
Do Not Own Computer	24	6	30
TOTAL	42	33	75

4. 20%
5. 30%
6. Yes. Possible explanation: Because 30% of middle school students have been outside of the United States and 20% of elementary school students have been outside of the United States, there is an association that the older a student is the more likely that the student has been outside of the United States.
7. Sarah found the ratio of a boy liking modern art to a boy not liking modern art instead of finding the ratio of a boy liking modern art to the number of boys surveyed. The correct relative frequency is $\frac{45}{120} = 37.5\%$.
8. 62.5%
9. 62.5%
10. No. Because the relative frequencies are equal, there is no association.

Skill 26: Two-Way Relative Frequency Tables

1.

Music	Rock	Country	Rap	TOTAL
Frequency	0.45	0.2	0.35	1

2.

Music	Rock	Country	Rap	TOTAL
Frequency	45%	20%	35%	100%

3.

	Peach	Pear	Strawberry	TOTAL
Students	46	21	13	80
Adults	32	24	24	80
TOTAL	78	45	37	160

4.

	Peach	Pear	Strawberry	TOTAL
Students	0.2875	0.13125	0.08125	0.5
Adults	0.2	0.15	0.15	0.5
TOTAL	0.4875	0.28125	0.23125	1

5.

	Peach	Pear	Strawberry	TOTAL
Students	28.75%	13.125%	8.125%	50%
Adults	20%	15%	15%	50%
TOTAL	48.75%	28.125%	23.125%	100%

6.

	Fractions	Decimals	Percents	TOTAL
Seventh Grade	10	20	10	40
Eighth Grade	15	25	20	60
TOTAL	25	45	30	100

7.

	Fractions	Decimals	Percents
Seventh Grade	0.4	$0.\overline{4}$	$0.\overline{3}$
Eighth Grade	0.6	$0.\overline{5}$	$0.\overline{6}$
TOTAL	1	1	1

8. Nick divided the number of juniors in track by the total number of students involved in track instead of by the number of juniors who are on varsity sports. Nick should have divided $\frac{27}{59} \approx 46\%$.
9. Possible answer: Of the students surveyed, 40% were seventh-grade students. Because each type of number is close to 40% with decimals going slightly over and percents slightly under, there is no association between numbers used and grade.

Skill 27: Absolute Value

1. 6
2. 8
3. 12
4. 8
5. 5
6. 9
7. $|-20| = 20$
8. Absolute values are positive, so $|-7| = 7$.
9. $>$
10. $>$
11. $<$
12. $<$
13. Less than 6 °F; Possible explanation: Adding 6 or more to a number greater than –6 gives a positive sum.
14. More than 10 points. Possible explanation: Adding 10 or less to a number less than –10 gives a negative sum.
15. 4.2
16. $6\frac{2}{3}$
17. 0.72
18. 3.6
19. $2\frac{1}{2}$
20. $\frac{5}{7}$
21. The statement is incorrect because the absolute values are opposites. Absolute values of the opposites $-3\frac{3}{4}$ and $3\frac{3}{4}$ are the same, so $\left|-3\frac{3}{4}\right| = 3\frac{3}{4}$.

Skill 28: Measures of Center

1. 92
2. 52
3. 36 and 48
4. There are two modes. Because 10 also occurs three times, the modes are 10 and 12.
5. 67.2
6. 64
7. 68
8. 60
9. Curtis did not order the numbers. When ordered, the middle number is 32.
10. 70
11. 47
12. Possible answer: Either measure can be used. There is no outlier, so both the mean of 90 or the median of 89 represent the data well.

Skill 29: Box Plots

1. 25
2. 18
3. 15
4. 13
5. 23
6.

80 82 84 86 88 90 92 94 96 98 100

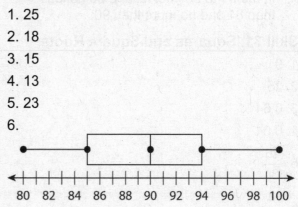

7.

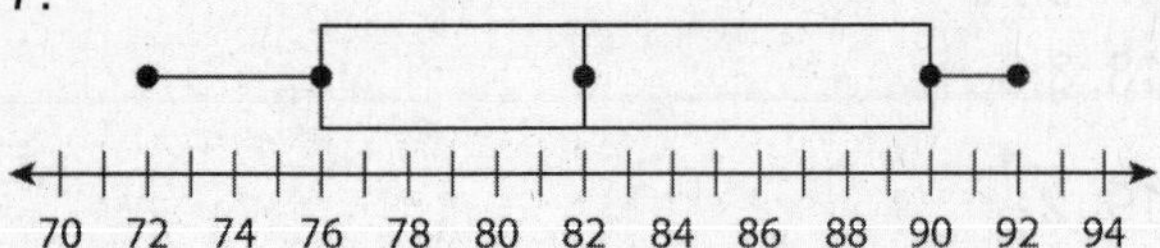

8. 20

9. 12

10. Caleb's error is that he subtracted the median from the greatest value. He should have subtracted the lower quartile, 62, from the upper quartile, 88. The IQR is 26.

Skill 30: Histograms

1. Histograms will vary depending on intervals used. Possible histogram is shown:

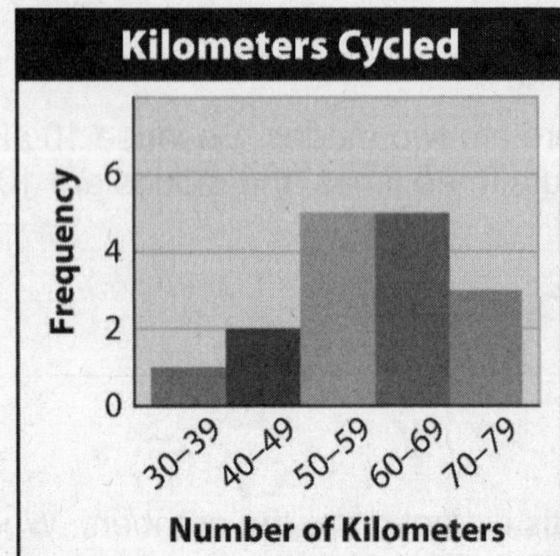

2. 60%

3. 65%

4. The median is the middle number in an ordered data set. There are 20 data, so the median is the mean of the tenth and eleventh values. Because there are only 8 values less than 81, the median must be in the 81 to 90 interval and be no less than 81 and no more than 90.

Skill 31: Squares and Square Roots

1. 9

2. 25

3. 0.64

4. 0.04

5. $\frac{16}{81}$

6. $\frac{4}{49}$

7. ± 9

8. ± 0.6

9. $\pm\frac{5}{8}$

10. The error is $\sqrt{100} = 10$ only. The symbol $\sqrt{}$ indicates the positive square root only.

11. Yes

12. No

13. Yes

14. 4.2

15. 5.7

16. 7.1

17. 8.7

Skill 32: Cubes and Cube Roots

1. 8

2. 512

3. 0.216

4. 0.027

5. $\frac{1}{729}$

6. $\frac{27}{1,000}$

7. 6

8. 0.2

9. $\frac{4}{9}$

10. No

11. Yes

12. Yes

13. Nate is incorrect because $1^2 = 1$ and $1^3 = 1$, so 1 is also a perfect square and a perfect cube.

14. 5 cm

15. 7 in.